The Legacy of Mesoamerica

History and Culture of a Native American Civilization

Second Edition

ROBERT M. CARMACK

State University of New York, Albany

JANINE GASCO

California State University-Dominguez

GARY H. GOSSEN

State University of New York, Albany

with contributions from
George A. Broadwell, Louise M. Burkhart, Liliana R. Goldin,
John S. Justeson, Brenda Rosenbaum, Michael E. Smith

PEARSON

Prentice
Hall

PRENTICE HALL, Upper Saddle River, New Jersey 07458

Library of Congress Cataloging-in-Publication Data

The legacy of Mesoamerica : history and culture of a Native American civilization /
[edited by] Robert M. Carmack, Janine Gasco, Gary H. Gossen.—2nd ed.
   p. cm.
  Includes bibliographical references and index.
  ISBN 0-13-049292-2
  1. Indians of Mexico—History. 2. Indians of Central America—History.
3. Mexico—Civilization. 4. Central America—Civilization. I. Carmack, Robert M.
II. Gasco, Janine. III. Gossen, Gary H.
  F1219.L44 2007
  972'. 00497—dc22

2006032568

Editorial Director: Leah Jewell
Publisher: Nancy Roberts
Supplements Editor: LeeAnn Doherty
Editorial Assistant: Lee Paterson
Full Service Production Liaison: Joanne Hakim
Marketing Director: Brandy Dawson
Senior Marketing Manager: Marissa Feliberty
Manufacturing Buyer: Ben Smith
Cover Art Director: Jayne Conte
Cover Design: Bruce Kenselaar
Cover Photo: © Akademische Druck-u. Verlagsanstalt

Manager, Cover Visual Research & Permission:
  Karen Sanatar
Director, Image Resource Center: Melinda Patelli
Manager, Rights and Permission: Zina Arabia
Manager, Visual Research: Beth Brenzel
Photo Coordinator: Debbie Hewitson
Full-Service Project Management: Jan Pushard/
  Pine Tree Composition
Composition: Laserwords Private Limited
Printer/Binder: R. R. Donnelley & Sons Company

Credits and acknowledgments borrowed from other sources and reproduced, with permission, in this textbook appear on appropriate page within text.

Pearson Education LTD., London
Pearson Education Singapore, Pte. Ltd
Pearson Education, Canada, Ltd
Pearson Education—Japan
Pearson Education Australia PTY, Limited

Pearson Education North Asia Ltd
Pearson Educación de México, S.A. de C.V.
Pearson Education Malaysia, Pte. Ltd
Pearson Education, Upper Saddle River, New Jersey

10 9 8 7 6 5 4 3 2 1
0-13-049292-2

Contents

Preface

Once again we invite our readers to share the urgency and passion that we feel toward the contents of this second edition of the *Legacy* book. We think the new edition is timely inasmuch as the native peoples of Mexico and Central America continue to attract the interest of scholars, students, and educated citizens. Indeed, since the publication of the first edition of this text interest in the topic shows no signs of abating.

THE SIGNIFICANCE OF MESOAMERICA FOR SCHOLARLY STUDIES

The encounter of the Old and New worlds, which commenced in a sustained fashion in 1492, can be said to have fundamentally changed the course of human history. This encounter not only provided the opportunity for the ascendancy of Spain and Portugal to the role of being the first truly global powers, but also, in a real sense, initiated the globalization of humanity under European hegemony, a pattern that for better or worse remains with us to this day.

Although the Caribbean Basin was the stage for the early and cataclysmic period of initial contact—it resulted in nothing less than the virtual annihilation of hundreds of thousands of Caribbean Indians, essentially the entire population by 1550—the institutionalization of Spain's New World enterprise took root only with the conquest of Mesoamerica and the creation of New Spain, and subsequently the parallel enterprise in Peru. By 1600, fundamental Western ideas and practices concerning modernity, social progress, "tutelage" of the vanquished, bureaucratic rationalism, and economic and political dependency under the global system we know as colonialism were firmly in place, complete with all of that system's atrocities and social asymmetries. Indeed, Mesoamerica's radically truncated and transformed Indian communities, forced to live under Spain's "missionary state," became what might be called prototypes of colonized peoples, a social condition that would eventually characterize much of Asia, Africa, North and South America, and the Pacific in the ensuing centuries.

Aside from the particulars of this period, which will be discussed elsewhere in this text, it should be remembered that the sixteenth-century theological and philosophical debates regarding the "moral status" of the Amerindians were in large part focused on data that came from New Spain (Mexico). These discussions, which came to influence not only Crown and

Church policy in America but also the very foundations of Western ideas about human nature, carried in their wake nothing less than the dawn of modern social science; that is, the attempt to understand human variation in what was the beginning of a truly global comparative perspective (Klor de Alva, 1988).

Sixteenth-century Mesoamerican data provided the first major, modern ethnographic reports, perhaps best exemplified by Bernardino de Sahagún's enormous corpus, in which we have a comprehensive and objective description of the customs, social organization, economy, and arts of the Nahuatl world, all of it set down in the native language with Spanish translation. This is not distant from the goals of modern ethnography. It was thus set down for all to see (although few saw the work since it was suppressed) that Spain had in fact encountered and destroyed a high civilization, comparable in some ways to Europe itself. Not only did Sahagún and others achieve a certain detachment of their descriptions from their missionary and political agenda; some also came to appraise the moral status of the colonial enterprise itself.

Father Bartolomé de las Casas, who had witnessed firsthand Spain's atrocities of the early Contact period in the Caribbean and later in what is now southern Mexico and Guatemala, wrote one of the most influential political treatises of sixteenth-century Europe *(A Brief Description of the Destruction of the Indies)* as a critique of his own country's systematic destruction and cruel exploitation of Amerindians in the Caribbean and in Mesoamerica. In this work, as in many other theological and political works of the period, we are able to discern a clear pattern of cultural critique and relativism, a distancing of the observer from his own culture.

Needless to say, men like Sahagún and Las Casas were exceptional individuals and their ideas were unpopular at the time. Nevertheless, it is important to note that these contemporary-sounding reports and reflections about human nature, the human condition, and human variation came from sixteenth-century Spaniards who were writing of Mesoamerica. Thus, in addition to the vast material wealth and enormously important food, fiber, and medicinal plant cultigens that flowed from the New World to the Old World, there also came from America the challenge to reflect upon the origins, interrelations, mutability, internal coherence, and moral value of myriad human social forms that were unfamiliar to the Old World.

To this brief sketch of what we believe to be the significance of Mesoamerica to the formative period of modern Western intellectual history, must be added the major contributions by colonial Spanish scholars to the lexicography, transcription, translation, and grammatical analysis of Mesoamerican and other Native American languages. This is noteworthy because it was a Spaniard, Father Nebrija, who in 1492 wrote the first grammar of Castilian; this was also the first grammar of any vulgate Latin language. Hence, Spain's influential Renaissance scholarship in philology and descriptive linguistics continued with major works on the languages of the New World, establishing—largely with Mesoamerican data—a remarkable corpus of written testimonies in native languages with sophisticated translations.

If we also consider that the ancient Mesoamericans themselves possessed several forms of pictographic, ideographic, and phonetic writing systems that date to at least the beginning of the Christian era, it becomes clear that, in terms of both native written testimony and early Contact period textual and linguistic materials, Mesoamerica has what are by far the oldest and most comprehensive written records of any region of the New World. It is therefore not surprising that scholars with an interest in problems of evolution and continuity of Native American civilization and of America's place in the whole flow of human history have found in Mesoamerica an extremely fruitful focus for such research.

The singular power of the region to elicit our scholarly and general human interest stems not only from the great diversity and temporal depth of its cultural forms, but also from the fact that Mesoamericans themselves have spoken eloquently and often of their own world. This testimony begins with the glyphic texts and calendrical notations that date from the Late Formative period (400 B.C. to A.D. 200) and continues vigorously into the present. This constitutes a written record, rendered in several different media and writing systems, that spans over 2,000 years.

If we also consider the massive contribution of modern archaeologists, epigraphers, ethnologists, linguists, and ethnohistorians to the construction of the cultural history of the region, it becomes clear that Mesoamerica ranks as the best-known and best-documented cultural tradition of the New World. This uniquely rich documentation confers upon the region the quality of a "benchmark" that makes it possible, using data from Mesoamerica, to mount credible comparisons on innumerable topics both within the Americas and with the Old World.

CONTRIBUTIONS OF MESOAMERICA STUDIES
TO CULTURAL STUDIES

Because of Mesoamerica's centrality in Western scholarly reflection and romantic imagination, it will come as no surprise to the reader to find that the region has played an important role in the history of cultural studies themselves. We use the phrase "cultural studies" in its broad sense, which includes both humanistic and scientific studies of human variation in time and space.

We have already observed that systematic ethnographic reporting can be traced back to Sahagún's pioneering work in the mid-sixteenth century. The comprehensiveness of his Mexican corpus and his commentaries on its meaning, together with his consistent attention to the importance of testimonies and texts written in the Aztec language, give his work a precocious modernity.

To the contributions already mentioned to modern cultural studies as a result of research on the Mesoamerican peoples, the following should also be briefly mentioned:

(1) *The ethnology of culture history*, beginning with Sahagún's efforts to elicit testimony from contemporary Aztec speakers for the purpose of reconstructing the recent and ancient past.

(2) *The theory of the evolution of state-level societies and empires*, their rise, decline, and transformation—in long historical perspective.

(3) *The theory of peasantry*, those tens of millions who have lived (and continue to live today) at the social, economic, political, and ideological peripheries of states.

(4) *The study of colonialism, ethnicity, syncretism, and social change*, that is to say how the native peoples cope with their new status as colonized subjects of European nations.

(5) *The uses of social science in the formation and implementation of public policy of European-modeled states toward their ethnic minorities.*

(6) *The fields of linguistics, epigraphy, and art history*, by which the Mesoamericans themselves tell us in their own writing systems what their world signifies to them.

(7) *The study of revolutions, ethnic nationalism, and transnationalism*, each of which will be fully illustrated in the chapters to follow.

IMPACT OF MESOAMERICAN CIVILIZATION
ON MODERN NORTH AMERICA

Why should we, as scholars and citizens of the New World, care about the cultural and social history of Mesoamerica as a segment of general knowledge? It is important to move beyond academic and intellectual concerns to observe that the region has already profoundly influenced the world that North Americans live in. Indeed, some of the most familiar tastes and sights that make up the everyday lives of North Americans derive from Native Mesoamerican and Mexican origins. For example, some of the staple ingredients in a McDonald's fast food lunch—french fries, ketchup, and chocolate shakes—come from plants that were domesticated by Native Americans—potatoes, tomatoes, and cacao. Chocolate (cacao) and tomatoes were native Mesoamerican cultigens, and potatoes were originally domesticated in Andean South America. Furthermore, the cattle that provide the beef to make the hamburgers are fed on maize (corn), the dietary staple of the ancient and modern peoples of Mesoamerica. The social and economic history of maize, a Mesoamerican plant domesticate, is extraordinary in itself. It has become the principal food crop of many nations of Africa and Asia. In our own culture it appears in many forms, from tacos and tortilla chips (taken from Mexican cuisine) and cornbread (adapted from North American Indians) to the corn syrup that is ubiquitous in our processed foods. Maize and products derived from it make a multimillion-dollar contribution to the annual U.S. export economy.

North American homes, too, have been influenced by Mesoamerican traditions. The "ranch-style" houses so common in modern U.S. suburbs were developed from the modest one-story ranch houses of northern Mexico, which in turn were derived from Spanish house styles, modified during the Colonial period by the use of Mesoamerican building materials. Both Spanish and ancient Mesoamerican architectural styles included public and private outdoor living spaces. North Americans have borrowed the names and concepts of "plaza" and "patio" and made them their own in the form of shopping plazas and backyard patios.

And around the world, what image is more associated with the United States than the Western cowboy? Time and again U.S. athletes choose to march into the Olympic Games wearing the familiar cowboy hat. Yet the mythical "cowboy culture" that North Americans celebrate as their own in literature, movies, and the arts bears the indelible imprint of its origins in northern Mexican cattle culture. The traditional cowboy outfit—broad-brimmed hat, kerchief, chaps, spurs, "cowboy" boots, and "Western" saddle—is of Mexican origin. And so are dozens of words, borrowed from Spanish, that are associated with cowboy life and culture: ranch *(rancho)*; corral *(corral)*; buckaroo (from *vaquero*, meaning "cowboy"); bronco (from *bronco*, meaning "hoarse," "resistant," "untamed"); and rodeo *(rodeo)*. To this list we must add "chili," the quintessential dish of Southwestern U.S. cuisine and mainstay of cattle drivers. This dish is nothing less than a slightly altered adaptation of a generic bean, chili, tomato, and meat stew that existed in Mesoamerica long before Spain invaded Mexico.

The list of influences from its southern neighbors on U.S. music, art, and other areas of our daily lives is long. Suffice it to say that many regions of the country have a long history of interaction with the peoples of Mesoamerica. This interaction began with the ancient trade networks between Mesoamerican and North American native groups, and it continued with the shared experience of exploration and efforts at colonization by Spain (large areas of our South and West were first explored by Spain between 1540 and 1570, decades before the founding of Jamestown). The pattern of close association continues with the current influx into U.S. cities of millions of Mexican and Central American immigrants and refugees.

The United States shares a highly permeable 2,000-mile border with Mexico, and the flow of people, goods, and ideas across it has had a powerful impact on that society. This is reflected in a simple but startling demographic fact: East Los Angeles ranks second only to Mexico City itself among Mexican urban populations. Mexican Americans make up the majority of what is the largest non-English-speaking population of the United States. Indeed, the United States is the sixth-ranking Spanish-speaking nation in the world. Furthermore, the Mexican Spanish-speaking segment of U.S. society is growing faster than any other minority or immigrant group in this country. All of this leads to the obvious conclusion that ancient and modern Mesoamericans have long been a significant presence in U.S. culture and society, a pattern that only increased in the past few years. Mesoamericans are, thus, literally and figuratively fellow Americans. There is every reason, then, to become well acquainted with them.

Canada, Mexico, and the United States formalized the North American Free Trade Agreement (NAFTA) in 1994, and the Central American states are in the process of becoming part of a similar free trade agreement (known as CAFTA). Modern Mesoamericans are joining the United States and Canada as members of one of the three major economic and trading blocs in the world: North America, Europe, and Asia. This trend suggests that the twenty-first century will inevitably bring Mexico and Central America, "distant neighbors" to the United States, into its very midst with a shared set of economic interests and opportunities. English-speaking North Americans will obviously have much to gain in appreciating and understanding the ancient and modern legacy of Mesoamerican civilization.

ACKNOWLEDGMENTS

The complexity of scholarship on Mesoamerica and the Mesoamerican cultural tradition itself was a compelling factor in our deciding to write this text as a collective effort. The editors of record in the first edition (Robert Carmack, Janine Gasco, and Gary Gossen) continue to be responsible in this second edition for ensuring the overall integration of the text. We also acknowledge the invaluable contributions by Edgar Martin del Campo, Jason S. R. Paling, and Bradley W. Russell in preparing the figures, bibliographies, and computation of the chapters in this second edition.

We are grateful to the original authors of chapters in the first edition: George Broadwell, Louise Burkhart, Robert Carmack, Jan Gasco, Liliana Goldin, Gary Gossen, John Justeson, Brenda Rosenbaum, and Michael Smith. And we are particularly grateful to the following additional scholars who have contributed to chapters in this second edition: Christine Eber, Walter Little, Marilyn Masson, and Rob Rosenswig.

We would like to thank the following reviewers for their helpful suggestions and useful insights: Victor Garcia, Indiana University of Pennsylvania; James McDonald, University of Texas at San Antonio; Ramona Perez, University of North Texas; John Bort, East Carolina University; Arthur Murphy, Georgia State University; and Ronald Waterburg, CUNY-Queens College.

Last, but certainly not least, we want to express our gratitude to Nancy Roberts, executive editor of Prentice Hall, and to this publishing company for their encouragement in the preparation of this second edition. Their backing was crucial to our making it a reality.

List of Figures

List of Boxes

Introduction

The Spanish explorers and conquistadors who first made contact with the Mesoamerican world were surprised by its complexity and grandeur, for they had become accustomed to the simpler ways of the previously subjugated natives of the Caribbean Islands. Their testimony constitutes an informative beginning place for our study of the Mesoamerican world, whose origins, conditions at European contact, and transformations resulting from colonization and (more recently) modernization are the subject of this text.

FIRST IMPRESSIONS OF MESOAMERICA BY THE SPANIARDS

As we will now see, the Spaniards were extremely impressed with the level of cultural development achieved by the Mesoamerican peoples. In reviewing the Spaniards' first impressions, the reader should take particular note of the complexity and diversity of Mesoamerica. We begin with Columbus and his fourth voyage to the New World.

Columbus Meets the Mayas during His Fourth Voyage

The first Europeans to make contact with Mesoamerican peoples were Christopher Columbus and his men during their fourth voyage to the New World. Columbus began the voyage in 1502. Departing from Spain, he touched down on the island of Española (present-day Haiti and Dominican Republic), and then sailed directly to the Bay Islands located off the coast of Honduras. While at harbor in one of the islands, a large canoe of "Indians" arrived, bearing merchandise brought from areas to the west. Many years later, Columbus's son Fernando described the canoe and its people as follows:

> [The canoe was as] long as a galley and eight feet wide, made of a single tree trunk. . . . Amidship it had a palm-leaf awning like that which the Venetian gondolas carry; this gave

complete protection against the rain and waves. Under this awning were the children and women and all the baggage and merchandise. There were twenty-five paddlers. . . . [The Admiral] took aboard the costliest and handsomest things in that cargo: cotton mantles and sleeveless shirts embroidered and painted in different designs and colors; breechclouts of the same design and cloth as the shawls worn by the women in the canoe, being like the shawls worn by the Moorish women of Granada; long wooden swords with a groove on each side where the edge should be, in which were fastened with cord and pitch, flint knives that cut like steel; hatchets resembling the stone hatchets used by the other Indians, but made of good copper; and hawk's bells of copper, and crucibles to melt it. For provisions they had such roots and grains as the Indians of Española eat, also a wine made of maize that tasted like English beer. They had as well many of the almonds [cacao beans] which the Indians of New Spain use as currency. . . .(Keen 1959:231–232)

Columbus was impressed by the cultural refinement of the natives in the canoe, for he had not seen a people like them before in the New World. He seized the leader of the boat, an old man named Yumbe, who became translator for Columbus with the peoples they later met along the coast of Honduras. Yumbe is a Yucatec Mayan name, which suggests that Columbus had stumbled on a group of Mayan long-distance traders from the Mesoamerican world.

Columbus apparently did not fully understand the significance of the Mayan traders nor the complex world from which they came, and as a result he sailed east toward lower Central America in search of the hoped-for passageway to the Orient. Farther south he encountered indigenous peoples culturally similar to the natives already known to him in Española and the other Caribbean islands. His decision to explore lower Central America established a pattern followed by subsequent explorers, who during the next two decades initiated the first permanent Spanish settlements in the area of southern Central America known today as Panama.

The Spaniards Make Contact with the Powerful Kingdoms of Mesoamerica

Exploration of the Mesoamerican region by the Spaniards began between 1517 and 1519 (for details, see Chapter 4), as first Hernández de Córdova, then Juan de Grijalva, and finally Hernán Cortés sailed around the Yucatán Peninsula and northward along the Gulf Coast of Mexico. In 1519, while Cortés and his men were camped with the Totonac Indians of Veracruz, they witnessed the arrival of a group of Aztec tax collectors. The Spaniards were astonished by the extreme deference with which the Totonac peoples received the Aztecs, and the Spaniards began to understand—perhaps for the first time—just how politically complex and culturally diverse the newly discovered world of native peoples really was. The point was driven home even more forcefully to the Spaniards as they began their history-making journey from the Veracruz coast to the Central Basin of Mexico. At each step along the way, they encountered economically richer, culturally more sophisticated, and politically more powerful peoples.

Beyond Totonac country, the Spaniards felt that they were entering "a different sort of country," one in which the gleaming plastered stone buildings of the towns and fortresses reminded them of Spain itself. In places like Tlaxcala, Cholula, and

Huejotzinco, the Spaniards were surprised to find cosmopolitan and highly politicized peoples. Their robust kingdoms were populated by over 100,000 subjects each, and they vied with one another for power by employing elaborate forms of diplomacy, intrigue, and warfare. Territories were defended with high walls and fortifications. Warriors numbering in the tens of thousands were organized into diverse ranks and squadrons, each with its own insignia and dress code. Cities as large as those in Spain bustled with people engaged in daily trade, administrative affairs, and religious ritual. The native societies were deeply stratified, not only between noble and commoner, but also between rich and poor, freeman and slave.

Cortés, perhaps exaggerating a bit in order to impress the Crown, nevertheless captured the cosmopolitan nature of these societies with the following description of Tlaxcala:

> The city is indeed so great and marvelous that though I abstain from describing many things about it, yet the little that I shall recount is, I think, almost incredible. It is much larger than Granada, and much better fortified. Its houses are as fine and its inhabitants far more numerous than those of Granada when that city was captured. Its provisions and food are likewise very superior—including such things as bread, fowl, game, fish and other excellent vegetables and produce which they eat. There is a market in this city in which more than thirty thousand people daily are occupied in buying and selling, and this in addition to other similar shops which there are in all parts of the city. Nothing is lacking in this market of what they are wont to use, whether utensils, garments, footwear or the like. There is gold, silver and precious stones, and jewelers' shops selling other ornaments made of feathers, as well arranged as in any market in the world. There is earthenware of many kinds and excellent quality, as fine as any in Spain. Wood, charcoal, medicinal and sweet smelling herbs are sold in large quantities. There are booths for washing your hair and barbers to shave you; there are also public baths. Finally, good order and an efficient police system are maintained among them, and they behave as people of sense and reason: the foremost city of Africa cannot rival them. (Cortés 1962:50–51)

The Tlaxcalas, Cholutecas, and other peoples of the area were able to describe for Cortés what the Aztec heartland was like. Nevertheless, the Spaniards were unprepared for what they saw when in November of 1519 they finally reached the Basin of Mexico and entered the Aztec capital of Tenochtitlan. Cortés later wrote glowingly of the Aztec capital (Figure A.1):

> The great city of Tenochtitlan is built in the midst of this salt lake, and it is two leagues from the heart of the city to any point on the mainland. Four causeways lead to it, all made by hand and some twelve feet wide. The city itself is as large as Seville or Córdova. The principal streets are very broad and straight, the majority of them being of beaten earth, but a few and at least half the smaller thoroughfares are waterways along which they pass in their canoes. (Cortés 1962:86)

Cortés, a boastful but astute observer, attempted to place the Aztec capital in the wider context of Mesoamerica as a whole and even of the Old World. He described in great detail the pomp and ceremony surrounding Motecuhzoma, the ruler of the Aztec empire, who, he said, rivaled "the sultans themselves or other eastern potentates." Cortés recounted how Motecuhzoma was attended by literally thousands

Figure A.1   The island city of Tenochtitlan at the time of Spanish contact. From a painting by Miguel Covarrubias in the Museo Nacional de Antropología, Mexico City.

of retainers, who were not permitted to wear sandals in his presence nor to see his face. The Aztec ruler changed attire four times a day, never wearing the same clothing more than once. Wherever he went he was carried on jewel-studded litters by men of the highest noble rank. Hundreds of young men and women served his meals, which included up to three hundred different dishes. Motecuhzoma conducted imperial business in the royal palace, amusing himself during breaks by strolling through the surrounding gardens and parks stocked with every variety of plant and animal known to the native world.

Motecuhzoma's wealth in gold and other metal pieces; precious stone jewelry; exquisite feather, stone, wood, and bone crafted items; beautiful cloths; and innumerable other objects so impressed Cortés that he was "doubtful whether any of all the known princes of the world possesses such treasures in such quantity." Cortés estimated the city's main market to be twice as large as the one in Salamanca. The quality of Aztec maize, in both grain size and taste, was said to be superior to that of "all the other islands or the mainland." The multicolored cotton cloth was as good as any in Spain, and on a par with the silks of Granada. Cortés also marveled at the number of commercial goods being exchanged in Tenochtitlan, brought there by thousands of canoes bound for the city from every direction along the network of canals. All goods that entered the city were taxed. In the marketplaces themselves, every conceivable item and service were available, from barbering to prostitution, and large numbers of skilled and unskilled laborers gathered there "waiting to be hired by the day."

In an attempt to put Aztec society (and his own exploits) into broader perspective, Cortés summarized his observations about the Aztec city as follows:

> Finally, to avoid prolixity in telling all the wonders of this city, I will simply say that the manner of living among the people is very similar to that in Spain, and considering that this is a barbarous nation shut off from a knowledge of the true God or communication with enlightened nations, one may well marvel at the orderliness and good government which is everywhere maintained. (Cortés 1962:93–94)

The Spaniards quickly determined that the Aztec empire was vast, extending for hundreds of miles in all directions, and that, as Cortés exaggeratedly claimed, "Motecuhzoma was feared by all both present and distant more than any other monarch in the world." Still, the Spaniards were well aware that they had seen only a small part of the Mesoamerican world, and that many other kingdoms, large and small, were yet to be explored and subdued.

With the fall of Tenochtitlan to the Spaniards in 1521 (see Chapter 4), Cortés began to send his captains on military expeditions from the Basin of Mexico to contact and, if necessary, conquer the diverse peoples and kingdoms of Mesoamerica. For example, expeditions were sent to the great province called Michoacan in the west and farther north from there to the province of Cihuatan, "which it is affirmed had an island inhabited solely by women"; and to the rebellious province of Huaxteca in the northeast. Other expeditions were dispatched to the southern regions of Mesoamerica, such as Oaxaca, Chiapas, and "the very rich lands" of Higueras (Honduras). One of the most important expeditions was entrusted to Cortés's courageous but ruthless captain, Pedro de Alvarado, who was sent to the "rich and splendid lands inhabited by new and different races" in the kingdoms of Utatlan and Guatemala.

DEFINING "MESOAMERICA" AND OTHER IMPORTANT TERMS

We have referred to the world encountered by Cortés and his band as "Mesoamerica." What do we mean by this term? And, to what will the term refer in the chapters to follow? In answering these questions, we should begin by noting that the term *Mesoamerica* has varied widely in meaning, even among scholars. In fact, perhaps no term is more debated in Mesoamerican studies than Mesoamerica itself. We do not propose to settle the debate, but rather to define terms as we use them in this text, and to try to employ them in clear and consistent fashion. We are aware that the native Mesoamericans themselves are sensitive about how such terms are employed, and in the chapters to follow we have tried to keep their interests in mind.

Literally, the term *Mesoamerica* means "Middle America," and it was at one time widely used to refer exclusively to the aboriginal cultures of the region, whether in their pristine pre-Hispanic or acculturated modern forms. That is to say, Mesoamerica had a geographic reference: the region where the ancient Mesoamerican peoples flourished prior to the coming of the Spaniards. This usage was problematic for mestizo, European, and even indigenous peoples who had little or nothing to do with the so-called Mesoamerican world but have resided in the region for centuries. There-fore, in this text for the most part, we avoid using the term strictly as a geographic region or culture area.

A more flexible and useful definition of Mesoamerica, we think, is to define it as a particular historical tradition of aboriginal cultures, and thus a "civilization." It is understood that this cultural tradition was constantly undergoing transformation prior to the coming of the Spaniards, and it has continued to experience even more radical change and adaptation since Spanish contact. The creators of this rich his-torical tradition—both in its original, pre-Hispanic version and in its post-Hispanic, modified versions—may properly be termed "Mesoamericans" (or "native" Mesoamericans).

From our perspective, Mesoamerica, whether past or present, cannot be ade-quately defined by a list of essential traits or ideas; rather, we need to examine the relationship through time between these cultural features and the social and mate-rial processes involved in their creation. Both the cultural traditions and the processes by which Mesoamerica has changed are worth tracing because they have profoundly influenced the participating peoples of Mexico and Central America, whether they be natives, mestizos, Africans, or Europeans.

It must be emphasized that Mesoamerica, as we employ the term, does not refer to a fixed or static cultural tradition. From at least 1000 B.C. onward, the Mesoamer-ican cultural tradition has consisted of a complex mix of regional and local cultures, and it has been in a state of continual flux. This was even more the case after Span-ish culture—and later other European and North American cultures—were imposed on the Mesoamerican peoples and further fragmented the Mesoamerican cultures. Nevertheless, the legacy of the Mesoamerican cultural tradition has been sufficiently cohesive, unique, and influential in the history of the region to warrant its identifi-cation with a special term: "Mesoamerica."

Despite the overall unity of the Mesoamerican cultural tradition, the Mesoamer-icans have perhaps never seen themselves as a single people sharing a common cul-ture. During pre-Hispanic times, the widest identifying social units for most Mesoamericans were the polities to which they were subject, whether empires, king-doms, city-states, or chiefdoms. Furthermore, most Mesoamericans have been locally oriented; and collective identities based on ethnic group, community, and lineage were probably stronger than those based on political affiliation. For millions of native Mesoamericans in the region, this trend continues to be true today, as their collective identity comes more from the village, hamlet, region, or language group to which they belong than from the nation-state in whose territory they reside. In most contexts and time periods, then, Mesoamericans have tended to see themselves mainly as first, members of a lineage; second, participants in a community; third, speakers of a com-mon language; and finally, if at all, as Mexicans, Central Americans, or Indians.

Like the term Mesoamerica, *Indian* is another controversial term debated within Mesoamerican studies. As is well known, this term was incorrectly applied to the na-tive peoples of Mesoamerica and elsewhere in the New World by Columbus and later Spanish explorers. The Spaniards continued to refer to the Mesoamericans during the colonial period as Indians (in the Spanish form, "Indios"), and its usage persisted within the nation-states of Mexico and Central America after independence. Therein lies the controversy, for many Mesoamericans today resent being called "Indians." The term, they say, is not only a misnomer but worse, a device employed by the ruling classes to keep the native peoples in a subordinate ("neocolonial") social position.

Various alternate labels have been suggested by scholars and Mesoamericans alike to replace the term "Indian," such as "aborigine," "indigene," "natural," "native," and "Native American." Some Mesoamericans prefer to be identified by either generic ethnic designations—such as "Mayas," "Nahuas," "Otomis," "Pipils"—or local community eponyms: for example, "San Juaneros" or "Ixtahuacanos" (people from the community of San Juan, or the community of Ixtahuacán). Given the controversy, the term "Indian" should be used with care and an effort made to determine how it has been manipulated to further the political and economic interests of both the Mesoamericans and their external oppressors.

An additional controversial term, especially for the Mesoamericans themselves, is "conquest." The Mesoamericans accept that they were invaded by Spaniards and defeated in wars against them, but insist that they were never "conquered" by the Spaniards nor anyone else. They argue that they did not willingly submit to domination by outsiders and that they have continued to struggle against the aggressors down to the present time. Considerable evidence will be presented in this text to support their claim, although, as the reader will discover, we nevertheless employ the term "conquest" in certain places to refer to the bloody clashes that took place during the sixteenth century between the Spaniards and Mesoamericans.

Although we are sympathetic to arguments made by Mesoamericans about the importance of terminology, terms like "Indian" and "conquest" are universally employed in North American scholarly discourse, and it seems to us that it would be overly pedantic to excise them completely from our account. Ironically, some native Mesoamericans insist on being called "Indians" in order to dramatize the oppression to which they have been subjected since initial contact with the Europeans. The word "conquest" is universally applied in the social sciences to refer to unequal military clashes like the ones that took place in Mesoamerica during the sixteenth century. We hasten to add, however, that "Indian," as we use the term, carries no connotation of racial or cultural inferiority, and that "conquest" does not mean that the native Mesoamericans have ceased to resist all means to subjugate them. We trust that it will be obvious to the reader of the pages to follow that our respect and admiration for the Mesoamerican Indians and their cultures are genuine and are grounded in a clear understanding of their history.

Finally, we wish to mention other, less controversial terminological problems. The most important of these, perhaps, has to do with orthography: how to spell or represent native terms and expressions. Linguists, of course, have a universal phonetic alphabet by which they record and analyze the diverse languages of the world, including those spoken by Mesoamericans. Other scholars, such as ethnologists, archaeologists, geographers, and historians have developed orthographies that do not always correspond perfectly with the linguists' phonetic system. In part this is a practical matter of being able to write native terms in the everyday alphabets of the scholars' home countries (English, Spanish, French, German, etc.). The countries of the

Mesoamerican region, especially Mexico and Guatemala, have stressed the importance of developing alphabets for the native languages that are easily adapted to Spanish. Recently, Mesoamerican Indians themselves have taken a renewed interest in developing their own ways of writing the native languages that are, after all, part of their own cultural heritage. Fortunately, a growing number of native scholars are being trained in the science of linguistics and consequently now express more of an interest in finding a universal graphic system to transcribe the Mesoamerican languages than in developing a unique "native" alphabet for each language.

In this text we attempt to follow linguistic usages adapted to Anglo-American forms in representing native terms and expressions, for example, by adding -s to pluralize the names of native peoples (Aztec-s or Maya-s) and -n when they are used in adjectival form (Maya-n). For the most part we avoid providing accent marks when native-language terms are used (for example, Tenochtitlan rather than Tenochtitlán). In general, Nahuatl (Aztec) words receive stress on the penultimate syllabus, whereas Mayan words receive stress on the final syllabus. We render Spanish terms and expressions—which have been incorporated into the Mesoamerican tradition in large numbers—with English glosses when first used. We also employ accent marks for words that are clearly Spanish rather than Mesoamerican, in part to help the reader pronounce the words correctly.

THE PHYSICAL SETTING
OF ABORIGINAL MESOAMERICA

Having seen how the Spaniards viewed the Mesoamericans, and having defined "Mesoamerica" and other terms, let us now turn to the physical setting in which the Mesoamericans developed their elaborate cultural tradition. In this section, we begin with a brief examination of the broad geographic conditions within which the Mesoamericans created their distinctive civilization, after which a series of special "natural areas" will be delineated. We will also briefly attempt to characterize the Mesoamericans in biological terms, arguing in the process that their physical features represent adaptations to the environmental conditions of the region.

The Highland and Lowland Division

Few regions in the world of equivalent size vary as much as the Mesoamerican region in its landforms, climate, flora and fauna, soils, and vegetation. Indeed, this geographic diversity is thought to be closely related to the origin of agriculture and evolution of the state within the region. The "natural areas" into which the region is subdivided provide widely divergent adaptive challenges to the inhabitants, whether aboriginal Mesoamericans or the modern mixed populations of Whites, mestizos, and Indians in Mexico and Central America. We are particularly interested in the responses to these environmental challenges through time by the native Mesoamericans, and the way that these responses help explain the social history and cultural features that will be reviewed in the chapters to follow. It is likely, too, that adaptations

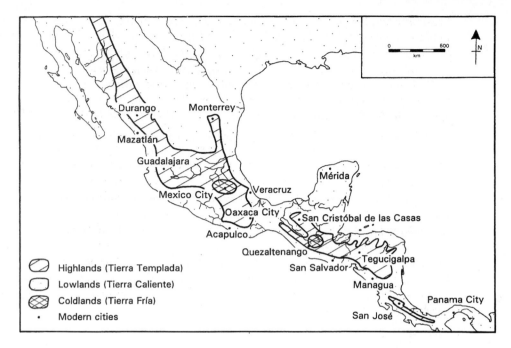

Figure A.2 Map showing the three major geographic zones of Mesoamerica. After Robert C. West, "The Natural Regions of Middle America," *The Handbook of Middle American Indians, Volume I: Natural Environment and Early Cultures,* volume editor Robert C. West, general editor Robert Wauchope. Austin, TX: University of Texas Press, 1964, p. 365.

to the more general features of the region's geography have provided the ecological basis for the many shared cultural features that gave the peoples of the Middle American region a common identity and set them apart from other native peoples in North and South America.

One useful scheme divides the region into three distinct geographic zones, as described in Box A.1 (see also Figure A.2). Generally speaking, the Mesoamerican peoples have adapted to the highland/lowland divide by means of two major adaptive or ecological regimes, defined in terms of their respective agricultural, demographic, and settlement patterns.

Box A.1 Three Geographic Zones of Middle America

Broad contrasts in elevation divide the region into the following three distinct geographic zones (Sanders and Price 1968:101–105) (see also Figure A.2):

Tierra Fría zone ("cold lands"), 2,000 to 2,800 meters in elevation.
Tierra Templada zone ("temperate lands"), 1,000 to 2,000 meters in elevation.
Tierra Caliente zone ("hot lands"), 0 to 1,000 meters in elevation.

(continued)

(continued)

These three zones can be further subdivided into geographically diverse subzones on the basis of variations in land elevation and the relative amount of rainfall received. The resulting zones and subzones define conditions that have greatly affected the production of the main cultivated plants in Mesoamerica, and thus played an important role in the history of the region. For example, the way maize (corn) is grown will vary considerably depending upon the subzones; in arid subzones, it usually will not grow at all unless irrigated. Similarly, cacao does not do well in Tierra Templada zones and requires irrigation in subhumid subzones or arid Tierra Caliente subzones. Cotton grows well only in arid and subhumid Tierra Caliente subzones.

It is customary to simplify the geography of the region by referring to both the Tierra Fría and the Tierra Templada zones as "highlands," and to the Tierra Caliente zone as "lowlands." This broad highland/lowland division is thought to have been historically the region's most fundamental geographic division.

Highlands.   The Mesoamericans associated with the highland ecological system have been concentrated mainly in the Central Plateau of Mexico, the mountainous areas of Oaxaca, and the intermontaine basins of Chiapas and Guatemala. The most fertile soils of the region are found in the highlands, especially within the larger basins, valleys, and plateaus. The soil fertility of the highlands is primarily the result of sedimentation in extinct lakes and of volcanic action. Periodic volcanic eruptions have carried ash and cinder into the numerous large valleys and basins of the highlands. Maize, beans, squash, amaranth, maguey, and other crops were produced in the highlands, by employing an intensive agricultural technology. In aboriginal times technological intensification took the form of terracing, irrigation, and short-term fallowing (dry farming).

Highland populations in the region have always been concentrated in the valleys and basins, at densities of 100 persons per square kilometer (km2) or more during the aboriginal period. They also have tended to be nucleated in urban centers, both "towns," with thousands of persons, and "cities," with tens of thousands of inhabitants. Population densities in the highland urban centers during aboriginal times were invariably greater than 2,000 persons per square kilometer (km2). Overall, the total population of the highland peoples of contact-period Mesoamerica may have numbered over 20 million persons, the vast majority of them residing in the highlands of Mexico.

Most of the minerals of importance to the aboriginal peoples of Mesoamerica occurred naturally in the highlands. Among these were metals (gold, silver, copper), obsidian, jadeite and other serpentine stones, amber, and volcanic stone for grinding tools. Salt, a necessary element in the diet of all peoples, came mostly from the lowlands, although there were a few briny sinks in the highlands from which salt could be extracted.

Lowlands.   The Mesoamerican peoples living in lowland ecological settings have been concentrated mainly along the eastern (Gulf of Mexico and Caribbean) and western (Pacific) coasts of the region. Soil fertility varies widely in the coastal lowland zones. Along the eastern coast, particularly in the Yucatán Peninsula, the limestone soils are generally thin and relatively infertile. The soils in the western lowlands tend to be more fertile as a result of volcanic deposition, especially in the piedmont areas. In general, the most fertile lowland soils consist of alluvial deposits formed by rivers flowing from the volcanic highlands down through the lowlands on their way to the two oceans.

The aboriginal inhabitants residing in lowland settings have usually adopted the slash-and-burn (swidden) system of horticulture. This system is based on an extensive technology in which the natural vegetation is cut and burned, after which maize, beans, and squash seeds are planted in holes punched by a simple digging stick. The Mesoamerican "trilogy" (maize, beans, and squash) is complemented in the lowlands by chiles, root crops (yucca, camote, sweet potatoes), and fruit trees (zapote, papaya, breadnut, cacao).

Lowland populations have tended to be more evenly scattered across the landscape than in the highlands, with overall densities in prehispanic times typically ranging from five to thirty persons per km2. The characteristic settlement pattern in the lowlands, even today, consists of a ceremonial-type center surrounded by dependent rural hamlets. Some urbanization has always existed in the lowlands, but generally in the form of towns rather than cities. At Spanish contact, the population of the lowlands together numbered around six million persons, roughly 20 percent of the total Mesoamerican population at that time.

The lowlands provided many exotic items of importance to the Mesoamericans. For example, bright feathers from tropical birds and pelts of the ocelot and other cats were obtained in large numbers. Hardwoods were available for construction and canoe making. From other trees rubber, copal incense, and dyes were extracted, whereas paper was manufactured from the bark of a large fig tree and an aromatic medicine was extracted from the balsam tree. There were many other dye plants in this area, including indigo, annatto, and genipap. Tobacco was cultivated and made into "rolled cigars," whereas the narcotic plant coca was grown in the far southern part of the lowland area.

It must be emphasized that the ecological zones of Mesoamerica, both past and present, were far more diverse than the general highland/lowland types just described. For example, research has shown that considerable intensification of agriculture—including terracing and "raised field" gardening—existed in some tropical lowland zones long before Spanish contact. Furthermore, within the highlands important ecological differences have always existed between temperate (Tierra Templada) and cold (Tierra Fría) zones. For example, in the cold highlands located at elevations above 2,000 meters, the maize growing season is shortened, whereas the pulque-producing maguey plant grows well. It is undoubtedly significant that the most powerful polities in the region, both past and present, have been located in the cold highlands.

Other important ecological differences result from the contrast between arid rather than humid lowland subzones. In the arid lowlands aboriginal Mesoamericans had to irrigate in order to obtain dependable maize production, whereas cacao could not be effectively grown even with irrigation. In contrast, cotton flourished in arid lowland zones. These and other ecological considerations help explain why some of the most powerful lowland polities of Mesoamerica were located in dry lowland subzones.

Natural Areas

With the basic highland/lowland division in mind, we will now briefly describe Mesoamerica's "natural areas," that is to say, subregional geographic divisions that define the critically important natural conditions for the inhabitants of the region. For the purposes of this study, five main natural areas warrant consideration (West 1964): (1) Northern Highlands, (2) Southern Highlands, (3) Gulf Coast Lowlands, (4) Pacific Coast Lowlands, and (5) Northern Mexico Dry Lands (Figure A.3). The geographic conditions of these five areas differ markedly from one another, and the peoples of the Mesoamerican region have had to adapt to them in fundamentally different ways.

Northern Highlands.   The Northern Highland area is composed of Mexico's Mesa Central, or Central Plateau, and the highlands of Oaxaca and Guerrero (Figure A.4). The Central Plateau has been a major focus of human activity within the Mesoamerican region for several thousand years. This remains true today: Mexico City is not

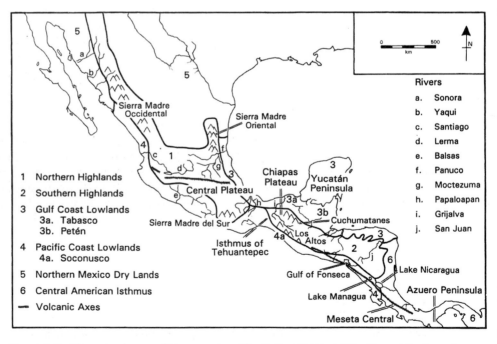

Figure A.3   The natural areas of Mesoamerica. After Robert C. West, "The Natural Regions of Middle America," *The Handbook of Middle American Indians, Volume I: Natural Environment and Early Cultures,* volume editor Robert C. West, general editor Robert Wauchope. Austin, TX: University of Texas Press, 1964, p. 368.

Figure A.4   Highland valley in Central Mexico. Photograph by the authors of the text.

only the largest and most important city of Mexico but is also now the second largest city in the world (only Tokyo is larger).

The Central Plateau is marked by volcanic features and unique hydrological patterns. A line of high volcanos, some of them still active, forms the southern rim; on the eastern flank is the Sierra Madre Oriental, whereas the Sierra Madre Occidental forms the western escarpment.

The plateau itself is pitted by both large, flat basins, many of which once contained lakes, and eroded volcanic peaks. Among the largest basins are Mexico, Puebla, Toluca, Guadalajara, and a series of linked basins that form the Bajío of Guanajuato. Many of the lakes no longer exist, some of them because of sedimentation and desiccation, and others—such as the five lakes in the Valley of Mexico—because of artificial draining. A few lakes, such as Lake Pátzcuaro in Michoacán, are still viable.

Much of the plateau itself lies in Tierra Templada, although the higher basins and surrounding mountains are Tierra Fría zones. Several of the volcanic peaks—such as Orizaba, Popocatepetl, Iztaccihuatl—are snow-covered year-round, and ice has been obtained from these peaks for centuries.

The Central Plateau is drained by three major river systems. With its headwaters in the Toluca Basin just west of Mexico City, the Lerma River flows west to the Pacific, forming the longest river system in the region. Tributaries of the Balsas River flow from basins in the southeastern portion of the plateau and drain into the Pacific Ocean. The Panuco River and its tributary, the Moctezuma River, form one of the largest drainage systems of Mexico's Atlantic watershed. Both rivers have their headwaters in the northeastern part of the Central Plateau.

The volcanic range that forms the southern boundary of the Central Plateau, overlooking the Balsas Depression formed by the Balsas River, defines the second highland zone of this area, composed of the Sierra Madre del Sur in Guerrero and the Mesa del Sur in Oaxaca. In contrast to the Central Plateau, there are few large, flat basins in this zone, which is instead covered by rugged mountain peaks and small, deep valleys. The Valley of Oaxaca, the largest basin, supported dense populations in the past and continues to do so today.

Much of the Central Plateau has been denuded of vegetation as a result of human activities. Once the area was covered with evergreen and deciduous oak forests. At higher elevations the mixed pine-oak forests gave way to stands of pines, firs, and junipers. At lower elevations grasses, scrub oak, cactus, acacia, and pirul (introduced from Peru in the sixteenth century) now dominate. The southern part of the Northern Highlands, like the Central Plateau, once supported cloud-forest vegetation, and in lower-lying arid valleys xerophytes (acacia and cacti) still predominate.

Neotropical (South American) fauna long ago invaded the Northern Highlands, including small numbers of such mammals as the peccary, tapir, spider monkey, jaguar, anteater, and armadillo. The Nearctic (North American) mammals native to the highlands include white-tailed deer, rabbits, squirrels, cougars, and pumas. The deer and peccary may have been the main mammals hunted and eaten in fairly large numbers in aboriginal times by Mesoamericans living in the Northern Highlands. Migratory birds (ducks, geese, teals), amphibians (frogs, salamanders), and small fish inhabited the many lakes of the Northern Highlands in times past, and were an important food source for aboriginal Mesoamericans.

Southern Highlands.   South of the Isthmus of Tehuantepec (Figure A.5) is a complex highland area framed by two mountain chains, a geologically older northern chain and a younger southern chain. The northern chain begins with the Chiapas plateau and continues southeast as the Cuchumatanes and Alta Verapaz mountains of

Figure A.5   Isthmus of Tehuantepec depression. Photograh by the authors of the text.

Guatemala. The intermontaine basins and plateaus formed by the northern chain—for instance, San Cristobal (Chiapas), Sacapulas (Guatemala)—are few in number and small (Figure A.6). The southern chain, volcanic in origin, begins with the Sierra Madre of Chiapas, continues southeastward as the Los Altos of Guatemala and the mountains of eastern Guatemala, Honduras, and northern Nicaragua. This southern chain provides the structural framework for numerous basins, valleys, and plateaus such as in Quezaltenango, Quiché, Guatemala, and Comayagua (the first three in Guatemala, the last in Honduras). In El Salvador and Nicaragua the southern volcanic chain is located in a transisthmian depression, and as a result the basins and valleys there are either low (for instance, Zapotitlán and San Salvador in El Salvador) or occupied by freshwater lakes (lakes Managua and Nicaragua in Nicaragua).

Most of the Southern Highlands fall into the Tierra Templada zone, although there is a small zone of Tierra Fría in Chiapas and western Guatemala. The highlands subzones are mostly subhumid, with fringes of humid pockets and a few arid river valleys (Grijalva in Chiapas, Motagua in Guatemala, and Catacamas in Honduras). In the western parts of the Southern Highlands, there is a distinct dry period (December through April), whereas in eastern parts rainfall tends to occur year-round.

Natural vegetation in the Southern Highlands mainly consists of mountain forest, typically made up of oaks and pines. Nearctic animals are less common in this area than in the Northern Highlands, whereas neotropical animals (tapirs, monkeys, etc.) are more common. Some bright-feathered trogan birds are found exclusively in the Southern Highlands, notably the quetzal.

Figure A.6   Highland mountains and valleys in Guatemala. Photograph by the authors of the text.

Gulf Coast Lowlands. This lowland area is part of a coastal plain that runs along the Gulf Coast of Mexico all the way to South America. The broad central zone is made up of the Tabasco Plains, the Petén Lowlands, and the Yucatán Peninsula. Narrower coasts are found to the north in Tamaulipas and Veracruz (Mexico) and south in Guatemala and northern Honduras. In the past the area was covered with dense evergreen rain forest, broken in places by savanna grasslands (as in eastern Tabasco, northern Yucatán, southern Petén).

In many places the coastal plains are cut by rivers flowing from the adjacent highlands, forming deltas and levees as the rivers slow down on their course to the Gulf of Mexico and the Caribbean Sea (especially in Tamaulipas, Tabasco, Belize, and the Gulf coasts of Guatemala and Honduras). Long stretches of the northern shoreline have "barrier beaches" that enclose lagoons and tidal swamps, whereas offshore sand bars and reefs are common, especially off the west coast of Yucatán and the coast of Belize.

The Gulf Coast Lowlands form part of the Tierra Caliente hot zone. Temperatures are high year-round, and rainfall is heavy. Most of the area is humid, and rain falls during all months of the year. Although humid, some zones such as the Petén, are drier during the first two or three months of the year. Northern Yucatán consists of a subhumid subzone to the east and an arid subzone to the west.

The natural vegetation of most of the Gulf Coast Lowlands is tropical forest. A canopy is formed by giant mahogany, ceiba, and wild fig trees, whereas below are found smaller but useful trees such as the palm, ramón (breadnut), rubber, mamey, sapodilla, and logwood. The patches of savanna are covered with grass and pines, except in northwestern Yucatán, where the vegetation is xerophytic scrub.

The fauna of the Gulf Coast area consists largely of neotropical animals. Most of the mammals and marsupials are arboreal—monkeys, sloths, opossums, coatis—but there are also ground dwellers such as tapirs, peccaries, brocket deer, and pacas. The main predators are jaguars, ocelots, and jaguarundis. Bright-feathered birds are numerous (some 500 species), including macaws, parrots, toucans, and trogons. Game birds, such as tinamous and cassarows, and numerous migratory waterfowl are common. Several varieties of poisonous snakes inhabit the area, whereas other reptiles like the iguana and marine turtle (five species) are good sources of food. The waters off the coast of the northern lowlands (especially off the coast of Tabasco, the west coast of Yucatán, and the coast of Belize) are rich in fish (for instance, mullets, grey snappers), crabs, shrimp, oysters, and manatee sea mammals.

Pacific Coast Lowlands. The Pacific coastal lowlands, starting in the north at Sinaloa and extending southward to the Nicoya Peninsula, form a second Mesoamerican lowland area. This natural area consists of plains, hills, and volcanic slopes, which in some zones, such as Soconusco and Guatemala, is divided into distinct piedmont and plains areas. The Pacific Coast Lowland area is generally traversed by relatively short, fast-flowing rivers that lay down smaller levee and delta depositions than in the Caribbean lowlands. The largest of these rivers are the Lerma-Santiago and Balsas of central Mexico. The coastline has many tidal swamp zones, the most extensive existing in El Salvador (Gulf of Fonseca, Jilquilisco Lagoon), Guatemala, and Soconusco. Some of the tidal areas form natural canals that were probably used as aquatic transportation routes in aboriginal times. High winds offshore make ocean travel very dangerous on the Pacific side, but the winds also stir up the coastal waters and enhance the availability of marine life.

The Pacific Coast Lowlands fall into the Tierra Caliente zone, but they receive less annual rainfall than the Caribbean lowlands and have a distinct dry season. Most of the area is subhumid, although the piedmont is largely humid and the coastal plain may vary from subhumid to arid. The rainfall pattern results in a natural deciduous forest cover of palm, broadleaf, fig, and dyewood trees. Savannas along the Pacific Coast are small and scattered, and may be artificial creations caused by human activities. In the piedmont and river floodplains, the natural vegetation has the appearance of rain forest, with giant guanacaste, ceiba, mahogany, and cedar trees. The natural vegetation of the coastal plains is deciduous forest, or thorny scrub in arid areas. The tidal swamp zones are covered by mangrove forests. The fauna of the Pacific Coast Lowlands is predominantly neotropical, similar to the animals of the Gulf Coast Lowlands already described.

Northern Mexico Dry Lands.   This area was the largest arid zone of the entire region, and stretched across the northern part of present-day Mexico on the eastern and western sides of the Sierra Madre Occidental. This area always served as a corridor between the Mesoamericans and the village farmers of the southwestern United States (for instance, the Pueblo peoples), although travel has never been easy in this desert country (Figure A.7).

The part of the Northern Dry Lands on the eastern side of the Sierra Madre Occidental is an extension of the Central Plateau, and topographically it consists of a long series of high desert basins. Some of the basins were once covered with lakes; but by the time of Spanish contact, most were dry, and many were caked with salt at their lowest points. Daytime temperatures tend to be very high in this zone, but nighttime temperatures often drop below freezing during winter. These temperature extremes, combined with very low precipitation, result in an extremely harsh environment. In the sections immediately adjacent to the Sierra Madre Occidental, the natural setting is more favorable, since daytime temperatures are lower, rainfall is higher, and numerous streams flowing from the foothills leave fertile alluvial deposits along the margins of the basins.

On the western side of the Sierra Madre Occidental, in the present-day Mexican states of Sonora and Sinaloa, is found a much lower extension of the Northern Mexico Dry Lands. Temperatures in this zone are higher than anywhere else in the entire region, even though winter frosts sometimes occur; and rainfall is even scarcer than in the higher zone on the eastern side of the mountains. The harsh environment is ameliorated somewhat by large rivers that flow westward across this desert zone from the Sierra Madre Occidental. The main rivers, the Sinaloa, Fuerte, Yaqui, and Sonora, create narrow valleys in which rich alluvial soils are deposited two times each year.

Vegetation on the eastern side of the Sierra Madre Occidental is xerophytic, made up largely of low, widely dispersed plants such as yucca, agaves, and cacti (including

Figure A.7   High plateau country of Northern Mexico. Photograph by the authors of the text.

the edible prickly-pear cactus). Clumps of mesquite (whose pods are edible) and yucca trees can be found in places with alluvial deposits. Peyote grows naturally in the zone. Adjacent to the mountains, the streams are lined with cypress, cottonwood, mesquite, and willow trees. In the low desert zone west of the Sierra Madre Occidental, the vegetation is more lush and arboreal. Furthermore, the rich river valleys there have been cultivated in maize, beans, and other crops since before Spanish contact. Nearctic animals such as deer and rabbits were once abundant in the more lush parts of the area, and they provided an important component of the inhabitants' diet in aboriginal times. A few neotropical animals were also present, such as the jaguar, peccary, and armadillo.

A sixth natural area, which largely falls outside the region occupied by the Mesoamericans but nevertheless has been important to them, is the Central American Isthmus. Its geographic features are described in Box A.2.

Biological Characteristics of the Mesoamericans

It needs to be stated from the outset that biological differences did not provide an important basis for social distinctions in the Mesoamerican world prior to the coming of the Spaniards. In general, the Mesoamericans themselves gave little social importance to skin color or biological features. Nor did the Spanish conquistadors observe major physical differences between the various Mesoamerican peoples,

Box A.2 The Central American Isthmus

The narrow territory of present-day Nicaragua, Costa Rica, and Panama forms a "bridge" that connects Middle America with South America, and this natural area has played an important role in the history of the Mesoamerican peoples. The Central American Isthmus is constituted by a central highland zone, which is formed by a continuation of the Southern Highland volcanic axis, flanked by Caribbean and Pacific lowlands that are structurally part of the Pacific Coast and Gulf Coast Lowlands already described. The most distinguishing natural feature of the area is its narrowness; it is less than 100 kilometers wide in many places. The highland strip occupies a relatively reduced part of the Isthmus area, and except for the Meseta Central of Costa Rica, the highland basins are relatively small and low in elevation. Furthermore, the Isthmus highlands are broken in several places, making coast-to-coast travel in the area relatively easy. The coastal lowlands on both sides of the Isthmus are more mountainous than in their northern extensions, and in many places the mountain cliffs drop off into the sea. These coastlines are also very irregular, with numerous peninsulas, gulfs, lagoons, cays, and reefs.

The Isthmus is predominantly a Tierra Caliente humid subzone, in both the highlands (except for the Tierra Templada zone of the Meseta Central in Costa Rica) and the two coastal lowlands. Some areas of the Caribbean and Pacific lowlands are the wettest in the entire region. Rain falls throughout the year in most of the Isthmus, although in southern Nicaragua, Guanacaste, the Meseta Central of Costa Rica, and the Pacific Coast east of Azuero in Panama there is a distinct dry period resulting in subhumid conditions.

It is not surprising that the natural vegetation of most of the Isthmus is tropical rain forest, the strip of highland mountain forest again being the major exception. Two important savanna zones are Guanacaste in northwestern Costa Rica and Panama's "interior," stretching west of the Canal zone and north of the Azuero peninsula. As might be expected, the Isthmus fauna is predominantly neotropical.

The Central American Isthmus area is endowed with important exotic natural resources that have long been of interest to the Mesoamerican peoples. Perhaps the most important of these in aboriginal times was gold, substantial veins of which exist in the Guanacaste, Osa, and the Chiriquí mountains. Other isthmian resources were typical of lowland areas: hardwoods, animal pelts, bright plumage, sea shells (including the murex shell from which a purple dye was extracted), salt, cacao, cotton, and special medicinal and narcotic plants (including coca).

certainly none comparable to the rather dramatic contrasts found in the Old World between Europeans, Africans, and Asians.

The Spaniards described the Mesoamerican peoples as being racially similar one group to another, made up of relatively small, brown-skinned peoples. For example, in one report by the first explorers of Yucatán, the Mayas were described as of "middle height and well proportioned," whereas the Emperor Motecuhzoma was portrayed by one of Cortés's soldiers as "of good height and well proportioned, slender and spare of flesh, not very swarthy, but of the natural colour and shade of an Indian." Both Spanish and native sources agree, however, that artificial alteration of physical appearance was of the utmost social importance in the Mesoamerican world. Social status was marked by facial painting; body scarification; hair styling; and pierced noses, ears, and lips, into which adornments were inserted.

Modern biological studies reveal that the Mesoamericans share important genetic features with Asian peoples. Nevertheless, the aboriginal Mesoamericans also had external physical features that differentiated them genetically from the Asians, as, for example, high frequencies of the convex nose type, absence of the mongoloid eye fold, and presence of wavy hair. Studies of genetically linked blood types have revealed that the aboriginal Mesoamericans lacked the Blood Type B found among Asians, and perhaps they were universally Blood Type O. This finding suggests that the Mesoamericans had long been separated from their distant relatives in Asia and that they were biologically rather homogeneous.

In aboriginal times, there must have been considerable genetic contact between populations within the Mesoamerican region but limited contacts outside of it. One modest biological variation that existed within the Mesoamerican region took the form of populations in the northern part being larger and stockier than those in the southern part. This difference may have been primarily due to the fact that on average, northern peoples inhabited highland settings, whereas their southern counterparts were widely distributed across lowland zones.

The arrival of the Spaniards to the region in the sixteenth century initiated a complex process of biological and demographic change in the native Mesoamerican populations. The indigenous populations were subjected to Old World diseases, against which they lacked strong natural immunities. At the same time, miscegenation (interbreeding) began to take place, creating new biological types with mixed genetic ancestry.

For the native populations of the Americas, including the Mesoamericans, contact with the Europeans and the African slaves resulted in demographic disaster. In many areas of the Mesoamerican region, 90 percent or more of the indigenous population died during the first decades of Spanish rule, leaving survivors with profoundly disrupted social worlds. Whereas in some areas the native populations began to recover by late in the sixteenth century, in other areas the recovery did not begin until the eighteenth century, and in still other places the Indian populations eventually disappeared altogether. The arrival of Spaniards and Africans, most of whom were men, led to unions with the native Mesoamericans throughout the region. This outcome resulted in postcontact populations made up not only of Spaniards and Indians, but also of a host of biologically mixed peoples ("mestizos") who did not fit neatly into either Spanish or Indian racial types. In time this process of miscegenation became even more complex, as new immigrants came to the region from other parts of Europe, Asia, and the Middle East.

The population of the Mesoamerican region today is a reflection of its demographic history. In many areas the population has remained predominantly Indian, and in certain cases the native Mesoamericans have expanded beyond their pre-Hispanic demographic levels. Thus, some 500 years after the demographic disaster initiated during the sixteenth century, the Indians of the Mesoamerican region appear to have finally surpassed their aboriginal population numbers (see Figure A.8).

The immigrant population as well as the mixed (mestizo) populations have grown at an even more rapid pace than the native Mesoamericans in the region,

YEAR	1520	1800	1900	1950	2000
Mexico	21	4	2	3	30
Central America	6	1	1	4	8
Totals	27	5	3	7	38

Note: All figures are approximations, especially for the pre-Hispanic period. For the 2000 figures, see *The World Almanac and Book of Facts*, 2005.

Figure A.8   Changes in native population size in the Mesoamerican Region (in millions of native persons).

especially in the urban centers, where a glance at a crowded street in Mexico or Central America reveals the complex biological makeup of much of its modern populations. The so-called mestizos and Whites now form the ethnic majority in these countries, rapidly approaching 100 million persons in total numbers.

PAST STUDIES OF MESOAMERICA

The summary of Mesoamerican history and culture to follow in this text builds on the labor of numerous scholars who have gone before us. Because the legacy of past studies is not one of information alone but is also of particular interpretations of that information, we have chosen to organize the following historical sketch according to the diverse approaches to Mesoamerica that have been taken through time. We warn the reader that space does not permit us to do justice to the full history of Mesoamerican studies and that the account here is meant to be illustrative rather than exhaustive.

Let us begin the review with the "Romanticists," writers who approached the study of Mesoamerica with preconceived notions, usually based on strong religious or philosophical views. Next we discuss the "Scientific Precursors," students of Mesoamerica who employed a more systematic and objective approach. They became particularly influential toward the end of the nineteenth century, and they began to replace religious ideas with scientific theories. A modern scientific approach emerged gradually during the twentieth century, carried forward at first by the "Culture Historians," and after 1950 by the "Cultural Evolutionists." The historical and evolutionary approaches continue to be influential in Mesoamerican studies today, and we will argue in the final section of this introduction that our own approach in general terms might be seen in part to be a synthesis of these two approaches.

Romanticists

From the time of Columbus to the present day, an unending stream of Western writers has concocted fanciful explanations for the origin and cultural achievements of the Mesoamerican Indians. We refer to them as Romanticists because their ideas have been highly speculative and for the most part have been based on preconceived religious notions about how they would like the world to be rather than how it actually is. Almost all these explanations are ethnocentric, rooted in the belief that cultural sophistication could be achieved only by Europeans, and therefore that Mesoamerica's cultural developments ultimately must have derived from ideas originating outside the region. The romantic explanations of Mesoamerica have not stood the test of time, but they continue to be proposed and to have ardent defenders even today.

Sundry priests, scholars, and dilettantes at one time or another have proposed nearly every conceivable place in the Old World as the original homeland of the Mesoamericans: Phoenicia, Egypt, Israel, India, China, Africa, Ireland, Germany, and even Rome. It is not surprising that most of the first Spanish priests who administered in the Mesoamerican region were of the opinion that the Indians were derived from biblical peoples. The most common view was that the Indians had descended from wandering Hebrews, and in particular the Lost Ten Tribes of Israel. This view was not universally accepted, however, as illustrated by the case of the erudite Franciscan priest Juan de Torquemada (A.D. 1564–1624). Torquemada (1943:I:25), who labored for many years in Mexico, rejected the claim that the Indians were descended from the Hebrews, noting that "if these Indians were Jews, why only in the Indies have they forgotten their language, their law, their ceremonies, their Messiah and finally their Judaism?" Nevertheless, Torquemada's own explanation of the Mesoamericans was both biblical and racist: As a dark-skinned people, they must have descended from Noah's son, Ham.

In more recent times, the Church of Jesus Christ of Latter Day Saints (the Mormons) teach as part of their official doctrine that certain descendants of Noah, Judah, and Joseph emigrated from the Middle East to the New World many centuries before Christ, laying the foundation for ancient Mesoamerican cultures of Mexico and Central America. The doctrine retains racist features, in claiming that the less righteous immigrants failed to prosper and became dark-skinned (the Lamanites), whereas the righteous prospered and remained light-skinned (the Nephites).

Quetzalcoatl, the Mesoamerican priestly ruler and feathered serpent deity, has been a particularly appealing figure for the Romanticists working within the biblical tradition. Some of the early Spanish and native documents describe Quetzalcoatl as a light-skinned, bearded, holy man. Catholic scholars have often identified him with St. Thomas or St. Bartholomew, who, according to tradition, traveled to India and beyond to the Americas to do missionary work. Mormon scholars find in Quetzalcoatl evidence for their belief that Jesus Christ visited the Americas in ancient times, citing as evidence the Mesoamerican tradition that Quetzalcoatl was a holy man whose symbol was the serpent (the Bible associates Jesus Christ with the serpent lifted up by Moses).

Almost as popular as the biblical tradition among Romanticists has been the idea that the Mesoamerican Indians came from continents that long ago sank to the bottom of the sea. It is noteworthy that the Lost Continent advocates share with the biblical Romanticists the belief that the Mesoamericans could not have independently developed their elaborate civilization. The most common version of the Lost Continent tradition held that a large continent known as Atlantis once existed in the ocean west of Europe, inhabited by an energetic people who created an advanced civilization (Figure A.9). Massive earthquakes and floods caused Atlantis to sink to the bot-

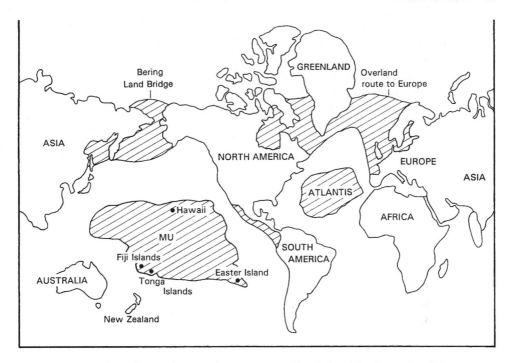

Figure A.9   Hypothetical map of ancient lost continents. After Robert Wauchope, *Lost Tribes and Sunken Continents: Myth and Method in the Study of American Indians.* Chicago, IL: University of Chicago Press, 1962, p. 37.

tom of the ocean, but not before its inhabitants escaped to America and other continents and then gave rise to the major civilizations of the ancient world. The story of Atlantis was an old one going back to Plato, who wrote that it had been told to Solon by Egyptian priests many years before. With the "discovery" of America by Columbus, interest in Atlantis was revived, some Spaniards claiming that America was the remains of the sunken continent mentioned by Plato. Box A.3 discusses some of the more interesting theories about the Lost Continent origin of the Mesoamerican peoples.

Box A.3   Lost-Continent Romanticists

The idea that the Mesoamerican and other advanced civilizations originated in Atlantis was popularized by a series of remarkably romantic figures. One of these was Ignatius T. T. Donnelly, a U.S. Congressman who in his 1880 book, *Atlantis: The Antediluvian World* argued that Plato's Atlantis was not only real but also was the original Garden of Eden and the place from which Mexico and all the continents were populated. By 1949, Donnelly's book had already undergone fifty printings!

(continued)

(continued)

An even more remarkable proponent of the Atlantis tale was the French physician and adventurer Augustus Le Plongeon. During visits to Yucatán, Mexico, Le Plongeon became interested in the Mayan culture. An erroneous reading of one of the Mayan codices (scroll books) led Le Plongeon to believe that he had found a lost history of Atlantis. The history allegedly described how Atlantis was split by civil war, the losing faction fleeing the continent and going on to found the Egyptian and Mayan civilizations. In contrast to other Romanticists, Le Plongeon argued that the Mesoamericans colonized Egypt rather than the reverse!

A few of the Atlantis advocates, such as the Scottish mythologist Lewis Spence (1925), attempted to square the tale with scientific findings. But most of the believers in Atlantis were hopelessly speculative. This was the case with Helena Blavatsky, the founder of the Theosophy religion, who claimed that one of the seven "Root Races" of humanity came from Atlantis. Upon fleeing the sinking continent, she said, the Atlantis race gave rise to various groups of people, among them Cro-Magnons, Semites, and the "handsome 8-feet tall" Toltecs of ancient Mexico!

The most outrageous of the Lost Continent Romanticists, however, was James Churchward, who created a continent in the Pacific Ocean out of whole cloth. "Colonel" Churchward's so-called "Continent of Mu" was said to measure 5,000 miles long and 3,000 miles wide. About 80,000 years ago its inhabitants began to emigrate in waves, headed for the utmost bounds of the world. One of these migratory groups, the so-called "Quetzals," was made up of "stalwart, young adventurers with milk-white skins, blue eyes, and light flaxen hair." They settled in Yucatán and gave rise to the great Mayan civilization.

The romantic tradition lives on today, most strikingly in the preposterous writings of Erich von Daniken. Von Daniken has achieved a large following by proposing that ancient astronauts from faraway galaxies visited the ancient Mesoamericans and introduced them to many technological and ideological innovations. A principal piece of evidence for von Daniken's theory is an image portrayed on the lid of a tomb at the Mayan site of Palenque, Mexico (Figure A.10). Von Daniken argues that this image can be none other than an ancient astronaut sitting at the controls, ready for takeoff! Like so many Romanticists before him, von Daniken seems to assume that the Mayas and other Mesoamerican peoples were incapable of creating complex cultures on their own, and so needed enlightenment from faraway places.

The old Romantic notion that ancient Mesoamerica was deeply influenced by peoples from Africa has resurfaced in a somewhat repackaged form. This may be seen as part of an effort to better understand the rich cultural heritage of Africa and to recognize the many contributions that Africans have made to Western civilization. For some zealous proponents of African culture, the effort has evolved into a form of Afrocentrism. They have speculated that the Mesoamerican cultures were influenced by Africans who came to the Americas before Spanish contact, introducing important elements of the African cultures to the Mesoamerican peoples. According to one claim, the main African influence occurred during the time of the Olmecs (ca. 900–400 B.C.), as suggested by the reputed African-like facial features of large stone heads carved by Olmec artists.

Like many other Romantic notions, the idea of an African origin for the Mesoamerican civilization stems more from ideological agenda than from scientific evidence. To date there is no credible evidence to support the claim that Africans somehow influenced the Olmecs or any other pre-Hispanic Mesoamerican peoples.

©1976 MERLE GREENE ROBERTSON

Figure A.10 Sarcophagus lid from the Classic-period Maya site of Palenque, Mexico. According to von Daniken, this carving portrays an ancient astronaut. Courtesy of Merle Greene Robertson, Copyright © 1973.

Scientific Precursors

Not all the early writers on the Mesoamerican Indians were Romanticists. For example, the famous sixteenth-century Dominican missionary Bartolomé de Las Casas (1958:105:69–72), rejected the Romantic notion that the Indians were descended from the Lost Tribes of Israel on the grounds that the languages and cultures of Mesoamerica were unlike those of the ancient Hebrews. He argued instead that the New World was an extension of the posterior part of Oriental India and that the Indians were thus "natural" to the American continent (Figure A.11). Another Spanish priest, the Jesuit José de Acosta (A.D. 1540–1600), also denied any connection between the American Indians and biblical peoples. Like Las Casas, Acosta (1987) concluded on rational grounds that the New World must have been connected to the

Figure A.11 Painting of the defender of the Indians, Fray Bartolomé de Las Casas. James A. Magner, *Men of Mexico,* 2nd ed. Salem, NH: Books for Libraries, Ayer Company Publishers, 1968.

Old World and that its first inhabitants immigrated there "by land, which might be done without consideration in changing little by little their lands and habitations."

Objective thinkers like Las Casas and Acosta, of course, were the exceptions until the nineteenth century, when more "positivist" scholars gradually began to push aside the highly fanciful and religious interpretations of Mesoamerica being put forward by the Romanticists. In growing numbers, the Scientific Precursors began to argue that the Mesoamerican peoples had developed their civilization independently from the peoples of the Old World or Lost Continents. Nevertheless, a truly scientific orientation came slowly, at first consisting mainly of applying somewhat more secular and systematic techniques to the study of Mesoamerica.

The forerunners to the scholars who would later produce modern accounts of Mesoamerica were people (and with few exceptions they were all males) like Alexander von Humboldt, John Lloyd Stephens, and Charles Étienne Brasseur de Bourbourg, to name a few. These men kept the study of Mesoamerican history and culture alive and provided new perspectives on the topic, although it is doubtful that they much advanced our knowledge beyond where the Spaniards had left it in previous centuries.

Humboldt, the son of a Prussian major, was perhaps the most renowned scientist of his time. He traveled throughout the Americas during the first years of the nineteenth century, making observations on geological and other physical phenomena of the two continents. In Mexico he studied firsthand numerous archaeological remains and native codices, which he correctly interpreted as "fragments of history." In Humboldt's (1814) account of his studies in Mexico, he concluded that the evidence failed to support the claim that the Mesoamericans had descended from biblical peoples. Rather, in physical appearance and culture they were closest to the Asians. He particularly called attention to the similarity between the ancient Mexican calendar cycle of fifty-two years and the Asian calendrical cycle of sixty years. In addition, six of the Mexican day signs corresponded to the Zodiac signs of Asia, namely, tiger, rabbit, serpent, monkey, dog, and bird. Humboldt's scientific credentials and objective methods of studying ancient Mesoamerica inspired all subsequent Scientific Precursors.

Another influential precursor was the North American lawyer John Lloyd Stephens. Traveling throughout southern Mexico and Central America between 1839 and 1841, Stephens and his artist colleague Frederick Catherwood made systematic observations, drawings, and maps of many of the most important archaeological sites in the southern Mesoamerican region (Stephens 1841). The drawings and descriptions provided new information on ancient Mayan architecture, settlement patterns, religious symbols, calendrics, and hieroglyphic writing. Although Stephens erroneously thought that most of the remains dated from the period of Spanish contact, he correctly concluded that the original sites were built by the ancestors of the natives who still inhabited the area in the nineteenth century. This conclusion motivated Stephens to record some customs of these native peoples—for example, their making ritual offerings inside caves—which in turn inspired subsequent students of Mesoamerica to search for persisting native customs as a way to reconstruct the aboriginal past.

Box A.4 recounts the contributions made by one of the key transitional figures between the Romanticists and the Precursors, the French scholar and priest Brasseur de Bourbourg.

Box A.4 Brasseur de Bourbourg, a Scientific Precursor

Brasseur de Bourbourg served as parish priest in Guatemala for many years in the mid–nineteenth century, during which time he also traveled extensively in Mexico. He obtained copies of numerous native documents important for studying the aboriginal Mesoamerican cultures. Brasseur was erudite, and he probably had access to more documentary and archaeological information on Mesoamerica than anyone else of his time. Unfortunately, many of his interpretations of history lacked objectivity and in some cases were downright speculative. For example, in Brasseur's (1857–1859) writings, petty Mesoamerican kingdoms were transformed into powerful empires, small towns into huge cities, minor priests into mighty prophets, and princely revolts into bourgeois revolutions. Nevertheless, Brasseur's general summary of events taking place in Mexico and Central America before the conquest was profoundly secular in orientation, and possibly constituted the most exhaustive historical treatise on the subject ever attempted up to that time. Unfortunately, during the last years of his life, Brasseur yielded to the lure of the Lost Continent of Atlantis tale in order to explain the origins of the Mesoamerican civilization. He died a broken man, his new "theories" rejected by the emerging scientific community in Europe and the United States.

The final decades of the nineteenth century and beginning decades of the twentieth century laid the groundwork for the development of a truly modern approach to Mesoamerican studies. The number of scholars engaged in this study rapidly expanded, and the methods of research became increasingly specialized. In particular, formal excavations of archaeological sites helped create a Mesoamerican "archaeology," while expertise in documentary texts and written native languages helped give rise to a Mesoamerican "ethnohistory." Most studies of aboriginal Mesoamerica have been carried forward in recent years by archaeologists and ethnohistorians, although other specialists such as linguists, epigraphers, geographers, historians, and ethnographers have also made major contributions. As already noted, many of these early scientific scholars at first applied a culture history model in their studies of ancient Mesoamerica.

Culture Historians

The approach to Mesoamerica taken by the Culture Historians represented an important advance over that of the Romanticists and Scientific Precursors, who tended to explain the aboriginal cultures as transplants (diffusions) from somewhere else, usually Asia, Europe, or a Lost Continent. Most Culture Historians, in contrast, accepted the indigenous source of the Mesoamerican cultures and concentrated on determining the origins and changes of cultures within the Mesoamerican region. Mesoamerica was viewed as a unified geographic area in which the diverse peoples shared distinctive customs or cultural traits. These traits set them apart from the peoples of other "culture areas." Culture areas were thought to have common historical traditions, the study of which would provide a way to explain the particular combination of traits that characterized each area.

The Mexican scholar Paul Kirchhoff (1943) provided the best-known application of the culture historical approach to the pre-Spanish natives of Mesoamerica. Kirchhoff placed most of the peoples of Mexico and Central America within the "Mesoamerican" culture area, and he defined the area by the languages spoken and the presence of a long list of cultural traits. Essential or diagnostic traits of the Mesoamerican culture area for Kirchhoff included the lake gardens (*chinampas*), cacao, bark paper, obsidian-edged swords, stepped pyramids, writing, solar calendars, ritualized human sacrifice, and long-distance trade. The native peoples in the northern part of Mexico, on the one hand, and the southeastern part of Central America, on the other, were said to have spoken different languages and to have exhibited distinct cultural traits. Thus, they constituted separate culture areas from Mesoamerica: namely, the "Southwest" culture area to the north, and the "Chibcha" culture area to the south (Figure A.12).

Much of the research on Mesoamerica by the Culture Historians centered on the so-called Olmec culture, initially reconstructed through excavations at the archaeological site of La Venta in Tabasco, Mexico. The Olmec culture provided the Culture Historians with a key to the origin of the Mesoamerican civilization. Olmec

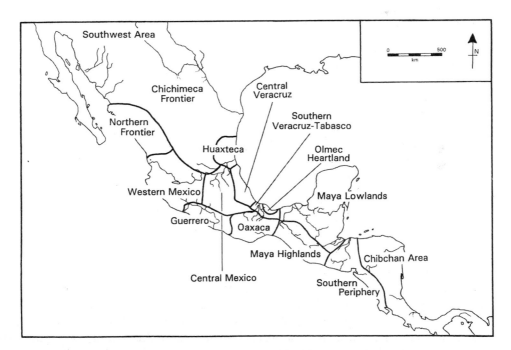

Figure A.12 Mesoamerican culture area and its main subareas. After Gordon R. Willey, et al., "The Patterns of Farming Life and Civilizations," in *The Handbook of Middle Americans, Volume I: National Environment and Early Cultures*, volume editor Robert C. West, general editor Robert Wauchope. Austin, Texas: University of Texas Press, 1964, p. 461.

culture was known to be very old (it was thought to have appeared around 900 B.C.), yet it already exhibited most of the essential traits of the Mesoamerican culture area, for example, pyramids, carved monuments, sacred calendars, exquisite jade pieces, and pottery craft items. Quite understandably, the Culture Historians concluded that the Olmec culture was the "mother culture" from which all other Mesoamerican cultures descended.

For several decades a focal point of Mesoamerican studies consisted of tracing the historical connections between the Olmec culture and other cultures appearing through time within the region. For example, the Mexican archaeologist-artist Miguel Covarrubias (1957) was able to demonstrate that the various Mesoamerican rain deities were derived from an original Olmec were-jaguar deity (Figure A.13). Other scholars found historical links between the Olmec calendrical system and those of the Mayas and Zapotecs. Special attention was given to Olmec religious, artistic, and intellectual expressions rather than to the material conditions that might have influenced the development of those cultural expressions. As one Culture Historian put it, "The most uniquely distinctive Mesoamerican features are not so much material as they are ideological, and it was this ideological realm—a kind of Mesoamerican world view" that was developed early on by the Olmecs and gave Mesoamerica its traditional unity (Willey 1966:108).

Another focus for the Culture Historians was the traditional Indian community of contemporary Mexico and Central America. Numerous "ethnographic" studies of individual Indian communities revealed that many of the Mesoamerican cultural traits had persisted into modern times. In an important summary of community studies, Sol Tax (1952) argued that the Mesoamerican culture area had remained largely intact despite modifications resulting from contacts with modern forces from the outside. In the 1960s and 1970s, a more general summary of over half a century of culture historical studies on Mesoamerica appeared in the twelve-volume *Handbook of Middle American Indians*. The *Handbook* essays dealt with both aboriginal and contemporary culture areas of Mesoamerica.

In retrospect, it is clear that the Culture Historians tended to see culture as primarily consisting of values and ideas, and thus their primary concern was with the *essential* features rather than the *material* determinants of the Mesoamerican cultures. For this reason the culture historical approach has been widely criticized as "idealist." Another tendency was to study contemporary Indian communities as isolated, self-contained units in which traditional cultural traits only gradually changed through contact with outside peoples, a process known as "acculturation." Eventually, it was recognized that the focus on isolated communities resulted in a perspective that was too static and thus insufficiently historical.

Cultural Evolutionists

By mid–twentieth century, a general turning away from culture history was taking place in Mesoamerican studies, partly because that earlier approach focused so much on ideas rather than behavior, and partly because it described cultural differences between peoples and areas without providing an explanation of these differences. There

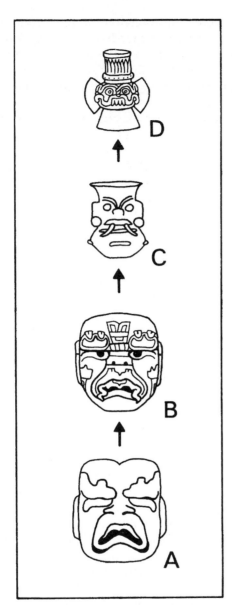

Figure A.13   Sequence (steps A–D) by which the Olmec were-jaguar motif was transformed into later religious motifs of Mesoamerica. Adapted from Miguel Covarrubias, *Indian Art of Mexico and Central America*. New York: Alfred A. Knopf, 1957, p. 62.

emerged in the social sciences a strong theoretical movement that focused attention more on behavior than on ideas, specifically, the behaviors by which human groups exploit their material environment. Cultures, according to this perspective, are best seen as adaptive mechanisms by which human populations conform to ever-changing environmental conditions. The adaptive changes engaged in by groups of people constitute cultural evolution, and they result in either divergence or convergence between cultures. Studies of particular cultural divergences are referred to as "specific evolution," whereas examples of cultural convergence—demonstrated by comparing different cases of adaptation around the world—are termed "general evolution."

An important early application of the cultural evolutionary approach to aboriginal Mesoamerica was carried out by the American anthropologist Julian Steward (1949). Steward presented an evolutionary sequence for Mesoamerica consisting of the following developmental stages:

> *Hunting and Gathering.* Simple food-gathering technology gives rise to bands of hunters and gatherers.
> *Incipient Agriculture.* Domestication of plants lays the foundation for settled village life.
> *Formative.* Increasingly intense farming provides the basis for the growth of villages into towns.
> *Regional Florescence.* Complex irrigation works promote population growth, cities, and highly stratified society.
> *Cyclical Conquests.* The use of metals and an increase in trade lead to conditions that promote endemic warfare between societies.

Steward compared the specific Mayan and Central Mexican evolutionary sequences in Mesoamerica with similar sequences in other regions of the world where ancient civilizations had developed, and he argued for their convergent evolution. He found the explanation for evolutionary convergences in the development of similar irrigation and other advanced subsistence technologies within similar ecological conditions. In particular, he applied his theory to the semiarid river valleys of Mesopotamia, Egypt, China, Peru, and Mexico. The Mesoamerican civilization, then, was defined not in terms of shared cultural traits but rather as a series of evolving evolutionary stages resulting from adaptive responses to a particular environmental setting.

Following Steward's lead, the evolutionary approach has been widely adopted in the study of Mesoamerican cultures. For example, whereas the Culture Historians had defined the aboriginal lowland Mayas as virtually unique in their cultural patterns and historical development, Cultural Evolutionists like William Sanders and Barbara Price (1968) argued that far from being unique, the Mayan advances were actually based on ecological adaptations common to Mesoamerica as a whole. Specifically, populations in Central Mexico had adapted to the semiarid conditions of the Teotihuacan Valley by constructing an elaborate irrigation system, and upon this material foundation the powerful, urban Teotihuacan civilization was constructed. Evolutionarily advanced Teotihuacán then became the material base for the development of advanced cultural features by the interconnected lowland Mayas located far to the south. The subsequent collapse of the Teotihuacan civilization around A.D. 700, followed by a transition to a new evolutionary stage in Central Mexico, was again used to explain the dramatic Mayan cultural collapse 200 years later in the southern lowlands. Sanders and Price concluded that without the evolutionary developments of Teotihuacan, Mayan cultural evolution would have remained at a chiefdom stage, which is precisely what happened to many of the peoples falling outside the Mesoamerican regional sphere.

The Cultural Evolutionists brought the Mesoamericans down to earth, so to speak, and forced scholars to see the region's cultures as rooted in material factors and as being generically similar to cultures throughout the world. Rather than cultural ideas and cosmologies determining behavior, behavior oriented to the production of food determines, or at least conditions, culture. The Cultural Evolutionists also shifted the focus of Mesoamerican studies away from isolated Indian communities to macrosocial units, such as ecologically diverse regions and nation states.

One manifestation of this shift was the adoption of "dependency" theory to explain the evolution of contemporary Indian cultures. Indian communities in certain regions of Mexico and Guatemala, for example, were now seen as being dependent on nation-state economic and political forces, which in turn were dependent upon world powers like the United States and Europe. From this perspective, Mesoamerican culture is perceived as an adaptive response to external political and economic forces rather than as primarily the legacy of ideas, rules, and values from the past.

THE THEORETICAL APPROACH TAKEN IN THIS TEXT

A few comments about the approach to Mesoamerica taken in this text need to be made. As should be obvious from the preceding review of past studies, romantic notions of Lost Tribes or Lost Continents to explain developments in Mesoamerica are eschewed. Nor is there a general adherence to strictly culture historical or cultural evolutionary arguments, although like most modern students of Mesoamerica, we have been influenced by those arguments. Broadly speaking, we have been guided by more recent theoretical perspectives that have emerged in the social sciences in general and Mesoamerican studies in particular.

The anthropologist Norman Schwartz (1983), in an insightful summary of Mesoamerican studies, notes the split mentioned earlier between studies that focus on the essential ideas of culture and those with a focus on the material determinants of culture. For the idealist students of Mesoamerica, the culture history model has evolved into the use of more sophisticated approaches of culture such as structuralism, semiotics, phenomenology, and more recently, discourse analysis. These scholars stress that Mesoamerican cultures, in both their pre-Hispanic and contemporary manifestations, are conceptual systems that cannot be explained as mere responses to underlying material or political conditions. As sets of integrated symbols and meanings, the Mesoamerican cultures have "inner logics" that fundamentally affect how they both persist and change.

The cultural evolutionary approach continues to be influential in Mesoamerican studies, but it also has undergone considerable modification. For example, neo-Marxists stress the importance of material production, but also the "superstructural" nature of Mesoamerican cultures. Similarly, ecologists, who derive their ideas from biology, treat Mesoamerican cultures as special behavioral responses to energy exchanges and demographic challenges. Dependency theory has largely given way to world-systems theory, according to which pre-Hispanic Mesoamerica is viewed as an interacting network of strong and weak societies, a "world" in its own right (for more on world-systems theory, see Chapter 3). Postconquest native Mesoamericans become participants in a worldwide class of exploited peasants and proletariats created by global capitalism. Even more so than the Cultural Evolutionists who preceded them, recent Materialists have tended to portray the Mesoamerican cultures as secondary derivations from behaviors oriented toward physical and political survival.

World-systems studies make it clear that we can no longer study the Mesoamerican cultures as isolated communities, nor can we ignore the impact of external powers on local Indian groups. Social classes based on the unequal distribution of economic means have always played an important role in determining the characteristics of the Mesoamerican cultures, both ancient and contemporary. As Schwartz (1983:355) points out:

> Identity, tradition, and culture become tactics in a game of power rather than primary irreducible determinants of change and continuity. [The Mesoamerican] tradition is no longer a manifestation of a particular world view but rather an expression of sectarian interests, a labile adaptation to an environment, and a dependent variable.

Nevertheless, cultures are not merely responses to material and political forces; they have their own internal logics and histories. Good theories should take into account both material and ideological factors, as well as microsocial and macrosocial settings. For Mesoamerica, as elsewhere, the "patterns of behavior and choices between alternatives are . . . the result of a complex interplay between ideas, rules, psychological and material resources, and situation circumstances" (Schwartz 1983:353; see also Gossen 1986). (Box A.5 provides a discussion of recent theoretical approaches to the study of native Mesoamericans in Guatemala.)

Box A.5   Recent Approaches to the Study of Mayan Peoples in Guatemala

The anthropologist John Watanabe (2000) has described the basic changes in theoretical approaches to Mayan community studies since the l960s. He refers to three dominant "themes" or directions taken by scholars in more recent Mayan studies, although clearly these three directions are interrelated and form part of a more general movement away from the study of cultural continuities toward the study of cultural reconstruction: "Rather than objectifying culture as consisting of essential traits that endure or are lost, anthropologists have come to treat Maya cultures in Guatemala as strategic self-expressions of Maya identity, motivated . . . by Maya propensities and possibilities in the present rather than by pre-Hispanic primordialism" (p. 4). The basic fault line ("sea change"), then, is between studies that objectified Mayan cultures and traits, seeing them as enduring, versus studies that focus on the strategic reconstruction of Mayan identity in the context of the wider, more dynamic political economy in which Mayas find themselves.

One important direction or approach in Mayan studies since the 1960s is the move away from the idea of persisting Mayan cultures, in favor of studying the changing social contexts in which they are created, along with the active processes by which Mayas reconstitute their ethnic identities despite these changes. A closely related theme or direction in Mayan studies emphasizes the transforming capacity of political economic forces (especially associated with capitalism). For example, in some accounts, Mayan culture and identity are seen as expressions of determinant class relationships. A sophisticated version of this approach calls for study not only of the impact

(continued)

of capitalism on Mayan communities but also of the counterreactions by Mayas in the form of market and labor systems that work against the outside domination. In some cases, such counterreactions have changed the nature of capitalism in the country as a whole. The result for the Mayas is "a world neither always as they imagined nor as others fully intended."

An additional directional change in Mayan studies consists of an attempt to interpret even the most traditional Mayan cultural patterns (ancestor worship, calendars, earth lord myths, milpa practices, etc.) as ". . . self-vindicating ideologies of ethnic continuity, autonomy, and resistance" (p.8). This emphasis shifts the approach from material factors to the ideological nature of Mayan cultures and identities, interpreting them as forms of political opposition to modernizing, exploitative institutions of conquest, colonialism, evangelization, capitalism, racism, violence, and war.

An important methodological modification associated with these more thematic and theoretical changes in Mayan studies is the application of a global dimension to the community approach taken in past studies. The community approach generally has focused on symbolism and on the "persistence of local patterns of meaning." In contrast, the global approach tends to focus on political economy, "rendering Maya cultural understandings as increasingly *ersatz* [fabricated] formulations."

In a final history-oriented statement, Watanabe claims that "understanding contemporary cultural formulations . . . necessarily entails knowing, not merely how they have changed over time, but, more precisely, how successive pasts have continued to inform succeeding presents, and how ongoing presents have repeatedly appropriated their pasts" (p. 27). This statement seems to offer a more dynamic approach than the scientific and the prescientific approaches of the past, or even the contemporary "constructivist" scholars who may deny the important weight that the past can have on the present.

Consistent with recent trends in theory, then, we attempt in this text to present the Mesoamerican cultures in terms of both the symbols and the meanings by which these cultures are constituted, and the material and behavioral contexts within which such ideas are created and transformed. We are interested both in *how* the Mesoamerican cultures have been created and in *what* they are like. We accept the important role of creative initiative on the part of the Mesoamericans, and where possible, we specify which individuals and groups created the social and cultural features under study and the reasons they did so. Our approach is therefore patently historical: We study the Mesoamerican cultures from their beginnings to their most recent manifestations. Finally, in taking account of world-systems perspectives, we also consciously relate local developments of Mesoamerican culture to regional, national, and global forces. Such approaches are in the best tradition of broadly defined recent theory, and therefore of Mesoamerican studies as now practiced.

ORGANIZATION OF THE TEXT

As already mentioned, the focus of this text is on native Mesoamericans and on the cultural traditions (civilizations) that they created and reconstituted through time. The reader will also find in the chapters to follow information on the non-Indian inhabitants of the Mexican and Central American region. Nevertheless, our emphasis is on the native Mesoamericans, their social institutions and cultural patterns, and the changing relations with each other and with the peoples surrounding them.

This emphasis on native Mesoamericans is by design, and it should not be interpreted as disinterest in the many millions of mestizos, Blacks, Whites, and diverse ethnic groups who now make up the majority of the regional Mexican and Central American peoples. We trust that the text will make clear that many of these non-Indian peoples have exercised controlling power over the native Mesoamericans for almost 500 years. This historical fact, of course, is well known, and has been stressed again and again in publications on Mexico and Central America.

This book carries the additional message that there existed a dynamic, highly developed Mesoamerican civilization before the coming of the Europeans; that the Mesoamericans resisted conquest from the beginning and have continued to resist assimilation of their cultures ever since; and that the peoples of the region, both Indian and non-Indian, continue to be profoundly influenced by the legacy of that civilization.

As pointed out in the new Preface to this text, this revised edition is primarily aimed at updating information on Mesoamerican culture and history. We have reorganized the chapters into four units, updated all the chapters from the first edition, and added two new chapters (chapters 3 and 10). The four units cover first, the pre-Hispanic period; second, the colonial and neocolonial period; third, the modern period; and fourth, accounts on key issues raised by the Mesoamerican civilization through its long history.

The three chapters of Unit I of this revised text provide an overview of the pre-Hispanic Mesoamericans, from their beginnings to the invasion of their territory by Spaniards. Unit II consists of four chapters that describe the impact of colonization and neocolonization (by "neocolonization" we refer to the continuing domination of the native Mesoamericans by Whites and mestizos all the way through the nineteenth century and into the first decades of the twentieth century). One of the chapters of this unit describes the nature of Mesoamerican literature produced during the darkness of the colonial period.

Unit III is constituted by three chapters that provide a historical overview of the native Mesoamerican peoples during the twentieth century and the first years of the twenty-first century (beginning with the Mexican revolution). The final chapter of this unit updates the situation of native Mesoamericans up to the present day through a detailed account of the Zapatista movement in Mexico and of its significance for the Indians of the region as a whole.

For each of the first three units, we describe the cultural characteristics of Mesoamerica, as well as the historical processes by which these characteristics were created and transformed through time.

The four chapters of Unit IV also take historical developments into consideration, but the primary focus is on a series of topics of current interest and special importance in Mesoamerican studies. In the chapters of this final unit, greater attention is paid to symbolic features of the Mesoamerican tradition than in the preceding units, particularly in the chapters on language, religion, and oral literature. Nevertheless, in each of these final chapters, attention is also given to the social and material forces that condition the cultural features under study.

We have dispensed with the Epilogue on the Zapatista movement found in the first edition, since an entire chapter devoted to that movement is included in Unit III on Modern Mesoamerica.

One of our main goals in writing this text is to ensure that the Mesoamericans' own perspectives on their history and world are represented throughout. Another goal is to summarize as fully as possible important scholarship available on Mesoamerica from the international scholarly community. We are also determined to integrate the scholarly findings on Mesoamerica into a useful text that is both cohesive and readable.

SUGGESTED READINGS

DÍAZ DEL CASTILLO, BERNAL 1956 *The Discovery and Conquest of Mexico, 1517–1521.* New York: Grove Press.

GOOSEN, GARY H. (ed.) 1986 *Symbol and Meaning beyond the Closed Community: Essays in Mesoamerican Ideas.* Studies on Culture and Society, Vol.1. Albany: Institute for Mesoamerican Studies.

GRAHAM, JOHN A. (ed.) 1966 *Ancient Mesoamerica: Selected Readings.* Palo Alto, California: Peek Publications.

HELMS, MARY W. 1982 *Middle America: A Culture History of Heartland and Frontiers.* New York: University Press of America.

HMAI 1964–1978 *Handbook of Middle American Indians,* vols. 1–15. Austin: University of Texas Press.

KENDALL, CARL, JOHN HAWKINS, and LAUREL BOSSEN (eds.) 1983 *Heritage of Conquest Thirty Years Later.* Albuquerque: University of New Mexico Press.

SANDERS, WILLIAM T., and BARBARA J. PRICE 1968 *Mesoamerica: The Evolution of a Civilization.* New York: Random House.

WAUCHOPE, ROBERT (ed.) 1962 *Lost Tribes & Sunken Continents: Myth and Method in the Study of American Indians.* Chicago: University of Chicago Press.

WEST, ROBERT C., and JOHN P. AUGELLI 1989 *Middle America: Its Lands and Peoples.* Englewood Cliffs, New Jersey: Prentice Hall.

WOLF, ERIC 1959 *Sons of the Shaking Earth: The People of Mexico and Guatemala, Their Land, History, and Culture.* Chicago: University of Chicago Press.

Chapter 1

Origins and Development
of Mesoamerican Civilization

At daylight the clouds still hung over the forest; as the sun rose they cleared away. . . . The branches of the trees were dripping wet, and the ground very muddy. Trudging once more over the district which contained the principal monuments, we were startled by the immensity of the work before us. . . . The woods were so dense that it was almost hopeless to think of penetrating them. . . . It is impossible to describe the interest with which I explored these ruins. The ground was entirely new; there were no guide-books or guides; the whole was a virgin soil. . . . We stopped to cut away branches and vines which concealed the face of a monument. The beauty of the sculpture, the solemn stillness of monkeys and the chattering of parrots, the desolation of the city, and the mystery that hung over it, all created an interest higher, if possible, than I had ever felt among the ruins of the Old World. (Stephens 1841:1:117–120)

With these words the nineteenth-century explorer John L. Stephens described his initial reaction to the ruined Mayan city of Copán. Stephens and his fellow traveler, artist Frederick Catherwood, were the first explorers to describe the lost cities of the Mayas to American and European audiences. These spectacular ruins, which had lain abandoned in the jungle for almost a millennium, excited the public's imagination (Figure 1.1), and a number of far-fetched theories arose attributing the construction of the cities to the ancient Greeks, Egyptians, Lost Tribes of Israel, and even refugees from the mythical continent of Atlantis (see the discussion of some of these "theories" in the Introduction). Against these popular notions, Stephens had the correct explanation from the start:

We are not warranted in going back to any ancient nation of the Old World for the builders of these cities. . . . There are strong reasons to believe them the creation of the same races who inhabited the country at the time of the Spanish conquest, or of some not very distant progenitors. (Stephens 1843:1:50).

These ancestral Mayan peoples and their contemporaries throughout Mesoamerica not only built the ancient cities discovered by Stephens and Catherwood, but they also forged a distinctive civilization whose legacy survives throughout Mesoamer-

FALLEN IDOL.

Figure 1.1   Ruins of the Classic Period Mayan city of Copán, Honduras, as captured in an 1843 engraving by artist Frederick Catherwood. Reprinted with permission of Dover Publications (*Incidents of Travel in Central America, Chiapas and Yucatan, Vol. I.* New York 1969, p. 154).

ica today. The antecedents of Mesoamerican culture can be traced back to the Pleistocene Ice Age over 10,000 years ago, when the first hunters and gatherers arrived in Central America. Sometime between 5000 and 3000 B.C., during the Archaic period, the descendants of the earliest inhabitants brought about what was probably the single most important innovation in Mesoamerican history, the domestication of maize or corn. The initial impact of maize cultivation was minimal, but after several thousand years, the crop had improved and people depended on the triad of maize, beans, and squash to fulfill most of their subsistence needs. The process of plant domestication was slow and uneven across Mesoamerica, and in most regions sedentary villages emerged before full agricultural dependence.

The Formative period (1800 B.C.–A.D. 200) saw the origin of Mesoamerica as a distinctive cultural entity. Widely scattered peoples speaking a variety of languages were united as Mesoamericans during the Early Formative (1800–900 B.C.) on the basis of sedentism, the use of ceramics, and of the construction of large-scale monumental facilities. During the Middle Formative (900–400 B.C.), people became dependent on agriculture, the earliest pyramids were built, and many societies developed complex social and political hierarchies. In the Late Formative (400 B.C.–A.D. 200), the first cities and states emerged in the New World. The following Classic period (A.D. 200–800) was characterized by the growth of cities and states. Mesoamerican societies became more complex, and they developed sophisticated writing, calendars, urban planning, state-sponsored cults, and other hallmarks of civilization. The final episodes of the pre-Columbian past, the Epiclassic/Terminal Classic and Postclassic periods

(A.D. 800–1519), saw a continuation of these patterns of social complexity. The large and powerful theocratic states of the Classic period, however, gave way to a majority of smaller, more secular and commercially oriented city-states (Figure 1.2).

Mesoamerica in 1519 had a distinctive cultural heritage shared by many diverse peoples. In this chapter we review the history of pre-Columbian Mesoamerica, starting with the arrival of Pleistocene hunters and ending with the era that followed the decline of the Classic civilizations. In Chapter 2 we focus on the Late Postclassic period, the last three centuries preceding the arrival of Europeans in 1519, and in Chapter 3 we turn to an examination of the ways that Mesoamerica was organized as an integrated world-system in the sixteenth century.

EARLY INHABITANTS OF MESOAMERICA.

Paleo-Indian and Archaic Hunter-Gatherers.

The earliest people to inhabit Mesoamerica arrived at the end of the Pleistocene epoch (also known as the Ice Age,) sometime between 30,000 and 10,000 years ago. Until recently, archaeologists thought that all of the early migrants walked to the New world over a land bridge called "Beringia" that linked Siberia and Alaska. Beringia was exposed when enormous glaciers were formed, causing sea levels to drop. New evidence has led some archaeologists to propose that early migrants may also have traveled from Asia to the Americas by boat along the Pacific coast (see Meltzer 2004 for a review of new evidence). At the end of the Pleistocene, glaciers that had covered much of North America melted, leading to a rise in sea levels and dramatic changes in vegetation, landforms, and surface water. One consequence of these changes was the extinction of many Pleistocene animals (including mammoths and mastodons) and modifications of the habits and ranges of many others. These changes had important effects on the new settlers.

These early settlers, using an elaborate stone tool technology, adapted to the varied late Pleistocene environments of the New World. Some populations traveled the length of the American continents as far as southern Chile. Archaeological sites from this time period represent the remains of hunting, butchering, quarrying, or temporary campsites of mobile hunter-gatherers. The most extensively studied Mexican sites were excavated by José Luis Lorenzo and Lorena Mirambell. El Cedral (in the Mexican state of San Luis Potosí) was a campsite at a freshwater spring in which stone and bone tools were found around a hearth. Tlapacoya, in the Valley of Mexico, was a settlement at the edge of a lake with remains of stone tools, animal bones, and hearths (Figure 1.3). At the site of Monte Verde in Chile, Thomas Dillehay has reported the earliest securely documented human occupation in the New World that is 13,000 years old. The diverse plant and animal remains recovered from this site indicate that the occupants had an intimate knowledge of their environment. Monte Verde is also the site of the first house in the Americas; its waterlogged condition helped to preserve compartments of wooden house foundations. A deeper occupation zone at Monte Verde that potentially dates to 33,000 B.P. is under further investigation, and it may provide evidence of much earlier human occupation.

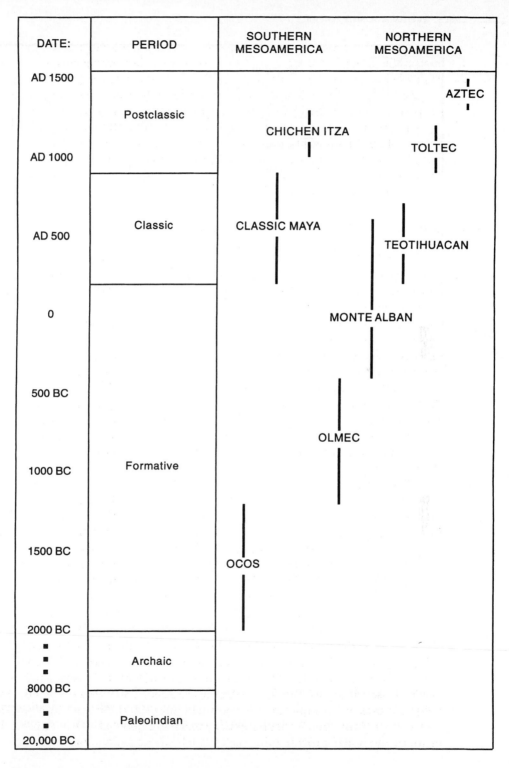

Figure 1.2 Pre-Hispanic chronology of Mesoamerica.

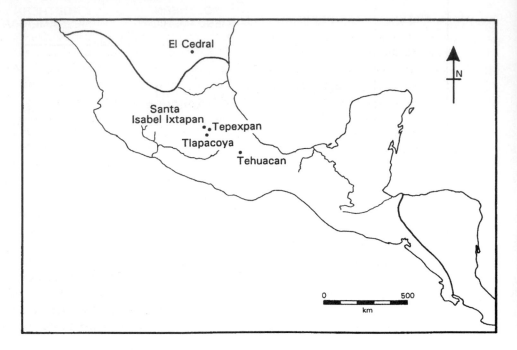

Figure 1.3   Locations of major Paleo-Indian and Archaic Period sites.

The latter part of the Pleistocene epoch saw the spread of the mammoth-hunting Clovis culture throughout North America and northern Middle America. Like Clovis sites in the United States, those in Middle America illustrate the proficiency of these ancient hunters, who used well-made stone tools to kill and butcher huge mammoths. The site of Santa Isabel Iztapan in the Valley of Mexico consists of the remains of two butchered mammoths together with the stone tools used to process them; the site is dated to sometime between 9000–7000 B.C. At nearby Tepexpan, a complete female skeleton dating to around the same time was preserved (although the excavation report called her "Tepexpan man"!).

The post-Pleistocene environmental changes after 9000 B.C.—rising sea levels, changing vegetation, and extinction of mammoths and other species—forced the Paleo-Indian peoples to modify their diets and activities, leading to an increased reliance upon plant foods. An important result of these modifications was the domestication of food plants, which led eventually to the start of farming in Middle America.

Plant Domestication.

Domestication is the process by which wild plants evolve into domesticated crops as humans select for traits that will make the plants more useful. Domesticated crops have a different genetic makeup than that of their wild ancestors, and generally cannot survive in the wild. Independent episodes of domestication took place in several parts of the world in the aftermath of the Pleistocene, including Middle America, the Near East, sub-Saharan Africa, southeast Asia, north China, the Andes, and the Amazon basin. Plant domestication in Middle America was particularly significant not only because it established a pattern for the development of later Mesoamerican cultures, but also because some of the resulting crops are among the most important food crops in the world today.

Domestication of Mesoamerican plants took place during the Archaic period. The earliest domesticate was squash, documented in the Valley of Oaxaca at 8000 B.C. and it was not for thousands of years after this that maize and beans were domesticated. Instead, chile peppers, bottle gourds (used as containers), amaranth, and avocados were the next early domesticates (see Table 1.1).

The earliest remains of maize are from Oaxaca and Tehuacán around 3400 B.C., by which time the crop (*Zea mays*) had evolved fully from its wild ancestor teosinte (*Zea mexicanus*) through processes of cultural selection and genetic mutation. The nutritional quality of maize was great, and when combined with beans it produces a complete protein. This combination was the basis of the Mesoamerican diet from early times until the present (see Box 1.1). In contrast to its variety of domesticated plants, Middle America was the home to very few species of domesticated animals. Only dogs, turkeys, and possibly bees, all used for food, were domesticated in the area.

Table 1.1 Mesoamerican Domesticated Plants

COMMON NAME	SCIENTIFIC NAME	COMMON NAME	SCIENTIFIC NAME
Grains		papaya	*Carica papaya*
maize	*Zea mays*	tuna cactus	*Opuntia*
beans	*Phaseolus (four species)*	mamey	*Calocarpum mammosum*
amaranth	*Amaranthus cruentus*	chicosapote	*Achras sapote*
sunflower	*Helianthus annuus*	Mexican cherry	*Prunus capuli*
chía	*Salvia hispanica*	hog plum	*Spondias mombin*
Tuber Plants		guava	*Psidium guajava*
jícama	*Pachyrrhizus erosus*	vanilla	*Vanilla planifolia*
Vegetables		Fiber Plants	
squash	*Cucurbita (four species)*	agaves	*Agaves (at least five species)*
tomato	*Lycopersicon esculetum*	Condiment Plants	
husk tomato	*Physalis xiocarpa*	chile pepper	*Capsicum (various species)*
chayote	*Sechium edule*	Dye Plants	
Fruits		indigo	*Indigofera suffruticosa*
avocado	*Persia americana*	Ceremonial Plants	
cacao (chocolate)	*Theobroma cacao*	copal	*Protium copal*

Note: Adapted from West and Augelli (1989:220).

Box 1.1   Maize

Why was maize so important to the ancient Mesoamericans, and why does it continue to be the primary food in modern Mesoamerica? The answer lies in a combination of the plant's nutritional qualities and the lack of domesticated animals in ancient Mesoamerica. In most areas of the world, traditional diets provide most of their calories through high-carbohydrate, low-protein, staple grains, but most rely on domesticated animals like cattle or pigs for their protein. This dietary strategy would not work well in Mesoamerica because of the paucity of domesticated animals (only turkeys and dogs were available). In order to meet their protein needs, Mesoamericans domesticated maize and then developed methods of preparing and serving the food to turn it into an adequate and complete source of protein.

Maize has high concentrations of most of the essential amino acids that the human body needs to synthesize proteins, but two are lacking and one is chemically bound and not readily available. In order to supply the missing amino acids, Mesoamericans eat beans with their tortillas (or other forms of maize); beans have high concentrations of the missing nutrients. To free the chemically bound acid, Mesoamericans soak their maize in an alkali solution (normally made by simply adding powdered lime—calcium carbonate—to water) before grinding the kernels. These two practices are deeply ingrained cultural traits that not only produce delicious meals but also ensure that maize provides adequate protein for human needs. The Mesoamerican diet, from Formative times until the present, is one of the few traditional world cuisines that can provide adequate protein without heavy supplements of meat or other animal protein sources.

Given the nutritional and cultural importance of maize, it is not surprising that Mesoamerican peoples long ago devised many different ways of serving the food. Tortillas, flat maize cakes roasted on a clay griddle, have been the most prevalent form of maize from the Classic period to the present day. In addition to being flavorful and easy to eat, tortillas have the advantage of portability—they can be cooked ahead of time and then carried to eat later, in the field or on the road. Tamales are balls of coarse maize dough steamed in large pots, often with chile or meat filling. This was probably the major way maize was eaten before the invention of the tortilla. Atole, a thin gruel of finely ground maize, often flavored with fruit or sugar, is a popular breakfast food; pozole, a soup made with large maize kernels (hominy), is a common evening food. Maize is also eaten fresh on the cob, but this method does not involve alkali soaking and therefore does not provide the nutritional benefits of the other maize foods.

The methods of tortilla preparation, well-documented in ethnographic accounts of modern traditional behavior, have probably changed little in 2,000 years. The ears of maize are typically left to dry on the plants. In the fall, the dried maize is harvested and then shelled; it is stored sometimes on the cob and sometimes as dried kernels. To prepare tortillas, the dried kernels are soaked in the alkali solution in a clay pot and then are ground by hand on a stone mill or metate. The moist ground flour or dough is then patted into shape by hand, and the tortillas are cooked on a clay griddle and stored in a basket or wrapped in cloth. Maize grinding stones are common artifacts at Mesoamerican archaeological sites, and clay griddles are typically either absent (at early sites) or ubiquitous (at later sites). This traditional method of food preparation is quite arduous; grinding the maize to make several dozen tortillas for the daily meals of a family of six requires four to five hours of physical labor. The domestic activities and schedules of women in traditional Mesoamerican societies are thus heavily conditioned by the requirements of maize grinding.

Although maize and the other food crops were available quite early, a fully agricultural economy did not develop in the region until the Middle Formative after 900 B.C. The hunter-gatherers of the Archaic period continued their nomadic lifestyle for several thousand years after the appearance of domesticates, merely adding these crops to their repertoire of wild resources. These groups had no pottery and used stone tools for land clearing and cultivation (Figure 1.4).

Sedentism emerged in some of the most productive coastal environments in Mesoamerica during the Late Archaic (3000–1800 B.C.) when reliance on marine fauna provided reliable resources on which to subsist. These sedentary villagers, along with their successors in the subsequent Early Formative, experimented with maize and developed more productive varieties. Because of its high sugar content, early uses of maize may have been for making beer or other alcoholic drinks. Today, much of the industrially produced sugar (in the form of fructose) is from corn.

The Beginnings of Village Life.

During the last 2,000 years of the Archaic period, peoples throughout Middle America gradually adopted a more sedentary lifestyle. The expansion of sedentism was one of the most far-reaching changes in ancient human history (in Middle America and elsewhere), as it set the scene for an agricultural way of life and the later evolution of cities and states. Over the same period, other important changes were taking place; populations were growing, people were becoming more and more dependent

Figure 1.4   Constricted adze from Caye Coco, Belize. Such tools were used during the second millennium B.C. by Late Archaic semisedentary gardening populations. Photo by M. Masson.

on domesticated plants, and villagers began storing food. Archaeologists believe that these changes were all linked.

The earliest evidence in the region for possible sedentism comes from lowland zones: the Pacific Coast, the Gulf Coast, and the Caribbean coast of Belize. A clay housefloor dating to between 3500 and 3100 B.C. has been found in a shell midden at the site of Tlacuachero in Chiapas. In coastal Veracruz, a preceramic village may have existed as early as 3000 B.C. at the site of Palo Hueco, and the remains of late Archaic camps have been found in northern Belize.

Other possible early village sites are found in certain regions of the highlands where environmental conditions existed that enabled people to become sedentary prior to dependence on agriculture. One such area is the Basin of Mexico, where villages may have existed along the shores of lakes and lagoons. Elsewhere in the highlands, in the Tehuacán Valley and in Oaxaca, evidence for sedentism also dates to the late Archaic period.

We know very little about these earliest villages. There does not appear to have been much variation among houses within villages, and within the various subregions there is no evidence of a hierarchy of communities. The general consensus among archaeologists is that the earliest Middle American villages were egalitarian and autonomous. Even though some of the earliest settlements were based on exploitation of wild resources in lowland zones, by the end of the Archaic period, populations in lowland as well as in highland areas were increasingly dependent upon cultivated plants, particularly maize and root crops. By around 1800 B.C., the village farming tradition was firmly in place in many parts of the region.

MESOAMERICA DEFINES ITSELF: THE FORMATIVE PERIOD.

The 2,000 years of the Formative period (1800 B.C.–A.D. 200) were a time of rapid and far-reaching cultural change throughout Middle America. Archaeologists usually divide this time span into three subperiods. The Early Formative period (1800–900 B.C.) saw the initial settlement of most areas of the region by sedentary peoples. In a few areas, early villages grew in size and complexity to reach the form of social organization known as the chiefdom. During the latter part of this period, a complex polity emerged on the Gulf Coast of Mexico at San Lorenzo, and a shared political and religious iconography spread throughout several regions.

The succeeding Middle Formative period (900–400 B.C.) is notable for three main historical developments: (1) complex chiefdoms and incipient states emerged in many parts of Middle America; (2) the first pyramid mounds were built, and (3) an adaptation completely dependent on agriculture and based on maize, beans, and squash, spread to most parts of Mesoamerica. In the Late Formative period (400 B.C.–A.D. 200), many Middle Formative polities collapsed, to be replaced by larger and more complex societies, the first fully developed Mesoamerican states. Formative period sites are shown in Figure 1.5.

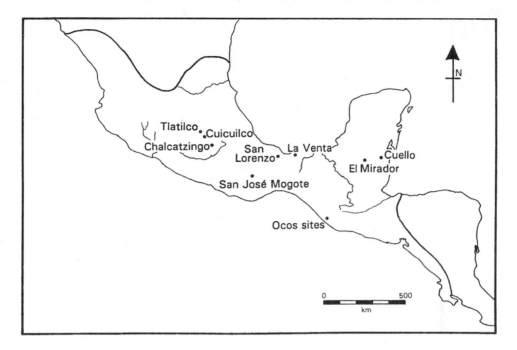

Figure 1.5   Locations of major Formative period sites.

The Early Formative Period.

The transition from the Archaic to the Formative periods was marked by the introduction of fired ceramics and the growth of sedentary villages. Both domestication and sedentism had existed in the Archaic period, but it was not until around 1800 B.C. that increased sedentism and the production of ceramics resulted in much more substantial sites. These two trends are logically linked. It is simply not practical for nomadic peoples to carry around ceramic pots, whereas sedentary peoples require a large number of sturdy vessels for food storage, and fired clay pots serve this purpose well.

Fired clay was also used to produce figurines—small images of persons, gods, and animals. These figurines were used in rituals, and most have been recovered from domestic contexts. Figurines from the Soconusco region of coastal Chiapas depict old, seated individuals wearing masks and young women standing without clothes (Figure 1.6). Figurine styles changed dramatically by the end of the Early Formative to depict so-called Olmec "baby-face" individuals whose age and sex are ambiguous (Figure 1.6).

The earliest documented pottery in Mesoamerica forms two traditions: the red-on-buff tradition west of the Isthmus of Tehuantepec and the Locona tradition to the east. Locona pottery proper is found along the Pacific Coast of Chiapas and

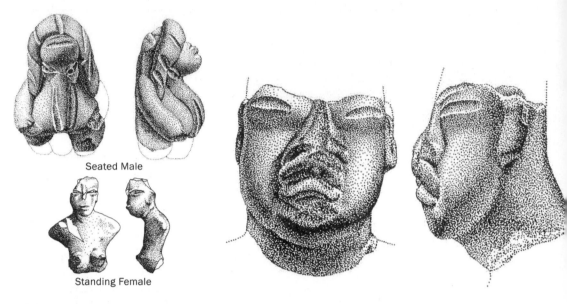

Seated Male

Standing Female

Figure 1.6   Early Formative figurines from Cuauhtemoc in the Soconusco region of coastal Chiapas: (a) Initial Formative old, seated, and young standing female figurines; and (b) late Early Formative "baby-face" figurines. Illustrations by Ayax Moreno (all but standing female) and Joseph McGreavy (standing female).

Guatemala, but Locona-related pottery also occurs across a wide area of Middle America, from the Gulf Coast of Veracruz to El Salvador and Honduras. This distribution suggests that for the first time, there was widespread contact and communication among regional villages, and pottery provides material evidence for the emergence of Mesoamerica as a distinctive culture in the Early Formative period.

Although most of the earliest Formative villages were small settlements with little evidence for social ranking or other elements of social complexity, recent research in the Soconusco region of coastal Chiapas by John Clark and Michael Blake suggests that simple chiefdoms arose early in this area. Evidence attesting to a society that had developed in the Paso de La Amada (Chiapas) vicinity beyond the level of other Early Formative groups in Mesoamerica includes (1) the presence of an elaborate central residence larger than others (probably of the chief), (2) the construction of Mesoamerica's earliest known ballcourt at Paso de la Amada, and (3) the existence of a two-tiered regional hierarchy of settlements.

West of the Isthmus of Tehuantepec, the red-on-buff ceramic tradition is documented in the highlands of central Mexico. In the Basin of Mexico, many Early Formative sites have been located in regional archaeological surveys, but few of these sites have been excavated. Excavations of burials at the site of Tlatilco in Mexico City (by both archaeologists and looters) reveals a tradition of sophisticated pottery vessels used as burial offerings. In the absence of excavations of houses and settlements, however, it is difficult to reconstruct the nature of Early Formative society in the area.

In the Valley of Oaxaca a long-term interdisciplinary archaeological project directed by Kent Flannery and Joyce Marcus has provided extensive information on Early Formative villages. A number of these sites have been excavated, revealing the rapid expansion of farming villages throughout the Valley. At the end of the Early Formative period, evidence for social complexity began to appear in Oaxaca, including large residences, public ceremonial buildings, and the beginnings of craft specialization.

In the last centuries of the Early Formative period and throughout the Middle Formative, the Olmec culture flourished along the Gulf Coast. At the site of San Lorenzo, a small farming village existed as early as 1500 B.C. In its early years the village at San Lorenzo was similar to villages elsewhere in the region, and its inhabitants used Locona-tradition pottery. Beginning around 1300 B.C., however, there is evidence for increasing cultural complexity at San Lorenzo. Most striking are the massive public works projects begun at this time, which involved the reshaping of the natural hill upon which the site of San Lorenzo rests. Large quantities of fill were used to turn the hill into a level plateau, and construction was begun on a symmetrical system of ridges that jut out from the main plateau. The investigations by Michael Coe, Richard Diehl, and Ann Cyphers have documented the tremendous labor mobilized by San Lorenzo rulers in constructing Mesoamerica's first major political center, which emphasized landscape modification rather than pyramid temples known from later periods.

By 1200 B.C. most of the features that characterized the fully developed "Olmec civilization" were present at San Lorenzo. These include colossal stone heads—thought to be portraits of rulers—for which the Olmec are most famous (Figure 1.7), as well as other stone sculptures, hollow ceramic figurines with baby faces (see Figure 1.6), ceramic vessels decorated with iconographic motifs, and a series of stone drains.

These characteristics indicate that by as early as 1200 B.C., a level of sociopolitical complexity was reached at San Lorenzo far beyond that which had previously existed. An elite group had emerged with the power to mobilize the labor force necessary for major public works projects and for the transport of stone for monumental sculpture. Although we do not know a great deal about these earliest Olmec leaders, the iconography on Olmec sculpture indicates that they were considered to be of divine descent and were imbued with supernatural powers (see Figure A.13 in the Introduction).

The Middle Formative.

San Lorenzo dominated the Olmec heartland for several hundred years, but by 900 B.C. its importance had faded, and the site of La Venta became a major Olmec center. Other Gulf Coast centers that may have been contemporary with La Venta were Laguna de los Cerros and Tres Zapotes, but less work has been done at these sites. At La Venta large quantities of stone sculpture as well as smaller portable artifacts such

Figure 1.7   Giant Olmec head from the site of San Lorenzo, Mexico. Photo by Robert Rosenswig.

as jade figurines and celts have been found (see Figure 14.1 in Chapter 14). Monumental architecture, rich tombs and offerings, and buried large mosaic masks all indicate that La Venta was an elite residential area as well as a ceremonial center. By the end of the Middle Formative period, La Venta was in decline and the extent of widespread Olmec influence on the emerging Mesoamerican cultural tradition was curtailed.

Linguists Lyle Campbell and Terrance Kaufman have postulated that the Olmecs spoke a Mixe-Zoquean language. Although these languages are limited to highland Oaxaca and the Isthmus of Tehuantepec today, in Olmec times Mixe-Zoque speakers were most likely distributed across a wide area of southern Middle America extending from the Gulf Coast, across the Isthmus of Tehuantepec, and down the Pacific Coast of Chiapas and Guatemala. In the Late Formative period, descendants of the Olmecs played a significant role in the development of the earliest Mesoamerican writing and directly influenced the evolution of the Maya writing system. An important key to this contribution is the recently discovered La Mojarra Stela 1 (see Chapter 11).

The Olmecs were not the only complex society in Middle Formative Mesoamerica. Chiefdoms emerged in various areas, and a network of trade and interaction linked the Olmecs with their contemporaries in Oaxaca, the Basin of Mexico, and the Soconusco. Olmec-style iconography appears at sites from El Salvador to the Valley of Mexico, and this distribution has generated a number of interpretations. Formerly, many scholars thought that the widespread distribution of these symbols indicated that the Olmecs had conquered or somehow controlled contemporaneous cultures in other parts of Mesoamerica. Recent fieldwork at sites that were supposedly Olmec "colonies" or "subjects" has produced a different view of these Formative cultures and the type of interactions among them.

During the last centuries of the Early Formative period, elites of several chiefdoms were in contact with one another through trade networks and personal visits, and the participants in this network used a common system of emblems and religious symbols to proclaim their positions and power. The Gulf Coast Olmecs were the most complex and powerful polity at the time and were emulated by elites across Mesoamerica at the time. Discrepancies in political organization were most evident during the late Early Formative when no other polity in Mesoamerica could compare with San Lorenzo in terms of the quantity of labor marshaled to fill in the massive plateau on which the site was built or to transport and carve huge stone monuments. During the Middle Formative, discrepancies were less obvious, not because La Venta was less impressive than San Lorenzo but because of the dramatic developments in other regions of Mesoamerica.

Two well-studied chiefdoms in the Mexican highlands were centered at San José Mogote in the Valley of Oaxaca, and at Chalcatzingo in Morelos. In these areas, important changes began to occur in the last centuries of the Early Formative period. These include the construction of public structures, the relatively rapid growth of villages, the development of craft specialization, increases in long-distance exchange, and the emergence of social stratification.

By the Middle Formative period, a hierarchy of settlements existed in the Valley of Oaxaca that consisted of the primary center of San José Mogote, a series of secondary centers with public architecture, and small villages with no public architecture represented the third, lowest tier in the regional system. Elites had access to valuable trade goods, they lived in larger houses than did the common people, and they were buried in more elaborate graves.

Chalcatzingo, a center in what is today the state of Morelos, is notable for its large civic-ceremonial precinct and its Olmec-style monumental stone art. Archaeologist David Grove argues that by the Middle Formative period, Chalcatzingo was ruled by a chief with close connections to the Gulf Coast Olmecs and other contemporary chiefdoms in the highlands. These connections included the exchange of goods, stylistic emulation, and perhaps marriage alliances. Variations in burial treatment at Chalcatzingo suggest significant levels of social stratification and hereditary social status.

The Soconusco region provides another example of cultural developments outside the Gulf Coast where the Locona Tradition had developed in earlier times. In this region, intensification of contact with the San Lorenzo Olmec correlates with the collapse of Paso de la Amada and the emergence of a new polity on the shores of the nearby Coatan River. With the collapse of San Lorenzo around 900 B.C., this entire part of the Soconusco was abandoned, and the polity of La Blanca emerged 50 km to the southeast. The La Blanca site sprang up around a 25m-high mound that was built during the first century of the Middle Formative (900–800 B.C.), making it the largest pyramid mound documented in Mesoamerica at this time. This site was the capital of a territory organized into a four-tiered settlement hierarchy.

In the Mayan lowlands, it is not until the Middle Formative period that the first good evidence for sedentary village life appears. Excavations by Norman Hammond, Patricia McAnany, and David Freidel at their respective sites of Cuello, K'axob, and Cerros in Belize have shown that early Mayan villages were inhabited by maize farmers who lived in pole-and-thatch houses with limestone plaster floors.

Toward the end of the Middle Formative period, population growth in the Mayan lowlands was rapid, and at sites in the Petén, the Yucatán Peninsula, and Belize, ceramics are quite similar, belonging to what is called the Mamon tradition. This uniformity in the pottery suggests that there was widespread contact across the region.

The first evidence for large public architecture in the Mayan lowlands occurs during the Middle Formative period. A ceremonial structure, consisting of three temples sitting atop a terraced platform, was constructed at the site of Nakbé in the northern Petén, Guatemala. There is little evidence for social ranking at these early Mayan sites. In the Mayan lowlands, very few Olmec-style artifacts have been recovered, and most Mayan villages did not participate in the network of interacting Middle Formative societies that included the Gulf Coast, Soconusco, Oaxaca, and Central Mexico.

Late Formative Developments.

After the collapse of Chalcatzingo and other Middle Formative Central Mexican chiefdoms, Cuicuilco and Teotihuacan became the preeminent polities. During the final two centuries B.C., each began construction of huge temple platforms, the first truly monumental buildings in Central Mexico. Cuicuilco, with its large circular-step pyramid, grew into a city of perhaps 20,000 inhabitants by 0 A.D.. Then in the first century A.D., a nearby volcano, Mount Xitle, erupted and buried the settlement under 20 feet of lava, leaving only the top of the pyramid visible. Archaeologists had to use dynamite to excavate parts of Cuicuilco, most of which remains covered with volcanic rock in the southern part of Mexico City. The destruction of Cuicuilco in the Late Formative period enabled Teotihuacan to become the dominant power in Central Mexico by the beginning of the Classic period.

During the Late Formative period in the Valley of Oaxaca, the organization of settlements underwent a major change as the hilltop settlement of Monte Albán was established. This urban center would serve as a regional capital until late in the Classic period, around A.D. 700. According to Richard Blanton, Monte Albán may have been established by a confederation of Valley chiefdoms. The site's founders, who probably came from many of the Valley's communities, established an administrative center in a neutral location. The hilltop site in the central part of the Valley was distant from the most productive farming lands, but it was centrally located and offered a commanding observation point for the entire valley.

At this time other changes also took place in Oaxacan society. Population grew at a rapid pace, a market system developed, agricultural intensification took place, and Monte Albán became an urban center and capital of the Zapotec state. Political domination by Monte Albán was achieved, in part, through violence: One building at the site is adorned with carved stones depicting over 300 prisoners who had been killed, and many of them had also been dismembered. Monte Albán was partially protected by defensive walls.

Along the Pacific coast of Chiapas and Guatemala, a series of early states emerged along the piedmont of the Sierra Madre mountains. The best known of these states are Izapa and Takalik Abaj; both are large sites with scores of mounds forming courtyards lined with carved stone stela and altars. The iconography found on these stone sculptures was obviously derived from the Olmecs and provides evidence that most of the conventions used in the subsequent Classic period, including a calendric system and writing (see Box 1.2 and Chapter 11), had already been established at this early time. Recent work has documented other large Late Formative centers along the piedmont, including Ujuxte and Chocola. Other centers, such as Chalchuapa and San Leticia, are located further south along the coast of El Salvador. Elsewhere,

---

Box 1.2   Mesoamerican Calendars

Beginning sometime in the Formative period, Mesoamerican peoples began making use of three distinctive calendars. The ritual or sacred almanac consisted of a combination of two cycles, one of thirteen numbers and a second of twenty named days, corresponding to deities, which together created a 260-day cycle (13 × 20). The specific names for the days varied from region to region, depending on the language spoken, but the meanings for the day names were similar across Mesoamerica. The 260-day sacred almanac was used (and still is used in some Maya communities) for religious and divinitory purposes. An individual's destiny was closely tied to his or her birthday as expressed in the ritual almanac.

The second Mesoamerican calendar corresponded to the solar year. The solar calendar was made up of eighteen months of twenty days plus an additional five-day period, which produces a solar year of 365 days. The months in the solar calendar had patron deities who influenced people and events.

For the ancient Mesoamericans, each day was named with reference to both the sacred almanac and the solar cycle. This method is not really so different from our own system, in which we have one cycle of seven day names (Monday through Sunday) and a second cycle of twelve months that have between 28 and 31 days. In our system, the most complete way to express a particular day is to say "Friday, September 23." Similarly, for the Yucatec Maya, for example, a particular day might be called "3 Imix" (for the ritual almanac) "15 Zac" (for the solar year). The combination of the ritual and the solar cycles created a third calendrical cycle called the calendar round, which was fifty-two years long. This arrangement means that a given combination of day designations from the ritual and solar cycles—for example, "3 Imix, 15 Zac" occurs only once every fifty-two years.

in the Isthmian region that had once been home to Olmecs, Late Formative developments include evidence for early use of long count dates and writing (see Chapter 11 and Figure 13.5).

The Late Formative period was a time of rapid population growth and cultural development in the Mayan lowlands. During this period most of the traits that would characterize Classic Mayan civilization developed. Communities that had been small-scale, egalitarian villages grew into centers with large populations and massive civic-ceremonial architecture.

The archaeological evidence from the Late Formative period is much more complete in the Mayan area than for earlier periods, and it provides us with clues for understanding the important changes that were taking place in Mayan society. During this period, the Mayas began to experiment with more intensive forms of agriculture, digging irrigation canals and reclaiming wetlands by constructing raised fields. Increased agricultural production allowed for even greater population growth. These agricultural projects also point to more centralized control over labor. At some centers massive construction projects were undertaken. At El Mirador the tallest structure ever built in the Mayan area, La Danta, which rose to a height of 70m, was built in the Late Formative period (see Box 1.3).

Box 1.3   Mesoamerican Technology

The Mesoamericans are sometimes described as having employed a "Stone Age" technology because of the prevalence of stone tools and the very limited and late development of metallurgy. Although this description is technically correct, it does not follow that Mesoamerican technology was crude or simple. A brief look at two areas of technology—tools and agriculture—illustrates some of the ingenuity and diversity of ancient Mesoamerican technological development.

With the exception of a small number of Postclassic cultures that used metal tools (see later), Mesoamerican peoples relied upon chipped stone for such cutting tools as knives, drills, scrapers, axes, arrow points, and swords, etc. The preferred stone was obsidian, a form of volcanic glass. The primary tool, known as a prismatic blade, was difficult to manufacture, and it took archaeologists many years of experimentation to figure out how the Mesoamericans produced them. The great benefit of prismatic blades was their sharpness; microscopic tests have shown that these blades are often sharper than a modern surgeon's scalpel (archaeologists who analyze obsidian blades can be recognized from the bandages on their fingers!). Because of the great skill required to make blades, obsidian knapping was probably a specialized occupation in ancient Mesoamerica. The study of obsidian is helpful to archaeologists not only for its insights into tool technology but also for the analysis of trade routes. Obsidian occurs only in a limited number of highland locations, and each geological source has a distinct chemical profile or fingerprint that allows artifacts to be traced to their point of origin.

Metallurgy was first developed in the New World in the Andes mountains of South America, where a tradition several thousand years old has been identified by archaeologists. The technology was introduced into Mesoamerica by contact with South American cultures. Gold and silver working were brought into southern Mesoamerica during the Classic period from craftspersons in Central America, and copper and bronze technology were introduced into western Mexico in the Early Postclassic period through sea contact with South America. Once Mesoamerican cultures had adopted metalworking, they developed new techniques to suit their interests. Most metallurgy was devoted to ornamental and ritual objects like plaques, bells, and jewelry. In western Mexico, however, a tradition of bronze tools (including axes, chisels, awls, and sewing needles) developed in the Postclassic period, and this tradition was spreading to Central Mexico at the time of Spanish conquest (Hosler 2003).

Some of the most impressive technological advances of ancient Mesoamerica were in the realm of agriculture. As populations grew and centralized states expanded in the Classic and Postclassic periods, Mesoamerican farmers responded by devising new, more productive farming methods. The primary methods—irrigation, terracing, and raised fields—produced more food per unit of land compared with simple rainfall agriculture, but at the cost of increased labor inputs per unit of food output. The process of devising and adopting such methods is known as agricultural intensification, and this process was associated with population growth, political centralization, and urbanization. Simple irrigation canals and dams were first used in the Middle Formative period, but widespread use of irrigation did not occur until Classic times. By the time of Spanish conquest, the Aztecs had achieved the ability to elevate canals on aqueducts to carry water over low areas, a difficult engineering task.

Raised fields, a method of reclaiming swamps for crop cultivation, were one of the most fascinating elements of Mesoamerican technology. Raised fields were first devised in the Mayan lowlands in the Formative period, and then they saw heavy use supporting the high population densities of the Classic period Mayas. The Aztecs later adopted this technology in the swampy lakes around their capital Tenochtitlán (Aztec raised fields are known as chinampas). Raised fields are constructed by piling up sediment and organic material from the swamp on long rectangular platforms, leaving canals filled with water between the fields. Crops planted on the field produce well, since they receive abundant water from the canals and the soils are fertilized by periodic applications of muck or organic matter from the swamp. This is a very highly productive agricultural method that was almost completely abandoned in the lowlands after the Maya collapse.

By the time archaeologists first recognized the remains of ancient raised fields in the Maya lowlands in the 1970s, there was only one place where this farming system was still practiced—in Xochimilco, just south of Mexico City. The Aztec system of raised fields had been used continuously since the Spanish conquest, and archaeologists looked to Xochimilco for clues as to how the method worked. They soon realized that raised fields in tropical lowland areas were somewhat different from the Central Mexican highland system, and archaeologists and agronomists began rebuilding Mayan raised fields to study their construction and use. A similar program of experimental raised field construction was being undertaken in the southern Andes of Peru and Bolivia, where the ancient Inca and Tihuanaco civilizations had also used raised fields. In both Mesoamerica and the Andes, the modern experiments not only provided clues to the ancient technology but also led to programs to reintroduce raised field cultivation as a sustainable agricultural method for modern peoples. This is a fascinating case of ancient technology providing a direct impetus for modern economic development.

Other evidence for the consolidation of religious and political power in the hands of the Mayan elite includes the large stucco masks that adorned the faces of many Late Formative temple-pyramids (Figure 1.8). Linda Schele and David Friedel interpret the masks as frameworks for performances of Mayan rulers who linked themselves with deities and supernatural powers. Many of these structures also served as the funerary monuments for Mayan leaders.

A spectacular discovery by William Saturno of Late Formative murals deep within a temple at San Bartolo, in the heart of the jungles of the Petén, Guatemala, provides new evidence for early Maya writing and religious beliefs that anticipate later

Figure 1.8   Temple-pyramid with stucco god masks at the Late Formative Period Mayan town of Cerros, Belize. Courtesy of David A. Freidel.

developments. Such features signal the growing link between political power and religion as Mesoamerican rulers took control over ritual and belief systems. The culmination of this trend came with the powerful states of the succeeding Classic period.

THE CLASSIC CIVILIZATIONS.

Beginning around A.D. 200, an era traditionally called the Classic period began (see Figure 1.2). This was a time of Mesoamerican cultural florescence (Figure 1.9). It should be pointed out that the use of the term "Classic" is not an altogether satisfactory term, given what we now know about cultural complexity of state societies in both the Formative and Postclassic periods. Despite some attempts to introduce more neutral terminology that might better reflect the historical stages in Mesoamerican prehistory, the current period names—Formative (or Preclassic), Classic, and Postclassic—are so embedded in the literature that archaeologists continue to use them extensively. These terms now refer to time periods rather than to developmental stages.

Teotihuacan.

The destruction of Teotihuacan's main rival, Cuicuilco, in the first century A.D. led to a period of explosive urban growth at Teotihuacan. The huge Pyramid of the Sun and Pyramid of the Moon were constructed, and the city's rulers laid out an entire city of 20 square kilometers following a regular grid pattern around the north-south axis of the "Street of the Dead." By A.D. 500, the city had grown to over 150,000 people and was the largest city in the world outside of China.

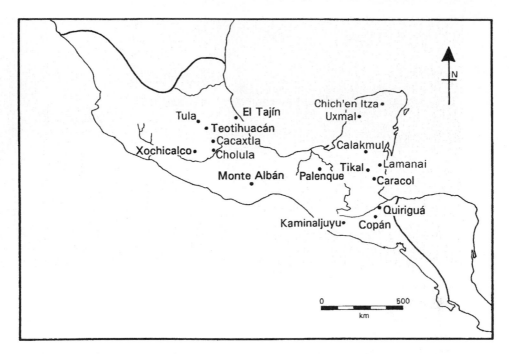

Figure 1.9   Locations of major Classic period, Terminal Classic/Epiclassic period, and Early Postclassic sites.

The names of structures, streets, and the city itself are words from Nahuatl, the language of the Aztecs; curiously, we do not know for certain who the people were who lived at Teotihuacan or what language they spoke. Almost a millennia after its demise, Teotihuacan, "city of the gods" in Nahuatl, was viewed as a sacred place by the Aztecs; and according to Aztec myths, this was the place where the sun was born.

Portions of Teotihuacan lie above a network of tunnels. The entrance to the largest of these is near the base of the central staircase of the Pyramid of the Sun, and it leads to a chamber directly under the top of the pyramid. Whereas it was once believed that this was a natural, if modified, cave, recent research suggests that these underground cavities were actually quarry sites created by early Teotihuacanos to provide construction material for the city's massive construction projects. Subsequently, the cavity under the Pyramid of the Sun was used for rituals. For Mesoamericans, caves had sacred qualtites; they were viewed as entrances to the underworld, and the sun, moon, and even humans were believed to have emerged from caves in the mythological past.

Settlement at Teotihuacan was laid out in a roughly concentric pattern. Major temples, elite residences, and civic buildings including a market were located along the Street of the Dead. These were surrounded by a zone of densely packed apartment compounds that housed the bulk of the city's populace, and this area was in turn surrounded by a zone of scattered huts that housed farmers (Figure 1.10).

Figure 1.10   Aerial photo of the Classic-period metropolis of Teotihuacan, Mexico. Courtesy of Companía Mexicana de Aerofoto, Mexico City.

Archaeologists have used evidence from apartment compounds to reconstruct aspects of ancient urban social organization. Apartment compounds were large, rectangular stone buildings with a single entrance leading to a central courtyard. Passages led off the courtyard to smaller residential units or apartments housing several families each. Some of the courtyards had small pyramid-temple models that served as shrines for religious offerings. Much of the craft production that took place in Teotihuacan was carried out within the apartment compounds. Archaeologists have found evidence for the specialized production of obsidian tools, ceramic vessels and figurines, and jewelry in many of the apartment compounds. Elites resided within more sumptuous apartment compounds that are primarily concentrated in the central part of the city.

With a population of some 150,000 persons, inhabiting over 2,000 separate residential structures, Teotihuacan needed a regular and abundant food supply. Many of the urban residents were farmers who had to walk out to their fields each day. The city was located in an area of natural springs, and water from these was channeled and used to irrigate highly productive agricultural plots at the edges of town.

Several lines of evidence point to a powerful government that regulated many aspects of life and society at ancient Teotihuacan. The city's regular grid plan signals a high degree of urban planning, which could have been accomplished only by a strong central authority. As the city grew in size early in the Classic period, many rural farmers were forced to abandon their homes and move into the expanding urban settlement. Although we are not sure of the reasons for this policy, it is likely that only a strong centralized government could carry out such a practice.

As Teotihuacan grew in size and complexity, its economic and political influence spread throughout much of Mesoamerica. The foreign influence of Teotihuacan was of three types: a political empire in highland Central Mexico that maintained key political contacts in distant lands, a trading network throughout much of Mesoamerica, and a sphere of ideological or religious influence even more widespread than the trade system.

Teotihuacan's armies conquered an empire that covered most of the central Mexican highlands. Within this area, formerly dispersed settlements were congregated into a small number of towns to facilitate administration and control of the conquered population. Many of these new towns were built in imitation of Teotihuacan itself, with a similar cardinal orientation (16 degrees east of north), grid plan, and use of a major central avenue.

Beyond the borders of its empire, Teotihuacan merchants engaged in an active trade and with many areas of Mesoamerica. Green-tinted obsidian artifacts from the Teotihuacan-controlled Pachuca source are found at Classic sites as far south as Honduras, and Teotihuacan-style pottery is abundant in many areas. At distant sites such as Kaminaljuyú in highland Guatemala, structures were built in the distinctive Teotihuacan style, perhaps as residences for merchants from the central Mexican city. At least one neighborhood of foreign merchants has been excavated at Teotihuacan itself, providing strong evidence for the importance of the city's international trade networks. The arrival of Teotihuacan officials at the Mayan center of Tikal in A.D. 378, documented in Tikal's hieroglyphic record, is linked to the establishment of a new major dynasty and suggests direct Teotihuacan intervention in the political affairs of distant lands. The ruling dynasty at Copan was also founded by an individual with strong links to Teotihuacan in A.D. 426.

The ideological significance of Teotihuacan as a major religious and political center was widespread and enduring. Iconographic symbols that emulate the military and religious art of Teotihuacan are found throughout the Classic period Mexican Gulf Coast, Pacific Chiapas, the Yucatan Peninsula, the Petén region of Guatemala, and Copán, Honduras. Feathered serpent symbolism and mythology so prevalent in the art of Teotihuacan became a primary focus of Terminal Classic and Postclassic mythology throughout Mesoamerica.

Teotihuacan's demise came rather suddenly in the seventh century A.D., when the city was burned and destroyed. Evidence indicates that burning was quite selective, with religious and administrative structures receiving the most damage and residences the least. This pattern suggests internal revolt rather than external invasion as the means of destruction, although the reasons or causes for the revolt are not known. Even after destruction of the major buildings along the Street of the Dead, a sizable population remained within the city, and people continued to inhabit the area through the Aztec period and up to the present.

The Classic Mayas.

We have seen that the antecedents of Classic Mayan civilization appeared in the Late Formative period, but in the southern lowlands the Classic period was a time of cultural florescence. During the Classic period, the population reached its peak, building construction was extensive, and there was widespread elaboration of a set of traits that were uniquely Mayan and associated with Mayan elites. These traits include sophisticated calendrical, mathematical, and astronomical systems, writing, and masonry architecture using the corbelled arch, an architectural innovation that formed a vault.

The Classic period in the Mayan area typically is subdivided into Early (ca. A.D. 200–600) and Late (A.D. 600–900) periods. This division reflects what is often called the Classic "hiatus," a period of 136 years (A.D. 557–692) in which there was a significant slowdown in the construction of buildings and the erection of stone monuments in the Tikal heartland. This decline may have been triggered by political competition and warfare initiated by Tikal's rival state, Calakmul, and the latter's ally, Caracol. Hieroglyphic records reveal evidence of the attack of Tikal, and rival cities prospered in conjunction with its hiatus. The beginning of the Late Classic period marks a new cycle of political dynamics and changes in ceramic pottery styles associated with this period. The vast majority of surviving hieroglyphic records were created during this time period.

A number of ideas once held about the Classic Mayas have been revised in recent years as new evidence has come to light. At one time the Mayas were perceived to be a peaceful people; commoners were thought to have lived in dispersed settlements, practicing simple slash-and-burn horticulture while a priestly class resided in empty ceremonial centers, conducting rituals based on an obsession with time. Archaeological fieldwork in the 1960s and 1970s followed by glyphic decipherment from the 1970s to the present day have modified this picture considerably.

We now know that Mayan cities, like other archaic states known in world history, were ruled by political elites who interacted in courts filled with intrigue, engaged in warfare, and were supported by a complex subsistence and luxury economy. The population in the lowlands was large, and many areas were densely populated. Agricultural systems were not limited to slash-and-burn techniques, as the discovery of features such as channeled wetland fields, terracing, arboriculture, and kitchen gardens have documented. Mayan centers once thought to be vacant ceremonial precincts are now known to have been true urban centers with a variety of functions (Box 1.4). The rural landscape was filled with towns and villages, and farmers and craftspeople produced surplus goods for exchange in local markets and as tribute payments to overlords.

Our understanding of the events of the Classic period in the Mayan lowlands has increased markedly in recent years as more of the Mayan writing system has been deciphered (see Chapter 11). Inscriptions appear primarily on stelae, but they also are found on stucco facades, on wooden or stone lintels above doorways, on stairways,

Box 1.4   Changing Views of Mesoamerican Cities

Forty years ago most Mesoamericanists believed that the Classic Maya did not have true cities. Sites with large architecture were thought to be "empty ceremonial centers" inhabited only by priests, and the Maya were mentioned along with Old Kingdom Egypt as the only ancient civilizations that lacked urban centers. Today nearly all Mesoamericanists would describe the Maya as an urban society with true cities and towns. This reversal of opinion came about partly as a result of archaeological fieldwork at Mayan cities and partly as a result of changes in our definition of the term "urban."

The fieldwork most responsible for showing that Mayan sites were indeed true cities was the University of Pennsylvania Tikal Project in the late 1950s and early 1960s. Most earlier archaeological work at Mayan sites had concentrated solely on the monumental architecture found in the centers of sites. The great innovation of the Tikal Project was to extend coverage outward from the site's center with a systematic program of mapping and excavations (directed by William Haviland and Dennis Puleston). Archaeologists learned that the jungle surrounding the pyramids and palaces was filled with low mounds that were the remains of commoner houses. Tikal was not an "empty" center at all but a city with a population of 50,000 or more. The fieldwork at Tikal was part of a larger reorientation of archaeological research in Mesoamerica and elsewhere in the 1960s, away from an exclusive concern with "temples and tombs" and toward a focus on ancient society and culture, including commoner households and rural areas.

Even after the residential neighborhoods of Mayan sites were identified, mapped, and excavated, some scholars still suggested that these settlements were not "true cities" like Teotihuacan or Tenochtitlán. This interpretation was based on a definition of cities as large settlements with very dense populations and complex social institutions. In comparison with Teotihuacan (Figure 1.10), Tikal (Figure 1.11) certainly had a smaller population, a far lower population density, and more limited expressions of social and economic complexity. But does this mean that Tikal was not really an urban settlement?

During the 1970s a new functional definition of urbanism was embraced by anthropologists and other social scientists. Rather than viewing cities as settlements with lots of people, the functional perspective defines cities as settlements that fulfill various functions or roles for a hinterland. These functions can be economic (the city as a center for manufacturing or trade), administrative (the city as a center for government), religious (the city as a setting for important temples), or cultural (the city as a center for the arts or education). This definition of urbanism leads to the notion that there are different types of cities, some of which have large, dense populations and others of which do not.

When the functional view of urbanism was applied to ancient Mesoamerica (initially by Richard Blanton and Joyce Marcus), it became obvious that there was more than one "type" of ancient Mesoamerican city. Tikal, Palenque, Copán, and other large Mayan centers were cities whose major functions were in the realm of administration (as shown by palaces) and religion (large temple-pyramids), whereas Teotihuacan was an urban center where economic functions predominated, although administrative and religious functions were also important.

Among Mesoamerican cities there is enormous variation in such features as city size, population density, degree of formal planning, amount of ceremonial space, presence of fortifications, topographic setting, and arrangement of housing, etc. (compare Figures 1.10, 1.11, 1.15, 2.9). But does this great variety of urban form mask an underlying similarity in urban function? Today many archaeologists believe that apart from a few exceptions, Mesoamerican urban centers functioned primarily in the realms of administration and religion. Nearly all Mesoamerican cities were built around a city center consisting of large buildings carefully arranged around one or more open public plazas. The most common types of central buildings were palace compounds and temple-pyramids. The central focus of the plaza and the size of temples and palaces relative to other structures point to the dominance of religion and administration.

(continued)

(*continued*)

In cases where written records provide clues to urban function (such as ethnohistoric descriptions of Aztec cities, or the content of glyphic inscriptions at Classic Maya cities), administration and religion also stand out, providing additional support for this model. Outside the city center, spatial patterns show considerable variation, but in most cases population density is not extremely high. The exceptions to this pattern are Teotihuacan and Tenochtitlan, Central Mexican imperial capitals with strong economic orientations and very large, dense populations. Nevertheless, these two cities were also important administrative and religious centers for their hinterlands, and the functional approach to urbanism provides insights into all of the urban centers of ancient Mesoamerica.

and on pottery. These inscriptions provide information on dynastic histories of Mayan rulers, the political alliances forged between and among centers, warfare, and ritual life. New publications such as *Chronicle of the Maya Kings and Queens* by epigraphers Simon Martin and Nikolai Grube (2000) have synthesized this information and made it available to the interested public.

Although cities across a wide area of the Mayan lowlands shared a common culture, the area was never unified politically. Instead, several regional states existed within the Mayan lowlands, with each region composed of a capital city and numerous smaller subject cities, towns, and villages. The composition of each region was fluid as centers were alternatively warring with each other and joining in alliances. Two superstates, Tikal and Calakmul, vied to manipulate the southern networks of alliances, which were not always geographically continuous. The Classic Mayan regional states were in a continuous process of expansion and contraction owing to changing fortunes in warfare, statecraft, and exchange.

For reasons that are still not completely understood, Classic Mayan civilization in the southern lowlands collapsed between A.D. 800 and 900. Although the popular image of the mysterious vanished Mayan civilization is not entirely accurate—Mayan peoples continued to live in certain areas within the southern lowlands after the collapse and to the present day—the state institutions that held society together during the Late Formative and Classic periods became obsolete at most cities by around A.D. 800. The first evidence for the impending collapse was the cessation of construction activity at sites in the western portion of the southern lowlands. No long count dates (see Box 1.5) were recorded at sites along the Usumacinta River after A.D. 840. All but a few centers were virtually abandoned by A.D. 900 or shortly thereafter.

The causes of the collapse of Classic Mayan civilization have eluded archaeologists for many years. It is now generally agreed that no single factor can account for the collapse; instead, several related factors contributed to the failure of elite institutions, and variation in the importance of these factors varied among different geographic areas. Demographic and ecological stress clearly played a role for some polities. The rapid increase in population in the lowlands meant that much more food needed to be grown to feed the population. In the fragile tropical ecosystem, the implementation of more intensive forms of agriculture may have upset an already delicate ecological balance and led to depletion of nutrients in soils in areas such as Copan. Skeletal ev-

Box 1.5   The Long Count Calendar

Sometime in the Late Formative period a system of dating was developed that we call the long count. The long count system allowed for much more precise dating than did other dating methods (such as the calendar round) because it was a linear count of days rather than a repeating cycle. The Classic Mayas made greater use of the long count system than did any other group, although the system was developed initially by non-Mayan peoples (probably Mixe-Zoqueans) before the beginning of the Classic period.

The long count system was based on a hierarchy of progressively larger units of time that were tied primarily to the vigesimal—or base 20—system of mathematics. To depict numbers from 1 to 20, a system of bars and dots were used, with a dot equalling 1, and a bar equaling 5. With a combination of bars and dots, numbers up to 20 could be recorded. Each Mayan long count date has five notations that represent the following units of time:

kin = 1 day
uinal = 20 days (or 20 kin)
tun = 360 days (or 18 uinals)
katun = 7,200 days (or 20 tuns) (approximately 20 years)
baktun = 144,000 days (or 20 katuns) (approximately 400 years)

Each long count date, then, tells us how many kin, uinals, tuns, katuns, and baktuns have passed since the beginning of the current "great cycle" (a period of approximately 5,128 solar years), which began on a mythical starting date of zero in 3114 B.C. in our own calendrical system. A long count date of 9.15.5.0.0 simply means that 9 baktuns, 15 katuns, 5 tuns, 0 uinals, and 0 kin have passed since the Maya zero date, or 3114 B.C. in our calendar.

The earliest long count dates currently known come from the sites of Chiapa de Corzo (36 B.C.) and Tres Zapotes (31 B.C.). But as we mentioned earlier, the Classic Mayas made the most extensive use of the long count system. Hundreds of long count dates appear on stelae during the eighth and ninth baktun cycles. The decline of the Classic Mayas of the southern lowlands took place during the ninth baktun cycle, and the last long count date of 10.4.0.0.0 (A.D. 909) was recorded at the site of Toniná.

idence from Copan indicates that Late Classic populations suffered from malnutrition and other chronic diseases. The environment simply could not sustain indefinitely the large populations of the Late Classic period.

A series of repeated droughts occurred between A.D. 760–910 around the time that southern cities were abandoned, and advocates of the "Great Mayan Drought" model argue that the droughts may have been the final straw for vulnerable portions of the Mayan lowlands. This factor cannot be universally applied across the Mayan area, as archaeological sites in northern Yucatán—an environment notoriously drier than the southern lowlands—did not suffer population declines during the drought interval. In some areas, strategies for subterranean water collection and variations in local rainfall may have buffered local populations from drought impacts.

Warfare was another significant cause of the Classic Mayan collapse. Evidence now suggests that warfare between Mayan polities increased during the Late Classic period in areas like the Usumacinta, the Petexbatun, and the Pasion, to the extent that it disrupted polities' abilities to function. In the Petexbatun region, extensive studies of environmental impacts and human ecology reveal that these factors were not significant for explaining collapse and abandonment.

Organizational changes may have been triggered by significant growth in the elite population. The art and writing of late monuments at many sites like Yaxchilan, Copán, and Palenque acknowledge powerful relatives, war captains, and queens who are largely absent in early dynastic records that were reserved for Mayan kings alone; and at Copán, nobles erected their own monuments. Late Mayan kings were forced to a level of inclusiveness that likely foreshadowed the council institutions that succeeded them in the northern Mayan lowlands at sites like Chichén Itza. Nobles were clearly challenging the institution of divine kingship in the decades prior to the southern Classic "collapse."

External pressures added to the disruptions of the ninth century. The intrusion of outsiders from the Putun or Chontal Mayas from the Tabasco region into the lowland Mayan area was once thought to have been a major factor in the Maya collapse. Evidence for foreign intrusion at some sites is clear, particularly in the western lowlands at the site of Seibal; but it is now believed that the intruders found an already unstable Mayan society and merely took advantage of an existing situation rather than being the main cause of the decline. Some combination of these factors was responsible for the collapse of Classic Mayan society in the southern lowlands, although it is likely that the precise combination of factors varied from region to region.

The collapse of Classic Mayan civilization in the southern lowlands did not mean that the area was left entirely uninhabited. The population decline was dramatic owing to both increased mortality rates and emigration, as elites and others apparently fled to areas near the Caribbean coast and northern Yucatán. Yet some of the population remained, choosing to live not in the abandoned cities but in the rural areas. By the Postclassic period a thriving, if smaller and radically reorganized, Mayan society survived with settlements such as the lake area of the central Petén, and at similar lagoons of northeastern Belize. Further north, in the Yucatán Peninsula, Mayan centers such as Chichén Itzá, Uxmal, Edzná, Sayil, and Labná thrived for one or more centuries after the southern decline.

A brief look at three of the largest and most intensively studied Classic Mayan cities—Tikal, Palenque, and Copán—will provide a fuller view of Classic Mayan culture and illustrate both similarities and differences among Mayan cities. The following discussion relies upon Martin and Grube's book, *Chronicle of the Maya Kings and Queens* for specific names and events of Classic dynasties.

Tikal. Tikal is the largest known Mayan center—the main residential area covers 23 square kilometers, and over 3,000 structures have been mapped—and it has been studied intensively by scores of archaeologists for many years (Figure 1.11). Located in the Petén jungle of Guatemala, Tikal had a population of 50,000 at its peak in the Late Classic period. From the numerous stelae and inscriptions found on buildings, epigraphers have been able to reconstruct the political and dynastic history of Tikal in some detail. An enduring dynasty ruled at Tikal from A.D. 378 to

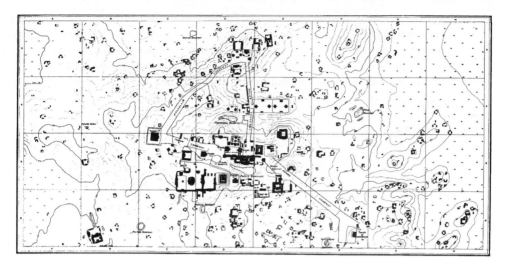

Figure 1.11   The central portion of the Classic-period Mayan city of Tikal, Guatemala. Courtesy of The University Museum, University of Pennsylvania.

the ultimate demise of the center, and we know the names of many of the rulers and some important events in their lives.

By the Late Formative period, Tikal was already developing into an important regional center. Following the involvement of Teotihuacan in founding a new dynasty, Tikal emerged as the dominant center of the Early Classic Period central lowlands. Hieroglyphic texts record the arrival of a military ambassador, Siyaj K'ak, at Tikal on January 31, 378, on the same day that the prior king, Chak Tok Ich'aak died; epigraphers view this as no coincidence. King Yax Nuun Ayiin I, installed by Siyaj K'ak over a year later, is the named descendant of a mysterious figure, Spearthrower Owl, who may have been the ruler of Teotihuacan. Texts declare that this boy king was overseen by Siyaj K'ak. Yax Nuun Ayiin was depicted in Teotihuacan attire, and his grave offerings included vessels with painted Teotihuacan mythological figures. Despite Teotihuacan's likely intervention with the Tikal line, local Mayan lineages allied with the new dynasty prospered from this circumstance. Yax Nuun Ayiin's son, Siyaj Chan K'awiil II, depicted himself in traditional Mayan costume in the splendid Stela 31, which also pays homage to Spearthrower Owl and portrays his father as a Teotihuacano. The Tikal nobility assimilated Teotihuacan elements and made them an important part of their founding mythology, and powerful local families likely married into this dynasty. Claiming foreign descent is a common cross-cultural strategy in ancient complex societies, and fusing exotic descent lines with powerful local ones draws upon two funds of social power that serve to legitimize aspiring rulers.

Elements of Teotihuacan symbolism are present in the art of many later Mayan sites, in reference to founding mythology or as components of kingly war gear. These elements include balloon headdresses, atlatls, square shields, Tlaloc (Mexican rain god) goggle-eyed figures, and the mosaic war serpent headdresses.

The pivotal events at Tikal in the fourth century A.D. subsequently entered the mythic history of the Classic Mayas and were regularly recycled to legitimize later dynasties. Opportunities presented by the dynastic interventions of Spearthrower Owl and his emissaries catapulted Tikal to prominence as one of the two major superpowers of the Mayan world.

Tikal's Classic hiatus began when it was attacked in A.D. 562 in a "star war" event timed with the motion of Venus. This action is recorded on an altar at Caracol, a large site in the Mayan Mountains of Belize, and Caracol was likely acting under the auspices of Tikal's rival city of Calakmul. Monuments are not recorded at Tikal for the subsequent 130 years (until A.D. 692), and nearby cities also suffer a similar depression. Calakmul, however, rose to power in the vacuum created by Tikal's demise. New information about the hiatus reveals that Tikal was not entirely crippled. Rich burials of otherwise silent hiatus kings attest to continued noble functions and dynastic succession at the city. Calakmul again attacked Tikal in A.D. 657 and sponsored other rivals of Tikal at this time.

King Jasaw Chan K'awiil I (A.D. 682–734) ended Tikal's hiatus and brought the city back to greatness in A.D. 695 by defeating Calakmul. He initiated massive construction projects including the city's famous twin-pyramid complexes, a ballcourt, Temple 2; and he revamped the city's huge palace compound known as the Central Acropolis. He revitalized the political and economic strength of Tikal, although the city's geographic sphere of political influence was still curtailed by a network of Calakmul's allies.

Jasaw's son, Yik'in Chan K'awiil (acceding in A.D. 734) continued major building projects at the city, including the final phase of Temple I, where his father was buried. He was a military hero, who expanded the kingdom to dominance in the Petén region through a suite of victories over major cities, including Calakmul, although it is not known how long he ruled. He was succeeded by a brief unnamed 28th ruler of two years (A.D. 766–768), followed by Yax Nuun Ayiin II (acceding in A.D. 768), who was the final great king of Tikal, although his regional control seems to have declined. Four other kings are named in the succeeding ninth century, during a time when southern lowlands dynasties were declining and cities were becoming depopulated. Tikal's final monument was erected in A.D. 869.

Palenque. Palenque occupies a dramatic natural setting, nestled in the hills of Chiapas overlooking the Gulf Coast plain. Much of what we see today at the site of Palenque was constructed during the reigns of its two most notable rulers: K'inich Janaab' Pakal I (A.D. 615–683), or Great-Sun Shield, and his oldest son, K'inich Kan B'alam II (A.D. 684–702), or Great-Sun Snake Jaguar. Pakal and Kan B'alaam ruled for most of the seventh century, although inscriptions at the site date the beginnings of Palenque's dynastic history to A.D. 431.

Palenque stands apart from other Classic Mayan sites for its unique architectural style and its beautiful bas-relief sculpture in both stone and stucco, which includes some of the longest Classic Mayan texts. The rulers of Palenque were particularly concerned with legitimizing their positions as rulers, and many of the texts focus on the foundations of royal genealogy in creation myths. Texts focusing on the concern for legitimacy has made it possible to reconstruct the complete dynastic history of the site. As a result we know that at least one queen-Lady, Yohl Ik'nal (acceding in A.D. 583), ruled at Palenque, and it is possible that Pakal I's mother, Lady Sak K'uk', also ruled for a brief three-year period before twelve-year-old Pakal acceded to the throne in A.D. 615.

Innovations by architects at Palenque enabled them to construct rooms with thinner walls and greater interior space, creating rooms that were lighter and better ventilated than the small, dark rooms found at other sites. At Palenque, unlike most other Classic Mayan centers, sculptors did not erect freestanding stone monuments or stelae, as their work could be displayed on building interiors.

Palenque was a smaller city than Tikal, yet it clearly was a prominent political and religious center in the Late Classic period. The site is dominated by the Temple of the Inscriptions, the funerary monument to Pakal, and a network of buildings called the Palace (Figure 1.12). Deep within the Temple of the Inscriptions is Pakal's tomb. His coffin, made of stone, is so massive that it had to be put in place before the pyramid was constructed. The sarcophagus lid is elaborately carved with a depiction of

Figure 1.12   Overview of the site of Palenque; the Palace compound is in the foreground at the right, and Pakal's Temple of Inscriptions is shown on the left. Photo by Robert Rosenswig.

Pakal's journey to the underworld (see Figure A.10 in the Introduction). The tomb was reached by climbing down a narrow, vaulted stairway that begins at the top of the temple.

Kan B'alaam built a triadic temple compound known as the Group of the Cross (see Figure 14.3), which features magnificent panels chronicling the supernatural sanctions of his accession to rule. His brother, K'inich K'an Joy Chitam II (Precious/Yellow Tied Peccary), added to Palenque's splendor in his modifications to the palace, but his reign was cut short when he was taken captive and presumably killed by the city of Tonina. He left no heir, and four kings followed from a new royal line at Palenque.

Recent investigations by Alfonso Morales and colleagues in Temples 18 and 19 behind the Group of the Cross have unearthed remarkable panels that show that these kings continued to frame their rule in the city's mythological origins. Significant military activity defined the reign of Ahkal Mo' Naab' III (acceding in A.D. 721), and the acts of a key war captain, Chak Suutz', is recognized in a panel commemorating events from A.D. 723–730. This war captain lived in a fine palace near Palenque's center, and his success illustrates the entry of nobles into dynastic records at the end of the Classic Period. Ahkal Mo' Naab' III's successor, K'inich Janaab Pakal II, is depicted in a magnificent panel from Temple 19 (Figure 1.13). Palenque's last

Figure 1.13   Newly discovered panel from The Instituto Nacional de Antropología e Historia, Mexico (INAH) investigations at Palenque depicting ruler K'inich Janab Pakal II, on exhibit at the Palenque Museum. Photo by Robert Rosenswig, courtesy of Alfonso Morales.

king acceded in A.D. 799, a fact recorded on a single pottery vessel. He erected no monuments. The city was suddenly depopulated during the early ninth century.

Copán. The Copán Valley, located in Honduras at the southeastern edge of the Mayan area, was first settled in the Early Formative period. The site of Copán grew into an important Mayan city in the Early Classic period, and most of what is visible at the site today are outer construction phases built during the Late Classic period. Situated in a highland valley at around 2,000 feet above sea level, Copán is one of the few Classic Mayan centers in an upland region. Copán has been the focus of extensive research in recent years; the ceremonial precinct and several outlying residential districts have been excavated, and epigraphers have made important advances in the decipherment of the numerous hieroglyphic texts at the site.

According to inscriptions at Copán, the ruling dynasty was founded in A.D. 426, and all subsequent rulers, sixteen in all, based their legitimacy on their descent from the first ruler, K'inich Yax K'uk Mo', or Great-Sun First Quetzal Macaw. Remarkably, his installment, like that of Yax Nuun Ayiin of Tikal, seems ultimately linked to Teotihuacan involvment in Early Classic period Mayan dynastic lines. The evidence for this pattern at Copán is impressive: Glyphic texts suggest that he was a nonlocal who arrived to take power from another location; he is most often shown wearing Teotihuacan Tlaloc goggles; his first funerary shrine (nicknamed Hunal by archaeologists) was a Teotihuacan style talud-tablero building covered with murals; and chemical studies of his bones link him to the Tikal area. In what is probably his wife's tomb, a beautiful vessel seems to portray him in Teotihuacan style, perhaps in death within his burial temple. Her bone chemistry indicates that she was locally born, and Yax K'uk' Mo's son rebuilt his father's funerary shrine in a more Mayan style. As at Tikal, the descendants of foreign-sponsored founders were quick to assimilate their exotic basis of legitimization into parallel local funds of power.

At Copán, like Palenque and Tikal, we know considerable details of Late Classic period dynasties. For most of the seventh century, Copán was ruled by its twelfth ruler, Smoke-Imix, a contemporary of Pakal I at Palenque and Jasaw Chan K'awiil at Tikal. Under Smoke-Imix, Copán expanded its territory to its greatest extent, bringing neighboring Quirigua and other centers into its orbit during his 67 years of reign. His successor and son, Waxaklajuun Ub'aah K'awiil (18 Images of K'awiil), was responsible for transforming much of Copán's ceremonial center into its currently visible form.

All of the stelae in the Great Plaza were erected by Waxaklajuun Ub'aah K'awiil between A.D. 711 and 736, and they portray him in the guise of various patron gods of the city. His impersonation of these deities emphasized his intermediary position between earth and the supernatural realm, and they dramatized his transformative capacities and ability to negotiate with supernatural entities on behalf of the living. These stelae are hailed for their artistic achievements in three-dimensional stone sculpture, which is primarily limited to modeled stucco in the Maya area (Figure 1.14).

Waxaklajuun Ub'aah K'awiil met an untimely end when he was captured and beheaded by the ruler of Copán's former subject city, Quirigua, in A.D. 738. As he had

Figure 1.14   Stela A at the Classic-period Mayan city of Copan, Honduras. Photo by Michael E. Smith.

installed this Quirigua ruler himself in 724, this was a treacherous betrayal. This act ended the creative works of Waxaklajuun Ub'aah K'awiil, and temporarily diminished the power of Copán's ruling dynasty: No structures or stelae were erected during the reign of his successor.

The death of Copán's ruler did not, however, result in any great changes in the everyday life of most of Copán's citizens; archaeologists cannot detect any changes in social and economic activities associated with this hiatus (A.D. 738–756). During the reign of the son of Waxaklajuun Ub'aah K'awiil's successor, Copán's ruling dynasty reestablished its position of strength, although this was not to last.

The sixteenth and penultimate ruler of Copán, Yax Pasaj Chan Yoaat, or First Dawned Sky Lightning God, came to power in A.D. 763. He began an ambitious building program at Copán, but he ruled in a time of crisis. By Yax-Pasaj's reign, overpopulation had put a strain on the valley's resources, and noble families were increasingly competing with the ruling family for power. His monuments differ from those of his predecessors in that they depict nobles alongside the king who share similar privileges of recognition and royal actions.

Nobles were erecting their own monuments in elite compounds during the late eighth century, representing a clear challenge to the royal family. When Yax-Pasaj died in the early ninth century, dynastic rule at Copán was close to collapse. His successor began to carve a monument commemorating his seating in A.D. 822, but it was never completed. Although the city center and outlying neighborhoods continued to be occupied for another hundred years or so, centralized political control and all of the activities it had engendered had come to an end.

A Classic Zapotec Civilization.

Although Teotihuacan and the lowland Mayas were the largest civilizations of the Classic period, several other areas of Mesoamerica also supported large state-level societies at this time. In the Valley of Oaxaca, the Zapotec hilltop city of Monte Albán became capital of a powerful state. Evidence from stone monuments indicates that the use of force was sometimes needed to subjugate neighboring as well as distant polities.

Monte Albán apparently had a good relationship with Teotihuacan. Depictions of what appear to be diplomatic meetings between Teotihuacan "ambassadors" and Zapotec lords were recorded on stone monuments at Monte Albán, and Zapotec merchants lived in their own barrio at Teotihuacan. After A.D. 600, however, Monte Albán suffered a period of decline, and its territory began to shrink as subject towns gained strength and broke away from its control. By A.D. 700, Monte Albán had lost its dominant position in the Valley; and by A.D. 800, portions of the site—including the Great Plaza—were no longer in use. Nevertheless, part of the site and the surrounding area continued to be used into the Postclassic period.

EPICLASSIC/TERMINAL CLASSIC AND EARLY POSTCLASSIC PERIODS.

A period immediately following the decline of Mesoamerica's Classic period civilizations, called the Epiclassic period in Central Mexico and the Terminal Classic period in the Mayan area, and the subsequent Early Postclassic period were times of transition and transformation in Mesoamerica. Because the dates attributed to these different periods vary from region to region and because developments at some of the sites discussed later do not fall neatly into one period or another, we consider this entire period—from the beginning of the eighth century to the twelfth century—in the following discussion.

The interval between the destruction of Teotihuacan and the rise of the Aztec empire over five centuries later saw the rise and fall of a succession of militaristic cities and states in northern Mesoamerica. After the fall of Teotihuacan, a number of large cities sprang up to fill the political and economic vacuum left by the fall of the Teotihuacan empire. Although some of these cities were important Classic period sites, they experienced a fluorescence in the Epiclassic period that followed Teotihuacan's decline.

A network of cosmopolitan world centers, which were engaged in extensive trade and ideological interaction with one another, extended from the Mexican highlands to the lowland Mayam area. In addition to the remnant city at Teotihuacan itself (still a major city of 30,000 inhabitants), impressive urban centers were found at Xochicalco in Morelos, Teotenango in the Toluca Valley, and Cacaxtla and Cholula in the Puebla-Tlaxcala area. These were mountaintop cities whose fortifications and iconography attest to the prevalence of warfare at this time (Figures 1.15 and 1.16).

The sites of El Tajin in Veracruz and Chichen Itzá in Yucatán represent nodes of this interaction sphere located in the Gulf Coast and Yucatan peninsula respectively. In Belize, the site of Lamanai is distinctive because it survived the southern Mayan collapse and maintained its position as a regional center through the Terminal and Early Postclassic Periods; it clearly prospered from its ties to the Epiclassic Mesoamerican world via a maritime Caribbean trade route.

Figure 1.15   The Epiclassic-period fortified, hilltop city of Xochicalco, Mexico. Courtesy of Companía Mexicana de Aerofoto, Mexico City.

Figure 1.16   Ritualized battle as depicted in a mural at the Epiclassic-period city of Cacaxtla, Mexico. Courtesy of Debra Nagao.

On the Gulf Coast, the center of El Tajín is an important site that gained prominence during the Classic period. Closely linked to Teotihuacan in the early part of the Classic period, El Tajín reached its peak of development after the fall of Teotihuacan. The site is noted for being a center of the ball game cult, with seventeen ballcourts mapped at the site, and many of the artifacts recovered during excavations at the site are paraphernalia used in the ball game (see Figure 14.4 in Chapter 14).

The Yucatán Peninsula: Chichén Itzá.

During the Late Classic through Early Postclassic periods, cities in the northern Yucatán Peninsula carried on much of the southern Classic Mayan tradition. These centers, which did not suffer the immediate effects of the southern collapse, are best known for their unique architectural styles. In the Puuc region, sites exhibit intricate mosaic designs on building façades and frequent depictions of Chac (rain god) masks over doorways and at the corners of buildings. Uxmal, Sayil, and Labná are the most elaborate examples of the Puuc tradition. These centers fell into decline within a hundred years of the collapse in the southern lowlands, perhaps for many of the same reasons.

Chichén Itzá is a unique Mayan city with combined architectural and artistic elements that reflect aspects of the more traditional northern Classic Period Puuc style as well as influences that point to contact with Central Mexico, indicative of what is called an "international" or "cosmopolitan" style. The traditional section of Chichén Itzá is located to the south of the Great Platform, while the architecture of the Great Platform reflects the International style with such notable features as "the Castillo"—a four-stair, serpent balustraded temple, the Great Ballcourt (one of the largest in Mesoamerica), the Mercado gallery-patio compound, and the Temple of the Warriors (Figure 1.17). Linked to the Great Platform and its massive central plaza by a stone road, or *sacbe*, is the Cenote of Sacrifice, an important pilgrimage locality, where many offerings and human remains were recovered.

Figure 1.17   Temple of the Warriors, a major administrative feature used for council meetings, ceremonies, and processions at Chichen Itza's Great Platform. Photo by Robert Rosenswig.

Features like those of the Great Platform are also located at key points within 2.5 km of the site's center, and the site has a total of thirteen ballcourts. Gallery-patio complexes are unique to this site, and it is likely that they represent key administrative halls maintained by major officials in the polity. The city was large and dispersed; networks of at least ten radial sacbes connect the city's center to its outlying groups. Notable earlier sites with similar radial sacbe networks include Calakmul and Caracol.

Chichén Itzá is a grand and resplendent site. Its buildings are elaborately decorated with more carved stone than any other city in Maya history. It was clearly the heart of an aggressive, expansionary polity that held major influence over the northern lowlands during its height. A surge in major construction programs occurred during the ninth century A.D., but this city's power waned by A.D. 1000 or 1100 at the latest.

Direct links between Chichén Itzá and Tula are suggested by both Central Mexican and Yucatec native histories and the striking architectural and artistic similarities between the two sites, but the precise nature of the relationship between the two centers is poorly understood and hotly debated. Long-standing difficulties with dating architecture at these sites have made empirical evaluation difficult, although recent research suggests that the sites are at least partially contemporaneous. In Central Mexico, in the tenth century or perhaps earlier, Tula emerged as the largest urban center since the fall of Teotihuacan, and by around A.D. 1150, it was abandoned (see the discussion that follows).

One view of the relationship between Tula and Chichén Itzá derives from central Mexican and Yucatec native histories, which claim that in A.D. 987, Topiltzín Quetzalcoatl, a high priest in the Quetzalcoatl (Feathered Serpent) cult at Tula, was expelled from Tula after a power struggle with Tezcatlipoca. Postclassic Mayan myths hail Kukulkan's arrival in the Mayan area (Kukulkan was the name for Quetzalcoatl in the Yucatec Mayan language). In this view, the architectural and artistic similarities between Tula and Chichén Itzá result from either the direct presence of Toltecs or else the influence of another Mayan group who had close contact with the Toltecs, who are generally assumed to be the Chontal or Putun Mayas of the Gulf Coast region. An alternative view proposes that Chichén Itzá was constructed prior to Tula, and that influence may have traveled in the opposite direction.

A more holistic view has been offered by William Ringle, George Bey, and Tomas Gallareta, who argue that Chichén Itzá embraced cultic icons in its art and architecture linked to the Feathered Serpent cult of interacting elites in the Epiclassic Mesoamerican world. The spread of this cult in elite culture fostered long-distance ties between cult centers that facilitated important trade flow through the same networks. Although iconographic similarities are greatest between Chichén Itzá and Tula, some of the same elements are found at many other major Epiclassic/Terminal Classic centers mentioned previously.

Recent considerations of the art of Chichén Itzá's ballcourt by Linda Schele and Peter Matthews reveal that the new cosmopolitan styles fused aspects of Classic Period traditional Mayan creation mythology (e.g., maize god and ball game sacrifice, agricultural fertility, world tree *axis mundi,* aged pauahtun/sky bearer gods) with innovative international elements shared with distant Mexican sites (e.g., solar disks, feathered serpents, atlantean warrior figures, chacmool statues). In addition to adopting key ideas and symbolism of international styles of the Epiclassic, the Mayan area also contributed to the mix. The use of foreign elements for royal legitimization was ubiquitous at Classic period Mayan cities long before Chichén Itzá arose to power.

Chichén Itzá exemplifies institutional transformations from the Classic to Postclassic periods. Although nobles were previously involved in affairs of royal courts, the art at Chichén Itzá reflects the involvement of multiple powerful factions to an extent that is unmatched by any other site in Mesoamerica. Inscribed panels and murals of the Great Ballcourt, hundreds of carved columns and inner murals at the Temple of the Warriors (see Figure 1.17), and many other programs show warriors, priests, captives, councils of officials, merchants, and other actors that celebrate the city's diverse and multiethnic segments. Elaborate outlying palaces and ballcourts, many connected to the center by radial sacbes (elevated roads) attest to the presence of a large noble class.

The administrative institutions of this city were complex and involved councils of political lords, priests, and warrior groups representing different political factions. Like other major contemporary cities in Mesoamerica, Chichén Itzá likely served as a cultic center where rulers of allied polities went to perform ceremonies that sanctioned their right to govern, as William Ringle has proposed.

Northern Mesoamerica.

In the tenth century, Tula emerged as the largest urban center since the fall of Teotihuacan. Tula was the home of the Toltecs, a group about which archaeology and ethnohistory are in disagreement. According to Aztec native historical accounts, the Toltecs were wise and great. They were devout, and they invented all of the useful arts and crafts. Their capital, Tula, was a magnificent metropolis with buildings constructed of precious stones. The Toltec dynasty was revered by the Aztecs and other Postclassic groups. Rulers of Late Postclassic Aztec city-states as well as Mixtec and Mayan elites traced their descent and legitimacy back to the Toltec kings.

Whereas the Toltecs of Tula were glorified by later groups, archaeology paints another picture. Tula had some impressive public architecture, but it was a far cry from the size and grandeur of the earlier Teotihuacan, and it had far fewer imported goods. Nevertheless, Tula was a large and an important capital city. It had one of the largest plazas in Mesoamerica, and its public architecture was arranged in a highly formal fashion around the plaza. A large pyramid, Structure C, stood on the east side of the plaza. Structure B on the north side was flanked by large colonnaded halls, an unusual form in Mesoamerica (this is one of the architectural similarities with Chichén Itzá noted earlier). Large ballcourts were built on the west side of the plaza and north of Structure B, and the south end of the plaza was filled out with several palaces. Numerous low-relief carvings at Tula depict scenes of battles, rituals, and trade.

Tula was an important city in Early Postclassic Mesoamerica, although its role was exaggerated by Aztec historians who looked back to Tula as the source of Aztec greatness. At some point around A.D. 1150, Tula was abandoned.

Elsewhere, beyond Mesoamerica's northern frontier, the trading centers of Alta Vista and La Quemada developed during the Epiclassic/Early Postclassic periods. Located in the modern Mexican state of Zacatecas, these sites were located in a region rich with minerals that were highly desired at Mesoamerican centers such as Tula. Alta Vista and La Quemada also served as important trade intermediaries between Mesoamerica and the American Southwest, and the valuable turquoise deposits there. By A.D. 1200, with many of the great Epiclassic/Termial Classic and Early Postclassic centers abandoned or in decline, the scene was set for the rise of the Late Postclassic polities (as related in Chapter 2 to follow).

SUGGESTED READINGS

BRASWELL, GEOFFREY E. (ed.) 2003 *The Maya and Teotihuacan: Reinterpreting Early Classic Interaction.* Austin: University of Texas Press.

CARRASCO, DAVID, LINDSAY JONES, and SCOTT SESSIONS (eds.) 2000 *Mesoamerica's Classic Heritage: From Teotihuacan to the Aztecs.* Boulder: University of Colorado Press.

CLARK, JOHN E., and MARY E. PYE (eds.) 2000 *Olmec Art and Archaeology in Mesoamerica*. Washington, D.C.: National Gallery of Art.

DIEHL, Richard A. 2004 *The Olmecs: America's First Civilization*. New York: Thames and Hudson.

DIEHL, RICHARD A., and JANET CATHERINE BERLO (eds.) 1989 *Mesoamerica After the Decline of Teotihuacan: A.D. 700–900*. Washington, D.C.: Dumbarton Oaks.

EVANS, SUSAN TOBY 2004 *Ancient Mexico and Central America*. New York: Thames and Hudson.

MARTIN, SIMON, and NIKOLAI GRUBE 2000 *Chronicle of the Maya Kings and Queens: Deciphering the Dynasties of the Ancient Maya*. London: Thames and Hudson.

MILLER, MARY ELLEN 2001 *The Art of Mesoamerica: From Olmec to Aztec*. 3rd ed. World of Art. New York: Thames and Hudson.

SCHELE, LINDA, and PETER MATHEWS 1998 *The Code of Kings: The Language of Seven Sacred Maya Temples and Tombs*. New York: Simon and Schuster.

SHARER, ROBJERT J. with LOA P. TRAXLER 2005 *The Ancient Maya*. 6th ed. Stanford: Stanford University Press.

SMITH, MICHAEL E. and MARILYN A. MASSON 2000 *Ancient Civilizations of Mesoamerica: A Reader*. Malden, Massachusetts: Blackwell Press.

Chapter 2
Late Postclassic Mesoamerica

To better understand the Late Postclassic period (A.D. 1200–1520) in Mesoamerica we benefit from having not only the archaeological record but also a wealth of documentary evidence from native sources (for pre-Hispanic and Colonial periods) as well as Spanish sources for the Colonial period. The analysis and interpretation of these written documents is known as "ethnohistory" (ethnohistoric sources are discussed at greater length in Chapters 3 and 6). In the first part of this chapter, we focus on Late Postclassic historical developments, relying primarily on archaeological evidence from several regions of Mesoamerica (Figure 2.1). Later in the chapter we turn to a more detailed view of three of the best known and important contributors to the Late Postclassic Mesoamerican world: the Aztec, Mixtec, and Mayan peoples. These profiles are designed to illustrate both the cultural features that defined Mesoamerica as a whole as well as the cultural variation that existed across the region.

HISTORICAL OVERVIEW OF THE LATE POSTCLASSIC PERIOD

The Late Postclassic period in Mesoamerica saw the continuation of general trends begun in the Early Postclassic period (see Chapter 1). One of these trends, the decentralization of political control over the economy, was linked to the expansion of market systems and long-distance exchange among Late Postclassic polities. The Aztec and Tarascan empires emerged as dominant powers in northern Mesoamerica in the Late Postclassic period, and the lowland capital of Mayapán exerted major influence throughout the lowland Mayan area. Beyond these core zones, the majority of Late Postclassic states throughout Mesoamerica were small in size and did not expand their territories in the same manner as the large Classic states like Teotihuacan or Monte Albán. At the same time, the boundaries between small polities became increasingly permeable to both commercial and cultural exchange and interaction. Art styles, for example, exhibit greater unity across all of Mesoamerica than ever be-

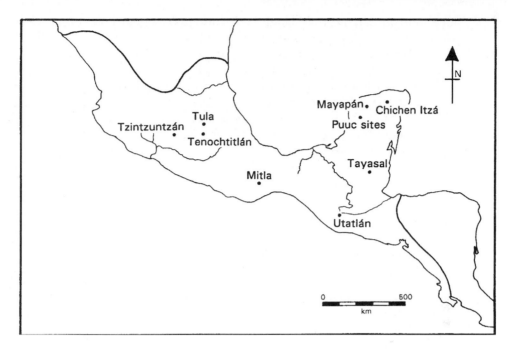

Figure 2.1   Locations of major later Postclassic Period sites.

fore, giving rise to the notion of an international or cosmopolitan art style—so named because it was an artistic style that was an amalgamation of elements from many regions of Mesoamerica, including Central Mexico, the Mixtec region, and the Mayan region (Boone and Smith 2003; see also the discussion of Mesoamerica as a "world-system" in Chapter 3 to follow this one). Technological innovations, such as the use of the bow and arrow and cotton-quilted armor, also were adopted throughout the region in the Late Postclassic period.

We now turn to a brief discussion of Late Postclassic historical developments within several of the major regions of Mesoamerica.

Oaxaca

Prior to the Postclassic period, the Oaxaca region had been dominated to a great extent by events taking place in the Valley of Oaxaca, an area populated by the Zapotecs. But in the Postclassic period, the Mixtecs, who inhabited much of Oaxaca outside the central Valley of Oaxaca, began to have a much greater influence on other Mesoamericans (see the Mixtec Profile later).

After the decline of Monte Albán, the Valley of Oaxaca was divided into a large number of independent city-states, none of which exercised absolute control over the valley, although the city-state of Zaachila was highly revered (see Chapter 3). The Postclassic occupation of Monte Albán was relatively small, but it had impressive architecture, and the site wielded considerable political power because it was home to an important Zapotec royal family. Mitla, also in the eastern part of the valley, is the best-known Postclassic site in the Oaxaca Valley.

Mitla was occupied continuously from the Early Formative period, but the center's florescence took place in the Postclassic period. It was during the Late Post-classic period that the most important, and beautiful, building complexes were constructed. Described in the sixteeth century as having two of the most impressive and famous buildings in New Spain, Mitla is noted for the intricate mosaic veneer on the façades of buildings and for its murals (Figure 2.2). Historical sources identify Mitla as a Zapotec religious center where oracles were housed that were the focus of pilgrimage and were consulted in the affairs of daily life. Mitla was a place where disputes were negotiated among rival factions and may have been a location where political rulers received sanctions of authority from Zapotec priests.

Many sites in the Valley of Oaxaca show evidence of Mixtec influence in the Postclassic period, although the precise nature of this influence is the subject of ongoing debate. By the early part of the Postclassic period, the Mixtecs were becoming an increasingly important and influential force within Mesoamerican (see the Mixtec profile that follows). This is particularly true of artistic styles. According to both Mixtec and Zapotec historical traditions, intermarriage between Mixtec and Zapotec noble families strengthened ties between the two groups, and this practice, rather

Figure 2.2   Stone mosaic façade of a palace building at the Postclassic-period city of Mitla, Mexico. Photo by Marilyn Masson.

than intrusive Mixtec populations, may best explain Mixtec presence and influence in the valley. The Mixtec pictoral codices chronicle foundation myths and historical events of Postclassic dynasties, and represent a rich corpus of historical indigenous documents for Mesoamerica at this time (Figure 2.3; see also Figure 6.5).

Yucatan. Mayapán succeeded Chichén Itzá as the primary center of the Yucatán Peninsula from around 1200–1441 (Figure 2.4). Mayapán dominated Yucatán for over two centuries, and its builders emulated some of Chichén Itzá's architectural features (colonnaded halls, feathered serpent column pyramids, round structures), and eliminated others (ballcourt, gallery-patio compounds). Native Colonial accounts claim that lords of Mayapán defeated Chichén Itzá and broke up its alliance network through an act of treachery, and founders of Mayapán claimed to revitalize some earlier Mayan traditions. Archaeologically, this is visible in the erection of stelae at the site (absent from Chichén Itzá) and in a Mayapán effigy censer tradition that portrayed many traditional Mayan gods recognizable from Classic period art (Figure 2.5).

Mayapán was organized quite differently from Chichén Itzá; unlike the latter it is a densely settled, highly nucleated urban center (4.5 square kilometers), largely contained within a circumferential outer wall. This Postclassic capital controlled much of the northwest peninsula, and its governors presided over councils of lords from affiliated territories. Mayapán maintained strong political and economic ties

Figure 2.3 Mixtec artist-scribe as portrayed in the Codex Vindobonensis. After Jill Leslie Furst, *Codex Vindobonensis Mexicanus I: A Commentary,* Publication No. 4. Albany, New York: Institute for Mesoamerican Studies, SUNY, 1978, p. 125.

Figure 2.4   The Temple of Kukulkan at the Postclassic Mayan political center of Mayapán. This edifice, with its serpent balustrades and four cardinal staircases, served as the central focus for political and religious activities at the site and was likely dedicated to Kukulkan, the Mayan manifestation of the feathered serpent deity. Photo by Robert Rosenswig.

with much of the Mayan lowlands, particularly the eastern and southern Yucatan peninsula, northern Belize, and the Petén Lakes of Guatemala. Like Chichén Itzá, it was an outward-looking polity with strong military, iconographic, and trading connections to the Mexican highlands through the Gulf Coast. Painted and stuccoed art programs in the city's center attest to these international ties in their incorporation of Mexican deities and artistic styles. Colonial documents claim that Mexican mercenaries resided within the city walls and aided in the establishment of at least one of the city's ruling regimes.

Mayapán's downfall was brought about through an internal violent attack, led by members of the Xiu lineage, and there is evidence that the city was sacked, burned, and rapidly abandoned. According to various chronicles, Mayapán fell in 1441. Mayapán was the last Yucatecan center that was able to dominate the peninsula. Subsequently, the region was divided into numerous small, independent polities (see Chapter 3). The best known of these were located along the Gulf and Caribbean coasts, where settlements continued to prosper by engaging in maritime trade until

Figure 2.5 Postclassic Mayan effigy censer from Mayapan depicting the deity Itzamna. This example was recently found by Carlos Peraza Lope of the Centro INAH–Yucatán during his investigations at the site center. Photo by Bradley Russell, courtesy of Carlos Peraza Lope.

the time of Spanish contact. Mayapán's long-distance economy, like that of Chichén Itzá, relied heavily on this network of sea-based commerce, which circled the Yucatan peninsula from Honduras to the Gulf Coast. The Island of Cozumel not only served as a center for trade but also was the site of an important shrine to Ix Chel, goddess of medicine and a patron deity of women and merchants. On the mainland, Tulum and Santa Rita Corozal were busy seaports whose buildings were adorned with colorful murals depicting ceremonies that may represent accession to political and religious offices (Figure 2.6).

Postclassic Mayan groups that remained in the southern lowlands following the Classic collapse have been intensively studied in the central Petén on the shores of a chain of lakes: Lakes Petén Itzá, Yaxhá, and Macanché. Similar Postclassic Mayan settlements have also been investigated in the lagoons of northeastern Belize, at the sites of Laguna de On and Caye Coco, and at the lagoon shore site of Lamanai, a Classic period center that never collapsed. In terms of both political organization and artifact and architectural styles, there were strong similarities in the architecture and

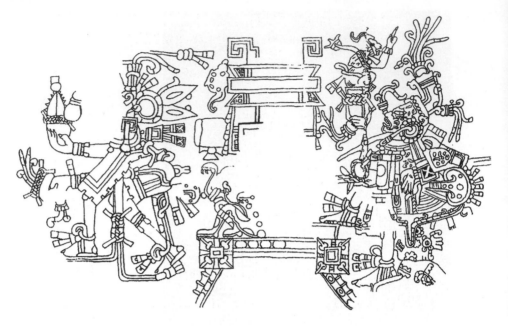

Figure 2.6   Segment of painted murals from Santa Rita, Corozal, Belize, located in the semiperiphery of the Caribbean Coast. The figure on the right holds up the head of the merchant deity opposite the drummer; he also wears a merchant deity mask (redrawn from Thomas Gann, Mounds in Northern Honduras, in the *Nineteenth Annual Report of the Bureau of American Ethnology*, 1987–1998, Part 2, Washington, D.C., 1900: Plate XXXI.

artifacts of the northern/eastern sites of Mayapán, Cozumel, and Tulum, and in the Late Postclassic centers in the Petén and Belize.

Ritual paraphernalia such as deity effigy censers and sculptured turtles linked to calendrical rituals are shared by Mayapán and its hinterland sites (Figures 2.5, 2.6, 2.7). The lagoons and rivers of northeastern Belize were well-populated during this period, likely because of an abundance of fresh water, rich agricultural soils, and riverine access to trading networks of the Caribbean. Some refugees from the collapsing Classic period centers of the interior likely resettled in these areas, and these southern aquatic localities have an enduring history of housing refugees during later exoduses of the Postclassic, Colonial, and Caste War periods (as discussed in Chapters 5 and 7 to follow). According to the Yucatecan chronicles, Itzá migrants from the fallen Chichén Itzá fled to the Petén and established a new capital on an island in Lake Petén Itzá (see Chapter 3). From their remote capital of Noh Petén (Tayasal), as it was called by the Spaniards, the Itzá came to dominate the southern Mayan lowlands' rebellious frontier during Colonial times, resisting conquest for nearly 200 years. But that story will be told in Chapter 4. Further details about the Late Postclassic Mayas appear in the Lowland Mayas profile that follows.

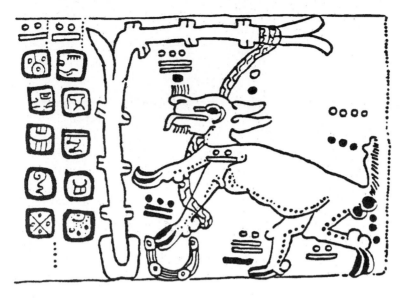

Figure 2.7   Scenes from the Codex Madrid indicate that hunting and sacrifice of deer were important in Postclassic rituals (after Villacorta and Villacorta 1971:XLIX).

The Highland Mayas

The Postclassic period in the highlands of Guatemala and Chiapas was a volatile time of warfare, migration, and social upheaval. Major settlements were located in defensible positions on ridgetops or plateaus and were surrounded with walls. Late Postclassic polities were influenced directly or indirectly by Central Mexican cultures, in some cases borrowing Nahua terms for kin groups, adopting elements of Central Mexican art styles (for example, in murals at Iximché and Q'umarkaaj, Figure 2.8), or adding Central Mexican deities to their pantheon. The ruling dynasties of many of these Postclassic Mayan states in the Highlands claimed descent from the Toltecs.

During the fourteenth and fifteenth centuries, the K'iche' capital of Q'umarkaaj (or Utatlan) was a large, nucleated city situated on an inaccessible plateau reachable only by a causeway and bridge from the east and a steep stairway from the west. The site consists of several plaza groups made up of an open courtyard bounded by a temple, a council house or an administrative hall, and a palace or residential building (Figure 2.9). The various plaza groups were occupied by the major K'iche' lineages as identified in ethnohistoric sources. Several adjacent plateaus—in equally defensible positions—featured hilltop centers that were settled by lineage groups integrated with Q'umarkaaj. Although individual highland Postclassic sites are small in size, they had the capacity politically to centralize under the authority of centers like Q'umarkaaj for military purposes. A system of rotating calendrical ceremonies helped to integrate political territories.

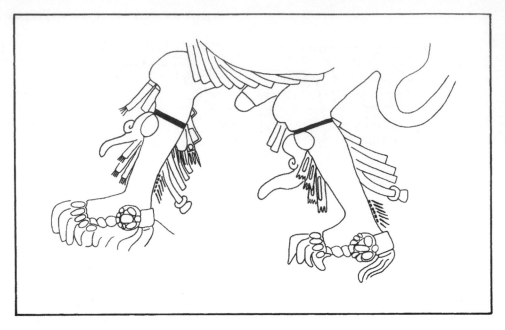

Figure 2.8 Monkey figure from a painted mural at the K'iche' Mayan capital of Utatlán, Guatemala. Redrawn from The Quiché Mayas of Utatlán: The Evolution of a Highland Guatemala Kingdom, by Robert Carmack. University of Oklahoma Press, 1981.

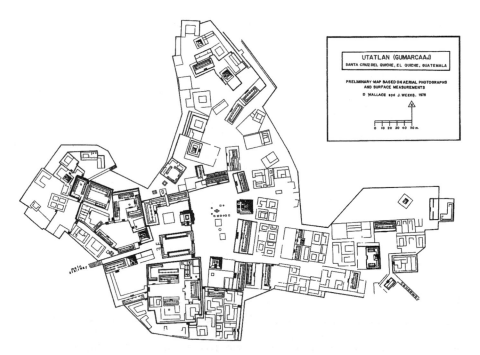

Figure 2.9 Map of Utatlán (Q' umarkaaj), the Postclassic K'ichean capital of highland Guatemala. Courtesy of the Institute for Mesoamerican Studies.

Several decades before the arrival of the Spaniards, the K'iche' empire began to break apart. By the late fifteenth century, K'iche' hegemony was seriously curtailed by the Kaqchikels, who had broken away and founded their own capital at the site of Iximché in the late 1400s (see Chapter 3). Like Q'umarkaaj, Iximché was situated in a defensible location, surrounded on three sides by steep ravines. Iximché remains an important symbolic center today for contemporary Mayan residents of highland Guatemala who are proud of their enduring heritage in this region (see Chapter 8).

West Mexico

In West Mexico, the Tarascan or Purépecha state ruled over a vast territory that rivaled the Aztec empire in territory. The Tarascans ruled from their capital at Tzintzuntzan on the shores of Lake Pátzcuaro in Michoacán. By the Late Postclassic period, Tzintzuntzan was an important city with as many as 35,000 inhabitants. Within the city were the burial-temple platforms of kings (Figure 2.10); other religious shrines; civil-administrative buildings; storehouses; artisan workshops; and the residences of elites, commoners, and foreigners.

Aztec attempts to conquer Tarascan territories were met with stiff resistance. The Tarascans had a well-trained military, and they maintained forts along their borders (see Chapter 3). West Mexico is well known for the metal goods produced there, including copper, bronze, and gold objects (see Box 1.3).

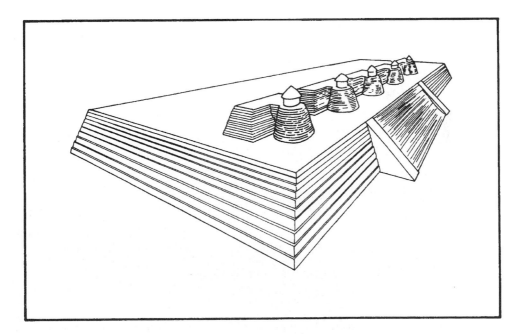

Figure 2.10   Temple mound at the Tarascan capital of Tzintzuntzan in West Mexico. After Ignacio Marquina, *Arquitectura prehispanica*, Mexico City, Mexico: Instituto Nacional de Antropología e Historia, 1951, p. 256.

The Rise of the Aztecs

We use the term "Aztec" to refer to the Nahuatl-speaking peoples of highland Central Mexico at the time of the Spanish conquest. There were several distinct Aztec ethnic groups, of which the Mexicas are the best known. These groups originated in northern Mexico, migrating south into the central Mexican highlands in the twelfth and thirteenth centuries. Scholars are divided as to whether these migrants' reported home, Aztlan, was a real or mythical place. When the Nahuatl-speakers arrived in Central Mexico after the fall of Tula, they founded towns and set up dynasties, leading to the development of a series of city-states that continued as the dominant political form through the time of the Spanish invasion. These new city-states were economically and politically successful, and this period witnessed a great surge of population growth caused by both immigration and natural increase. Calixtlahuaca was one such city-state, located in the Toluca Valley (Figure 2.11).

Like other Mesoamerican city-state systems, such as the Mixtecs and the Classic Mayas, the Aztec polities interacted with each other through a combination of peaceful and aggressive practices. By the early fifteenth century, several Aztec polities had succeeded in establishing small-scale empires consisting of networks of conquered city-states. These included Texcoco, capital of the Acolhua ethnic group in the eastern Valley of Mexico; Azcapotzalco, capital of the Tepanecs in the western Valley; and Cuauhnahuac, head city of the Tlahuicas in Morelos.

Figure 2.11   Aztec round temple from the site of Calixtlahuaca. Such round temples were dedicated to Ehecatl, the wind god manifestation of Quetzalcoatl (the feathered serpent). Photo by Michael E. Smith.

The Mexica, who were to become the dominant polity by the end of the century, were originally vassals of the Tepanec king. Their tribute to the Tepanecs was service as mercenaries in their wars of conquest. In 1428, the Mexicas banded together with the Acolhuas and several other groups to overthrow the Tepanec empire and establish an alliance of three polities: Tenochtitlan (the Mexica capital), Texcoco (the Acolhua capital), and Tlacopan (capital of a dissident Tepanec polity). This "Triple Alliance," known today as the Aztec empire, began a systematic campaign of militaristic expansion soon after 1428. The combined armies began by conquering areas in the Valley of Mexico, and then moved beyond to incorporate ever-greater areas of Mesoamerica. When Cortés and the conquering Spaniards arrived in Mexico in 1519, the Aztec empire covered much of Mesoamerica, and areas not conquered by the empire were influenced by the Aztecs through trade and other institutions. A more detailed look at Aztec society appears in the Aztec profile that follows. Further details about the organization of Mesoamerica in 1519 is the theme of Chapter 3.

PROFILES OF THREE LATE POSTCLASSIC MESOAMERICAN PEOPLES

We turn now to a closer look at the social and cultural features of three Late Postclassic Mesoamerican peoples. Information on these three Mesoamerican groups derives primarily from documentary sources, both native and Spanish. In the case of the Aztecs and Mixtecs, the native documentary corpus includes numerous pictorial codices, as well as texts written in the native languages (using Latin characters taught to them by the Spanish friars) and in Spanish. The Mayas produced similar documents, but they also painted hieroglyphic texts that contain additional information. Descriptions by the Spaniards of these peoples were written primarily by Spanish missionaries, such as Bernardino de Sahagún in Central Mexico (see the Introduction and Figure A.10) and Diego de Landa in Yucatan. But many other Spanish sources rich in information are also available, produced by the Conquistadors and later administrative officials (see Chapter 6 for illustrations and a full description of these documentary sources). Archaeological studies of the sites occupied by these three peoples, as well as by other Mesoamerican peoples, provide an additional useful source of information upon which the accounts to follow are based.

Given the limitations of space, it will be necessary to focus on only a few of the multitude of features that characterized the complex societies and cultures of these three Mesoamerican peoples. We have chosen to concentrate on three basic topics that are universally recognized as being particularly critical for an understanding of any culture: economics, politics, and religion. For information on other topics related to the Aztecs, Mixtecs, and Mayas, as well as to other Mesoamerican peoples discussed in this text, the reader should consult the suggested readings at the end of this chapter.

The Aztecs of Central Mexico

As we have seen, the Aztecs were heirs to earlier Central Mexican civilizations that included the powerful Classic period Teotihuacanos, and especially the Early Post-classic period Toltecs. Most Aztec peoples insisted that their dynastic lines and religious beliefs were handed down from the Toltecs, although scholars have pointed out that their cultural legacy probably extended much farther back than the Toltec period. An early phase of Aztec history (ca. A.D. 1200–1325) was dominated by migrations of partially Mesoamericanized Aztec peoples from the north into the valleys of Central Mexico. Stimulated by influence from surrounding Mesoamerican peoples and competition with each other, the Aztec peoples began to create fledgling city-states that were established in such places as the Basin of Mexico, Tlaxcala, Cholula, Morelos, and Toluca (Smith 2003:34–37).

It was during the next phase of Aztec history (ca. A.D. 1325–1519) that the Aztec peoples were able to create powerful city-states, and in some cases empires. The Mexicas, for example, established a city-state on the island of Tenochtitlan, and in 1372 they proclaimed their first "Toltec" ruler (*tlatoani*). In 1428 the Mexica state entered into an alliance with the Texcocan and Tlacopan states to form a powerful confederated empire. Subsequently, under the direction of energetic rulers such as Motecuhzoma I and Axayacatl, the Mexicas rose to dominance in the confederacy and expanded imperial reach far beyond Central Mexico. Motecuhzoma II, a hardline elitist ruler, held the reigns of power over the empire at the time the Spaniards finally reached Tenochtitlan in 1519 (Smith 2003:37–55).

The cultural features to be described next largely refer to this last phase of Aztec history, and particularly to the Mexica version of it.

Aztec Economy. Although the Aztecs utilized a technology that was largely "Stone Age," their material productive capacity was truly astounding. They provided food for approximately 200,000 inhabitants in the city of Tenochtitlan and more than one million persons residing in the Central Basin. They erected monumental structures in the numerous cities of the basin. As described in Box 2.1, the stone and mortar constructions in Tenochtitlan included thousands of public buildings; a huge hydraulic system of dikes, causeways, canals, and aqueducts; and an extensive system of irrigation channels in the hilly country surrounding the central lake area (Figure 2.12).

The Aztecs were heirs to centuries of Mesoamerican developments with respect to food production (see Table 1.1, Box 1.1, and Box 1.3). The many cultigens available to them included maize, beans, squash, chile, chía, amaranth, and maguey. Domesticated dogs and turkeys and wild game provided a supply of meat, although diet for commoners was predominantly vegetarian, especially maize and beans. Swidden agriculture (*tlacolol*) was practiced along the foothills, whereas the flat areas and river beds were worked into complex irrigation systems of agriculture, and agricultural terraces were constructed on hillsides. Especially productive were the lake gardens (*chinampa*), which began to fill in much of the southern shoreline of the great lakes. The chinampas could produce seven crops per year, and it has been estimated that they may have provided over half of the basic food needs of Tenochtitlan, the other half coming from

Box 2.1   The Mexica Capital Tenochtitlan

The Aztec imperial capital Tenochtitlan was founded in A.D. 1325 on a swampy island in Lake Texcoco. According to Aztec history, the wandering Mexica people chose the city's site upon receiving an omen from their god Huitzilopochtli: An eagle would be seated on a cactus eating a snake (this image is now the national symbols of Mexico). Tenochtitlan's island location in the densely settled Valley of Mexico provided excellent opportunities for commerce, and the city prospered and grew. It became the imperial capital after the formation of the confederated Aztec empire in 1428. By 1519 the city covered thirteen square kilometers and boasted a population of around 200,000 persons. Much of Tenochtitlan was destroyed when the Spaniards invaded, and colonial Mexico City was built over the ruins.

Tenochtitlan was criss-crossed by many canals that were traversed by busy canoe traffic. Dikes kept the salty waters of Lake Texcoco separate from the fresh water surrounding the city, permitting cultivation of *chinampas*, "raised fields," on the outskirts (see Box 1.3). Urban residents included nobles and commoners engaged in a variety of occupations including artisans, merchants, bureaucrats, farmers, and priests. The great marketplace at Tlatelolco, Tenochtitlan's smaller twin city, was attended daily by over 60,000 persons. Political and religious activities were centered in the Sacred Precinct, a large walled compound crowded with temples, palaces, and other civic buildings including the "Templo Mayor" (the latter an impressive temple-pyramid that was the symbolic center of the Aztec empire and cosmos). The precinct formed the nucleus for the rest of the city, whose streets, canals, and buildings were all built with a common grid orientation matching that of the Sacred Precinct.

The rulers of Tenochtitlan drew on older Mesoamerican traditions of urban planning as they designed the city, but they also innovated. The great size, dense population, and strict grid layout were features that mirrored the earlier imperial capitals of Teotihuacan and to a lesser extent Tula. The Aztecs also called upon an older Mesoamerican urban tradition not evident at the earlier site of Teotihuacan by founding a sacred city constructed around a central ceremonial precinct dominated by large pyramids and shrines. In this respect, Tenochtitlan resembled the great sites of Tikal, Monte Albán, or Xochicalco more than Teotihuacan (see Box 1.4).

Tenochtitlan exceeded Teotihuacan and other earlier Mesoamerican cities in size, scale, and the importance of marketplaces and trade. Tenochtitlan's merchants, traveled farther and traded a wider variety of goods with a greater number of foreign towns than any previous merchants, and the number and size of marketplaces in Tenochtitlan and Tlatelolco far surpassed those of other Mesoamerican cities. The Templo Mayor, although not as massive as the Pyramid of the Sun at Teotihuacan, was far more elaborately decorated and contained many times the number of rich offerings than earlier temple-pyramids. The richness of the construction and offerings at the Templo Mayor reflects the opulence and prosperity of Tenochtitlan, a prosperity that was created and sustained by both commercial activity and tribute payments coming from conquered provinces.

Today Tenochtitlan lies buried under Mexico City. In recent decades, archaeologists have made numerous discoveries in connection with the expansion of the Mexico City underground metro system. By far the most spectacular archaeological finds have come from the excavations between 1978 and 1988 of the Templo Mayor, in the heart of Mexico City. The Templo Mayor and its elegant museum, open to visitors year-round, are impressive testimonies to the grandeur that was Tenochtitlan in 1519.

Figure 2.12 Central Basin of Mexico, showing the system of dikes and causeways that undergirded the Aztec capital of Tenochtitlan. From Geoffrey W. Conrad and Arthur A. Demarest, *Religion and Empire: the dynamics of Aztec and Inca expansionism*, p. 12. Copyright © Cambridge University Press 1984. Reprinted with the permission of Cambridge University Press.

foods brought in as tribute from the imperial provinces. Agriculture was supplemented by hunting game in the hinterlands, along with fish and migratory water birds from the lakes. The Aztecs also gathered locusts, grubs, fish eggs, lizards, honey, "a green like scum formed by water fly eggs," and the spirulina algae. The flesh of human sacrificial victims was consumed, too, primarily by members of the ruling class.

The Aztecs' agricultural system underwrote a highly advanced industry of craft manufacturing. The most complex of the manufactures—featherworking, metallurgy, painting, and lapidaries—were worked by artisans of guildlike organizations whose members lived together in special residential wards. These master artisans manufactured exquisite adornments and objects used by the noble class, as well as constructing the ornate and architecturally fine buildings that gave the cities of the central Basin their impressive, metropolitan aura.

In Aztec society, the ruling class exercised considerable control over the production of these goods and the means to produce them. The ruling class demanded the agricultural surpluses from producers in the basin and beyond, expropriated the labor of commoners in order to build monumental public works, and accumulated masses of raw materials and artisan goods from the peoples in the imperial provinces. Control over the main means of production—lands, raw materials, laborers—by the Aztec ruling class was especially evident in the Central Basin, whereas in the provinces to a much greater degree the means of production remained under the control of local rulers and the producers themselves (see Box 2.2).

The tributary system, along with the commercial markets, dominated the Aztec exchange economy. Most commodity producers, including farmers working the lake

---

Box 2.2   Archaeology and Mesoamerican Peasants

It is only natural that archaeologists studying the complex societies of Mesoamerica and elsewhere have focused most of their attention on cities and urban centers. These are the largest archaeological sites, they contain the most impressive architectural remains, and they exhibit the most complete evidence for ancient social complexity. Nevertheless, in the past two decades an increasing number of archaeologists have turned their attention to rural areas that were the hinterlands of ancient cities. Archaeological fieldwork on rural areas has taken two forms. First, regional settlement pattern surveys that became common in the 1960s and 1970s following initial projects that were directed by Gordon Willey and William Sanders provided information on the number, size, and location of rural sites across the landscape. More recently, archaeologists such as David Webster and Michael Smith have furnished more detailed data on rural life by excavating peasant houses in Maya and Aztec hinterland areas.

This growing archaeological attention to peasants and rural areas is important for rounding out our view of ancient Mesoamerican societies. Peasants are rural farming peoples who are part of larger state-level societies. They typically provide labor, food, and other products for urban elites and state institutions. Research around the world shows that in some ancient states, peasants were heavily exploited, had little freedom, and lived a hard, dull life, whereas in other cases peasants were well-off economically and had considerable control over their own lives and destiny. One of the goals of archaeological research on Mesoamerican peasants is to document the conditions of peasant households and communities in order to provide more complete interpretations of ancient Mesoamerican societies.

A comparison of Teotihuacan and the Aztecs illustrates some of the variation among Mesoamerican peasants. As urban settlements, Teotihuacan and Tenochtitlán shared many characteristics, but their overall societies were quite different politically and economically, and these differences influenced the nature of rural settlement during the Classic and Late Postclassic periods. Teotihuacan was a powerful polity whose rulers dominated their subjects in both city and countryside. Many rural villagers had been forcibly moved into the city early in the Classic period, leaving a small number of scattered peasant villages in the hinterland. Excavations at one of these villages suggest a meager standard of living, with villagers imitating urban styles in both artifacts and architecture. There is little evidence of economic activities apart from food

(*continued*)

(continued)

production. These were poor peasants with few independent economic resources or opportunities.

Rural conditions in the Aztec period were quite different. Archaeological surveys located many more rural sites, with a nearly continuous distribution of hamlets and villages in some areas. Compared with Teotihuacan, Aztec city-states had less power to dominate or exploit their commoners, and the growth of market systems gave rural Aztecs ready access to goods and exchange opportunities. Excavations at two rural sites in Morelos reveal thriving rural economies where peasant households obtained large numbers of exotic goods including obsidian, foreign pottery, and bronze tools. In addition to growing maize and other food crops using agricultural terracing, farmers cultivated cotton, which was spun and woven into cloth for both tribute payments (to nobles and city-states) and exchange in the marketplace (textiles served as a form of money for the Aztecs). Although these peasants lived in small adobe houses with stone floors (Figure 2.13), they were well-off economically in the commercialized city-state economy of Aztec Central Mexico.

Knowledge of Aztec peasants is important not only to provide a complete picture of Aztec society but also to understand the nature of change after the Spanish conquest. Aztec cities were destroyed by the Spaniards, states and empires were dismantled, and the Aztec nobility were co-opted into the Spanish colonial system (see Chapters 4 and 5), leaving rural peasants as the repositories of the Mesoamerican cultural tradition. These people were accustomed to paying tribute to nobles and to conforming to the laws of states. Age-old peasant strategies of surviving within the context of states and empires served them well under Spanish rule, when tribute and law continued as institutions controlling peasant life. In fact, for many rural Aztecs, the Spanish conquest had only a minimal effect on their lives—one set of overlords was simply replaced by another. The peasant lifeway had a long history in ancient Mesoamerica, and archaeological research is now bringing to view these previously ignored rural Mesoamericans.

Figure 2.13 Remains of an Aztec peasant house excavated at the Late Postclassic Period village of Capilco, Mexico. Photo by Michael E. Smith.

gardens near the cities, obtained essential goods from the central markets. Tribute payers residing in more distant places also acquired food, raw materials, and other necessary goods in local and regional markets. The full-time Aztec merchants exchanged a wide variety of goods in both regional markets and distant ports, apparently providing for their own subsistence needs in local markets. Rights to land, slaves, carriers, and luxury items all circulated to some extent in the markets, although always within limits laid down by the ruling class.

The main tribute takers formed a nobility (*pipiltin*) whose status could be inherited from either parent (or both). Nevertheless, some tribute rights were specifically attached to administrative offices, and others may have been purchased (that is, were personal property). Many of the lands, tributary goods, and labor services were grants from the king and other high officials to noblemen and, in a few cases, to commoners of high achievement (*quauhpipiltin*) in war or other state activities. The tribute payers were hereditary commoners (*macehualtin*) who formed the bulk of the lower-class residents of the town and country wards (*calpulli*). They were "free" artisans and peasants, subject to the demands of public officials, including the priests, noble houses, and perhaps, in some cases, private landlords. Some commoners were so closely tied to certain parcels of land that as tenants, they were included in any transferral of these lands. Students of Aztec society have determined that a sharp division did not exist between free and tenant commoners, at least for the last decades of the precontact period. Virtually all lands, including those within the calpulli districts, came under control of the noble class, and the internal organization of commoner wards and hamlets fell under the direct authority of these nobles.

Free commoners could sell themselves as slaves (*tlacotin*), but they were also subject to being made slaves for criminal acts or capture in warfare. Slavery was not rare, and a thriving slave trade existed in Central Mexico. Slaves did not pay tributes, but their labor and subsistence were subject to direct control by the overlords. Commoners as well as nobility could own slaves. Slaves could even have other slaves subject to them, and they could marry and procreate children free of slave status. The carriers (*tlameme*), so critical to a commercialized world without draft animals, were in some cases hired laborers, but many of them must have been slaves or tenant commoners who were assigned this onerous service obligation.

The full-time merchants (*pochteca*) and artisans (*tolteca*) were also subject to tribute and payments, but of commodities and services rather than subsistence goods or manual labor. They could achieve a rank just below noble status, which allowed them to own private property, accumulate wealth, wear fine clothing, and carry out rituals involving human sacrifice. Nevertheless, the professional merchants were carefully supervised by the ruling class, and were required to demonstrate public humility and obeisance in the presence of true nobility.

Aztec Politics.   The basic political unit of the Aztecs was the city state (altepetl), whereas the emerging empires were greatly enlarged versions of this unit. It is estimated by Aztec scholars (Smith 2003:148) that there were some fifty city states in the central basin of Mexico alone, and another four-hundred-and-fifty outside the basin that were subject to imperial authority. In the center of each city-state was constructed a palace, the symbol of political authority, along with temples and a marketplace. The urban center was divided into wards (capulli), whose inhabitants were required to provide services to the palace and labor on public projects. Beyond the center itself were subject rural villages and scattered peoples also obligated to pay tributes to the state rulers.

Relations between the city states were multidimensional, and they included marital exchanges between rulers and other members of the noble class, extensive trade, ceremonial visits, and diplomacy. Nevertheless, warfare between the city-states was also endemic, the primary goals being extraction of tributes from defeated city-states and the capture of enemy warriors for purposes of carrying out human sacrifice (by taking captives, warriors achieved elite Eagle and Jaguar military rankings). The supreme ruler of the Aztec empire and the rulers of the empire's constituent city states bore the title of *tlatoani* (plural, *tlatoque*). The Tlatoani was primarily a secular figure who ruled over the affairs of state from the palace. One of the key symbols of the Tlatoani's supreme authority was a throne covered with reed mats or jaugar skins. The Tlatoani had many ritual obligations as well, especially in relation to the patron of rulers, Tezcatlipoca, for whom he was the chief spokesman. Nevertheless, religious theology and most daily ritual were left largely in the hands of a full-time priesthood.

The Tlatoani was above all a military leader, and his first act upon taking office was to launch a military campaign in order to demonstrate military prowess by capturing prisoners. Furthermore, he was in charge of a government largely dominated by military men. Most of the highest positions in the state hierarchy were military, especially a council of four commanders to which the Tlatoani had belonged before his "election" as supreme ruler. Functionaries in charge of other matters of state participated in much larger but less prestigious councils, each subject to the dictates of the Tlatoani and his military commanders.

In addition to the important economic, military and ritual functions of the Tlatoani, he was also the highest arbitrator in a well-organized Aztec legal system (Offner 1983). At the ward or district corporate level (*calpulli*) of Aztec society, a type of common-law judicial process operated, but it was always subject to higher state agents who made sure that it conformed to the centralized and hierarchical legal structure. The Aztec Tlatoani had almost absolute judicial authority, not only because he was the judge of ultimate appeal but also because he had the right to name lesser judges and to reform the laws.

According to Aztec and Spanish sources, the Aztec judicial hierarchy at Texcoco consisted of the Tlatoani at the top, and two superior judges who together with the supreme ruler formed a supreme council that met each ten to twelve and eighty days. Below them were twelve judges who functioned in six state-level districts. The state-level judges were specialists in the law and were economically supported (and carefully watched) by the state. Below this legal hierarchy were numerous provincial judges, all subject to the higher political officials (Figure 2.14).

Aztec procedural and substantive laws were complex and well developed, and they were expressed by means of a rich and subtle Nahuatl vocabulary. They were said

Figure 2.14   A pictorial portrayal of the political hierarchy, including judges, within the Texcocan city-state as in the Mapa Quinatzin (based on a drawing by Susan Toby Evans 200l Aztec Noble Courts. From *Royal Courts of the Ancient Maya, Volume One*, pp. 237–273, Takeshi Inomata and Stephen Houston. Copyright © 2001 by Westview Press.

to have the legitimacy of being laid down by the heads of state. Accordingly, the laws themselves were thought to be powerful and thus dangerous, and for that reason had to be administered with wisdom and seriousness. Furthermore, the Aztec legal system was quite secular and relatively free of input from the kinship groups; it even employed the concept of "the reasonable man" as a way to decide cases in which the evidence was insufficient. Besides the many specialized judges, numerous other officials participated in the system, including scribes, "lawyers", and a special type of policeman. Justice was swift, sure, and severe, and an elaborate suite of sanctions could be applied to the guilty. (Box 2.3 describes the process by which adultery was adjudicated within the Texcocan legal system.)

Significant political changes were taking place in the Aztec empire during the final years preceding the Spanish invasion. For example, the selection of the Tlatoani in the powerful Mexica state had fallen into the hands of a small coterie of royal lineage officials. During an earlier phase of Mexica history, this selection had required

---

Box 2.3   The Application of Aztec Law to the Crime of Adultery

The Aztecs placed great emphasis on criminal laws because these were essential to maintaining the social order. According to a detailed analysis by Offner (1983:260ff), adultery was considered a serious crime, and in most cases it resulted in the penalty of death. Factors considered by the judges in such cases included whether the guilty parties were commoners or lords, whether the evidence was direct or indirect, whether the initiator of the proceeding was a man or woman, or whether the adulterer was military rather than civilian.

The actual sanctions applied depended on the preceding factors. With the exception of soldiers, all the guilty were executed, but the manner of their execution—whether by stoning, strangulation, burning, or crushing the head with stones, etc.—depended upon the degree of disgrace involved. The punishment for soldiers took the form of their being sent to an active war front.

---

the approval of the rulers of the Texcoco and Tlacopan, as well as rulers from other city-states under the authority of the confederated empire. Then, in A.D. 1503, Motecuhzoma II was selected supreme Tlatoani (*huehuetlatoani*) without participation by the other rulers. He thus became the "monarch" of an Aztec empire that represented "the beginnings of a new, higher level of political and social control and integration" Smith (2003:157). A greatly enlarged bureaucracy numbering in the thousands was created and was restricted almost exclusively to persons of noble status. Control over subject city-states by the Aztec empire was tightened in order to boost tribute payments needed to support the enlarged bureaucracy and to ensure that regional markets would provide the strategic commodities demanded by rulers in the imperial center. As part of these political "reforms," subject city-states outside the central basin were organized into "tributary provinces" with the express purpose of improving tribute collection. By 1519, fifty-five provinces of this type had been organized (Berdan et al. 1996). In addition, as a response to the threats from other imperial powers that the Aztec imperialists were unable to defeat in warfare (especially the Tarascans and Tlaxcalans), "client states" were established along the frontier zones with these competitors. The client states were freed from paying tributes, instead providing such services as "low-intensity" warfare against enemy peoples and supplying Aztec garrisons located along the disputed borders with personnel.

Aztec Religion.   Some scholars claim that what made the Aztec political economy effective was an ideology that tied the ancient religious traditions of Mesoamerica to the expansionist strategies of the emerging city-states and empires (Conrad and Demarest 1984). This ideology was created by the first leaders of the empire, such as Itzcoatl and Tlacaelel, who in A.D. 1428 burned the ancient books in order to erase the memory of the past and begin to reorganize Central Mexican myth, ritual, and history. They "rationalized" the entire religious system, making it more supportive of the new political order. While the modifications were designed primarily to legitimize the authority and tributary rights of the new more authoritarian leaders,

Aztec religion took on a life of its own and influenced developments within the empire and the Mesoamerican world as a whole.

A rich source of information on the beliefs and practices of the Aztecs is the corpus of pictorial documents that originated with the Nahutal-speaking peoples of Central Mexico in the pre-Columbian and Early Colonial periods (see Chapter 6 and Figures 6.2, 6.3, and 6.4).

The central figure in the Aztec religion was Huitzilopochtli, the hero-deity of the Mexica. The Huitzilopochtli ("humming bird on the left") persona was melded with the ancient Mesoamerican war and hunting gods, such as Tezcatlipoca ("smoking mirror") and Tonatiuh ("he who goes forth shining," the sun), and so he was thus moved to the center of the cosmos as patron of war and human sacrifice. Huitzilopochtli thus symbolized the Aztecs' responsibility for maintaining the life of the Sun by feeding it sacrificial blood. The implication of this practice was that the Aztecs were required to relentlessly take captives through warfare and to sacrifice them before the gods in order to preserve the universe from the threat of cosmic destruction. Between A.D. 1428 and Spanish contact in 1519, these powerful ideas were expressed in newly inscribed books, carved and painted in art works, and taught at the elite schools (*calmecac*).

The myth of the solar struggle gave the Aztec peoples a religious orientation that may have significantly differed from many of the other Mesoamerican states, at least at first; it was a religious ideology that was manipulated to justify the Aztecs' aggressive military expansion. Political economic goals, such as outdoing other states in the competition for tributes, marched in step with ideological goals, imbuing Aztec warriors with the cosmic mission of winning sacrificial victims to feed the gods. Virtually all aspects of Aztec religion helped serve the interests of the ruling class because imperial policy and sacred cosmology were thoroughly integrated. Major events, such as important conquests or succession to the highest political offices, were draped in the sacred trappings of the cosmos: Rulers dressed in the attire of deities, dancers moving in the cosmic counterclockwise direction, and dates of political importance identified with universal cycles of time, etc. Aztec religion, of course, expressed concerns besides the political ones, but interests of the state were inevitably present in every aspect of myth and ritual.

According to Aztec mythology, creation was a cyclic process, consisting of a series of periods, or "Suns," each ending in destruction (Figure 2.15). The most recent Sun was to end by earthquakes. Ometeuctli ("lord two") and Omecihuatl ("lady two"), the dualistic (male-female) creator couple, were said to have initiated creation by bringing forth four active deities associated with the cardinal directions: Tezcatlipoca (north), Xipe Totec (east), Quetzalcoatl (west), and Huitzilopochtli (south). These deities then created human beings and the other elements of the world. Human sacrifice began when a lowly god with pustules (Nanahuatzin) cast himself into the fire at Teotihuacan, followed by an arrogant rich god (Teccistecatl), both then rising to the sky as Sun and Moon. They were given orbital movement by the auto-sacrifices of the other gods and a strong wind provided by Ehecatl, the wind god.

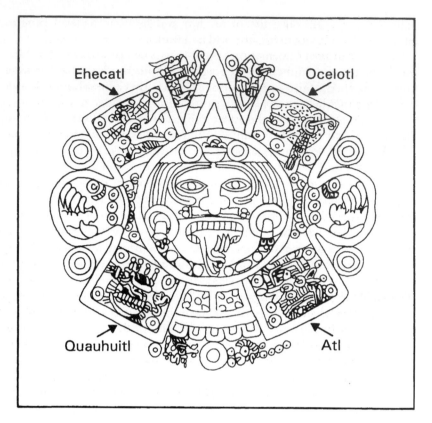

Figure 2.15   Central element of the Aztec calendar stone, denoting the Sun deity, the cyclic creations of the world, and the ascension to power of the Aztecs in A.D. 1427. After Richard F. Townsend, *State and Cosmos in the Art of Tenochtitlan*. Washington, D.C.: Dumbarton Oaks, 1979, p. 64.

The Mexican historian Miguel León-Portilla (1963) has argued that myths of this kind were synthesized out of preexisting myths by certain Aztec priestly wisemen (*tlamatinime*), who claimed to be adding to the original ideas of the Toltec priest-ruler, Topiltzin Quetzalcoatl. The Aztec wisemen were able to determine the origin of the world, its stabilization through dualistic balancing, and its cyclic transformations with the passage of time. They further conceptualized the world as being composed of four basic elements, namely earth, wind, fire, and water, spatially divided into four quarters (each associated with one of the cardinal points). As they conceived the world, it was not a tranquil place but an arena in which diverse and powerful sacred forces were in perpetual struggle for supremacy.

As already indicated, the "metaphysical" elements in Aztec religion were not solely the philosophical speculations of sages, but were also elements of a practical ideology being promoted by hardened military rulers. Thus, for example, the universalism associated with abstract creative powers might be seen as an expression on a highly symbolic level of the imperial quest for universal domination of the known Mesoamerican world. The violent destruction and reconstruction of the Suns or cosmic periods—especially associated with the emerging Fifth Sun when a homely god jumps into the fire and initiates the obligation to feed the Sun with blood—recapitulated in symbolic form the history of the Aztec peoples, at first as obscure wanderers from the North who went on to military greatness. We should note, too, that a cosmology in which a myriad of deities and other forces competed for supremacy was consistent with the real Central Mexico world of struggling ethnic peoples, city-states, and empires.

The cosmological division of the world into four sections, each associated with a cardinal direction, was an ancient pattern in Mesoamerica (see Chapter 14). As the Aztec specialist Richard Townsend (1993) has pointed out, the Aztecs used the idea of the four cosmic quarters as a general model of the Mesoamerican world and the empire's relationship to that world. In particular, the cosmological Eastern quarter, which was associated with warmth and fertility, was associated with the empire's most successful provincial units to the east (see Figure 6.4). The Northern and Western quarters, cosmically linked with cold, death, and the underworld, were associated with the enemies of the Aztec peoples, specifically the hated Tarascans to the west and the recalcitrant Chichimecs to the north. The Earth itself (Tlaltecuhtli) was cosmically viewed as the back of an alligator floating on a great sea, its life-giving heart being the very center of the world. It is not surprising that the Aztecs associated their glorious capital of Tenochtitlan with the "heart" and center of the reptilian earth. The Aztecs' cosmic view of a world divided into thirteen celestial and nine underworld levels might at a more general level been seen as symbolic expressions of the highly stratified nature of Aztec imperial society and the Mesoamerican world as a whole.

Aztec society had other dimensions besides the imperial one, of course, and the complex pantheon of Aztec religion must have provided symbolic expression of the diverse groups and categories present in that highly pluralist society. For example, the Huitzilopochtli deity was the patron of warriors, and as such came to represent the highly militarized ruling class as well as the military units themselves. As noted before, this deity provided the main rationale for conducting military actions, collecting tribute, and ritually sacrificing human beings—three important preoccupations of the Aztec peoples. Other Aztec war deities with ancient genealogies in Mesoamerica were Tonatiuh (the Sun, also an aspect of Huitzilopochtli), Mixcoatl (the Milky Way), and the all-powerful, all-seeing warrior and sorcerer of the night, Tezcatlipoca.

Tlaloc, the Aztec rain deity, was patron of the agriculturalists, largely made up of commoners. Tlaloc's consort, Chalchiuhtlicue, was conceptualized as the woman with a jade skirt. Tlaloc's helper-children were known as Tlaloque, the little sprinklers. Tlaloc's domain was said to be located in the Eastern paradise, hovering over the mountain tops. Tlaloc was depicted with goggle eyes and a snarling upper jaw, symbols that linked him to rain gods present in the most ancient of Mesoamerican religious traditions (see Box 6.2). Tlaloc shared a spot alongside Huitzilopochtli atop the main temple of Tenochtitlán, presumably to provide legitimization of the critical but unequal relationship between the ruling and commoner classes. Together these deities symbolically expressed the Aztecs' propagandistic claim that they had achieved cosmic balance between noble and commoner, warfare and agriculture, life and death, civilization and barbarism.

Little children were sacrificed to the rain deities because of the magical relationships between their teardrops and rain, as well as their small size and the diminutive Tlaloque sprinklers. In general, both human and vegetative fertility were closely associated with commoners and women in Aztec religion. The ancestral "mothers" and "grandmothers" of the Aztecs were patron goddesses of earth, birth, and curing (Teteo Innan, Toci, Coatlicue, Xochiquetzal). The red deity Xipe Totec represented the renewal of the vegetation layer at springtime, and he was more masculine and militant than the fertility goddesses. Victims sacrificed in Xipe's honor were flayed, and the skins ceremonially donned (for the origin of this deity in Yopitzinco, see Box 3.2 in Chapter 3).

Quetzalcoatl, the "feathered serpent" deity, was patron of priests (Figure 2.16). To the Aztecs, this deity shared an identity with Topiltzin Quetzalcoatl, the legendary priest-ruler of the ancient Toltecs. According to Aztec history, Topiltzin left Central Mexico in the ninth century for the east coast, where he is alledged either to have died and been apotheosized as the Morning Star or to have set sail on the ocean with a promise to return. The legitimacy of the Aztec rulers was based on their claimed genealogical right to stand in for Topiltzin. As patron of the priests, Quetzalcoatl symbolized the abounding wisdom, knowledge, and art of the Toltecs, handed down through the priesthood. "He embodied all that the Mexica characterized as 'civilization'" (Berdan 1982:130). The Aztecs usually portrayed Quetzalcoatl as wearing a mask with a bird's beak, conical headdress, and garment bearing a sea shell. Ehecatl, the Aztec wind and rain deity, was another aspect of Quetzalcoatl, and Ehecatl's temple at Tenochtitlán was cylindrical in shape like a coiled serpent.

The professional artisans and merchants also had patron deities that bore the special symbols traditionally associated with these two "middle-level" occupations. Yacatecuhtli, the most important patron deity of the merchants, was portrayed as a traveler, usually carrying a staff and backpack. Yacatecuhtli was represented as having a long nose, the nose symbolizing the merchants moving forward during their extended trading journeys. Some of the Aztec wise men apparently went beyond the otiose creator deities to conceptualize an even more abstract universal creative force. This was a dualistic force, having both male and female aspects, sometimes associated with the creator couple and sometimes with Tezcatlipoca, the source of all natural force and human strength. As the ethnohistorian H. B. Nicholson (1971:411) explains: "In the conception of the leading religious thinkers, all the deities may have been considered merely aspects of this fundamental divine power." With this omnipresent, abstract creative force we are brought once again to the issue of religion and political ideology. Although some scholars consider this abstraction to be a projection of Christian ideas back onto Aztec religion, it may well have been an indigenous religious expression of the Aztec dream to create a "universal" empire out of the intangible but socially very real Mesoamerican world.

Figure 2.16   The Aztec deity, Quetzalcoatl, the "Feathered Serpent." After the *Codex Borbonicus.* Graz, Austria: Akademische Druck- und Verlansanstalt, 1974, folio 22.

The Mixtecs of Southern Mexico

The Mixtecs live in the western part of what is today the Mexican state of Oaxaca, an area called La Mixteca (Figure 2.17). The term "Mixteca" is a Nahuatl word for "people of the cloud place." The Mixtecs call themselves *tay ñudzahui,* or "people of the rain place" (Terraciano 2001:1). The Mixtec region is geographically and ecologically diverse, extending from the hot and humid coastal zone in the south (Mixteca de la Costa or Ñundehui) to the semiarid and topographically varied Mixteca Baja (Ñuiñe), and to the cool highland valleys and rugged mountains of the Mixteca

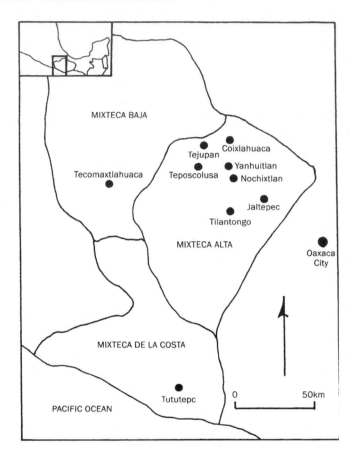

Figure 2.17   Map of the Mixtec region, showing the Mixteca Alta, Mixteca Baja, and Mixteca de la Costa.

Alta (Ñu Dzahui Ñuhu). In the Postclassic period the Mixtecs, particularly those who lived in the Mixteca Alta, experienced a cultural fluorescence, and their influence was felt across many regions of Mesoamerica.

During the Postclassic period, Mixtec artisans were noted for their brilliant pictographic manuscripts (Figure 2.3; see also Figure 6.5), their spectacular polychrome pottery, and their fine metalworking and lapidary skills. Mixtec artists are at least partly responsible for creating an artistic style that is often called the Mixteca-Puebla style; it is linked to the Postclassic international art style mentioned above, and is found in codices, polychrome ceramics, and murals. The style was adopted across a broad area of Mesoamerica where it "served as a common idiom for the validation of authority among the leaders of this wide area" (Byland and Pohl 1994:6).

The Postclassic also was the time when population in the Mixtec area reached new heights, both in terms of total population and in number of settlements. Much of our evidence for Postclassic Mixtec society and culture comes from information in codices and other documents, but archaeological research at Mixtec sites, particularly work in the Nochixtlan Valley and at Tilantongo and Jaltepec, also has provided critical data for understanding the ancient Mixtecs.

Mixtec Economy.   The agricultural foundation for Mixtec society was based on the cultivation of maize, beans, and squash, which were supplemented by other crops grown locally and imported from elsewhere, and by hunting wild game and collecting wild plants. In the fertile highland valleys, agricultural production was carried out along the alluvial plains of rivers and on the terraced hillsides through the use of run-off irrigation. The resources needed to produce a number of basic household goods such as pottery, manos and metates, mats and baskets, stone tools, and textiles were not evenly distributed across the Mixteca, and many of these items could be produced only in certain regions. Inter-community and inter-regional trade was well-developed, however, and communities across the Mixteca had access to a wide range of goods.

Mixtec society was highly stratified, perhaps the most stratified society in Mesoamerica. Social divisions were tightly regulated, and these divisions were reflected in economic and political organization and in ideology. The Mixtecs were divided into two major hereditary social strata, the nobility and the commoners, and each of these had two or more subdivisions. The nobility included the ruling class (*yaa tnuhu*) and a lesser nobility (*tay toho*). Commoners included free commoners (*nanday tay nuu, tay yucu,* or *tay sicaquai*); landless tenants who functioned as serfs or servants (*tay situndayu*); and slaves who had been captured in battle, acquired as tribute, purchased, or born to a slave. Free commoners were allowed access to less-productive lands in return for tribute and service to the nobility, and landless tenants and slaves were under the direct control of the nobility.

Mixtec social divisions were rigid, social mobility was virtually nonexistent, and class endogamy prevailed. Among the high-ranking royalty, marriage between closely related individuals was not uncommon, and there are numerous examples of males in ruling families marrying half- or even full-siblings, their siblings' daughters, or cross- or parallel-cousins. The ruling nobility controlled productive agricultural lands and other resources, they demanded tribute and the labor of the commoners under their control, they oversaw religious activities, they controlled craft production, and they enjoyed a number of other exclusive privileges. Because rulers exercised such complete authority and rarely delegated power, the Mixtecs did not develop an administrative bureaucracy in the same way that the Aztecs did.

The Mixtecs are noted for their extraordinarily high-quality gold, silver, and stonework, polychrome ceramics, and manuscript paintings. In contrast to the way the Aztecs organized craft production, in which artisans were members of guildlike groups who lived and worked together in special residential wards, Mixtec artisans were members of the royal families, and they lived and worked in the royal courts. The organization of trade for the Mixtecs also stands in contrast to the Aztec system of trade described above where a professional merchant class (the *pochteca*) engaged in long-distance commercial exchange. The Mixtecs did not have a specialized merchant class. Instead, members of the lesser nobility traded on behalf of the rulers, traveling to distant locations to acquire the raw materials needed to produce manufactured goods. Materials like turquoise and gold were brought to the royal courts where royal artisans created fine stone and metal objects. Highly skilled artisans who were part of the royal courts also created polychrome ceramics and painted manuscripts.

Mixtec Politics.   The Mixtec rise to prominence in the Postclassic period is often linked to relationships between Mixtec ruling dynasties and the Toltecs or other Central Mexican polities. Early in the Postclassic period these dynasties may have stepped in to fill a power vacuum following the decline of Toltec power. Several major Mixtec dynasties in the Postclassic period claimed Toltec or Central Mexican ancestry and dynastic histories, portrayed in Mixtec codices that depict founders of these dynasties making the journey to Tula or other Central Mexican centers to receive a nose ornament that was a symbol of authority (see Box 2.4).

Postclassic Mixtec society was divided into numerous small competing independent city states (kingdoms) or chiefdoms (*ñuu* in Mixtec) governed by hereditary rulers. There was no formal centralized political organization above the level of the state or chiefdom, but alliances were often forged between kingdoms creating confederacies that worked together to pursue common interests. Elaborate gift exchanges, feasting, and marriage ties between royal families served to maintain these alliances. Generally, the territory of a Mixtec polity was small enough to walk across in a day. Typically these territories consisted of a centrally located palace and associated buildings that were home to the ruler's family, and the surrounding countryside where the dependent communities and agricultural lands populated by commoners and governed by the lesser nobility were found.

Some of the major Mixtec city states and chiefdoms in the Late Postclassic period (see Figure 2.17) included centers in the Nochixtlan Valley and others such as Teposcolula, Tejupan, Coixtlahuaca, and Tilantongo. The Mixteca Baja has not been systematically surveyed, but evidence from sites like Tepexi and Tecomaxtlahuaca suggest that settlements were similar to those in the Mixteca Alta. In the Mixteca de la Costa, the best-known center is Tututepec, but as with the Mixteca Baja, much work remains to be done in this region.

In the Late Postclassic period, Mixtecs began to expand into Zapotec territory in the Valley of Oaxaca. This expansion does not appear to have been entirely the result of military conquest. To a large extent, the Mixtec presence in the Valley of Oaxaca was based on strategic marriage alliances between Mixtec and Zapotec royalty. Mixtec brides (or grooms) who married into Zapotec royal families apparently brought with them not only finely crafted goods produced by Mixtec artisans—ceramics, metal objects, and other materials—but also Mixtec serfs or servants (the *tay situndayu,* discussed before). Spectacular examples of Mixtec craftsmanship were found in royal tombs at Monte Alban (Tomb 7) and at Zaachila (Tombs 1 and 2). These tombs were filled with exquisite Mixtec-style gold and silver jewelry, pottery, and carved bones.

At the site of Mitla in the Valley of Oaxaca (Figure 2.2), we find further evidence of Mixtec influence in the valley. Although Mitla was fundamentally a Zapotec cen-

Box 2.4   The Story of Lord Eight Deer and His Legacy

Lord Eight Deer was a great Mixtec leader whose rise to power, his ultimate demise, and his legacy are depicted in Mixtec pictorial records including the Codices Zouche-Nuttall, Colombino, and Becker I. The saga of Eight Deer is filled with tales of love, war, ambition, and political intrigue; but beyond the drama, it also provides us with insights about political transformations and changing strategies for the establishment of political legitimacy during a critical period of Mixtec history.

Eight Deer, named for the day of his birth in the 260-day calendar and typically pictured with eight dots and the head of a deer, was born in A.D. 1063. The son of a high priest and an adviser to the King of Tilantongo, Eight Deer grew up during a time of violent dynastic conflict among various Mixtec kingdoms in and around Tilantongo and Jaltepec in the Mixteca Alta. In the midst of this conflict, and during a time when different factions were struggling for control over the Tilantongo throne, Eight Deer was sent to the coastal center of Tututepec where he and his troops secured and expanded Tututepec's realm.

Several years later, as factional fighting continued and with the death—possibly the murder—of the young prince who was the legitimate heir to the Tilantongo throne, Eight Deer began to take the steps that would lead to his own ascendancy to the Tilantongo throne. As a usurper, with no legitimate claim to rule the Tilantongo kingdom, one of Eight Deer's strategies was to appeal to outside forces who could legitimize his claim.

Among Nahua-speaking groups (sometimes called the "Tolteca-Chichimeca") to the north of the Mixteca Alta, at centers like Cholula and Tlaxcala, high-ranking leaders, often heads of lineages, underwent a nose-piercing ritual and subsequently wore a distinctive turquoise nose ornament that symbolized their high office and their new title of *tecuhtli*, a title that signified head of a lineage or a royal estate. Mixtec codices portray Eight Deer traveling to one of the Tolteca-Chichimeca centers where he had his nose pierced and was granted the title of tecuhtli, and in all subsequent images, Lord Eight Deer wore the unique nose ornament that indicated his new status and provided him with the legitimacy he sought. Eight Deer also was able to gain the support of other Mixtec royal families, and he soon ascended to the throne as King of Tilantongo.

With Eight Deer in power, rival dynasties continued their efforts to gain power over Tilantongo, and soon Eight Deer's brother was assassinated by sons of Eleven Wind, king of a place called Red and White Bundle. To revenge his brother's death, Eight Deer destroyed Red and White Bundle, and during the battle Lord Eleven Wind and his wife, Lady Six Monkey (of the Jacaltec dynasty) were killed, although their children were spared. To further solidify his position, Lord Eight Deer later married one of the daughters of Eleven Wind, thereby linking his own dynasty with that of Red and White Bundle. Lord Eight Deer ruled his kingdom for the next twelve years, but dynastic conflicts did not end. In 1115, Lord Four Wind, the son of Lord Eleven Wind and Lady Six Monkey, avenged the death of his parents by killing Lord Eight Deer. Subsequently, Four Wind married a daughter of Eight Deer, thus ensuring an enduring legacy for Lord Eight Deer.

When Spaniards arrived in the Mixteca Alta over 400 years later, virtually all of the Mixtec royal dynasties claimed descent from Lord Eight Deer, Lord Eleven Wind, or Lady Six Monkey. (For further details about Lord Eight Deer, see Byland and Pohl 1994.)

ter initially founded in the Early Formative period, by Late Postclassic times it had become a regional religious center for the Zapotec and Mixtec nobility.

Late in the fifteenth century a number of Mixtec and Zapotec centers in Oaxaca were conquered as part of the expansion of the Aztec empire. Subsequently these towns were obliged to pay annual tribute to the Aztecs, and Mixtec artisans were moved to Tenochtitlan where they were required to produce goods for their Aztec overlords.

We can learn much about the origins and histories of royal Mixtec families from the surviving Mixtec codices that tell epic tales of strategic alliances, heroes and villains, wars, political intrigue, and tragedy (Box 2.4; see also Chapter 6). Research that integrates Mixtec history as it is presented in the codices with on-the-ground archaeological data has now demonstrated that many of the events depicted in the codices correspond to changes identified in the archaeological record. This finding has led some scholars to conclude that the Mixtec codices do not record mythical events, but historical ones. Of course, because of the main subject matter of the codices—that is, dynastic history—the codices cannot provide us with a comprehensive understanding of Mixtec history, but they do highlight key historical events and people and they provide insights into how the Mixtecs themselves viewed their own history.

Mixtec codices are made of long strips of deer hide, covered with a thick white gesso, painted, and then folded accordion-like to make a "screenfold" (note that codices from other parts of Mesoamerica were made of other materials, including paper from the bark of the *amate* fig tree or from maguey fiber, and they were sometimes rolled or left flat). Screenfolds can be easily stored and transported, and then unfolded to reveal the painted pages that tell the story. They may have also served as pictorial devices for performers who reenacted the stories through drama, dance, and song in the royal courts.

Mixtec writing, like Aztec writing, is pictorial in that it uses images that resemble what is being represented. With the exception of the Codex Vienna, which deals with Mixtec cosmogony, the Mixtec codices record the origins, achievements, and conquests of royal families, an indication of just how important genealogical history was to these families. Clearly, their right to authority was based on ancestry (see Box 2.4). In addition to the major Mixtec codices, other pictorial manuscripts from the Colonial period have survived, including maps, *tiros* (pictorials on rolled paper), and lienzos (pictorials on large, flat sheets of cloth) (for more on this topic, see Chapter 6).

Mixtec Religion.   The Mixtec belief system was based on the notion that the supernatural and natural worlds were inextricably interrelated. Natural features such as caves, mountains, rivers, and heavenly bodies were venerated, and forces of nature such as the sun, wind, rain, lightning, clouds, fire, and certain animals were given supernatural identities as spiritual beings or deities.

The Mixtec spiritual pantheon included spirits associated with powerful natural forces and places as well as the spirits of ancestors. The Mixtec word for "sacred being" was *ñuhu,* a word that Spaniards in the Colonial period translated as "idol," reflecting the fact that many spiritual beings were represented by images made of stone, jade, or turquoise. Deities included the rain god, Dzahui, the Mixtec version of the Nahua deity Tlaloc and the Mayan deity Chac, and the god of merchants, Xiton or Xitondodzo. In many Mixtec communities there may have also been a male deity for the men and a female deity for the women. Moreover, there were numerous local deities associated with specific towns or regions.

The spirits of deceased ancestors of ruling families also played important roles in the Mixtec belief system. Sacred places included temples and shrines associated with royal palaces and civic centers as well as spiritually significant natural places (e.g., caves and mountaintops) away from population centers. These remote locations often were the places where the founders of Mixtec dynasties were believed to have emerged miraculously from natural features like trees and stones. The mummy bundles of these divine ancestors were often kept in nearby caves, and periodically, royal families and their entourages would make pilgrimages to these sacred sites to honor their ancestors.

Humans were expected to respect nature and the spirit world, and they had to carry out appropriate activities—rituals, offerings, and sacrifices—in order to maintain the proper balance among humans, nature, and supernatural forces. Proper ritual activities were carried out in the household and in the community.

Mixtec creation myths reflect the link between humans and the natural world. The Mixtec ancestors emerged from the earth itself, from the underworld, a stream, or the roots of trees (see the account from the Codex Vienna below). In contrast to other Mesoamerican groups, Mixtec origin stories did not involve multiple human creations or the cyclical creation and destruction of previous worlds. The origin myth presented in the Codex Vienna to follow, explains the creation of the Mixtec's supernatural, natural, and cultural features.

Beginning in the celestial realm, ritual and ceremony existed before anything else. Then a primordial couple, Lord One Deer and Lady One Deer performed a series of rituals that culminated in the creation of a number of natural and cultural features. Eventually, as other beings continued to make offerings, the Mixtec culture hero, Lord Nine Wind (the Mixtec equivalent of the Aztec Quetzalcoatl-Ehecatl) was born (see Figure 6.5). Lord Nine Wind is credited with bringing into being the accouterments of political authority: features like royal costumes and the staff of office that would serve the later Mixtec rulers. He also brought over 200 towns and villages into being, including many that would figure in later Mixtec history. He created important spiritual beings, and he caused the first humans to be born from a tree, including certain lineage ancestors. Lord Nine Wind and his human creations continued to make offerings that led to the creation of additional humans and natural features as well as deities, sacred architecture, and ritual activities. Finally, the sun rose after Lord Nine Wind's work was finished. In the final section of the Vienna, the Mixtec world was organized, political units were established, and foundation rituals were carried out, setting the stage for and legitimizing subsequent dynastic authority (from Boone 2000:89–96).

Like other peoples of Mesoamerica, the Mixtecs used the 260-day ritual calendar and the 365-day solar calendar. For the 260-day ritual calendar, the Mixtecs recognized the same 20 day signs as the Aztecs; that is, the names of the days were identical as was the sequence. There were also other similarities between the Aztec and Mixtec calendars. In the Postclassic period, the Mixtecs and Aztecs named each year (of the 365-day solar calendar) based on one of four possible year names: rabbit, reed, flint, and house. These names represented either the name for the last day of the previous year or the first day of the new year. The years were grouped into periods of 13 years, so that the name for any year included the numbers 1 to 13 along with the year name. The sequence of year names would have been as follows: 1 Rabbit, 2 Reed, 3 Flint, 4 House, 5 Rabbit, 6 Reed, 7 Flint, and so on. This method of combining the numbers 1 to 13 with four year names constituted another way to create the 52-year cycle or Calendar Round (as explained in Box 1.2). Calendrical specialists kept track of the calendar and also maintained specialized knowledge of astronomical cycles. They had divinatory powers and provided counsel to the ruling families.

Religious specialists, *naha nine* or *tay saque,* were under the direct authority of the ruling nobility. These practitioners oversaw a variety of activities including feasting, sacrifices, making of offerings, marriages, funerals, fertility rituals, and religious training. Boys as young as seven years old entered formal religious training. In some cases these boys came from both social strata (nobility and commoners), whereas in other cases they came only from the noble class.

From this brief summary of Postclassic Mixtec society, we can see that the Mixtecs played an important role in Postclassic Mesoamerica. Mixtec artisans were highly regarded, and Mixtec crafts—gold, silver, and turquoise jewelry and ornaments and polychrome ceramics—were greatly desired by elites across much of Mesoamerica. The so-called Mixteca-Puebla art style, linked to the international Mesoamerican art style, was influenced by Mixtec artists, and was popular in many parts of Mesoamerica during the Postclassic period. Yet, in spite of the obvious links between Mixtecs and other Mesoamerican groups, we have seen that in several respects, Mixtec society was distinct. Their political, economic, and social systems were based on the supreme authority of the royal families, and the supernatural origins and political legitimacy of these families were recorded in the famous Mixtec codices.

The Lowland Mayas

The Mayan lowlands of the Yucatan Peninsula, Belize, and Guatemala comprised a vast terrain of fragmented city-states at the time of Spanish arrival. About seventy years before Spanish contact (in A.D. 1511), this region had been structured differently. A primary capital city, Mayapan, had centralized polities of the northwest Yucatan under a confederate style council (*mul tepal*) and paramount lord. Beyond the northwest peninsula, Mayapan extended its influence among more loosely organized autonomous states across the Mayan area by maintaining an extensive trade network, engaging in religious proselytization, exercising military strength, and building political alliances. Towns of the Gulf and Caribbean coasts, along with the Peten Lakes region, have well-documented connections to Mayapan. Many of these towns continued to prosper after Mayapan declined from power, because of a thriving maritime commercial economy that connected them to a larger world of exchange with Central Mexico and Honduras. Mayapan fell from power in A.D. 1441, as a result of factional divisions among its principal noble families.

The historian Matthew Restall (1997) refers to the A.D. 1441 (post-Mayapan) to 1542 (year of Spanish contact) period as the "segmented century," and a wealth of contact period documents inform our understanding of Mayan society at this time. Initial Spanish visits to cities like Ecab, Campeche, and Champoton were met with hostility, and the northern peninsula resisted defeat until 1542. Spanish control over the northern Mayan realm was ultimately enabled by the political treachery of rival factions descended from Mayapan: the Xiu and the Cocom. These are the same factions who had, a century earlier, broken up the Mayapan confederacy.

For another 155 years, southern Mayan groups in Belize and the Peten resisted the Spaniards in regular, episodic rebellions. It was not until Spanish troops built a road to Lake Peten Itza and conquered the rebellious island polity of the Itza that the Spanish conquest was completed. Notably, indigenous rebellions on local or regional scales have arisen periodically in the Mayan area to this day. The following discussion provides details on the main features of the lowland Mayan peoples during the Postclassic and early Colonial periods.

Mayan Economy.   Slash-and-burn (milpa) agriculture, timed with the annual cycle of rainy and dry seasons, supported Mayan society at Spanish contact and still forms the basis of village agriculture today. Crops such as corn, beans, squash, and peppers are planted when the rains start in late May or June. Fruit trees, along with other crops, are grown in domestic gardens in Mayan houselots, where animals are also raised. Hunting game and wild fowl provide important supplements (Figure 2.7).

A lively trade in subsistence goods existed on the peninsula between coastal and inland towns, which exchanged fish and salt for game and fruit. Across the Mayan lowlands, the peoples specialized in the production of specific goods for export, although this was not an exclusive pattern. Products such as honey and wax, wooden canoes (and other wood products), cacao, copal (incense), and cotton textiles were exchanged between polities located in different ecological pockets of the lowlands.

Large groves of cacao were cultivated in well-watered, agriculturally fertile areas of the eastern and southern lowlands. Cacao was grown in lesser quantities in the northwest peninsula, in *cenotes* (sinkholes) or other wet depressions that offered suitable moisture and greater soil depth. Northern production was not sufficient to meet the demand of centers like Mayapan, which acquired large quantities of it through trade and tribute from southern polities. Cacao was used as a currency in marketplace exchange. The cacao beans were counted in units, including a *contle* (400 beans), *xiquipile* (1,800 beans), and a *carga* (2,400 beans). A Spanish *real* coin was worth 200 beans (half a contle). Other forms of money included copper bells and axes, red stone or shell beads (*kan*), and other precious stones.

The exchange economy during the Postclassic period was complex, and it involved gifting, tribute taking, long-distance trading, and market exchange. Postclassic lords and priests sponsored numerous feasts and ceremonies, many of which were associated with gift giving among hosts and guests. Mayapan did not demand heavy tribute from its vassals; modest quantities of maize, turkeys, cotton mantles, salt, honey, fish, and other basic goods were requested. Military service was also expected from the Mayapan city-state, and succeeding local rulers likely maintained this custom.

Market exchange, which had also been important during the Classic period, was amplified in scale and significance during the final 300 years before Spanish arrival. Nobles performed the bulk of distant trading expeditions, but several tiers of lesser-ranked merchants served local and regional needs. Some settlements had specialized functions as market towns (notably, Chauaca, Conil, Ecab). It is likely that periodic regional markets were held at all major central places, perhaps timed with key calendrical/religious events that drew pilgrims, as David Freidel and Jeremy Sabloff document for the sites on Cozumel Island.

Long-distance merchants maintained agents, support groups, and facilities in towns that they visited regularly. Large, heavily laden, twenty-five-foot-long trading canoes voyaged from the Gulf Coast port of Xicalanco to the Bay of Honduras. Warehouse facilities have been documented for some major trading sites in Honduras, Quintana Roo, Mexico, and Veracruz. Long-distance connections linked the Mayan area, through the Gulf Coast port of Xicalanco, to peoples of Central Mexico, including the Aztecs. Exports from the Mayan lowlands included salt, cacao, wax, honey, cochineal, achiote, indigo, cotton, and slaves—this list is known only from historic documents as none of these perishables can be recovered from archaeological sites. Mayan groups received colorful thread made of rabbit fur (*tuchumitl*), as well as woven cloth, and ornaments—all likely paid for in cacao currency.

Goods obtained from distant localities were used for daily activities in elite and commoner Maya households, thus indicating the importance of market exchange. Earlier precedents for this are known in the Classic period; for example, pottery made in the Terminal Classic period of northern Yucatan, utilized widely by all social classes, was tempered with volcanic ash. The nearest volcanoes are in the Mayan highlands of Guatemala, and important interregional dependencies were clearly created, on the basis of the preferences of pottery makers and users. This situation occurred despite the fact that local, nonvolcanic tempering materials were available. Volcanic products are highly suitable for evaluating long-distance economic relationships, because they are durable and identifiable with respect to their limited-source areas. The amount of imported obsidian, a volcanic glass used for stone tools, is another indicator of distant dependencies. While the major centers of Classic period Tikal and Mayapan had comparable amounts of obsidian, Postclassic commoner sites in Belize had much greater quantities than their earlier analogs.

Although trade was important, local economies were well developed, and settlements achieved a considerable degree of self-sufficiency in terms of providing for basic needs. This strategy was wise and provided insurance against trading disruptions due to interpolity conflict. Farmers worked in agricultural fields that surrounded Mayan towns. Large workshops for stone-tool-making found at Mayapan indicate that local craftsmanship was geared to meeting the needs of this relatively large city.

Meat was plentiful as indicated by abundant quantities of deer, turkey, peccary (wild pig), and dog at sites like Mayapan, or fish at sites on Cozumel Island. Although hunting was the most common means of securing wild game such as deer and peccary, at Mayapan, deer were raised in captivity. Dogs and turkeys were domesticated by Mesoamerican peoples long before the Postclassic period, and the degree to which dogs were a food source varies strikingly according to region. Along with other animals, they were commonly used for ritual sacrifice.

Despite efforts toward self-sufficiency, communities were limited by the degree to which resources were unevenly distributed. Sometimes settlements within a polity depended on each other for raw materials; for example, Mayapan flint-knappers obtained raw chalcedony cobbles from another town, since no outcrop was located near the city. Craftspersons who made shell ornaments at inland towns depended on coastal towns for the marine shells themselves.

Family and community land ownership is documented for the lowland Mayan peoples. Sites such as Mayapan and Cozumel (along with earlier sites) are divided by a maze of houselot boundary walls. Field walls are also documented that delineated agricultural plots belonging to specific social groups, as Freidel and Sabloff (1984) argue for Cozumel. Nobles owned valuable orchards, particularly those with cacao or edible fruits. Although towns held some land in common, improvements to property (e.g., orchards) were probably privately owned, as Ralph Roys (1957) suggests.

Mayan Politics.   Matthew Restall's (1997) ethnohistoric research indicates that the *cah,* or community, was the principal unit of social and political affiliation. The *cah* represented a town and its agricultural landholdings, a political unit of governance, and the center of social identity for its members. Two other primary units of identity were social classes and the *ch'ibal,* an out-marrying extended family (or lineage) group. The *ch'ibal* provided a basis for sociopolitical subunits and economic organization within the *cah.* Specific, allied *ch'ibal* groups would often maintain marriage alliances with each other, and this practice helped to preserve social-class standing across generations.

Mayan society had three primary social classes: nobles (*almehen*), commoners (*macehual*), and slaves, although a range of social statuses was possible within these categories. Restall has identified four levels of social status within the Colonial period: *almehenob* and four levels within the *macehualob* (this status division probably had pre-contact precedents). Nobles comprised about 25 percent of society. Female slaves (*munach*) and male slaves (*ppentac*) were common in Yucatec Mayan society. Warfare was often performed for the purpose of raiding for captives, some of whom were sacrificed, whereas others became slaves. Slaves were used in the local economy and were also exported to Central Mexico.

Ethnohistorian Ralph Roys identified sixteen distinct Mayan polities during the sixteenth century, and one other polity has been proposed by Grant Jones in the central/northeastern Belize area (Figure 2.18). These polities were referred to by the Mayan term *cuchcabal,* which signified a town's geographic jurisdiction. The organization of these polities varied from those that had a three-tier political hierarchy, led

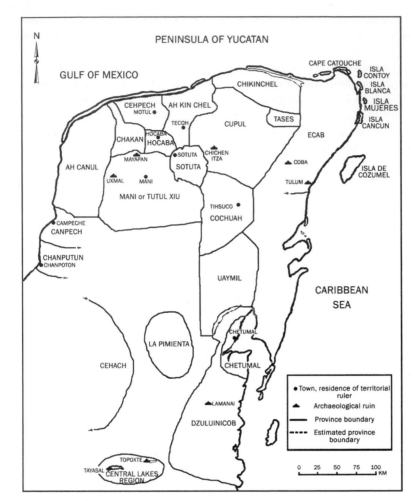

Figure 2.18 Mayan polities in the Yucatan at the time of Spanish conquest and location of important Postclassic Mayan sites mentioned in the text. (From Ralph L. Roys 1962 Literary Sources for the History of Mayapan, In *Mayapan, Yucatan, Mexico,* by Harry E. D. Pollock, Ralph L. Roys, Tatiana Proskouriakoff, and A. Ledyard Smith, Carnegie Institute of Washington Publication 619, p. 24, and Grant D. Jones 1989 Maya Resistance to Spanish Rule, University of New Mexico, Map 2).

by a lord, or *Halach Uinic,* who resided in the political center and oversaw secondary officials knowns as *Batab.* Other less-centralized polities lacked the *Halach Uinic* office, and the *Batab* official was the highest authority. Interior, less populous, and loosely organized zones were not governed by a *Batab.* There is some evidence of a hierarchical relationship between polities, as the lord of Acalan (in the interior of Campeche) extracted tribute from the polity of Chetumal (southern Quintana Roo/Belize coast) following a military expedition.

In addition to political rulers, other specialized offices included: *Holpop* (mat official with festivity/administrative duties); *Kaluac* (supplier who procured resources for overlords); *Nacom* (war leader); *Ah Kin* (high priest); *Ah Kanob* (speaker); and *Ppolom yok* (merchant). Commoners had various occupations as craftspeople, farmers, free laborers, and slaves. Another class of secondary officials, the *Ah Kulel* and the

Ah Kuch Cab, were in charge of neighborhood divisions (*kuchteel*) of particular towns; they coordinated the logistics of barrio tribute obligations, military service, and ceremonies.

The term *kuchteel* likely refers to a vassal social group and their landholdings. Sergio Quezada (1993) suggests that they were taxation units. Under Spanish rule, principal men were incorporated into town councils known by the Spanish term *cabildo.* Matthew Restall (1997) claims that these included precontact principles of community oligarchical rule and were significantly different from the Spanish institution of the same name. Above the *cabildo,* a *Batab* was appointed to rule the towns. Up to fifty officials (including religious offices) were members of the largest town *cabildos.*

During the Colonial period, important factions within the community were based on membership in patronymic groups and social class standing; little evidence for geopolitical ward or barrio divisions has been found. This situation may have changed from precontact to Colonial times, as numerous accounts suggest that towns were conceptually quartered into four divisions and that four major entrances to towns were marked by stone structures. At the walled city of Mayapan, *ch'ibal* lineage groups are named as the guardians of three cardinal gates, although the city actually had twelve gates (eleven of these are thought to have been in use simultaneously).

Efforts to identity quadripartite organization in the archaeological remains of precontact Mayan cities have thus far been unsuccessful, and such divisions may have been more important for ritual and cosmological purposes than for defining political and settlement sectors. Neighborhoods can be identified archaeologically by settlement clusters that share adjacent houselot walls, and cenotes or roads (*sacbe*). The presence of outlying administrative or ritual architecture that is dispersed among commoner neighborhoods may also testify to the presence of barrio administrators such as the *Ah Kuch Kab.*

Political officials shared authority with councils of pricsts, who were also hierarchically organized and specialized according to ritual responsibilities. In the Peten Lakes, ethnohistorian Grant Jones (1999) has documented an institution of paired rulership, in which secular lords and high priests governed together over political territories. This institution was likely widespread and had considerable time depth, extending backward in time to at least the site of Chichén Itza. Throughout Mesoamerica, Epiclassic and Postclassic political officials received the vestments of governorship from priestly officials, and councils of political and religious authorities administered the affairs of major cities.

This system created a complex and complementary system of power sharing. For the Mayan area, it represented a major departure from the Classic period institution of divine kingship, in which secular and religious authority was centralized under the single office of the king. Postclassic political and religious realms were not entirely separate as political officials drew upon ritual and mythological bases for legitimation, and they participated in ritual occasions. Conversely, priests meddled continually in political affairs; in fact, the fall of Mayapan may have been instigated by the actions of one high priest, Ah Xupan Xiu, whose political clout also enabled him to help found the post-Mayapan polity of Ah Kin Chel. The prevalence of the twin institutions of priesthood and rulership in late Mayan politics is likely due to the growth of the noble class and efforts to achieve greater regional integration by inclusive, complex, ranked institutions.

Some secondary political offices rotated according to the calendrical cycle, as illustrated in the succession of "katun lords" documented by Bruce Love (1994) in the Paris codex. This arrangement provided further opportunities for members of local polities to participate in governance. The scenes depicted on the murals of Tulum and Santa Rita Corozal, which show human actors interacting with supernatural impersonators, most likely record accession into rotating or permanent community offices. The Santa Rita figures are linked to one-year (*tun*) intervals (see Box 1.5 in the preceding chapter). Bishop Landa claimed that Yucatan was conceptually segmented into 13 divisions, paralleling the 13 K'atun cycle of 256 years, and communities rotated the honor of celebrating these calendrical divisions by erecting stone monuments and sponsoring rituals involving idols, priests, and prophesies linked to the interval. Prudence Rice (2004) has recently argued that this custom has its roots in the Preclassic Mayan period and may have helped to structure shifting centers of political power among Classic Mayan kingdoms.

Mayan Religion.   Religion in Postclassic Mayan culture, much like the Classic Mayan period before it, was centered on a pantheon of deities of varying importance. Each deity was linked with specific kinds of actions and associations in mythology and cosmology. The four surviving Mayan codex books are a primary source for understanding these deities, where they are shown performing rituals related to a complex array of calendrical and astronomical events, including New Year's ceremonies, twenty-year K'atun intervals, various almanacs, and planetary cycles (see Figure 6.6). The primary gods, such as K'awil (Lightning god), Chac (Rain god), Maize god, and old gods (Pauahtun) originate earlier in Mayan history and were prevalent in Classic period art. The most prominent deity in the Postclassic pantheon was Itzamna, a god of sorcery and priestly activities (Figure 2.5). The Merchant God (Ek Chuah) was also popular. In addition, there were two Postclassic goddesses, an older Ixchel, associated with childbirth and merchant pilgrimages, and a younger female deity. Some effigies lacking deity identifiers may portray customized patron family gods and/or deified ancestors.

At Mayapán, the elaborately crafted effigies were partly molded and partly modeled and hand-painted by skilled artisans working for noble families. Deities wear intricate headdresses and are adorned with representations of shell and greenstone jewelry as well as finely woven and embroidered cloths. Effigy censers are found at all lowland Postclassic sites, although their size, diversity, quantity, and complexity decrease with distance from Mayapan, the nucleus of this tradition.

A few representations of foreign deities from Central Mexico are found within the Maya area, although only at Mayapan. Xipe Totec is the most common foreign deity at this site, associated with sacrifice and agricultural renewal. This deity was found in contexts at that site along with a range of traditional Mayan gods. Murals of Mayapan, Tulum, and Santa Rita Corozal (Figure 2.6) are portrayed in an international style used throughout Mesoamerica at this time, although many specific elements within them (e.g., pottery forms, specific deities, reptile mouth portals, calendrical glyphs) are local to the Mayan area.

An important founding deity for Mayapan and other Postclassic cities was Kukulkan. This god is analogous to the Quetzalcoatl Feathered Serpent hero of Central Mexican mythology. The close ties to the two areas are illustrated by the presence of (Central Mexican style) bird-beaked human effigy sculptures at Mayapan. One aspect of Quetzalcoatl and Kukulkan was the bird-beaked anthropomorph known as *Ehecatl,* associated with the wind. Architecture linked to both the Feathered Serpent and *Ehecatl* includes round temples, quadripartite staircase temples with serpent balustrades, and serpent column temples, all of which are present at Mayapan.

According to Mayan mythology, Kukulkan came to the Mayan area on multiple occasions to establish new dynasties and shrine centers, including at Mayapan. He was a hero priest who taught important aspects of ritual knowledge to local nobles. Indeed, one temple mural program at this site depicts four serpent mouths framing miniature stucco temples. This theme likely celebrates founding myths proclaiming that the "four divisions" were united at this polity. Quadripartite serpent balustrade temples dedicated to Kukulkan also attest to cosmological foundations of political authority at centers such as Chichén Itza and Mayapan.

Rituals associated with religious celebrations often included bloodletting (of ears or tongue), human or animal sacrifice, hunting or warfare, incense burning, gift-giving and offerings of precious items, and the manufacture of specific deity effigies who were patrons of festival events. The sacrifice of slaves, war captives, or other persons who possessed little social capital was commonplace in the Spanish Colonial period. At Mayapan, mass graves next to major monumental buildings and in special burial shaft temples also attest to sacrifice and conflict in pre-Hispanic times. Mass graves at this city show that bodies were usually disarticulated, probably chopped apart, and effigy censers likely portraying the patron gods of the deceased were also smashed and deposited with them.

Various assumptions made by scholars since the 1950s about changes in Mayan religion from the Classic to Postclassic periods have persisted, despite archaeological evidence to the contrary. The Carnegie Institution's investigations at Mayapan recovered a large number of effigy censers in ritual, administrative, and elite domestic contexts. These investigators inferred that Mayan religion had "degenerated" to the level of household worship, in contrast to the Classic period kingdoms where art and effigies were concentrated heavily in noble contexts. Subsequent research has revealed that, in fact, effigies are also concentrated in elite features at Mayapan; the bulk of the effigies there come from structures of the Main Plaza and a few nearby noble palaces or outlying administrative complexes. At the site of Tulum, effigies are also concentrated in elite buildings. At the northeastern Belize settlements of Laguna de On and Caye Coco, effigies were discarded at special shrines away from domestic contexts. We now know that Postclassic Mayan priests and lords controlled ritual knowledge and material paraphernalia, as they did in earlier times. Commoners, however, embraced many basic religious concepts, and they commemorated key events at the household level with less elaborate material representations as their ancestors had done since the Formative period.

Contact-period Mayan society comprised a hierarchical set of complex economic, political, religious, and social institutions. Like earlier periods, there were distinct social-class divisions, and local nobles vied for position to control ritual knowledge and luxury material exchanges to distinguish them from commoners. Oligarchical structures were well developed during the Postclassic and early sixteenth century compared with earlier times (prior to Chichen Itza), with multiple priestly and political offices and councils that supported the leadership of *Batabilob* or *Halach Uinicob* paramounts.

Trade, which was widespread and well developed, provided opportunities for surplus exchange in thriving regional markets, but communities did not give up their efforts to produce their own food supply and meet essential needs. Interregional contact with Central Mexico involved substantial trafficking of basic and luxury items across long distances, and this intense contact is reflected in the ideological realm of Mayan centers. Foreign influence is detected in the use of international stylistic conventions (popular in Central Mexico) in Mayan art and the adoption of certain Mexican deities. The lowland Mayan peoples were integrated into a larger Postclassic Mesoamerican world of commerce and information exchange (for more on this larger Mesoamerican world, see Chapter 3 to follow).

SUMMARY OF MAJOR DEVELOPMENTS IN PREHISPANIC MESOAMERICA

As we have seen in Chapters 1 and 2, Mesoamerican civilization was forged by processes of change among many different peoples over a time span of millennia. The developments listed below stand out as the key features that shaped the course of Mesoamerican history.

First, the domestication of maize provided a secure nutritional and agricultural foundation for the emergence of Mesoamerican civilization.

Second, the rise of settled village life and the spread of early religious concepts brought about the coalescence of Mesoamerican culture in the Formative period.

Third, the development of state-level societies characterized by writing, cities, social stratification, and powerful kings signaled the development of truly complex civilizations in the Classic period.

Fourth and finally, the Postclassic period witnessed the continuing political and economic development of these societies, particularly the emergence of smaller polities (city-states) in which markets and commercial forces came to the fore as dominant institutions.

By the time of the arrival of Cortés and the Spanish conquerors in 1519, Mesoamerica was a distinct cultural tradition whose heritage shaped the continuing historical development of the area in the colonial, national, and modern epochs. Before we turn to these later developments, however, it will be important to explore the Late Postclassic (Contact period) Mesoamerican world in terms of the ways that it was organized and integrated into a world-system at the time of the Spanish invasion. That is the subject of Chapter 3 to follow.

SUGGESTED READINGS

BERDAN, FRANCES F. 1985 *The Aztecs of Central Mexico: An Imperial Society.* New York: Holt, Rinehart and Winston.

BERDAN, FRANCES F., RICHARD E. BLANTON, ELIZABETH H. BOONE, MARY G. HODGE, and MICHAEL E. SMITH 1996 *Aztec Imperial Strategies.* Washington, D.C.: Dumbarton Oaks.

BOONE, ELIZABETH HILL 2000 *Stories in Red and Black: Pictorial Histories of the Aztecs and Mixtecs.* Austin: University of Texas Press.

BYLAND, BRUCE E., and JOHN M. D. POHL 1994 *In the Realm of 8 Deer: The Archaeology of the Mixtec Codices.* Norman: University of Oklahoma Press.

CARRASCO, DAVID, LINDSAY JONES, and SCOTT SESSIONS (eds.) 2000 *Mesoamerica's Classic Heritage: From Teotihuacan to the Aztecs.* Boulder: University of Colorado Press.

EVANS, SUSAN TOBY 2004 *Ancient Mexico and Central America.* New York: Thames and Hudson.

JONES, GRANT D. 1999 *The Conquest of the Last Maya Kingdom.* Stanford: Stanford University Press.

LANDA, FRIAR DIEGO DE 1941 *Landa's Relaciones de las Cosas de YUCATÁN.* Translated by Alfred Tozzer. Papers of the Peabody Museum of Archaeology and Ethnology 18. Cambridge: Harvard University Press.

LOVE, BRUCE 1994 *The Paris Codex: Handbook for a Maya Priest.* Austin: University of Texas Press.

MASSON, MARILYN A. 2000 *In the Realm of Nachan Kan: Postclassic Maya Archaeology at Laguna de On, Belize.* Boulder: University of Colorado Press.

MILLER, MARY ELLEN 2001 *The Art of Mesoamerica: From Olmec to Aztec.* Third Edition. World of Art. New York: Thames and Hudson.

RESTALL, MATTHEW 1997 *The Maya World: Yucatec Culture and Society, 1550–1850.* Stanford: Stanford University Press.

SMITH, MICHAEL E. 2003 *The Aztecs.* Second Edition. Oxford: Blackwell Publishers.

SMITH, MICHAEL E., and FRANCES F. BERDAN (eds.) 2003 *The Postclassic Mesoamerican World.* Salt Lake City: University of Utah Press.

SMITH, MICHAEL E., and MARILYN A. MASSON 2000 *Ancient Civilizations of Mesoamerica: A Reader.* Malden, Massachusetts: Blackwell Press.

SPORES, RONALD 1984 *The Mixtecs in Ancient and Colonial Times.* Norman: University of Oklahoma Press.

TAUBE, KARL A. 1992 *The Major Gods of Yucatan.* Studies in Pre-Columbian Art and Archaeology No. 32. Washington, D.C.: Dumbarton Oaks.

TOWNSEND, RICHARD F. 1993 *The Aztecs.* London: Thames and Hudson.

WEAVER, MURIEL PORTER 1993 *The Aztecs, Maya, and Their Predecessors.* Archaeology of Mesoamerica. New York: Academic Press.

Chapter 3
The Mesoamerican World at Spanish Contact

The Mesoamerican world that confronted the Spanish conquistadors at the beginning of the sixteenth century was extremely complex, the result of a long development as outlined in the two preceding chapters. In this chapter we consider the extent to which Mesoamerica formed an interconnected world where events taking place in one social unit affected those in another, however distant they might have been from one to the other. Such an approach will help simplify for us the complexity of Mesoamerica, while also casting into relief the underlying cohesiveness and unity that has allowed the peoples of the region to resist cultural destruction during the centuries following Spanish contact. We will begin our discussion of Mesoamerica at Spanish contact with a brief description of its social and cultural complexity, and then turn to an analysis of Late Postclassic Mesoamerica as a world system.

The reconstruction of contact-period Mesoamerica to follow is based primarily on archaeological and ethnohistoric (documentary) studies. These two approaches often yield quite different information, but together they make possible a more rounded and complete view of the Mesoamerican peoples. They also provide a meaningful connection between the preceding Chapters 1 and 2, and this chapter. Many of the archaeological studies upon which the account is based—especially those dealing with the remains of Mesoamerican settlements that flourished at the time of Spanish contact—are cited and discussed in Chapter 2.

The two most important types of documentary sources employed in this chapter consist of Spanish accounts, provided by the first explorers, conquerors, and colonizers of the region; and written accounts left to us by the Mesoamericans themselves (see Chapter 6 for a full discussion of these latter documents). Useful supplementary information comes from studies of linguistic and cultural features that the descendants of those original Mesoamericans successfully preserved through five difficult centuries of "colonization." Based on these various sources of information, we attempt to answer the question of what the Mesoamerican world was like on the eve of contact with the Spaniards.

SOCIOCULTURAL COMPLEXITY
OF THE MESOAMERICAN WORLD

Let us begin our account with a brief review of the social and cultural diversity that characterized the contact (Late Postclassic) period Mesoamerican world. At this point, our goal is to portray the complexity of Mesoamerica in extremely broad terms, building upon the description of various regions, archaeological sites, and peoples discussed in Chapter 2.

City-States and Empires

Most scholars argue that the fundamental building blocks of the Mesoamerican world at contact were towns or cities and their dependent rural communities. The rural communities were made up of kinship groups, often patrilineal in descent, which together formed a commoner class of peasants. The elite ruling class and its attendants resided in the politically dominant urban centers where they exercised authority over the rural commoners. Scholars have long debated whether these units in Mesoamerica constituted chiefdoms or states. It now seems clear, however, that chiefdoms and states are best understood as models we use in an attempt to understand a continuum of ancient Mesoamerican political groups, and that no specific feature can demarcate one polity as chiefdom or another as state. Any given political unit in Mesoamerica, then, might fall toward either the chiefdom or the state end of the continuum, depending upon the degree to which the ruling group's authority was accepted as superior to all other forms of internal authority.

Many political units in Mesoamerica at the time of contact fell on the chiefdom end of the continuum where kinship relations (especially lineage relations) were dominant; but the majority of them—numbering perhaps several hundred—fell on the state end where military and recognized central authority relations prevailed. The latter are usually referred to by scholars as "city-states." Each city-state had a ruler or joint rulers, appointed by the "royal" lineages to act as the supreme authority over the political center and dependent rural communities. For example, at least fifty city-states existed in the Valley of Mexico alone, each supreme ruler being identified by the title *tlatoani* ("he who speaks"; plural, *tlatoque*). In the case of highland Guatemala, to give another example, some thirty city-states flourished, each maximum ruler bearing the title of *ajpop* ("he of the mat," "councilman").

Mesoamerica, however, did not consist simply of a large number of equal and autonomous city-states. Throughout the region powerful imperial states (empires) used conquest along with other means to subjugate formerly independent chiefdoms, city-states, and even empires. The Mexica or Aztec empire is the best-known imperial state, but there were perhaps another ten to twenty notable examples in Mesoamerica from the contact period. Many of these empires were modeled on the legendary Toltec empire of Central Mexico, which had collapsed 300 years before the coming of the Spaniards (for details on the Toltec empire, see Chapter 1). Several successor states became "epigonal" Toltec city-states and empires, employing conquest and tribute collection as part of a mission to civilize Mesoamerica in the name of great

Toltec rulers of the past such as the priest-ruler Quetzalcoatl ("Feathered Serpent"). At least some of the imperial rulers claiming Toltec connections were actually usurpers who had ruled over small city-states or even chiefdoms located on the margins of Mesoamerica. Driven at first to expand in order to survive, these upstart rulers later created elaborate militaristic political visions, synthesizing ideas derived from both their own marginal political units and the more "civilized" Mesoamerican political tradition.

Imperial states like the Aztec empire were influential throughout Mesoamerica, and they were able to affect in significant ways the political units falling outside their direct control. A form of dependency relationship was created by the aggressive actions of such entities, and the resulting unequal relationships became a defining characteristic of Mesoamerica at the time of Spanish contact (see the discussion on the Mesoamerican world-system that follows).

Ethnic Groups

Mesoamerica is often described as a single "culture area," defined by a long list of cultural "traits" supposedly shared by the peoples of the area. Indeed, broad cultural patterns were common to the peoples of Mesoamerica, but it must also be emphasized that there was much cultural diversity within the region as well (additional social and linguistic diversity is discussed in Chapter 11).

A great part of the cultural diversity of Mesoamerica was an expression of an incredibly complex ethnic mosaic found throughout the region. Mesoamerican ethnic groups—often referred to in the account to follow as "peoples"—were often defined on linguistic grounds. Nevertheless, other important criteria were used to define ethnicity in Mesoamerica, such as occupation (for instance, groups of merchants or artisans), style of life (rustic vs. civilized), relations of descent (different lineage affiliations), religious cult (shared patron deities), and historical origins (such as emigration from a common sacred homeland). Ethnic "peoples" existed by the thousands throughout Mesoamerica, and they influenced all aspects of social life there.

Many of the Mesoamerican city-states had their origins in ethnic groups, and each group's particular language, deity, and general vision of the world continued to be influential long after political relations had become dominant over ethnic ties. For example, in Central Mexico most of the city-states were organized by "Chichimec" groups, the term *chichimec* being an ethnic designation that meant something like "nomadic peoples from the north." The Aztecs and several other Chichimec groups spoke Nahuatl, but some ethnic Chichimecs spoke other languages such as Otomí and Tarascan. In contrast, the ethnic groups that formed the Mayan city-states of highland Guatemala were usually referred to as *amaq'*, their defining criterion being emigration from a common homeland in the "East." The Mayan Amaq' groups spoke diverse languages, but they shared a common identity through affiliation in lineage systems that united them into kin groups of variable size.

Most city-states and all imperial states of Mesoamerica were multiethnic, thus raising the question of the extent to which state religion and ideology superseded internal ethnic cultural differences. Scholars have pointed out that Mesoamerican states such as the Aztec empire did not actively seek to impose their own gods and particular cultural practices on other peoples. Recent research indicates, however, that the ruling ethnic groups tended to reformulate their particular patron deity cults to promote religious ideologies that supported broader imperial interests. Ideologies stressing war and human sacrifice were widely promoted by states throughout Mesoamerica, although the particular features of each ideology varied considerably. We also know that ethnic ideas and symbols within the core areas of the larger states were often assimilated to the dominant imperial culture, whereas in the marginal areas, ethnic groups usually remained segregated as culturally distinct peoples.

Regional Networks

Beyond the cultural variation in Mesoamerica based on ethnic and political organization, broader sociocultural differences were of regional importance; the regional networks gave rise to expanded cultural expressions that are sometimes referred to in the literature as "civilizations." Archaeologists in particular have called attention to this regional diversity and have shown that it existed in Mesoamerica long before Spanish contact. Each regional network was characterized by distinctive language and cultural features promoted by highly influential polities that dominated the regional network. A prototypical case would be the Zapotec peoples who built the Monte Albán city and later nearby towns in the Valley of Oaxaca, in the process promoting a regional sociocultural network inherited by the peoples of the Oaxaca region at the time of Spanish contact.

The most important regional networks and corresponding cultures of Mesoamerica, according to one prominent scheme, were associated with the following geographic regions of Mesoamerica: highland Guatemala, lowland Yucatan, lower Central America, southern Veracruz-Tabasco, Oaxaca, Central Mexico, central Veracruz, northeastern Mexico, Guerrero, western Mexico, and northernwestern Mexico (see the section on ecology in the introductory chapter for the geographic characteristics of these regions). Some of the specific sociocultural features of these regions will be described next in conjunction with the positions that their peoples occupied within the wider Mesoamerican world-system.

In summary, Mesoamerica at the time of Spanish contact was composed of highly diverse component parts: numerous city-states, empires, ethnic groups, and regional networks.

MESOAMERICA AS A WORLD-SYSTEM

In this section we attempt to describe the unity of Mesoamerica despite the sociocultural diversity just outlined. One way that scholars attempt to simplify and make sense out of sociocultural diversity and complexity is to apply a world-system perspective to it. This perspective, as originally elaborated by Immanuel Wallerstein (1976) in order to explain historical developments in Europe, posits that for several thousand years the societies of the Old World were embedded in large intersocietal networks known as "world-systems." Europe in the fifteenth and sixteenth centuries was in the process of being formed into a "modern" world-system, the consequences of which have been felt ever since in all regions of the globe. The coming of the Europeans to Mesoamerica truly initiated a clash of "worlds," because, as we shall now see, Mesoamerica also had formed its own world-system at the time it was "discovered" by the Europeans.

A first step in seeing Mesoamerica as a world-system at the time of contact with Europe is to recognize that some of its component societies were dominant over others, and that as a result its diverse social units formed an integrated but stratified world. A second step is to understand that the Mesoamerican region was not under the political control of any single state, but instead it was an arena of competing political and economic (social) units. The most powerful Mesoamerican state at the time of Spanish contact was the Aztec empire, yet it controlled less than half of the territory in the Mesoamerican world. Furthermore, as already noted, other powerful, independent empires coexisted with the Aztecs. Mesoamerica at contact was tied together in important ways through economic bonds and thus constituted a "world economy" rather than a "world empire," despite occasional claims by the Aztecs that they were rulers over the entire "civilized" world known to them.

Students of Mesoamerica recognize that Central Mexico was the most influential area, or in world-system terms, the dominant core. As we have seen, however, the Mesoamerican world had other *core zones* in West Mexico, Oaxaca, Yucatan, and Guatemala. Adjacent to the core zones were located the socially dominated *peripheral zones* of Mesoamerica, in such regions as northwestern Mexico, northeastern Mexico, and southeastern Central America. The main *semiperipheral zones* of the Mesoamerican world-system can be identified primarily with zones specialized in trade and other commercial activities. These so-called semiperipheral zones functioned to bind the Mesoamerican world into a common economic system, largely by mediating between the unequal core and peripheral units. The most important semiperipheral unit in Mesoamerica at contact was probably Xicalanco on the Gulf Coast of southern Mexico, but other key semiperipheral units existed in northwest Mexico and along the Caribbean and Pacific coasts of Central America (Figure 3.1).

Relationships between core, periphery, and semiperiphery in the Mesoamerican world-system were determined to an important extent by the flow of luxury goods such as cotton garments, jade pieces, cacao beans, animal skins, rare tropical bird feathers, and gold ornaments. These "preciosities" were the lifeblood of the core states, for they were used to legitimize the authority of the rulers and reward the loyal cadres of warriors and state officials who dominated the intersocietal networks. The peripheral peoples were pressed by the core societies to yield their precious resources. The mechanisms employed in this unequal exchange process included ceremonial gift-giving and mediated trade within semiperipheral zones, as well as military threat, outright conquest, and tributary demands.

The exchange of goods between core and periphery societies, which underwrote the stratified relations of the Mesoamerican world-system, has been summarized as follows:

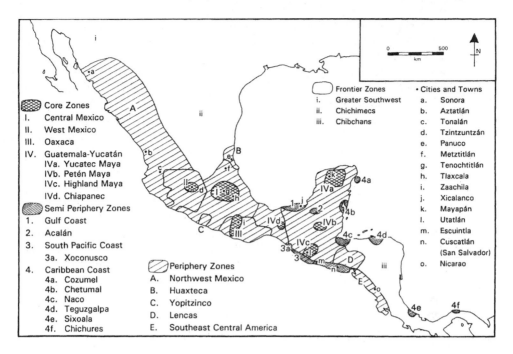

Figure 3.1   Core, semiperiphery, and periphery zones of the Mesoamerican world-system.

. . . a consequence of the growth of powerful core states in ancient Mesoamerica was a widespread stimulation of trade, a reorientating of priorities in many places toward production and exchange in the world-system arena . . . [A]s powerful core states develop they must stimulate increased production of the luxury goods used to reward cadre. These heightened demands ripple outward, beyond territories conquered by the emergent cores, influencing production strategies over a broad area and thus incorporating more and more local groups into [the periphery of] a Mesoamerican world economy. (Blanton and Feinman 1984:678)

The core states of Mesoamerica expropriated not only the preciosities of the peripheral peoples but also their labor. In the core zones, most subject commoners were required to specialize in the production of bulk goods, especially "grains" such as maize, beans, and amaranth. In the peripheral zones, the demand for preciosities forced the peoples there to expand production of these precious items or of other items that could then be traded down the line for the desired goods. In particular, the prodigious demand for cotton garments by the core societies—it is estimated that over 3 million articles of cotton cloth flowed into Central Mexico alone each year—meant that much of the labor-intensive cultivation of cotton, spinning of it into thread, and weaving of the thread into cloth were shifted away from the core to the periphery.

It is likely that at the time of Spanish contact all societies located within the territorial boundaries created by the Mesoamerican world-system, however small or undeveloped, had been incorporated into the exchange network either as core, periphery, or semiperiphery. Outside the boundaries of Mesoamerica were found *frontier* peoples, divided into hundreds, perhaps thousands, of smaller, less complex social networks. Although few, if any, of the frontier societies were so small or isolated as to qualify as simple bands ("minisystems," in world-system terms), many of them were organized on a tribal level of development (including chiefdoms in some cases) and were politically weak. In general, the frontier peoples were of limited economic or political interest to the Mesoamericans, in part, no doubt, because they controlled few luxury items and in part because their fragmented social networks would have made it difficult to subdue and incorporate them into the Mesoamerican world-system.

Nevertheless, the frontier peoples to the north and south of Mesoamerica were influenced by, and in turn exercised some influence on, the Mesoamerican world, although their relationships with Mesoamerican peoples were neither systematic nor definitive. To the north of Mesoamerica, the frontier consisted largely of peoples speaking languages of the Uto-Aztecan family (Cora, Huichol, Piman, Mayo) and were widely known to the Mesoamericans as Chichimec peoples. To the south, the frontier peoples mainly spoke Chibchan languages (Paya, Sumu, Huetar, Talamanca, Boruca, Guaymi). It is not known whether the Mesoamericans had a special term by which they referred to these Chibchan peoples, but they were undoubtedly considered culturally foreign and socially backward.

The world-system view of pre-Hispanic Mesoamerica just presented represents a highly simplified version of that framework, and other scholars have suggested more elaborate versions. For example, Smith and Berdan (2003) argue that the major world-system zones can be subdivided into a more complex set of sociocultural units than the simplistic core, semiperiphery, and periphery units. For example, they point to such additional world-system units as "Affluent Production Zones," "Resource-Extraction Zones," "Exchange Circuits," "Style Zones," and "Unspecialized and Contact Peripheral Zones." Nevertheless, for the purposes of this introduction to the Mesoamerican world-system, we will confine our discussion to the three main structural units: core, semiperiphery, and periphery. We begin with the core states.

Mesoamerican Cores

Although the Aztec empire was clearly the most powerful and influential core unit within the Mesoamerican world-system at the time of Spanish contact, there were other core states that competed with the Aztecs for military, economic, and cultural dominance. Like the Aztecs, these polities were organized into states with imperial tendencies and thus were able to fend off adjacent strong states while exploiting (peripheralizing) the hundreds of less-powerful city-states and chiefdoms that dotted the landscape throughout the Mesoamerican region.

Competition among core states was intense and resulted in the most complex intersocietal networks, localized in four special geographic subregions of Mesoamerica, which we shall refer to as "core zones." The strongest of the four, Central Mexico, was built upon the foundation of the ecologically rich Basin of Mexico, the Mesoamerican zone most agriculturally fertile and free of physical barriers to communication. The Nahuatl (Aztec) language was spoken by the majority of inhabitants in the zone, and this practice facilitated intercommunication between the many states making up this interacting network.

Although the other three core zones were less ecologically propitious than Central Mexico, they were also areas with favorable ecological conditions. The West Mexico core zone had a strong ecological base in the "symbiotic" relationships established between the highland Lake Pátzcuaro basin and the lowland Balsas river system. The Tarascan language (also known as Purépecha) was spoken throughout most of the subregion, and this practice facilitated the thorough domination of the zone by the Tarascan empire. The Oaxaca core zone was also ecologically diversified and was founded on the economic integration of a highland area (Mixteca Alta), a large highland river valley (Valley of Oaxaca), and two important lowland plains (Oaxaca Pacific Coast and Isthmus of Tehuantepec). The Mixtec and Zapotec languages were widely spoken in Oaxaca, and their historical connection, while somewhat distant, provided at least a minimal basis for intercommunication throughout the zone at the time of contact.

The Mayan core zone was located in the northern region of Central America, stretching from Guatemala to Yucatán. It too was an ecologically diversified subregion made up of southern highland river basins (Highland Guatemala and Chiapas), a central area of lakes and tropical lowlands (the Peten), and northern lowland plains (Yucatan, Campeche, Quintana Roo). Virtually all the peoples of this zone spoke languages belonging to the Mayan family; moreover, these languages, despite many differences, shared enough common features to permit limited but crucial intercommunication between the numerous states of the Mayan core zone.

We will now examine more closely each of the four main core zones of Mesoamerica (see the map in Figure 3.1).

Central Mexico Core Zone. The Central Mexico core zone was dominated by a confederated empire composed of the allied Mexican, Texcocan, and Tlacopan states (see Chapters 1 and 2) (see Figure 3.1). The Mexican state achieved dominance over its two confederated states, and its city of Tenochtitlán, inhabited by approximately 200,000 persons, became the capital of the empire. The Aztec empire ruled over some fifty city-states (*altepetl*) within the Basin itself. The subordinate city-states (for example, Culhuacan, Huexotla, Azcapotzalco) shared many of the institutions, benefits, and liabilities of the empire, and even though they had tribute obligations, they are properly seen as core units within the Central Mexico zone. At the time of contact with Spaniards, most of the peoples in the Basin spoke Nahuatl, the language of the empire.

The Aztec empire ruled over some 250 additional city-states located outside the Basin, which were administered as thirty-eight tribute-paying provinces (Hodge and Smith 1994). Most of the provinces were close to the Basin of Mexico, but a few of them, such as Yoaltepec (Guerrero coast), Coixtlahuacan (Oaxaca highlands), and Xoconusco (Chiapas coast), were far removed from the imperial heartland. The lingua franca of the provinces was Nahuatl, but the majority of the peoples there spoke other Mesoamerican languages such as Otomí, Mazatec, Matlazinca, Totonac, Mixtec, and Zapotec. Roughly 100 additional city-states located outside the Central Basin were subject to Aztec political and military controls as "client states," and they were probably in the process of being organized into provinces. Some client states paid tributes to the empire, but their main imperial role was to serve as buffers against the empire's chief military competitors. The peoples of the client states were as linguistically diverse as those in the provinces. Both the formal provinces and the client states can be seen as peripheral units in terms of their relations with the Aztec empire and the Central Mexico core zone as a whole.

There was considerable competition among the states that made up the Aztec empire, and this was manifested in the form of wars from time to time. But the sharpest conflicts within the Central Mexico core zone took place between the Aztec empire and a series of politically independent states located adjacent to the Basin. The most important competitors to the Aztec empire were Tlaxcala, Huejotzinco, and Metztitlán. These states shared basic imperial and cultural features with the Aztecs (for example, they had similar origin myths, deities, and calendar systems), but nevertheless they were engaged in protracted military struggles with the Aztec empire and with each other. They also participated in ritual warfare ("flower wars") with one another, staging battles designed to provide captives for sacrifice to their respective patron deities. The rulers of the hostile states in the Central Mexico core zone attended each other's important ceremonies, at which times they exchanged elite gifts and other prestations. They also intermarried, although most elite marriages probably took place within the imperial domains.

Huejotzinco, Tlaxcala, and Metztitlán were located in mountainous areas quite close to the center of the Aztec empire. Although relatively poor in natural resources, they stood in the way of the empire's access to the resources of the rich coastal lowlands to the east. Tlaxcala had traditionally been active in trade with the Gulf Coast peoples, and the Aztecs were apparently determined to take control of their trading routes.

The Aztec armies attacked these three states on numerous occasions, sometimes in alliance with one or the other of the confederacy, but were never able to militarily dominate them (Huejotzinco apparently fell to the Aztecs shortly before Spanish contact). In part this failure was as a result of the defensive nature of these states' mountain strongholds, but it was also related to the fact that internally they were profoundly militarized, unified, and determined to maintain political independence. All three states had within their ranks fierce mercenary warriors, especially from Otomí and Chalca ethnic groups, who had previously been driven from their homelands by the Aztec warriors. The peoples of Huejotzinco and Tlaxcala spoke Nahuatl, the Aztec language, whereas Otomí appears to have been the primary language of the people of Metztitlán.

There is some indication that the Aztecs may have considered all-out war against these hostile states to have been more costly than the limited tributes they would gain in return. The Aztecs' strategy appears to have been increasingly one of isolating the three states by conquering their weaker neighbors, while engaging the states themselves in a kind of low-intensity, highly ritualized warfare. Nevertheless, relations between these states and the Aztec empire were profoundly competitive, and they set a tone that pervaded the entire Mesoamerican world-system.

West Mexico Core Zone.   Like Central Mexico, West Mexico was dominated by a single empire, which we will refer to as the Tarascan empire. The West Mexico core zone, however, was unique in that its empire had no serious competitor states. The boundaries of the Tarascan empire corresponded roughly with the modern Mexican state of Michoacán, a vast territory of mountains, plateaus, river basins, and coastal plains enclosed by the Balsas and Lerma-Santiago river systems. The capital of the empire was Tzintzuntzan, a city of only some 35,000 inhabitants located in the highland Lake Patzcuaro Basin.

The Tarascan empire was originally formed through the political and military unification of some eight city-states located within the Patzcuaro Basin. Later, it expanded by conquering an additional seven city-states adjacent to the Basin and eventually took control of many other political groups located in more distant areas. The Tarascan empire was more centralized and unified than the Aztec empire, and its subjugated city-states retained little autonomy. Administration of the empire was divided into four regions, with its authorities ruling directly over the local units rather than through a provincial organization. Nevertheless, several client states located along the frontiers of the empire, especially the eastern borders, were allowed to retain their own authorities. They were considered by the empire to be allies rather than subjects, and their tributary obligations took the form of military service and provision of captive slaves and sacrificial victims. Together, the tribute-paying units of the four regions, along with the client states, made up an important part of the periphery of the West Mexico core zone.

The Tarascan language and culture were dominant in the Patzcuaro and surrounding basins, and were being assimilated by most of the peoples of the empire. The strong ethnic character of the empire is thought to have been a response by the imperial heartland to the relatively limited ecological base of the Patzcuaro Basin and, therefore, the need to ensure access to resources over a much wider area through cultural assimilation. Nevertheless, some ethnic "segregation" existed within the empire. A few foreign enclaves (for example, Cuitlatecs and Nahuatls) within the core zone provided special services in the form of artisanry, trade, and spying. Along the imperial frontiers the client states tended to be multiethnic, made up mainly of Otomi, Mazahuan, Matlazincan, and Nahua groups.

Competition and conflict within the West Mexico zone was muted, especially when compared with the Central Mexico zone. The Tarascan empire had no major rivals in the region, and its highly centralized political system kept internal conflict at a minimum. There were no powerful states north or east of the empire, although smaller city-states such as the Nahua-speaking Coca, Tecuexe, Cazcan, and Zacaluta (in the present-day Mexican states of Jalisco, Colima, and Guerrero) were able to contain Tarascan advances in these areas.

The principal rivals of the Tarascans were the Aztecs, and this intense *external* rivalry undoubtedly helps explain the relative *internal* cohesiveness of the West Mexico core zone: A unified empire was necessary if the Tarascans were to compete successfully with the powerfull, more numerous Aztecs. The Tarascans became one of the most militarized states of all Mesoamerica, and they more than held their own in many wars fought against the Aztecs. To the south and west, where the Tarascan empire abutted Aztec provinces and client states, fortifications were constructed and client states organized to defend against Aztec incursions. Even though Tarascan rulers at times attended Aztec ceremonies in Tenochtitlán, and presumably vice versa, nonmilitary contacts between the two great powers were minimal. As far as we know, there was no intermarriage between the respective royal families, and direct trade was virtually nonexistent (nevertheless, considerable trade through intermediaries flourished). Long-distance merchants from the two empires could not cross each other's imperial boundaries, and even ambassadors under royal escort entered the other's territory at great risk to their personal safety.

The West Mexico core zone, then, was a special case within the Mesoamerican world-system. Its imperial state was militarily powerful but was more inward-looking than its Aztec rivals. Beyond the Aztecs and other close neighbors, the Tarascans appear to have shown limited interest in the rest of Mesoamerica. They were not renowned as traders, although they produced superb metal objects that may have been traded over great distances within Mesoamerica (in part, perhaps, by sea along the Pacific Coast). Tarascan culture shared many of the characteristics of the Mesoamerican "world" culture, but it was also parochial compared with other imperial states. Many of the Tarascan religious beliefs and art forms differed significantly from the rest of Mesoamerica and, surprisingly, the Tarascans had no established writing system.

Oaxaca Core Zone.   The core zone in what is today the state of Oaxaca, Mexico, contrasted dramatically with the Central and West Mexican core zones in that there was no dominant imperial state. Rather, the zone was divided into some fifty small kingdoms or city-states, whose territorial boundaries and political alliances were constantly shifting. These states were concentrated in roughly equal numbers in the Mixtec highlands and the Valley of Oaxaca. The highland city-states were made up primarily of Mixtec speakers, whereas the peoples of the Valley of Oaxaca mostly spoke Zapotec (however, an important minority of the Valley inhabitants spoke Mixtec). The Mixtecs also controlled or were confederated with additional city-states in the eastern and coastal lowlands, as were the Zapotecs with polities in the Isthmus of Tehuantepec lowlands. Other ethnic peoples residing in the zone spoke languages that were neither Mixtec nor Zapotec: Chocho, Chinantec, Mixe, Zoque, Chatino, and Amuzgo. For the most part, these peoples remained outside the direct control of the core states, forming a periphery to the Oaxaca Mixtec and Zapotec city-states of the core zone.

Within the Mixtec highlands the ruling lines of city-states such as Tilontongo, Yanhuitlan, and Jaltepec were considered to be ancient and particularly prestigious; moreover, the rulers of many of the other states in the area traced royal genealogy from them. The Mixtec codices make special reference to a ruler, 8 Deer "Tiger Claw," who seized the Tilantongo throne, conquered many towns and peoples in the region, and established the important kingdom of Tututepec on the coast. He was later killed by a lineage rival named 9 House. The sharing of a common royal lineage and similar funerary rites (centered on past mummified rulers) provided the Mixtec states with considerable cultural unity, a unity reinforced by extensive intermarriage between the diverse ruling families. Despite such bonds, warfare between the Mixtec states was widespread.

In the Oaxaca Valley many of the Zapotec states recognized Zaachila as the most revered and powerful of the allied city-states there. The Zaachila rulers collected tributes from several polities in the valley, and in a few areas they established provinces by appointing regional authorities to govern over the local peoples. As in the case of Tilontongo in the Mixtec area, Zaachila's prominence appears to have been limited and was based more on cultural respect than military domination. Both the Zaachila state and other Zapotec city-states were probably heirs to the historic Monte Albán Zapotec political system, and as such they were characterized by an especially close blending of politics and religion.

Archaeological evidence indicates that the highland Mixtec states were able to dominate and perhaps peripheralize many of the Valley Zapotec peoples (see Chapters 1 and 2). For example, members of the royal family from the Mixtec kingdom of Yanhuitlan gained a measure of control over the Zaachila state through marriage into its dynastic line, whereas other Zapotec city-states were conquered and either ruled over or confederated with Mixtecs states from the mountainous highlands. Mixtec ceramics, metalwork, carvings, and painted figures have been found at many sites in the Valley of Oaxaca, most notably at Monte Albán (Tomb 7) and Zaachila. It is likely that relations between the highland Mixtecs and valley Zapotecs were a complex mix of military threat and political confederation. The result was a creative synthesis of the Mixtec and Zapotec cultures in this core zone.

The Oaxaca zone developed a network of relationships with states in the other core zones of the Mesoamerican world-system. The Mixtec kings claimed descent from the Toltec ruling line and maintained political ties with rulers of city-states in Central Mexico who were making similar claims. The Aztec warriors conquered many Mixtec and Zapotec states, organizing them into the tribute-paying provinces of Coixtlahuaca and Coyolapan. The Aztecs set up a garrison at Guaxacac (from which derives the name Oaxaca) in the Valley, intermarried with the ruling families of important Mixtec and Zapotec kingdoms, and made Nahuatl the lingua franca for the zone's ruling classes. Nevertheless, control over the zone by the Aztec empire was weak, and rebellion against Aztec rule—carried out by the Mixtec and Zapotec city-states, often in alliance with one another—was widespread at the time of Spanish contact.

The Oaxaca core zone was famous for its artisans, who, working within the so-called "international" Mesoamerican art tradition, produced some of the most exquisite and widely distributed preciosities of the Mesoamerican world (see Figure 2.3). Various cities of the Central Mexico core zone had wards of resident Mixtec artisans, who not only manufactured crafts but also taught their skills to Aztec artisans.

In addition, Oaxaca polychrome ceramics, gold pieces, bone carvings, and other objects circulated widely throughout the larger Mesoamerican world-system.

Mayan Core Zone.   This southernmost core zone comprised diverse city-states and empires occupying the areas of present-day Guatemala and the Yucatán Peninsula. Like the Central Mexico zone, the Mayan states exercised powerful influence over a large area of Mesoamerica (in the Mayan case, the northern part of the Central American region). One of the Mayan zone's main characteristics was that its constituent peoples, in both the core and the periphery, were overwhelmingly Mayan in language and culture. Another defining characteristic was the relative weakness of ties between its highland and lowland core states, although important political and economic exchanges between them did take place.

Broadly speaking, the Mayan core states were distributed in three geographic areas: the southern highlands (present-day Chiapas and Guatemala), the central lake and tropical lowlands (Petén and Belize), and the northern lowlands (Campeche, Yucatán, and Quintana Roo). More than thirty distinct Mayan languages were spoken in these three areas, the majority of them in the southern highlands (for example, Tzotzil, Jakaltec, Mam, Ixil, K'iche', Kaqchikel, and Poqomam). The languages of the central lake area and northern lowlands were fewer in number and more similar to one another (Lacandon, Chol, Mopan, Itza, Chontal, and Yucatec). Most of the core states incorporated speakers of diverse Mayan languages and, in some cases, non-Mayan speakers as well.

The political organization of the Mayan core states in the southern highlands has been the subject of considerable dispute. Some scholars have seen them as alliances between lineages and larger factions, and thus not centralized states. However, a detailed study of the K'iche' polity (Carmack 1981), historically the most imortant polity in the zone, indicates that it was similar in organization to the city-states and empires of Central Mexico and the other core areas of Mesoamerica.

The K'iche' Mayan state was centered on its capital of Q'umarkaaj (also known as Utatlan), an urban center of perhaps 10,000 to 15,000 residents. Through conquest the K'iche' imperialized most surrounding Mayan and non-Mayan city-states, organizing them into approximately thirty tribute-paying provinces. The K'iche' empire also competed in military and economic terms with other Mayan core states of the southern highlands, such as the Kaqchikel and Tzutujil states.

The highland Mayan imperial states were able to peripheralize numerous less powerful city-states and chiefdoms through warfare, trade, and aggressive diplomacy. Most of these peripheral peoples were also Mayan speakers: Tzotzils, Tzeltals, and Mams to the west; Ixils and Poqomams to the north and east. To the south the peripheral peoples mainly consisted of non-Mayan-speaking Pipils (Nahua) and Xinkas. The Mangue-speaking Chiapanecs formed perhaps the only non-Mayan imperial state within this core zone. The Chiapanecs, from their capital city near Chiapa de Corzo, dominated Zoque-speaking peoples on their western flank and applied military pressures against the Tzotzil Mayas to the east.

Core states were not as numerous in the central lake and northern lowland areas as in the southern highlands, and many of the Mayan peoples there occupied peripheral and semiperipheral positions within the larger zone. Perhaps the only core state within the central area was that of the Itza-Mayas, whose capital of Taj Itza was built on an island within Lake Peten. The Itza rulers collected tribute from dispersed farming groups residing on the mainland surrounding the lake. The Itza language was very similar to Yucatec-Mayan, and these two language groups engaged in extensive trade (using the Mopan Mayas of Belize as intermediaries). Less powerful Mayan peoples who spoke Chol and Lacandon languages were located in the territory surrounding the Itza state. They were apparently peripheralized by the Itza through threats of war and actual military encounters.

In the northern lowlands of Yucatan, most of the peoples at one time had been subject to the powerful Mayapan "empire," centered on a small city of some 11,000 inhabitants in the northwestern part of the peninsula. By the time of the Spanish conquest, however, the Mayapan state had fragmented into smaller political units. Some sixteen of the independent units (for example, Mani, Sotuta, Chanpoton) were able to organize small core states that competed with one another for power and tribute goods. They probably peripheralized other, more simply organized political groups in the Chakan, Chikinchel, and Uaymil "provinces."

Most interaction between the southern highland and northern lowland Mayan core states primarily took the form of trade, especially long-distance trade carried out by specialized merchants who moved merchandise both by land and by sea. Jade, obsidian, grinding stones, metals, and quetzal feathers from the highlands were exchanged for textiles, pottery, slaves, honey, and cacao from the lowlands. Relations between the highland and lowland areas were difficult to maintain, in part because travel through the dense tropical jungle of the Petén and surrounding environs was so arduous. The Itza were perhaps reluctant mediators between the southern highland and northern lowland sections of the Mayan core zone. Nevertheless, some direct contacts existed, for rulers of the highland core states claimed genealogical ties with "Mayan-Toltec" rulers in the Tabasco and Yucatan areas, and they periodically sent ambassadors to those places in order to bolster their own authority.

Both the southern highland and northern lowland Mayan states traded extensively with the Oaxaca and Central Mexico core zones, mostly through the mediation of outside long-distance merchants. Mayan and Aztec merchants traveled to special markets on the coasts of Guatemala and Tabasco, where they exchanged goods under highly formal conditions. The Aztecs and K'iche's probably engaged in military skirmishes, as when they struggled for control over the Xoconusco area. As a result, considerable military tension existed between the Aztec and K'iché empires, and marriages between their royal families may have been arranged in order to help ease the tensions. Trade between the Mayan core states and the peripheral peoples southeast of the Guatemala-Yucatan zone involved direct exchanges carried out under the auspices of Mayan merchants. Apparently, the Mayan states were also able to apply considerable military and political pressure on the peoples of the southeastern periphery.

Mesoamerican Semiperipheries

Societies that help mediate unequal relations between core and periphery form the semiperiphery. According to world-system theory, semiperipheral units tend to be innovative in the development of social institutions, in part because they assimilate cultural patterns from both core and peripheral peoples. Within the Mesoamerican world-system, the societies that specialized in arranging and promoting trade between foreign peoples can be seen as the key semiperipheral units. Zones where open trade takes place are often referred to as "ports of trade," although "international trade centers" have been suggested as more appropriate terms (Smith and Berdan 2003:12). In the Mesoamerican trading centers, exotic religious cults often flourished and served to attract pilgrims from near and far. Trade and religion went together especially well in the Mesoamerican semiperiphery.

Most of the Mesoamerican semiperipheral zones were located away from the core centers, in some cases on the borders between different core zones and in most cases adjacent to large peripheral areas. Thus, for example, the famous international trade center in the southern Gulf Coast of Mexico was situated near the boundaries of the Aztec empire to the west and the Mayan core states to the east. In contrast, the Casas Grandes trading center (destroyed around A.D. 1350) was located far to the north of the Mesoamerican core zones but near important peripheral peoples of that area. The monumental architecture of Casas Grandes included workshops, warehouses, a large marketplace, apartment buildings, and a ball court. Local products such as painted ceramics, copper ornaments, and exotic feathers attracted traders from afar, who in turn brought to Casas Grandes luxury items such as turquoise and other rare stones desired in the Mesoamerican core zones. A cult dedicated to the Quetzalcoatl deity apparently existed at Casas Grandes, perhaps making it a "holy city."

A few semiperipheral societies may have existed within the core zones themselves, although surrounded by powerful core states it was no doubt difficult for them to maintain political independence. Most of them, in fact, were incorporated into empires and thus lost or radically altered their ability to mediate relations between core and periphery. For example, Tlatelolco, a merchant city-state that maintained considerable independence even within the Aztec empire, eventually was subjected to the full weight of Aztec rule (in A.D. 1473).

We turn now to the main semiperipheral zones of Mesoamerica and their individual trade centers (see the map in Figure 3.1).

Gulf Coast.   The area of the present-day Mexican state of Tabasco was the setting for the largest and most important semiperipheral zone in Mesoamerica. This international trade zone was situated on a major transportation route where the Grijalva, Usumacinta, and Candelaria rivers and numerous lagoons made travel by canoe highly efficient. A series of small city-states in the area functioned as trade centers, beginning with Coatzacoalco to the west and extending eastward to Xicalanco and beyond that to Champoton (Campeche). Foreign merchants visited these trade centers from all directions: Aztecs from Central Mexico, Tzotzil and K'iche' Mayas from highland Chiapas and Guatemala, Chontal Mayas from Acalan, and Yucatecan Mayas from the Peninsula. Gulf Coast merchants have been referred to as "Putuns," a name probably taken from the people of Putunchan, one of the important ports of trade located in the central part of the zone near Xicalanco.

Much of the trade within the Gulf Coast consisted of formal exchanges between merchants representing the interests of hostile core states, mediated by the ruling officials of the trade centers. Trade of this kind usually involved exchanging manufactured goods (cloth, pottery, gold ornaments, precious-stone jewelry) for valuable raw materials (feathers, jade, skins, salt, slaves). There were regular marketplaces in the zone as well, where considerable trade of a more "open" exchange took place. The local peoples produced large quantities of cacao beans, which allowed them to profit handsomely from the trade zone. They also traveled long distances by canoe to exchange merchandise in trade centers elsewhere, especially in Yucatan and along the Caribbean coast.

The international trade centers were politically independent and were oriented toward trade rather than war and conquest. The governing class was made up of merchants organized into political councils. Women could reach high positions of authority, although male relatives are said to have exercised their administrative duties. Foreign merchants formed residential wards in the trade towns and no doubt exercised influence in political matters. This was especially true of the Aztec merchants residing in Xicalanco, who apparently served on the governing councils and had the backing of fellow warriors stationed in the area. Nevertheless, political neutrality was an important characteristic of the trade centers, for without it the trade between merchants from powerful competing states would not have been possible.

The Chontal Mayan language was spoken by most peoples in the Gulf Coast, and it also served as one of the commercial languages employed by the merchants and officials doing business in the zone. Nevertheless, Nahuatl was also spoken by most members of the merchant class, and native Nahuatl and Pipil speakers resided in the trade center. In eight of these towns (the largest was Cimatan), native Nahuatl speakers made up the majority of the residents.

The peoples of the Gulf Coast zone were considered by their neighbors to be particularly wealthy, cosmopolitan, and friendly toward outsiders. The merchant class surrounded itself with fine works of art, such as painted codices, pottery, jewelry, murals, and statues, all executed in the current Mesoamerican "international" art style. We know little about their religion, except that it bore many similarities to the religion of the Yucatecan Mayas.

Box 3.1 describes the semi-peripheral trading zone of Acalan, similar in many ways to Xicalanco.

South Pacific Coast. The Pacific Coast from Xoconusco southward formed a long strip of land in which a string of trading centers were located. Unfortunately, we know little about this zone at the time of contact, and some scholars question

---

Box 3.1   The Trading Center of Acalan

Acalan ("the place of canoes") was an independent city-state that specialized in trade and was located along the tributaries of the River Candelaria in what is today Campeche, Mexico. The capital of Acalan, Itzamkanac, was a merchant town of perhaps 10,000 inhabitants. This town was too far inland to have been a true seaport, but its merchants were Putuns, middlemen who traveled far and wide to link up with vital trading routes. The Acalan merchants regularly moved by canoe to the Gulf Coast area in order to engage in trading, and perhaps from there around the Yucatan Peninsula to still more distant international trade centers. They also trekked overland to trade with Yucatecan-Mayan peoples to the north, and to the south at least as far as the small Nito trading center on the Caribbean coast. At Nito the Acalans had their own permanent commercial agents and residential ward.

The Acalan city-state was governed by an independent merchant class. The paramount ruler was also the leading merchant, and he was subject to the will of merchant councils representing the interests of the four wards into which the capital was divided. The merchant class oversaw the production of portable trade goods, such as cacao, cotton cloth, dyes, body paint, and pine resin.

The native tongue of the Acalan people was Chontal Maya, but many members of the ruling class had Nahuatl names and could speak the Nahuatl language. The Spaniards claimed that the Acalans were better proportioned and more refined than their neighbors. The patron deity of the ruler of Itzamkanac was Kukulchan (the Chontal equivalent of Quetzalcoatl). Patron deities of the town's four quarters were also prominent in the Acalan pantheon: Ikchaua, patron of cacao and merchants; Ix Chel, patroness of weaving, childbirth, and women; Tabay, patron of hunters; and Cabtanilcab, of unknown identity. The goddess Ix Chel was of special importance, and the Acalans sacrificed maidens especially raised for that purpose in her honor.

---

the presence there of true international trade centers. Xoconusco itself (Soconusco, the coastal part of Chiapas, Mexico) had been a neutral trade zone where merchants from the mutually hostile Aztec and K'iche' Mayan empires could engage in administered trade. About fifty years before the coming of the Spaniards, the K'iche's and Aztecs began to vie for political control over the Xoconusco area. The K'iche' conquered some of the eastern towns (Ayutla, Tapachula, Mazatan), but shortly thereafter the Aztecs gained control over the entire Xoconusco area. Aztec historical sources indicate that the latter conquests were carried out by long-distance merchants from the Tlatelolco city-state who had previously been attacked by the native peoples of Xoconusco.

Even though Xoconusco became a tributary province of the Aztec empire, apparently it continued to function as a trading zone. Aztec merchants traded there and, despite Aztec political control, so did merchants from Oaxaca, Chiapas, and Guatemala. The Aztec merchants also used the zone as a base for launching trading expeditions farther south along the Pacific Coast.

The Xoconuscan peoples themselves produced large quantities of cacao and were actively engaged in trade. Archaeological remains in the area suggest that Xoconuscan society was less stratified or politically centralized than the societies of the core zones. They may have been organized as chiefdoms rather than states. Most of the inhabitants of the zone spoke Mixe-Zoquean languages, although Mangue- and Pipil-speaking minorities were also present. At Spanish contact, Nahuatl was the lingua franca of the Xoconusco zone.

Suchitepequez on the western coast of Guatemala, like Xoconusco, was an area of cacao production and trade. Aztec merchants traveled there not only to trade their wares but also to spy for the empire. The special trading centers that existed in Suchitepequez were necessary because Aztec merchants were not welcome in the highland capitals of the Mayan core states to the north. The situation may have been the reverse of that in Xoconusco: In Suchitepequez, the coastal trading centers were subject to K'iche' political authority, but Aztec and other foreign merchants were permitted to visit for purposes of trade. The K'iche's established colonies of Nahua speakers in the area, no doubt to better exploit the trade networks that had long operated there.

Documentary sources indicate that both Aztec and Mayan long-distance traders passed through Escuintla in the central part of the Guatemalan coast on their way to points farther south. Additional trade centers existed along the Pacific Coast of eastern Guatemala, El Salvador, and Nicaragua. Unfortunately, our historical sources do not provide details on the locations of most of these centers nor on their forms of political organization.

Caribbean Coast.   A series of trading centers were located along the Caribbean coast of the Yucatan Peninsula and the Central American Isthmus, and together they made up still another important Mesoamerican semiperipheral zone. The Caribbean trading centers were established in strategic locations so as to exploit local resources and link up the core zones of Mesoamerica with the large southeastern periphery and, beyond that, the lower Central American frontier. Gold was one of the main precious items that moved through this network, circulating all the way from Panama to Yucatan and from there to the rest of Mesoamerica.

The island of Cozumel just off the Caribbean coastline of the Yucatan Peninsula was organized as a small trade center at the time of Spanish contact. Special platforms were built at various locations on the island so as to be out of reach of the floodwaters and thus to provide safe storage for trade goods. In addition, causeways extended from the water's edge to the central town, where it is thought that the formal trading activities took place. This central town was probably the site of the famous Ix Chel goddess's shrine, to which religious pilgrimages were directed.

Archaeologists excavating at the island sites argue that the inhabitants of Cozumel were a pragmatic people. They invested in warehouses, stone streets, and modest residences rather than in massive temples, shrines, or palaces. Even the Ix Chel cult had a practical dimension, for its "speaking" idol was thought to issue flexible instructions to meet the changing needs of the trade-oriented Cozumel inhabitants. As might be expected of an international trade center, the people of Cozumel for the most part received the first Spanish visitors in a friendly manner and tried to trade with them. They even requested "letters of recommendation," which they hoped would bring commercial benefits from subsequent Spanish visits!

Located farther south along the Caribbean coastline were two other well-known trade centers, Chetumal and Nito. Both were strategically placed for receiving goods from the interior by way of major river systems and for providing easy access to the Caribbean Sea. They were also cacao-producing areas. Murals found at the Chetumal site were painted in a local version of the Mesoamerican international art style; and Ikchaua, the merchant god, was among the deities prominently portrayed in the mural scenes (see Figure 2.6). As noted in Box 3.1, the Nito trading center had resident merchants and agents from Acalan and elsewhere.

The largest and most important of the international trade zones along the Central American coast was found in the Ulua river valley of present-day Honduras. Ulua was similar in many ways to the Gulf Coast zone, in that travel was mostly by canoe and abundant cacao was produced in the environs. One of the most important trade centers in the zone was located at Naco in the Chamelecon Valley just south of the Ulua delta. Naco apparently served as a crossroads for merchants from Yucatan to the north, highland Guatemala to the west, and traders from Central American trade centers farther to the south. As an inland port, Naco received goods such as obsidian, gold, jade, cacao beans, and feathers from both overland and sea routes. The commoner population of Naco most likely spoke Chol or Chorti Maya, both languages being close relatives of the Chontal-Mayan language spoken in the Gulf Coast and Acalan. Archaeologists working at Naco have suggested that an enclave of Nahuatl speakers or Nahuatl-influenced Mayas governed this trading town (Figure 3.2).

Other trading centers were located south of the Ulua zone along the Caribbean coast of Central America. One possible trade center in the Teguzgalpa area of eastern Honduras the zone was Papayeca, established near the Agalta Valley gold deposits. The rulers of Papayeca spoke a language similar to the Aztec language (Pipil),

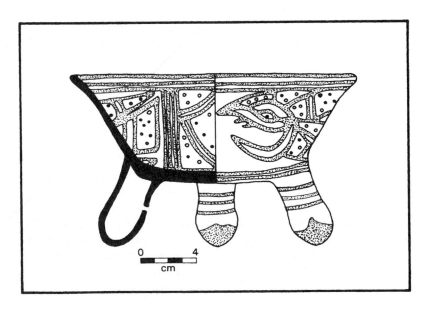

Figure 3.2 Painted ceramic vessel from Naco, Honduras, in the northern part of the Central American periphery. After Anthony Wonderley, "Imagery in Household Pottery from 'La Gran Provincia de Naco,'" in *Interaction on the Southeast Mesoamerican Frontier*, ed. E. Robinson, BAR International Series, 327. Oxford, England: BAR, 1987, p. 310.

and they apparently exchanged "gold and other valuables" directly with Aztec merchants. Still farther south along the Caribbean coast in the Sixoala Valley of present-day Costa Rica was another trade center of Nahuatl speakers, known to the Chibchan-speaking peoples of the area as Siguas ("foreigners"). The ruler of the Siguas bore the Aztec name of Iztolin and was said to be a "Mexica-Chichimeca." The Siguas moved gold taken from the Sixoala riverbeds to the Aztecs, either directly by means of Aztec merchants or indirectly through Putun seaborne merchants.

Finally, we have tantalizing evidence of a group of people living near Nombre de Diós (the place where the Panama Canal now flows into the Caribbean Sea) who, according to the Spanish conquistadors, in precontact times had traveled in canoes from the Honduras area to colonize the center. They spoke a different language from the other natives of Panama and were called "Chuchures." The Chuchures were probably traders, most likely Chontal or Nahuatl speakers. If so, they must have formed the southernmost outpost of semiperipheral peoples operating within the Mesoamerican world-system.

Mesoamerican Peripheries

Mesoamerican peripheral peoples actively participated in the economic, political, and cultural life of the Mesoamerican world, but from a weak, subordinate position. Whether through military conquest or threat of conquest, forced political alliances, or unequal ceremonial and market exchanges, the peripheral peoples were subservient to the core states of Mesoamerica. The powerful empires and kingdoms that so impressed the Spaniards could not have continued to function without the many peripheral peoples who provided the labor, raw materials, and sacrificial victims that sustained the complex Mesoamerican core zones.

Many peripheral peoples, as we have already seen, were incorporated into the imperial states as subject provinces. In these cases, they were exploited and peripheralized in a direct manner in the form of tributary obligations. Other peoples of Mesoamerica retained varying degrees of political independence, yet were subject to indirect and more subtle forms of domination. Most of them confronted unrelenting military pressure from the core states, as well as exploitation through economic exchanges. The "meddling" by the core states kept the peripheral peoples, whether administered provinces or dependent societies, politically weak, economically exploited, and by Mesoamerican standards, culturally "backward".

As already noted, the Mesoamerican periphery should be distinguished from the so-called frontier areas, which were made up of peoples outside the Mesoamerican world-system located primarily in northern Mexico and southern Central America. The frontier peoples were politically and economically influenced but not structurally transformed by the Mesoamerican world. Frontier peoples, however, could affect developments in Mesoamerica, not only by making war on its peripheral peoples but also by exposing them to new ideas and practices. The Aztecs originally were a frontier people who were later integrated into the Northwest Mexico periphery; subsequently migrated to Central Mexico, where they became a core state and finally organized the dominant imperial state of the Mesoamerican core (see Chapters 1 and 2).

We will now briefly examine a sample of the most important peripheral zones of the Mesoamerican world-system, beginning with Northwest Mexico (see the map in Figure 3.1).

Northwest Mexico Periphery.   Northwest Mexico was an area rich in resources of interest to the Mesoamerican core peoples, especially its copper, gold, and silver; turquoise and other precious stones; cotton; seashells; aquatic birds; salt; peyote; and other desert flora and fauna. These valuable raw materials were extracted and processed by peripheral peoples in the Northwest and were exchanged for manufactured goods coming from the core zones of Mesoamerica. The raw materials were concentrated in two main areas of the Northwest: one along the Pacific Coast, the other along the eastern flanks of the Sierra Madre mountains.

At the time of Spanish contact, the peoples who extracted and processed the raw materials were concentrated in greater numbers along the coast than on the eastern side of the mountains. They were generally organized as polities that were transitional between chiefdoms and city-states, and shared many Mesoamerican cultural features. Their closest ties to a core zone were probably with West Mexico and the Tarascan empire. Trade with the Aztec empire and other Central Mexico core states may have been partly impeded along the coast by the Tarascans, but it continued to operate fully along the Sierra Madre route.

The most powerful city-states of the Northwest area were in the southern part, in what are today the Mexican states of Jalisco, Colima, and Nayarit. Most of the peoples there spoke languages related to Nahuatl. City-states like Tonalan (Guadalajara) and Cazcan were relatively large and highly militaristic. They could take to the battlefield with several thousand warriors and may have built urbanlike towns occupied by up to 10,000 inhabitants. They shared several "advanced" Mesoamerican features such as copper hoes, obsidian-blade swords, markets, and public buildings and houses constructed of stone. Their religious pantheons featured familiar Mesoamerican deities, and human sacrifice and cannibalism were part of the ritual system.

The city-states under discussion received strong military and economic pressure from the Tarascan empire just to the south, and many of the previously mentioned Mesoamerican features may have been responses to Tarascan meddling. The Tarascans no doubt found ways to drain off the scarce goods produced in the area, especially cotton, metals (gold, silver, copper), salt, honey, and cacao. The southern part of the Northwest periphery, then, was rather directly dominated by the Tarascan core state.

City-states farther to the north, such as Chametla, Aztatlan, and Culiacan, were made up of peoples speaking Cora and Cahita languages, both close relatives of the Nahuatl language. These peoples probably had limited direct contact with the Tarascans, and therefore they were perhaps more influenced by indirect means from other Mesoamerican core zones. Apparently, they traded with the core societies of Central Mexico, as suggested by the polychrome ceramics and copper and gold ornaments fashioned within the Central Mexico art style found at archaeological sites in the area. Although these polities were smaller than the ones southward, some of the military units may have numbered a few thousand warriors. Political rulers in the area were carried about on litters and enjoyed high (noble) status.

In general, the peripheral peoples in the northern part of the zone supplied the Mesoamerican world with similar products to those yielded by their neighbors in the southern part. In return they received manufactured goods, and in the process they assimilated Mesoamerican cultural features. Their craft goods, rendered in the late Mesoamerican international art style, and complex religious ideas about deities and human sacrifice were typically Mesoamerican (Figure 3.3). It is noteworthy, however, that the northern peoples failed to produce stone architecture or to sculpt monuments.

Scholars once thought that the line between Northwest Mesoamerica and the non-Mesoamerican frontier was located along the Rio Fuerte in Sinaloa. Recent historical and archaeological evidence indicates, however, that the Mesoamerican periphery extended into the main river valleys of present-day Sonora. The Opata-speaking inhabitants of Sonora were organized as transitional chiefdoms and city-states similar to the other polities of the northern periphery. They must have

Figure 3.3 Figure painted on a pottery vessel from Sinaloa, Mexico, in typical Mesoamerican style. After Charles J. Kelley, "The Mobile Merchants of Molino," in *Ripples in the Chichimec Sea*, eds. Frances Joan Mathien and Randall McGuire. Carbondale, IL: Illinois University Press, 1986, p. 87.

provided an important connecting link between the Northwest Mesoamerican periphery and the frontier peoples of what is today the southwestern United States.

Some archaeologists argue that the Northwest periphery at one time extended all the way to the southwestern United States, from where socially complex peoples such as the Hohokam and Anasazi exported turquoise and cotton cloth to Mesoamerica. In the process these southwestern peoples took on selected Mesoamerican features, and according to some scholars, became peripheral units of that world-system. Trade between the Northwest periphery that we have been describing and the Greater Southwest area remained intact at the time of Spanish contact, but it had been reduced to sporadic exchanges best characterized from a Mesoamerican perspective as frontier relations.

Huaxteca.   The peoples of the Huaxteca formed a special periphery in the northeastern part of Mesoamerica. Although Nahua speakers inhabited the northern and southern parts of the Huaxteca, most inhabitants of the area spoke Huaxtec, a distant linguistic relative of the Mayan family. It is surprising to find Mayan speakers so far removed from their sister languages to the south, but some scholars think that the Huaxtecs at one time inhabited the entire east coast of Mexico and had been geographically contiguous with the Mayan zone to the south.

The Huaxtecs seem to exhibit certain "archaic" cultural features, suggesting that their entry into the Mesoamerican world-system may have happened relatively late. Core peoples like the Aztecs considered the Huaxtecs to be exotic. The Huaxtecs were distinguished by such characteristics as painting their hair different colors, filing their teeth, wearing a kind of conical head cover, and revering shamanistic and other magical practices (Figure 3.4).

Furthermore, well-known Mesoamerican gods were conceptualized by the Huaxtecs in anachronistic ways. For example, Tlazolteotl, the Aztec goddess of sensuality, was for the Huaxtecs a primeval mother fertility goddess. The Huaxtecs are mentioned in an ancient Mesoamerican myth that describes the settling of Mexico by peoples who came from across the sea and landed at the Huaxtec port of Panuco. Whether or not there was any historical basis to the myth, it suggests that in the minds of Mesoamericans the Huaxtecs were a remnant of their civilization's ancient past.

From the perspective of Mesoamerica as a world-system, the Huaxtecs were rather typical peripheral peoples. They inhabited a somewhat isolated area and were in close contact with frontier Chichimec peoples falling outside the civilized world. Nevertheless, the area was rich in exotic materials of interest to the core societies, especially rubber, bark cloth, turtle shells, animal skins, feathers, and shells. The Huaxtecs were politically weak, being fragmented into numerous small chiefdoms rather than consolidated into centralized states. Nevertheless, larger polities existed on the borders with Metztitlán, a core state with which the Huaxtecs were at times allied. Huaxtec public architecture mirrored the political situation: It was relatively small and unimpressive except for a few larger, well-fortified sites along the southern border in the Metztitlán area. As far as we know, the Huaxtecs had no writing system.

Figure 3.4 Huaxtec carved statue of an unclothed man with tatoos on one side of his body. Drawing by Ellen Cesarski.

Even prior to the emergence of the Aztec empire, there was considerable direct exploitation of the Huaxtecs by the Central Mexican city-states. The Aztecs themselves are said to have first attacked the Huaxtecs during the reign of Motecuhzoma I (A.D. 1440–1468), in retaliation for the Huaxtecs' having killed merchants trading in the area. The Huaxtecs apparently relied heavily on magical rites to win this battle; they were defeated, however, and many men, women, and children were killed by the victorious Aztec warriors. Only when the Huaxtec chiefs agreed to pay handsome tributes to the empire did the killing stop. Wars between the Huaxtecs and Aztecs continued, in part because many Huaxtec political groups remained independent and in part because others rebelled against imperial rule. The wars were opportunities for the Aztecs to carry off booty, slaves, and sacrificial victims. Like other peripheral peoples, the Huaxtecs were subjected to degrading stereotypes: The Aztecs referred to them as disgusting drunkards and sodomists.

The Yopes and Lencas, described in Boxes 3.2 and 3.3, are best seen as peripheral peoples similar in their relations with the core centers to the Huaxtecs and Northwest peoples described above.

Box 3.2 Yopitzinco

Yopitzinco, an isolated mountainous zone located in what is today the state of Guerrero, was similar in some ways to the Huaxteca peripheral zone described in the text. Guerrero, which was perhaps the region of greatest linguistic diversity in all Mesoamerica, included peoples speaking Nahua, Tarascan, Tlapanec, Cuitlatec, and other languages now extinct. The Yopes, inhabitants of Yopitzinco, spoke the Tlapanec language. Most of Yopitzinco's neighbors, including other Tlapanec speakers, were conquered by either the Aztecs or the Tarascans. Some of these peoples paid regular imperial tributes, whereas others were required to man military garrisons established on the borders between the two hostile empires. The Aztecs also colonized one of Guerrero's northern provinces with 9,000 families from Central Mexico.

In Mesoamerican terms, the inhabitants of Yopitzinco were a rather unsophisticated people. As a mountain folk, they were famous for their hunting prowess and use of the bow and arrow. Until marriage neither men nor women wore clothing. They were known to be fierce warriors who beheaded and flayed the skins of captives. Politically, the Yopes were organized into loose chiefdoms or "tribes" rather than centralized states, and they totally lacked urban centers. The Yope were identified as the people of Xipe Totec, the red god of the Eastern sun and vegetative renewal. In Xipe's honor gladiatorial rituals were performed, during which sacrificial animals and humans were flayed and their skins donned by red-painted ritual specialists. Xipe Totec was an important deity throughout Mesoamerica at the time of Spanish contact and was especially revered by the Aztec emperors. The Yopes were given special religious status because of their close association with the Xipe deity.

The Yopitzinco area was poor in the kinds of raw materials that interested the Mesoamerican core peoples, although jaguar, lion, and wolf pelts extracted from the area circulated in the wider exchange network. The Yopes were only weakly incorporated into the periphery of the Mesoamerican world-system, in part, no doubt, because of the dearth of resources in the area. Culturally, they lacked many of the features common to other peoples of Mesoamerica. Nevertheless, as noted, they were the source of important religious ideas and practices that apparently were taken over and used for imperial purposes by the core states. Yopitzinco was also a source of slaves and sacrificial victims for the more powerful societies of Central and West Mexico.

Strategically located along the border between the Aztecs and the Tarascans, the Yopes were subject to political manipulation by these two imperial powers. The Aztecs, in particular, regularly invited the Yope chiefs to witness their bloodiest and most impressive sacrificial celebrations in Tenochtitlán, at which times they would shower their rustic guests with expensive gifts. The underlying political message must have been clear to the visitors: It would be useless to oppose the Aztecs, and therefore they should hold the line against the Tarascans. As with other peripheral peoples, the Aztecs employed ethnic stereotyping to keep the Yopes in place, referring to them as untrained barbarians: "just like the Otomí only worse"!

Box 3.3   The Lencas

Scholars have long debated the position relative to Mesoamerica of the Lencan peoples of south-western Honduras and eastern El Salvador. Some scholars think that they were part of the Mesoamerican world, others a buffer or frontier to Mesoamerica, and still others part of an entirely different cultural world. Although the Lencan language shares some features with the major language families of Mesoamerica, it appears not to have demonstrable genetic ties with any of them. Nevertheless, the Lencas had a long history of interaction with Mayan peoples from the Guatemala-Yucatan core zone of Mesoamerica, and at Spanish contact they shared important cultural features with the Mesoamerican world (for example, city-states, the 365-day solar calendar with its eighteen "months," high temple mounds). From a world-system perspective the Lencas are best seen as forming a relatively independent peripheral zone of Mesoamerica, similar in important ways to the Huaxtecs and Yopes.

Politically, the Lencas were organized as chiefdoms and small city-states, each political unit exercising authority over a single river valley. The political ruler, high priest, chief justice, and other officials formed a Lencan ruling class that was internally united by bonds of kinship and marriage. Nevertheless, the various polities engaged one another in warfare, in never-ending struggles to increase territorial holdings, tribute goods, and slaves. Still, in some areas certain periods were set aside during which warfare was banned. In many cases the Lencan political divisions were correlated with language dialects, each dialect providing a degree of ethnic homogeneity. At the time of Spanish contact, for example, the Care dialect was spoken around Gracias a Diós, the Colo dialect in the Agaltec Valley, and the Poton dialect in eastern El Salvador and northern Nicaragua. These and other "languages" mentioned in the documentary sources were apparently variants of the same Lencan language.

The Lencas shared features typically associated with peripheral peoples throughout Mesoamerica. They were politically fragmented, limited in power, and transitional between chiefdom and state levels of development. Archaeologists have shown that Lencan monumental public structures were relatively small and few in number, except for military fortifications, and most construction was of adobe rather than stone. Many Lencan peoples inhabited isolated mountain zones adjacent to non-Mesoamerican tribal peoples such as the Jicaques, Peches, and Sumus.

Lencan territory was relatively poor in resources of interest to the Mesoamerican world, although it yielded some honey and cacao. Because the Lencas were numerous—they may have numbered over 500,000 persons at the time of Spanish contact—they may have been an important source of slaves for neighboring Mayan and Pipil core states. In the northeastern part of Honduras, the Lencas occupied strategic territories with important gold and other mineral deposits.

Unfortunately, we have little information about the processes by which the Lencas were integrated as periphery into the Mesoamerican world-system. They apparently fought wars on unequal terms against the neighboring Mayan and Pipil city-states. No doubt the Lencas also engaged in trade with semiperipheral peoples in the ports of trade at centers like Naco and the Pacific Coast. In order to have commodities to trade for the salt and manufactured goods they desired, the Lencas must have intensified the labor that went into the production of larger quantities of honey, animal skins, and woven cloth. A more direct form of exploitation of the Lencas occurred in the Olancho and Agalta mining areas, where under the authority of Nahua-speaking overlords they labored to extract gold and other precious metals.

Southeastern Central America Periphery. The southeastern periphery of Mesoamerica comprised a string of chiefdoms and city-states occupying the Pacific Coast zone from the eastern part of Guatemala down to the Nicoya Peninsula of Costa Rica. The northern section of this zone, what are today Guatemala and El Salvador, was occupied mainly by groups speaking Pipil, a language closely related to Nahuatl. The southern section, along the coasts of Nicaragua and Nicoya, was inhabited by groups speaking the Chorotega and Subtiaba languages as well as additional groups of Pipil speakers (the Nicarao). The closest linguistic relatives of these three languages (Chorotega, Subtiaba, and Pipil) lived far to the north within the Mesoamerican core zones.

There has been much confusion over the relationship between the southeastern peoples and Mesoamerica. They have been variously referred to as "buffer," "frontier," or "intermediate" peoples relative to Mesoamerica. The evidence suggests, however, that those residing along the Pacific Coast as far south as the Nicoya Peninsula were integrated into the Mesoamerican world-system as peripheral peoples. They were subject to political and economic pressures from the Mesoamerican core states, and they shared many typical Mesoamerican characteristics. In particular, they were under pressure to provide the Mesoamerican world with raw materials and unprocessed goods such as cotton, cacao, feathers, animal skins, dyes, and gold.

Politically, most peoples of the southeastern periphery were organized as city-states and advanced chiefdoms. These polities engaged in continual struggles with one another over power and position relative to the more powerful core states. The largest city-states were found among the Pipils in such places as Escuintla, Mita, Izalco, and Cuzcatlan. The Pipil city-states interacted more directly with the neighboring Mayan core states than did the other peoples of the southeastern periphery, and correspondingly they assimilated more corelike features. South of these Pipils the polities were smaller, often described by scholars as chiefdoms, exemplified by the Chorotegas and Nicaraos located along the Pacific Coast of Nicaragua and the Peninsula of Nicoya, Costa Rica.

In most cases, the southeastern polities were governed by a ruler of noble status, who was subject to advice and consent from political councils made up of older men chosen for set periods of time. Together, the rulers and councils selected war chiefs to lead the people in times of war. This somewhat decentralized form of government differed from the generally more centrally organized core states of Mesoamerica. The southeastern town centers were also smaller and less nucleated than their counterparts in the core zones. Architectural differences existed too, as exemplified by the fact that most of the public buildings in the Southeast were constructed of earth rather than stone.

Some scholars have argued that the Nicaraos and Chorotegas engaged in external relations primarily with non-Mesoamerican peoples to the south rather than with the Mesoamerican peoples to the north. This theory has been particularly suggested for the Chorotegas, who were politically weaker than the Nicaraos and were considered by the Spaniards to be "crude . . . and subject to (the rule of) their women" (Chapman 1960:86). Nevertheless, the cultural ideas and practices of the Chorotegas appear to be fully Mesoamerican, and their peoples actively engaged other Mesoamerican peoples in trade, political alliance, and warfare. In short, they formed part of the southeastern periphery of Mesoamerica.

The Nicaraos were clearly tied into the Mesoamerican world-system. Many of their cultural features—such as the 260-day calendar system, elaborate pantheon of deities, and ritual human sacrifices—were virtually identical to their Aztec counterparts. Cultural similarities of this kind with the rest of Mesoamerica would not have been possible without continuing interaction between the Nicaraos and the core units of the larger Mesoamerican world. This conclusion is confirmed by maps shown to the Spanish conquistadors that portrayed routes used by Aztec and Putun merchants who traveled all the way down to "Nicaragua" in order to engage in trade. Indeed, the Nicaraos had well-developed markets, where the most important Mesoamerican preciosities circulated, including cacao money. The Nicaraos traded with merchants from the Mesoamerican core states, most likely in international trade centers located along the Pacific Coast.

As noted before, the Nicarao and Chorotega societies were politically weaker than the Pipil city-states farther to the north. Nevertheless, whether organized as chiefdoms or states (or more likely, transitional forms between the two), both the Nicaraos and Chorotegas had well-established tributary systems and standing warrior units. Furthermore, as with the core states, noble status was required for holding the highest public offices.

On the Caribbean side of lower Central America (Honduras, Nicaragua, Costa Rica, and Panama), to the east of the Pipil, Chorotega and Nicarao polities, were located peoples who fell outside the Mesoamerican world-system. From the perspective of Mesoamerica, they constituted its southeastern frontier. Most of these peoples spoke Chibchan languages and were linked together into small social networks of their own. Generally, their political organizations took the form of tribes or chiefdoms, organized largely through kinship (lineage) ties. Their elite leaders traveled throughout the area exchanging gold and other valuable objects with one another. As frontier peoples to Mesoamerica, they exercised some influence on that world. For example, the Nicarao custom of chewing coca was probably borrowed from the Chibchan frontier peoples. Nevertheless, cultural influence came mostly from Mesoamerica to the peoples making up the Chibchan worlds of the Central American Isthmus, rather than vice versa.

REFLECTIONS ON THE MESOAMERICAN WORLD

We began the chapter by defining the sociocultural diversity that characterized the contact period expression of the Mesoamerican world. Next, we adopted a world-systems perspective in an attempt to demonstrate that the Mesoamerican world during its final phase had formed a political-economic network that both unified its component parts and provided the network for its broadly shared culture (civilization).

It seems reasonable to conclude from the preceding account that, despite the great sociocultural diversity (or perhaps in part because of it), the Mesoamerican peoples indeed had established an integrated world-system at the time of Spanish contact. Accordingly, we defined the Mesoamerican (1) core zones in which powerful states exploited weaker polities and interacted with one another in highly competitive ways; (2) peripheries, made up of peoples subject to exploitation, whether directly under imperial rule or indirectly through diverse forms of domination; and (3) semi-peripheries of trading zones where hostile core states as well as core and peripheral peoples could actively engage one another in economic exchanges. Despite the broad hegemonic power of the Aztec empire, there were many independent states in the Mesoamerican world-system, including other powerful empires.

The Mesoamerican world-system then, was more a "world economy" than a "world empire," to use Wallerstein's terms. Its relationships of widest scope were the economic ones of trade, gift exchange, forced production, and market control. As we noted, however, political relations also extended outward, binding together the diverse peoples of the Mesoamerican region. The city-states and empires exercised influence on one another through never-ending struggles for power and relative economic advantage. Cultural patterns corresponding to the individual city-states (as well as to core, periphery, and semiperipheral units) existed, although the extent to which a Mesoamerican-wide culture ("civilization") emerged is more difficult to determine than the economic and political dimensions of that world-system.

Having argued that the Mesoamerican case conforms reasonably well to the world-system model, certain caveats are in order. It is particularly important to keep in mind that we are employing extremely broad world-system categories. Concepts such as "core," for example, allow us to discuss together highly disparate political groups, from the huge Aztec empire to the rather small Mixtec city-states of highland Oaxaca. There is much to be gained from viewing these societies together as components of a larger regional network that defined much of social life in ancient Mesoamerica. It cannot be denied, however, that the differences between the individual societies were also important for understanding social life in ancient Mesoamerica, and some of these differences are discussed in the specific profiles of three Mesoamerican peoples in Chapter 2. The "periphery" is an even broader concept, for we have applied the term to peoples of vastly different political organization (from tribes and chiefdoms to city-states), and with highly diverse connections to Mesoamerica as a whole (from imperial provinces to largely independent peoples such as the Lencas in Central America).

It can be argued that our account of Mesoamerica unduly stresses economic and political relations over cultural features. Nevertheless, our approach clearly does not leave out culture; and, in fact, a focus on political and economic relations provides an essential context for the analysis of Mesoamerica's diverse cultures. Furthermore, even at the broadest level of the Mesoamerican world-system, we would expect to find cultural expressions that could be understood only in their widest world-system context.

The Aztec case is particularly relevant to the issue of a pan-Mesoamerican culture or civilization, since it suggests the possibility that certain Aztec intellectuals (and probably their counterparts in other Mesoamerican core societies) had generated the idea of highly abstract, invisible powers transcending the complex pantheons of deities that characterized Mesoamerica's diverse religions. By taking this first step in the creation of universal sacred symbols, the Mesoamericans were perhaps engaging in a kind of cultural "rationalization" that must have been inspired in part by the quite rational economic and political relationships binding Mesoamerica into a unified world-system.

The issue of cultural rationalization leads to questions about where the Mesoamerican world was headed at the time it so violently collided with the emerging modern world-system of which Europe was the core. In the history of the Old World, ancient world economies similar in type to the Mesoamerica one were often transformed into world empires, as powerful states managed to dominate all others in key regions and thereby gain political control over the entire regional network. The rulers of the Aztec empire certainly were aware of the possibility of gaining hegemonic control over the larger Mesoamerican world, and they boasted at times of already having accomplished just that.

As we have seen, however, the Aztecs failed in their attempts to create a universal empire, and there is good evidence that they were far from ever doing so. After all, even close neighboring states in Central Mexico were able to maintain political independence from the Aztec empire, and more distant imperial powers such as the K'iche' Mayas of Guatemala were probably more than equal to the task of preventing Aztec domination of the highland Mayan core zone. Even political groups already incorporated into the provincial structure of the Aztec empire—for example, city-states in the Oaxaca area—were a constant threat to regain political independence through military means. There is some evidence, too, that the Aztecs had come to realize that subjugation of the semiperipheral trading zones might have been profoundly crippling to the larger economy. Perhaps their military takeover of the Xoconusco port of trade zone taught them that valuable lesson.

It seems likely, then, that Mesoamerica was destined to remain a world economy for many years to come, politically and socially divided by its numerous ethnic identities, city-states and regional networks. Of course, inevitably changes would take place in the relative position of the individual polities and regional networks within the Mesoamerican world-system. New core states would emerge, old ones would drop down to peripheral or semiperipheral positions, and former frontier peoples would be incorporated into the periphery. Unfortunately, we shall never know the transformations that might have taken place, and instead we are left to ponder the legacy of an incredibly vibrant world that has reverberated down through the corridors of time in Mexico and the countries of Central America.

SUGGESTED READINGS

BYLAND, BRUCE E., and JOHN M. D. POHL 1994 *In the Realm of 8 Deer: The Archaeology of the Mixtec Codices.* Norman: University of Oklahoma Press.

CARMACK, ROBERT M. 1981 *The Quiché Mayas of Utatlan: The Evolution of a Highland Guatemala Kingdom.* Norman: University of Oklahoma Press.

EVANS, SUSAN TOBY 2004 *Ancient Mexico and Central America: Archaeology and Cultural History.* London: Thames and Hudson.

FLANNERY, KENT V., and JOYCE MARCUS 1983 *The Cloud People: Divergent Evolution of the Zapotec and Mixtec Civilizations.* New York: Academic Press.

FOWLER, WILLIAM R. JR. 1989 *The Cultural Evolution of Ancient Nahua Civilizations: The Pipil-Nicarao of Central America.* Norman: University of Oklahoma Press.

HODGE, MARY G., and MICHAEL E. SMITH (eds.) 1994 *Economies and Polities in the Aztec Realm.* Albany: Institute for Mesoamerican Studies.

NEWSON, LINDA. 1986 *The Cost of Conquest: Indian Decline in Honduras under Spanish Rule.* Boulder: Westview Press.

POLLARD, HELEN P. 1993 *Tariacuri's Legacy: The Prehispanic Tarascan State.* Norman: University of Oklahoma Press.

SCHOLES, FRANCE V., and RALPH L. ROYS 1968 *The Maya Chontal Indians of Acalan-Tixchel: A Contribution to the History and Ethnography of the Yucatan Peninsula.* Norman: University of Oklahoma Press.

SMITH, MICHAEL E., and BERDAN, FRANCES F. (eds.) 2003 *The Postclassic Mesoamerican World.* Salt Lake City: University of Utah Press.

TOWNSEND, RICHARD F. 1993 *The Aztecs.* London: Thames and Hudson.

VOORHIES, BARBARA (ed.) 1989 *Ancient Trade and Tribute: Economies of the Soconusco Region of Mesoamerica.* Salt Lake City: University of Utah Press.

Chapter 4
Mesoamerica and Spain:
The Conquest

For three centuries, the Mesoamericans were part of a vast colonial empire ruled by Spain. Spanish domination profoundly altered the culture and history of Mesoamerica's indigenous peoples. Old World infectious diseases, combined with violence and exploitation, killed millions of people; new technologies and new plants and animals had a deep impact on local economic and ecological adaptations; and new social and religious customs were imposed. Spanish rule also introduced new categories of people into the social scene: Spaniards and other Europeans; the Africans they brought as slaves; and people whose heritage mixed Indian, European, and African ancestry in every possible combination. The native people who survived these upheavals found themselves at the bottom end of a new social hierarchy, with power concentrated in the hands of the foreigners and their descendants.

In this chapter we present a historical overview of the Spanish invasion, in order to explain how this small European nation came to rule over the densely populated, socially complex, and highly militarized Mesoamerican world described in the preceding chapters (Figure 4.1). Particular attention is given to the beliefs and motivations of the actors on both sides of the conflict. We begin by examining events in Spain's history that led up to the country's colonial enterprise and affected its course in many ways.

THE ORIGINS OF SPANISH IMPERIALISM

Spanish imperialism grew out of the Christian "reconquest," or *reconquista,* of Spain from the Moors. The Moors were Muslims of North African descent, whose Arab and Berber ancestors had conquered most of the Iberian Peninsula between A.D. 711 and 718. The Moorish rulers in Spain presided over a cosmopolitan, multiethnic society in which Jews and Christians were tolerated and permitted to practice their religions. Many Spanish Christians, however, found rule by these foreign "infidels" unacceptable,

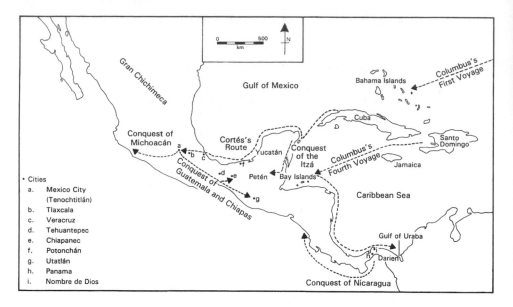

Figure 4.1   Map showing the main routes by which the Spaniards conquered the Mesoamerican world.

and bands of independent Christians challenged Moorish rule from their bases in mountainous northern Spain.

During the ninth century, the originally united Muslim state fractured into many small and competing kingdoms. Thereafter, Christian armies from the north were able to confront their Muslim enemy one faction at a time. Between A.D. 850 and 1250 the balance of power gradually shifted until the only remaining Moorish kingdom was Granada, a wealthy mountain stronghold in the south of Spain. The rest of the peninsula was dominated by the Christian kingdoms of Portugal in the west, Castile in the north and center, and Aragon in the northeast.

For the Christians, the conflict with the Moors was a holy war: The Islamic religion was seen as evil and the Muslim way of life as sinful. Spanish soldiers believed that Saint James, the patron saint of Spain, not only sanctioned their quest but also often appeared before them on a white horse, leading them into battle. Religious faith and military zeal went hand in hand; these in turn were barely distinguishable from political and economic ambitions. That Christ's soldiers should enjoy the material spoils of victory, appropriating the wealth and property of vanquished Moors, was seen as no more than their due reward.

Over the centuries of the *reconquista,* Spanish Christian society came to glorify military achievement. Lacking ancestral ties to particular pieces of territory, the aristocracy was highly mobile, counting its wealth in herds of domestic animals rather than in agricultural land. The knights who conquered a territory would move in as its new over-lords, being rewarded for their military service with rights to tribute and labor from the subject population. Soldiers recruited from the peasant class would be given parcels of land in the new territory, which they owned outright (in contrast to the serfdom pre-vailing elsewhere in Europe). The Christian kings found their power always circum-scribed by the need to placate the nobles, on whose military prowess they depended for the conquest of additional lands; as a result, there was constant tension between the central authority of the monarch and the local concerns of the feudal lords.

After a long hiatus marked by the Black Death and by factional disputes within the Christian kingdoms, the reconquest resumed in 1455 under King Henry VI of Castile. In 1469, Henry's eighteen-year-old half-sister and heir, Isabella, married seventeen-year-old Ferdinand, heir to the throne of the much weaker kingdom of Aragon. After much political intrigue, including a civil war in Castile, the couple emerged as the powerful rulers of a united Spain. They succeeded in limiting the in-fluence of both their own nobles and the pope. Themselves very pious, they used re-ligion as an effective means of promoting national unity. They established the Spanish Inquisition as a tool for enforcing religious conformity among Spanish Christians, in-cluding increasing numbers of *conversos,* or converts from Judaism, and *moriscos,* or Christianized Moors, thousands of whom would be executed as heretics. The couple's close ally Francisco Jiménez de Cisneros, a Franciscan priest and Isabella's confessor, raised the standards of orthodoxy and austerity among the religious orders, espe-cially the Franciscans, and sought to revitalize the religious faith of the entire pop-ulace. Appointed Archbishop of Toledo in 1495 and Inquisitor General in 1507, Cisneros was the most powerful individual in Spain apart from the king and queen themselves. He twice served briefly as regent of Castile, following Isabella's death in 1504 and Ferdinand's in 1516.

Isabella and Ferdinand sponsored scholarship in the humanities, earning an in-ternational reputation as patrons of learning. Among their circle of learned associ-ates was Antonio de Nebrija, a *converso* scholar who in 1492 published the first grammar of a modern, spoken language, as opposed to Latin and Greek. Nebrija's *Grammar of the Castilian Language* elevated Castile's dialect of Spanish to a privileged position previously restricted to those ancient languages. It thus helped to legitimize Castile's supremacy over the rest of Spain, and beyond: When first presented with the book, Isabella reportedly asked its purpose; the Bishop of Ávila, speaking on Ne-brija's behalf, explained, "language is the perfect instrument of empire."

His words were apt, for the year 1492 launched Spain on its way toward becom-ing the world's most powerful state. Early that year, Isabella and Ferdinand had seen the *reconquista* come to an end: The forces of Christian Spain marched victorious into Granada on January 2. With the Moorish frontier closed at last, Spain's heavily militaristic and aristocratic society might have settled down to focus on internal eco-nomic development. The towns were already dominated by a middle class of trades-people and entrepreneurs; production of certain goods, especially wool and leather, was in the process of industrialization. However, other events of 1492 steered the na-tion onto a different track.

On March 30, 1492, Isabella and Ferdinand signed a decree demanding that all Jews be expelled from Spain within four months. A campaign to force Muslims to convert began in 1499, with an edict of expulsion following in 1502. Prior to the fall of Granada, Jews actually had fared better in Spain than elsewhere in Europe. Spanish Christians knew that any Jews or Muslims expelled from Christian-held territory would have been welcomed in Moorish lands, where their skills and assets would only strengthen the power of the Moorish rulers. But after the conquest of Granada, there was no longer any such refuge, and in the climate of religious fervor that accompanied the culmination of the *reconquista,* Spain's rulers opted to impose their faith on all their subjects.

Between 120,000 and 150,000 Spanish Jews left the country; today's Sephardic Jews are descended from these exiles. Thousands more, like the majority of the Moors, chose to convert to Christianity, at least in name, rather than leave their homes and property. As *conversos,* the descendants of Jewish families often continued to practice at least some Jewish customs in secret, and they were always at risk of being tried by the Inquisition for real or alleged Judaic practices. Some were attracted to Christian religious orders, such as that of the Franciscans, that were somewhat compatible with their own traditions of scholarship, prophecy, and mysticism. Scholars from *converso* families contributed significantly to the sixteenth-century flowering of Spain's universities.

The departure of the majority of Spain's Jews took a tremendous toll on Spain's economy. Jewish merchants and financiers had dominated the middle class; without their skills and trading networks, Spain's commerce was devastated. Jewish traders were replaced not by upwardly mobile Spanish Christians but by foreigners who took their profits out of the country. What had been a thriving and industrializing commercial system sank into centuries-long stagnation.

On August 3, 1492, a Genoese mariner named Christopher Columbus set sail from Spain on a voyage sponsored by Isabella and Ferdinand. The goal of the enterprise was to discover a westward route to Asia and to claim Spanish sovereignty over any previously unknown lands found along the way. For the Spanish rulers, such a route—and their control over it—would facilitate trade for such items as silk and spices as well as giving them access to whatever riches might lie in undiscovered lands.

Their interests were more than economic, however, for Columbus and his Spanish patrons envisioned a worldwide religious crusade. They hoped that with a Spanish-controlled route to Asia, the struggle against Islam could be continued beyond Spain's borders. The abandoned medieval crusade to establish Christian control over the Holy Lands, which were then part of the Ottoman Empire of the Turks, could be restarted under Spanish leadership, financed by new wealth from the western trade. In effect, a westward passage would allow Christian armies to sneak up on the Turks (and other Islamic peoples) from behind, rather than having to battle their way eastward through the Turks' formidable defenses. Furthermore, the non-Islamic peoples of Asia might be converted to Christianity. Not only would such conversions be pleasing to God, but also the new converts, potentially numbering in the millions, would swell the ranks of the Christian armies as they passed westward toward what might be the ultimate battle between the followers of Christ and the followers of Mohammed.

But on October 12, Columbus and his men stumbled upon an island in the Caribbean. That island proved to be one of many lying adjacent to two large continents. Instead of establishing new links to Asia, Isabella and Ferdinand found themselves presiding over a massive project of exploration, invasion, and conquest, as the lands Columbus mistook for the "Indies" were forcibly transformed into colonies of Spain.

SPAIN'S COLONIAL ENTERPRISE BEGINS

The leaders of Spain believed that they had a God-given right to dominate non-Christian peoples and to bring to them the word of Christ; the fact that the "new" lands were revealed to Columbus while he sailed under the Spanish flag was proof enough of divine intent. Spanish claims were further legitimized by Pope Alexander VI, himself a Spaniard, who issued a papal bull in 1493 giving Spain the right to explore westward and southward and to claim any territory not already under Christian rulership.

This act ran afoul of Portugal, which was engaged in expeditions in the eastern Atlantic and along the coasts of Africa. In 1493, Spain and Portugal agreed to divide between themselves the right to explore and conquer unknown parts of the world. This Treaty of Tordesillas declared a line of demarcation, which passed through the Atlantic Ocean 370 leagues west of the Cape Verde Islands (which Portugal already claimed). Spain had rights to everything to the west of this line and Portugal had rights over all lands to the east. Spain, though intending to claim all of America, had inadvertently yielded to Portugal the eastward-projecting mass of Brazil.

Once Spain's rights to American territory had thus been formally recognized, the process of invading and conquering these lands could be treated juridically as a process of pacification. Native peoples who declined to recognize Spanish dominion were by definition rebelling against their lawful rulers and thus inviting violent retaliation and suppression. Native groups that submitted peacefully to Spanish rule were merely performing their duty as Spanish subjects. This "myth of pacification" served to justify the Spanish invasion and mask its accompanying brutality behind a façade of legitimate statecraft.

The *reconquista* had won back previously Christian territories from the descendants of Muslim invaders. The conquest of America was an aggressive campaign against peoples who had never heard of, let alone threatened, Spain. However, for many Spaniards the invasion of America was a logical continuation of their struggle against the Moors, led, like that campaign, by their warrior patron Saint James. The new frontier provided new employment for soldiers and new opportunities for sons of the aristocracy to rule over territory and subjects that they had helped to conquer. Spain had been purged of Jews and Muslims, and the new lands also would be uniformly Christian. Indeed, the prospect of converting the native peoples of America was compatible with the plan to convert Asia: The Church would be that much more fortified against the Muslim threat.

Also, the economic decline of Spain could be temporarily stalled by an influx of wealth from America. Although the cities of gold that filled Spanish dreams never materialized, Spanish colonists extracted enough silver, gold, and other precious substances to enrich their homeland. However, the result of flooding Europe's markets with American silver was similar to what would happen if a modern nation sought to offset economic problems by printing additional currency: It set off a cycle of inflation that only furthered Spain's long-term decline.

Even though millions of pounds of silver poured into Spain, its New World colonies were never profitable. Under the Habsburgs, Spain concentrated its energies and wealth on expensive military campaigns throughout Europe instead of developing successful commercial and industrial enterprises as the northern European powers were doing. The Dutch, British, and French, unhappy with the Pope's having essentially given the New World to Spain and Portugal, sought to gain America's wealth through control of commerce and banking, as well as through outright piracy. In the end, Spain's royal coffers were nothing more than a funnel through which New World silver flowed on its way to the pockets of northern European merchants and bankers.

Spanish attention, following the example of Columbus's voyages, focused at first on the Caribbean islands, especially the island of Hispaniola—today shared by the nations of Haiti and the Dominican Republic—where the settlement of Santo Domingo was established in 1496. The native inhabitants of the islands, divided among many small polities with no standing armies or other organized defensive forces, were ill-prepared to ward off the Spanish invasion.

Spain's rulers rewarded successful conquerors with rights to tribute in goods and labor from the native people. This reward system, which had precedents in the reconquista, was called encomienda; an individual who held an encomienda grant was an encomendero. Encomenderos comprised a colonial aristocracy that from the beginning found its interests often in conflict with those of both the Spanish Crown and the Church. Encomenderos were officially charged with seeing to the religious instruction of the native peoples entrusted to them; the *encomenderos'* frequent indifference to this demand was one source of friction between them and their rulers.

The consuming purpose of the early colonists was the search for gold, which overrode any concern for the long-term integrity of a colonial society. The islands contained some placer deposits of gold, and the native people were compelled to work the gold fields for the enrichment of their new overlords. Already facing massive population loss owing to disease, these people saw their survival further threatened by this forced labor and other abuses: beatings, rapes, and murders. They also suffered from a nutritional crisis resulting from the disruption of their agriculture, hunting, and fishing.

Such problems only made the people more susceptible to the Old World infectious diseases that European invaders and their African slaves inadvertently introduced to the Americas. Never having been exposed to these bacterial and viral agents, the native peoples had no natural immunity to the diseases they caused. Mortality rates when a new disease first struck were as high as one-third of the population, with the sickness affecting healthy adults as severely as children and the elderly. Owing to a combination of brutality, exploitation, and disease, within three decades of Columbus's first landfall very few native people of the islands were left alive. (See Box 4.1 for a more extensive account of the demographic consequences for the Mesoamericans of the European contact.)

Box 4.1   The Demographic Consequences of European Contact

A precontact indigenous population that some estimate as high as 27.1 million in Mexico alone was reduced to around 1.2 million in the first century of Spanish rule, after which it began a gradual rebound (see the Introduction for estimated figures). During the conquest years, warfare was directly responsible for the deaths of many Indians, and in the years immediately after the conquest, slavery and the harsh treatment of Indians in the mines and in other Spanish enterprises accounted for many more deaths. Random acts of torture and murder, whether for the purpose of "sport" or to maintain a state of terror, were responsible for additional deaths. In terms of sheer numbers, however, most of the deaths were the result of infectious diseases previously unknown in the Americas. The biggest killers were smallpox, measles, typhus, bubonic plague, yellow fever, and malaria. In many areas, native populations were already weakened by early epidemics before they had to fight the Spanish invaders.

The process of *mestizaje* also affected native demographics. Mestizos were neither Spanish nor Indian: They were the children of unions between Spaniards and Indians (usually a Spanish father and an Indian mother). Indians and Africans also formed unions, giving birth to children who were classified as mixed-race rather than natives. Thus, Indian populations declined in areas where *mestizaje* was high, even if Indian mortality rates were relatively low.

Within colonial Mesoamerica there was significant variability in demographic patterns in different regions. Generally, populations in the lowland regions suffered greater declines than did the highland populations, although the causes for this difference are still not well understood. Throughout much of colonial Mesoamerica this pattern has had a long-term impact, and today Indian populations are typically much greater in highland areas than in the lowlands. Thus, in the highlands of Oaxaca, Chiapas, and Guatemala, Indians still constitute the majority of the population.

The impact of high mortality rates in the years just preceding and following the Spanish conquest was profound. In many areas as much as 90 to 95 percent of the native population died within the first fifty to seventy-five years following contact, such that all aspects of native life were disrupted. Communities were left with no legitimate leaders, children were without parents or even close relatives to care for them, and entire families died out.

Spaniards often explained the epidemics as punishment wrought by God. Native practices before the conquest—the worship of false gods, human sacrifice, polygyny, and so forth—were now being avenged. Certain sympathetic priests, however, asserted that it was the Spaniards who were being punished for their ill treatment of the native people. The Indians, now baptized as Christians, would go to heaven, but the rapacious colonists would be deprived of a native population to labor for them.

It is difficult to determine how the Mesoamericans themselves explained these diseases. At least some insight is provided by the answers to a questionnaire that Spain's King Philip II sent to all the communities in the colony in the late 1570s, just after a particularly severe epidemic. Asked about the health of their people, elders in a number of Indian towns blamed the high mortality rate on the changes in lifestyle that had followed the Spanish conquest. People no longer followed the strict behavioral regimen of their ancestors. They ate too much meat, dressed

(continued)

(continued)

too warmly, married too young. Behaviors such as these caused people to become weak and easily susceptible to illness. Indirectly, these elders were blaming the Spaniards, who had introduced domestic animals like sheep and pigs, wool (for warmer clothing and blankets), and previously unknown garments such as shirts and coats. Similarly, Catholic priests, trying to prevent premarital sex, encouraged the Mesoamericans to marry in their midteens. The ancestors' way of life had been more rigorous and virtuous. In contrast to the Spanish idea that the Indians were being punished for the "sins of the ancestors," these Indians blamed their decline on the adoption of Spanish ways.

Some native documents provide particularly vivid descriptions of epidemics and their effects on the population. The Mayan *Book of Chilam Balam of Chumayel,* from the Yucatán Peninsula, speaks as follows:

> There was no sickness then;
> They had no aching bones then;
> They had no high fever then;
> They had no pustule fever [smallpox] then;
> They had no burning chests then;
> They had no abdominal pains then;
> They had no consumption then;
> They had no headaches then;
> The course of humanity was orderly then;
> The foreigners made it otherwise
> When they arrived here.
> They brought shameful things
> When they came. (Roys 1933:22)

In the *Annals of the Cakchiquels* an epidemic that struck in 1519 is described in equally vivid terms:

> It happened that during the twenty-fifth year [1519] the plague began, oh, my sons! First they became ill of a cough, they suffered from nosebleeds and illness of the bladder. It was truly terrible, the number of dead there were in that period. . . . Little by little heavy shadows and black night enveloped our fathers and grandfathers and us also, oh, my sons! when the plague raged. . . . Great was the stench of the dead. After our fathers and grandfathers succumbed, half of the people fled to the fields. The dogs and the vultures devoured the bodies. The mortality was terrible. Your grandfathers died, and with them died the son of the king and his brothers and kinsmen. So it was that we became orphans, oh, my sons! So we became when we were young. All of us were thus. We were born to die! (Recinos 1980:119–120).

The status of native people under Spanish colonial rule was inherently problematic. At first treated unambiguously as potential slaves—Columbus being the first to enslave Indians—under Isabella's orders they were soon declared citizens of the Spanish Crown with corresponding legal rights. However, since the Crown had the right to tax its subjects and also had somehow to reward conquerors for their service, it was considered acceptable to require tribute from these new subjects. But heavy tribute requirements could amount to virtual slavery. Furthermore, an illegal slave trade flourished, and slavery long remained a legal option when dealing with peoples who resisted Spanish domination or who were believed to practice cannibalism. False accusations of cannibalism were used to justify slave-raiding campaigns. The nature and extent of service that Spaniards could legitimately extract from Indians remained a major issue of contention.

Christian evangelization was a second major issue. Religious fervor played such a key role in promoting Spanish unity and legitimizing Spanish imperialism that the conversion of the Indians was a top priority for the Crown, especially for pious Isabella. How could the Indians be brought to the faith? Were they capable of becoming fully Christian? How could the material needs and desires of Crown and colonists be reconciled with the spiritual needs of the native people? So rapidly were the island natives decimated that these questions were barely considered before it was too late.

In Spain, Isabella's death in 1504 ushered in another era of factionalism and instability. After a series of deaths in the royal lineage, Isabella and Ferdinand's daughter, Juana, inherited the throne of Castile. Juana was married to Archduke Philip of Burgundy, a member of Europe's powerful Habsburg dynasty. Philip's father, Maximilian, was ruler of the Holy Roman Empire, a confederation of feudal states in Central Europe whose princes traditionally elected their so-called "emperor."

Many Spanish nobles allied themselves with Philip in order to curtail Ferdinand's claims to his dead wife's dominions and to boost trading links with Habsburg possessions in the Netherlands. The ensuing disputes are too complex to be treated in detail here, but the upshot was that, with Philip's death in 1506 and Juana's alleged insanity, after Ferdinand died in 1516, the Spanish crown passed to the eldest son of Philip and Juana, young Charles of Ghent.

Charles, born in 1500, had grown up in the Netherlands. He did not speak Spanish and had never set foot in his mother's homeland until he arrived as king in 1517, bringing with him a bevy of Flemish advisers. Two years later, Charles's grandfather Maximilian died, and Charles was elected to succeed him as Holy Roman Emperor. This event further linked Spain to the fortunes of other European lands, lands that would soon be torn apart by the religious wars of the Protestant Reformation. A man of the Renaissance, Charles opened Spain's closed and conservative society to humanistic influences from elsewhere in Europe. Not all Spaniards wished to see this virtual foreigner upon their throne, however, and he did not secure his control over the Crown until 1522.

By 1520, the limited quantities of gold that the Caribbean islands had held were nearly gone. Lacking both gold and the native laborers to extract it, the Spanish colonists had to turn to new enterprises. As the native population dwindled, trade in African slaves had become widespread. With Africa as the new source of forced labor, an economy based on livestock ranching and agriculture began to develop. The Spanish settlers, descendants of the original *encomenderos,* came to constitute a landed gentry, a small, elite group living off of the work of a large subject population of African slaves and free African and mulatto wage laborers.

Some Spaniards, however, unwilling to settle for the increasingly limited options offered by the island colonies, looked toward the vast, unconquered mainland as a potential source of new opportunities. On his fourth voyage in 1502, Columbus had encountered an elite Mayan merchant and his entourage sailing near the coast of Honduras, their large ocean-going canoe laden with rich goods (see the Introduction for an account of this historical event). Since then, Spaniards had known that the mainland was home to peoples whose societies were more complex and whose material goods more sophisticated than those of the island natives.

The Spanish conquest and occupation of the mainland was staged from strongholds in Central Mexico and Panama. Most of Mesoamerica was brought under Spanish control by Spanish forces radiating out from Central Mexico. But even before their struggle with the Aztecs in Central Mexico had begun, the Spaniards already had established towns in Darién and the Panamanian Isthmus.

The Spanish occupation of the mainland began in 1510 with the foundation of Santa María de Antigua del Darién (in modern Colombia). In 1519, six years after Santa María's founder, Vasco Núñez de Balboa, first saw the Pacific Ocean, the new settlement of Panama was established on the Pacific side of the isthmus, a short distance from the Caribbean port of Nombre de Dios. Spanish treatment of the native population was harsh. Under the brutal leadership of governor Pedro Arias de Ávila (Pedrarias), Spaniards raided native settlements for gold and slaves, and soon the indigenous population had virtually disappeared.

Spanish expansion into Nicaragua, Costa Rica, and Honduras was carried out primarily by forces based in Panama. The native peoples of these regions also suffered from heavy-handed treatment by their conquerors. Indians throughout lower Central America were captured and sold as slaves during the first decades of colonial rule, but nowhere was the slave trade as lucrative as in Nicaragua. Tens of thousands of Nicaraguan Indians were taken as slaves; most were transported to Peru, but large numbers died en route. In 1542, Indian slavery was officially outlawed, although Indians continued to be enslaved in subsequent years. When the Indian slave trade died out around 1550, its cessation was not because the Spaniards were concerned about the legal ramifications of their actions but because there were so few Indians left.

Once the slave trade had died out and the Isthmus and the rest of lower Central America were firmly under Spanish control, the Caribbean and Pacific port cities in Panama served primarily as a locus of movement of people and goods from Spain, New Spain, and the Caribbean to Peru and the rest of Pacific South America.

THE DEBATE OVER INDIAN RIGHTS

The disastrous effects of Spanish rule in the Caribbean caused a small number of contemporary observers to question Spain's right to govern these lands. How could Christians, charged with bringing the Word of God to these fellow humans, justify their presence in the face of such widespread suffering and abuse? In 1511, a Dominican priest named Antonio de Montesinos preached a famous sermon to the

Spanish colonists of Hispaniola. He asked them, "Are these Indians not humans? Do they not have rational souls? Are you not obliged to love them as you love yourselves?" The *encomenderos* were outraged that a priest would dare to criticize their behavior. And thus was born a campaign for the human rights of the Indians.

An alliance between priests and the powerless that foreshadowed the Liberation Theology movement of the late twentieth century, this campaign was phrased in terms of Christian religion and tended to take a paternalistic view of the Indians as helpless victims. Nevertheless, the arguments of Montesinos and his followers speak across the centuries to anyone concerned about human rights and the survival of indigenous peoples.

The most influential convert to Montesinos's views was the Spanish adventurer-turned-Dominican-priest Bartolomé de Las Casas. Las Casas would come to view the entire Spanish enterprise in America as unjust and illegal. Although he would also play an important role among the native people of Mesoamerica as a missionary and the first bishop of Chiapas (see Chapter 5), he is most famous for his activities in Spain, where he publicized the brutal effects of Spanish colonialism. In Spain he found an ally in Francisco de Vitoria, a Dominican priest who was one of the country's foremost theologians. Although Vitoria never visited America, he lent his immense knowledge of Classical philosophy and Medieval theology, plus his skill in logic and rhetoric, to the cause of Indian rights. He concluded that the Indians were civilized people with full rights to their own territories. They were not irrational or otherwise mentally deficient. Customs that offended Spanish sensibilities were not unknown among Old World civilizations and, however shocking, did not provide grounds for invasion and conquest.

Las Casas's own writings went beyond Vitoria's careful reasonings and into polemical, sensationalized accounts of Spanish brutality. His treatise entitled "A Brief Relation of the Destruction of the Indies" was printed in several European languages and helped give rise to the so-called "black legend" regarding the injustices associated with Spanish domination (Figure 4.2). To these European readers, the tract was less relevant as a description of the distant colonies than as a warning about their own possible fate, given Charles V's control over Habsburg and Holy Roman Empire lands outside Spain and his intentions to enlarge these holdings. Las Casas's work thus helped to stir up anti-Spanish (and in Protestant territories, anti-Catholic) sentiment throughout Europe.

Las Casas never went so far as to doubt that the Indians would benefit from the Christian religion. He argued, however, that the only proper way to introduce them to that faith was through peaceful contact and that there was no justification for violent conquest. In his book entitled "Of the Only Way to Attract All Peoples to the True Religion," he proposed that missionaries should enter Indian territory unarmed and unaccompanied by soldiers. If they were welcomed and permitted to preach, the Indians—being as intelligent and rational as any other people—would soon be persuaded that Christianity was indeed superior to their own forms of worship. And if not, then so be it; the priests should depart in peace and hope that future ventures might prove more successful.

Figure 4.2   Illustration from Las Casas's "Brief Relation on the Destruction of the Indies," Spanish edition, Seville, 1552. *Source:* Courtesy of the John Carter Brown Library at Brown University.

Charles V, troubled by the assertions of Las Casas and Vitoria, summoned a group of theologians to present arguments on both sides of these issues. This famous debate occurred at Valladolid, Spain, in 1550 and 1551. Las Casas was the spokesman for the anticolonial side. His opponent was Juan Ginés de Sepúlveda, a distinguished theologian and historian. Sepúlveda based his arguments on the ancient Greek philosopher Aristotle's theory of natural slavery. He claimed that the Indians were by nature brutish and irrational and therefore inferior to Europeans. Not only did Europeans have the right to conquer and enslave them, but also the Indians would actually benefit from their own subjection by being provided with superior behavioral models. Las Casas countered that the Indians were fully rational, of equal or superior capacity to all other peoples. Since the judges of the debate did not leave a record of their decision, we do not know who was considered the winner.

The pro-Indian movement, despite the stir it caused in Europe, did little to improve the lot of native people in the colonies. Las Casas and his allies had some impact on official Spanish policies, but these efforts to mollify the damage wrought by colonial rule were often ignored by the colonists who were supposed to enforce them. The whole controversy over whether the conquest was justified was little more than a game of words, since almost all of Mesoamerica was already under Spanish control by the time of the Valladolid debates, and there was no way that the conquerers were going to pack their bags and return home. Franciscan priests criticized Las Casas for focusing on these philosophical debates instead of living among the native peoples and helping to defend them against their more immediate Spanish neighbors.

Some scholars have claimed that the pro-Indian movement of Las Casas and his allies indirectly promoted African slavery. Since their efforts contributed to the outlawing of Indian slavery (in law if not always in practice), Spanish colonists who wanted to own slaves had to look elsewhere. The African people sold as slaves by Portuguese traders were, for these colonists, a convenient source of forced labor.

It is true that Las Casas and Vitoria saw nothing inherently wrong with the enslavement of Africans; Vitoria even admitted that he would be willing to own such a slave. The pro-Indian movement's most effective argument against Indian slavery was not based on a belief in human equality. Rather, it was based on legalistic principles. Spain could not claim jurisdiction over the Indies and simultaneously enslave their inhabitants, any more than the Spanish king could arbitrarily enslave citizens of his own nation. In Africa, however, where Spain had no territories and claimed no jurisdiction, Portuguese treatment of the native people, whether benign or brutal, was of no concern to Spain. African peoples had no legal rights that were recognized by Spain. Thus, if an African person had the misfortune to end up transported to the Indies, she or he had no legal grounds on which to claim mistreatment.

Although the movement for Indian rights was of limited benefit for the natives of the Spanish colonies—and did nothing to promote fair treatment of Africans—it did have a long-range impact on European intellectual currents. The efforts by Las Casas and his allies to describe and analyze native cultural patterns, in order more effectively to defend them, were among the first attempts to create systematic accounts of other cultures. Their insistence that these cultural patterns were valid in respect to the societies that practiced them was an early expression of cultural relativism, the idea that any particular cultural trait must be understood in relation to the rest of the culture within which it makes sense.

In a broad sense, as Europeans learned about the Americas, the Europeans were led to question many of their traditional assumptions about human nature. The very existence of a "New World" forced radical adjustments to a mindset that had always assumed that the world was composed of a trinity of continents: Europe, Africa, and Asia. A theology that explained everything in terms of the Bible and the accrued contemplations of medieval scholars was hard pressed to reduce all of the new knowledge to its traditional categories of thought.

Accounts of the native cultures were often highly distorted, alternately exalting and vilifying indigenous customs; nevertheless, they challenged Europeans to think in new ways about their own cultures and their own social structures. It became possible to imagine that one's own cultural patterns were arbitrary and might be changed. The accomplishments of native American civilizations were admired; at the same time, the native peoples were envied for their (presumed) freedom from some of the restrictions that circumscribed life in Europe. Critiques of European customs were phrased in terms of comparisons with native America. For example, Michel de Montaigne's essay "On Cannibalism," though based on an inaccurate conception of native Brazilian peoples, nevertheless constituted a brilliant satire of the author's sixteenth-century French society. As much as any other factor, the existence of America and its peoples helped drive European thought out of the Middle Ages and into the modern age.

It was the Aztec civilization, with its sophisticated art and oratory, its centralized state and extravagant court life, and its bloody rituals of human sacrifice and cannibalism, that provided European commentators with their most frequently cited examples of both American accomplishments and American depravity. Both Las Casas and Sepúlveda drew principally on Aztec ethnographic data in constructing their arguments for and against the legitimacy of native cultures. The need to justify the Aztec practices of human sacrifice and cannibalism was perhaps the greatest challenge that Las Casas faced in the debate. He insisted that the number of victims (Sepúlveda claimed 20,000 a year) had been grossly exaggerated, otherwise the land could not have been so populous as it was when the Spanish first arrived. Las Casas asserted that the number must have been less than 100 or even less than fifty. And even a century's total of victims amounted to fewer native lives than the Spaniards had sacrificed to their precious "goddess of greed" every year since their conquests began.

THE CAMPAIGN AGAINST THE AZTECS

We now turn to the Spanish campaign against the Aztecs. Hernán Cortés's victory over the Mexica capital of Tenochtitlan brought with it military control over a massive part of Mesoamerica, already organized into a tribute-producing empire. The story of this campaign is one of the great dramatic narratives of European colonial expansion; as such, it quickly accumulated elements of legend, with Cortés potrayed as a military hero and the native peoples depicted as too paralyzed by their fatalistic religious beliefs to mount an effective resistance. Some native accounts blamed the emperor Motecuhzoma for the defeat and also claimed that various supernatural omens preceded the Spaniards' arrival.

A common misconception is that the Aztecs failed to resist because they believed Cortés was the god Quetzalcoatl returning at a prophesied time, but this is a legend that developed after the Conquest. This legend assumes that the Spaniards were smarter and more rational than the Mesoamericans, who were too blinded by their religious beliefs to realize what was going on and to respond appropriately. The Aztecs did resist, and they and their fellow Mesoamericans did not really view Cortés or other Spaniards as gods. For Spaniards, denying Indian resistance made it easier to pretend that a small group of clever white men was responsible for the fall of the great Aztec Empire, when in fact the Aztecs were militarily overwhelmed by fellow Mesoamericans whose uprising against them was led and organized by the Spaniards. For native people, interpretations of the Conquest as having been preordained by omens and prophecies helped them, after the fact, to justify their own defeat. Because of the many contradictions among the various versions of this story, both Spanish and native, it is not possible to construct one single "true" account of what really happened. The following synopsis is based on a critical examination of native and Spanish sources.

In February 1519, Hernán Cortés left the colony of Cuba on an expedition to explore the nearby mainland. Cortés had come to the Caribbean in 1504 from Extremadura in western Spain. He had participated in the campaign to take control of Cuba and had served as secretary to Diego Velásquez, Cuba's first colonial governor. The 1519 expedition, funded largely with Cortés's own money, consisted of eleven ships and over 500 men, sixteen horses, and a few cannon. The first landfall was the island of Cozumel off the east coast of the Yucatán Peninsula. Here Cortés discovered Gerónimo de Aguilar, a Spaniard who had survived a shipwreck eight years earlier. Held captive by the local Mayas on the mainland in the intervening years, Aguilar had learned to speak the Yucatec Mayan language. After he joined Cortés, he became an interpreter for the expedition. Another Spaniard who had survived the shipwreck was Gonzalo de Guerrero. Guerrero, however, had married a Mayan woman and was living as a Maya. Unlike Aguilar, Guerrero had no interest in rejoining his compatriots; instead he chose to fight the Spanish invaders, and he reportedly died fighting on the Mayan side.

After sailing westward around the Yucatán Peninsula, Cortés's expedition stopped at Potonchan, near the mouth of the Grijalva River in what is today the Mexican state of Tabasco. After initial hostilities, the local leaders offered Cortés gifts, including several young women. One of these women was a native speaker of Nahuatl whose mother and stepfather had sold her into slavery among the Tabascan Indians, from whom she had learned the local Mayan tongue. She was given the Christian name Marina, or Malintzin in Nahuatl (she is often called Malinche or La Malinche). She and Aguilar were able to translate for Cortés's group from Maya to Nahuatl to Spanish (and vice versa). Marginalized by her own people, Malintzin threw her lot in with the Spaniards and proved an invaluable assistant to Cortés, especially as she quickly mastered Spanish (see Box 4.2).

On Good Friday, April 19, 1519, Cortés landed near what is today the city of Veracruz. Here he had his first encounter with representatives of Motecuhzoma, the Aztec ruler. According to a native account written down in the 1550s and already influenced by some of the developing legends, Motecuhzoma's emissaries brought gifts to Cortés, which included complete costumes of three of the Aztecs' most important deities: Quetzalcoatl, Tezcatlipoca, and Tlaloc (see the discussion of these deities in Chapter 3). These costumes were made up of headdresses of precious gold and feathers; masks of turquoise; and ornaments of jade, gold, and seashells (Figure 4.3). Motecuhzoma may have been seeking to establish a social relationship with the strangers through the exchange of gifts, while impressing them with his wealth. The Nahuatl account says that the messengers dressed up Cortés in the costume of Quetzalcoatl, but it is highly unlikely that the Spaniard actually permitted this. In any case, his subsequent behavior diverged sharply from the model of the wise and priestly

Box 4.2   La Malinche

La Malinche today is a figure of folklore. On the one hand, she is detested as a traitor of her people and as a whore for the Spanish invaders, a beautiful but evil woman who lusted after the white man Cortés's virility and power. On the other hand, she is glorified as Cortés's equal and the first mother of the mestizo Mexican nation. What do we know about the real woman behind these conflicting images?

She was a native speaker of Nahuatl living among the Chontal Mayas of coastal Tabasco, to whom her mother and stepfather had given or sold her (or she may have been stolen into slavery). Her original name was never recorded. She was one of the first Mesoamericans to be baptized a Christian, by Cortés's companion priest Bartolomé de Olmedo during the Spaniards' interactions with the Chontals in 1519. She was given the Spanish name Marina as her Christian, baptismal name. Nahuatl does not have the sound "r," and Nahuatl-speakers changed this sound to "l" when they pronounced Spanish words. The suffix "-tzin" shows respect or affection. Thus, Malintzin means "honored Marina" or "dear Marina." The name "Malinche" originates in a Spanish mispronunciation of this respectful name.

We do not know how old Malintzin was when the Chontal Mayas gave her to Cortés's party, but she was likely still a teenager. She was first given as a servant, and possibly as a forced mistress, to Alonso Hernández de Puertocarrero, one of the leaders of the expedition. But Cortés took her back a few weeks later, when he realized her usefulness as a Maya- and Nahuatl-speaking interpreter. She learned Spanish quickly and was indispensable to Cortés in his negotiations and communications with Nahuatl-speaking enemies and allies.

In serving Cortés, Malintzin was not betraying her "race" or her "people." As readers of this textbook by now realize, the native peoples of Mesoamerica belonged to many different ethnic and linguistic groups, with shifting patterns of alliance and warfare. Nahuatl-speaking peoples were divided into many groups, and some were bitter enemies of the Aztecs. Malintzin, though a native speaker of Nahuatl, was not an Aztec and had no reason to feel any loyalty to the Mexica state in Tenochtitlan. She was more likely to sympathize with the provincial peoples who paid tribute to the Aztecs and who sought, by allying with Cortés, to throw off that burden. Neither she nor the thousands of other native people who supported Cortés knew what Spanish colonial rule would be like. After being a slave, she might have felt empowered by her vital role among the Spaniards and their allies, but she was not seeking revenge.

Malintzin became Cortés's lover and bore him a son, Martín (named after Cortés's father), in 1522, ten months after the fall of Tenochtitlan (by which time he was certainly not the first mestizo baby!). The timing of Martín's birth suggests that the couple might have delayed having sexual relations until after that victory; pregnancy and new motherhood would have hampered Malintzin's ability to campaign with Cortés. Whether Cortés forced her into this relationship or she was willing, we cannot know, but it probably would have been difficult for her to refuse him.

Cortés had a wife in Cuba, who came to Mexico a few months after Martín's birth but who died within months of her arrival. He did not then marry Malintzin; as conqueror of Mexico, he likely envisioned a more elite second marriage. But Cortés did make her part of his household in Mexico City, and he brought her along, in her old job as interpreter, on his 1524 expedition to Honduras. Early in the expedition she married another Spaniard, Juan Jaramillo. When she returned from Honduras in 1526, she was pregnant with Jaramillo's child, a daughter who was baptized María. In 1527, Malintzin died; the cause of her death is not known.

When Martín was six he traveled to Spain with his father, who successfully petitioned the Pope to legitimize the mestizo boy (i.e., have him recognized as his father's legal son). When his father returned to Mexico with a new and high-born wife, Martín stayed behind. He became a knight in the Order of Saint James, married a Spanish noblewoman, and in middle age returned to Mexico, where he was implicated in a plot to oust the Spanish viceroy and put his half-brother, the son of Cortés and his second wife, in power. Martín was tortured and then, banished from Mexico, returned to his military career in Spain. María grew up with her father and his second, Spanish wife. When Jaramillo died and left that wife the *encomienda* (see Chapter 5) Cortés had granted to him and Malintzin upon their marriage, María, by then married to a Spaniard, spent years litigating to establish her claim to the property, eventually winning partial rights to it. She died in 1563. (The preceding account is based on Karttunen 1994; Restall 2003.)

Figure 4.3   Motecuhzoma's emissaries present gifts to Cortés. To Cortés's left stands his Nahua interpreter, Malintzin. *Florentine Codex,* Book 12, folio 8v. Reprinted with permission from Fray Bernardino de Sahagún, *Historia General de las cosas de Nueva España,* Códice florentino. Facsimile of the Codex Florentinus of the Biblioteca Medicea Laurenciana, supervised by the Archivo General de la Nación (AGN) de México, Florence, Italy, 1979.

Quetzalcoatl: Rather than reciprocating with rich gifts of his own, Cortés had the messengers shackled and then demonstrated the power of the Spanish guns.

When the emissaries returned to Motecuhzoma, they described the Spaniards' weapons, armor, horses, and personal appearance:

> . . . the guns went off at [the Spaniards'] command, sounding like thunder, causing people actually to swoon, blocking the ears. And when it went off, something like a ball came out from inside, and fire went showering and spitting out. And the smoke that came from it had a very foul stench, striking one in the face. And if they shot at a hill, it seemed to crumble and come apart. And it turned a tree to dust; it seemed to make it vanish, as though someone had conjured it away.
>
> Their war gear was all iron. They clothed their bodies in iron, they put iron on their heads, their swords were iron, their bows were iron, and their shields and lances were iron.
>
> And their deer that carried them were as tall as the roof. And they wrapped their bodies all over; only their faces could be seen, very white. Their faces were the color of limestone and their hair yellow-reddish, though some had black hair. They had long beards, also yellow-reddish (Lockhart 1993:80).

Motecuhzoma sent more emissaries, and wizards found that their magical spells had no effect upon the strangers.

While the native people wondered who the Spaniards were, the Spaniards themselves were beset with internal dissensions. Many in Cortés's party were eager to continue to the Aztec capital, but others were dissatisfied with Cortés, believing that he had exceeded his orders, and still others had fallen ill. Cortés managed to have himself declared leader of the newly founded Spanish town of La Villa Rica de la Vera Cruz ("the rich town of the true cross," today's Veracruz), and as such, he claimed that he was no longer subject to Cuba's governor, Velásquez, but instead responsible directly to the king of Spain. The newly established *cabildo* (town council) of Vera Cruz sent emissaries to Spain to lobby for Crown support for Cortés at the same time that Velásquez was asserting new powers for himself on the mainland and continuing his efforts to contain Cortés. With several of Cortés's men threatening to desert and return to Cuba, Cortés took bold steps: He had two of the men executed, and he sank his ships.

Before moving inland, Cortés made his first alliance with a native group, the Totonacs who lived in the town of Cempoala and who were weary of Aztec domination. In August 1519, the expedition began its journey toward Tenochtitlan, accompanied by a large party of Totonacs. Within two weeks Cortés's party was in Tlaxcala, a powerful independent state that had never fallen to the Aztecs (see the account of these events in the Introduction). The Tlaxcalans decided to ally themselves with Cortés, and they provided him with several thousand warriors (Figure 4.4). The party moved next into Cholula, where they were initially received favorably, but it soon became clear that the Cholulans were preparing an ambush. The Spaniards, however, captured Cholulan leaders and then reportedly massacred thousands of Cholula warriors. Subsequently the Cholulans declared their loyalty to the Spanish king.

Shared enmity toward the Aztecs was the most important reason why these and other indigenous polities allied themselves with Cortés. Having themselves been taken by surprise by Spanish weapons and Spanish tactics, they recognized that these could be a potent force against their own enemies. In allying himself with these groups, Cortés began the process that would lead to his ultimate victory. His small party of Spaniards had no hope of conquering Mexico. What he did was organize and oversee a joint uprising of the Aztecs' traditional enemies and subject states that were tired of paying tribute to Aztec overlords.

In early November 1519, Cortés' party, now made up of around 350 Spaniards and several thousand Tlaxcalan warriors, made the last leg of the journey to Tenochtitlan. As they approached the city, Motecuhzoma sent Cortés more rich gifts. But instead of feeling humiliated that they had nothing of like value with which to reciprocate, the Spaniards only longed for more. Their reaction to the golden treasures is described in a native account:

> They gave [the Spaniards] golden banners, banners of precious feathers, and golden necklaces.
> And when they had given the things to them, they seemed to smile, to rejoice and be very happy. Like monkeys they grabbed the gold. It was as though their hearts were put to rest, brightened, freshened. For gold was what they greatly thirsted for, they were gluttonous for it, starved for it, piggishly wanting it. They came lifting up the golden ban-

Figure 4.4   Two of Tlaxcala's four principal lords declare their alliance with Cortés. The scrolls in front of the faces represent speech. *Florentine Codex*, Book 12, folio 21v. Reprinted with permission from Fray Bernardino de Sahagún, *Historia General de las cosas de Nueva España*, Códice florentino. Facsimile of the Codex Florentinus of the Biblioteca Medicea Laurenciana, supervised by the Archivo General de la Nación (AGN) de México, Florence, Italy, 1979.

ners, waving them from side to side, showing them to each other. They seemed to babble; what they said to each other was in a babbling tongue. (Lockhart 1993:96, 98)

Bernal Díaz del Castillo, one of Cortés' companions, later penned a lengthy account of his experiences. When he and his fellows caught their first glimpse of the Basin of Mexico, they thought it looked like something out of Spain's popular romances of chivalry:

. . . when we saw so many cities and villages built in the water and other great towns on dry land, and that straight and level Causeway going towards Mexico, we were amazed and said that it was like the enchantments they tell of in the legend of Amadis, on account of the great towers and cues [temples] and buildings rising from the water, and all built of masonry. And some of our soldiers even asked whether the things that we saw were not a dream. (Díaz del Castillo 1956:190–191)

On November 8, 1519, Cortés and his party entered the great city of Tenochtitlan, and Cortés and Motecuhzoma met face-to-face (Figure 4.5). Motecuhzoma welcomed the Spaniards, treating them as honored guests and allowing them to reside in the imperial palace of his father, Axayacatl. Despite the later accounts that depict him as extremely fearful, it is unlikely that at this point he felt insecure: At a word from him, his armies could have conquered the Spaniards and Tlaxcalans or driven them out of the city.

Figure 4.5   The first meeting between Motecuhzoma and Cortés. The native artist highlights the crucial role of Malintzin, Cortés's Nahua interpreter. *Florentine Codex,* Book 12, 26r. Reprinted with permission from Fray Bernardino de Sahagún, *Historia General de las cosas de Nueva España,* Códice florentino. Facsimile of the Codex Florentinus of the Biblioteca Medicea Laurenciana, supervised by the Archivo General de la Nación (AGN) de México, Florence, Italy, 1979.

Some accounts say that Cortés soon took Motecuhzoma prisoner and held him in the Spaniards' quarters, while he pretended to reside there willingly. This treatment may be untrue, but somehow the presence of the Spaniards and their allies, something between invaders and guests, was tolerated for several months. In April 1520, the situation changed when it was learned that a fleet of eighteen ships sent by Governor Velásquez had landed on the Gulf Coast. The leader, Pánfilo de Narváez, had orders to arrest Cortés and bring him to Cuba to stand trial. Cortés's response was to try to win over Narváez and his men to his side through a combination of bribery and armed attack. The latter was accomplished when a force, led by Cortés, attacked Narváez's men as they slept. Narváez was captured, and his men surrendered to Cortés, thus increasing the size of Cortés's force.

Meanwhile, in Tenochtitlan, Pedro de Alvarado, whom Cortés had left in charge, was losing control of the situation. Alvarado flew into a rage upon hearing of the celebration of a traditional Aztec festival in honor of Huitzilopochtli that was to include human sacrifice, even though he had initially given permission for the ceremony to take place. Alvarado ordered his men to attack the defenseless participants, and hundreds of Mexica were massacred. This act prompted retaliation against the Spaniards: There were attempts to burn the palace where they were housed, and several Spaniards were killed. At this moment, Cortés and his entourage, which included several thousand Tlaxcalan warriors, returned to Tenochtitlan. The Mexica allowed them to join Alvarado, but attacks on the Spanish compound continued.

In the midst of growing tension, members of the Mexica ruling elite, who had long opposed Motecuhzoma's cooperation with the Spaniards, decided to depose Motecuhzoma and elect his brother Cuitlahuac to succeed him. In late June, Motecuhzoma was killed. Spanish accounts claim that he was stoned by his former subjects; native accounts claim that he was murdered by the Spaniards. The situation for the Spaniards was grim, and Cortés decided to retreat (Figure 4.6).

The night of the Spaniards' retreat, usually identified as June 30, 1520, has come to be called the *noche triste* (the night of sorrows) because of the high casualty figures on both sides of the conflict. As the Spaniards and their Tlaxcalan allies attempted to flee the island of Tenochtitlan on the causeways, they were attacked by Aztec warriors. Many were killed, and many others drowned in the lake, some of them weighed

Figure 4.6 The *noche triste*. The Spaniards, with their Tlaxcalan allies, begin their flight from the city. A man standing atop a temple and a woman drawing water from a canal raise the alarm. *Florentine Codex*, Book 12, 42v. Reprinted with permission from Fray Bernardino de Sahagún, *Historia General de las cosas de Nueva España*, Códice Florentino. Facsimile of the Codex Florentinus of the Biblioteca Medicea Laurenciana, supervised by the Archivo General de la Nación (AGN) de México, Florence, Italy, 1979.

down by the gold they had looted from Motecuhzoma's treasury. What was left of Cortés's troops made their way back to the safety of Tlaxcala.

In the following months, Cortés strengthened his position east of the Basin of Mexico by carrying out raids and making new allies. Several hundred Spanish reinforcements arrived from Jamaica and Cuba, and a garrison founded along the road to Veracruz established control over routes to the south. By late December, Cortés and his troops were making the final preparations for an assault on Tenochtitlan. By now Cortés had a force of over 700 Spaniards and an estimated 75,000 Tlaxcalan allies as well as eighty-six horses and fifteen cannon.

In the meantime, the people of Tenochtitlan may have experienced their first encounter with an Old World infectious disease: smallpox (Figure 4.7). It is not entirely certain that this epidemic struck in 1520. The accounts of Cortés and other conquistadors do not mention it; it is possible that the epidemic did not occur until after Spanish control was established the following year. However, the principal na-

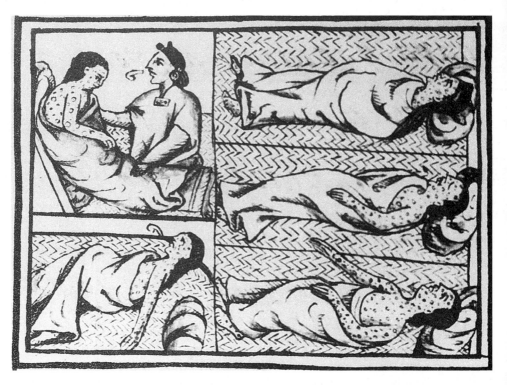

Figure 4.7   The smallpox epidemic. A woman, possibly a doctor, attempts to comfort a sick man; other sufferers lie helpless on their sleeping-mats. *Florentine Codex*, Book 12, 53v. Reprinted with permission from Fray Bernardino de Sahagún, *Historia General de las cosas de Nueva España*, Códice Florentino. Facsimile of the Codex Florentinus of the Biblioteca Medicea Laurenciana, supervised by the Archivo General de la Nación (AGN) de México, Florence, Italy, 1979.

tive history of the conquest, as well as other native documents and an important chronicle written by a Spanish priest in 1541, place the smallpox outbreak in 1520 after the *noche triste* retreat and before Cortés's final campaign. In addition to causing population losses, the epidemic could have had a severely demoralizing effect on the survivors, who had never before experienced widespread suffering from infectious disease. The native chronicle gives this account of the disease's progress:

> They could no longer walk about, but lay in their dwellings and sleeping places, no longer able to move or stir. They were unable to change position, to stretch out on their sides or face down, or raise their heads. And when they made a motion, they called out loudly. The pustules that covered people caused great desolation; very many people died of them, and many just starved to death; starvation reigned, and no one took care of others any longer.
> On some people, the pustules appeared only far apart, and they did not suffer greatly, nor did many of them die of it. But many people's faces were spoiled by it, their faces and noses were made rough. Some lost an eye or were blinded. (Lockhart 1993:182)

This account is an accurate description of how smallpox afflicts its victims. The most severely ill, those with a great many pustules, are unable to move about. If a whole family or neighborhood is stricken, such that no one is able to tend to the ill, people are as likely to die of thirst or starvation as of the virus itself. People with relatively few pustules are likely to survive but may be left scarred by pockmarks or even blind.

The new Mexica ruler, Cuitlahuac, also died between the *noche triste* and the Spanish assault. It has often been assumed that he died of smallpox, but no source states this cause explicitly. Cuitlahuac was succeeded by Cuauhtemoc, a nephew of Motecuhzoma selected for his prowess in war. Cuauhtemoc led a valiant resistance against Cortés and his allies. Cortés's strategy for the final assault on Tenochtitlan involved first subduing settlements along the lakeshore, which effectively isolated Tenochtitlan. A blockade kept fresh water and food from reaching the island city. People had to drink the briny water of the lake, and when their food stores ran out, they were reduced to eating such things as marsh grass and worms. The final blow was struck through a combined force by lake and land. Spaniards and Tlaxcalans who approached Tenochtitlan by foot along the causeways were aided by thirteen sailing vessels that had been constructed under Spanish supervision, disassembled, and then reconstructed on the shore of Lake Texcoco (Figure 4.8).

The final battle for Tenochtitlan lasted for almost three months. Differences between Spanish and native military tactics, as well as the element of surprise fostered by Spanish horses, huge dogs, cannon, and guns (which were so clumsy and inaccurate that they caused relatively few actual casualties), had favored the Spaniards in their earlier battles against native groups. The goal of native warfare was not to kill or maim the enemy upon the battlefield but to seize uninjured prisoners to take home as captives. The native soldiers fought one-on-one, seeking to display their individual prowess rather than to maximize the other side's casualties. In contrast, the Spaniards fought as a closed and, to native warriors, impenetrable rank, while indiscriminately killing and wounding warriors and even unarmed civilians. On an open battlefield, a small group of Spaniards was able to vanquish a much larger native army.

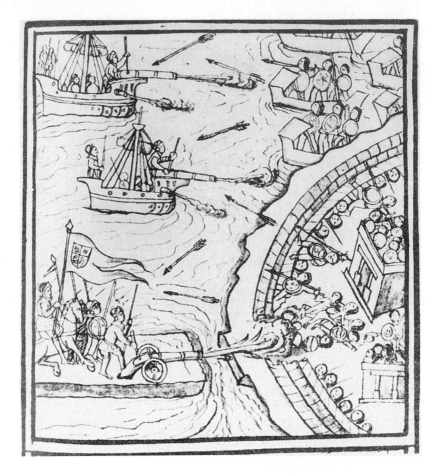

Figure 4.8 The siege of Tenochtitlan. The Spaniards attack from their ships, while Mexica soldiers fight back from canoes and from the city's walls and rooftops. *Florentine Codex*, Book 12, 56r. Reprinted with permission from Fray Bernardino de Sahagún, *Historia General de las cosas de Nueva España*, Códice florentino. Facsimile of the Codex Florentinus of the Biblioteca Medicea Laurenciana, supervised by the Archivo General de la Nación (AGN) de México, Florence, Italy, 1979.

The conquest of the island city, however, posed a greater challenge. In the narrow streets there was no space for Spanish fighters to close ranks. Horses had limited footing. It was difficult to move cannon around, and equally difficult to find clear targets amid the tangle of streets, canals, and buildings. Mexica warriors could carry out guerrilla-style attacks on isolated parties of Spaniards and their allies, then disappear along the familiar alleyways (Figure 4.9). They also learned quickly how to dodge cannon fire and how to kill horses with their obsidian-bladed swords. Captured Spaniards—and even horses—were sacrificed atop the great pyramid and their heads displayed on a rack, to the distress of fellow Spaniards.

Figure 4.9 Fighting in the city streets: Mexica warriors unhorse and kill a Spanish soldier. *Florentine Codex*, Book 12, 58r. Reprinted with permission from Fray Bernardino de Sahagún, *Historia General de las cosas de Nueva España*, Códice florentino. Facsimile of the Codex Florentinus of the Biblioteca Medicea Laurenciana, supervised by the Archivo General de la Nación (AGN) de México, Florence, Italy, 1979.

To conquer Tenochtitlan, Cortés and his allies had virtually to level it. They proceeded bit by bit, tearing down buildings and filling in canals in order to provide a flat surface on which they could move freely and challenge their enemies to open combat. The city's defenders, weakened by the lack of food and fresh water, resisted as long as they could but were gradually driven back. Finally, on August 13, 1521, the day One Serpent in the native calendar, Cuauhtemoc surrendered to Cortés. As starving, ragged people fled the city, Spaniards searched their bodies for valuables and selected women to rape. Cortés's first act as victor was to demand that all remaining gold be brought to him.

With the defeat of the Aztec capital, virtually all of the territories of the Aztec empire also were now under de facto Spanish rule. The native allies who joined with Cortés in order to free themselves from Mexica rule would now find themselves subject to overlords whose demands were even more burdensome.

THE CONQUEST OF MICHOACÁN

Once the Aztec empire was firmly under Spanish control, the Spaniards began their expansion to other areas of Mesoamerica. To the west and north of the Basin of Mexico, in what is today the state of Michoacán, was the powerful Tarascan or Purepecha state. From their capital at Tzintzuntzan on Lake Patzcuaro, the Tarascans maintained an independent polity that had successfully resisted every attempt by the Aztecs to impinge upon its territory (for details, see Chapters 1 and 2).

Before any official contacts between Tarascans and Spaniards took place, a small-pox epidemic hit Michoacán, and one of its first victims was the Tarascan ruler or Cazonci, Zuangua. He was succeeded by one of his sons, Tzintzicha Tangachoan, and as the new Cazonci, this young man was faced with difficult decisions about how he would respond to the Spaniards. The first face-to-face contacts between Spaniards and the Tarascans took place in February 1521, before Tenochtitlan had fallen. A year later Cristóbal de Olid was sent by Cortés to explore in the region. Initial contacts be-tween the Tarascans and the Spaniards were friendly, although Olid ultimately failed to subdue the region. In 1525, the Cazonci converted to Christianity, formally ac-cepted Spanish domination, and requested that friars be sent to Michoacán. The Ca-zonci apparently hoped that peaceful acceptance of Spanish rule would result in his maintaining some degree of autonomy. But this was not to be the case.

In 1528, Nuño de Guzmán, who would earn a reputation as one of the most ruthless conquistadors and treasure-seekers in New Spain, took the office of President of the Audiencia of Mexico, the colony's first ruling body. Early on, he began press-ing the Cazonci to turn over more gold and silver, and he had the Cazonci impris-oned in Mexico City on more than one occasion, holding him for ransom. But what must have at one time seemed an inexhaustible source of gold and silver was now in short supply. In 1529 to 1530, Guzmán organized a large expedition, made up of both Spaniards and Indian allies, to bring Michoacán more firmly under Spanish control.

Guzmán's expedition quickly made its way from Mexico City to Tzintzuntzan, leaving looted and burned towns and tortured victims in its wake. Shortly after ar-riving in the Tarascan capital, Guzmán took the Cazonci prisoner, and he was put on trial for a number of offenses, the most serious being interference with the *encomienda* system and ordering the killing of several Spaniards. After being tortured by Guzmán, the Cazonci confessed guilt. His sentence was harsh: He was to be dragged through town behind a horse and burned at the stake. With the death of the Cazonci, the great Tarascan kingdom ended.

THE MAYAN AREA

A situation quite different from that of Central Mexico confronted the Spaniards in the Mayan region, where no single group dominated large territories (see Chapter 3). Within the Mayan area were numerous small polities that were often at war against each other. Here, the Spaniards faced a more protracted battle. It was simply not possible to gain control of the Mayan area except through a series of campaigns that could subjugate each region one by one. This process took over 175 years.

In Chiapas initial contact with the Mayas there may have occurred as early as 1522, but it was not until 1524 that a small group of Spaniards, led by Luis Marín, made a concerted effort to bring the Tzotzil Mayas and the neighboring Chiapanecs, a non-Mayan people, under Spanish control. Although the Spaniards apparently achieved some military success, their failure to establish a Spanish community in the region rendered any military victories meaningless.

The definitive conquest of the area occurred during the 1527 to 1528 campaigns of Diego Mazariegos, in which the Zoques, the Chiapanecs, and the Tzotzil and Tzeltal Mayas were pacified. By 1535, a Spanish town, Ciudad Real (today San Cristóbal de Las Casas), was established in Chiapas, and within a few years the outlying areas also were under Spanish control.

The Yucatán Peninsula was not brought under Spanish control until 1547, although initial contacts between Spaniards and Mayas there had taken place several years before Cortés's arrival in Central Mexico. Early expeditions were received with hostility and did not succeed in establishing any permanent Spanish presence. There is good evidence that the peninsula was hit by a series of epidemics before the first party of conquistadors, under Francisco de Montejo, arrived in 1527. Initially, Montejo and his men were received in peace, but within months they met with considerable opposition. After two years Montejo left to renew supplies and enlist more men.

Montejo's second campaign took place between 1531 and 1534. This time, he concentrated more on the west coast of the peninsula. After some initial successes, this campaign, too, met with defeat. Toward the end of the campaign, word reached the expedition of the riches to be found in Peru. By this time it was clear that there was no gold in Yucatán, and most of Montejo's men abandoned him to go to Peru. Now left vulnerable to attacks by the Mayas, Montejo was forced to withdraw.

The final campaign to "pacify" Yucatán was carried out by Montejo's son, Francisco de Montejo the Younger, from 1540 to 1547. Although much of the Yucatán Peninsula was under Spanish control by 1545, uprisings occurred for the next two years. Even then, Spanish control was not complete, for many Indians fled south to the Petén. The Mayas in the Petén would successfully resist Spanish domination for another 150 years.

The Spanish invasion of Guatemala was preceded by a smallpox epidemic in 1520. Three years later, in December 1523, Pedro de Alvarado was commissioned by Cortés to lead a group of over 400 Spanish soldiers and hundreds of Tlaxcalan warriors south to Guatemala. En route Alvarado and his troops successfully subdued Mixtecs in Oaxaca, Zapotecs in Tehuantepec, and Mixe-Zoque groups in Soconusco.

As in Central Mexico, the Spaniards were aided in Guatemala by a polarized situation that had been created by the existence of a powerful and expansionist state ruled by the K'iches. The K'iche' Mayas had made many enemies during the course of expansion; by 1523, their power was waning, and many groups that had once been subjugated by them were willing to join with the Spaniards to ensure their defeat.

Alvarado's first encounters with the K'iche' warriors came in early 1524 in battles on the Pacific piedmont and in the highlands of western Guatemala. During hostilities near Xelaju (today Quetzaltenango), the K'iche' leader, Tekum, was killed (Figure 4.10). A passage from a K'iche' document, the *Títulos de la Casa Ixquin-Nehaib*, describes in vivid detail the personal battle between Tekum and Alvarado. Told from

Figure 4.10   Conquest of Quetzaltenango, the place where the K'iche' Mayan leader, Tekum, was killed by the Spaniards. From the Lienzo de Tlaxcala. Guatemala, CA: Dirección General de Cartografía (DGC), Editorial del Ejército, 1963.

a K'iche' point of view, this version casts the encounter in mythological terms. In attacking Alvarado, Tekum is transformed into a valiant eagle; in death he becomes a resplendent quetzal bird whose beauty astonishes the Spanish leader. Even in defeat the native hero is glorified (see Box 4.3 for the full text on the death of Tekum from the K'iche' perspective).

After this defeat, the K'iches invited the Spaniards to return with them to their capital, Q'umarkaaj or Utatlán. Once there, Alvarado realized that the Spaniards had been led into a trap, and he and his men slipped away, taking several K'iche' lords prisoner. Alvarado then fought to bring the area surrounding Utatlán under control, and Utatlán itself was burned. Here the Spaniards were aided by the Kaqchikel Mayas, enemies of the K'iches.

Box 4.3   The Death of Tekum

The account to follow is based on a Spanish version of the original K'iche' Mayan text.

. . . this captain [Tekum] brought many people from many towns, ten thousand Indians in all, all came armed with their bows and arrows, slings, lances and other arms. And Captain Tekum, before leaving his town and in front of the chiefs, demonstrated his courage and his spirit and he put on wings with which he flew and his two arms and legs were covered with feathers and he wore a crown, and on his chest he wore a very large emerald which looked like a mirror, and he wore another on his forehead. And another on his back. He looked very gallant. This captain flew like an eagle, he was a great nobleman and a great sorcerer. . . .

. . . [after a battle of many hours] the Spaniards killed many Indians, there was no count of those whom they killed, not a single Spaniard died, only the Indians who had been brought by Captain Tekum and much blood ran from all the Indians. . . . And then Captain Tekum flew up, he came like an eagle full of feathers that grew from his body, they were not artificial; he wore wings which also sprang from his body and he wore three crowns, one was of gold, another of pearls and another of diamonds and emeralds.

This Captain Tekum came with the intention of killing Tunadiu [Alvarado] who came on horseback and he hit the horse instead of the Adelantado and he cut off the head of the horse with one lance. It was not a lance of iron but of shiny stone and this captain had placed a spell on it. And when he saw that it was not the Adelantado but the horse who had died he returned to fly overhead. . . . Then the Adelantado awaited him with his lance and he impaled this Captain Tekum with it. . . .

. . . [Captain Tekum] appeared covered with quetzal feathers and very beautiful plumes, for which reason this town of Quetzaltenango ["Quetzal fortress"] was given its name, because here is where the death of this Captain Tekum came to pass. And immediately the Adelantado called to all his soldiers to come and see the beauty of the quetzal Indian. Then the Adelantado told his soldiers that he had never seen another Indian as gallant and as noble and covered with such beautiful quetzal feathers, in Mexico, nor in Tlaxcala, nor in any of the towns that he had conquered. . . .

And as the rest of the Indians saw that the Spaniards had killed their captain, they fled, and immediately the Adelantado Don Pedro de Alvarado, seeing that the soldiers of this Captain Tekum were fleeing, said that they also should die, and the Spanish soldiers pursued the Indians and caught up with them and killed all of them. There were so many Indians that they killed that they made a river of blood . . . all the water became blood and the day became red because of the great bloodshed that day. (Recinos 1984:89–94)

With the conquest of the K'iches complete, Alvarado founded the first Spanish capital in Guatemala at the Kaqchikel city of Iximché on July 25, 1524. At first the Kaqchikels welcomed the Spaniards, but Alvarado's increasing demands soon led the Kaqchikel to revolt. In fact, a general revolt against the Spaniards took place in 1526. One by one, the other Mayan groups of the Guatemalan highlands fell to the Spanish invaders. The Tzutujils, the Mams, the Poqomams, the Ch'ortis, and others were all under Spanish control within a few years.

For almost 200 years after the first contact between the Spaniards and the Mayas of the Yucatán Peninsula, the dense forests of the Petén served as a zone of refuge for

Mayas fleeing Spanish rule in the northern part of the peninsula. In fact, the move-ment of peoples between northern Yucatán and the Petén had begun well before the arrival of the Spaniards (see Chapters 1 and 2). The Itzas were one of the groups who, according to native tradition, fled to the Petén lakes region after the demise of Chichen Itza and/or Mayapan. There they established a capital, Noh Peten, on the island where the modern town of Flores lies today. In the sixteenth century, the Itza polity was composed of a confederacy of four territorial groups, with the Canek lin-eage in control of the most powerful group.

The Spaniards showed little interest in the Petén during the sixteenth century, but several attempts were made in the seventeenth century to bring the Itzas under Spanish rule. The Spaniards were not successful until 1697, and the fascinating story of the final conquest of the Itza is worth recounting.

For many years the influence of Mayan prophecies in the conquest of the Itzas has received attention. It has been argued that the Mayan view of cyclical history meant that certain events were destined to be repeated at specific dates within cal-endrical cycles. The year 1697 has long been thought to be one such date, a date that was destined to bring political collapse. According to this view, the conquest of 1697 was inevitable; the Itzas simply surrendered knowing that any attempt to resist the Spaniards would be futile. Recent research by ethnohistorian Grant Jones has led him to call into question this interpretation, suggesting that the situation was, in fact, more complex.

Jones does not deny that the Itzas were influenced by prophecies and a cyclical view of history but argues that, in the case of the events of 1697, the Spaniards, in par-ticular a certain Franciscan priest, took advantage of their knowledge of Mayan be-liefs to try to negotiate a peaceful surrender. Subsequent events make it clear that, contrary to some reports, these efforts did not succeed.

The Itzas put up a valiant fight, and it was only after the Spaniards slaughtered huge numbers of Indians that they succeeded in taking the city. One report states that the Spaniards killed "such an innumerable quantity that the dead bodies of the In-dians appeared as an island in the lake."

If the Itzas did not surrender to the Spaniards peacefully, then what was the role of prophecy in these events? Jones suggests that internal struggles within the con-federacy had disrupted the existing balance of power in which Canek (leader of the ruling lineage) enjoyed a dominant position. The year 1697 was, in fact, seen by the Itzas as a year of political collapse foretold by the prophecies, but it was interpreted as the time when the local ruling dynasty would change, not the time to submit to Spanish rule. Canek's lineage had ruled over the Itzas for 256 years, which constituted an entire calendrical cycle, and rival lineages sought a change of command. Canek himself, it seems, had agreed to surrender in the hope that the Spaniards would let him remain in power as governor. But his strongest rivals had effectively seized power, and they were the ones who put up the resistance to the Spanish army. Thus, despite the decades of cautious negotiations aimed at a peaceful surrender, the last inde-pendent Mesoamerican kingdom came to a violent end. Canek, his hopes of alliance shattered, ended up a prisoner in Guatemala City.

SUGGESTED READINGS

CLENDINNEN, INGA 1987 *Ambivalent Conquests: Maya and Spaniard in Yucatan, 1517–1570.* Cambridge: Cambridge University Press.

COLUMBUS, CHRISTOPHER 1989 *The Diario of Christopher Columbus's First Voyage to America, 1492–1493.* Edited and translated by Oliver Dunn and James E. Kelley, Jr. Norman: University of Oklahoma Press.

CORTÉS, HERNÁN 1986 *Letters from Mexico.* Edited and translated by Anthony Pagden. New Haven: Yale University Press.

DÍAZ DEL CASTILLO, BERNAL 1956 *The Discovery and Conquest of Mexico.* Edited and translated by A. P. Maudslay. New York: Farrar, Straus and Giroux.

GIBSON, CHARLES 1966 *Spain in America.* New York: Harper and Row.

HANKE, LEWIS *1949 The Spanish Struggle for Justice in the Conquest of America.* Philadelphia: University of Pennsylvania Press.

JONES, GRANT 1998 *The Conquest of the Last Maya Kingdom.* Stanford: Stanford University Press.

LAS CASAS, BARTOLOMÉ DE 1992 *The Devastation of the Indies: A Brief Account.* Edited by Bill Donovan. Translated by Herma Briffault. Baltimore: Johns Hopkins University Press.

LEÓN-PORTILLA, MIGUEL 1992 *The Broken Spears: The Aztec Account of the Conquest of Mexico.* Boston: Beacon Press.

LOCKHART, JAMES (ed. and trans.) 1993 *We People Here: Nahuatl Accounts of the Conquest of Mexico.* Berkeley: University of California Press.

RESTALL, MATTHEW 1998 *Maya Conquistador.* Boston: Beacon Press.

RESTALL, MATTHEW 2003 *Seven Myths of the Spanish Conquest.* Oxford: Oxford University Press.

SCHWARTZ, STUART (ed.) 2000 *Victors and Vanquished: Spanish and Nahua Views of the Conquest of Mexico.* Boston: Bedford/St. Martin's.

WARREN, J. BENEDICT 1985 *The Conquest of Michoacán: The Spanish Domination of the Tarascan Kingdom in Western Mexico, 1521–1530.* Norman: University of Oklahoma Press.

Chapter 5
The Colonial Period in Mesoamerica

Despite the trauma of the conquest and the demographic collapse that occurred over the course of the sixteenth century, the native peoples of Mesoamerica survived. Their populations eventually rebounded, and at the end of the Colonial period, they still accounted for the majority of the region's inhabitants.

Ruled by Spain for three centuries, the peoples of Mesoamerica underwent the usual fate of a colonized people: They were systematically impoverished, with their resources and productive capacity redirected toward the enrichment of the invaders and their descendants. However, in some ways Spain pursued a policy of indirect rule, allowing the native people to run many of their own affairs within limits set by the colonizers.

This chapter begins by describing how Spain ruled and administered its Mesoamerican territories and then discusses the colonial institutions that had direct impact on the native people, with particular attention to the role of the Catholic Church. We then examine colonial society, first giving an overview of the social makeup of the colony as a whole and then focusing on the way of life that developed in the surviving native communities.

THE COLONIAL REGIME

The Spanish king was, in all respects—economic, political, and religious—the supreme ruler over Spain and its territories. A portion of all the wealth generated in the Indies was destined for the royal treasury. The king and his advisers also had ultimate political power, overseeing the appointment of all high-ranking colonial officials. In addition, the Crown had been granted extraordinary privileges by the pope, meaning that the Spanish king controlled all the ecclesiastical affairs in his domain. But despite all this power and the vast wealth of the empire, the "golden age" of Spain was fleeting.

Crown strategies for controlling and profiting from its empire were based on maintaining strict monopolistic powers over the movement of goods and people between Spain and its colonies. Ideally, the colonies would provide raw materials as well as ready markets for goods manufactured in Spain. The House of Trade (*Casa de Contratación*) was created in 1503 to grant licenses to all ships and merchants bound for the Indies, to monitor imports and exports, and to provide permits to all passengers traveling to the New World.

The first years of Spanish colonial rule in the Mesoamerican region were marked by power struggles over the spoils of victory. The Crown, always fearful that the development of an aristocracy in the colonies would threaten its own power, actively sought to create a highly centralized colonial government directly under its control. But from the beginning of Spanish occupation, intense rivalries developed among the many Spanish factions over control of the vast resources that the New World offered, whether they be precious metals or Indian labor. Strong animosities existed between the Crown and the conquistadors, between Crown-appointed officials and colonists, and between members of the clergy and colonists. Arguments raged over the status of the native population: Were Indians to be treated as humans? Could they be enslaved? The implementation of various laws intended to protect the Indians provoked outraged responses from colonists.

The most notorious example of this situation was the attempted implementation of the New Laws of 1542 to 1543, a set of laws that had been heavily promoted by the Dominican activist Bartolomé de Las Casas (see Chapter 4). These laws were intended to end certain abuses against the native people. At the heart of the New Laws was a new attempt by the Crown to regulate and ultimately to eliminate the *encomienda* system.

We have already seen that the *encomienda* system had originated in medieval Spain and had been introduced in the Caribbean, where it was at least partially responsible for the demise of much of the native population there. On the Mesoamerican mainland, as elsewhere, the *encomienda* system consisted of rewarding Spaniards (initially the Conquistadors) for service to the king by "commending" or entrusting to them the tribute and labor of a given group of Indians, usually the Indians of a specific town. The Spanish *encomenderos* were charged with the Christianization of the Indians in return for their goods and labor. The merits of the *encomienda* system on the mainland—after its disastrous effects in the Caribbean—were hotly debated, with the Crown opposed to it on principle but grudgingly allowing Conquistadors to be given *encomiendas* as rewards for their part in the conquest.

A few *encomiendas* were granted to very high-ranking Indians, in recognition of their status and in an attempt to pacify individuals who might otherwise pose a challenge to Spanish rule. For example, doña Isabel de Motecuhzoma was granted the important town of Tlacopan (or Tacuba) in *encomienda*. She was the eldest surviving child of the Aztec emperor Motecuhzoma with his principal wife. According to some accounts, she was also the widow of Cuauhtemoc. The last of her three Spanish husbands made a prolonged but ultimately unsuccessful effort to secure the perpetual continuation of her *encomienda* rights for the couple's descendants, on the grounds that his wife was the legitimate heir of her father's throne.

The New Laws prohibited slavery of Indians, regulated the tribute that could be paid by Indians to their *encomenderos,* and, of most importance, forbade the granting of any new *encomiendas* and prohibited the inheritance of those already in existence. Throughout the colonies, the New Laws were met with outrage on the part of the Spanish colonists. In Peru their implementation resulted in the death of the viceroy and a civil war. In New Spain the portion of the New Laws that prohibited new *encomiendas* and the inheritance of *encomiendas* was simply not enforced.

After several years of instability, a governing apparatus was put into place that was based on the organization of government in Spain. Sixteenth-century Spain did not recognize a separation of church and state. The Spanish, as well as the Spanish colonial, government, was divided into five branches: civil, judicial, military, treasury, and ecclesiastical. The jurisdictional units for the five branches of government were not necessarily the same, and the powers of officials—the king as well as some lower-ranking officials—were broad, often crosscutting the various branches. We will briefly outline the civil and ecclesiastical administrations.

The Spanish Crown ruled its American colonies with the help of the Council of the Indies, which was charged with overseeing Spain's New World possessions. In the colonies, royal power was delegated to viceroys. By the 1540s, there were two viceroyalties in the Americas, New Spain and Peru. Within the viceroyalties were smaller jurisdictions called Audiencias, ruled by a group of Crown-appointed judges or *oidores.* Different regions of Mesoamerica fell under the jurisdictions of the Audiencias of Mexico, created in 1527; Guatemala, created in 1543; and Guadalajara, created in 1548 (Figure 5.1).

Smaller political units were kingdoms *(reinos)* and provinces *(provincias),* which were ruled by governors; even smaller units, called *corregimientos* and *alcaldías mayores,* were governed by lesser-ranking officials, *corregidores* and *alcaldes mayores,* who were subordinate to the governors. A special category of *corregidor,* the *corregidor de indios,* was responsible for the administration of Indian towns. Finally, municipalities, both Spanish and Indian, were governed by a group of officials collectively called the *cabildo,* or town council. In addition to this hierarchy of officials, the Crown regularly appointed royal inspectors *(visitadores)* who conducted inspections *(visitas)* and filed reports directly to the king. The king also was kept informed about the performance of colonial officials through a program of investigations *(residendias)* whereby testimony was given by any interested party about the behavior of officials during their term of office.

In the eighteenth century, after the French Bourbon dynasty replaced the Habsburg dynasty on the Spanish throne, the administrative organization of Spain and its colonies was overhauled. In the colonies one of the changes made by Bourbon King Charles III was the introduction, in 1786, of the intendancy system developed in France to strengthen royal control. This change resulted in the creation of new jurisdictions that replaced, and in many cases crosscut, previous divisions. Similarly, the new office of intendant replaced the offices of governor, *alcalde mayor,* and *corregidor.* The intendancy system was introduced in order to bring governance in the colonies under more direct control by Spain: Intendants were to be Spanish-born, and they reported directly to officials in Spain.

Figure 5.1   The main Spanish colonial jurisdictions established in Mesoamerica during the sixteenth century. After Howard F. Cline, "Introductory Notes on Territorial Divisions of Middle America," *The Handbook of Middle American Indians, Volume 12: Guide to Ethnohistorical Sources, Pt. 1,* volume editor Howard F. Cline, general editor Robert Wauchope. Austin, TX: University of Texas Press, 1972, p. 25.

The ecclesiastical administration of Spain's colonies was carried out by two groups within the Roman Catholic Church: the secular clergy (so-named because they live in the world at large), made up of clerics in the ecclesiastical hierarchy that extends from the Pope to parish priests; and the regular clergy (so-called because they live according to a rule or *regla*), which comprises the mendicant orders (those who live from donations and alms, such as the Franciscans, Dominicans, Augustinians, Mercedarians, etc.) and the Society of Jesus, or Jesuits.

For most of the Colonial period, the entire region of the pre-Hispanic Mesoamerican world fell within the Archdiocese of Mexico, headed by the Archbishop of Mexico, although after 1745, portions of southern Mesoamerica became part of the newly created Archdiocese of Guatemala with its own archbishop. Diocesan divisions within Mesoamerica included, at various times, Guadalajara, Michoacán, Mexico, Tlaxcala, Antequera (Oaxaca), Chiapa, Yucatán, Verapaz, Trujillo, and León, each administered by a bishop. Within the dioceses were smaller divisions, the parishes, administered by parish priests.

The regular clergy came to the Spanish colonies with the specific mission of bringing Christianity to the Indian communities. In the New World, members of the religious orders lived primarily among the Indians, learning the native languages and ministering to the native peoples through missions, schools, and hospitals. Originally the regulars were expected to return to Spain once the conversion of the Indians was completed; but, with the exception of the Society of Jesus, whose members were expelled from Spain's colonies (and Spain itself) in 1767, the religious orders remained in the colonies throughout the Colonial period and into the Neocolonial (Republican) and Modern periods.

In 1571, the Holy Office of the Inquisition was established in Mexico City to investigate and punish religious crimes. Native people were exempt from prosecution by the Inquisition. Inquisition-like proceedings carried out by bishops in Mexico and Yucatán during the 1530s and 1540s had, it was thought, gone too far, with Indians being tortured and even executed. By 1571, the opinion prevailed that the Indians had been brought into the Catholic faith too recently to be held to the same standards as Spanish Christians. This policy would remain in effect until the Inquisition was dissolved at the end of the Colonial period.

Spaniards of Jewish ancestry who may have hoped that their move to the colony might grant them some religious freedom found themselves once again under perpetual scrutiny and suspicion. People from European countries where Protestantism was common, such as the French printers who ran some of Mexico's first publishing houses, were also viewed with suspicion. And people of African and mixed descent were subject to investigation, even though they might have much less familiarity with Christian teachings than the Indians around them. The Inquisition's *autos de fe,* or rituals of penitence and reconciliation, became a feature of New Spain's public life, and those convicted of religious crimes were occasionally burned at the stake.

CIVIL-RELIGIOUS INSTITUTIONS AFFECTING THE NATIVE POPULATION

For the Spaniards the wealth of the Indies was not confined exclusively to precious metals and other goods; the large Indian populations themselves were viewed as a valuable resource. As a result, many of the institutions imposed by the Spaniards were designed to allow Spanish colonists to use native labor. Ultimately, any wealth generated by Indian labor (or by any other means) would benefit the king of Spain, since he was guaranteed to receive one-fifth of anything coming out of the Indies.

In establishing official policies regarding the treatment of the Indians, the Crown was torn between what was genuinely felt to be an obligation to promote the well-being of the Indians, on the one hand, and its ultimate desire to generate revenues from the colonies, on the other. Unfortunately for the Indians, even when Crown policies were clearly intended for their benefit, local officials often failed to implement them out of indifference, if not open hostility. The unwillingness of Crown officials to enforce the laws is well-illustrated in the phrase *obedezco pero no cumplo* ("I obey but do not execute"); the speaker acknowledges the king's authority but refuses to carry out his commands. Cortés reportedly uttered this phrase when he received orders from Charles V that, among other things, explicitly forbade him from distributing *en-*

comiendas in Central Mexico. He may have been the first to express this sentiment in colonial Mesoamerica, but he was certainly not the last.

One of the earliest Spanish institutions to have a direct economic impact on the Indians was the *encomienda* system. Initially, *encomiendas* were a great source of wealth for Spaniards, with native communities furnishing large amounts of goods to their *encomendero*. An *encomendero* of the highland Guatemalan town of Huehuetenango received the following items in tribute in 1530 to 1531 (Kramer, Lovell, and Lutz 1991:274):

800 lengths of cotton cloth
400 loincloths
400 jackets
400 blouses
400 skirts
400 sandals
400 reed mats
400 woven mats
unspecified amounts of corn, beans, chile, and salt
108–126 large jugs of honey
2,268 turkeys

The Crown repeatedly tried to eliminate the *encomienda* system, but with little success. In some areas the Crown was successful in revoking *encomiendas;* in these cases an Indian town or province became, in effect, an *encomienda* of the Crown. In other areas, however, *encomiendas* held by generation after generation of Spaniards persisted until well into the eighteenth century.

In the 1550s, Indian slavery was abolished, and that act, together with a new policy that prevented *encomenderos* from demanding labor from the Indians they held (they could still receive goods), presented the Crown with a serious dilemma: Who was going to provide the labor required for the various colonial enterprises? The *repartimiento* system was implemented to solve this problem. *Repartimiento* was essentially a system of forced labor that provided the Spaniards with a new means for exploiting native people. Under *repartimiento,* Indian communities were required to provide labor for public projects such as building and road construction and maintenance, for agricultural work, for work in the mines, and for work as porters. The law required that *repartimiento* laborers be paid. The system was easily abused, however, with Spanish officials and their friends using the labor drafts for private endeavors and finding ways to cheat the Indians out of the wages they had earned.

A variation of the *repartimiento* of labor was the *repartimiento* of goods, in which the Indians were forced to purchase goods from unscrupulous Spanish officials at exorbitant prices. Often these were items the Indians neither needed nor wanted, such as Spanish shoes, although sometimes the goods were actually the raw materials that the natives needed to produce items for tribute payments. For example, a native community that was charged tribute in textiles might be forced to purchase at high prices the cotton or wool needed to produce the textiles. Another variation of this form of *repartimiento* consisted of Spaniards' providing raw materials (such as raw cotton) to Indian weavers in return for the right to purchase the finished product, and often the purchase price was well below market value.

Among the most disruptive of the Spanish institutions was the program of *congregación* or *reducción*. These forced resettlement programs were instituted throughout New Spain in the sixteenth century. They were intended to aid the clergy in "civilizing" previously dispersed native populations by congregating them into new, densely populated villages where the activities of the natives could be more easily monitored.

In addition to providing their *encomenderos* with goods and labor and providing labor for *repartimiento,* native communities also were taxed through the colonial tribute system. Indians, as vassals to the king, were required to pay annual tribute either directly to the Crown or to their *encomenderos*. In the latter case, a portion of the tribute collected by the *encomendero* was paid to the king. Initially, tribute payments were made in goods, but gradually payments in money replaced payments in goods. By the mid–eighteenth century, payment in goods was made illegal.

We saw in Chapters 2 and 3 that at the time of Spanish contact, expansionist powers like the Aztecs collected tribute from conquered regions. In fact, some of the earliest colonial tribute assessments may well have been based on existing Aztec tribute collection documents. But eventually the tribute demands of the Spaniards were much more debilitating than pre-Hispanic tribute payments. The demographic decline meant that there were fewer and fewer Indians, but reductions in tribute payments usually lagged far behind population decline. In colonial documents we find many examples of native communities requesting that they be excused from tribute payments because they simply did not have the resources to pay.

In addition to the many abusive policies forced upon the Indians, many Spanish economic enterprises in colonial Mesoamerica affected the native populations. Among the enterprises that would have the greatest impact on native societies were mining, the hacienda system, and the textile factories or *obrajes*.

From the beginning, the Spaniards were obsessed with a desire to obtain gold and silver, and by the mid–sixteenth century, large deposits of silver were being mined in several areas of Mesoamerica, primarily in the north in the areas around Zacatecas, Guanajuato, San Luis Potosí, and Pachuca. Mining was one arena where the Crown and the colonists were of one mind; no holds were barred to ensure that the mines were as productive as possible. Beyond the wealth generated by the silver itself— even after the king had received his fifth—fortunes also could be made by the entrepreneurs who provided the food and other goods for the mining camps. Labor for the mines was provided largely by the Indian population, at first through *repartimiento* labor and later through wage labor. Wages were good, but the risks were high, and many natives lost their lives as they toiled in the unhealthy atmosphere of the mines.

With the gradual demise of the *encomienda* in many parts of Mesoamerica, Spanish access to large tracts of land shifted to outright ownership of landed estates called haciendas. In less-populated areas, primarily in the north, haciendas were large and focused primarily on livestock. In other areas they were often smaller and more diverse with livestock and agricultural components. In many regions, the growth of the haciendas was achieved at the expense of the native communities as Spaniards took control of what were formerly Indian lands. In theory, official policies prevented Spaniards from taking Indian lands, but in practice, Spaniards were able to acquire these lands through a variety of means. Indian leaders sometimes willingly sold community properties to Spaniards. Another common practice involved the Crown policy of selling what were deemed to be vacant lands to make money for the royal treasury. The demographic collapse of the native population left many areas with low population densities. Lands that were underpopulated—even though they might be used for hunting and other activities by native communities—could be declared vacant and then legally sold to Spaniards.

The labor for haciendas was often supplied by native workers who had left their communities. A situation of debt-servitude frequently developed when these people were given wages in advance and were then required to remain on the hacienda until the debt was paid off. In other cases, however, a share-cropping arrangement existed whereby laborers were provided with access to a portion of the hacienda lands to cultivate in exchange for handing over part of their crop and perhaps providing the owner with other services. In still other cases, natives temporarily left their communities to work on haciendas to earn the cash they needed to meet their tribute demands.

Obrajes were textile factories that produced coarse cloth for consumption within New Spain. Finer cloth was imported. The *obrajes* tended to be located in the cities in Central Mexico, and they had little impact outside this area. The bulk of the workforce in the *obrajes* was made up of Indians who had left their communities. Working conditions were unhealthy, and treatment of native workers was harsh (Figure 5.2).

EVANGELIZATION: ISSUES AND IMPLICATIONS

The colonial institution that had the most profound effects upon indigenous life in colonial Mesoamerica was the Catholic Church. Most Spanish colonists were content to enrich themselves by the Indians' labor, satisfied if the Indians stayed peaceful and displayed some minimal evidence of Christianity. But men of the Church sought to extend colonial authority into the most intimate aspects of native life, from the selection of marriage partners to the expression of sexual desire.

Many books have been written about the Christian evangelization of Mesoamerica. Current scholars question a number of common assumptions, especially the notion that Mesoamerica was "spiritually conquered" by Christian missionaries, and these scholars see the native people as playing an active role in formulating their own understandings of Christianity. Rather than include here a detailed discussion of missionary methodologies—the subject of numerous previous studies—we have chosen to discuss some of the broader political and social issues involved in the evangelization of colonial Mesoamerica.

The missionary friars of the mendicant orders had tremendous influence and prestige during the early decades of Spanish rule in Mexico. The recent reforms initiated

Figure 5.2   Indian textile workers in an *obraje*. This illustration by a native artist is from the *Codex Osuna*, a set of documents prepared in 1565 as a report on the Spanish and native governments of Mexico City. *Códice Osuna*. Mexico City, Mexico: Instituto Indigenista Interamericano, 1947, p. 258.

in Spain by Jiménez de Cisneros had filled the religious orders with well-educated men who took their vows and duties seriously. They enjoyed the favor of a king who was determined to prevent a repetition of the disastrous colonization of the Caribbean. And, for the most part, these men found themselves welcome among the native people. A few friars, who dreamed of being martyred by savages, were actually disappointed by the graciousness and generosity with which they were received (Figure 5.3).

Were these missionaries mere tools of Spanish colonialism, helping to transform Mesoamericans into compliant colonial subjects, or did they sincerely believe that the native people would benefit from their preaching of the Christian gospel? Just as we cannot fully separate the Spanish conqueror's lust for gold from his desire to glorify his God, we must understand that, even though these distinctions may be meaningful to us, people of the sixteenth century did not think in these terms. Most of the

Figure 5.3   Indo-Christian art: A native artist painted this portrait of fray Martín de Valencia, the leader of New Spain's first official mission of Franciscan friars, in the Franciscan friary at Tlalmanalco (southeast of Mexico City); it probably dates to the late 1580s. Photo provided by authors.

missionaries believed that the Spanish "conquest," despite its attendant evils, was justified precisely because, and to the extent that, the native people were brought into the Christian fold.

Many friars supported Spanish rule in principle and condoned the military conquest, but they objected to the actual colonization of these territories by large numbers of Spaniards. They hoped to insulate the native people from what they saw as the corrupting influence of Spanish colonists, whom the friars did not consider model Christians. These friars hoped that New Spain might remain a predominantly Indian society, but one that was Christianized by the friars and ruled by a viceroy appointed by the Spanish king. These concerns led the friars often to side with New Spain's viceroys against the settler aristocracy and against the secular ecclesiastical hierarchy, which sought to administer New Spain according to the same system of tithes and parishes that operated in Spain. Many native peoples adhered to the position of these friars, declaring loyalty to the king—to them a distant but potentially benevolent figure—while objecting to specific policies and to particular abuses perpetrated by local Spaniards.

Opposed to this majority opinion was the more radical position taken by Bartolomé de Las Casas and some of his fellow Dominicans. As discussed in Chapter 4, Las Casas believed that the end, Christian evangelization, did not justify the means: violent conquest. Missionaries should do their work without the assistance of invading armies. Las Casas convinced Charles V to allow him to try out his program in Tuzulutlan, an as yet unconquered area of Guatemala. During the 1540s he and other Dominicans succeeded in bringing the area under Spanish control without military intervention, while introducing Christianity among the indigenous peoples. In recognition of the Dominicans' achievement, Charles changed the region's name from Tuzulutlan, which means "the land of war," to Verapaz, or "true peace." He granted the Dominicans full administrative authority over this district, which for the next three centuries remained a theocratic ministate operating within the larger colony.

The situation in Verapaz was an extreme example of a pattern that emerged throughout colonial Mesoamerica: an alliance between the religious orders and the native communities. This is one dimension of a colonial political scene that was far more complex than a simple struggle of Spaniards against Indians. The ties that bound friars and Indians to one another were often phrased in terms of kinship, with the friars represented as stern but compassionate fathers to their innocent but oft-misguided Indian children. This terminology helped to obscure what was in reality a relationship of mutual dependence. The Indians fed and clothed the friars, built their convents and churches, and provided a power base to back up the friars' various political intrigues, many of which, such as a campaign to prevent the ecclesiastical hierarchy from forcing the Indians to pay tithes, benefited both friars and Indians.

The friars taught the native nobles to read and write and to master the forms of rhetoric with which they could petition Crown or Council on their own behalf. Since they sometimes petitioned for more friars, or to prevent friars from being removed from their communities, such skills worked also to the friars' advantage. The friars trained commoners to exploit the new tools and technologies introduced from Europe, to the frustration of Spanish artisans who had hoped to monopolize these industries. They acted as advocates and interpreters before the colonial government. Sometimes the friars resorted to corporal punishment to impose their will, and occasionally they were guilty of economic and sexual exploitation, but far less frequently than other Spaniards, including the secular clergy. It is no wonder that the native people, shrewdly appraising the friars as the best friends they were likely to find among the emigrants from Europe, welcomed their presence.

But what about conversion? Did the Indians become Christians? Perhaps the best answer to that question is both "yes" and "no." Yes, they were baptized, almost all of them within a few decades after their particular territory had been brought under Spanish rule. Yes, they participated in Christian worship and eventually came to think of themselves as Christian people who no longer worshipped the gods of their ancestors. Yes, Christian churches replaced the old temples as the centers of community religious life (Figure 5.4). Yes, they were sincerely devoted to the sacred beings of Catholic Christianity: Christ, the Virgin Mary, the various saints.

Figure 5.4   Colonial church in the town of San Pedro y San Pablo Teposcolula, Oaxaca. The resident Dominican friars ministered to the town's native population from the large, arcaded open chapel, now partially ruined. Photo provided by authors.

But they did not undergo a conversion experience, in the sense of responding to a personal spiritual crisis by consciously and intentionally replacing one entire belief system with another. The fact that in Mesoamerica the social structure of the native communities generally remained intact, with local leaders retaining control over community affairs, probably helped to keep people from experiencing the transition to Spanish rule as a traumatic crisis in their own lives. Traditional religion was more a matter of collective, community rites and celebrations than of an individualized, personal faith. Christianity too would be above all a collective, public enterprise associated with the identity of the community, now centered on a patron saint rather than a tutelary divinity.

The native people interpreted Christianity in terms that were more or less compatible with their own cultures. This process was facilitated by the fact that the friars preached to them in their own languages. Friars, in collaboration with native assistants, produced many books and manuscripts in the native languages (Figure 5.5). The process of translation subtly altered Christian concepts and brought them more in line with indigenous understandings. For example, in the Nahuatl language the word *tlahtlacolli* was used to convey the Christian concept of "sin." The Nahuatl word meant "error" or "crime" or "destruction" in a much broader sense and alluded to a general process of disintegration and decay that affected all social and natural

¶ Confessionario ma
yor, Instruction y Doctrina, para el que
se quiere bien confessar: compuesto por el reverendo pa
dre fray Alõso de Molina de la orden de señor sant
Francisco: traduzido y buelto enla lengua de
los nauas, por el mismo autor.

I La ynicocatzin sanctissi
ma trinidad, tetatzin, te
piltzi, yua espiritu sancto. Mi
can ompeua yn neyolmelaua
loni, yn oquimotlahli yn oqui
motecpanili padre fray Alon
so de Molina, sant Francis
co reopixqui: ynipan oquimo
cuepili yn nauatlatolly.

O El nombre de la sanctis
sima trinidad, padre, hi
jo, y espiritu sancto. Aqui co
mien ça vn confessionario, que
compuso y ordeno el R. padre
fray Alonso de Molina, de la
orde de señor sant fracisco: tra
duzido en legua de los nauas
por el mismo autor.

¶ Tlatolpeuhcayotl .

Ni la
copiltze .
{ in ça ço
acteuatl}
tymoma
qrtizneq,
in vel tiqc
nopilhuiz
neq cemi
cac yuliliz
tli, cenca
motech
moneca in
timiquima
tiz

¶ Prologo.

O Ama
do hijo.
{ qualqe
ra q tu se
as, q pre
tedces fal
uarte}pa
ra que pu
edas al
cat çar la
vida eter
na, te es
muy ne
cessario ,
que

a iij

Figure 5.5   The first page of a 1565 confession manual printed in both Spanish and Nahuatl. The woodcut depicts a Franciscan friar accompanied by Indian children. From Alonso de Molina, *Confessionario mayor, en lengua Mexicana y Castellana.* Courtesy of the John Carter Brown Library at Brown University.

orders. The translation thus had the effect of watering down the Christian notion of personal moral responsibility and relating individual behavior to broader processes that were not seen as necessarily evil (for more on this topic, see Chapters 6 and 14). Also, native peoples had no concept of a "religion" or a "faith" as such, as a clearly defined entity separable from the rest of culture, and thus they did not comprehend what it was they were supposed to be giving up and taking on. Priests were too few and too awkward in the native languages to explain to everyone the theological and philosophical underpinnings of Christianity in terms they would understand; most religious instruction occurred on a rudimentary level.

To the native people, Christianity appeared to be primarily a set of practices, many of which resembled their traditional practices of prayer, offerings, processions, dramas, fasting, and the use of sacred images. It was on these expressive and often collective behaviors that the native people focused, sometimes with notable enthusiasm. Christianization proceeded as a process of addition and substitution within the existing repertoire of devotional practices. Priests who lamented that instead of a thousand gods the Indians now had a thousand and one, the Christian god having simply been added to the native deities, had indeed perceived an aspect of this process. Over time, new prayers, new images, new songs, new penances, and new festivals were adopted whereas many of the old practices were abandoned. But there was never a sudden and total substitution of a new *faith* for an old.

Given that Christianity was not perceived as a spiritually compelling new faith, what motivated people to make even these changes in their traditional devotions? With the exception of the native priesthood, most people had little to lose and much to gain by joining the Church. We have already seen that the presence and support of the friars benefited the native communities. Other factors may also be noted. The Spaniards attributed their military success to their god, just as native people did when they were victorious in warfare. The conquest itself thus was a compelling endorsement of the efficacy of Christian worship. The new god was obviously more powerful than the old ones, and many people came to accept the Christian view that their old deities were demons unworthy of service (Figure 5.6).

Another important factor was the Spanish policy regarding indigenous rulers. The native nobles were allowed to retain their rank and position and to hold government offices at the city and town levels. However, Spanish officials were more

Figure 5.6   This relief by a native sculptor decorates a sixteenth-century chapel in San Andrés Calpan, now in the state of Puebla, Mexico. It shows the archangel Saint Michael's victory over the Devil. This story was told to native people as an explanation for the origin of their gods, whom the friars claimed were really devils. Photo provided by authors.

willing to support and cooperate with local rulers who showed themselves to be devotees of Christian worship. Those who failed to accept Christianity soon found themselves passed over in favor of young men from the friars' schools, who knew how to read and write and could speak some Spanish. Some of these upstarts were not even born into noble rank! Within a generation, the indigenous nobility had been brought into the Church, and the common people tended to follow the example of their leaders.

Some scholars have suggested that Mesoamericans were relieved to give up the more bloody aspects of their religion, such as human sacrifice, and to turn from their cruel gods to the compassionate figures of Christ and the saints. There may be some truth in this view, but it is difficult to assess how much of a factor this was. For one thing, human sacrifice had been most closely associated with the cult of war, which became obsolete as Spanish rule turned traditional enemies into peaceful neighbors. Many of the old gods had been relatively benevolent providers of water, food, health, and children. The relationship between the native communities and their new Christian patron saints retained, and still retains today, a contractual character, according to which the community provides service in exchange for the saint's protection and support: No reward is bestowed without adequate payment.

But we can say one thing with more certainty. As the native people became more and more impoverished and oppressed, the Christian teachings that made a virtue of poverty and promised an easier existence after death became meaningful to people whose ancestors had never thought in those terms. Indian Christianity developed into a religion of the poor, and the words with which Jesus of Nazareth had challenged the status quo of an earlier colonial regime became readily available tools of protest.

Similarly, the Virgin Mary's compassionate, entirely benign, maternal character was new to native religion but struck a chord among people who desperately needed a friend in high places, someone to present their case in heaven just as lawyers did in the colonial courts to which people took their earthly disputes. Devotion to her also allowed people to perpetuate some degree of the gender complementarity and nature-based symbolism (light, flowers, birds) that had characterized their earlier religion (for the Mesoamerican view on women, see Chapter 12). One advocation of the Virgin, Our Lady of Guadalupe, developed during the colonial period into a principal devotional focus. The colonial history of this devotion is outlined in Box 5.1.

The missionary friars, though at first thrilled at the Indians' enthusiastic reception of Christian worship, soon were disillusioned by what they perceived as a superficial conversion. To them, all Indian worship was either Christian or pagan; either the Indians had truly converted, or they remained in thrall to the Devil. They did not understand that the Indians could be perfectly sincere in their devotion to Christ and yet continue to mingle with their Christian practices elements that the friars considered to be idolatrous. Nor did they understand the extent to which Christian devotions took on indigenous characteristics when translated across cultures, just as native practices labeled as pagan took on new meanings when redirected toward Christian figures. They did not understand that native spirituality was closely linked

Box 5.1   The Virgin of Guadalupe

The popular story associated with this cult asserts that it began in 1531 when the Virgin appeared several times to a Nahua commoner named Juan Diego. Intercepting him as he walked past the hill of Tepeyacac, on the lakeshore north of Mexico City, she spoke to him in Nahuatl and told him to go to the bishop, who at the time was the Franciscan friar Juan de Zumárraga, and to ask that a shrine be built for her on that site. The bishop did not believe Juan Diego and insisted that he bring some sign from the Virgin. She then had Juan Diego gather into his mantle the flowers that were blooming on the hillside. When he shook out his mantle in front of the bishop, the Virgin's image appeared miraculously impressed upon the cloth. Zumárraga kneeled before it, and soon a new shrine was built to house the image. According to tradition, this cloth image is the same one revered today at the basilica at Tepeyacac, which now lies in the northern part of Mexico City's huge urban sprawl.

Controversy has long surrounded the origins of this cult, for authentic sixteenth-century documents supporting the Juan Diego story have never been found. The date of the shrine's origin is unclear, though it was surely founded by Spanish devotees of the original Virgin of Guadalupe, Spain's principal shrine to the Virgin Mary. The cult image at the Spanish shrine is a statue of the Madonna and Child. The first cult image in Mexico may have been a copy of this statue, later superseded by the cloth image known today. In contrast to Spain's Guadalupe, this image depicts the Virgin of the Immaculate Conception: She stands alone, hands joined as if in prayer, upon a crescent moon and surrounded by beams of light.

The Mexican shrine first became popular in the mid-1550s, when significant numbers of Spaniards from the city started going there to worship. One document states that the cult image that these Spaniards were revering had recently been painted by a native artist. Stylistically, the cult image does closely resemble the work of native artists from the mid- to late sixteenth century, much of which was based on woodcuts imported from Spain. These artists sometimes painted religious images on cloth. By the late sixteenth and early seventeenth centuries, people were claiming that the image had miraculously cured various illnesses and injuries.

Another popular claim, that the shrine stood on the site where an Aztec mother goddess named "Tonantzin" had previously been worshipped, such that the identity of this goddess merged with that of the Virgin, is also impossible to substantiate. Tonantzin is not the name of any goddess but rather an honorific title ("our dear mother") that Christianized Nahuas used for the Virgin Mary. It is possible, though, that some preconquest shrine did stand on this site. It was by no means unusual for colonial chapels and churches to be built on or near the ruins of preconquest temples.

The Juan Diego story was first published in Spanish in 1648 and in Nahuatl the following year. Both editions were the work of creole priests; the author of the Nahuatl version, Luis Laso de la Vega, may have had some assistance from a native speaker of the language. The basic outline of the story bears a strong resemblance to European legends about miraculous images. Apparently, this basic legend form was adapted to fit the Mexican context and an image that already existed, and to which people were attributing various miracles.

Despite the popular belief that the shrine immediately became a focus of native religious devotion, it appears from historical records that Indian participation in the cult was limited until priests began, in the later seventeenth century, to propagate the cult in native communities. Until this time, as James Lockhart has noted, Indians would have had little interest in a saint's cult whose focus lay outside their own communities and whose shrine was not under native jurisdiction. Native people participated avidly in devotion to the Virgin, but they preferred their own local images housed in their own churches and tended by their own confraternities.

However, by the late seventeenth and eighteenth centuries, the old community boundaries were weakening; many Indians spoke Spanish as well as their native language; and many were spending long periods outside their own communities, working as wage laborers. Away from

(continued)

(continued)

home, they interacted as individuals with Spaniards and with Indians from other communities. When their priests encouraged them to take up the Guadalupan devotion, they could now identify with a cult that represented the larger colonial society centering on the capital city, and that spoke to them as individuals and as Indians rather than as members of local ethnic groups.

During Mexico's struggle for independence, the cult began to serve as a focus of national identity. Today, the Virgin of Guadalupe is viewed as a mestizo or Indian woman, the "dark" *(morena)* virgin. The story of her apparition to a humble Indian is an important national myth, symbolizing the merging of Spanish and Indian cultures, under divine sanction, into the Catholic and mestizo nation. Papal decrees have named Guadalupe the queen and patroness of Mexico and empress of the Americas. John Paul II canonized Juan Diego in 2002. (See Chapter 14 for more on the cult.)

to collective experiences generated by elaborate ritual, rather than to private prayer and contemplation.

The friars attributed the shortcomings they saw in native religion to shortcomings of the Indians themselves. They characterized the Indians as weak and sensual, childish, more attracted by outward appearances than by inward meanings. Blind to the spiritual aspects of native religion, they concluded that the Indian personality lacked a spiritual dimension. Recall that the friars holding these views were the Indians' staunchest defenders, far less prejudiced against them than were most other Europeans in the colony, many of whom equated the Indians with brute animals.

This view of the Indians echoed the attitude that many urban and educated Europeans took toward people of the lower classes, especially rural peasants. By labeling the Indians in this way, the friars placed them into a familiar category. They could then talk about, preach to, and interact with Indians according to the same tactics they would use with uneducated peasants in their European homelands. They could thus, in a sense, deny the immense cultural differences separating them from the native peoples.

The friars' attitude had other important implications. Of most significance, the belief that the Indians were spiritually inferior justified a policy of keeping them out of the priesthood. With very rare exceptions, Indian men in colonial Mesoamerica were not allowed to become priests. Indian women were only rarely allowed to become nuns, even though some chose to live like nuns and even entered convents as servants and companions to the more privileged daughters of Spaniards. This policy reinforced the colonial status quo, helping to keep the Indians in a dependent, inferior position relative to Europeans and their descendants (the same exclusionary policy applied to persons of mestizo and mulatto background).

COLONIAL SOCIETY

The social structure of colonial Mesoamerica was based on the hierarchical ranking of categories of people who were defined in ethnic and racial terms. We have seen that in the wake of the *reconquista* in Spain, the Spaniards became increasingly intolerant of anyone who was not Catholic, and from this intolerance the doctrine of *limpieza de sangre* (purity of blood) was born. In Spain, anyone who could not demonstrate that he or she was descended from pure Christian stock, untainted by Jewish or Moorish blood, was unable to hold noble status and was prohibited from taking part in many other activities.

In the New World this intolerance translated into legal discrimination against people of mixed ethnic ancestry, and a complex nomenclature was developed to deal with the wide array of possible backgrounds that any individual might have. During the course of the Colonial period the number of categories soared, perhaps numbering in the hundreds. These different categories were called *castas,* or castes (Figure 5.7). Skin color was of prime importance in the ultimate determination of one's status, and the possibilities for upward mobility were certainly higher for individuals with lighter skin.

We should point out, though, that these discriminations were based not on a biologically or genetically based concept of "race" but on legalistic categories. As the colonial overlords of the land, Spaniards enjoyed the highest level of legal privilege. Indians, as the original inhabitants of the land, had claim to legal rights, including some special privileges. African slaves had no recognized legal rights, but free persons of African or partially African descent were citizens of the colony with some legal status. Determining the status of persons of mixed ancestry was a thorny legal problem. Since the darkness or lightness of a person's skin happened to correspond, to some extent, to these status levels, it became a convenient index to a person's place in the social and legal hierarchy.

Historian Magnus Morner has reduced the number of *castas* to six broad categories: Peninsular Spaniards, Creoles, Mestizos, Mulattoes–*Zambos*–Free Blacks, Slaves, and Indians. At the top of the *casta* hierarchy were pure-blooded Spaniards who had been born in Spain. Referred to as "peninsulars," because they had been born on the Iberian Peninsula, members of this group almost always held the best positions, in both civil and religious life, and they were the most prestigious members of the community.

Creoles had the same ancestry as the peninsular Spaniards, but because they were born in the New World, they were relegated to a lower status than were peninsulars. This secondary status reflected the belief among Europeans that the American climate and general environment was detrimental, rendering anyone born there inherently inferior, even if one's parents were from Europe. This belief functioned, we may note, to help maintain the Spanish king's power, since he could continue to appoint administrators whom he personally knew and trusted. As a result, few creoles ever attained the highest church and government positions. Despite this secondary status, they enjoyed a privileged position in colonial society and belonged to the ranks of the colonial aristocracy, particularly in the more provincial areas.

Ranking well below the creoles in social status were the mestizos, the offspring of Spanish and Indian parents. In most cases, mestizos had a Spanish father and an Indian mother. During the years of Spanish exploration and invasion, it was quite common for Spanish men to take Indian women as lovers and occasionally as wives

Figure 5.7 These paintings are from a series illustrating different *castas*, or social and ethnic categories, in eighteenth-century New Spain. (A) A Spanish man with an Indian woman produce a mestizo child; (B) the child of a Spanish man with an African woman is a mulatto; (C) a man of African descent and his Indian partner produce a *sambaigo*, a category also called *zambo* or *sambo*. Pedro Alonso O'Crouley, *A Description of the Kingdom of New Spain*, ed. and trans. by Seán Galvin. San Francisco, CA: John Howell Books, 1972.

(particularly when the woman came from a noble Indian family). But from the beginning, mestizos were discriminated against: They were prohibited from holding *encomiendas,* and they were not allowed to hold certain public offices. Generally, they were not allowed to enter the priesthood. Although some mestizos—primarily those descended from prominent conquistadors—held comfortable positions in colonial society, the large majority were poor and uneducated.

Mulattoes, the offspring of Spanish and African parents, occupied a lower position in colonial society than did mestizos. For many legal purposes, mulattoes occupied the same position as did free Africans and so-called *zambos,* who were the offspring of Africans and Indians.

Occupying the bottom rungs in society were the African slaves. The holding of enslaved Africans remained legal in New Spain until independence from Spain was won in 1820, although the slave trade diminished after the mid–seventeenth century. Most Spanish and creole families throughout the colony had African slaves in their households; large numbers were exploited as laborers in coastal plantation regions and in mining areas.

Where Indians fit into this hierarchy is somewhat problematic. In some places and times, they were treated even worse than slaves. For example, Indians were sometimes worked to death in the mines, their lives being considered of no value; owners of slaves would, at the very least, seek to protect their investment by keeping their workers alive. For the most part, however, the status of black slaves was, indeed, lower. In fact, members of the native nobility sometimes had African slaves in their households.

Although Indians had low social status and were looked down upon by anyone who could claim at least some Spanish descent, they did have some legal rights and protections not available to other residents of the colony. For example, they were able to govern their own communities, they maintained community ownership of land, and they were exempt from prosecution for religious crimes. They also were obliged to pay tribute to the Crown, which other persons, though subject to Church tithes and other taxes, did not have to do. Indians had a unique status in the colonies: They were, in effect, wards of the Church and Crown, and as such were to be protected from unscrupulous colonists to the extent that this was possible.

Although all Indians were included in this single legal category, there were complex internal divisions within native society. The Spaniards, coming from a hierarchical society themselves, were quick to recognize the existence of a native nobility. Particularly in the early part of the Colonial period, the Spaniards relied heavily on native elites to implement colonial policies. In return for their cooperation, members of the native nobility were given special privileges that set them apart from the common people. They were granted coats of arms and were allowed to wear Spanish dress, to carry firearms, and to ride horses.

LIFE IN THE CORPORATE COMMUNITY

Under colonial rule, the Mesoamerican region remained culturally diverse, its native people speaking many languages and pursuing a wide variety of local customs. Native communities were all subjected to similar influences from the Church and the colonial administration, but the ways that they responded—accepting some of these influences, reshaping others, and rejecting still others—varied considerably across colonial Mesoamerica.

Our knowledge of indigenous life in colonial Mesoamerica has been greatly expanded over the last few decades, thanks to pioneering studies of original documents written by Indians in their own languages. These sources include historical annals, city council records, wills, bills of sale, and court testimony. The largest number of documents are in Nahuatl, but important records exist in many other languages as well. (See Chapter 6 for a more extensive discussion of native-language texts).

Historian Nancy Farriss has described Indian life under colonial rule as "the collective enterprise of survival" (Farriss 1984). This phrase is useful because it focuses our attention on two points. First, for those Indians who remained in the native towns, life remained very much oriented toward the community as a corporate entity. Most land was held in common by the community as a whole or by its constituent wards. Government officials were selected by the community and were expected to use their office for the community's benefit, not for personal prestige or financial gain. The most important religious events were community affairs.

Perhaps of most significance, people drew their primary sense of identity from their membership in a particular community. The concept of community was very strong; that is, the "idea" of community was highly developed and associated with powerful emotional ties. This social and territorial unit, which the Nahuas called the *altepetl,* the Yucatec Mayas called the *cah,* and the Mixtecs called the *sina yya,* had deep roots in preconquest times. Though often referred to in English as a "city-state," the traditional corporate community was often not very large or very urbanized. What was more important was the idea of a group of people who shared ancestral rights to a particular piece of land, which they occupied as a settled and permanent community. They shared an identity based on their association with this particular place. Most people married within their own community. People thought of themselves not as Indians, or Nahuas, or Zapotecs, but as Teposcolulans, or Tlapanecans, or Pantitecans, depending on whatever their home community happened to be called.

The second point is that these corporate communities were engaged in a struggle to survive. Spanish colonization had devastating effects not only on population levels but also on all aspects of native life. The political system was reorganized so that native people had no power beyond their own communities. The economy was reorganized in order to siphon wealth away from the native people and into Spanish hands. A European worldview and Roman Catholic religion made significant inroads, even though they never completely supplanted native belief systems. In order to survive, native peoples had to make tremendous changes and adaptations in their lifestyle and to develop complex strategies of self-defense and mutual support. This is not to say that life in native communities was always harmonious, with everyone working together for the good of the community. Conflicts within communities—between individuals, kinship groups, or political factions—over access to power and resources were common.

But the native communities did survive through the Colonial period and in many cases up to the present day. We can attribute at least part of that success to their collectivist orientation. By working together for their mutual support and often presenting a united front against outside forces, the townsfolk helped to ensure the survival of the community as a whole. At the same time, however, this strong community affiliation tended to prevent people from reaching across their borders and forming broader alliances to address common problems.

Community Government

The colonial authorities grouped the native communities into townships called *municipios*. The largest settlement in each *municipio* was designated as the *cabecera*, or head community. The other communities then became subjects, or *sujetos*, of this head community. For administrative purposes, jurisdiction trickled down to the subject towns through the governing officials of the *cabecera*. In turn, tribute payments, legal disputes, and other matters passed first from the subject towns to the *cabecera* and from there to higher, Spanish-controlled, levels of administration. It is interesting that although Spanish administrators viewed this organization in terms of a hierarchy of greater and lesser towns, native people took a different view. For them, each town was essentially an equal and independent unit of the same type. The *cabecera* had certain rights and duties for the sake of convenient administration, but generally it was not seen as inherently dominant over the other towns around it.

The colonial administration, by incorporating the native community into its structure, helped ensure the survival of that institution. One could argue that the Spanish rulers caused it to survive, that they kept the native communities intact precisely because their existence facilitated the colonial program of indirect rule. It was easier for the Spanish authorities to allow the native communities to govern their own local affairs than it would have been to introduce an entirely new sociopolitical organization at all levels of native society. For Indians to identify with their local communities, rather than uniting more broadly along class or ethnic lines, also served the Spanish strategy of "divide and conquer."

But we can also look at this arrangement in another way. The native people probably would not have tolerated the complete dissolution of their communities. The Spaniards would have had to contend with constant rebellions and uprisings; perhaps they would have been driven out of Mesoamerica completely. The system that developed was a compromise. Native people gave up the intercommunity, regional patterns of integration that had existed at the time of the conquest, which were inherently weaker than local affiliations and were quickly undermined by colonial policies. But the Spaniards acknowledged the status of the individual community as a self-governing entity with rights to its communal property. If they had not, there might have been no colony.

In the early colonial years, political power within native communities was wielded by members of the traditional ruling families, descendants of the pre-Hispanic *tlatoque* in Nahua regions, the *halach uinic* in Yucatán, and the *yaa tnuhu* in the Mixtec area, as well as members of other high-ranking noble families. These leaders came to be called *caciques* by Spaniards who had learned this word for "chief" from the Arawaks of the West Indies and applied it to the leaders of native communities throughout the Spanish colonies. Within a few decades of the conquest, however, the Spaniards imposed a system of community government that was based on the model of town government in Spain.

By the mid–sixteenth century, native communities were governed by a municipal council called a *cabildo* (Figure 5.8). The *cabildo* consisted of a hierarchy of offices. Men from the community were elected to these offices, typically for terms of one year. In theory, all tribute-paying men of the community, that is, all married men and widowers, had the right both to hold office and to vote in *cabildo* elections. In many cases, however, the traditional ruling families managed to hold a monopoly on the highest community offices. Similarly, elites often were able to manipulate elections, sometimes by limiting voting rights to those who already held office, or by allowing only members of the nobility to vote.

The most prestigious office was that of *gobernador,* or governor. After him came the *alcalde,* or judge, of which there were one or two, followed by two to four *regidores,* or councilmen. Below these there were several variously named lesser offices, whose incumbents served as notaries, constables, policemen, wardens of the town jail, church stewards, tribute collectors, and messengers. A municipal building, constructed on the town's central plaza opposite or adjacent to the church, housed the *cabildo* offices and the jail.

Figure 5.8   The members of Mexico City's native *cabildo* receive staffs of office, plus advice on good leadership, from Luis de Velasco, viceroy of New Spain from 1551 to 1564. *Códice Osuna.* Mexico City, Mexico: Instituto Indigenista Interamericano, 1947, p. 198.

At first, the traditional office of hereditary ruler was combined with the new office of governor, with no abrupt change in leadership. However, the political structure did change as the *cabildo* system took shape. The governor had to share his power with the other officials. And since *cabildo* officials were subject to yearly elections and the local priest and the local Spanish *corregidor* or *encomendero* could veto *cabildo* appointments, men who hoped to remain in office had to cooperate with the colonial administration. Unlike preconquest rulers, colonial governors often served only for short terms. But some managed to hold office for many years. For example, Antonio Valeriano, a noted Nahua scholar who spoke Latin and collaborated on some of the great works of sixteenth-century Nahuatl literature (see Chapter 6), served for eight years as governor of his hometown of Azcapotzalco and then became the Indian governor of Mexico City for twenty-three years, retiring only when his health failed. A commoner by birth, Valeriano was able to pursue this political career thanks to his marriage to a member of Mexico City's traditional royal dynasty.

According to law, *cabildo* officials were supposed to be Indians from the community. But mestizos, typically the sons of local Mesoamerican noblewomen who had married Spaniards, were occasionally elected, their ability to function in both Spanish and Indian worlds being seen as an asset by their Indian supporters. And sometimes outsiders would move into a community and gain office through aggressive politicking, as we know from court cases in which disgruntled locals challenged the authority of these usurpers.

The *cabildo* members had jurisdiction over all affairs that were internal to the community. They could imprison offenders, impose taxes and fines, assign community lands to needy families, rent out community lands to raise money, and grant permits allowing individual merchants or craftspeople to pursue their trade in the community. They could allocate community funds to such projects as building roads, maintaining the town hall and the church, and financing religious festivals. Non-Indians who wished to take up residence in the town had to petition the *cabildo* for permission, which was often denied. *Cabildo* officers also had the unpleasant tasks of collecting tribute payments and assigning local men to the labor drafts required under the *repartimiento* system. For an example of a *cabildo* in action, see Box 5.2.

If a legal dispute crossed community lines—perhaps a Spanish rancher was running cattle on community land, or people in one town were diverting water from irrigation canals claimed by another town—the case would move up to the Indian courts run by the Spanish colonial administration. Indians saw these courts as legitimate arbiters of their disputes, and their suits were often successful, even against Spanish defendants. The Indians quickly gained a reputation of being excessively litigious, ready to run before the court after the slightest injury.

Social Structure and the Family

Throughout the Colonial period, the basic division of native society into nobles and commoners remained intact. It was reinforced by the colonial government's recognition of the nobles' right to govern and to receive tribute from their vassals. Although the degree of wealth differentiation between nobles and commoners shrank over time, status differences within native society continued to be important

Box 5.2   Ana Gets a New House Site: San Miguel Tocuillan, 1583

An unusually detailed Nahuatl record of a land transfer provides insight into how colonial town government operated. This document comes from the town of San Miguel Tocuillan, a lakeshore community located near the larger town of Texcoco, to the east of Mexico City. Written by the town notary, this record was intended for local use; it is not directed to Spanish officials and assumes that the persons mentioned are known to the reader.

The text tells of a woman named Ana who, along with her husband, Juan, and their small son, also named Juan, has been staying for a month in the home of her older brother, Juan Miguel, who is a member of the town's council or *cabildo*. It is possible that they lost their former residence because of flooding: The brother's house is described as being on high ground. Ana decides to petition the council for a plot of land on which she and her husband can build themselves a new home. Her brother goes off to gather four other members of the town council, telling his sister the following: "Don't worry, younger sister. Let me go and get them right away, and you be making a tortilla or two. There's nothing for you to worry about; there's *pulque* for them to drink when they come."

Juan Miguel returns with the councilmen, and Ana invites them in and serves a snack. After they have eaten, she asks them for a piece of the town's communal land, which she describes as belonging to the town's patron saint. Following the customary rules for polite speech, she expresses herself very humbly in this way: "I have summoned you for a negligible matter. Here is what we beg, that we might apply for a bit of the land of our precious father the saint San Miguel, for we want to put up a little hut there. I don't have many children; the only one I have is little Juan alone. May we?"

The councilmen agree to grant her request, and the entire group immediately heads out to find a suitable piece of land. Ana chooses the spot, and a square lot is measured out. The rest of the proceedings are recorded as follows:

Then Ana said, "Thank you very much; we appreciate your generosity."

Then the rulers said, "Let it begin right away; don't let the stone concern you, but let it quickly be prepared to begin the foundation."

Then Ana said, "Let's go back and you must enjoy a bit more *pulque*."

Then the rulers said, "What more do we wish? We've already had enough." And Ana wept, and her husband wept, when they were given the land.

Then Ana said, "Candles will be burnt, and I will continue to provide incense for my precious father the saint San Miguel, because it is on his land that I am building my house."

Then Juan Miguel said, "We thank you on behalf of your precious father. Let it always remain this way."

When all five lords had spoken, everyone embraced.

The notary and all five councilmen signed the document. All six men have simple Spanish saints' names as their surnames, such as Juan Miguel, but all claim for themselves the noble title "don."

An indigenous perspective pervades this account. Rather than just summarizing the results, the notary has meticulously recorded the words spoken (or allegedly spoken) by the parties involved throughout the process. This reflects the continuing importance of oral expression in native life: Written documents exist to record what people say, not to replace the spoken word with impersonal prose.

The conduct of public life is highly ceremonialized: People do not simply carry on a conversation, but give formal little speeches. The parties share food and drink before getting down to business. They treat one another with much respect. The successful petitioners weep in a ritualized display of humility and gratitude. All parties embrace at the close of business.

Religious beliefs are closely tied up with this economic transaction: The land "belongs" to Saint Michael; Ana promises to make offerings to the saint as if in fulfillment of a religious vow; and her brother invokes San Miguel as the symbolic father of the *cabildo* members.

Finally, we also see a native woman acting independently and negotiating the local political scene to her own and her family's advantage. True, as sister of a councilman Ana had an "in" with the officeholders, but rather than letting her older brother speak for her, she presents her own case. Her husband stands by and lets her do the talking. She knows the right things to do and say, and is duly rewarded: Having asked for land on which to build a "little hut," she is allowed to choose the site herself and is promised a sturdy house with a stone foundation. (Adapted from Lockhart 1991:66–74)

throughout the Colonial period. The nobility saw their wealth diminish as they lost control over resources to Spaniards and as community lands were appropriated by non-Indians. Also, some of the wealthier nobles were siphoned off into mainstream society as high-ranking women wed Spaniards and raised children who identified with the dominant culture. But in many parts of colonial Mesoamerica, marked status differences between nobles and commoners were retained (Figure 5.9).

Another long-term effect of colonial rule was the breakdown of traditional family systems in favor of a nuclear family model promoted by both Church and state. This process proceeded at different rates in different areas, with some aspects of extended family and lineage organization surviving to the present in rural regions.

Colonial authorities believed that the Indians would be easier to supervise and control if divided into small nuclear households. The authority of the elders would be reduced if their adult children were separated from their influence. Also, since tribute levels and labor drafts were assessed on the basis of how many male heads of household resided in the community, it worked to the Spaniards' advantage if young Indian men married and set up their own homes. Priests, seeking to keep young people from engaging in premarital sexual relations, also encouraged them to marry young, in their midteens, or even younger for girls. With the Church controlling the wedding ceremony and imposing new restrictions on the choice of marriage partners, family elders found their authority over kin even further undermined (Figure 5.10).

Colonialism also had an impact on gender relations. The trend toward male-headed nuclear families reduced some of the autonomy that native women had traditionally enjoyed as members of extended kin groups. The age difference between wives and husbands widened. A young girl of fourteen or fifteen, living alone with a husband a few years older, did not have the same power base as a woman of twenty wed to a man her own age and surrounded by a network of supportive relatives. Over a period of generations, the balance of power shifted somewhat in favor of male dominance. However, gender relations in native communities tended to remain more egalitarian than those that prevailed in Spanish and mestizo contexts.

This shift can be seen, for example, in Nahuatl documents from Central Mexico analyzed by anthropologist Susan Kellogg. Records from the sixteenth century show Nahua women being very active in the colonial courts, acting as plaintiffs in lawsuits and presenting their own testimony. In their wills, they pass property to a wide variety of relatives including siblings and cousins, that is, members of their own family who were not related by blood to these women's husbands. In the seventeenth cen-

Figure 5.9 These paintings from 1774 show the differences in dress between (A) Indian *caciques*, or members of the native elite, and (B) commoners. Pedro Alonso O'Crouley, *A Description of the Kingdom of New Spain*, ed. and trans. by Seán Galvin. San Francisco, CA: John Howell Books, 1972.

208

Figure 5.10 This woodcut from 1565 depicts a Franciscan priest presiding over a native wedding ceremony. The bridegroom wears the traditional native-style cape knotted over his colonial-style tunic; the bride wears the long, loose blouse and skirt characteristic of Nahua women before and after the Spanish conquest. From Alonso de Molina, *Confessionario mayor, en lengua Mexicana y Castellana,* folio 57r. Courtesy of the John Carter Brown Library at Brown University.

tury, women rarely pursued lawsuits in their own right but instead were represented in court by their husbands or fathers. And in their wills, they left nearly all of their possessions to their husbands and children, following Spanish patterns that favored nuclear family ties over broader networks of kin relations.

At baptism, every Indian child received a Spanish first name. These were always the names of Catholic saints, some of which were so popular that a small town might have many Anas, Isabels, Juans, and Pedros. Other names used by native people reflect differences in rank and the degree of Spanish influence operative in any given area. Native names came into use as individual surnames; some then became established as family surnames. These native names were passed down from one's ancestors or from preconquest naming traditions. For example, before the conquest the Nahua often referred to their daughters according to their order of birth: Tiacapan for the eldest, Tlaco for the middle one, Xoco for the youngest, and Mocel for an only daughter. In the colonial records appear women with such names as María Tiacapan, Barbara Tlaco, Ana Xoco, and Angelina Mocel. Other names derived from the day-signs of the traditional calendar: hence, Martín Ocelotl (Martin Jaguar). Some native nobles chose to use traditional lordly titles as their second names. In general, the farther people were from the centers of Spanish power, the greater the extent to which these indigenous names were maintained.

The historian James Lockhart has found that when native people did take on Spanish surnames, their usage tended to correlate with social status. High-ranking noble families sometimes adopted a name associated with the Spanish nobility, such as Mendoza, Velasco, or Pimentel. Nobles also made frequent use of the Spanish title "don" (or "doña" for women), prefixing this to their name: For example, don Diego de Mendoza was the native ruler of Tlatelolco from 1549 to 1562. Somewhat less prestigious were Spanish surnames derived from the Catholic religion, such as de la Cruz ("of the Cross") or San Miguel. And people of humbler status, or even nobles in smaller towns (such as the *cabildo* members discussed in Box 5.2), might have as their second name a typical saint's name (without the San or Santa), such that in effect they had two first names: Ana Juana, Pedro Martín. Last names of this sort were less likely to be passed along as family surnames.

One European institution that proved enormously popular with native Mesoamericans was the Catholic custom of godparenthood. In standard Church practice, a child is sponsored at baptism by a couple who then share the parents' responsibility for the child's religious education and, if necessary, material needs. As this institution was adapted by Mesoamericans, these ritual kinship ties came to focus less on the relationship between child and godparents and more on the relationship between the two adult couples. The practice is therefore called *compadrazgo*, or "coparenthood." Adults linked in this manner call each other *compadres*, "coparents" or "cofathers," and *comadres*, "comothers."

We can easily understand why this institution proved useful to the native people. The recurrent epidemics left many people widowed or orphaned. Men were often away from home for long periods because of *repartimiento* obligations or wage labor; some died or became disabled while working at dangerous tasks such as mining. *Compadrazgo* gave families a mechanism for helping to ensure their mutual survival. Parents knew that if one or both of them died, they could rely on their coparents to look after the children. It also gave people more economic security: If the whole family should fall into need, their coparents could be relied on to share whatever resources they might have. Coparents also helped to pay the costs of the children's courtship and wedding.

It was to a family's advantage to have many coparents and to have close ties with them. A pattern developed by which, instead of a child's having only the godparents who sponsored her or him at baptism, additional sponsors would be chosen at other important rituals in the child's life, especially confirmation and marriage. Parents could manipulate the system in various ways, choosing to intensify ties with a small circle of ritual kin (for example, by having the same couple sponsor a number of their children), or to develop more extensive ties by involving as many other couples as possible. They could also choose whether to seek alliances with people of their own socioeconomic status, thus promoting solidarity among equals, or to invite people of higher rank, such as local nobles or wealthy non-Indians, into their circle. This practice had economic advantages, for one could then approach this wealthier couple if in need of a loan, and they might help their sponsored child to find a job. For the higher-ranking couple, to be sought out in this way was a source of prestige.

In a sense, the native people used these forms of ritual kinship, which were approved by the Church, to compensate for the loss of their more traditional patterns of extended kinship ties. *Compadrazgo* relationships were marked by a great deal of formality and respect, and thus provided a context in which customs of polite behavior and formal speech-making, developed to the status of a fine art in preconquest times, could continue to flourish.

Economy

The economic activities that members of native communities engaged in varied tremendously across colonial Mesoamerica, reflecting both the traditional differences that had existed at the time of the Spanish invasion and the variable influence of Spanish interference in local affairs. At one end of the spectrum are the more isolated, usually highland communities, where subsistence agriculture—little changed from the pre-Columbian past—remained the dominant activity of most residents. At the other extreme are communities whose economies were transformed because they were located near Spanish population centers or in areas where Spanish enterprises came to dominate the local economy. In these cases, the introduction of new crops and new technologies, together with a foreign work ethic—reliance on wage labor—thoroughly disrupted traditional economic relations. The experience of most native communities, of course, lies somewhere between these two extremes.

The traditional agricultural system, with its reliance on the cultivation of maize and other indigenous crops, prevailed in many communities throughout the Colonial period, but it was quickly supplemented with the introduction and ready acceptance by the natives of European fruits and vegetables. Similarly, European animals, particularly chickens, pigs, and goats, were quickly adopted by Indian families. In some areas simple European agricultural technology, such as the ox-driven plow, became essential to native agriculture.

The *repartimiento* system of forced labor was clearly a disruptive influence within the Indian communities, but the concept of what was essentially a labor tax was not a foreign one for Mesoamerican Indians. As with tribute, communities had been compelled to provide labor to dominant powers, whether they be regional capitals or the powerful Aztec or K'iche' empires, in pre-Columbian times. It does seem likely, however, that the levels of forced labor under the Spaniards increased and were much more burdensome, particularly in light of the disastrous population decline that reduced the size of the potential labor force so precipitously. The decline of the *repartimiento* system cleared the way for what was a truly new form of economic relationship: wage labor.

The idea of selling one's labor for money must have seemed strange to most Mesoamerican natives when it was first introduced. We do not know what proportion of the Indians participated in this system by the close of the Colonial period, but surely a large number were compelled to work for others at one time or another. Many who had managed to survive and support families by growing enough food for their own sustenance found the situation increasingly difficult in the eighteenth century. By the mid–eighteenth century, communities that had paid tribute for over 200 years in the goods they produced were now forced to pay tribute in money. At the same time, pressures on land were also increasing, owing to larger Indian (and non-Indian) populations and increased Spanish takeovers of Indian lands. In the face of such pressures, many Indians were forced to turn to Spanish enterprises such as the local hacienda, sugar plantation, or textile factory in order to make ends meet.

Religion

Indian parishes were called *doctrinas,* or "doctrines," rather than the usual Spanish term *parroquia.* This difference in terminology highlights the continuing sense, on the part of the Spaniards, that the native people were still in the process of being indoctrinated and were not fully comparable to Spanish Christians. In general, only the larger native communities had resident priests. Smaller communities would receive occasional visits from priests who lived in other towns. On these visits the priest would celebrate Mass, baptize new babies, conduct marriage ceremonies, and hear confessions. Native people often complained about priests who neglected their duties and rarely showed up in the smaller towns, or who acted abusively, such as charging exorbitant fees for administering the sacraments, beating people, and molesting women. Priests fluent in the languages of their native parishioners were always in short supply.

The native people were able to exercise considerable control over their own religious life. Persons from the community handled many day-to-day affairs and also organized the community festivals. The most important religious official was called the *fiscal.* He acted as an assistant or deputy to the priest. The *fiscal* oversaw local matters such as teaching the catechism to children; making sure that everyone attended Mass; and keeping records of baptisms, marriages, and burials. Today these parish record books are valuable sources of information on demography, family structure, and naming patterns.

Other religious officials included the sacristan, who supervised the maintenance of the church building and its ornaments. A choirmaster, or *maestro de coro,* was in charge of musical performances (Figure 5.11). Music was such an integral part of native worship that this position brought considerable status. The choirmaster and the members of the choir, both singers and musicians, sometimes enjoyed special privileges, such as exemptions from paying tribute or the payment of a salary. However, these salaries were only a small fraction of what choir members in the Spaniards' churches received. Other minor officials, often designated even in non-Nahua areas by the Nahuatl term *teopan tlaca,* or "church people," were responsible for such tasks as preparing bodies for burial and digging the graves, cleaning the church grounds, and providing fresh flowers and other decorations. The carrying out of these various religious duties was often hampered when people had to leave their communities to find wage labor.

The most important institution in native religious life was the *cofradía,* the religious brotherhood or confraternity. Like *compadrazgo,* this was a European institution that native people took over and adapted to their own purposes. The *cofradía* was a voluntary organization; that is, members joined by their own choice. Each confraternity was devoted to some aspect of Catholic belief and was responsible for the

Figure 5.11 Two Nahua *cantores,* or choir members, rehearse their music in this native painting from the *Florentine Codex*. Native choirs sang Latin chants during Church services and also prepared music for religious festivals, when native-language songs were sung to the accompaniment of drums and other traditional instruments. *Florentine Codex,* Book 10, folio 19r. Reprinted, with permission, from Fray Bernardino de Sahagún, *Historia General de las cosas de Nueva España,* Códice florentino. Facsimile of the Codex Florentinus of the Biblioteca Medicea Laurenciana, supervised by the Archivo General de la Nación (AGN) de México, Florence, Italy, 1979.

public celebration associated with its designated devotion. A town might have one or more confraternities devoted to the Virgin Mary in her various forms (such as the Assumption, the Rosary, or the Immaculate Conception); one devoted to the Souls in Purgatory; another devoted to the Passion of Christ; another devoted to the Eucharist; and another devoted to Saint Francis or some other saint. A small village might have just two or three of these organizations, but a larger town might have a dozen, and a city would have several attached to each of its neighborhood churches.

Members of a confraternity contributed yearly dues to a communal coffer. The funds were used to pay for the funerals of any members who passed away (not a trivial matter in times of epidemic disease); to finance Masses for the souls of the dead; and to purchase the candles, flowers, costumes, and other paraphernalia needed for religious festivals that the group sponsored. The members also took care of the holy images housed in the local church. They manufactured ornate vestments and processional platforms to be used when the images were brought out of the church during festivals. They acted in a general sense as mutual aid societies, caring for impoverished or orphaned members.

Cofradías were formally instituted and overseen by the Catholic Church: The native people were not free to invent their own. However, as they operated at the local level, these organizations did allow people to organize their religious celebrations much as they chose. The collective orientation undoubtedly appealed to the native people, allowing them to come together in groups dedicated to a common purpose. The confraternities counterbalanced the authority of the priest—an isolated foreigner—with that of local groups who controlled their own funds and whose ceremonial rights and duties were inscribed in official statutes. Confraternities were especially important for women, whom the priests barred from offices such as *fiscal* and choirmaster. They were able to take on leadership roles within the confraternities; some confraternities were for women only. Thus, they could gain prestige in their communities while participating actively in religious celebrations.

The Catholic saints were regarded as community sponsors and protectors. The name of each town's patron saint was combined with the town's traditional name to yield a composite designation; for example, San Miguel Tocuillan or San Andrés Calpan. The town's identity became linked to that of the saint in the minds of its residents, as seen in the land document in Box 5.2 where the saint is treated as the owner of the town's communal property. The centering of religious devotion around community patron saints makes sense in a context where the community was the most important unit, although devotion to the Virgin Mary and Jesus was widespread (Figure 5.12).

Because they did not see any necessary contradiction between Christian worship and their own traditions, native people supplemented their Christian devotions with many other practices that were more indigenous in character or that freely combined Christian and native elements. This practice was particularly true in regard to concerns that were not adequately addressed within the rudimentary form of Christianity that the native people were taught. Issues of personal, family, and group survival were the most prevalent concerns. These were dealt with through rituals surrounding the birth of a child; through a wide range of curing techniques; and through rites intended to ensure success in agriculture, hunting, or other subsistence pursuits. Curers, midwives, and conjurers of the weather—people who were credited with control over winds, rain, and hailstorms—enjoyed considerable prestige and operated as informal religious authorities.

From the viewpoint of the Catholic priests, such practitioners were in league with the Devil. The practitioners themselves, however, often claimed that their powers were given to them by God or a saint, whom they encountered in a vision. They used formulas from Christian prayers in their incantations, and sometimes they explained misfortune in reference to Catholic supernaturals, claiming, for example, that the sick person had angered a particular saint. At the same time, they invoked preconquest deities, often using complex metaphors that masked these deities' identity behind a kind of secret language. They sometimes used psychogenic substances, such as peyote or hallucinogenic mushrooms, in their quest for supernatural knowl-

Figure 5.12 Title page from the first published Nahuatl account of the Our Lady of Guadalupe apparition legend. The title reads: "By means of a great wonder appeared the royal noblewoman of heaven, Saint Mary, our precious mother, here on the outskirts of the great city of Mexico, in the place called Tepeyacac." From Luis Lasso de la Vega, *Hvei Tlamahviçoltica . . .*, 1649. Courtesy of the John Carter Brown Library at Brown University.

edge. They made offerings at ancient shrines and in some areas continued to observe the ancient 260-day ritual calendar. Many non-Indians thought that Indian practitioners had authentic magical powers as witches and magicians, and sought them out when they wanted charms or potions, paying them for their services.

At the household level, religious devotions centered around a family altar, which in Nahuatl was called the *santocalli,* or "saints' house." Here again, Christian worship is combined with non-Christian customs. Images of saints, crucifixes, rosaries, and other religious objects were purchased and treated with reverence. But the saints' images might share the altar with an ancient figurine that had been passed down from the family's ancestors or that someone had discovered somewhere. Even an oddly shaped stone someone happened to dig up in his or her field might be placed on the altar as a manifestation of divine essence. These altars were tended with offerings of food, flowers, and incense, and the space around them was carefully swept.

One final aspect of native religious life that needs to be addressed is the ritual use of alcohol. This is a sensitive subject, because the stereotype of the "drunken Indian" is a powerful one throughout the Americas and carries with it connotations of laziness and violence that contribute to prejudices against native people. But we should not gloss over a significant issue just because it has been so often misused and misunderstood.

During the Colonial period, Spanish observers frequently expressed dismay at the disorderly public drunkenness they saw in the native communities. Priests strove to curb such behavior by preaching against it and punishing participants. But such efforts had little impact on a behavior pattern that was becoming an integral part of native religious festivals. The communal experience of religious ceremony was expressed and enhanced by collective drinking: Sharing drinks with one's fellows reinforced community ties, whereas the drunken state itself transported one beyond the mundane level of nonritual life, providing a sense of being temporarily taken over by a sacred force beyond one's control. Catholic figures—in particular, certain images of the Virgin Mary—became associated with the maguey plant, whose fermented juice, *pulque*, was the most important native brew.

Spaniards consumed substantial quantities of alcohol themselves, but they admired the man who could "hold his liquor," who might partake on a daily basis but never showed signs of losing his self-control. Indians did not share the European ideal of the independent, rational, self-determining, and self-controlled individual. They exploited alcohol's capacity to alter and dissolve people's sense of individual identity, and they chose to get riotously and publicly drunk on special occasions rather than drinking "moderately" and in private. This difference in the use of alcohol may have had more to do with the image of the "drunken Indian" than actual levels of consumption.

That alcohol provided some solace to the oppressed and some escape from daily hardships may also be assumed. We may further note that, given Spanish attitudes toward the Indians' drinking, this behavior was a form of resistance against colonialism, a refusal to obey the Spaniards' rules and to act the way the Spaniards wanted Indians to act. People who were too drunk or too hung over to labor effectively for their Spanish masters were, after all, refusing to cooperate with their own exploitation.

Unfortunately, this was a behavior pattern that also took a toll on the lives and health of native people. Traditional alcoholic beverages such as *pulque* were low in alcohol content and rich in vitamins. The Spaniards introduced wine and hard liquor, which had much higher levels of alcohol and provided little or no nutritive benefit. They also introduced the technique of distillation, which would turn maguey juice into the much stronger mescal and tequila. In the presence of these stronger drinks and in the absence of preconquest social controls over drinking, it was all too easy for native peoples, also faced with the hardships imposed by colonial rule, to become addicted to alcohol. Alcohol sometimes brought out aggressive behavior that would be directed against one's fellow Indians, often women. The corporate community was not always a peaceable place.

Native people who remained in the corporate communities faced an often diminishing resource base and onerous demands for tribute and labor. Their own officials sometimes ruled them unfairly. But they had the advantage of various support structures that helped to ensure that, although they might share their neighbors' poverty, they would be able at least to survive. Emotional ties within the community, reinforced by marriage patterns, ritual kinship, and collective religious life, provided a potent psychological armature that helped people to defend themselves against pressures for assimilation to the dominant culture.

Legal protections granted to the native communities under colonial law—most significant, the rights to their communal lands—gave them some economic security, even though they often had to go to court to defend those rights. People who left their communities merged into the burgeoning mass of Spanish speakers of mixed Indian, African, and Spanish descent; their children ceased to identify with Indian cultures or to speak the native languages. After the end of the Colonial period, many native towns also would gradually lose their indigenous character and merge into the dominant mestizo or ladino society, a process that continues to the present day. But where indigenous people do survive today, their colonial ancestors lived in these corporate communities and engaged in the collective enterprise of survival that we have described.

NATIVE REBELLIONS

Native response to the imposition of Spanish colonial rule was never passive, and in much of this chapter we have seen how Indians coped with Spanish domination in creative ways, holding on to elements of their pre-Hispanic heritage and adapting Spanish institutions to meet their own needs. But throughout the Colonial period, and right up to the present day, native groups in many parts of Mesoamerica have openly rebelled against authorities when their situations became intolerable. The following are just a few examples of native revolts that took place during the Colonial period.

We saw in Chapter 4 that the Itza Maya of the Peten effectively resisted Spanish rule until the closing years of the seventeenth century. East and northeast of Itza territory, in the area that today makes up central and northern Belize, the Spaniards also encountered strong Mayan resistance. This region initially came under Spanish control in the early 1540s, but local Mayas joined in a widespread revolt throughout the Yucatán Peninsula in 1546 and 1547. The Spaniards were determined to maintain control of the region, however, resettling rebellious Mayas into *reducción* settlements. Again, in the 1630s, rebellions broke out, culminating in a major revolt in 1638 that was orchestrated by the Indians of Tipu. Over the next forty years, Mayan communities were deserted, and the entire region was virtually free of Spanish control. Spaniards regained control of the area in the late 1670s; but for a variety of reasons, most of the Mayan population was moved to Lake Peten Itza following the Spanish conquest of the Itza. The entire region eventually came under British control.

In the town of Tehuantepec (Oaxaca), an abusive Spanish *alcalde mayor* was stoned to death in 1660 by angry Zapotecs. The rebels burned municipal buildings

Box 5.3   The Tzeltal Revolt, Chiapas, 1712

One day in May 1712, María López, a thirteen-year-old Tzeltal Mayan girl from the town of Cancuc, was walking along the outskirts of her town when she experienced an apparition of the Virgin Mary. As Agustín López, María's father, later described the encounter, the Virgin said to the girl, "María, you are my daughter." María responded, "Yes, Lady, you are my mother." The Virgin then told her, "Daughter, make a cross on this place and mark the earth. It is my will that a shrine be made here for me to live in with you." When María told her husband and parents what had happened, her mother encouraged her to tell the townspeople of the miracle, and her father erected a cross on the site that the Virgin had designated. With the support of the town's native leaders, the whole populace turned out to help build a small chapel on the site. The Virgin continued to visit María, appearing to her in a hidden room within the chapel.

María's apparition experience followed a standard European pattern: The Virgin Mary or another saint appears to a worshipper, often a shepherd boy or a young woman, on the edge of town and asks that a chapel be built on the spot. However, in eighteenth-century Chiapas, there was little chance that an Indian girl's personal religious experience would be considered authentic by the local Spanish ecclesiastical authorities. In June, Fray Simón de Lara, the Dominican priest in charge of Cancuc, heard of these events and came to investigate. He denounced the new cult as the work of the Devil and flogged María and her father with forty lashes each. However, he did not dare to anger the townspeople by tearing down the chapel.

Later that month, sixteen citizens from Cancuc went to see the bishop of Chiapas. They told him of the miracle and requested permission to maintain the chapel and have a priest say Mass there. The bishop had them imprisoned in Ciudad Real, the capital of Chiapas, and declared that he would send soldiers to burn the shrine if the townspeople did not tear it down. The religious authorities' next step was to imprison some of Cancuc's town officials and install more obedient replacements.

Meanwhile, people from other native towns were flocking to Cancuc to make offerings at the chapel and listen to María convey messages from the Virgin. María's father organized an inner circle of cult leaders. These included men from other villages, some of whom had held religious offices and had had negative experiences with Spanish priests. One, a Tzotzil man named Sebastián Gómez from the town of San Pedro Chenalho, carried with him a small statue of Saint Peter. Gómez claimed that he had gone to heaven and had spoken with the Holy Trinity, the Virgin Mary, Jesus Christ, and Saint Peter. Saint Peter had given him the authority to ordain literate Indians as priests and had told him that the Indians were now free from Spanish rule and no longer had to pay tribute. What had apparently begun as a local attempt at community religious revitalization within the framework of the Catholic Church was—because of the authorities' repressive responses—escalating into a rebellion against the Church and the Spanish colonial state. Warned that his life was in danger, Fray Simón de Lara fled the town.

The imprisoned Cancuc officials escaped and returned home, ousting the men who had been appointed in their places. The townspeople removed the religious images from their main church and took them to the new chapel. Using ceremonies that imitated the Mass and the rite of baptism, Sebastián Gómez took on the role of Indian bishop and began ordaining rebel priests. The new priests, and María herself, dressed in priestly vestments taken from the old church. María became known as María de la Candelaria, after the Virgen de la Candelaria (Candelaria is a Spanish name for Candlemas, the feast of the purification of Mary). Cancuc was renamed Ciudad Real Cancuc, symbolizing that the town was to replace the Spanish city of Ciudad Real as the political center of the region.

In early August the cult leaders sent a letter, written in Tzeltal Mayan language, around to the leaders of other communities in the region. The letter read, in part, as follows:

> I, the Virgin of Our Lady of the Rosary, command you to come to the town of Cancuc. Bring all the silver from your church, and the ornaments and bells, with all the coffers and drums, and all the books and money of the confraternities, because now there is neither God nor King.

The letter was signed, "The Most Holy Virgin Mary of the Cross."

That the cult leaders framed their call to war as orders from the Virgin Mary demonstrates how the political rebellion continued to be conceived in religious terms. Throughout the revolt, the participants held to the ceremonial forms and institutional structures of the Catholic Church. The rebel priests conducted Masses, baptisms, and marriages; the communities celebrated Catholic festivals with processions and other customary practices. The rebels were attempting to legitimize their movement by associating it with the objects, behaviors, and words that they had learned to consider sacred, while also usurping control over these symbols of authority as a way of declaring independence from Spanish rule. The attempted power reversal is well illustrated by María López's role as the cult's spiritual leader: An Indian girl represented the antithesis of the adult male Spaniards who controlled the colonial Church and government. The cult simultaneously drew on older Mayan beliefs about the supernatural; for example, one source indicates that some of the men chosen as military leaders were shamans believed to have powerful *naguales,* or spirit guardians.

In all, people from twenty native towns joined Cancuc in the revolt. Thirteen of these shared Cancuc's Tzeltal Mayan language; five were Tzotzil, and two were Chol. Two of the Tzotzil towns, Santa Marta and San Pedro Chenalho, had seen local miracle-based cults discounted and forcibly suppressed by the Church only the preceding year.

Because of the prevalence of Tzeltal speakers, the movement is often called the Tzeltal Revolt, even though some Tzeltal communities remained loyal to the Spanish king. The rebels began raiding non-Indian communities, killing priests and militiamen. Some of the women were taken back to Cancuc, where they were forcibly married to Mayan men: The Virgin had declared, through María, that in the future there would be no difference between Spaniards and natives. The rebels also attacked Indian towns that refused to join the uprising. At one point, Spanish defenders claimed to have faced an army of 6,000 Mayas, but this estimate was probably exaggerated.

An army of Spanish, mixed-race, and native militiamen eventually suppressed the revolt. Toribio de Cosío, president of the Audiencia of Guatemala, came to Ciudad Real in September 1712 to oversee the campaign. After he issued an offer of amnesty in November, a number of the rebel villages put down their arms; others were forcibly occupied by the Spanish-led army. In February 1713, the last of the rebel soldiers abandoned the cause. Cosío then supervised the execution of dozens of captured rebel leaders and the floggings of many more. Others were exiled or barred from future public office. New officials were appointed in all of the towns. Cancuc was destroyed, and its residents were forcibly resettled on a new site.

Cosío attempted to prevent further violence by issuing a series of edicts. Native leaders were forbidden to publicize any new miracles or to purchase gunpowder. The economic situation of the Chiapas highlands was also addressed: Several of the edicts were intended to limit and better regulate the economic exploitation of the Indians by, for example, reducing the *repartimiento* labor drafts imposed on some of the towns and demanding that cattle ranchers sell beef to the Indians at fair prices. These and later reform efforts had little effect, however. Ethnic relations remained polarized, and the native population remained impoverished.

Toward the end of the revolt, María López had fled Cancuc. She and other members of her family had gone into hiding near the rebel town of Yajalon. They spent the next three years in hiding, growing food for themselves, their presence known only to a few people from Yajalon who remained loyal to the cult. María continued to commune daily with the Virgin in a small chapel built by her father. Early in 1716, she died from complications brought on by her first pregnancy. Two weeks after her death, the hiding place was discovered. María's father and two other family members were arrested and executed, the last of the rebels to be put to death. Sebastián Gómez, the rebel bishop who claimed to have visited heaven, was never found. (Based on Gosner 1992:122–159; see also Bricker 1981:59–69.)

and captured Spanish weapons. With an Indian government installed in Tehuante-pec, the uprising spread to other towns, nearby Nejapa and the highland towns of Ixtepeji and Villa Alta. Indian supporters of the revolt may have numbered as many as 10,000 in over twenty towns. In a letter to the viceroy, leaders of the rebellion explained that they remained loyal to the king of Spain but were unwilling to submit to harsh treatment, excessive tribute, and the demands of *repartimiento*. Within a year, the revolt had been violently suppressed; the leaders were condemned to death, their bodies quartered and displayed in prominent places within the communities.

Priests perpetually feared that the Indians would rebel against Christianity and revert to their pagan ways. But when religious uprisings did occur, their participants usually did not try to revive the native cults of the ancestors but instead sought to form their own versions of Christianity, with their own priests. These movements sometimes began as reactions against particularly abusive or negligent priests. This desire to give an Indian face to Christian religion has its roots in the failure of the early mission Church to integrate Indians into the priesthood.

Perhaps the most well-known colonial religious rebellion is the so-called Tzeltal Mayan rebellion of highland Chiapas in 1712. This rebellion was the culmination of events that began several years earlier with roots in the almost two centuries of economic abuse by Spaniards and the development of a native Christianity that horrified some members of the Spanish clergy. Beginning in 1706, the Virgin Mary appeared to Tzotzil and Tzeltal Indians in several highland communities. In each case the Virgin offered to help the Indians, and a cult was created around her image. These apparitions happened at a time when Spanish friars and priests were increasingly intolerant of any deviation from Spanish Catholicism. Church response to the Virgin cults was swift and decisive; church officials destroyed chapels dedicated to the Virgin, images of the Virgin were removed, and Indian devotees were punished. See Box 5.3 for a fuller account of this revolt.

There were numerous other native rebellions in colonial Mesoamerica. None of them was successful for very long, and many never received widespread support. Spaniards always maintained an advantage, since they controlled the weapons, and punishment for rebels was always severe.

SUGGESTED READINGS

BURKHART, LOUISE M. 1989 *The Slippery Earth: Nahua-Christian Moral Dialogue in Sixteenth-Century Mexico*. Tucson: University of Arizona Press.

CHANCE, JOHN K. 1989 *Conquest of the Sierra: Spaniards and Indians in Colonial Oaxaca*. Norman: University of Oklahoma Press.

CLINE, S. L. 1986 *Colonial Culhuacan, 1580–1600: A Social History of an Aztec Town*. Albuquerque: University of New Mexico Press.

FARRISS, NANCY M. 1984 *Maya Society under Colonial Rule: The Collective Enterprise of Survival*. Princeton: Princeton University Press.

GOSNER, KEVIN 1992 *Soldiers of the Virgin: The Moral Economy of a Colonial Maya Rebellion*. Tucson: University of Arizona Press.

GRUZINSKI, SERGE 1989 *Man-Gods in the Mexican Highlands: Indian Power and Colonial Society, 1520–1800*. Translated by Eileen Corrigan. Stanford: Stanford University Press.

HILL, ROBERT M. 1992 *Colonial Cakchiquels*. Fort Worth, Texas: Harcourt.

JONES, GRANT D. 1989 *Maya Resistance to Spanish Rule: Time and History on a Colonial Frontier*. Albuquerque: University of New Mexico Press.

KELLOGG, SUSAN 1995 *Law and the Transformation of Aztec Culture, 1500–1700*. Norman: University of Oklahoma Press.

LEWIS, LAURA A. 2003 *Hall of Mirrors: Power, Witchcraft, and Caste in Colonial Mexico*. Durham, North Carolina: Duke University Press.

LOCKHART, JAMES 1992 *The Nahuas After the Conquest: A Social and Cultural History of the Indians of Central Mexico, Sixteenth through Eighteenth Centuries*. Stanford: Stanford University Press.

LOVELL, W. GEORGE 1985 *Conquest and Survival in Colonial Guatemala: A Historical Geography of the Cuchumatán Highlands, 1500–1821*. Montreal and Kingston: McGill-Queen's University Press.

PATCH, ROBERT 1993 *Maya and Spaniard in Yucatan, 1648–1812*. Stanford: Stanford University Press.

POOLE, STAFFORD 1995 *Our Lady of Guadalupe: The Origins and Sources of a Mexican National Symbol, 1531–1797*. Tucson: University of Arizona Press.

RESTALL, MATTHEW 1997 *The Maya World: Yucatec Culture and Society, 1550–1850*. Stanford: Stanford University Press.

SOUSA, LISA, C. M. STAFFORD POOLE, and JAMES LOCKHART (ed. and trans.) 1998 *The Story of Guadalupe: Luis Laso de la Vega's* Hueitlamauiçoltica *of 1649*. Stanford: Stanford University Press.

SPORES, RONALD 1984 *The Mixtecs in Ancient and Colonial Times*. Norman: University of Oklahoma Press.

TAYLOR, WILLIAM B. 1979 *Drinking, Homicide, and Rebellion in Colonial Mexican Villages*. Stanford: Stanford University Press.

TERRACIANO, KEVIN 2004 *The Mixtecs of Colonial Oaxaca: Nudzahui History, Sixteenth Through Eighteenth Centuries*. Stanford: Stanford University Press.

Chapter 6
Indigenous Literature
from Colonial Mesoamerica

Mesoamerican peoples living under Spanish colonial rule produced a great trove of documents written in their own languages. We have relied on some of this documentation in preparing the preceding chapters on the conquest and the Colonial period. To more fully appreciate the quantity and variety of these texts and the insight they provide into the history and culture of their authors, we here devote a chapter to the native textual genres of the Colonial period.

Literacy is something that Mesoamericans had in common with the Europeans who conquered them. This mutual recognition is well illustrated by an anecdote included in one of the first European books that told of Spanish experiences in America. Peter Martyr of Anghiera, who interviewed returning Spaniards and published their stories, heard the following account from a Spaniard named Corrales who, in Panama around 1514, had met a man from the Mesoamerican interior:

> Corrales was reading. The native jumped, full of joy, and by means of an interpreter, exclaimed: How is this? You also have books and use painted signs to communicate with the absent? And saying this, he asked to see the book in the belief that he was about to see the writing he was familiar with, but he discovered it was different. (León-Portilla 1992:317)

The native person's utterance—"you also have books"—conveys his sense of his own culture as a literate one and the importance he placed on this fact. He and the Spaniard, unlike the native people of Panama among whom they found themselves, understood the nature and value of books.

The roman alphabet would transform Mesoamerican literacy, even though writing remained the province of elites and stayed closely tied to oral performance. Alphabetic writing was a more efficient, though less aesthetically appealing, method of recording the spoken word than the traditional pictorial systems. The friars who taught the alphabet to their native students adapted it as well as they could to the sounds of the native languages, though features such as tone and vowel length were often omitted. Native people used the same words for books, documents, scribes, paint or ink, paper, and the act of writing whether pictorial or alphabetic conventions, native or European paper, were employed. As they did with other aspects of European culture introduced by the colonizers, Mesoamericans took alphabetic writing and made it their own, adapting it to their own needs and employing it as a tool for their own survival.

Before looking at colonial texts, we will look briefly at surviving pre-Columbian literature.

PRE-COLUMBIAN LITERATURE

In Mesoamerica's tropical environment, paper decays quickly if discarded or buried. A handful of texts painted on paper survives from the Postclassic period. The only texts that survive from more ancient times are those inscribed on more durable media: stone; ceramics; bones; shells; and the walls of caves, tombs, and buildings. The largest corpus of such inscriptions is that of the Classic Mayas. Classic Mayan texts deal primarily with historical information, particularly the genealogies and exploits of rulers. This concern with elite personages extended to the inscribing of their personal effects with messages like "this is Ruler So-and-so's chocolate cup." Such a text hardly constitutes a work of literature, but some Mayan inscriptions include hundreds of glyphs. The Hieroglyphic Stairway at the ancient city of Copán, Honduras, the longest stone inscription in the Americas, has approximately 1,300 glyphs.

Mayan scribes set their human protagonists into grand cosmological schemes that span millions of years. The texts tie the actions of actual Mayan leaders to those of primordial deities and to the movements of the moon, stars, and planets. The rulers claim to be descended from deities and to share their birthdays. They assert that their deceased parents and other ancestors have themselves been deified. At the same time, actual historical events such as accession to the throne or the designation of an heir are recorded with precise historical dates. Such glorification of human rulers obviously functioned as political propaganda. But the texts also reveal ancient Mayan views of the cosmos and the nature of their historical consciousness, which cast human history in mythological terms. One such text is shown in Figure 6.1.

Only fifteen books, or fragments of books, are known to survive from preconquest Mesoamerica. Most of these were taken to Europe soon after the Spanish invasion of Mesoamerica and preserved as curiosities. Eventually they found their way from private hands into libraries in England, France, Germany, Austria, and Italy.

These manuscripts are usually called codices (singular, codex). The term "codex" originally meant a manuscript with its pages sewn together on one side. But since the late nineteenth century, scholars of Mesoamerica have used this term to designate any pictorial (or combination written and pictorial) manuscript executed in an indigenous artistic style. Early colonial pictorial manuscripts are included in this designation.

Figure 6.1 This Classic Mayan relief sculpture, carved at the ancient city of Palenque in A.D. 722, shows the apotheosis, or transformation into a deity, of Kan-Xul, a ruler of Palenque. Kan-Xul is depicted dancing his way out of the underworld to join his mother and father in the heavens. Dumbarton Oaks Research Library and Collections, Washington, D.C.

Each codex has a name derived from its location, discoverer or former owner, place of origin, or some other criterion.

The codices were constructed of paper made from the bark of a type of fig tree, or of deer hide. The paper or leather was coated on both sides with a layer of gesso or plaster of paris. This provided a smooth, white surface on which to paint. Each codex consisted of a single long, rectangular strip, made by attaching together numerous pieces of paper or hide. This strip, called a "tira," was painted on both sides and then was either rolled up like a scroll or, more frequently, folded up accordion-style into a type of book known as a screenfold. A cover made of wood or leather protected the book.

The fifteen preconquest codices divide into three groups based on their style and area of origin. Five of them comprise what is known as the Borgia Group, named after its largest and most beautifully executed member, the *Codex Borgia*. These codices come from somewhere in central Mexico, probably to the south and east of the Mexico City area and very likely a Nahuatl-speaking region. They date to shortly before the Spanish invasion. All of them are screenfold books of ritual and divinatory character. Their content focuses on the 260-day ritual calendar, its use in prognostication, and the deities and religious rites associated with the different days (Figure 6.2). Other calendrical cycles are also represented, particularly the cycle of the planet Venus, which was identified with the deity Quetzalcoatl.

One of the codices in the group, the *Codex Laud,* includes a series of twenty-five pictures to be used for advising couples who planned to marry (Figure 6.3). Each picture shows a man and a woman, depicted with different features, poses, and gestures and accompanied by different objects. The diviner would add together the numerical signs of the prospective bride's and groom's birth dates in the 260-day ritual calendar. This would yield a number from 2 to 26. He or she would then consult the corresponding picture in this section of the codex and make a pronouncement regarding the couple's future prospects. Given the ambiguous nature of the pictures, the diviner could make a wide variety of predictions combining the interpretation of the signs with knowledge of the two individuals and their families.

Another of the codices, the *Fejérváry-Mayer,* shows on its first page a map of the world, as Mesoamericans conceived of it (Figure 6.4). Space is divided among four quadrants representing the four directions. In the space at the middle stands the fire deity, who stands at the *axis mundi* or center of the cosmos, just as the hearth lay at the center of the Mesoamerican home. Each of the four directional quadrants

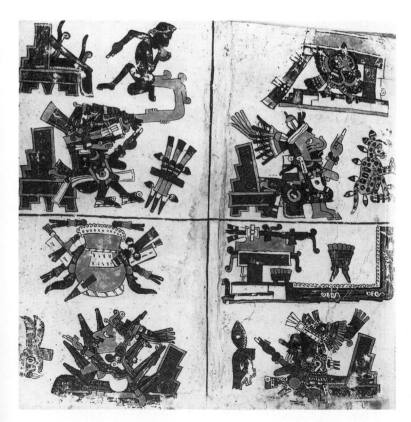

Figure 6.2 *Codex Borgia.* On this page of the screen-fold book are depicted the deities associated with four of the twenty day-signs in the 260-day calendar. Reprinted with permission from *Codex Borgia.* Graz, Austria: Akademische Druck- und Verlagsanstalt, 1976, folio 12.

Figure 6.3   *Codex Laud*. A page from the marriage prognostication tables. Reprinted with permission from *Codex Laud*. Graz, Austria: Akademische Druck- und Verlagsanstalt, 1966, verso of folio 11.

contains a male-female pair of deities, one of the sacred world-trees that held up the sky, and a sacred bird representing the heavens. Additional trees stand at the inter-cardinal points. The day signs of the 260-day ritual calendar are arranged about the perimeter. Five of the twenty signs are associated with each of the four directions; 260 small circles represent the individual days in the count. In such a manner, time and space, history and geography, were united in a single vision of creation.

The second group of surviving codices comes from the Mixtec civilization in what is now the Mexican state of Oaxaca. There are six of these, and they are known, after one of their number, as the Nuttall Group. Two of these manuscripts, the *Codex Nuttall* and the *Codex Vienna,* are believed to have been sent by Hernán Cortés to Emperor Charles V. Two others, the *Codex Colombino* and the *Codex Becker I,* remained in Mixtec hands until they were used as evidence in legal suits over land rights, the *Colombino* in 1717 and the *Becker* in 1852. Another, the *Codex Selden,* continued to be added to during the Colonial period, up to about 1560.

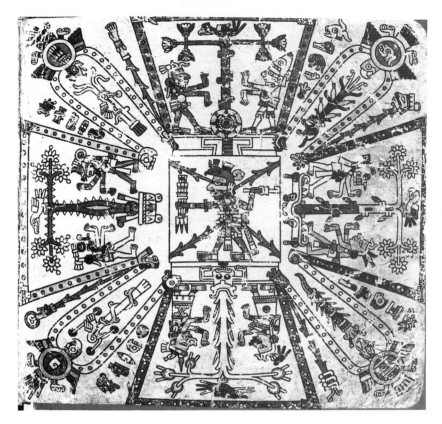

Figure 6.4 The frontispiece of the *Codex Fejérváry-Mayer,* depicting the layout of the earth and the spatial distribution of the ritual calendar's 260 days. Reprinted with permission from *Codex Fejérváry-Mayer.* Graz, Austria: Akademische Druck- und Verlagsanstalt, 1971.

These Mixtec codices are predominantly genealogical and historical in content. They tell the history of the ruling dynasties of particular towns and cities in the Mixtec region, including the exploits of various individual rulers, both male and female. These histories, however, include many elements of myth and ritual. The historical personages are shown engaging in religious rites and consulting priests and diviners. The mythological origins of the dynasties are also represented, with the lineage founders being, for example, born out of trees or out of the earth. An exception to this pattern is the *Codex Vienna,* which is genealogical on one side but on the other is devoted to mythology, particularly the story of the deity Nine Wind, the Mixtec version of the god that the Nahuas called Quetzalcoatl (Figure 6.5).

The third group consists of four manuscripts that come from the Mayan region. One of these, the *Codex Madrid,* consists of two parts that were formerly considered to be two separate manuscripts. Another, the *Codex Grolier,* emerged from a private collection in 1971. It had reportedly been discovered by looters in a dry cave, and

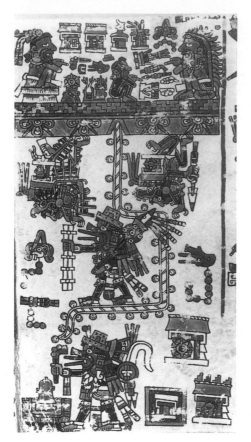

Figure 6.5   This scene from the *Codex Vienna* depicts part of the story of Nine Wind, the Mixtec equivalent of the Aztec deity Quetzalcoatl. Reprinted with permission from *Codex Vindobonensis Mexicanus I*. Graz, Austria: Akademische Druck- und Verlagsanstalt, 1963, folio 48c.

some scholars believe that it may be a forgery. The Mayan codices, like the Borgia Group, are ritual and divinatory in content. The most famous and complete one, the *Codex Dresden,* is thirty-nine leaves in length and is believed to date to the thirteenth century A.D. (Figure 6.6). It is particularly notable for its complex and very accurate astronomical calculations relating to lunar and solar eclipses and the cycles of Venus and Mars.

Thousands more of these Precolumbian books might have come down to us if not for the repressive policies of the Spanish colonial regime. Colonial authorities confiscated and burned many native books, thinking that the Devil's hand lay behind the strange pictures and unfamiliar writing. The religious rituals that went along with some of the texts were also suppressed. With no one performing these rituals, there was no incentive to replace the confiscated texts. Native peoples who wanted to keep their ancient books had to hide them. In these hiding places the books often rotted away or were eventually forgotten. In some places, though, books of divination survived along with the shamans who consulted them.

Figure 6.6 *Codex Dresden.* Venus rises in the east as morning star. At bottom is the maize deity, sacrificial victim of the vengeful star: Crop failure may be expected at this time. Reprinted with permission from *Codex Dresdensis.* Graz, Austria: Akademische Druck- und Verlagsanstalt, 1975, folio 48.

THE COLONIAL CODICES

Native people continued to create pictorial manuscripts during the Colonial period, especially through the sixteenth century. Four major changes occur in the tradition. First, ritual and divinatory codices cease to be produced except when commissioned by Europeans seeking ethnographic information on native religion, mainly for the purpose of recognizing and eradicating "idolatry." Such manuscripts resemble their pre-Columbian models but functioned in entirely different contexts. Second, alphabetic writing invades the pictorial text, first complementing the pictures and gradually replacing them. Third, the native artists adopt some conventions of European art, introducing perspective, landscape, and three-dimensionality into their paintings while still maintaining a representational style easily distinguished from that of European artists. Fourth, entire new genres of pictorial manuscript are created under European sponsorship.

Although religious manuscripts were largely suppressed, or at least driven underground along with the native rituals and priesthood, there continued to be a need for other kinds of manuscripts that had long been in use. The Spanish colonial government tolerated and even encouraged the maintenance of these traditions, for a lot of information useful to Spaniards as well as natives was recorded and preserved in such texts. Spaniards accepted native documents as accurate representations of dynastic genealogies, imperial organization, and local history.

Probably the largest genre of these nonritual manuscripts that continued to be made by native people for their own use were historical accounts recording the history of a particular community. The account would deal with the origins of the group (often mythological); its migration to its current home; the founding of the community; and notable events in its subsequent history, such as the deaths and successions of rulers, wars, temple dedications, crop failures, comets, and earthquakes.

In much of Mesoamerica, these local historical chronicles took the form of a year count. A calendrical symbol representing each year would be painted along the margin. Adjacent to this the scribe would paint whatever significant event(s) happened to occur that year. For example, in central Mexican manuscripts a portrait of a seated ruler accompanied by his name glyph represented the accession of a new king; a depiction of a corpse wrapped in white cloth labeled with the same name glyph was painted for the year that that ruler died. A military victory was shown as a burning temple labeled with the name of the defeated town. A comet was represented as a smoking star, and an earthquake as a plot of ground with the calendrical symbol *ollin*, "movement," above it. If nothing noteworthy happened in a particular year, the space would be left blank. Captions in alphabetic writing may explain or elaborate upon the information shown in pictures.

Perhaps what is most striking about these year-counts is the matter-of-fact way in which they deal with the transition to Spanish colonial rule. The count passes unbroken from preconquest to colonial times. The only difference is that the noteworthy events begin to include the coming of Spaniards, baptism by Catholic friars, deaths and successions of viceroys and bishops as well as local native governors, epidemics, the building of churches, and other previously unimagined occurrences. The scribes simply copied the earlier annals and appended recent events to the traditional account. This practice shows, perhaps as effectively as any other evidence, that for most native people the Spanish conquest did not represent an end to or even a transformation of their sense of their own identity and history (Figure 6.7).

Maps are another pictorial genre that colonial authorities accepted. Native maps showed the layout of a community and the locations of its boundaries and neighbors. Artists often emphasized the local churches as the symbolic center of each town or neighborhood, and also—like preconquest documents that mapped historical information across a representation of space—often incorporated some historical and dynastic information. Such maps were sometimes prepared for use in legal disputes over boundaries or access to natural resources, or in response to government surveys (Figure 6.8).

The colonial codices that are most widely studied are those that were produced for Europeans seeking to know more about native culture and history. These manuscripts tell us not only about pre-Columbian traditions but also about the adjustments—in their daily lives and in their interpretations of the past—that native people were making as they learned to cope with their colonial circumstances.

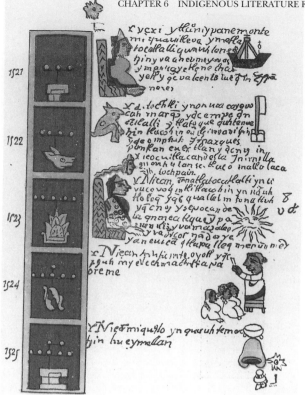

Figure 6.7 A page from the *Codex Aubin,* a year-count chronicling Mexica history from A.D. 1168 to 1608. This page records events of the years 1521 to 1525, including the succession of Cuauhtemoc as Mexica ruler, the occupation of the city by Spaniards, activities of Cortés, a solar eclipse, the coming of the Franciscan friars in 1524, and Cuauhtemoc's death. Reprinted with permission from Charles E. Dibble, ed., *Codex Aubin: Historia de la nación mexicana.* Madrid, Spain: J. Porrúa Turanzas, 1963, p. 87.

Nearly all of these "ethnographic" codices come from the Nahuatl-speaking region of central Mexico, mainly from Mexico City and its environs. This area was conquered and evangelized earlier and more pervasively than the rest of Mesoamerica. The center of the former Aztec polity as well as the Spanish colony, it was home not only to many artists but also to the Spanish priests and officials who commissioned these works. Close working relationships between friars and native artists and consultants were possible here, especially in the schools and college that the Franciscans founded. The result was a florescence of manuscript painting during the mid– to late–sixteenth century.

Most of these codices are organized around the calendar: the 260-day ritual calendar, the 365-day year (broken into eighteen "months" of twenty days each), year counts, or a combination of these. Emphasis is on the deities and ceremonies associated with each calendrical period, sometimes with additional information on non-calendrical rituals or other aspects of native culture. Pictures painted by native artists are accompanied by written glosses, usually in Spanish. A number of these calendrical books are related to one another and derive from now-lost prototypes ultimately based on the work of a Franciscan friar, Andrés de Olmos, who began his

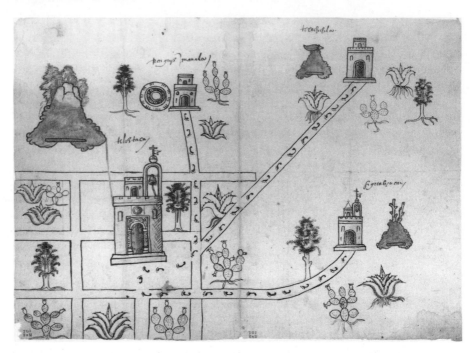

Figure 6.8 A native artist's map of the Nahua town of Tetlistaca, painted in 1581 in response to a royal questionnaire. Tetlistaca and three subject communities are represented by their churches; their names are given in alphabetic and glyphic form. Footprints mark the routes from the outlying settlements to the main town square. The local vegetation is depicted in native style, showing the roots (see also Figure 12.15). Photo courtesy of the Benson Latin American Collection, The General Libraries, The University of Texas at Austin (JGI xxv–12).

ethnographic research in 1533. Box 6.1 provides an example of one of these calendrical codices from the Colonial period.

The *Codex Mendoza*, thought to have been commissioned in the early 1540s by the colony's first viceroy, is one of the most beautiful and informative of colonial codices (Figure 6.11). Illustrated by a master artist and glossed in Spanish by a priest, the codex comprises three parts. The first two are pre-Columbian in style and based on earlier documents: One is a history of the Mexica rulers and their conquests, the second is a catalog of all the tribute those rulers demanded from each of their subject provinces. Such information was of obvious value to Spaniards wanting to know what riches they could wrest from their new territories.

The third section is unique. It deals with the life of the Mexica (Aztec) people: the upbringing of male and female children from birth to marriage (Figure 6.12), the different professions for young men, the military and the priesthood with their various ranks, the conducting of warfare, and the operation of the courts of law and the royal palace. To create this pictorial ethnography, the artist had, in a sense, to stand outside his own culture and look at it analytically, to play the role of interpreter between his own people and the foreigners who now ruled over them. The portrait

Box 6.1   Codex Borbonicus

One of the earliest colonial codices is the *Codex Borbonicus,* once thought by some to be pre-Columbian. Most colonial codices are bound along the left-hand margin like European books, but the *Borbonicus* retains the screenfold format. The first part is a 260-day calendar, painted in a style that is purely pre-Columbian except for the fact that space has been left next to the painted symbols in order that Spanish glosses may be written in, as they are in some instances (Figure 6.9).

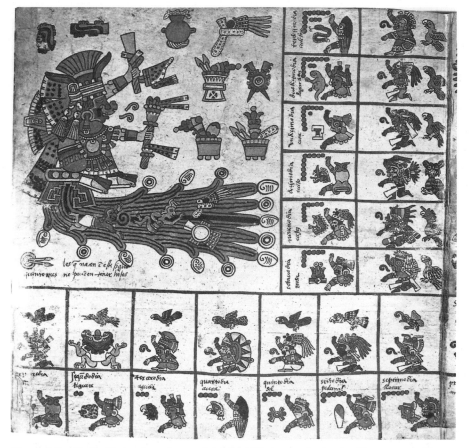

Figure 6.9   *Codex Borbonicus.* A page from the 260-day ritual calendar. The water goddess Chalchiuhtlicue, "She of the Jade Skirt," presides over the thirteen-day period commencing with the day One Reed. Reprinted with permission from *Codex Borbonicus.* Graz, Austria: Akademische Druck- und Verlagsanstalt, 1974, folio 5.

(*continued*)

(continued)

A later section of the *Borbonicus* consists of depictions of the ceremonies performed for the months of the 365-day calendar and the New Fire Ceremony, performed every fifty-two years. This was not something that pre-Columbian codices ordinarily included, so there were few conventions regarding how such a document should look. The paintings are spread out across a blank background with much space left empty; this arrangement contrasts to the very dense and even distribution of figures across the page in pre-Columbian manuscripts. Also, the artist makes some tentative and not altogether successful attempts to show perspective (Figure 6.10). The back of the screenfold is left blank, an unlikely circumstance had the manuscript been made for actual native use.

Figure 6.10   *Codex Borbonicus.* The New Fire Ceremony: Every 52 years all fires were extinguished, and a new fire was kindled in a temple near the Aztec capital. Here four priests bring wood to feed the new fire. The lower two appear to stand on the temple stairs while the upper two float in space. The artist has only partially adopted European conventions of landscape and perspective. Reprinted with permission from *Codex Borbonicus*. Graz, Austria: Akademische Druck- und Verlagsanstalt, 1974, folio 34.

he drew presents an orderly, disciplined, hierarchical society of a sort that Europeans of the time would be able to respect. The document is both a nostalgic, somewhat idealized recollection of the preconquest social order and an attempt to persuade Spanish viewers of the legitimacy of native society. Sent to Charles V, it was transported to France after French pirates attacked the Spanish fleet; eventually it ended up in the Bodleian Library at Oxford University.

Figure 6.11 Drawing of the frontispiece of the *Codex Mendoza*. The main scene represents the founding of the Mexica (Aztec) capital, Tenochtitlan, on an island in Lake Texcoco. Below this scene, two of the Mexicas' early military victories are represented. Courtesy of Frances F. Berdan. Reproduced with her permission from Frances F. Berdan and Patricia Anawalt, eds. *The Codex Mendoza, Volume 4: Pictorial Parallel Image Replicas of Codex Mendoza.* Berkeley, CA: University of California Press, 1992, p. 9 (folio 2r).

Figure 6.12 *Codex Mendoza.* Drawing of the wedding ceremony: The bride and groom sit on a new mat in the groom's house, their clothing knotted together to symbolize their union, while elderly men and women offer advice. Below, the bride is carried to the groom's house by a woman doctor while other women light the way with torches. Courtesy of Frances F. Berdan. Reproduced with her permission from Frances F. Berdan and Patricia Anawalt, eds. *The Codex Mendoza, Volume 4: Pictorial Parallel Image Replicas of Codex Mendoza.* Berkeley, CA: University of California Press, 1992, p. 127 (folio 61r).

The greatest monument of sixteenth-century ethnography is the work of a Franciscan friar named Bernardino de Sahagún. From the 1540s to the 1580s, Sahagún and a number of indigenous students and collaborators produced a series of ethnographic studies combining pictorial and textual materials, the latter not in Spanish but in Nahuatl. They interviewed experts in different fields, such as medicine, divination, rhetoric, and the ancient ceremonies. Sahagún's goal was to create an encyclopedia of native culture that not only would assist priests in eliminating "pagan" religion but also would serve as an extended lexicon for the language and a record of native knowledge that was good (in his estimation) and useful. The native collaborators, like the artist who painted the *Codex Mendoza*, wanted to present an orderly and a respectable image of their rapidly changing culture.

The culmination of the project is a document known as the *Florentine Codex*, completed in 1577 and now housed in the Laurentian Library in Florence, Italy. Its twelve books are written in Nahuatl, with an accompanying Spanish text summarizing and commenting on the Nahuatl. Though primarily a written rather than pictorial document, the small paintings by native artists found throughout the text are integral to the work as a whole. The *Florentine Codex* is the longest text in a native language from

Figure 6.13 *Florentine Codex.* A merchant family is hosting a party to celebrate the birth of a child. Women guests receive gifts of flowers and tobacco, enjoy a meal of tamales and turkey, and dance in honor of the new baby. *Florentine Codex,* Book 4, folio 69v. Reprinted with permission from Fray Bernardino de Sahagún, *Historia General de las cosas de Nueva España, Códice florentino.* Facsimile of the *Codex Florentinus* of the Biblioteca Medicea Laurenciana, supervised by the Archivo General de la Nación (AGN) de México, Florence, Italy, 1979.

Figure 6.14   *Florentine Codex.* Aztec nobles play *patolli,* a game similar to Parcheesi. The playing pieces are black beans; the men gamble on the outcome by betting their ornaments of jade, gold, and feathers. *Florentine Codex,* Book 8, folio 19r. Reprinted with permission from Fray Bernardino de Sahagún, *Historia General de las cosas de Nueva España, Códice florentino.* Facsimile of the *Codex Florentinus* of the Biblioteca Medicea Laurenciana, supervised by the Archivo General de la Nación (AGN) de México, Florence, Italy, 1979.

anywhere in the Americas and the most complete description of a native American culture created before the advent of professional anthropologists (Figures 6.13 and 6.14).

Another unique colonial document is the *Codex Badianus* or *Cruz-Badiano.* An illustrated book of herbal remedies, it explains the cures for various ailments and depicts the plants to be used in preparing the medicines. It was produced in 1552 at the Franciscan college in Tlatelolco. A native doctor named Martín de la Cruz wrote the text in Nahuatl on the basis of his own medical knowledge, which already shows some European influence. This Nahuatl text was then translated into Latin by a Nahua student at the college, Juan Badiano. Only this Latin version was included in the finished book. An unknown native artist painted the 184 pictures of plants. Sent to Spain as a gift for Charles V, the document was discovered in the Vatican Library in 1929 (Figure 6.15).

COLONIAL TRANSCRIPTIONS OF ORAL LITERATURE

Many literary compositions that had formerly been passed along through pictorial writing, oral transmission, or a combination of the two were, during the Colonial period, transcribed using alphabetic writing. As a result, we have access to a great deal of verbal art reflecting native experience before and during Spanish rule. Much of this literature is probably very similar to versions used before the Spanish invasion.

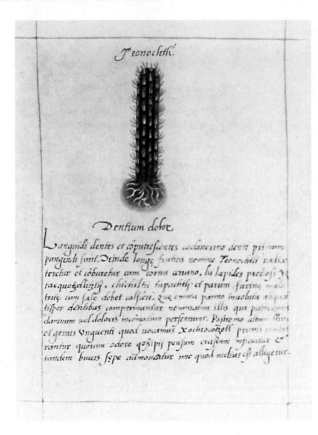

Figure 6.15   A page from the *Codex Badianus*. A species of cactus is employed in a cure for toothache. Reprinted with permission from Emily Walcott Emmart, ed. and trans., *Badianus Manuscript (Codex Berberini, Latin 241), Vatican Library: An Aztec Herbal of 1552*. Baltimore, MD: The Johns Hopkins Press, 1940, folio 17v.

However, since the texts were transcribed during the Colonial period, we can never rule out the possibility that the performers have adapted them in light of their current experiences. Nor should we assume that there was one original or correct pre-Columbian version, for all of these texts may have developed and changed over time and existed in multiple versions.

From this rich trove of literary treasures—oratory, poetry, song, myth—we have selected three works representing different regions, different literary genres, and different production contexts. We will describe these texts and give some brief excerpts in English translation.

In some cases, alphabetic transcriptions of traditional literature were executed by native people for their own use and kept within the native community. This is the case with our first example, the *Popol Wuj*, "Book of the Mat" or "Book of Counsel," of the K'iche' Mayan people of highland Guatemala. The single most important mythological text from Mesoamerica, this sacred book was written down by K'iche' noblemen between 1554 and 1558, on the basis of a native text and oral tradition. Statements made within the text imply that these men wished to preserve the story while the original version and the ability to read it still existed, but they also needed to keep the work hidden from Spanish eyes, since they lived "in Christendom now" and could no longer perform the text in its traditional ritual contexts. At the beginning of the eighteenth century, a friar working among the K'iche' made a copy of the text. This copy, the only version of the text known to have survived, eventually found its way to the Newberry Library in Chicago.

The *Popol Wuj* tells the history of the world and of the K'iche' people from the time of the earth's creation to the early decades of Spanish rule. At the beginning exist only the sky and the primordial sea:

> There is not yet one person, one animal, bird, fish, crab, tree, rock, hollow, canyon, meadow, forest. Only the sky alone is there; the face of the earth is not clear. Only the sea alone is pooled under all the sky; there is nothing whatever gathered together. It is at rest; not a single thing stirs. It is held back, kept at rest under the sky.
>
> Whatever there is that might be is simply not there: only the pooled water, only the calm sea, only it alone is pooled.
>
> Whatever might be is simply not there: only murmurs, ripples, in the dark, in the night. (Tedlock 1996:64)

Then Heart of Sky, Plumed Serpent, and other deities come together and converse in the primordial sea:

> "How should the sowing be, and the dawning? Who is to be the provider, nurturer?"
>
> "Let it be this way, think about it: this water should be removed, emptied out for the formation of the earth's own plate and platform, then comes the sowing, the dawning of the sky-earth. But there will be no high days and no bright praise for our work, our design, until the rise of the human work, the human design," they said.
>
> And then the earth arose because of them, it was simply their word that brought it forth. For the forming of the earth they said "Earth." It arose suddenly, just like a cloud, like a mist, now forming, unfolding. Then the mountains were separated from the water, all at once the great mountains came forth. By their genius alone, by their cutting edge alone they carried out the conception of the mountain-plain, whose face grew instant groves of cypress and pine. (Tedlock 1996:65–66)

The gods endeavor to create human beings who will appreciate the gods' work, live orderly lives according to the days of the calendar, and pray to them. First they create the animals, but these wander about aimlessly and are incapable of articulate speech. Two more attempts, one using wood and the other mud, also fail to yield the kind of beings the gods have in mind.

The text then digresses into what probably was originally a separate myth. This myth tells how a pair of magically conceived twin brothers defeat the nasty lords of the underworld, gods of death and sickness, and other primordial monsters. These beings had to be destroyed or constrained before the earth could be safe for human society. At the climax of the story, the twins appear in the court of the underworld lords disguised as roving acrobats. They dance and do magic tricks, which include sacrificing first animals and then people and bringing them back to life. Swept away in the excitement, the underworld lords beg that they too may be sacrificed and brought back to life. The boys kill them, but do not bring them back!

The narrative then returns to the gods who are still trying to create human beings. On their fourth try they are successful. They use a dough made from white and yellow corn, ground up by a female deity and mixed with water in which she has rinsed her hands: The oil from her skin turns into the body fat of the four men who are formed from the dough. These four men thank their creators with the following prayer. The text is built with a variety of parallel constructions, with the same or similar ideas expressed in two or more ways. For the K'iche' and other Mesoamericans, mastery of this poetic strategy signaled good literary style:

> *Truly now,*
> *double thanks, triple thanks*
> *that we've been formed, we've been given*
> *our mouths, our faces,*
> *we speak, we listen,*
> *we wonder, we move,*
> *our knowledge is good, we've understood*
> *what is far and near,*
> *and we've seen what is great and small*
> *under the sky, on the earth.*
> *Thanks to you we've been formed,*
> *we've come to be made and modeled,*
> *our grandmother, our grandfather. (Tedlock 1996:147)*

These very articulate men of corn are actually superior to what the gods intended, for they are able to see and know everything that is in the world. They are too similar to the gods themselves, and a bit too familiar, addressing them as grandparents! The gods therefore dull the men's vision, so that they are able to see only things that are close to them. As compensation, the gods create four women to be the men's wives, and the men are happy once more.

These four couples become the ancestors of the K'iche' people. The rest of the *Popol Wuj*, approximately half of the total text, deals with the migrations, wars, settlements, and ruling lineages of the K'iche'. Myth passes gradually into history, and we come at the end to the middle of the sixteenth century.

Many other works were written down at the behest of Europeans, with the resulting documents removed from native hands. Some such transactions occurred in an atmosphere of cooperation, as in the case of Sahagún's project: The friar was popular among the native people, and teams of native researchers and consultants worked together on the texts. Even in contexts like this, however, the native consultants knew that much of their traditional culture—especially in regard to religious beliefs—was considered by the Spanish priests to be idolatrous or immoral.

Book Six of Sahagún's *Florentine Codex* preserves a collection of Nahuatl orations pertaining to a genre of oral literature the Nahuas called *huehuehtlahtolli*, "ancient words" or "speech of the elders." These were formal speeches delivered on special occasions. They are packed with moral philosophy, religious teachings, and poetic devices such as metaphors and parallel constructions. The speeches were first transcribed around 1547, probably in Tlatelolco, the northern part of Mexico City.

One set of orations concerns childbirth and is particularly valuable as a window into the lives of women. Here are some excerpts from the speech that the midwife would make to the newborn baby, welcoming it to its loving family and warning it about the hardships and brevity of life on earth:

> *You have come into the world, my little one, my beloved boy, my beloved youth.*
> *(If it is a girl she said: "My beloved girl, my little one, noble lady.")*
> *You have wearied yourself, you have fatigued yourself.*
> *Your father, the lord, Tloque Nahuaque, Creator of People, Maker of People has sent you.*
> *You have arrived on earth*
> *where your relatives, your kin, suffer hardships, endure affliction,*
> *where it is hot, it is cold, it is windy.*
> *It is a place of thirst, a place of hunger,*
> *a place without pleasure, a place without joy,*
> *a place of suffering, a place of fatigue, a place of torment.*
> *O my little one, perhaps, for a brief time, you shall shine as the sun!*
> *By chance are you our reward, our recompense?*
> *By chance shall you look into the faces, upon the heads,*
> *of your grandfathers, your grandmothers, your kinsmen, those of your line?*
> *And by chance shall they look into your face, upon your head?*
> *. . .*
> *Here are your grandfathers, your grandmothers who have been awaiting you.*
> *Here, into their hands, you have come.*
> *Do not sigh, do not sorrow.*
> *. . .*
> *May Tloque Nahuaque, your mother, your father, the Maker, adorn you, provide for you!*
> *And we who are parents, shall we, perhaps, regard ourselves worthy of you?*
> *Perhaps wee as you are the Maker shall summon you, shall call to you.*
> *Perhaps you shall merely pass before our eyes.*
> *Perhaps we have had only a brief glimpse of you.*
> *Let us await the word of our Lord, my beloved child. (Sullivan 1980:46–47)*

Excerpts from another of these orations, a prayer to the rain god Tlaloc, are presented in Box 6.2.

Sometimes the transcription of oral literature involved coercion. Early in the seventeenth century, a priest named Hernando Ruiz de Alarcón ran an antisorcery campaign among Nahuas living to the south and west of Mexico City, in what is now the states of Morelos and Guerrero. This was a rural context compared with the Basin of Mexico, where most of the codices and other ethnographic documents were produced.

Box 6.2   The Prayer to the Rain God Tlaloc

The following excerpt describes the earth languishing in need of life-giving rain. The "elder sister of the gods" is the corn, sister of the rain gods. "He of the Near, He of the Nigh" is the important deity Tezcatlipoca. By the time the text was transcribed, this title was also being applied to the Christian God. Tlaltecuhtli is the earth deity.

And here it is true,
today the crops lie suffering,
the elder sister of the gods lies dragging herself along.
The crops already lie covered with dust,
already they lie wrapped with spider webs,
already they suffer, already they are weary.
And here are the vassals,
the tails, the wings [the common people],
already they are perishing,
for their eyelids are swollen, their lips are parched,
they are bony, they are bent,
they are emaciated.
They are just thin-lipped, pale-throated,
the tails, the wings.
With pallid eyelids go about the little children,
The little babies,
they who toddle, they who crawl,
they who pile up earth and potsherds,
they who sit on the surface of the earth,
and they who lie on the wooden plank,
they who lie on the cradleboard.
And already every person knows torment, exhaustion;
already every person sees anguish.
And there is none whatsoever who is left out,
for already all the little creatures are suffering.
The troupial bird, the roseate spoonbill,
they just drag their wings along,
they tumble over, they fall on their heads,
they open and close their beaks.
And the animals, the four-footed ones
of He of the Near, He of the Nigh,
they just wander about,
they just rise up upon us,
in vain they lick the surface of the earth.
And already they go crazy for water,
already there is dying of thirst,
already there is perishing,
already there is destruction.
Already the vassals, the animals perish.
And here is the one who is our mother, our father,
Tlaltecuhtli.
Already her chest is dry,
no longer can she nourish, no longer can she feed,
no longer is there anything with which she might suckle

> *that which germinates, that which lies germinating,*
> *that which is the maintenance, the life, of the vassal.*
> *And that which is life,*
> *there is no more,*
> *it has gone away, it has perished. (Sahagún 1950–1982: VI, 35–36; trans. by L. Burkhart)*
>
> The final appeal to the rain gods at the end of the oration goes as follows:
>
> *Oh master, oh precious noble, oh giver of gifts,*
> *may your heart concede it, may it do its job,*
> *may you console the earth,*
> *and all that live upon it,*
> *that travel about on the surface of the earth.*
> *I call to you, I cry out to you,*
> *you who occupy the four quarters,*
> *you the green ones, you the givers of gifts,*
> *you of the mountains, you of the caves!*
> *May you carry yourselves here,*
> *may you come, may you come to console the vassals,*
> *may you come to water things on the earth!*
> *For they lie watching, they lie crying out,*
> *the earth, the animals, the herbs, the stalks.*
> *For they all lie trusting in you.*
> *May you hurry, oh gods, oh our lords! (Sahagún 1950–1982:VI, 40; trans. revised by L. Burkhart)*
>
> The repetition, the elaborate imagery, and the tone of desperation serve not only the aesthetic purpose of creating beautiful and moving poetry. Such a text would have the power also to get Tlaloc's attention and oblige him to send the rains.

Ruiz de Alarcón arrested and punished Nahua religious practitioners, men and women who he believed were in league with the Devil. He understood enough Nahuatl to write down many of the chants these specialists used in their rites of curing and divination. The result is an invaluable collection of Nahuatl ritual poetry, though one gained under unfortunate circumstances.

The chants employ a specialized vocabulary characterized by elaborate metaphors. The practitioners personified the various phenomena involved in the ritual. They granted identities, for example, to the patient's injury or illness, the medicines being used, the fire and the offerings of incense and tobacco that were made to it, and the curer's own hands and fingers. They invoked mythological precedents for the situation at hand, thus casting it in grandiose terms and bringing the sacred power of the myth to bear on the problem.

One of the simplest of the ritual cures is this procedure that a woman named María Salome used for curing eye problems. First she addresses the pain, personifying it as a series of serpents and thus giving a concrete form to the patient's sensations.

She then threatens the serpent with the water she is about to use to wash the eye. "Jade-Skirted One" is the Nahuatl name for the female water deity: The water here is being treated as a supernatural force.

> *Well now, please come forth,*
> *1 Serpent,*
> *2 Serpent,*
> *3 Serpent,*
> *4 Serpent:*
> *Why do you harm*
> *The enchanted mirror,*
> *The enchanted eye?*
> *Lie down I know not where,*
> *Remove yourself to I know not where.*
> *But if you do not obey me,*
> *I shall call the Jade-Skirted One,*
> *The Jade-Bloused One:*
> *For she will scatter you,*
> *She will disperse you,*
> *Upon the plain*
> *She will leave you dispersed. (Coe and Whittaker 1982:234)*

In a spell for setting broken bones, a curer named Martín de Luna cast himself in the role of the god Quetzalcoatl. According to a myth recorded in the sixteenth century, this god had stolen one or more bones from the Lord of the Underworld with which to create the human beings of the present age of creation. In one version of the myth, quail startle the fleeing god and he stumbles, breaking the bones. The spell seems to allude to such an episode:

> *I am the Priest,*
> *I am the Plumed Serpent,*
> *I go to the Land of the Dead,*
> *I go to the Beyond,*
> *I go to the Nine Lands of the Dead;*
> *There I shall snatch up*
> *The bone of the Land of the Dead.*
> *They have sinned—*
> *The priests,*
> *The dust-birds;*
> *They have shattered something,*
> *They have broken something,*

But now we shall glue it,
We shall heal it. (Coe and Whittaker 1982:268–269)

The curer identifies the patient's broken bone with this primordial bone over which gods fought and from which humanity was formed. Ruiz de Alarcón dismissed these chants as a combination of superstitious nonsense and diabolical deception. However, it is now recognized that symbolism such as this can work upon the mind and yield healing effects. At the very least, such cures boost the patient's morale, which in turn contributes to recovery.

NATIVE AND MESTIZO HISTORIANS

We saw earlier that the keepers of year-count annals gradually supplemented and eventually replaced their picture-writing with alphabetic texts. But some native historians began to think about their history not as a sequence of separate episodes but in terms of a more continuous narrative, such as European historians—following a pattern established in ancient Greek and Roman times—tended to produce. Instrumental in the development of this new historical consciousness were the native men who were educated according to European models, particularly at Franciscan and Jesuit institutions. Literate in Latin, these men read the same classical sources as learned Europeans.

A few native scholars took the old pictorial chronicles and began to convert them into narrative histories that told the story of a people. Like both the pictorial records and the Old World models, these histories focused on politics and warfare, telling of the glorious deeds of the great men of the past. They also reflect the kinds of issues with which native people were especially concerned: the founding of noble lines and their dynastic history, the granting and inheritance of special titles, the patronage of deities, and the building of temples.

The authors were motivated by a desire not only to preserve information about the past but also to seek legitimacy in the present. The authors play up the roles of their own ancestors and their own communities. They sometimes seek to downplay, or to blame on other groups, practices such as human sacrifice. Some of them wrote in Spanish, clearly intending that their accounts be read by nonnative people. They present their history in a style and format that Europeans will understand and respect.

The most prolific historian to write in a native language is a Nahua who gave himself the imposing name Don Domingo de San Antón Muñón Chimalpahin Quauhtlehuanitzin. His writings—eight historical chronicles, a diary, and miscellaneous shorter pieces—comprise the largest body of native-language texts from colonial Mesoamerica that can be attributed to a single author. Most of his work dates to between 1600 and 1620. Chimalpahin was born in 1579 in the town of Chalco Amaquemecan (today's Amecameca de Juárez) in the southeastern corner of the Basin of Mexico. He spent his adult life in Mexico City, employed as a steward or sacristan at a small church. He based his writings on older documents and on interviews with relatives and acquaintances.

Chimalpahin's histories cover a time span from the twelfth century to 1620. Like other native historians, he treats this known period of the past as an unbroken sequence of years, those following the arrival of Cortés not qualitatively different from the preceding span. His accounts focus on his hometown and nearby communities, but also include extensive information regarding the Mexica (who conquered Chalco in the mid–fifteenth century), the Spanish conquest, and events in the colonial capital. Some of his writings take the form of year-count annals.

In some cases men of mixed parentage, products of unions between native noblewomen and Spanish men, wrote histories of the native communities to which they bore maternal ties. Don Fernando de Alva Ixtlilxochitl's father and maternal grandfather were Spaniards, but through his mother he was descended from Ixtlilxochitl, a Texcocan lord who supported Cortés, and also from Nezahualcoyotl, a long-lived fifteenth-century ruler of Texcoco who was an important ally of the Mexica rulers in Tenochtitlan (on Texcoco, see Chapter 3). His family had a large collection of native historical manuscripts, and on the basis of these, Don Fernando wrote several Spanish-language chronicles during the early seventeenth century. It is not surprising that he extols Texcoco and emphasizes Texcocans' alliances with the invading Spaniards. He also glorifies Nezahualcoyotl along the lines of the Old Testament's David or Solomon: Nezahualcoyotl becomes an almost superhuman patriarch, poet, philosopher, law-giver, judge, and prophet; he is even said to have believed in only one god. Other important mestizo historians are Diego Muñoz Camargo, who wrote a history of Tlaxcala between 1576 and 1595, and Juan Bautista Pomar, author of a 1582 history of Texcoco.

A particularly interesting genre of historical document comes into existence later in the Colonial period, becoming especially popular in the eighteenth century. These documents, known as *títulos primordiales,* "primordial titles," give an account of a community's founding, history, and original boundaries. They often include pictures done in a native, although not pre-Columbian, style. Some are made from particularly coarse and ragged native paper. Both the pictures and the rough paper were intended to make the documents look ancient (Figure 6.16).

In essence, these are late-colonial attempts to reclaim a historical tradition that many communities had lost. The ancient-seeming documents are meant to make it look as if the community has preserved these records ever since the early Colonial period. But the information they contain is characterized by inaccurate dates, events placed out of chronological sequence, mythological events, and other events that could not have occurred as described. Authors tried to make the community look good in Spanish eyes: The ancestors allied themselves with the Spanish invaders, and they welcomed the friars and were baptized immediately. Authorities such as Cortés or early Spanish viceroys are said to have granted the community permanent rights to certain lands.

For example, see how smoothly a Mixtec *título* from the town of San Juan Chapultepec, produced in the 1690s but "backdated" to 1523, describes the arrival of the Spaniards:

Figure 6.16   A page from an eighteenth-century "primordial title," from a Nahua village called Santa María Tetelpan, which was used to help defend the village's property in a land dispute. The four men are supposed to be ancestors who founded the community. *Coyoacan Codex, Codex Indianorum 1.* Courtesy of the John Carter Brown Library at Brown University.

When our Lord Cortés first arrived with a crowd of white people, he came to our ñuu chayu [town]. Then he came out to meet us and to name us. He received and named our yya [ruler] don Diego Cortés Dzahui Yuchi.

. . . The yya don Diego Cortés was baptized and, second, all the nobles were baptized and, third, all the commoners were baptized. . . .

. . . Then we lived together in peace with the white people, the great ones, and we gave them a place to build the big church. (Sousa and Terraciano 2003:371)

These documents are an excellent source of insight into how native people viewed their own history during these later colonial times. They show how people could absorb the Spanish conquest into their histories, remembering it not as a trauma or crisis but using it to confirm their community identity and their property rights.

The primordial titles proliferated at a time when many native communities were experiencing a serious shortage of resources owing to population growth. In the wake of the early colonial demographic collapse, lands that once belonged to these communities were appropriated by Spaniards. When population levels finally rebounded, communities found themselves in dire need of more land. Most of these communities had no authentic early documents that could help them reestablish their claims to these lands. Primordial titles were sometimes presented in court to back up such claims. However, Spanish defendants and judges could easily dismiss them as inauthentic by noting their factual inaccuracies.

The Mayas of the Yucatán Peninsula continued throughout the Colonial period to keep books of history and prophecy organized around one of the native calendrical systems. Several of these books, known as the *Books of Chilam Balam,* survive in copies written down just after the end of the Colonial period. "Chilam Balam" means priest or spokesperson of the jaguar; this title refers to the official Mayan prophet whose words these books purport to represent. These books are written in a highly specialized form of poetic language, full of metaphors and other figures of speech; this usage makes them quite difficult for scholars to interpret.

The *Books of Chilam Balam* are based on the *katun* calendar. One *katun* corresponded to 20 *tuns,* or "years" of 360 days each; hence, one *katun* was equal to 7,200 days, or 100 days less than 20 of our 365-day years. Thirteen *katuns* comprised a *may,* a unit of 260 *tuns,* or 160 days short of 256 years. The Mayas believed that each of the *katuns* within the *may* was characterized by certain kinds of events. To compare this with our calendar, imagine that in every century the decade of the twenties was associated with invasion, the thirties with sickness, the forties with prosperity, the fifties with changes in government, and so forth.

As with the more straightforward chronicles kept by other peoples, these Mayan books do not treat the Spanish invasion as a significant discontinuity in history. The coming of the Spaniards is recorded in the same manner as invasions by other native groups and is sometimes confused or conflated with these other conflicts, all of which were remembered as occurring during a certain *katun.* However, sufferings associated with the Spanish invasion are recalled quite eloquently in the *Book of Chilam Balam of Chumayel:*

> Herein was the beginning of our misery. It was the beginning of tribute, the beginning of tithes, the beginning of violent purse-snatching, the beginning of violent rape, the beginning of violent crushing of people, the beginning of violent robbery, the beginning of forced debts, the beginning of debts from false testimony, the beginning of violent hair-pulling, the beginning of torture, the beginning of violent robbery. This was the origin of service to the Spaniards and to the priests, of service to the *batabob* (Mayan municipal governors), of service to the teachers, of service to the public prosecutors [*fiscalob*] by the boys, the youths of the *cah,* while the poor people were made to suffer greatly. (Restall 1998:135)

INDO-CHRISTIAN LITERATURE

During the Colonial period, a tremendous quantity of textual material was written for use in the context of the Catholic Church. This includes catechistic materials for teaching Catholic doctrine to native people and devotional texts, such as prayers and songs, for native people to use themselves. Some of these works were published. Indeed, the first text ever published in the Americas was a Nahuatl catechism issued in 1539.

Most of this Christian literature was authored by priests. However, even those who were fairly fluent in the native language being used relied extensively on native assistants and interpreters, to the extent that what we really have are collaborative texts in which natives and nonnatives participated to varying degrees. In some cases, native style and imagery are so prevalent that we may consider the texts to be works of native literature. Excerpts from two very native-style songs are given in Box 6.3.

Christian preaching often drew on knowledge of native culture, sometimes denigrating it to argue that Christianity was superior, sometimes using native imagery to make Christian teachings more appealing. For example, Bernardino de Sahagún and his Nahua students compare the pious Saint Clare to the native noblewomen described in his ethnographic work:

> Noblewomen highly esteem decorated blouses, quail blouses, coyote fur blouses, various precious blouses. But God's beloved Saint Clare just put on an itchy mantle, called a hair shirt.
> . . . They make themselves up, they paint their faces with red powder, they paint their faces with yellow ochre, they color their teeth with cochineal, the sinful women. But God's beloved Saint Clare went about with her face lowered. (Burkhart 1989:139)

Juan Bautista, a Franciscan who, like Sahagún, worked closely with Nahua assistants, encourages devotion to the Virgin Mary by using native-style parallel constructions and emphasizing her associations with flowers and gardens in this text for the Feast of the Conception:

> And now may you know, oh my precious children, that the flower garden, the flowery enclosure, our Lord's place of consolation, his place of repose, is really she, the precious noblewoman, Saint Mary, whose festival we celebrate this very day. She is really our advocate, really our appeaser. It is true that it is she who is our lord God's flower garden. The way that in God's flower garden there lie gathered together many flowers that are very good, very wondrous, just like that is the noblewoman, Saint Mary. Many things that make one good, that make one proper lie gathered together with her, and the boons, the gifts, of the Holy Spirit. And sacred sweetness, sacred fragrance—which means, the signs of good living—lie gathered together with her. And God placed them with her, they grew with her, so that people would take her as a mirror, take her as a measuring stick. (Burkhart 2001:15)

Another collaborative genre was theater: Native actors performed plays with Christian subject matter, written or translated by priests and/or their native assistants. These range from simple Bible stories to three-act extravaganzas based on works of Spain's

---

Box 6.3 Nahua-Christian Songs

A collection of Nahuatl songs transcribed during the later sixteenth century contains several songs with predominantly Christian subject matter. These are undoubtedly of native authorship. The following is the opening stanza of a Christmas song composed in 1553 by a Nahua nobleman named Don Francisco Plácido:

> May he be prayed to! Uncover your sacred jewels of turquoise, your compassion, oh you children! May there be jewels of jade, jewels of gold, your rosary beads! With these may we entertain the one who lies now in Bethlehem, the savior of the world! Let us go! Come on! Hurry! May we depart from the place of waiting, oh our nephews, oh our brothers! Red popcorn flowers are scattering, there where God's compassion has descended to the world!
>   In a house of quetzal feathers by the side of the road, there you are, you maiden, Saint Mary. Right there you have given birth to the child of God. With various jewels may he be prayed to!
>   You are simply exalted, as if you surround yourself with jewels. Now he is in your arms, God the child, various jewels! (Bierhorst 1985:254; trans. revised by L. Burkhart)

Bernardino de Sahagún and four of his Nahua assistants composed a collection of Nahuatl songs for Christian festivals, published under the friar's name in 1583. In much of the work, the friar seems to take a back seat to the literary skill and creativity of the native authors. A song for Easter morning conjures up a vision of a beautiful garden populated by native species of flower, tree, and bird:

> You green-corn flower, you heart flower, you cacao flower, you red jar flower: put forth a shady ring of fronds, send forth boughs! You have come to arrive in your place of sprouting.
>   You ceiba tree, you cypress, you fir, you pine: why do you still stand sadly? It is the time, it is the moment for you to renew your flowers, your leaves, for you to send forth boughs, for you to bloom! You oriole, you blue grosbeak, you mockingbird, you hummingbird: Where had you gone? Where had you entered? And all you various spoonbills, you various troupials, come! Let there be flying, let there be unfolding, let there be unfurling of wings! May your speech resound! May there be chattering, may your songs resonate like bells!
> (Sahagún 1993:108; trans. by L. Burkhart)

Later in the song this sacred place is identified as the churchyard, the flowers representing the worshipping women, the trees representing the men, and the birds representing visiting angels circling above.

---

theatrical "Golden Age" or the story of Juan Diego and Our Lady of Guadalupe. Passion plays brought the central narrative of Christianity to life with native performers. Morality plays reinforced the friars' moral teachings by showing sinners being examined by Jesus Christ and hauled off to hell by demons. Demon characters tempt people to ignore the Church's moral strictures, saying, for example:

> Enjoy yourself for now. Are you an old man already? Do penance and whip yourself when you are an old man. Do you not see the multitude of young men who go about enjoying

the things of youth, who go about speaking of and thinking of their pleasures? For they just say, "when we are old men we will stop, we will engage in spiritual activities." (Sell and Burkhart 2004:275)

Those who do live proper lives receive onstage assurance that the Virgin Mary will indeed help them after they die:

SAINT MARY: You, Jesus Christ, my beloved honored only child, I cast myself down before you on account of your creatures who are suffering in the place where people are purified by fire, purgatory. O my beloved honored child, have pity on them, show them mercy. See my weeping and tears and sorrow, for while they still lived on earth, O my beloved honored child, they never forgot you, they always followed you for at the time they remembered it was on account of your suffering that you saved them.

JESUS CHRIST: O maiden eternal, O my beloved mother, do not cry for your servants because while they still lived on earth they always trusted in me, relied on me. They will be defended, helped and saved with my protection, and they recognized my beloved Father, God. When they cry out to me I will hear what they say, their prayers when their hearts are anguished, when they are unwise and in great pain and affliction. As for me, I will console them, make them famous, honor and exalt them. They will live forever, content, and I will reveal to them my bliss [glory]. (Sell and Burkhart 2004:179–181)

Pre-Columbian religious rituals were highly dramatic, with costumes and role-playing, but were not "theater" in the sense of a staged reality with a written script and "actors," as opposed to a sacred, ritual reality with impersonators who were thought actually to become the deities they represented. Thus, colonial religious theater, a hybrid product of colonial evangelization and native performance traditions, was the first true theater in the Americas. Colonial scripts are limited in number, far outweighed by sermons, but give precious insight into a mode of religious performance much valued in native communities. That some of the scripts we have are eighteenth-century copies of sixteenth- or seventeenth-century compositions shows that some plays were passed along over many generations.

CIVIL OR NOTARIAL LITERATURE

The office of scribe or notary was a standard part of native town government throughout the Colonial period. The records of local and municipal affairs kept by these scribes and other literate individuals comprise a corpus of documents in native languages that provide many details about daily life in the colonial community. These texts include wills, records of town meetings, records of land grants, petitions and letters, and other genres, even such things as a note from 1684 that a Mixtec man left on his wife's body after he murdered her. The note accused her of having an affair with the sacristan of the town's church (Terraciano 1998). The wealth of information in these texts is best demonstrated by showing some examples. In Box 5.2 of the previous chapter we presented one particularly detailed land grant document. A few other genres are excerpted next.

Cochineal is a type of cactus-dwelling insect that Mesoamericans crushed to make a red dye. In the Colonial period, Europeans sought this dye for paints and cosmetics, creating a lucrative export industry. But in 1553, the town council of Tlaxcala met to discuss the negative impact of this industry on local food supplies and local morals. The notaries recorded the discussion:

> Everyone does nothing but take care of cochineal cactus; no longer is care taken that maize and other edibles are planted. For food—maize, chilis, and beans—and other things that people need were once not expensive in Tlaxcala. It is because of this (neglect), the cabildo members considered, that all the foods are becoming expensive. The owners of cochineal cactus merely buy maize, chilis, etc., and are very occupied only with their cochineal, by which their money, cacao beans, and cloth are acquired. They no longer want to cultivate their fields, but idly neglect them. Because of this, now many fields are going to grass, and famine truly impends. Things are no longer as they were long ago, for the cochineal cactus is making people lazy. And it is excessive how sins are committed against our Lord God. These cochineal owners devote themselves to their cochineal on Sundays and holy days; no longer do they go to church to hear mass as the holy church commands us, but look only to getting their sustenance and their cacao, which makes them proud. And then later they buy pulque and then get drunk. . . . And he who belonged to someone no longer respects whoever was his lord and master, because he is seen to have gold and cacao. This makes them proud and swells them up, whereby it is fully evident that they esteem themselves through wealth. (Lockhart, Berdan, and Anderson 1986:81)

The councilmen decided to ask the viceroy to let them limit the number of cochineal-producing plants any one person would be allowed to keep. Communities also faced a crisis when the local priest turned out to be a predator. This was the case in Jalostotitlan, northeast of Zacatecas, in 1611, when Juan Vincente, a town official, petitioned for the removal of the priest, Francisco Muñoz. Here are just a few of the abuses he described:

> Three times he has given me blows and knocked me down, and I fainted. And he broke my staff into pieces there in the church, in the sacristy . . . and I said to him: Father, why are you beating me, you have broken my staff into bits. Then he said, Yes, I beat you and splintered your staff, and I will break your whole head.
> . . . Another time there was a boy, a sacristan, eight years old; he whipped him very severely, he stripped off much of his skin, and he fainted. He lay in bed for a week; when he got up, then he ran away.
> . . . Once my daughter Catalina Juana went there to the church in the evening to sweep, and there in the church our father seized her and wanted to have her. She would not let him, and there inside the church he beat her.
> . . . And also, he does not teach us the divine words, the sermon, but only hates us and mistreats us constantly. When the vicar-general wrote him, saying: Console the commoners, for they are your children, as soon as he read it, he said: Why am I to console and love them as my children? They are children of the devil, and I will mistreat them. (Anderson, Berdan, and Lockhart 1976:167–173)

Although we don't know the outcome of this case, you can see here how native people used writing to defend themselves against mistreatment. Wills yield a wealth of information: By seeing to whom people leave their property, we learn about family structure, inheritance, and naming customs; by seeing what goods and land people owned, we learn about their economic status, including class and gender differences; by reading their declarations of Christian faith and seeing what people leave to the Church, we learn about their religion. Here is one such will, from the Yucatec Mayan town of Ixil, where, in 1765, a woman named Antonia Cante lay on her deathbed:

> In the name of God the Father, God the Son, God the Holy Spirit three persons one true God almighty, the paper of my final statement in my testament will be seen, inasmuch as I am Antonia Cante, the daughter of Martin Cante and child of Bernardina Canche, residents here in the cah [native town] of Ixil. Although my life is ending on this earth, I wish my body to be buried in the holy church. Likewise, I supplicate our blessed lord the Padre, that he say one said mass for my soul, that he send a prayer in the mass that will assist my soul in the sufferings of purgatory. The fee shall be given, six tomines and two tomines for Jerusalem. Likewise one chest for my infant Juan Canul. Likewise one bed that is now the property of Pedro Canul. Likewise one shirt and one measure of yarn, the inheritance of my husband, Lucas Cuouh. One beehive with bees for Juana Canul, one beehive with bees is Juliana Canul's, one to Viviana Canul, one to Maria Canul, one to Marta Canul, one to Pedro Canul. This is the truth, the end of my statement in my will. (Restall 1995:31)

She designated a local nobleman to see to the mass, and the priest later wrote down that he had performed it. We see from her will that Antonia wished to conform to Roman Catholic customs concerning mass and burial; that she had been recently widowed and remarried, as her seven children, including an infant, have a surname different from her husband's; that she earned money by keeping bees (as some people in Ixil still do today); and that she tried to divide her modest property equitably among her husband, two sons, and five daughters.

With the end of the Colonial period, this tradition of local native-language record-keeping almost completely vanished along with the administrative structure that had fostered it in most of the Mesoamerican regions. Thus, with few exceptions, native people literate in their own languages disappear from Mesoamerica until the twentieth century. Although people's words are not recorded, their traditions of speech and performance were passed along orally, and would reenter the written record when anthropologists, folklorists, and linguists arrived on the scene in the twentieth century (see Chapters 11 and 13).

SUGGESTED READINGS

ANDERSON, ARTHUR J. O., FRANCES BERDAN, and JAMES LOCKHART (eds. and trans.) 1976 *Beyond the Codices: The Nahua View of Colonial Mexico.* Berkeley: University of California Press.

BIERHORST, JOHN (ed. and trans.) 1992 *History and Mythology of the Aztecs: The Codex Chimalpopoca.* Tucson: University of Arizona Press.

BURKHART, LOUISE M. 1996 *Holy Wednesday: A Nahua Drama from Early Colonial Mexico.* Philadelphia: University of Pennsylvania Press.

CARMACK, ROBERT M. 1973 *Quichean Civilization. The Ethnohistoric, Ethnographic, and Archaeological Sources.* Berkeley: University of California Press.

COE, MICHAEL D., and GORDON WHITTAKER (eds. and trans.) 1982 *Aztec Sorcerers in Seventeenth Century Mexico: The Treatise on Superstitions by Hernando Ruiz de Alarcón.* Albany: Institute for Mesoamerican Studies.

EDMONSON, MUNRO (ed. and trans.) 1982 *The Ancient Future of the Itza: The Book of Chilam Balam of Tizimin.* Austin: University of Texas Press.

HASKETT, ROBERT 2005 *Visions of Paradise: Primordial Titles and Mesoamerican History in Cuernavaca.* Norman: University of Oklahoma Press.

KARTTUNEN, FRANCES, and JAMES LOCKHART (eds. and trans.) 1987 *The Art of Nahuatl Speech: The Bancroft Dialogues.* Nahuatl Studies Series, 2. Los Angeles: UCLA Latin American Center.

KELLOGG, SUSAN, and MATTHEW RESTALL (eds.) 1998 *Dead Giveaways: Indigenous Testaments of Colonial Mesoamerica and the Andes.* Salt Lake City: University of Utah Press.

LEÓN-PORTILLA, MIGUEL 1969 *Pre-Columbian Literatures of Mexico.* Norman: University of Oklahoma Press.

RECINOS, ADRIÁN, DIONISIO JOSÉ CHONAY, and DELIA GOETZ (eds. and trans.) 1953 *The Annals of the Cakchiquels and Title of the Lords of Totonicapán.* Norman: University of Oklahoma Press.

RESTALL, MATTHEW 1998 *Maya Conquistador.* Boston: Beacon Press.

ROYS, RALPH L. 1967 *The Book of Chilam Balam of Chumayel.* Norman: University of Oklahoma Press.

SAHAGÚN, BERNARDINO DE 1950–1982 *Florentine Codex.* Edited and translated by Arthur J. O. Anderson and Charles E. Dibble. 12 vols. Santa Fe and Salt Lake City: School of American Research and University of Utah.

SELL, BARRY D., and LOUISE M. BURKHART (eds.) 2004 *Nahuatl Theater Volume 1: Death and Life in Colonial Nahua Mexico.* Norman: University of Oklahoma Press.

SMITH, MARY ELIZABETH 1973 *Picture Writing from Ancient Southern Mexico: Mixtec Place Signs and Maps.* Norman: University of Oklahoma Press.

TEDLOCK, DENNIS (ed. and trans.) 1996 *Popol Vuh: The Mayan Book of the Dawn of Life.* New York: Simon and Schuster.

WOOD, STEPHANIE 2003 *Transcending Conquest: Nahua Views of Spanish Colonial Mexico.* Norman: University of Oklahoma Press.

Chapter 7
Mesoamericans in the Neocolonial Era

Any effort to synthesize the neocolonial history of the Mesoamerican Indians—from independence to the beginning of the modern era—must necessarily be carefully framed and qualified. Although the beginning of this period is clearly marked by political and state-level events that established the region's independent nations that we recognize today, it could be argued that the end of the period—the radical break symbolized by the emblematic Mexican Revolution (1910–1940)—did not occur in all of the region at the same time or in the same ways or on the same scale.

In Guatemala, for example, typically nineteenth-century neocolonial political and social forms appeared to find closure with the revolutionary events of the mid–twentieth century. Thus, in this chapter we are considering nineteenth-century and early-twentieth-century social and political adjustments to the postcolonial order that evolved in similar ways throughout the region, but with decidedly different chronologies and national characteristics. For the most part, we will examine the general trends and patterns of the region as a whole rather than on the basis of individual countries.

In keeping with the overall theme of the text, our focus is on the biological and cultural descendants of ancient Mesoamerica, a world whose coherent social system, as we have seen, was broken into a hundred pieces by the Spanish colonial regime. The Mesoamerican Indians were segregated into isolated rural communities during the colonial period, where they were deprived of native leadership at regional and national levels and sorely exploited by the colonial ruling class. The new creole and mestizo leaders of the neocolonial period, and the liberal reforms that many of them advocated, resulted in exploitation of the Mesoamerican Indians as severe as that by the Spanish colonialists. Indeed, these so-called liberals were perhaps even less sympathetic to the native cultures than had been the Spaniards.

Our story of the native Mesoamericans in the neocolonial period, then, cannot be a saga of glory or triumph. Nevertheless, it will be shown that the Mesoamerican cultural tradition continued to provide an important reservoir from which the native peoples of the region could draw in their struggle to survive as ethnically distinct peoples within the independent states of Mexico and Central America. We will learn, too, that the Mesoamericans contributed in concrete ways to the important social movements of the region far more than is generally recognized.

NINETEENTH-CENTURY SOCIAL HISTORY: FROM INDEPENDENCE TO DICTATORSHIP

The Break from Spain

The emergence of the modern states of Mexico and Central America between 1810 and 1825 came through a dominolike set of events, many of which began violently in Europe and reached America almost as a distant echo. The close of the eighteenth century brought the last gasp of the millennium-old vision of the Holy Roman Empire. Underwritten by the waning idea of the divine right of kings to hold both political and religious authority on behalf of universal Roman Catholic Christendom, France and Spain in the late-eighteenth century were besieged by the rising economic and political power of the Protestant nations of northern Europe, particularly Britain, and by the perceived threat of the Russian and Ottoman empires in the east. The U.S. independence movement beginning in 1776 was also being watched with the greatest of interest by Spanish-American creole leaders and intellectuals.

These external political and economic forces, together with the growing favor being enjoyed by Enlightenment ideals of individual and collective rights and freedoms under secular state authority, led to a violent end to the eighteenth-century political order of Europe. The French Revolution of 1789 and the subsequent continental firestorm of the Napoleonic Wars brought with them the fall, in 1807, of the faltering Bourbon monarchy of Spain. Carlos IV's abdication, the Napoleonic occupation and defeat, followed by the restoration in 1817 of a greatly weakened Spanish monarch, Fernando VII, created a full decade of political vacuum that enabled most of Spain's vast empire in America to mobilize for a clean break from Europe.

The ideologies of the American and French revolutions were conscious models for Latin America's independence movements (1810–1825), yet it is important to note that the "Nationalist period" of Latin American history was dotted with early pan-national experiments, notably Iturbide's Mexican–Central American empire (1822–1823) and Simón Bolívar's confederation of Gran Colombia (1819–1830). These experiments failed, but the ideology of unity persisted even when unity could not be achieved, notably in the case of the Central American Federation, which lasted from 1823 to 1839 (Figure 7.1).

Nationalism in Mexico and Central America was intimately linked with the effort of creoles to forge a home for themselves in a region divested of the authority of the Spanish Crown. The creoles, who were left in power when Spain departed, naturally sought to stay in power. They accomplished their goal by creating states in which it made sense—at least to themselves and to Europe and to the United States—that

Figure 7.1 Political divisions of Mexico and Central America shortly after Independence. Based on Jorge L. Tamayo, *Geografía Moderna de México*, 2nd ed. Mexico City, Mexico: Editorial Trillas, 1981, p. 365.

they should be the heirs apparent of the Spanish colonial order. The creole ascendancy effectively produced the map of the modern Mesoamerican region.

The seat of the colonial viceroyalty of Mexico became the dominant new nation. The colonial Captaincy General of Guatemala, however grudgingly, was broken into the lesser nations of Guatemala, Honduras, El Salvador, Nicaragua, and Costa Rica.

If the first quarter of the nineteenth century witnessed the forging of the political identity of the modern nations of the Mesoamerican region, their essential ethnic composition long antedated their existence as nations. Mexico emerged from the Colonial period as the quintessential mestizo core of New Spain, with significant enclaves of unmixed Spanish settlements in the north, and large parts of the central, southern, and western sections of the region effectively segregated into Indian and mestizo communities. In particular, the Mexican states of Yucatán, Chiapas, and Oaxaca contained many thousands of ethnically Indian hamlets and villages. This demographic pattern continued into Guatemala, where the northwestern and central highlands were overwhelmingly Indian, with large towns and cities being mestizo and creole (Figure 7.2).

Pacific and Caribbean Guatemala was of mixed Indian and mestizo composition. By 1800, the colonial southern provinces of New Spain, under the jurisdiction of the Captaincy General of Guatemala—El Salvador, Honduras, Nicaragua, and

Figure 7.2   Spreading coffee beans for drying on a Guatemalan plantation in the nineteenth century. Courtesy of E. Bradford Burns. Reprinted from E. Bradford Burns, *Eadward Muybridge in Guatemala, 1875: The Photographer as Social Recorder.* Berkeley, CA: University of California Press, 1986, p. 118.

Costa Rica—had acquired the essential mestizo character that persists today, with the exception of a major presence of mixed Afro-Americans along the eastern coasts of Honduras, Nicaragua, and Costa Rica.

Oscillation Between Centralism and Federalism

The administrative centers of the Mesoamerican region's new nations, once formed, typically did not enjoy effective territorial and political sovereignty. One of the reasons for this situation was demographic. Most of the new nations of the region had a series of noncontiguous heartland settlement areas, separated by vast hinterlands. This noncontiguous, nucleated settlement pattern led to various political expressions of regionalism, for authority systems were in effect local, not national. To some extent, then, the new nations were fictions, and central governments had neither the communication and transportation systems nor the political control to exert effective national authority.

Regionalism was thus related to the important current of federalism as a model for governing. The powerful creole elites, however, lived in the old capital cities and provincial capitals. This old aristocracy of land, army, and church interests was linked by ties of kinship and common interests in such a way that their power bases—the national and provincial capitals—expressed a political preference for central authority, which was usually conservative, proclerical, and favorably disposed to large landholding interests. The political expression of centralist elements was also conservative, holding that power and tradition beget wisdom and, for this reason, ought to rule.

Alliance with the army became an important part of the centralist political strategy, for military coercion was an effective way of enforcing the right of conservatives to rule. The more liberal "federalists" were skeptical of the centralist vision and generally followed U.S. models of regionally based consensus, with the central government being more a bureaucratic and ceremonial than a policy-making entity. Federalism tended to be politically liberal in the sense of valuing individual and regional expressions of self-interest. This political form meant that social and economic sectors beneath the landholding aristocracy were entitled to political expression, the acquisition of property, education, and general participation in "social progress."

Federalism and liberalism, most typically associated with the presidencies of Benito Juárez of Mexico (1854–1862; 1867–1872) (Figure 7.3) and Justo Rufino Barrios of Guatemala (1873–1885) (Figure 7.4), also tended to favor the secular state and

Figure 7.3 Painting of Benito Juárez, the great Liberal reformer of Mexico. James A. Magner, *Men of Mexico*, 2nd ed. Salem, N.H.: Books for Libraries, Ayer Company Publishers, 1968.

Figure 7.4 Justo Rufino Barrios, the Liberal strongman of Guatemala. Source unknown.

diminished legal and economic power for the Catholic Church. So great was the antipathy of the Mexican conservative elite for the liberal reforms that they looked in desperation for help from abroad, which led France, for reasons of its own, to help install a short-lived and ill-fated monarchy in Mexico (1867–1872) under the Archduke Maximilian of Austria.

The oscillation between federalist and centralist models was the great leitmotif of nineteenth-century political life in all of the region from Mexico to Costa Rica, and was one of the dominant features of neocolonial Mesoamerica. The pattern of oscillation yielded periods of liberal "reform," such as the eras of Juárez and Barrios, in which liberal, federalist models encouraged diffusion of economic and political authority from central to regional governments. The oscillating pattern of centralism and federalism also tended, during centralist periods, to emphasize development of urban centers and their access to port cities. This lack of interest in the hinterland, beyond its economic utility, had an obvious result: The hinterland was never fully incorporated into national cultural and political life.

The social and economic relations between city and countryside became progressively more unidirectional, with wealth flowing out of the countryside into the cities and abroad, thus concentrating status and privilege and development priorities in the urban centers. This phenomenon had a great deal to do with Mexico's loss, under the long rule of centralist President Antonio López de Santa Anna, of half its national territory to the United States in 1848. It is useful in understanding the origins of the U.S. Hispanic Southwest to realize that Santa Anna and his conservative followers regarded the far north and its inhabitants as irrelevant to the national interest, for both economic and demographic reasons. Their priorities lay with the urban heartland and the agricultural, ranching, and mining resources of Mexico's Central Basin.

The poles of centralism and federalism were also related to other themes in national life in the region. Under the centralist mode, the emphasis was on economic development and creation of a commercial infrastructure (communication and transportation) in the already dominant urban areas and in those areas suitable for large-scale, capital-intensive, and labor-intensive agricultural production. Under the federalist program, the emphasis was instead on the extension of political and social participation to broader sectors of society. Yet both centralism and federalism coincided in their commitment to the "positivist" agenda of progress via economic growth and applied science. If anything, both models created new opportunities for the creole establishment to dominate national life, both in the capitals and in the provinces. The rural and urban poor, largely of mestizo and Indian background, found themselves economically and socially more marginalized under both these neocolonial systems than they had been in the closing years of the Colonial period itself.

Although the constitutions of the new nations generally followed French and U.S. models, the political traditions of the region's states were not strongly democratic. Rather, they were personalistic and authoritarian, with a strong military infrastructure that often became one with the political system. The long-lived regimes of dictators Rafael Carrera (1844–1865) of Guatemala and Porfirio Díaz (1872–1910) of Mexico exemplified this tradition. It is easy to find the roots of this system in the structure of the older colonial society, whose strong infrastructure was actually appropriated by the new creole *caudillos* ("strong men"). In the colonial system as well as its derivate neocolonial forms after independence, both liberal and conservative, the military was always at the disposal of the political authorities to safeguard and underwrite their right to rule.

This tradition of authoritarian, personalistic rule allied with military force was based on the charismatic leadership qualities of one individual, the *caudillo*. The support from the army was usually obtained through reciprocal favors. The compliance of the army in supporting the *caudillos* was encouraged by the opportunities for social and economic mobility for mestizos that were available through military careers. This was a singularly successful way—often the only way—for ambitious mestizos to penetrate the relatively impermeable social networks of the creole aristocracy and new professional classes. The creoles needed the army to guarantee their own positions of political and economic power. The cost to the creoles consisted of granting privileges:

Substantial salaries as well as access to their own family networks through intermarriage. In this manner, upwardly mobile mestizo army officers became economically, politically, and socially allied with the creole elite. The local expression of *caudillo* was the *cacique*, a small-scale version of the nondemocratic, authoritarian ruler at the community level (not to be confused with the native elite class of the Colonial period, also known as *caciques*).

The cacique system of personalistic local authority characterized both mestizo and Indian communities, and often, in the latter case, involved the descendants of the old Indian elite families who had enjoyed, during the Colonial period, privileges and exemptions from the tribute system in exchange for serving as intermediaries, labor provisioners, and tribute collectors for the Crown. As these small-scale strongman fiefdoms developed in the region, it was often the case (as it was at the regional and national levels with the system of *caudillos*) that reciprocity greased the system through favors from the caciques such as loans, legal assistance, marriage arrangements, jobs, and scriptorial services.

Caudillos and caciques were also involved in ritual kinship links with their subalterns through the system of *compadrazgo*, whereby the caudillo or cacique would become godparent, patron, and protector of the client's child in the ritual of baptism. The client, in turn, owed absolute loyalty to his patron in all matters pertaining to defending his privileges and right to absolute political authority in local affairs. This neocolonial mode of local political authority, while often informal, nevertheless proved to be an effective way of guaranteeing local stability in the ebb and flow of national politics.

Positivism and Early Attempts at Development

The intellectual universe of the independence movement and the subsequent formulation of national agendas and priorities were strongly influenced by French positivism. It was a world view and policy template that emphasized the ideal of inevitable progress and modernization through science and reason. Following closely the ideals of general social evolution, the models to be emulated were European. Latin America was "behind" in the world hierarchy of power, progress, and prosperity and felt obliged to "catch up." These ideals, as interpreted by creoles in Mexico and Central America, could best be achieved through economic development of their backward regions. Thus, capitalist development, with relatively few regulatory constraints, became the policy focus of most nineteenth-century governments of the region, both liberal and conservative. Whatever brought economic growth, urban development, increased production for export markets, and "civilization" was good. This outlook meant that education and expanded social inclusion for skilled technicians were desirable, but not so much so as to keep "progress" from favoring the privileges of the old creole elite.

Although the old creole elite did not lose out on the direct and indirect benefits of the fever for economic development and modernization, the mestizo and Indian poor turned out to be the big losers. Increasingly, the power structure totally excluded these elements of the population, even though they comprised an overwhelming majority of the population. In contrast, the newly arrived *científicos* ("scientists," "technicians") did extremely well. In some cases, their success eclipsed the privileges of the old creole elite. It was not uncommon at the end of the nineteenth century to have railroad and telegraph facilities wholly in the hands of North American and English companies.

Guatemala's enormous expansion of coffee production included vast tracts that were owned by newly arrived German immigrants. North American corporations and individuals controlled much of Mexico's rail infrastructure and a majority of the henequen plantations in Yucatán. Even Costa Rica permitted Minor Keith—a North American engineer who built the railroad that linked the highlands to the Atlantic port city of Limón—to acquire almost full economic control of it. Whose party was it? Certainly not the sharecroppers and plantation workers down the road.

The ideologies of liberalism and positivism, operating in the name of social progress and economic growth, displaced millions of the region's rural poor, both mestizo and Indian. Their traditional land base eroded, facilitated by government policies that encouraged privatization of communal property and easy alienation of it for cash. The frenzy for development of export production also led to government policies that facilitated encroachment on and outright appropriation of small landholdings of Indian and mestizo peasants. Land that had hitherto been deemed marginal suddenly became prime land for coffee, henequen, banana, and beef production for the export market to the United States. Once the rural poor saw themselves without a source of subsistence, millions of them became attached to large cattle ranches and commercial agriculture operations in what was essentially a return to colonial forms of debt peonage. Their wages were never sufficient to pay their debts for housing, food, and emergency cash needs. The company store became an agent of bondage.

It hardly comes as a surprise, therefore, that the truncated and impoverished Indian communities that managed to survive these predations retrenched and retreated from other than obligatory contact with national institutions. In particular, in both Guatemala and Mexico, renewed emphasis was placed upon the highly local, ethnically segregated civil and religious community organizations that developed during the Colonial period in accordance with Crown dictates. It is worth noting the irony that the very institutional formulas that were intended to *integrate* Indian communities into colonial society became defense mechanisms that facilitated their exclusion from participation in national life in the neocolonial postindependence period.

Nevertheless, scholars have pointed out that the so-called "closed corporate" Indian community was a form of social organization that was never fully closed during the Colonial period and that it was becoming even less closed during the turbulent years of the nineteenth century. If it ever existed, the option for the Indians of isolation within closed communities, shielded from the dramatic political and economic changes being promoted by liberal dictators like Porfirio Díaz in Mexico, was rapidly disappearing.

For those displaced rural people who were already outside the confines of Indian communities, the main option was migration to the cities, either directly from their eroded communities or indirectly via the haciendas and plantations. Great numbers fled to the anonymity of the cities, especially the major cities and provincial capitals, which indeed had been the main beneficiaries of the economic "progress" that was created by the priorities of both centralist and federalist governments. In and around the cities were to be found real (and sometimes fictional) sources of employment in the manual labor and service sectors of the economy. Thus, one of the fruits of neo-colonial positivism and liberalism was the creation of a new rural and urban prole-tariat.

It was thus in this period that the Mexican and Central American cities took on their current mosaic of elite cores and suburbs, with interlaced working-class and slum barrios. It was also during this period that because of the new transportation net-works, deliberately built by the United States to link Mexico to U.S. markets, the United States became a popular destination for the displaced rural and urban poor, particularly from Mexico.

They found employment largely in the growing commercial agriculture economies of the southern, western, and southwestern parts of the United States. The greatly expanding U.S. rail network also provided employment opportunities for Mexican laborers, creating sizable Mexican-American communities in places like Denver, Chicago, Philadelphia, and Kansas City. It is clear, therefore, that the events we are discussing in this chapter came to influence quite directly the demography of many U.S. cities as well as the vast region that would become known in our time as the Sun Belt.

On the wave of positivism, and with the economic development that accompa-nied the expansion of agricultural export production, came a huge flow of foreign capital to Mexico and Central America. Frequently the production units themselves (cattle ranches, and the henequen, banana, cotton, and coffee plantations), as well as the processing and shipping facilities, were completely controlled by foreigners or by newly arrived, wealthy immigrants. Governments, whether centralist or federalist, conservative or liberal, tended to look benignly on this phenomenon. Why? Because foreign control seemed a small price to pay for the economic transformation and commercial infrastructure—railroads, power plants, and telegraph systems—that would bring progress. The irony, of course, is the very one that continues to haunt much of the region to this day: It was development that mobilized a continent to provide raw materials, fiber, food, meat, and minerals to supply industrial Europe and the United States without creating the capacity for self-sufficiency in the production of industrial goods and technical skills on which they had become dependent.

MESOAMERICANS AND THE INDEPENDENCE MOVEMENTS

The independence movements in Mexico and Central America were led primarily by creoles in order to retain political control over the Indian peasants and mestizo masses who, it was feared, might otherwise rebel against colonial rule and usher in genuinely revolutionary changes. This was a justified fear from their perspective, since by the time of independence, there were over two million mestizos and almost five million Indians in the Mesoamerican region, compared with only some 120,000 creoles. Indeed, as we shall now see, shortly before independence in Mexico, Indians and mestizos by the thousands participated in major uprisings that threatened to become class wars between the haves and have-nots, and similar uprisings on a smaller scale broke out in Central America around the same time.

Hidalgo and the Mexican Independence Movement

The great hero of the independence movement in Mexico was Father Miguel Hidalgo, whose name is recalled each September 15 when from the balcony of the National Palace the president of the republic repeats Hidalgo's legendary cry: "*Mexicanos, viva México*" ("Mexicans, long live Mexico"). In September 1810, Hidalgo, priest of the Dolores parish in the Bajío (just north of the Central Basin), incited his followers to rebel against the French usurpers of the Spanish Crown and to strike for independence. Father Hidalgo was a creole (his father was a Spaniard), and his call to independence was part of a popular creole plan to replace the ruling *peninsulares* (Spaniards, also known as *gachupines*) with the creoles themselves.

The band of men who made up Hidalgo's followers on that day in 1810, as well as the tens of thousands who joined his cause in the ensuing months, were made up largely of Indians and mestizos, and their goal was much more radical: to end tributes, forced labor, discrimination, landlessness, and political subjugation (Figure 7.5; for places mentioned in the account to follow, see the map in Figure 7.1). In many ways their goals were consistent with the liberal constitution being created in Spain at the time as explained in Box 7.1.

Hidalgo seized the image of the Virgin of Guadalupe as his banner and led several hundred men in the takeover of Dolores, followed by the capture of San Miguel, the hometown of Hidalgo's creole military chief, Ignacio Allende, and shortly thereafter the town of Celaya. At this time Hidalgo assumed the title of "Captain-General of America," and with a force that had swelled to over 25,000 men he marched on the rich mining center of Guanajuato. The Spaniards of Guanajuato retreated to the protection of the town's granary *(alhóndiga)*, which was stormed and overrun by the furious Hidalgo "horde." The rebels had lost at least 2,000 men in the assault, which they soon avenged by hacking to death some 400 to 600 men, women, and children found inside the granary. The town was sacked, everything of value being carried off by Hidalgo's rude warriors. Shortly thereafter, Hidalgo's band took Valladolid (later renamed Morelia), as their numbers swelled to around 80,000 men.

At this point Hidalgo turned his warrior band toward Mexico City, the capital and main stronghold of the Spanish establishment. The rebels met a small but well-trained Spanish contingent in the mountains between Toluca and Mexico City. The Spanish forces inflicted very heavy casualties on the rebels (2,000 to 4,000 rebel warriors were killed). Hidalgo decided not to march on the capital. Instead, he directed his followers to Guadalajara, which was taken without a fight. In Guadalajara, the rebels quietly executed hundreds of *gachupines* (Spaniards), while recruiting thousands of new rebel fighters from the surrounding Indian communities and creole haciendas.

Figure 7.5 Mural painting of Miguel Hidalgo and his band of followers. Mural by Juan O'Gorman. Courtesy of the Organization of American States, Columbus Memorial Library.

After the capture of Guadalajara, events began to turn against Hidalgo. Most creoles had come to see the movement as a "caste war," a life-and-death struggle between Indians and poor mestizos on one side and Whites on the other. The creoles rallied to the side of the Spaniards, among them men who had originally joined Hidalgo's movement. The Spanish forces under the ruthless General Félix Calleja retook Guanajuato, where they proceeded to slaughter anyone suspected of being

Box 7.1   Napoleon, the Great Horned Serpent

Developments in Spain during the period of the Napoleonic occupation had important reper-
cussions for the Spanish colonies of New Spain and Central America. Among these was the formation of a constitutional assembly (*cortes*), and the creation of a constitution designed to be
applicable to both Spain and its American colonies. The constitution, ratified in 1812, was a profoundly liberal document, granting "sovereignty" to the people, dividing power between the
government agencies, eliminating the privileges of nobility, and promoting the economic and social welfare of all peoples, including the native Mesoamericans in the overseas colonies.

That same year a proclamation was sent to the American colonies, explaining why the constitution was necessary and pointing especially to Napoleon's deceitful invasion and heavy-
handed rule over Spain, along with the capture and exile of King Ferdinand VII. According to
the anthropologist Robert Laughlin (2003:191), the constitution and the previously mentioned
proclamation were a source of political inspiration to many of the creoles in Mexico and Central
America. Of particular interest to Laughlin, however, is the fact that the proclamation was translated into a few of the Mesoamerican native languages as part of an attempt to gain the support
of the Indians for the continuation of Spanish authority in the American colonies. One of the
translations was from Spanish to the Tzotzil Mayan language spoken in the Chiapas province of
Guatemala. Although it is likely that the Tzotzil version of the proclamation was never read to a
single Tzotzil Indian, manuscript copies of the translation have been preserved and analyzed by
Laughlin in an attempt to decipher their coded messages relative to Napoleon, Ferdinand, and
the new constitution.

Laughlin concludes that the translator of the proclamation into the Tzotzil language must
have been a Spanish friar. This conclusion is made clear not only by the fact that the grammatical use of Tzotzil does not appear to have been that of a native speaker, but also by the many
references to religion and the Catholic church, references that do not appear in the original Spanish proclamation. Nevertheless, the friar employed numerous Tzotzil terms and metaphors in
order to make the proclamation understandable to the Tzotzil Mayan people of Chiapas. Most
notably, while the Spanish proclamation paints Napoleon as a "tyrant," in the Tzotzil version he
becomes the "Great Horned Serpent," as well as a "jaguar," "lighted fire," "thunderbolt," and
"whirlwind."

The allusion to the great horned serpent no doubt drew upon images from the Book of
Revelations, but as Laughlin points out, it also was a key symbol in ancient Mesoamerica standing for "the god of the earth's center." Indeed, in one of the hamlets of Zinacantán, Chiapas,
where Laughlin has recorded Tzotzil tales, "horned serpents are believed to have gouged out the
ravines with their horns and to cause earthquakes when they emerge from the underworld"
(p. 160). The Tzotzil version was far more paternalistic toward the Indians than the original Spanish text, the former always referring to the Spaniards and creoles as "fathers, elder brothers" of
the Indians. In contrast, the original Spanish proclamation refers to the Indians as "that beautiful portion of humankind that inhabits America."

During the following years, the kind of liberal thinking expressed by the priestly translator
of the proclamation helped inspire the independence movements, although in the end the creoles' more paternalistic ideas about the Indians came to prevail. For this reason, as Laughlin
points out (p. 191), Indians such as the Tzotzils of Chiapas continued to perceive of their historical destiny as one of *ik'ti' vokol*, "torment, suffering"!

sympathetic to the rebel cause. Next the Spaniards marched on Guadalajara, which Hidalgo decided to defend with the full force of his vast following. While fighting on the grassy plains outside the city, a Spanish cannonball struck one of Hidalgo's ammunition wagons, which blew up, killing many of the rebel fighters and setting fire to the plains. Hidalgo was forced to retreat, losing over 1,000 men as well as control of Guadalajara.

The rebel forces fled to the north, where Allende stripped Hidalgo of his military command, and began to seek support from friends on the U.S. side of the border. At this point, both Hidalgo and Allende were betrayed by a former rebel lieutenant, who led them into a trap laid by the Spanish forces. The two leaders were captured at a small desert village named Our Lady of Guadalupe Baján. Hidalgo was taken to Chihuahua, where he was tried, stripped of his priesthood, and executed in July 1811. Hidalgo was then beheaded, along with other rebel leaders, and his head placed in an iron cage hung on one of the four corners of the granary roof at Guanajuato. The main threat of the "caste war" had ended for the time being, even though the idea of independence remained very much alive.

Hidalgo's rebellion was viewed generally as an Indian uprising at the time, which is one of the reasons why the creoles abandoned the movement so quickly. The term used to refer to the Indians, "indios," was highly ambiguous (indeed, it still is in Mexico), and under this rubric were included poor, underclass, rural mestizos. Indeed, Hidalgo's ragged "army" was made up of mestizos, mulattoes, and poor creoles, as well as Indians. Nevertheless, it is noteworthy that tens of thousands of Indians from the Bajío and western Mexico did take up arms under Hidalgo. We know little about the ethnic identities of these Indians, but most of them appear to have been Nahua and Otomí speakers. Enemies of the movement referred to Hidalgo's Indians as "Chichimecs," arguing that they were wild savages very different from the civilized Indians in the central and southern zones of Mexico. More likely, however, they were descendants of aboriginal peoples who had once been part of the pre-Hispanic Mesoamerican world, albeit the northwestern periphery of that world (see Chapter 3 for information on that periphery).

The native peoples to the south of the Bajío in central and southern Mexico largely rejected Hidalgo's call to arms. The historian John Tutino (1986) claims that this rejection helps explain the failure of the Hidalgo forces to take Mexico City: The rebels were not supported with either warriors or supplies by the Indians in areas like Toluca and Morelos on the road to the capital. The Indians in these areas had retained traditional community organizations, and they had worked out a stable symbiosis with neighboring haciendas. While these Indians provided much of the labor needed to work the haciendas, the haciendas in turn protected the Indians' local autonomy and, within limits, community lands. Thus, the Indians nearer to the capital were able to maintain strong peasant communities and traditional Mesoamerican cultures. They provided a sharp contrast to the Indians of the Bajío and Guadalajara area who joined with Hidalgo. The latter had been subjected to irresistible commercial forces that disrupted their communities, proletarianized the able-bodied men, and shattered the traditional Mesoamerican cultures. Such Mesoamerican

Indians were attracted to Hidalgo's movement and had considerably less to lose from joining it than the communities of Indians located adjacent to the Basin of Mexico.

The thousands of Indians from the north and west who followed Hidalgo saw him as a charismatic religious leader whose message was sympathetic to their repressed social condition (Hidaglo was not unlike the friar in Chiapas who translated the Spanish constitutional proclamation into the Tzotzil language as recounted in Box 7.1). As noted, Hidalgo played to the Indians' religious inclinations by adopting the Virgin of Guadalupe as the movement's key symbol, a symbol deeply meaningful to the Indians. On a more practical level, as priest of Dolores, Hidalgo was widely respected for having promoted a series of "development" projects to help the Indians. Among the projects—managed by the Indians themselves—were commercial pottery making, cultivation of silkworms, and the growing of grapes for wine and olives for oil.

Hidalgo struck a responsive chord with the struggling Indians of the Bajío when he spoke of his movement as a "reconquest," undoing some of the wrongs inflicted on the Indians by the Spanish conquistadors. He pronounced in favor of eliminating the hated tribute payments and of returning lands to the Indians (Hidalgo's Indians were allowed to keep properties taken from Spaniards during the war). Hidalgo was not a revolutionary, and we must not exaggerate the extent to which his movement was carried out on behalf of the Indians. Yet, the Indians believed he was on their side, and they became faithful, even fanatical, followers.

Hidalgo's independence movement in Mexico was carried on after his death by others, particularly by another parish priest from the Michoacán area, José María Morelos. Morelos's followers were primarily mestizos and mulattoes rather than Indians, recruited largely from among the peons working on haciendas in the lowland areas of Michoacán and Guerrero. Morelos, in fact, forbade his followers to use the term "indio," which he felt helped perpetuate the colonial caste system. Nevertheless, he was strongly supported by Mixtec Indians in the military takeover and plundering of Oaxaca (Reina Aoyama 2004:96ff). Morelos came to envision a Mexican nation that would revere its Mesoamerican ancestry and give the native peoples their rightful place within it. Thus, at a rebel constitutional assembly in Chilpancingo (Guerrero) in 1813, Morelos issued the following proclamation:

> Spirits of Motecuhzoma, Cacamatzín, Cuauhtemoc, Xicotencatl, and Calzontzín! Take pride in this August assembly, and celebrate this happy moment in which your sons have congregated to avenge your insults! After August 12, 1521, comes September 8, 1813! The first date tightened the chains of our slavery in Mexico-Tenochtitlán; the second broke them forever in the town of Chilpancingo. . . . We are therefore going to restore the Mexican Empire! (Cumberland 1968:125)

Morelos's warrior band was much smaller than Hidalgo's, and it never posed a serious threat to the Spaniards and their creole allies. Like Hidalgo, Morelos attempted to strike against Mexico City, but he also failed to find support from the Indian peasants in the areas surrounding the Central Basin. Even in the area of the present-day state of Morelos (named after this independence hero), which 100 years later would become the center of the Mexican revolution, the Nahuatl-speaking Indians there remained ensconced within their communities and generally did not support the independence rebellion. Morelos was captured and executed by the Spaniards in 1815.

Following the death of Morelos, Mexico's independence movement fell into the hands of more conservative creole leaders, who feared not only "revolutionary" rebels like Hidalgo and Morelos but also liberal reformers in Spain. These creoles convinced the remaining rebel leaders that their own more moderate plan for independence would include social justice for Indians and mestizos. Under the leadership of a creole military official, Agustín de Iturbide, the creoles finally took possession of Mexico City in September 1821 against only token opposition from the Spaniards. Mexico was now in the hands of "Spanish Americans," some of whom (the conservatives) would try to revive the very colonial system that leaders like Hidalgo and Morelos and their Indian and mestizo followers had struggled so hard to eliminate.

The Independence Movements in Central America

The independence movements in Central America were more responses to external factors than in Mexico, and they produced no large-scale civil war. As in Mexico, however, conservative creoles led these movements, in part out of opposition to the liberal policies emanating from Spain but also because they were inspired by Iturbide's imperialization of Central America. They declared independence in Guatemala on September 15, 1821, and five months later under pressure from Iturbide accepted annexation by the Mexican "empire." Opposition to these decisions came largely from liberal creoles and mestizos concentrated in the southern provinces of Central America, where resentment of political dominance by Guatemala was strong. Rebellious Salvadorans eventually had to be brought into line by Iturbide's troops.

At this point, events in Mexico once again determined the fate of Central America, as the Mexican empire crumbled and Central Americans declared independence for a second time in July 1823 (this time Chiapas decided to remain with Mexico). Subsequently, the Federation of Central American States was founded under the leadership of creole and mestizo liberals. Although no large Hidalgo-type national movement broke out in Central America, many smaller Indian rebellions erupted prior to independence, and they indirectly contributed to the eventual successessful independence rupture. These uprisings not only demonstrated the weakness of the Spanish regime but also convinced the creoles in the region that if they did not take matters into their own hands, a popular "revolution" might ensue. As one scholar has observed (Jonas 1974:119): "It is frequently said that Central American independence was an achievement of the *criollos* alone. Insofar as *ladinos* and Indians participated in various phases of the movement, and insofar as their participation forced the *criollos* to take up the cry for independence, this was not the case."

Indian uprisings in the decade prior to independence were focused on the issue of tribute payments, which had been abolished by the liberal Spanish assembly in 1811, but were reimposed in 1814, only to be again removed in 1820. Many Indian communities refused to pay tributes after 1811, and their inhabitants violently resisted attempts by Spanish and Crown officials to force them to comply. Rebellion against the reimposition of tributes became endemic throughout the highlands of Guatemala during these years, and spread through El Salvador and Nicaragua.

The rebellions by Indians in Nicaragua were particularly threatening to Spanish rule there. Between 1811 and 1812, bands of rebels numbering over 12,000 in number (mostly Subtiaba and Pipil Indians from León, Masaya, and Rivas, Nicaragua) were able to temporarily seize the reins of local government from the ruling Spaniards and creoles. The rebel leaders, among them several priests, formed more extended but weaker alliances. The rebels armed themselves and demanded an end to such hated colonial practices as tribute payment, forced labor, and slavery. The movement was all but destroyed in 1811, however, when local creole collaborators jumped sides and aided contingents of Spanish soldiers sent from Olancho (Honduras), San Miguel (El Salvador), and Cartago (Costa Rica) to put down the rebellion. Nevertheless, led by a Subtiaba Indian priest, Tomás Ruiz, the Nicaraguan rebels participated in the so-called Belén "conspiracy" in Guatemala (1813), which was designed to free their incarcerated comrades, initiate a colonywide military uprising, and declare independence.

The Atanasio Tzul Rebellion. The Central American rebellion from the independence period that perhaps has received most scholarly attention was initiated just prior to independence from Spain by an Indian leader named Atanasio Tzul, from Totonicapán, Guatemala. For details of the uprising, see Box 7.2; see also the map in Figure 7.1 for the location of places mentioned in connection with the Tzul rebellion.

The Tzul rebellion has been largely discounted in scholarly discussions of Central America's independence movements. Some have argued that it had nothing to do with independence from Spain but was merely another "colonial riot" against abuses by the Spaniards and their creole collaborators. Even its nativistic features have been denied, with the argument that Atanasio Tzul was only assuming the role of the deposed regional Spanish authority and dramatizing his loyalty to the Spanish king by taking the crown of a Catholic saint (McCreery 1989). It has been noted too that the rebellion was restricted to the Totonicapán area and hence should be seen as the product of a colonial system that had forced the Indians into relatively closed, isolated communities. These are all important points, and it must be conceded that Tzul and his followers were heavily influenced by Spanish institutions, did remain respectful of the Spanish Crown, and indeed were unable to marshal enough broad support to keep the movement going for very long.

The Guatemalan historian Daniel Contreras (1951), however, has argued persuasively that the Tzul rebellion must be seen as part of the larger independence movement of 1821. After all, he says, in their own way the Indians were struggling to be liberated from the repression of the Spanish system and thus added their "grain" to the success of the larger movement. He points out that the creole officials on the scene considered the rebellion to be not a mere local riot but a true, premeditated conspiracy that could easily become a general insurrection. Those creole officials

---

Box 7.2   The Atanasio Tzul Rebellion

As with so many other native uprisings in Guatemala of the time, the immediate cause of the Tzul uprising was the refusal of the K'iche' Mayan Indians of San Miguel Totonicapán to pay tributes. Already in 1816 the community's Indian alcalde, Atanasio Tzul, had refused to collect the prescribed tributes for the Crown, and in subsequent years as governor he had personally traveled to the colonial capital (Santiago de Guatemala) in order to obtain official papers exonerating the Indians from further payments. Atanasio was considered to be a cacique in Totonicapán, a status that gave him particularly strong legitimacy among the Indians of that community. Furthermore, he was the head of a large and powerful clan located just to the northwest of the town center, and he was a direct descendant of royal officials who in aboriginal times had been sent from the capital of the K'iche' empire to rule over the Totonicapán province.

By 1820, the Indians of the greater Totonicapán area had rebelled against further payment of tributes. Atanasio Tzul became the focal point of the resistance, assisted by Lucas Aguilar, a Totonicapán Indian of commoner status. Leaders from surrounding Indian communities such as San Francisco El Alto, Chiquimula, and Momostenango coordinated efforts with Tzul to do away with the tribute payments, and if necessary to cast aside the regional Spanish officials. On July 5, Tzul and his followers drove out the leading regional Spanish official *(alcalde mayor)*, threatened and then deposed the local native authorities, and took charge of regional government. In an elaborate ceremony celebrated with processions, dancing, and music, Atanasio Tzul was crowned "King of the K'iche'" under a feathered canopy, and Aguilar was named "President." Tzul's crown was taken from Saint Joseph's statue, and he also donned Spanish pants, shoes, and sword. His wife Felipa was named Queen and given the crown of Saint Cecilia. Messages sent to Tzul from Indians in the surrounding towns clearly indicate that Atanasio's crowning was taken seriously by thousands of K'iche' Mayan Indians, who began to address him with such honorary titles as "Our Lord" and "Your Grace."

Atanasio Tzul's reign as king of the K'iches was short-lived. The Spaniards organized an army of over 1,000 men made up of soldiers from Spanish towns in the highlands, and they marched on Totonicapán almost exactly one month after Tzul's crowning. The town was taken without opposition, although rebels from surrounding communities attacked the Spanish soldiers with slings, stones, and machetes from positions in the mountains above the road leading into Totonicapán. The Spanish soldiers looted many homes in Totonicapán, and dozens of Indians were whipped and threatened. Tzul, Aguilar, and other native leaders were carried off as prisoners to Quetzaltenango, where they were tried for sedition. Although found guilty, Tzul and the other K'iche' leaders were pardoned seven months later.

---

understood, too, what some modern-day scholars tend to overlook: The Indians had never lost the desire to be free of colonial rule and thus had persisted as a partially digested Indian "nation," not strictly autonomous but nevertheless culturally distinct from the Spanish, creole, and mestizo peoples who dominated them. Too often, Contreras observes, Indian rebellions are seen as "caste wars," racial vendettas, rather than the liberation movements that they were. Contreras concludes:

> . . . it is not possible to deny the similarity in goals between the creole and Indian groups: a change in the political, economic, and social regime. Therefore, if one wants to obtain the complete picture of the total historical development of our political emancipation (Central American Independence), one cannot forget the Indian rebellions (p.69).

The Tzul rebellion, like others from this time period in Central America, was inspired in part by the past Mesoamerican cultural world, despite denials by some scholars and even by Atanasio Tzul himself in testimony to Spanish magistrates (under the circumstances, it is understandable that he would deny trying to organize a countergovernment to the royal colonial regime!). The rebellion suggests that the idea of restoring the old K'iche' Mayan kingdom was very much alive among the Indians of the western highlands 300 years after the Spanish invasion, as proven by the widespread acceptance of Atanasio Tzul as "King" by Indians from other communities. Furthermore, subsequent to independence these same Indians continued to struggle to establish their own native "King." Even though Atanasio Tzul did not seem to express in his persona all the characteristics typical of the prophet-leaders of independence movements in Mexico, his royal Mayan ancestry was still revered and must have been a source of enormous legitimacy. And, despite the many Spanish elements that found their way into Tzul's coronation ceremony, we can be certain that most of the deeper meanings associated with the processions, crowning, and ritual language employed in Totonicapán were profoundly K'iche' Mayan, and hence part of the Mesoamerican legacy.

MESOAMERICAN INDIANS UNDER CONSERVATIVE AND LIBERAL RULE

The profound changes described earlier for Mexico and Central America during the century following the independence movements and collapse of Spanish rule resulted in major transformations in the social life and cultures of the remnant Mesoamerican peoples. The question arises as to just how, in fact, the Mesoamerican Indians were affected by the turbulent conditions of the postindependence (neocolonial) period. As we shall now see, the situation of the Indians under creole rule remained highly oppressive and became progressively worse as liberal policies were periodically implemented.

Creating Ethnonational Identities

The postindependence struggles between individual power-seeking creole *caudillos,* each supported by Indian and mestizo dependents, became political "schools" for the mestizos and, to a lesser extent, the Indians. The mestizos especially took advantage of the unusually chaotic conditions after independence to become acquainted with regional power, and to achieve their first positions of political leadership. Eventually, *caudillos* from the mestizo sector would achieve power at the national level, notably in the cases of Benito Juárez and Porfirio Díaz in Mexico, and Rafael Carrera in Guatemala.

In his classic book *Sons of the Shaking Earth* (1959), the anthropologist Eric Wolf points out that relative gains in power by mestizos after independence, as compared with the Indians, were correlated with the contrasting cultural systems that guided the two ethnic groups in their struggle for survival. The mestizo culture placed stress on entrepreneurial skills, and also the drive for power and self-improvement. The

Mesoamerican Indians' culture was based more on traditional Mesoamerican principles, and in some ways was in dialectical relationship with the mestizo system. Compared with the mestizos, for example, the Indians were less open to change, less willing to take risks, less socially ambitious, more oriented to collective than individual goals, and far less articulate in the Spanish language. These differences provided the mestizos with a comparative advantage over the Indians as the two groups struggled against creole repression during the long neocolonial period.

The differences between mestizos and native Mesoamericans, of course, were partly based on their respective social class positions. The mestizos shared a common social alienation and exclusion, and thus formed a marginal lower-class status within Mexican and Central American society. They functioned in a wide variety of low-prestige occupations, as petty officials, small ranchers, low-level priests, humble artisans, petty traders, half-employed paupers, cattle rustlers, and town thieves. The Mesoamerican Indians also shared a common alienation within the dominant creole world, but their lower-class status was more clearly defined for them in ethnic terms—and at times legally—as members of the inferior native caste. The Indians were less economically diversified than the mestizos, most of them working in agriculture either as peasant cultivators or hacienda peons.

The differences between the Indian communities in language and custom made it more difficult to unite into larger political groups on the basis of common class or ethnicity. Only on a few occasions were the Mesoamerican Indians able to challenge the creole establishment: As described later, by means of neocolonial nativistic movements.

The identification of the mestizos and Indians as culturally distinct sectors in neocolonial society theoretically made both of them eligible candidates to serve as symbols for the emerging nations of Mexico and Central America. In Mexico during the early years following independence, a few enlightened creoles proposed that the new nation adopt the native Mesoamericans as the central identifying ethnic symbol. One creole leader even suggested that a descendant of Motecuhzoma be crowned emperor of a new Mexican empire, after which the monarch should take a wife from among the "Whites," thus binding the races together. These suggestions did not prevail, and, as might be expected, the Spanish and creole Whites emerged as the dominant ethnic identity. For example, Hernán Cortés was glorified and hailed as the true founder of the Mexican nation.

Later, when upwardly mobile mestizos began to challenge creole leadership in Mexico, the creole rulers hit upon the idea of fomenting a massive immigration of Europeans (particularly the French) and North Americans as a means of preserving the country's ethnically White identity (and not coincidentally, preserving the creole's political control). Of this policy, a modern Mexican scholar has remarked: ". . . it seems inconceivable that our creole liberators were willing to hand us over to the North Americans or English rather than accept an Indian (identity) for Mexico" (Aguirre 1983:328). In the end the mestizos could not be denied, and during the Porfirio Díaz dictatorship they began to replace the creole Whites as the symbol of national race ("raza"). Consistent with Díaz's liberal positivism, however, ethnicity came to be seen more in cultural than in racial terms. The Mexican mestizo was said to combine the progressive traits of the Whites and the fighting spirit of the Indians.

In Central America a national identity based on the image of the White creole remained strong throughout the entire neocolonial period, and even mestizos (or, as they were generally called, "Ladinos") found it hard to gain ethnic recognition within the budding national cultures. Indian ethnicity was totally discounted, creating a pathetic situation in which the Mesoamericans and other native peoples of Central America had become foreigners in their own land.

Impact of Liberal Reforms on the Mesoamerican Indians

Even before independence was achieved from Spain, beginning with the Bourbon reforms toward the end of the Colonial period and continuing through the entire nineteenth century and into the early twentieth century, the Mesoamerican Indians were under pressure from the liberal faction of the creoles, and especially mestizos, to assimilate into the wider colonial and later national society. Liberal attempts to "reform" the Indian communities were specifically aimed at forcing them to adopt the Spanish language, practice orthodox Catholicism, work for wages, and generally replace native practices and beliefs with Western ways.

In contrast, the conservative creoles believed that they benefited from maintaining the Indians as an inferior "caste," and therefore they tended to oppose reforms that would transform the natives' social condition. This difference helps explain why most Mesoamerican Indians preferred conservative "centralism" to liberal "federalism." The conservative creoles were interested in freezing the Indians in their inferior castelike colonial status. As long as the Indians paid tributes in the form of goods and services, the conservatives were largely content to let them organize their rural communities as they pleased. As the Mexican writer Octavio Paz (1961) points out, in postindependence Mexico the conservative *caudillos* were heirs to the old Spanish order, and they actually employed Spanish colonial law in dealing with the Indians. Among other things this meant that the Indians would be legally distinct from both the creoles and the Mestizos, and as a result would occupy a secure but inferior position in society.

Liberal reform programs were stronger in nineteenth-century Mexico than in Central America, especially during the final fifty years. The pivotal Mexican liberal figure was Benito Juárez, a Zapotece Indian from Oaxaca (see Box 7.3 for a description of Juárez's Indian ancestry and attitude toward the Indians of Mexico). Juárez attempted to establish a more just society in Mexico, one based on law and equal rights for all Mexicans. He courageously resisted the American invasion of the national territory, spearheaded the effort to establish an enlightened national constitution (1857), and led the military struggle to overthrow the conservative-backed Maximilian monarchy.

Juárez's successor, Porfirio Díaz (Figure 7.6), further solidified liberal rule, brought order to Mexico, and greatly increased national integration. Nevertheless, as Paz (1961:133) explains, the political philosophy behind the liberal reforms negated Mexico's Indian past, and therefore was necessarily sterile and empty: "The

Box 7.3   Benito Juárez, Mexico's Greatest Indian Hero

Benito Juárez was born into a Zapotec Indian family of noble descent in a small town of Oaxaca. As a boy he spoke only the Zapotec tongue and served as a shepard of his uncle's sheep. At around twelve years of age he moved to Oaxaca city, with the idea of learning Spanish and seeking a better future. There he studied philosophy, theology, and eventually law at the Institute of Arts and Sciences. Eventually he became the director of the Institute and a member of the city council. At the age of thirty-seven he married a woman of creole descent, and the children he had with her were recognized as mestizos.

Benito's wisdom and knowledge of law led to his being named governor of Oaxaca, whereby he gained considerable legtimacy by basing his governance on the rule of law. He remained close to the Church at this time, although later on his liberal policies brought deep opposition from the priesthood and their conservative supporters. According to one historian (Krauze 1997:164), underneath Juárez's legalism and serious demeanor "[h]e resembled a Zapotec idol, an imperturbable god, stonelike, dressed always in a dark frock coat" (p. 164). Gobernor Juárez's opposition to President Santa Anna—he forbad the President to visit Oaxaca—elevated his stature to national heights, especially after the President sent him into exile (to New Orleans). His stature continued to move upward by his playing a key role in writing the liberal Constitution, followed by his leadership of liberal forces in the civil war against conservatives who opposed the constitutional reforms. Juárez became president of the Republic in 1861.

During Juárez's long political career, he chose not to issue policies that directly favored the Indians. In fact, he was often opposed by Indian rebels in areas such as Nayarit, the Yaqui valley, Yucatán, and Chiapas. Many Indians even supported the imposed emperor Maximilian rather than Juárez. Like other liberals, Juárez believed that the mestizos were the future of Mexico, and he opened the door to their rise to national power. Nevertheless, in supporting the liberal ideas of law, constitution, and reform, he is reputed to have applied "the instinctive knowledge of his forefathers." Furthermore, it is claimed that his "innermost and religious longing . . . [was to] save the Indians, 'our brothers,' from the clergy, from ignorance, from servitude from 'torpid poverty'" (Krause 1997:204).

past returned, decked out in the trappings of progress, science, and republican laws . . . (an) imposition of juridical and cultural forms which not only did not express our true nature but actually smothered and immobilized it."

It is not surprising that the Indians of Mexico reacted negatively to the recurring liberal reforms. Many of them supported the imperial rule of Maximilian, and Indian rebellions during the liberal period were endemic, sometimes led by *caudillos* who claimed Mesoamerican ancestry. These rebellions should be seen as violent rejections of the repressive effects of reform policies, and thus might be considered true liberation movements. The rebellious Indians were inspired by such noble goals as community autonomy, preservation of land rights, and cultural preservation. The creoles understood just how radical the Indian rebellions were to their own long-range goals, and this fact helped push the conservative and liberal factions into common cause and in the end tipped the balance toward the liberal policy of Indian assimilation.

The liberal reforms had similar consequences in Central America, although the native rebellions there were smaller in scope and came later in time. The most important uprising took place in Guatemala, where the mestizo *caudillo* Rafael Carrera

Figure 7.6   Porfirio Díaz, mestizo caudillo and liberal dictator of Mexico. James A. Magner, *Men of Mexico*, 2nd ed. Salem, N.H.: Books for Libraries, Ayer Company Publishers, 1968.

led a massive movement against the liberals. He was supported not only by poor mestizos from the eastern part of the country but also by tens of thousands of Mayan Indians from the western highlands (Figure 7.7). The Carrera rebellion led to thirty years of conservative rule in Guatemala, which in turn elicited relative peace from the Indians. Finally, in the latter part of the nineteenth century, the *caudillo* Justo Rufino Barrios was able to reestablish liberal rule in Guatemala, and this change again touched off widespread native rebellions in that country as well as similar conflicts in El Salvador and Nicaragua.

The dramatic liberal programs introduced by Barrios and other dictators in Central America have been hailed by many as laying the foundation for nationhood in the region. However, from the perspective of the Mesoamerican Indians, these

Figure 7.7   Rafael Carrera,
conservative dictator of Guatemala.
Source unknown.

programs were repressive, sterile impositions. As in Mexico, the Central American liberal regimes applied excessive force against the Indians and lower-class mestizos in
an attempt to ensure the availability of cheap labor for the burgeoning capitalist enterprises (coffee and banana plantations) being established in the region.

Conservative Followed by Liberal Rule in the Mayan Community of Momostenango.
The specific case of a native Mesoamerican community in nineteenth-century
Guatemala will help us understand the impact that liberal reforms had on local
Indian communities in Mexico and Central America during this phase of
neocolonial history. The community, Santiago Momostenango, was one of
approximately 700 Indian communities subjected to Spanish rule within the colonial
Captaincy General of Guatemala. Even though Momostenango's tributary
obligations to their colonial overlords had not been particularly onerous, the Mayan
Indians there considered tributes to be an undesirable burden, and the local
inhabitants rose up in open rebellion against them toward the end of the colonial
period.

Following independence, the Momostenango Indians rallied behind the mestizo *caudillo* Rafael Carrera, and during the 1840s they helped him seize the presidency of the Republic and then maintain dictatorial hold over it. The Momostecans considered Carrera to be their personal patron lord and served him faithfully as client warriors and tributaries. In return, the conservative Carrera allowed the Momostecans to retain considerable political and cultural autonomy. Social conditions for the Indians of Momostenango under Carrera's rule are clearly revealed by a series of court cases dating from that period of time, the records of which are now preserved in the community's archives (Carmack 1995).

The court records show, for example, that as late as the 1860s the ancient K'iche' Mayan pattern of rural clans and districts had remained intact. Customary native law was still operating in Momostenango, and it enjoyed the respect of all the Indian sectors of the community. The Momostenango Indians were able to reconstitute these cultural traditions despite the fact that the municipal and regional authorities were now either creoles or mestizos (the latter were referred to as "Ladinos" in the court records). Special Indian judges were introduced in important legal cases, as during the colonial period, and Spanish colonial laws relative to the Indians were still in use. Consistent with conservative thinking, the Indian judges dealt with the natives in highly paternalistic ways. One judge, for example, stated that the Indians had the right to receive special treatment because they were "ignorant, not ever having been taught the Gospel."

As a result of the liberal reforms carried out in Guatemala in the 1870s under the *caudillo* Justo Rufino Barrios, the Indians in Momostenango lost nearly half of their best agricultural lands, and this event facilitated the forced labor of hundreds of Momostecans on the new coffee plantations in the Pacific Coast. Liberal creole and mestizo authorities were now put in charge of virtually all activities in Momostenango, in a drastic reduction of the autonomy that the community had enjoyed during the Carrera years. Momostenango's Indians rose up against the liberal authorities in 1876 and fought a bitter guerrilla war to preserve their traditional privileges as Indians. The liberal armies ruthlessly quashed the native rebellion, after which they executed several rebel leaders and burned the homes of collaborators. Momostenango's Indians were thenceforth subjected to years of suffocating control under a series of subseqent liberal dictators.

The social conditions of the Momostenango Indians under the repressive liberal regimes were dramatically cast into relief by a murder that took place in the community in the early morning hours of a day in February 1899 (Figure 7.8). As an Indian named Timoteo attended the wake of his sister at the house of his in-laws, an Indian militia lieutenant named Fermín led a patrol of soldiers into the house, where he embraced Timoteo and then plunged a knife into his heart. Lt. Fermín was taken into custody a few hours later by the mestizo *alcalde* (mayor). Acting as justice of the peace, the alcalde had the body examined by an "expert," took testimony from the many witnesses to the stabbing, and remitted the case and the prisoner to the Court of First Appeal in the regional capital of Totonicapán (Atanacio Tzul's home community). Timoteo's father employed the services of a highly skilled and educated

Figure 7.8 Parade of local police and militia in the town center of Momostenango, 1968. Photograph provided by authors.

mestizo lawyer to prosecute the murderer, whereas Lt. Fermín's defense was made by an educated local Indian. The court proceedings lasted for eight months and resulted in a guilty verdict for Fermín. He was sentenced to ten years in prison for murdering Timoteo, and an appeal to a higher court was rejected. In less than two years, however, liberal President Manuel Estrada Cabrera pardoned Fermín, and he was freed from prison in 1904.

This case reveals that most of the Indians involved in the dramatic events were active participants in the local militia organization. Besides Lt. Fermín and his Indian patrol members, it appears that Timoteo, his male in-laws, and the local Indian "lawyer" were also militiamen. All the principal Indian actors appear to have been significantly acculturated to ladino ways: They spoke Spanish, were active in commerce, had familiarity with the legal system, and depended more on ties of friendship than on kinship relations. Even the manner in which the crime was committed—in a public setting, using a knife—was a mestizo rather than an Indian pattern, for murder in rural Momostenango usually was interpreted by the K'iche' Indians there as an act of witchcraft. Nor were the motives behind the crime traditional native motives, but instead the more typical mestizo motives of jealousy over women or insults against

Box 7.4 Tepoztlán, Mexico, and the Liberal Reforms

The anthropologist Oscar Lewis's classic account of Tepoztlán, Mexico, *Life in a Mexican Village* (1963), provides a brief but insightful social history of that community during a liberal phase of the neocolonial period.

In pre-Hispanic times, Tepoztlán had been a city state within one of the Aztec provinces, paying tributes largely in the form of paper, lime, cotton cloth, and turkeys. During the Colonial period, Tepoztlán was subjected to Spanish governors residing in Cuernavaca. Tributes were paid in maize and money, as well as in the form of onerous labor in the mines of Taxco and nearby sugar haciendas. A large number of local officials, including *caciques* who were descended from the pre-Hispanic ruling class, were also supported by tribute payments.

Conditions for the common people worsened following independence. The *caciques*, Church, and haciendas all increased their monopoly hold on the land properties of the area, and the "tithes" now demanded by the Church surpassed in amount what the Tepoztecans had paid as tributes during the Colonial period. The local *cacique* Indians collaborated with the ruling creoles, enhancing the former's wealth and power over the local population. Most Tepoztecans became poor peasants, forced to labor part-time on plantations as peons for pitifully low wages. The liberal reforms of Benito Juárez divided the community, most of the inhabitants siding with the conservative Church, which had lost properties. A few, however, sided with the liberal government and formed a military unit that fought bravely in the war to drive Maximilian and the French out of Mexico.

Nevertheless, under continued liberal rule the *caciques* grew ever more powerful while the Tepoztlán Indian peasants became poorer. Rebellious actions by the Indians was common, but most rebels would be quickly rounded up, imprisoned, and either banished from the community or forced to serve in the army. By the time of the Porfirio Díaz period, the vast majority of the Tepoztlán Indians had become landless. They were not permitted to use the communal lands, and thus had no alternative but to labor on the nearby sugar plantations, mainly as indebted peons. These native peons were positioned at the bottom of a highly stratified society, exploited not only by the upper-class mestizos and creoles of the region but also by the local cacique rulers. The old custom of collecting religious taxes was reinstituted, as was obligatory participation in an elaborate calendar of religious ceremonies and fiestas. As a result, many of the poorer Tepoztecans became increasingly critical of the Church, a clear prelude to the strong anti-Church ideas that erupted later in connection with the Mexican revolution.

An account of what life was like for the Indians during the Díaz period was recited to Lewis by a small landholder who still remembered those years. The account provides a graphic view of Tepoztlán during the liberal periods (Lewis 1963:95):

> The thing that was truly scarce was work. And so during the difficult times from January to May and from August to September the stronger among us went to work on the sugar plantations . . . in the state of Morelos. The owners of the plantations were *gachupines* (Spaniards), and they mistreated the Indians, kicking and insulting them. These plantations also robbed the nearby villages of their lands. This is what happened to Tepoztlán. We lost some of our best lands. The rich here had their lands and produced good crops, but the poor had no lands. The poor ate chile and salt and some beans. Meat was had once a month at best. . . . The local government was in the hands of *caciques*. [Cacique] Vicente Ortega held power for many years, with the support of the state authorities among whom he had ties of *compadrazgo* [ritual kinship relations]. There were no political parties or opposition groups allowed. . . . Anyone who opposed his rule might be sent to prison in Quintana Roo.

As this description makes clear, the Indians of Tepoztlán were profoundly exploited by the Mexican liberal regimes, and in the process they were becoming secularized and losing many of their Mesoamerican cultural ideas and practices.

personal dignity. The court record also indicates that the law being applied by the authorities in this case no longer made legal distinction between Indians and mestizos. In fact, the Indian defender of the accused presented an elegant argument to the effect that "moral" considerations were not relevant, only legal ones, as befitted "[liberal] modern legislation." It is evident, too, that some Indians were active participants in the liberal establishment itself, including Lt. Fermín, the militia head, and the educated Indian who acted as the victim's legal defense.

Liberal reforms in Guatemala introduced major changes into Indian communities such as Momostenango. The Indians were being transformed in thought, language, custom, and social position. The great majority of them had been subordinated to the political control of creole and mestizo authorities and were being severely exploited economically on the coffee plantations and cattle ranches where they were forced to labor. That the impact of liberalism on the Indian communities of Mexico was similar to that of Momostenango and other Central American communities, is illustrated by the case of Tepoztlán, Mexico, summarized in Box 7.4. (See the map in Figure 7.1 for the location of Tepoztlán.)

NATIVIST MOVEMENTS
BY MESOAMERICAN INDIANS

Exploitation of the Mesoamerican Indians by the conservative, and ever more so by the liberal rulers of Mexico and Central America, coupled with their peripheralization by U.S. and European powers, was bound to elicit a radical response from the millions of Mesoamerican Indians who survived into the postindependence period. Without access to the written word, these poor and marginalized peoples were nevertheless quite aware of what was happening to and around them. Employing quite rational logic, they took advantage of "openings" in national and regional events (such as the U.S.–Mexico war between 1846 and 1848) to mount massive and vigorous movements in support of their native ethnicities and in protest against their degraded social condition.

Mexico and the Central American countries experienced hundreds of these rebellious movements on the part of the native Mesoamerican communities. The movements typically addressed longstanding economic and political grievances against the local representatives of the national powers, and they nearly always advocated their causes by demanding religious and political autonomy as well as recognition of their respective native ethnic identities. A few of the movements created national panic, as when masses of Mayan Indians in Yucatán rebelled against national rule just at the time that Mexico was losing large parts of its northern territory to the United States (see the account to follow on the "Caste War of Yucatán"). Indians from one community would rise up in arms against the creole and mestizo oppressors, usually joined by those from other communities in the region, especially where the Indians comprised the majority populations in their respective regions. The Indians frequently justified this militancy by mobilizing Mesoamerican symbols in the name of native separatism, and for this reason the rebellions are often referred to as "nativist" movements.

Most nativist movements were violently suppressed by state military mobilization, as happened in the case of the independence movements led by Hidalgo and Morelos. Nevertheless, some of them proved to be rather long-lasting. They expressed in poignant terms the reality of certain regions with hidden "majorities" of Indians, especially those living within rural communities but also many now living outside the communities who had begun to participate in national economic and political life as servants to the ruling creole class.

The nativist movements of nineteenth- and early twentieth-century Mexico and Central America were not just cathartic expressions of "tradition," for they also provided a basis on which the Indians could adapt their own social and cultural traditions to the social changes being forced upon them by liberal reformers. Through time, these movements tended to expand in territorial scope and assimilate more of the dominant creole-mestizo culture. We have the paradox, then, of movements that helped the Mesoamerican Indians preserve their cultural heritage, at the same time that they united them in larger political organizations and incorporated more creole and mestizo culture than ever before.

Nativist movements as we are employing the terms here are not revolutionary movements. Their proponents marshal local kinship and village groups behind charismatic leaders, in contrast to revolutionary movements in which great classes of peasants or proletariats are united under the leadership of radical modernizers. We agree with social scientists like Frantz Fanon (1968), however, that nativist movements may prepare the way for later revolutions by creating hope, solidarity, and politicization among exploited native peoples. As we shall see in the next chapter, such a transition from nativist to revolutionary movements is precisely what occurred in the Mexico and Central America during the twentieth century.

We turn now to examples of prototypical nativistic movements carried out by the Mesoamerican Indians during the post-independence period, starting with a review of the most successful nativistic movement of the Mesoamerican region, the caste war of Yucatán, Mexico. This will be followed by a brief description of an important movement in Central America, the Nonualca rebellion of El Salvador.

The Caste War of Yucatán

In Nelson Reed's classic study, *The Caste War of Yucatán* (1964), he describes conditions in Yucatán during the first half of the ninteenth century that were typical of Indian areas during that period in Mexico and Central America. After independence, the creole *caudillos* of Yucatán competed with one another for regional power, rationalizing personal conflicts as contests over liberal versus conservative ideals. The contests particularly pitted *caudillos* from the city of Campeche against their counterparts in the capital city of Mérida. Large numbers of Mayan Indians were recruited as soldiers in the *caudillo* armies, and fighting alongside the mestizos they received on-the-job training in warfare and other creole practices.

The liberal *caudillos* of Yucatán began to push hard to expand plantation agriculture, especially the henequen industry, in the western part of the Peninsula as well as sugar in the eastern part. Under the auspices of liberal reform, the land and labor of the huge Mayan peasantry inhabiting the Peninsula were exploited. Thousands of Mayas were trapped on the plantations as peons (indebted workers); thousands of others fled to the Quintana Roo frontier zone, where they established independent peasant communities and became known as the Huites ("the loincloth people"). The Catholic Church was suppressed by the liberals too, and this diminished the ruling creoles' control over the Mayas and hence gave greater freedom for the latter to perservere in their traditional Mayan religious practices.

Around midcentury (1850), over 100,000 of the Huites in the eastern frontier finally rose up against liberal rule, and a "caste war" ensued with the Indians on one side and the now-united creoles and mestizos on the other. For the Mayas, the goal was liberation from what had become an intolerably repressive system of rule. The Mayan rebels succeeded in liberating a large area of Yucatán from Mexican control, but eventually they retreated to Quintana Roo where they established a separate "nation," which was called the "Empire of the Cross." This independent Mayan "empire" survived for over fifty years. The rallying symbol in both war and political organization for the Mayas was a series of sacred crosses dressed in *huipils* (native cotton "dresses"), which they claimed had suddenly appeared near a sacred well (*cenote*) in Chan Santa Cruz. It was believed that the crosses spoke to the charismatic leaders of the movement and instructed them on how to make war against the Whites.

The movement's message was strongly nativist, and it was a rejection of the liberal attempt to destroy the identity and culture that the Mayas had struggled to preserve throughout the centuries of domination, first by the Spaniards, and later by the peninsular creoles. The society created by the rebellious "people of the cross" was a fascinating syncretic creation, comprising a surprisingly large number of cultural features similar to those of the pre-Hispanic Mayas. Political leadership was vested in a prophet ruler (Tatich) who was said to have received messages from the talking idols (the crosses). The Mayan society was stratified into the ancient division between lords, commoners, and slaves (the slaves were white captives); and the traditional Mayan dispersed settlement pattern was instituted, consisting of a politico-ceremonial center surrounded by numerous small agricultural villages (Figure 7.9).

Important cultural features from the creole world were also woven into the rebel institutions. For example, creole-type military companies became important units of the social system; public administration was performed by secretaries and ecclesiastical officials similar to those found in creole society; and a Spanish-type cathedral was constructed on the spot where the crosses had first appeared. Within the church, masses and rituals dedicated to the saints were regularly conducted by Mayan priests.

In the creole and mestizo areas of Yucatán beyond the Empire of the Cross, the henequen industry greatly expanded and the nonrebellious Mayas were drawn further into the liberal system as indebted laborers. Finally, after Porfirio Díaz came to power in Mexico, the central government was able to gain control over the caudillo struggles in Yucatán by appointing loyal military leaders as governors of the state. General Bravo, one of these governors, defeated the hapless warriors of the Mayan empire around the turn of the century and once again incorporated Quintana Roo into Mexican territory. Despite their defeat, the rebel Mayas had succeeded in making an im-

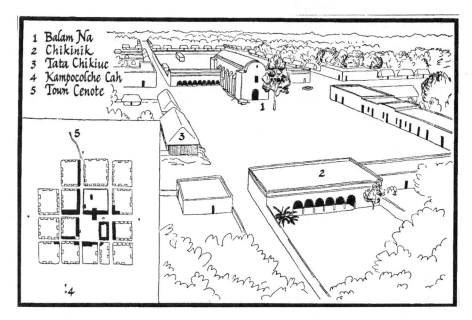

1 Balam Na
2 Chikinik
3 Tata Chikiuc
4 Kampocolche Cah
5 Town Cenote

Figure 7.9   Drawing of the town layout at Chan Santa Cruz, the capital of the rebellious Mayas of Yucatán. Reprinted from *The Caste War of Yucatan* by Nelson Reed with the permission of the publishers, Stanford University Press. © 1964 by the Board of Trustees of the Leland Stanford Junior University.

portant political point as a result of their fifty-year struggle: They were determined to survive as Mayas in spite of all attempts by Mexican overlords to destroy their way of life.

In a recent study of the Caste War of Yucatán, Terry Rugeley (1996) points out that one of the main differences between Yucatán and other parts of Mexico is that in Yucatán there was a particularly close relationship between the Catholic priests and the landlords on the one hand, and the liberal politicians on the other hand. When the Liberals reimposed the Church tax system on the Mayas, the Indian rebels "seized upon the opportunity to end their participation in the Spanish Catholic system altogether" (p. 182). As with the Hidalgo independence rebellion in northern Mexico, creole divisions in Yucatán had created a power vacuum. By bringing the peasant and peon Indians and mestizos into the frey, the liberals were prepararing these underclasses for a complete break with the state government: ". . . leaders who began separatist revolts soon found themselves overtaken by newer and more radical movements" (p. 184). The Mayan Indians in Yucatán, like the Otomí Indian followers of Hidaglo, were just acculturated enough to adopt nontraditional social means, but sufficiently near frontier zones to be free of excessive creole vigilance and to have access to weapons and areas of refuge.

For an account of an additional nativist movement in Mexico, see Box 7.5 on the Yaqui rebellions.

Box 7.5 The Yaqui Rebellions

The Yaqui Indians of Sonora, Mexico, have a long history of rebellious activity against outside rule (see the map in Figure 7.1 for the location of the Yaquis during the period under discussion). Occupying the banks of the Yaqui River, they formed part of the northwest periphery of Mesoamerica in pre-Hispanic times. They fiercely resisted conquest by the Spaniards, and remained outside colonial control until voluntarily submitting to the authority of liberal Jesuit missionaries in the early part of the seventeenth century. For 120 years the Yaquis lived peacefully in model villages organized by the Jesuits, governed by their own native authorities. With the increasing encroachment of Spanish, creole, and mestizo miners and ranchers into their territory, however, in 1740 the Yaquis joined with the neighboring Mayo Indians in a violent and bloody uprising against the Spaniards. Later, after the Jesuits were expelled from Mexico (in 1767), the Yaquis dispersed widely throughout the northwest area and thus evaded effective Spanish control. Consequently, they did not take sides, nor did they participate directly in Mexico's independence movements.

Creole liberal policy toward the Yaquis throughout the nineteenth century and into the early twentieth century called for their assimilation into Mexican society, access by outsiders to their fertile river lands, and expropriation of their labor for use in the adjacent mines and cattle haciendas. The Yaquis never acceded to these policies and repeatedly resisted every attempt to dominate them. Preservation of Yaqui identity, language, religion, and political system provided the underlying nativist inspiration for their unrelenting struggle against outsiders.

The first major Yaqui rebellion following independence took place in 1828 in response to an attempt by Mexican liberals to subject the Yaquis to local, regional, and national authorities, and to divide their lands into individual plots. The rebellion was led by a highly charismatic Yaqui leader, "Captain General" Juan Banderas, who rallied the native forces in the names of Father Hidalgo, the Virgin of Guadalupe, and Motecuhzoma. Banderas sought to unite all the native groups of the northwest in order to drive the Mexican Whites out of the area. The rebellion was interpreted by Mexican creoles and mestizos as a "race war." Banderas and his forces were effective in preventing the liberals from carrying out reforms in Yaqui country, and they managed to roam throughout Sonora, terrorizing the resident white settlers. Organized Yaqui militant actions ended, however, when Banderas was captured and executed in 1833.

The following decades saw renewed efforts by the liberal governments of Mexico to put the Yaquis under political control, but continued opposition by the organized Yaqui militias blocked all such attempts. Nevertheless, the area eventually became surrounded by Mexican mines, haciendas, and ranches, and the Yaquis increasingly were drawn away from their communities into wage labor (but not peonage). In 1873, a new charismatic leader named Cajeme emerged from among the Yaquis and led them once again into open rebellion.

Cajeme, who had previously served in the state militia, was a good organizer and helped the Yaquis to rebuild their communities and become more self-reliant. Under Cajeme the Yaquis regained political and territorial control over the river valley that had always defined their homeland. They adopted an openly nativist strategy to revitalize the ancient communal land tenure system, calendar of rituals, and council form of government. Many of these practices actually dated from the Colonial period, but since the Jesuit missionaries had originally allowed the Yaquis to blend Spanish with aboriginal ways, the revitalized patterns also had roots in the pre-Hispanic cultures of the area.

Yaqui claims to autonomy were totally rejected by the Porfirio Díaz regime, which had important commercial plans for developing the area. Contingents of the Mexican army launched military campaigns against the Yaquis beginning in 1879, and they finally captured and executed Cajeme in 1887. The Yaquis continued the struggle through guerrilla warfare after that, until in 1903 Díaz turned to the ultimate solution of the Yaqui problem: The mass deportation of thousands of Yaqui men, women, and children to Yucatán and other select areas of southern Mexico. Many Yaquis fled to the cities of the northwest and exile communities near Tucson, Arizona. In the meantime, the Yaqui homeland was resettled by mestizo colonists and prepared for large-scale, irrigated commercial agriculture. The liberals had finally gained control over the Yaqui river valley, although the remarkable Yaqui people never willingly yielded to liberal authority.

A Pipil Movement in Central America

Nativist movements in Central America during the neocolonial period can be illustrated by a movement carried out by the Pipil Indians of Nonualco in El Salvador a few years after independence (see the map in Figure 7.1 for places mentioned in the account to follow).

Nonualco was an important province within the southeastern periphery of Mesoamerica in pre-Hispanic times. Located in a valley of the central piedmont zone southeast of present-day San Salvador, Nonualco probably exercised political control over the Jiquilisco Bay on the Pacific Coast. Its population was made up of over 5,000 Pipils (speakers of a Nahua language) and perhaps some Lencas as well (see Chapter 11 for information on the Pipil and Lenca languages). Nonualcans produced maize, beans, and chiles; extracted fish, salt, and cotton as tribute goods from their coastal subjects; and traded for other items such as cacao, honey, and obsidian.

At the time of the Spanish invasion, Nonualco had apparently been subjugated by the Pipil city-state of Cuzcatlan, whose capital was near present-day San Salvador. Nonualcans no doubt paid tributes to the Cuzcatlan rulers in the form of foods, including fish, and cotton cloth.

Following the conquest, the Nonualcans were concentrated into several more compact communities, among them Santiago, San Pedro, and San Juan Nonualco, and were forced to pay tributes to Spanish *encomenderos* (overlords). During the sixteenth century, cacao beans were one of the main tribute items paid by Nonualcans to the Spaniards. The indigo plant, which produced a blue dye, soon replaced cacao as the main commercial crop in the area, and the Nonualco Indians were forced to provide labor on the Spanish and creole indigo plantations. These indigo estates disrupted community life in Nonualco by encroaching on communal lands and draining off labor.

Toward the end of the Colonial period, the population of the three Nonualcan communities numbered over 4,000 persons, about 700 of them mestizos. These communities were surrounded by at least nine indigo and sugar-producing plantations. Relations between the Indians and the plantations were tense, and in 1789, the Nonualcans rose up in opposition to the low wages being paid by the indigo plantation owners. The rebellion was quickly put down, however, by the Spanish authorities. Between 1812 and 1814 the Nonualcans again rebelled, this time to protest the reinstatement of tributes by the Spanish Crown and the forced recruitment of Nonualco men into the creole militias organized to help El Salvador sever its ties with Guatemala.

Despite the many disruptions, the Nonualco communities survived the colonial period surprisingly well, and they confronted the postindependence liberal reforms with many traditional institutions reasonably intact. The Pipil language was still widely spoken, although Spanish had become the language of public discourse. The system of ancient kinship-based districts *(calpulli)* continued to operate in the communities, some districts having over 200 members. Native leadership was still in place, based in part on a continuation of the ancient noble and commoner status distinction. Lands had been lost to the indigo estates, but a significant portion of the communal lands was preserved. Trade was flourishing, and the Nonualcans were considered to be "rich" Indians.

By the 1830s, the liberals had been in power for several years in El Salvador, and their policy of favoring the indigo plantations was viewed by the Indians as highly oppressive. The Salvadoran province was on the verge of civil war, pitting the liberal creoles against the conservative creoles. The Indians were forced to fight for interests in which they had no stake. Thus, in 1833 the Nonualcans rebelled against the local creole authorities and plantation owners. They were led by Atanasio Aquino, a commoner Pipil Indian from Santiago Nonualco who had worked as a peon on the indigo estates. From the beginning, the uprising had strong nativist features, as Aquino assumed traditional Pipil titles and dress. He called for an end to creole domination over the Indians and mobilized the Indians and many mestizos from surrounding communities. The rebels quickly overpowered the main creole towns and estates of the area, as well as in the adjacent area of San Vicente.

Aquino's forces soon swelled to 3,000 warriors and easily beat back several military contingents sent by the government to put down the rebellion. Aquino adopted the title of "General Commander of the Liberation Forces," proclaiming a free and an autonomous Nonualco territory. He replaced the creole authorities with Indians and laid down a severe legal code to govern the affairs of the nearly independent territory (for example, thieves were to have their hands cut off!). It is generally conceded by scholars that Aquino's rebels could have taken the Salvadoran capital had they wished. Aquino, however, made no attempt to extend his control beyond the Nonualco area, not even to other Indian communities in the west that were sympathetic to his movement. A commission of Mayan Indians as far away as highland Guatemala came to negotiate with Aquino over the possibility of a pan-Indian union, but apparently Aquino's political vision was decidedly local rather than regional.

The Salvadoran creoles and most mestizos were profoundly frightened by Aquino and his Indian "terrorists." They regrouped, and reinforced by soldiers from Guatemala, managed to raise a force of 5,000 men who marched on Nonualco. The rebels were quickly routed and Aquino captured. The rebellion had lasted less than four months. Aquino was imprisoned, and after the formality of a trial, he was executed. Like Hidalgo in Mexico, his head was cut off, put in a stone cage, and placed on high for all to see (in Aquino's case, on a prominent hilltop).

Atanasio Aquino was a remarkably charismatic leader. He was deeply religious, and medallions of the saints dangled from his neck. His Christian beliefs were tightly interwoven with native "superstitions." He was an extremely brave warrior and excellent horseman. His fighting prowess was enhanced, he claimed, by a secret narcotic (probably coca) that he chewed in battle. Like Atanasio Tzul twelve years earlier and later the leaders of the Caste War of Yucatán, Aquino had himself crowned "king" (adopting Saint Joseph's crown for this purpose). There is some evidence that Aquino believed in the ancient Mesoamerican concept of companion animals (naguals) and that his nagual was the tiger (*ocelot*). He used a tiger skin as a saddle, and while in prison referred to himself as "a tiger without claws or fangs." During his rise to power, Aquino was able to integrate in his persona both native and Spanish cultural elements, and consequently to become an archetypical nativist prophet.

Events calmed down in Nonualco after the death of Aquino. By midcentury, coffee replaced indigo as El Salvador's main export crop and has remained so ever since.

In 1879, the liberals passed laws that made it possible for coffee owners to acquire additional lands from the Indian communities. Even though the Nonualco area largely fell outside the coffee zone, its native inhabitants were adversely affected by the new laws, and so they joined in widespread Indian rebellions in 1885. The center of native rebellion, however, had begun to shift to the western Izalco area, where Indian unrest there would again turn into a major conflagration in 1932 (as explained in Chapter 8).

U.S. MEDDLING AND OTHER ANTECENDENTS TO THE MODERN ERA

U.S. interference in the affairs of Mexico and Central America has a long history, extending back to the last decades of the colonial period and continuing on into the twentieth century. As early as 1786, Thomas Jefferson expressed the official U.S. attitude toward the region: "Our confederacy must be viewed as the nest, from which all America, North and South, is to be peopled" (Cockcroft 1983:49). Late in the eighteenth century, U.S. merchants and contrabanders broke through the Spanish trade monopoly to sell their wares at huge profits in Mexico and Central America. U.S. commercial representatives began to appear in the major ports of trade of the region, and U.S. political agents engaged in military intrigue, pressuring the colonies to cast aside Spanish control.

No sooner had Mexico and Central America achieved independence than U.S. (along with British and other European) merchants were aggressively maneuvering to monopolize trade with these countries at the expense of British and other merchants. Political meddling immediately increased as well: The first U.S. ambassador to Mexico referred to the Mexicans as "ignorant and debauched," and correspondingly tried to tell them how to run their government. In Central America the postindependence federation was based on the U.S. model; and on one or two occasions, states like El Salvador, Honduras, and Nicaragua went so far as to request admission to the U.S. union.

Despite President Monroe's warning to the European powers in 1823 to stay out of the region, Mexico and Central America were repeatedly invaded during the nineteenth century by European powers, especially England. The other major offender was the United States. Texas was annexed in 1845, and in 1846 the United States invaded Mexico with the excuse that it was collecting debts owed to its citizens from the time of the independence wars. U.S. soldiers succeeded in occupying Mexico City, at the cost of some 50,000 Mexican lives, and forced the Mexican government to cede almost half of its territory (in the "Treaty" of Guadalupe).

In Central America William Walker, the filibusterer from California, invaded Nicaragua in 1855, and ruled it as a slave state for two years with U.S. official recognition. In 1861, at a time when the United States was preoccupied with its Civil War, Spain invaded Mexico, only to be replaced in 1862 as invaders by the French. The French occupied the country until 1867, when they were driven out by Benito Juárez's nationalist forces. Veterans of the U.S. Civil War aided the Juárez forces, and Juárez offered important concessions to the United States in exchange for its recognition of the new Mexican government.

The most important concessions to the United States, however, were made by liberal dictators in Mexico and Central America after the 1870s. Porfirio Díaz not only made it legal for U.S. citizens to own property in Mexico but also personally saw to it that U.S. companies were given contracts to build the major rail lines throughout the country. With Díaz's open-door economic policies, U.S. investors soon dominated mining, oil production, and export agriculture in Mexico. Even the textbooks used in Mexican schools were written by U.S. authors and published by the Appleton Publishing Company (Cockcroft 1983:88).

Díaz was himself part Indian, but like other so-called liberal dictators of the region, he did not give favorable treatment to the native Mesoamericans. As described in Box 7.6, Díaz believed in the need to assimilate the Indians into national society through the same process that had created his own social persona; that is, through *mestizaje* (racial and cultural mixing).

In Central America, the United States intervened almost at will in the region's governmental affairs. For example, in 1906, the United States forced a Guatemalan dictator to end his war with the other Central American countries; in 1909, it coerced a Nicaraguan dictator to resign from office when he dared challenge U.S. power; in 1912, it appointed an acting president of Honduras in order to protect U.S. banana interests; and in 1917, it ousted a Costa Rican president who refused to make special concessions to U.S. banana and oil companies. As a direct result of these interventions, the Central American countries became known as "Banana Republics" (La Feber 1983).

The liberals opened the door to foreign investment during the nineteenth century, and in the early part of the twentieth century their successors allowed the United States and other foreigners to take virtual control of the political and economic affairs of the states in the region. U.S. investments in Central America were primarily concentrated in mining, oil, and agriculture. As might be expected, the investments were oriented toward production for exports, especially to the United States. But the investments were also accompanied by the heavy infusion of advanced technologies—especially machine-driven tools and infrastructural improvements—mainly in railroads, shipping, irrigation systems, and building construction. In northern Mexico, mining was stepped up, largely under the auspices of U.S. companies such as Anaconda, and by 1911, the country had become the second leading producer of silver in the world

The exploitation of Mexican oil was dominated by U.S. and British companies (Figure 7.10). As of 1921, production of crude oil in Mexico accounted for about one-fourth of the world's supply, and 70 percent of it was in American hands. Most of the eighty largest industries of Mexico in 1911 were U.S.-owned, many of them specialized in commercial agriculture. U.S. companies, for example, owned and operated the majority of the sugar plantations of Morelos, the most productive sugar cane area in the world, and the lucrative henequen (fiber) plantations of Yucatán. Largely because of foreign mining and agricultural operations, foreigners succeeded in gaining rights to almost 20 percent of Mexico's total land surface. Also, early in the century Mexico became linked to the U.S. market through a vast network of railroad lines, built and controlled by U.S. investors.

Box 7.6   Porfirio Díaz and the Indians of Mexico

The Mexican historian Enrique Krauze begins his lively book on Mexico (*Mexico, Biography of Power,* 1997) with an account of the centennial celebration in 1910 of Independence from Spain and the eightieth birthday of President Porfirio Díaz. Visitors from all over the world arrived at a refurbished Mexico City to pay honor to the man who had brought peace to Mexico, presided over unprecedented economic development, and reached accommodation with world powers that in the past had intervened in the country's affairs (especially, Spain, France, and the United States). The Paseo de la Reforma avenue had been renovated to reflect Díaz's negative attitude about the country's colonial past, in contrast to his glorification of its postindependence liberal modernization. Monuments dedicated to Spanish conquistadors and colonial rulers were put aside in favor of majestic monuments to such liberal heroes as Hidalgo, Juarez, and Díaz himself. A monument was also erected in honor of Cuauhtemoc, the fallen Aztec leader who, like the other "liberal" heroes, had fought against external invaders of Mexico.

President Díaz was the "quintessential mestizo." His mother was a Mixtec Indian, his father a working-class creole. Díaz had renewed his Indian ties while serving as the liberals' military leader in Tehuantepec, Oaxaca, among the highly militant Mixe and Zapotec peoples of that area. As he rose to national power, however, he cast aside his Indian heritage, adopting the liberal mantra that mestizo identity should provide the means to national unity. As the supreme caudillo of Mexico, his policies toward the Indians were extremely harsh. He claimed that they were generally "docile and grateful," and thereby had contributed in only a minor way to the social and economic progress that had been made. Indians who were not docile and grateful, such as the Yaquis and Mayas, were dealt with severely. In 1902, Díaz sent 8,000 soldiers to Yaqui country, where they slaughtered Yaqui women and children, and deported the men to the south as virtual slaves. Shortly thereafter, his troops "overwhelmed" the rebellious Cruzob Mayas of Yucatán and exiled many of them to a deep canyon in Oaxaca (the "Valley of Death") where, like the Yaquis, they were forced to carry out slave labor.

Despite Díaz's shedding of his own personal Indian identity and his advocacy of cultural assimilation for the Indians, Krause claims that in his person and actions he continued to be influenced by his Mesoamerican heritage. The French priest Brasseur de Bourbourg, who visited with Díaz in Oaxaca, described his physical appearance as "the most handsome indigenous type that I had ever encountered . . . in all my travels" Krauze 1997; (p. 208). Furthermore, there is evidence that the way Díaz expressed himself in Spanish, as well as the intonations in his use of the language, "seemed to stem from his Indian inheritance" (p. 210). But most of all, his personal style of governing was similar to that of past Mesoamerican rulers: His figure as a protective father, the aura of godlike powers, the reliance on "command" and authority (some eighteen forms of command existed in the Aztec's language). But as a mestizo, Díaz's political actions also manifested a Spanish colonial legacy, including caudillo traits and "a new kind of 'enlightened despotism' similar to the policies of the [Spanish] emperors of the eighteenth century" (p. 218).

Díaz saw the centennial celebration of 1910 as the culmination of his rule and the zenith of Mexican history. His experiences in the many wars and rebellions of the neocolonial period should have tipped him off to the impending social explosion in Mexico. And he most certainly should have known that "the Indians of Mexico (and the much larger body of mestizo peasants—the *campesinos*) were not really broken beyond any possibility of violent action" (p. 220). Despite the portents, in 1910 Porfirio Díaz had himself reelected for the eighth time.

The Mexican revolution broke out that same year, and the following year Díaz fled into exile in Paris, France. In 1915, he died and was buried in France, never to have his remains returned to his beloved *patria*.

Figure 7.10 Oil fields of Veracruz, Mexico, around the turn of the twentieth century. Source unknown.

In Central America, coffee became the leading export item, accounting for over 50 percent of the area's export values in 1917, and foreign investors increasingly monopolized its production, processing, and shipping (Figure 7.11). As in Mexico, mining was foreign owned and operated in Central America, although with the exception of the Nicaraguan gold mines near Puerto Cabezas, the yields were not substantial. U.S. control of the area's economy was most visibly manifested in the growing power of the United Fruit Company (UFCO). Formed around the turn of the century as a U.S. exporter of bananas, UFCO eventually came to monopolize not only banana production in Central America but also the area's railroad, shipping, and communication systems. The UFCO received huge land concessions from all the Central American countries and exercised enormous influence over economic and political matters there, even though the company was exclusively U.S.-owned, and its substantial profits were largely remitted to the parent company in Boston.

Politically, the countries of the region were ruled by dictators manipulated behind the scenes by foreign powers. Populist slogans helped create an image for the

Figure 7.11   Carts for transporting coffee from the Pacific coastal plantations to the seaports in nineteenth-century Guatemala. Courtesy of E. Bradford Burns. Reprinted from E. Bradford Burns, *Eadward Muybridge in Guatemala, 1875: The Photographer as Social Recorder.* Berkeley, CA: University of California Press, 1986, p. 126.

dictators of the strong father figure, and this image was used to keep the poorer sectors in line. Nevertheless, dictators throughout the region created large armies and highly coercive rural police forces that they could call upon if necessary to maintain the status quo. One observer has referred to the Díaz regime in Mexico around 1910 as "not so much a nation as a company store." The regime made Mexico safe so that U.S. investors and other foreigners could reap huge profits.

The role of Porfirio Díaz as keeper of the store in Mexico applies equally well to such Central American dictators as Manuel Estrada Cabrera (1898–1920) and Jorge Ubico (1931–1944) in Guatemala; Maximiliano Hernández (1931–1944) in El Salvador; Tiburcio Carías Andino (1932–1948) in Honduras; Anastasio Somoza García (1936–1956) in Nicaragua; and even the somewhat more democratic Cleto González and Ricardo Jiménez (1906–1936) in Costa Rica.

Dictatorial rule does not mean that peace and harmony reigned at the top of the political "store," and, as noted, the United States intervened on many occasions in order to orchestrate developments in the Mesoamerican region. Some of the political problems originated from local capitalists who opposed domination by foreign investors, others from conflicts between manufacturing and agricultural interests, and still others from middle-class intellectuals and professionals blocked from power by the dictatorial regimes. The dictators themselves often outlived their usefulness to the foreign powers, and the latter did not hesitate to negotiate their downfall. In Mexico, for example, the United States facilitated Porfirio Díaz's departure from power in 1911, later maneuvering behind the scenes to have him replaced by the wealthy creole Francisco Madero. Failing at this attempt, the United States landed the marines in Veracruz in 1914 in an effort to bring down Victoriano de la Huerta, who was being supported by its British competitors.

Political intervention by the United States in the first three decades of the twentieth century was even more blatant in the case of the Central American countries. The pattern was set early on in Panama, where in 1903, with the backing of President Theodore Roosevelt, U.S. troops negotiated Panama's political separation from Colombia and concessions for U.S. ownership and construction of a canal connecting the two oceans (the canal was completed in 1914). An even more egregious U.S. intervention took place in Nicaragua, which was occupied by the U.S. marines between 1912 and 1933 (except for a short period between 1925 and 1927 when the marines were withdrawn).

The U.S.-dominated capitalism of early-twentieth-century Mexico and Central America brought dramatic economic growth to the region, but it failed to promote the well-being of common people. Peasants by the hundreds of thousands were drawn into wage labor, much of it required as debt cancellation and all of it miserably low-paying. Most of these rural workers were people of color: mesoamerican Indians, mestizos, and Blacks. They profoundly resented the economic exploitation to which they were subjected and the racist discrimination heaped upon them by the foreign and national capitalists. The United States, for its part, seemed to show no interest in the plight of the Indians or other exploited peoples from whom its entrepreneurs extracted exorbitant profits. Neither did it recognize that increasingly this rural sector—part peasant and part proletariat—was becoming a tinderbox waiting to burst into flames.

Even the industrial workers, most of whom had emigrated from the rural zones to occupy the manufacturing jobs in the burgeoning cities of the region, were subjected to severe economic exploitation and racial discrimination. In Mexico many of them labored in mining and textile manufacturing, and already by 1910 they made up around 15 percent of the economically active population. Influenced by intellectuals in the city, the workers began to be radicalized, and toward the end of the Díaz period they engaged in dozens of (illegal) strikes.

In Central America the urban workers constituted a smaller percentage of economic society, perhaps 10 percent of the labor force in the 1920s. But they were sorely repressed by the Central American regimes, and by the 1920s began to form radical unions and engage in wildcat strikes. They were soon joined by rural laborers from the United Fruit Company's banana plantations, who in the 1930s became the premier radical sector of Central American society.

In retrospect, it seems clear that already in the early part of the twentieth century, the societies of the region under powerful U.S. influence were developing conditions that would lead to revolutionary actions more radical than the nativist movements of the nineteenth century. "Revolution," in contrast to "reform," refers to those violent actions by which socially dominated classes seek to break the bonds that hold them down and in the process cast aside the ruling classes. If in reform, the change comes from above (led by the upper classes), in revolution it comes from below (the lower classes take the lead). The modern era was initiated in the region by the twentieth century's first "socialist" revolution, which like a volcano erupted in Mexico's countryside in 1910. But that is a topic for the chapter to follow on native Mesoamericans in the Modern Era.

SUGGESTED READINGS

CARMACK, ROBERT M. 1995 *Rebels of Highland Guatemala. The Quiche-Mayas of Momostenango.* Norman, Oklahoma: University of Oklahoma Press.

JOSEPH, GILBERT M., AND TIMOTHY J. HENDERSON (eds.) 2002 *The Mexico Reader: History, Culture, Politics.* Durham, North Carolina: Duke University Press.

KATZ, FRIEDRICH (ed.) 1988 *Riot, Rebellion, and Revolution: Rural Social Conflict in Mexico.* Princeton: Princeton University Press.

LA FEBER, WALTER 1983 *Inevitable Revolutions: The United States in Central America.* New York: W. W. Norton.

LAUGHLIN, ROBERT M. 2003 *Beware the Great Horned Serpent. Chiapas under the Threat of Napoleon.* Albany: Institute for Mesoamerican Studies.

LEWIS, OSCAR 1963 *Life in a Mexican Village: Tepoztlán Restudied.* Urbana: University of Illinois Press.

McCREERY, DAVID J. 1989 Atanasio Tzul, Lucas Aguilar, and the Indian Kingdom of Totonicapán. In *The Human Tradition in Latin America: The Nineteenth Century,* edited by J. Ewell and W. H. Beezley, pp. 39–58. Wilmington, Delaware: SR Books.

PAZ, OCTAVIO 1961 *The Labyrinth of Solitude.* New York: Grove Press.

REED, NELSON 1964 *The Caste War of Yucatan.* Stanford: Stanford University Press.

SMITH, CAROL A. (ed.) 1990 *Guatemalan Indians and the State: 1540–1988.* Austin: University of Texas Press.

Chapter 8

Native Mesoamericans in the Modern Era

Globally, the twentieth century has been a time of reaping the harvest of seeds sown by nineteenth-century and early-twentieth-century capitalism and the liberal reforms used to justify them. This has been as true for the native Mesoamericans of Mexico and Central America as for native peoples elsewhere. Liberal programs from the neocolonial period evolved into more sophisticated and carefully planned modern "development" strategies, while widespread opposition to the injustices accompanying residual old-fashioned liberalism and the new developmental reforms led to "revolutions" throughout the region.

The revolutionaries and development agents of twentieth-century Mexico and Central America have not always taken the native Mesoamericans into account in their haste to create modern nation-states, although they have at least paid lip service to the preservation of their surviving cultural traditions. Even the "indigenist" programs sponsored by agents of the modern world were largely designed to assimilate the native Mesoamericans as underclass minorities. It is not surprising that the Indians have resisted the loss of their cultural heritage.

Revolution has been one common path to modernization in the twentieth century, and another was development. The Mexican author Octavio Paz (1985) has commented that there are two kinds of revolution, one resulting *because of* development, as in England and France, and one from the *lack of* development, as in Russia and China. The developmental approach to change is more gradual than the revolutionary approach, and it tends to be more conservative. It may avoid most of the violence associated with revolution, but it has costs, particularly the costs of devisive social inequalities and widespread poverty.

Attempts in Mexico and Central America to modernize through both revolution and development are the main topic of this chapter. Our focus will be on the reaction to and the participation in these historical events by the native Mesoamericans. The first section to follow will deal with revolutionary movements in Mexico and later in Central America. The second section will provide an account of the developmental reforms that succeeded revolutionary actions in these same countries. A third and final section will describe more recent attempts by native Mesoamericans to mobilize their peoples in order to create "multicultural" national societies. The primary context for such ethnic and national movements was provided by neoliberal economic and political programs that often work against the Indians' perceived interests.

NATIVE MESOAMERICANS AND THE MEXICAN AND CENTRAL AMERICAN REVOLUTIONS

"Revolution," as we define the term here, refers to violent movements by underclasses attempting to cast aside their overlords and radically transforming the oppressive conditions of society. Comparative studies of revolutions in the twentieth century—especially the Russian, Chinese, and Vietnamese cases—have given us a much better understanding of the social forces that lead to revolutions and the key participants in them. The anthropologist Eric Wolf (1969) has suggested three common features of revolutions that seem relevant to an understanding of twentieth-century violent uprisings taking place in the homeland of the Mesoamerican Indians.

One of these features points to the fact that revolutions tend to take place in societies in which large peasantries have been negatively affected by capitalist forces. These forces break down the old landlord-peasant ties and then free up modernizing peasants to participate in revolutionary actions. A second feature concerns the pivotal leadership role played by middle-class radicals—teachers, military officers, merchants, bureaucrats—who have become frustrated by barriers to their attempted rise in social status. These leaders and their urban followers meet up with the rebellious peasants in the countryside, from where they march to battle, usually under "socialist" banners. The third feature has to do with the presence of corrupt regimes that are highly dependent on outside powers. Such regimes lack legitimacy, and therefore easily crumble in the face of determined internal opposition. The fallen regimes create political vacuums that revolutionaries try to fill.

In the account to follow, it will be shown that these three conditions have consistently arisen in the Mexican and Central American region during the twentieth century, and that the native Mesoamerican peasants have provided the powder, and at times the leadership as well, that led to revolutionary explosions in the region (Figure 8.1).

We turn first to the Mexican revolution, followed by the Central American revolutions, particularly the Guatemalan and Nicaraguan revolutions.

The Mexican Revolution

Revolution first broke out in Mexico in 1910 with the electoral challenge to the dictator Porfirio Díaz by the conservative reformer Francisco Madero. The conflict was initially between different factions of the ruling class, and it led to the overthrow of Díaz and the replacement of Madero by another conservative, Victoriano de la Huerta. These events eventually unleashed genuine revolutionary forces under the leadership of Pancho Villa in the north (Figure 8.2) and Emiliano Zapata in the

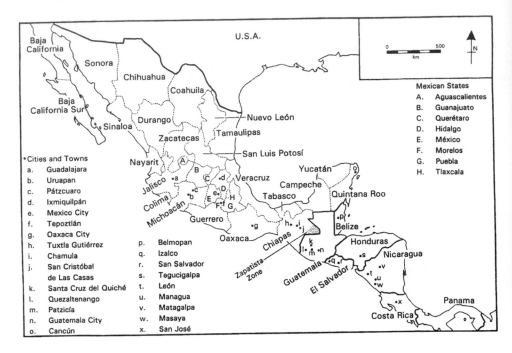

Figure 8.1   Map showing the states of modern Mexico and Central America; also shown are places mentioned in the text.

south (Figure 8.3). Venustiano Carranza and Alvaro Obregón led two other somewhat more moderate forces. These various factions captured the government in 1914 but then began fighting among themselves. The Carranza and Obregón factions formed an alliance, and by integrating their armies in 1920 they finally achieved victory over Villa and Zapata after years of bitter warfare (see the map in Figure 8.4 for places mentioned in connection with revolutionary actions in the region).

The conditions just mentioned that characterized twentieth-century revolutions around the world were conducive to the revolutionary explosion in Mexico. The driving force of the revolution, particularly in its early stages, were the peasant Indians, the majority of whom lined up behind Zapata. These peasants generally had been forced off their lands and made to work for capitalist enterprises, especially sugar plantations in the case of Zapata's followers. The Villa forces tended to be more "proletarianized" (engaged in wage labor), and many of them were not peasants at all but cowhands, miners, and migrant farmworkers. Most of the revolutionary leaders themselves were middle-class, as in the case of Zapata and many captains of the Villa, Carranza, and Obregón forces. Villa himself came from the lower class, but Carranza and Obregón, whose movements were more reformist than revolutionary, had strong ties to the landlord class.

It is clear, too, that the Mexican revolution was precipitated by the weakness of the dependent Díaz regime and was further fomented by the clumsy attempts on

Figure 8.2 Pancho Villa, leader of the revolutionary forces in northern Mexico. Courtesy of Culver Pictures.

Figure 8.3   Emiliano Zapata, leader of the peasant revolutionary forces in southern Mexico. Courtesy of the Organization of American States, Columbus Memorial Library.

the part of the United States and England to name his successor (first Madero, then Huerta, and finally Carranza). Not only did the collapse of authority at the center create a vacuum into which the revolutionaries rushed but also outside meddling gave the movement a strong antiforeign and pronationalist tint. The idea of Mexico as an independent, "revolutionary" country provided political legitimacy for the new government in the years that followed.

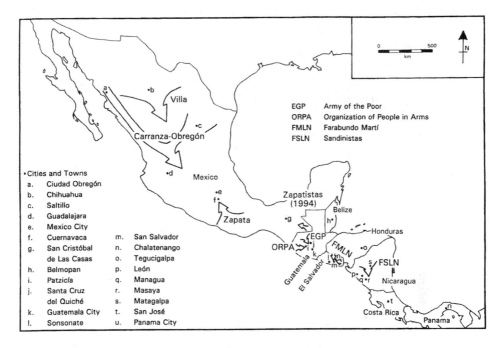

Figure 8.4   Places and regions of action in the Mexican and Central American revolutions.

The Mesoamerican Indians actively participated in the Mexican revolution, but not to the same degree in every region; and overall, their impact, although important, was not decisive to the outcome. The expansion of haciendas and plantations in the rural areas during the Porfirio Díaz period had greatly affected the native peoples of Mexico on the eve of the revolution. In the northern states, the native Mesoamericans had lost most of their best lands, and this outcome forced them to labor as peons on the large estates. Communities were destroyed and native identities lost. In the central and southern states, the Mesoamericans survived with more of their communities and native cultures intact. Even in the latter cases, however, the surrounding commercial plantations tended to exert strong pressure on the native communities to yield their lands and laborers.

The Zapatista wing of the early revolutionary movement in Mexico was the primary recipient of backing from the Mesoamerican peasant communities. In contrast, the Villista wing was supported primarily by rural proletariats, most of whom no doubt had native ancestry but now identified "racially" and culturally with the mestizos. The more moderate constitutionalist wing of Carranza and Obregón received much of its support from hacienda peons, rural middle-class farmers, and eventually urban workers. It is not coincidental, then, that the Zapatistas were the most radical of the revolutionary bands, nor that they placed the greatest stress on the Indian heritage. They became the only revolutionary group at the time to represent the

---

Box 8.1   Lázaro Cárdenas and the Indians

Lázaro Cárdenas is considered by many to have been Mexico's most beloved and successful president. He was born and raised in Michoacan, a state famous for its large and rebellious Tarascan Indian people. Cárdenas came from a middle-class mestizo family, but he was very fond of an aunt, also his godmother, who was of Indian descent. As a young man he worked in a printshop but soon joined the revolutionary forces, where he quickly rose to prominence as a military leader. Early on he fought against both Villistas and Zapatistas, and he became a protégé of the Sonoran General Plutarco Elías Calles.

Cárdenas became governor of Michoacan at the age of thirty-two, where he successfully organized popular agrarian, political, and educational groups in order to carry out socialist-oriented policies. He gained solid support from the Tarascan Indians through his agrarian reforms and open sympathy for their struggle against the Catholic priests and landlords. The Indians affectionately referred to him as "Tata Lázaro" (Father Lázaro), a term that the Tarascans had used to refer to revered Catholic monks during the Colonial era.

Cárdenas was chosen by Calles to replace him as president, a selection that autmatically guaranteed his election in 1934. As president, Cárdenas became famous for his radical policies: support for organized labor (he soon integrated the workers into a single state-backed organization known as Confederation of Mexican Workers, CTM); and the expropriation in 1938 of the rich oil fields in the Huasteca area (for which he was wildly cheered by the Mexican people). But his boldest policy was a vast agrarian reform. He confiscated huge tracts of lands from the rural landlords (*hacendados*), many of them former revolutionary leaders, and redistributed the land in the form of state-owned *ejidos* to over one million peasants.

The historian Enrique Krause (1997:452) claims that Cárdenas always had a "genuine love" and "special connection with the Indians." One of the main goals of his agrarian reform, in fact, was to allow the Indians to recoup native lands they had lost through the centuries. He insisted that the Indians were not a hindrance to "progress." Accordingly, two of the most important early redistributions of lands took place in Indian areas: the first in the La Laguna area of Coahuila, and the second in Yucatán. Of the land reforms of 1937 in Yucatán, Cárdenas is reported to have said (Krause 1997:463):

> . . . we will move on to totally resolve the agrarian problem in Yucatán, that has dragged on for long years and we must finish with it so that we can save the indigenous peoples—the majority of the peons in the sisal-growing zone—from their misery.

Cárdenas also founded the first Department of Indian Affairs in order to provide education, health care, and economic improvement for the Mexican Indians (see the section to follow on "development" in Mexico). Finally, after retiring from the presidency, Cárdenas returned to his home in Michoacan. Like a "village priest" attending to his flock, he continued to receive, and mediate disputes among, the common Indian and mestizo peoples of the region.

---

interests of the native Mesoamericans, despite the fact that Zapata himself was a mestizo and that many Mesoamericans failed to join his movement.

Many of the radical social changes mandated in the Constitution of 1917 were implemented by President Lázaro Cárdenas, a later revolutionary leader who gained widespread support from the Indians and poor mestizos. Cárdenas curtailed the power of the Church, although much more modestly than his predecessors; confiscated the oil fields being exploited by foreign companies (especially U.S. companies); and centralized the authority of the presidency. His most radical change, however, was to carry out an aggressive agrarian reform, redistributing lands to the peasants and rural proletariats. Lands were turned over to the villages in the form of "ejidos," state properties to which use rights were legally granted to the landless. By the end of Cárdenas's term in 1940, approximately two million people in 15,000 villages had received lands and now controlled production on some 50 percent of Mexico's croplands. The peasants seemingly had gained the lands for which they had fought so long and hard, and among them were many thousands of Indian families.

(See Box 8.1 for an account of Lázaro Cárdenas's attitude and actions toward the Indians of Mexico.)

The Zapatista Revolutionaries of Morelos.   Followers of Zapata were scattered throughout Mexico, but the core area of the movement was the state of Morelos. Morelos society on the eve of the revolution was still deeply divided between the "civilized people" and the "*macehuales*," that is to say, the mestizos and the Indians. Most of the Indians by then spoke Spanish, but Nahuatl was the language of the elders, and in some communities it continued to be the everyday language (in 1910 about 9 percent of the population in the state spoke a native tongue). Dress was an important social marker, the Indian men wearing breeches and coarse cotton shirts, the Indian women wraparound skirts and huipils (blouses). The Indian villages had their own traditional ways, expressed in elaborate ceremonies in honor of the saints, and accompanied by food, drink, and music. Large families—in reality, lineages—provided the essential internal relations for the Indians, as did innumerable *compadrazgo* (fictive kinship) ties actuated during ceremonial occasions.

New economic barriers between the mestizos and Indians were being erected that were less rigid than the traditional ones, but effective just the same. The estate owners, government administrators, merchants, and professionals were all considered to be civilized, whereas the *milpa* farmers and part-time peons on the plantations were thought to be uncivilized Indians. Permanent peons residing on the plantations were distinguished from the Indians, dubbed "little creoles." Most of the middle-level farmers and moneylenders were mestizos, but a few Indians also engaged in these economic pursuits. Through social climbing, Indians could in theory become "civilized." In fact, it was not uncommon for well-to-do Indians to wear trousers rather than breeches and to move from the rural villages to the town centers, although they were subject to ridicule by the poorer Indians.

The Zapatista movement in Morelos was led by mestizos from the middle level who had close connections with the Indian communities. The Zapata family was made up of merchants and horse breakers, whereas other revolutionary chiefs worked as ranchers, artisans, storekeepers, and one as a Protestant preacher. Their followers, who swelled to well over 40,000 soldiers at one point, were Indian peasants who tilled communal lands and worked part-time as peons on the large sugar plantations (Figure 8.5). In most cases, entire communities of young Indian men (and some women) would join one of the revolutionary bands as a group, although later

Figure 8.5 Zapatista revolutionaries fight the federal troops at Milpa Alta, Federal District of Mexico. From *Life and Death in Milpa Alta: A Nahuatl Chronicle of Díaz and Zapata*, translated and edited by Fernando Horcasitas. Copyright © 1972 by the University of Oklahoma Press.

individual switching from one band to another took place. The upper-class mestizos of Morelos, of course, opposed the Zapatistas from start to finish, even though at first they tried to reach some kind of an understanding with them. Later on, members of the Mestizo elite were forced to abandon Morelos, taking with them as much wealth as they could. Many of the middle-level mestizos served as intermediaries between the wealthy elite and the rebellious communities during the military period, but most of them personally opposed the revolution. The permanent peons on the plantations were too compromised to turn against their bosses, and for the most part they did not support the revolutionary cause.

The Zapatistas were not strongly motivated by abstract ideology. The early uprisings were highly practical affairs, directed against greedy plantation owners and government officials who had made it impossible for the peasants to live off the land or maintain community autonomy. The initial fighting helped bring down Porfirio Díaz as well as affecting other far-reaching political developments, but despite important victories the Zapatistas were generally content to retreat to Morelos and institute the kind of local land and political reforms for which they had rebelled in the first place. These actions revealed the peasant base of the movement, and the practical but limited nature of the Zapatista goals. Later, pro-Díaz and then pro-Carranza constitutionalist armies brutally retaliated against the Zapatistas in Morelos for their rebellious actions. Men, women, and children were killed by the thousands, and other thousands were carried off in exile to cities and faraway areas. The Indian communities were ransacked, looted, and burned; cattle were slaughtered, and fields destroyed. The Zapatistas were moved to battle again, and once more for explicitly practical reasons: to defend their very lives and homes in the face of possible extermination at the hands of the government forces.

The Zapatista movement became widely known in Mexico for its nativist character. One overt symbol employed was the image of the Virgin of Guadalupe, carried on battle flags and sewn into wide-brimmed hats. To them Guadalupe stood for the preservation of Indian identity and the inviolate linkage between native peoples and the land. Opponents of the movement used the nativist character of the movement to raise the specter of a new "caste war" and invasion of the capital by "savages" from the south.

Zapatista nativism, however, was quite general in character, as might be expected of a movement led by mestizos and supported by native Mesoamericans who had been strongly influenced by modern forces. Much of the nativism that can be detected was implicit rather than explicit. For example, native cultural features were manifested in the Zapatistas' sense of moral outrage at being deprived of ancestral lands and self-sufficiency; in the unswerving efforts to restore communal property and political autonomy; in the legitimization of military authority on the basis of community service and personal ties to *cacique* leaders; in the integration of religious ritual and political action (Zapata set aside village lands to be worked in support of rituals to the saints); in the guerrilla form of warfare, in which the fighting was always closely articulated with the milpa cycle and community life; and in the use of discussion and consensus in making decisions.

The assassination of Zapata in April 1919 ended the movement as an effective revolutionary force. Perhaps the excessive reliance on Zapata as a father figure by the Morelos peasants should be seen as still another nativist feature of the movement. At any rate, the Zapatistas were defeated, and there seemed little to show for their long and bloody struggle. Most of the plantation owners were able to recoup lands and privileges with the help of the constitutional authorities in Mexico City. The villagers were left landless, their communities ravaged, and the population depleted by one-half as a result of deaths in the war and forced migrations. The Indians had demonstrated their willingness to fight for their native identity and way of life, but powerful acculturation forces were unleashed in the process of their fighting under Mestizo leaders against mestizo enemies. By the time President Cárdenas restored lands to the impoverished peasants of Morelos in the 1930s, it was too late to prevent the further transformation of remaining Mesoamerican cultural elements.

Reaction to the Zapatista movement was very different in other Mexican states that had large Indian populations, as illustrated by the case of Oaxaca (described in Box 8.2).

Central American Revolutions

Full-scale revolutions erupted in Central America half a century later than in Mexico, although several aborted revolutionary movements broke out shortly after events finally began to calm down in Mexico (for example, the Sandino rebellion in Nicaragua; see Figure 8.6). At this time in Central America (early twentieth century), the three revolutionary features mentioned earlier apparently were not as fully developed as in Mexico. In particular, capitalist penetration into the peasant Indian communities was more localized and not as ubiquitous. Middle-class ladino (Mestizo) leaders

---

Box 8.2   Revolution in Oaxaca

The Zapatistas of Morelos proved to be the most consistently radical Mesoamerican group of the Mexican Revolution. There were many native Mesoamerican recruits to the Zapatista movement from surrounding states such as Puebla, Tlaxcala, and Guerrero, but in such states the native Mesoamericans' militancy tended to be sporadic and kept under control by local conservative caudillos. In other states, such as Michoacán, revolutionary activity on the part of the native Mesoamericans was largely confined to postwar conflicts over lands being redistributed as part of the agrarian reforms. Revolutionary actions were notably weak or absent in the southern states of Mexico, where native Mesoamericans made up higher percentages of the population. In fact, most of the native peoples in the south adopted a conservative stance relative to the radical wing of the revolution. The Oaxaca case can serve as an illustration of the conservatism of Mesoamericans in such southern states as Chiapas, Tabasco, and Yucatán.

Oaxaca on the eve of the Mexican Revolution had a huge peasant population (approximately 87 percent of the total state population), made up mostly of Mesoamericans who spoke the Zapotec, Mixtec, Cuicatec, and other indigenous languages. Except for scattered local uprisings in 1911, however, the Oaxacan Indians failed to respond positively to the revolutionary call. Many of them joined a conservative movement that opposed radical change while calling for state sovereignty. The Indian recruits to the sovereignty army were organized along Zapatista lines by village units, each with its own chief, but the causes and consequences were totally different. In fact, Carranza's constitutionalist army, against which the Oaxacans were supposedly fighting, was able to recruit soldiers from among these very same peasant Indians.

Ronald Waterbury (1975) has observed that the contrast in responses to the revolution by native peasants in Morelos on the one hand and the Oaxaca natives on the other can be traced to the profoundly different economic and cultural conditions in the two areas. The haciendas and plantations of Oaxaca were much weaker and less capitalist than in Morelos, and as a result the Oaxaca Indians had retained far more of their lands, languages, and customs. Organized native communities existed in both areas but were more internally cohesive in Oaxaca than in Morelos. Economic conditions in Morelos left the Indians with little choice but to rebel, and their years of experience working on the plantations had resulted in extravillage relations and ideas that made a regional movement feasible. The Indians of Oaxaca, in contrast, generally retained the lands and resources necessary to survive on their own, and they closed themselves off to the outside by re-creating small cultural worlds with roots extending back into the Mesoamerican past. They had more to lose than to gain from joining the revolution, and in the end they rejected the Zapatista call for radical change.

---

commanded much smaller followings among the urban working classes than in Mexico. Certainly, corrupt and dependent political regimes abounded in Central America at the time, and successions from one dictator to another brought on periods of considerable confusion and instability. In general, however, military caudillos, usually with U.S. help, were able to fill these periods of political void in Central America, thereby restoring "order" more effectively than in the case of Mexico.

By the 1960s and 1970s, conditions for revolution in Central America had greatly increased, and full-blown revolutionary actions broke out in the area. In Central America, as had been the case in Mexico, Indian peasants played a major role in these revolutionary events, mediated by middle-class Marxist radicals and their working-class supporters from the urban zones. Corrupt military regimes lacking

Figure 8.6 Augusto Sandino, the Nicaraguan rebel. Courtesy of Bettman Archives.

broad legitimacy were precipitating factors, along with blatant political meddling by the United States. Castro's Cuba, backed by the Soviet Union, provided a new element that figured into the revolutionary equation, serving as both model for socialist revolutions "Latin-American style" and source of military and economic aid to the Central American revolutionaries.

The revolutionary movements in Central America differed in detail from one another, including the degree to which the native Mesoamericans participated in them. In the case of Guatemala, Indian involvement in the phase of the revolution that began in the second half of the 1970s was pervasive and profoundly important. Contemporaneous revolutions in El Salvador and Nicaragua, in contrast, had relatively less to do with the Indians—especially in the Salvadoran case—either as direct participants or as inspiration for the struggles. This dissimilarity raises the question as to whether or not the presence or absence of the native Mesoamericans made a significant difference in the outcome of the Central American revolutions. For example, did the Guatemalan Revolution, where the participation of native Mesoamericans was pervasive, differ from the revolutions in El Salvador and Nicaragua where Indian participation was limited? The answer to this question is decidedly "yes," as is indicated by the solemn fact that the Guatemalan Revolution was the bloodiest and lasted longer than the other two (it led to perhaps double the loss of human life than in the Salvadoran and Nicaraguan revolutions).

The prolonged and extremely violent struggle in Guatemala can be attributed partly to the racist, "ethnic cleansing" policy of the government forces in the country. We should note, too, that the ideology employed by the Guatemalan revolutionaries was more idiosyncratic and less rigidly Marxist than in El Salvador and Nicaragua. The Guatemalan insurgents had to accommodate to the important Indian component in society, and this necessity resulted in serious attempts to incorporate nativist ideas into the revolutionary program.

The Central American revolutionary wars dominated political developments during the 1970s and 1980s, and have had lasting impact on them up to the present time (Spence 2004). This outcome is understandable, given the disasters that the wars wrought in these countries (especially in Guatemala, El Salvador, and Nicaragua). Tens of thousands of lives were lost, their economies were devastated, the gap between the rich and poor widened, and dependence on outside world powers and nongovernmental organizations (NGOs) increased dramatically.

The peace accords—finalized in 1996 in Guatemala, in 1992 in El Salvador, and in 1990 with free elections in Nicaragua—ended the Central American revolutionary wars and played a key role in transforming developmental patterns in the region: The agreements laid the groundwork for a series of positive developmental changes that in an uneven way have gradually taken place during the past decade and a half. The most notable achievements have been the demise of the military dictatorships and the emergence of a variety of democratic governments in all the Central American countries (only Costa Rica had a genuine democracy prior to the 1990s).

In Guatemala, El Salvador, and Nicaragua, the revolutionaries have organized political parties that now participate in the electoral process and the governing legislatures (the URNG party in Guatemala, FMLN in El Salvador, and FSLN in Nicaragua). In all three cases, too, the power of the military has been greatly curtailed (of the three, the military remains the strongest in Guatemala). Conservative parties have dominated the recent political scene, but in every case they have been strongly challenged by more liberal and even radical parties (the strongest radical party being the FSLN, the Sandinista party of Nicaragua).

Let us now look more closely at the role of the native Mesoamericans in two major revolutionary movements in Central America: the Guatemalan and the Nicaraguan.

Guatemalan Revolution. In many ways the Guatemalan revolution can be understood as the legacy of the U.S.-orchestrated overthrow of the country's legitimate government in 1954, and subsequent U.S. backing of a long succession of corrupt military regimes. The Guatemalan army virtually took over the state, serving the interests of foreign and local capitalists and its own generals, who increasingly used political office to acquire personal wealth. As the state became more repressive, opposition from the lower and middle classes intensified. In the 1960s a group of young army officers broke with their commanders and formed bands of revolutionary guerrillas in the eastern zone of the country. They were joined by proletarianized mestizo peasants there, and together they achieved widespread popularity throughout the country.

The military government went on to create a permanent state of terror in Guatemala, losing any legitimacy it might have enjoyed and creating dissidence from all social sectors, even from members of the upper class. Toward the end of the 1970s, guerrilla fighting erupted again, this time in the western highlands where the majority of Mayan Indians resided. Most of the guerrilla leaders were urban Marxists affiliated with the earlier movement in the East, but now they were joined by several thousand Indian soldiers and aided by hundreds of thousands of sympathizers from the Indian communities.

The two most important guerrilla organizations in Guatemala—the Guerrilla Army of the Poor (EGP) and the Organization of the People in Arms (ORPA)—were established squarely in Indian zones, and the bulk of the guerrilla soldiers and most civilian support of a logistical nature came from the Indian sector. At the high point of guerrilla activity around 1980, a few thousand Indian soldiers joined the insurgent forces, and up to a quarter of a million civilian Indians provided them with support of various kinds. Furthermore, most of the civilians killed in the counterinsurgency war were Indians (estimated at over 200,000 persons for the entire civil war period), as were almost all of the refugees, both inside Guatemala (estimated at around one million persons) and outside the country (some 200,000 in Mexico alone) (Jonas 2000:24).

The guerrilla leaders, most of them ladinos (mestizos) from the urban middle class, recognized that the Indian presence was a major factor in Guatemala's revolution. One of the guerrilla spokespersons wrote that the Guatemalan revolution was "unique" because the Indians were heirs to highly developed pre-Hispanic native cultures, and in the face of weakly developed colonial capitalism they were able to reconstitute through time many of their native organizational and cultural patterns. Therefore, this guerrilla leader went on to explain, orthodox Marxist revolutionary ideology about class warfare was an inappropriate model for the revolution because "'ethnic-nationalism' constitutes one of the essential factors for any possible revolutionary change."

The counterinsurgency forces organized by the Guatemalan military establishment not only recognized but also exaggerated the importance of the Indian factor in the revolution. According to interviews with army officers fighting against the guerrillas, the army's most critical task was to eradicate the Indians' "worldview" and replace it with a modern, "cosmopolitan" view. Beginning in the mid-1980s, the army began to lay down a structure of civil patrols, model villages, and development poles in the Indian areas in an attempt to transform the thinking and behavior of Guatemala's Indians. This highly repressive military apparatus constituted concrete evidence of the importance that Guatemala's political establishment attached to the Indians and their involvement in the ongoing revolutionary war.

Scholars have pointed out that the peasants most strongly identified as Indians were at the very center of revolutionary actions in Guatemala, and it was thought that their joining one side or the other would probably be decisive to the eventual outcome of the war. The majority of the over five million Guatemalan Indians in the country at the time were Mayas. They spoke Mayan languages and were cultural heirs to the Mesoamerican traditions of the past. But they had become highly diversified in social status, and Mayas from these social divisions responded differently to the revolutionary struggle. Although the individuals making up the diverse sectors were all identified as Indians in Guatemala, in varying degrees they had retained elements of the Mayan cultural tradition and tended to manifest divergent "affinities" for revolutionary action.

The largest social sector of Mayas were peasants who inhabited tightly integrated communities. They tended to hold to traditional native cultures, which clashed on most points with revolutionary ideology. For these Mayas, power was expressed more as a supernatural than as a secular force. Their enemies were defined in local rather than national terms, and often were identified as neighboring lineages, hamlets, or villages; furthermore, social change was conceptualized in terms of cyclic rather than linear time. It is understandable that the "traditional" Indians of this sector were unlikely to be receptive of revolutionary ideas; and, in fact, with few exceptions they did not join the guerrilla movements.

Indians from other sectors held to versions of Mayan culture that seem better suited to revolutionary action. For example, it is well known that Indian leadership within the guerrilla organizations was largely provided by a much smaller sector of urbanized, educated Mayan Indians. One example would be Pablo Ceto, an Ixil-speaking Mayan Indian who attended high school in the town of Santa Cruz del Quiché during the 1970s and who later became a leader in an EGP guerrilla unit. While in Santa Cruz and before joining with the guerrillas, Ceto organized a study group of town Indians intent on discovering their Mayan roots. Anthropologists were invited to help Ceto's group identify nativist elements consistent with the needs of the embattled Indians. Ceto went on to take a leadership role in the Committee for Peasant Unity (CUC), a political organization made up mostly of Indian and poor ladino peasants and workers. At first, CUC's work was devoted to organizing and educating rural workers and peasants in an attempt to improve their general social conditions, but under relentless attack from the army and death squads, the organization went underground and merged with the guerrilla movement.

Indian leaders like Ceto came to understand that remnants of the ancient Mayan culture could serve as powerful symbols for the revolution. One important source of Mayan symbolism was the *Popol Wuh,* the so-called "bible" of the K'iche' Mayas (for a discussion of this important Mayan document, see Chapters 6, 13, and 14). The Popol Wuh, for example, tells the story of a greedy and pompous giant macaw bird claiming to be the sun. The bird is brought down from its high perch by humble orphan twins who mortally wound it with pellets from a blowgun. Cast in the emerging nativist ideology of the revolution, the self-aggrandizing bird metaphorically could stand for the wealth-seeking military rulers of Guatemala, whereas the orphans who humbled that arrogant bird could represent the poor Indians fighting against the military regime. Metaphors of this kind had enormous motivational power among both the educated and the peasant Mayas of Guatemala.

Perhaps even more important than the educated town Indians for the Guatemalan revolution were the rural proletarianized Mayas. Jeffrey Paige (1983) noted that, as in the Vietnam revolution, the insurgents in Guatemala enjoyed their greatest success in gaining recruits precisely in rural areas where the Mayan Indians had previously been transformed "from hacienda to migratory labor estate and from Indian to proletarian." The evidence available on the revolutionary ideas that motivated these proletarianized Indians came in part from the powerful Mesoamerican cultural tradition. This effect is made clear from a soliloquy delivered by a K'iche' Mayan guerrilla leader who appears in the documentary film on the Guatemalan revolution entitled "When the Mountains Tremble":

> Guatemala is at war. The road that led to that war is over 400 years old. It led us up into the mountains when the Spaniards invaded and tried to wipe out our Indian culture. Our ancestors preserved our customs. We grew corn and our numbers increased. We say that every road has a coming and a going, a leaving and a returning. Now we're coming down out of the mountains. We're going back down to the towns and cities. We are reclaiming our rights. But we don't travel this road alone. There can be no returning unless everyone, Indians and non-Indians go together. All of us together will make a new Guatemala. All of us together will reclaim our rights. The road is returning. Together we will win.

This leader and the people to whom he addressed the speech were representative of the hundreds of thousands of Mayan peasants who had recently become wage laborers on the coffee, sugar, and cotton plantations of Guatemala. In his eloquent phrases we hear echoes of both their recent travails and the memory of ancient Mesoamerican traditions. In particular, the metaphor of the modern Indian's history as a "road" takes us back to the Popol Wuh and to a prayer recited there that refers to the journey of life as a dangerous "Green road, the Green Path" trod by both the ancient and the modern Mayas, despite its many pitfalls and snarcs.

(See Box 8.3 for a discussion of the testimony on the role of the Mayan Indians in the Guatemalan revolution by the Nobel Peace Prize recipient, Rigoberta Menchú.)

Nicaraguan Revolution. The essential factor leading to revolution in Nicaragua was the highly corrupt, U.S.-dependent regime of Anastasio Somoza Debayle. Somoza used the government for personal gain, as he and his relatives and cronies amassed huge fortunes in property and business holdings. The Somoza regime lacked legitimacy among the important social sectors of Nicaragua; even the capitalists resented his personal meddling in the country's commercial affairs. Political control was maintained by means of a highly corrupt National Guard and the unfailing support of the United States government. The

---

Box 8.3   Rigoberta Menchú, A Mayan Witness to the Guatemalan Revolution

Rigoberta Menchú was born into a K'iché Mayan Indian family in the highlands of Guatemala. In her youth she worked alongside her family on the coastal plantations picking coffee, and later she joined a labor organization seeking to improve the working conditions of Indian and mestizo rural workers. Her family eventually espoused the guerrilla cause, for which her father, mother, and brother paid with their lives. Rigoberta herself barely escaped the same fate by fleeing Guatemala for exile in Mexico. Later, during a visit to France she dictated her life story (*I . . . Rigoberta Menchú*), recounting the atrocities committed against the Indian peoples of Guatemala and their struggle to retain the Mayan heritage.

In the 1980s as the civil war raged on in Guatemala, Rigoberta became the chief spokesperson for the Indians of Guatemala under siege, testifying on their behalf before the United Nations and other international fora. She attempted to return to Guatemala in 1988 but was seized by security officials and forced to return to Mexico. In 1992, Rigoberta entered Guatemala triumphantly as the Nobel Peace Prize winner for that year, finally protected against assassination by the international acclaim given to her as one of the world's foremost peacemakers. She remains a leading political figure in Guatemala, despite continual attempts by enemies from the ladino sector to disparage her on the grounds of her personal appearance and unfailing defense of Indian rights.

The anthropologist David Stoll (1999), in his provocative book on Rigoberta Menchú's role in the revolutionary war, claims that she "turned herself into a composite Maya" who symbolized the genocide perpetrated against the Mayan peoples by the Guatemalan state and its military forces. On the basis of Stoll's own research on the war, he presents evidence that Menchú seriously distorted the facts about what happened to her own family and the reasons why her small community became involved in the war. Stoll asserts that Menchú was used by human rights activists, scholars, and leftists in general to promote the cause of the revolutionaries, despite the fact that most of the Indians and Guatemalans in general had long ceased to support that radical movement.

Despite Stoll's criticism of Rigoberta's testimony, he recognizes that she has become an important "national symbol" for both Mayas and many Ladinos in Guatemala. Furthermore, he thinks that "[h]er story has helped shift perceptions of indigenous people from hapless victims to men and women fighting for their rights. The recognition she has won is helping Mayas become conscious of themselves as historical actors." (p.283)

Nicaraguan National Guard was a 7,000-strong army and police force directly under Somoza's control (his sons usually held its highest command posts).

The National Guard used terror and extortion to keep the Nicaraguan people in line, and as a result the guardsmen were greatly resented. Besides the National Guard, other precipitating factors leading to the revolutionary explosion against the Somoza regime were the devastating earthquake in 1972 (Somoza was accused of personally profiting from the incoming foreign assistance); Somoza's fraudulent re-election in 1974, and the assassination in 1978 of his leading political opponent, newspaper editor Pedro Joaquín Chamorro (it was widely believed that Somoza was responsible for Chamorro's death).

Revolutionary opposition to the Somoza regime started as early as 1961, with the founding of the Sandinista National Liberation Front (FSLN) by a group of middle-class radicals from the Matagalpa Highlands. Following the Cuban model, the small band of revolutionaries engaged in guerrilla-like attacks against the National Guard and gradually won to their side large numbers of Nicaragua's rural workers and peasants. By the 1970s the FSLN was able to recruit several thousand middle-class youth and urban workers to its cause, and it began to launch bold military offensives against the regime. For example, in 1978 the rebels seized the National Palace and forced Somoza to accede to several exorbitant demands. Finally, the FSLN forces initiated attacks on all the major cities of Nicaragua, preceded in almost every case by local insurrections (Figure 8.7).

The FSLN revolutionary army launched a final offensive from Costa Rica in 1978, and in July 1979 Somoza fled to Miami as the Sandinistas occupied the capital of Managua. The victorious Sandinistas then attempted to establish a socialist state in which both private enterprise and civil liberties would be respected. They were opposed at every step by the United States, which cut off all aid and organized a counterrevolutionary group of dissident National Guardsmen and Nicaraguan peasants known as the Contras.

Figure 8.7   Masks worn by Sandinistas during the 1978 insurrection at Monimbó, Masaya, Nicaragua. Photograph by the authors.

Through the mediation of Mexico, Costa Rica, and other countries, the Sandinistas and Contras finally agreed to a cease-fire in 1988. New elections were held in 1989, and the Nicaraguan Opposition Party (UNO) candidate, Violeta Chamorro (the wife of the newspaper editor who had been assassinated in 1978), was victorious over Daniel Ortega of the FSLN party, winning almost 60 percent of the vote. President Chamorro agreed to allow the Sandinistas to retain control over the army, and a degree of reconciliation began to take place in Nicaragua after thirty years of civil war.

The peoples identified as Indians in Nicaragua today for the most part are the Miskito, Sumu, and Rama of the Caribbean coast, descendants of tribal peoples who lived outside the pre-Hispanic Mesoamerican world. Making up about 4 percent of the national population, these coastal Indians form a small minority of relatively isolated natives similar to indigenous groups such as the Talamanca and Kuna found in the countries of Costa Rica and Panama. In Nicaragua, these native groups took no part in the revolutionary war against the Somoza regime, and later they vigorously resisted attempts by the Sandinista government to integrate them into the emerging socialist society. MISURASATA (Miskito-Sumu-Rama-Sandinista), the organization set up by the Sandinistas to bring the Indians into the revolutionary fold, was taken over by Indian leaders like Steadman Fagoth, whose goals were Indian self-determination rather than national integration. When MISURASATA began to cozy up to the Contras, the Sandinista government declared it a counterrevolutionary force and began resettling the Indians inland, away from their coastal villages. This move further alienated the Indians, and despite later gestures of goodwill the Sandinistas were never able to gain their confidence.

Nicaragua's native Mesoamerican population located on the Pacific coastal side of the country had become largely invisible by the time of the Sandinista revolution. Perhaps 20 percent of the population retained Indian biological features and traces of the Mesoamerican cultural heritage, but they were generally identified as mestizos rather than Indians. Nicaragua's revolutionaries concluded that these Indians had already lost their communal lands and native identity by the time Augusto Sandino launched a rebellion against the occupying U.S. Marines toward the end of the 1920s. In the process of their becoming mestizo peasants, it was thought that the Indians had developed greater revolutionary "consciousness" than their Indian ancestors.

According to the ideology of the Sandinista revolutionaries, Indian identity was a vestige of colonialism and an impediment to the creation of a socialist state. Once in power, the Sandinista government created a program that called for the emancipation of peasants, workers, women, blacks, and the repressed peoples of Asia, Africa, and Latin America, but not of their own native Mesoamericans. They made reference to the non-Mesoamerican indigenous groups of the Caribbean coast in policy statements, but only in the context of the need to incorporate them into national life.

Despite being ignored, in the 1970s thousands of people who still thought of themselves as native Mesoamericans resided in communities in and around the cities of Managua, Masaya, Granada, and León. These people could no longer speak the Mesoamerican languages previously spoken in the area (Pipil, Chorotega, Subtiaba), but they had reconstituted certain traditional cultural practices in craftsmanship, political organization, and ritual. In a surprising development, they inserted themselves into the ongoing revolutionary struggle in dramatic fashion by spearheading a series of insurrections against the Somoza regime. The most dramatic uprising took place in the city of Masaya in 1978, when the National Guard interrupted a funeral sponsored by the Indian community of Monimbó (a "barrio" in the city of Masaya) in honor of the slain newspaper editor Pedro Joaquín Chamorro. Over two thousand Monimbó "Indians" attacked the Guard with stones and fireworks, and during the following weeks barricaded the streets and fended off assaults from the Guard. The National Guard finally attacked in mass, supported by heavy weapons and aerial bombing. Monimbó was taken only after intense house-to-house fighting, and at the cost of hundreds of lives on both sides.

Similar insurrections led by Indians in Diriamba and the Subtiaba community in León were also crushed after heavy fighting and the loss of numerous civilian lives. Students of the Nicaraguan revolution agree that these insurrections, especially the one in Monimbó, were symbolically important for the eventual success of the revolution. What is remarkable is that they were spearheaded by native Mesoamericans who supposedly did not exist as an identifiable people.

The Sandinista mestizo guerrilla fighters, whose participation in the events of Monimbó and Subtiaba had been extremely limited, praised the role of the Indians in the revolutionary struggle. As a result, nativist elements began to be incorporated into the revolutionary ideology for the first time. The new Ministry of Culture sought to rediscover the country's indigenous roots through preservation of archaeological remains and promotion of native foods and crafts. Mesoamerican dishes made out of corn, such as tortillas and tamales, were touted as substitutes for wheat products, and the production of pre-Hispanic-type pottery and filigree gourdwork was encouraged by the government. Nevertheless, attempts to recognize the contributions by native Mesoamericans to Nicaraguan national culture have been modest, and they pale in comparison with the rich symbolism and lore built up around Sandino and the heroes and events of the revolution itself. Under the revolutionary government, Nicaragua remained a profoundly mestizo society, its roots in the ancient Mesoamerican tradition largely unappreciated.

DEVELOPMENT AND NATIVE MESOAMERICANS IN MEXICO AND CENTRAL AMERICA

"Development," as we use the term, consists of planned change, especially change resulting from economic measures taken by governments and collaborating capitalists. As we will see in this section, the developmental approach to modernization has been widely applied in the region of Mexico and Central America; and as elsewhere in the world, its costs have been significant. The specific application of the developmental agenda to the Indians of the region is known as "indigenismo" (Indianism). Indigenismo as applied to the native Mesoamericans was largely a program of assimilation, of fully integrating them into the economic, political, and cultural life of national society as "citizens" rather than as "Indians."

Development in Mexico

The Mexican revolution, according to Paz, was caused by the lack of development. Indeed, even after the immensely important changes brought about by the Mexican revolution, as of 1940 an estimated 60 percent of the peasants in Mexico still did not have enough lands to sustain themselves, and 50 percent of all cultivable lands remained under the control of large landowners (*latifundistas*). Industry continued to be dominated by foreigners, despite the fact that majority ownership by law had to be in the hands of Mexicans.

Under the guidance of the Institutionalized Revolutionary Party (PRI), Mexico launched development programs of such magnitude and success that they resulted in what became known as the "Mexican Miracle." Goals were shifted from public welfare to economic development, and during the 1950s and 1960s, economic growth exceeded 6 percent per year. Urbanization proceeded apace as peasants streamed into the cities to work in the factories, especially in Mexico City. By 1960, the urban workers and middle classes made up 40 percent of the total population of the country. Mexico was becoming modern, and new ideas about progress as measured by the consumption of material goods were replacing the earlier revolutionary goals of social equality through class conflict.

Changes after 1940 were also taking place in the political field. Following the radical policies initiated by Cárdenas, the ruling party and its administrative organ, the Mexican state, took on more authoritarian, corrupt, and repressive characteristics. As Octavio Paz (1972) describes it, the system became a veritable "pyramid" of power. The presidents of Mexico, chosen and essentially appointed by PRI, thoroughly dominated the legislative and judicial branches. The party and the army closed ranks, and even after the army became more professional and less politically active, powerful military, police, and paramilitary units were organized to control, by terror if necessary, opposition to the state and its "institutionalized revolutionary" policies. Indeed, in 1958 a large strike in Mexico City was ruthlessly put down by the army; and again in 1968 a crowd of 400,000 antigovernment demonstrators in the Tlatelolco Square was brutally fired upon by security forces, killing some 300 or more persons (Figure 8.8).

The Mexican revolution was ostensibly fought on behalf of the Indians, while its agrarian reforms, though not specifically formulated with the Indians in mind, were thought finally to have restored the lands that the liberals had taken from the Indian communities in times past. After the 1940s, however, Mexico began to turn from radical change to economic development and the creation of a modern nation-state. It became clear that the Indian peoples were lagging behind. In many of the more isolated areas of Mexico, prerevolutionary conditions continued to prevail: The Indians were enclosed in communities where they reconstituted through time their traditional Mesoamerican languages and cultures, while still being exploited by surrounding mestizo and creole landowners and merchants. Furthermore, the Indians and rural mestizos continued to be socially segregated by means of local caste-like inequalities. Mexican anthropologists termed such Indian areas "refuge regions" and argued that they negated the advances of the revolution by perpetuating colonial

Figure 8.8   Demonstrators confront the Mexican army near the Plaza of Three Cultures, Tlatelolco, Mexico, in 1968. Courtesy of Bettman Archives.

conditions. The refuge regions could not be allowed to persist unchanged if Mexico was to fulfill the goal of creating a modern nation-state.

Development of modern Mexico was to be accomplished through industrialization, political reform, and formation of a national identity. Mexican anthropologists such as Manuel Gamio and Alfonso Caso argued that the creation of a modern Mexico required a common national culture, which in turn depended upon a common language, an ethnic identity, and a set of customs. The development of nationalism was to be achieved through a process of "acculturation," the blending (*mestizaje*) of the different races, ethnic groups, languages, and customs into a unified "Mexican" people. This process meant that the refuge regions would have to be broken down and their Indians integrated into national life.

The policy that emerged in Mexico, "indigenismo," was officially enunciated in 1940 by President Lázaro Cárdenas at the First Inter-American Indigenist Congress in Pátzcuaro, Mexico. The program was later institutionalized in Mexico through the formation of the National Indigenist Institute (INI) under the direction of Alfonso Caso. Mexico, Caso argued, "could opt for no other way than to incorporate the indigenous cultures into the great Mexican community" (García Moray Medina 1983:179). For the most part, the intellectual leaders of the indigenous development program were students and advocates of the Indian cultures, and they labored diligently to enhance appreciation of the Indians in Mexico. They believed that integration of the Indians, and hence their development, could be achieved through managed acculturation: a selective blending of elements from both the Indian and the mestizo cultures, mediated by indigenist agents. Nevertheless, the overriding indigenist goal was for the Indians to adopt the fundamental ideas and institutions of modern Mexico.]

The indigenists set up coordinating centers in the main refuge regions of Mexico, beginning in 1951 with the Tzeltal-Tzotzil Mayan center in highland Chiapas. Gonzalo Aguirre was installed as the first director of the center in Chiapas. Aguirre used his position to investigate the social features of refuge regions like highland Chiapas, particularly the highly unequal relationships that existed between the local Mesomaerican Indians and the dominant mestizos. The indigenists also tailored programs in education, health, agriculture, and community development to suit the needs of the Indians. The precedent was established that modernization of the Indians would be carried out with due regard for the special social and cultural conditions of the Indians and in a fair and comprehensive fashion. In the following years, coordinating centers were set up among other native groups such as the Mixtecs, Zapotecs, and Mixes of Oaxaca; Mayas of Yucatán; Mazatecs and Tlapanecs of central and western Mexico; Otomís of Hidalgo; and Tarahumaras of northern Mexico.

It must be noted, however, that during this same time period the Indians of Mexico were subjected to developmental forces even stronger than those emanating from the National Indigenous Institute (INI) centers. Agrarian industries, for example, were established in most of the refuge regions, resulting in the expropriation of lands and other resources from the Indian communities. At the same time, the Mexican government vigorously sought to modernize politics throughout the country, establishing branches of the Institutional Revolutionary Party (PRI) in the native communities and reforming traditional political structures such as the Indians' local governing hierarchies. The Catholic and Protestant churches were also active modernizing agents among the Indians, as they proselytized to replace traditional native beliefs and practices with doctrinal systems more in line with Mexico's increasingly secular society.

By the 1970s, Aguirre, now director of INI, could assert that the main goals of the indigenist program were being achieved. The Indians had been largely "Mexicanized," the census of 1970 revealing that only about 10 percent of the population could now be classified as Indians. Furthermore, the Indians had been largely "Christianized," the culmination of a process begun centuries earlier with the arrival of the first Spanish missionaries. Most important of all, it was claimed, the Indians were being integrated into national life without being subject to racial or ethnic prejudice. Because of indigenismo the Indians had avoided becoming ethnic "minorities" in Mexico; that is to say, cultural groups seeking separate national status. Finally, under President Luís Echevarría (1970–1976), the indigenist program was expanded even further, as thousands of additional bilingual teachers and development agents were assigned to the refuge regions.

Despite Aguirre's optimism over the successes of Mexico's indigenist program, it came under severe attack from two fronts: the Indians themselves, and scholarly critics of its underlying assimilation goals. For their part, the Indians had shown far greater interest in retaining their native identities than expected, as well as resisting specific features of the programs designed to integrate them into the Mexican nation. In 1970, at least three million people in Mexico still claimed to be Indians, and about one-third of them identified far more with their traditional communities than with the nation as a whole. Much of the resistance to the indigenist programs by Indians took the form of either indifference or careful monitoring of proposed changes from the outside.

Resistance also took more violent forms during the 1970s and 1980s, as hundreds of thousands of rural Indians joined radical peasant movements in order to recoup lands lost to agrarian capitalists. Guerrilla warfare broke out in states like Hidalgo, Guerrero, Oaxaca, and Chiapas; and hundreds, perhaps thousands, of Otomís, Huastecs, Tarascans, Zapotecs, and Mayas were tortured and killed by government and private security forces. In some cases, such as the Yaqui and Mayo seizure of lands in Sonora, the government supported some of the Indian demands, but overall the response to Indian militancy was extremely harsh.

Scholarly critique of indigenismo became acrimonious far beyond what might be expected of an academic debate. It split anthropologists and other Mexican social scientists into two hostile and opposed camps: The defenders of the indigenist and other programs for the "development" of Indians were pitted against those who favored radical change through renewed revolutionary actions. The opponents of indigenismo in Mexico included illustrious students of Indian history and culture. They argued that the indigenists define the Indians too much in cultural terms, a process that is misleading: first, because it falsely assumes that Mexican national culture represents a more progressive evolutionary stage than the Indian cultures; and, second, because the focus on Indian culture diverts attention away from the Indians' exploited class condition as rural proletariats. Such critics claimed that the indigenist program was actually destructive to the Indians because it "modernizes their exploitation;" that is to say, it makes the Indians more accessible to capitalist exploiters.

Critics further point out that the Indians could no longer be culturally distinguished from the Mestizo peasants and rural proletariats of Mexico. Both were said to be fundamentally Western in culture and increasingly subject to U.S. influences. It was the Indians' profound dependence on the Mexican nation-state, which in turn was dependent on outside capitalist countries such as the United States, that to this day makes discussion of the "Indian problem" so volatile among Mexican scholars. The fundamental issue at stake was the same issue that led to the original revolutionary struggle in Mexico: liberation from dependency on foreign powers (the issue of national sovereignty). Unfortunately, as Aguirre argued, even should the problem of Mexico's dependency on outside powers be resolved, this solution probably would not have eliminated the so-called Indian problem because the Indians continued to demand to be recognized as culturally distinct peoples with rights of self-determination (this point is further discussed in the final section that follows).

The historian Alexander Dawson (2004) insists that one of the main consequences of the indigenist project was the emergence of "*indígenas capacitados,*" bilingual and bicultural Indians who mediated between the state agencies and the local communities they represented. Through time these educated Indians were able to make the indigenist programs conform more with local native traditions and interests, and in the long run this outcome helped create more pluralist relationships between the Indian communities and the state. But many of these Indian leaders also acquired local power, becoming "caciques" who promoted their own personal interests.

The successes and, more significantly, the many failures of the indigenist developmental program in Mexico can be illustrated by the the case of the native Otomís of the Mezquital Valley in the state of Hidalgo, Mexico.

The Mezquital Otomí Indigenist Project.   Mezquital is located close to Mexico City, and beginning in the 1930s, the area became a testing ground for the theories of the postrevolutionary government on how both to modernize and to "revindicate" Mexico's native peoples.

The large Mezquital Valley occupies over 3,000 square miles of territory, and it is located at an altitude that varies between 5,000 and 10,000 feet. Most of the valley is arid and relatively unproductive, except for a small zone along the Tula River where irrigation is possible. The Otomí Indians are scattered across the valley floor, as well as in small villages in the upland zones. The focus of the project was on four communities inhabited by some 36,000 Otomís, most of them monolingual speakers of the Otomí language. They engaged in subsistence farming, relying heavily on the maguey plant, which supplies *pulque,* the daily beverage, as well as fibers for weaving coarse cloths (*ayates*) and leaves for roof thatching (Figure 8.9). The indigenist offi-

Figure 8.9   A maguey plant of the type found in the Mezquital area. Photograph provided by the authors.

cials referred to them as a "poor race that has been dejected and enslaved since the Aztecs" (Dawson 2004:129).

The Otomí Indians along with other peasants in the Mezquital Valley had previously joined with the Zapatista and Villa forces during Mexico's revolutionary war. Their struggle had been directed against the landlords of large irrigated estates in the valley who had taken over Otomí lands and converted them into productive farms. To make matters worse, in 1900, the Díaz regime diverted Mexico City's sewage waters to the Mezquital Valley to be used by elite landlords there for irrigation purposes. The Mezquital revolutionaries succeeded in driving out the landowners, and with the help of Zapata and Villa, they recovered some of their lands in the form of ejido grants (despite the efforts by Carranza to return the lands to the same wealthy landlords). The struggle for land continued, however, as mestizo caciques and their gunmen fought it out for control over the ejidos. As elsewhere in Mexico, the strongest caciques assumed the office of ejido "commissaries" and usurped many of the best lands for themselves and their clients. The disastrous history of the Otomí Indians made them ideal subjects for the postrevolutionary indigenous models.

Through the years major investments were made by the Mexican government to develop the Valley, including the founding of cooperatives, credit banks, schools, irrigation projects, workshops on weaving, other hand-industries, and cattle ranching. In 1952, the indigenist program was given the title of Indigenous Patrimony of the Mezquital Valley (PIVM) and underwent reorganization along the lines of the INI coordinating centers located in other Indian areas of Mexico. Elaborate PIVM headquarters were built in the town of Ixmiquilpán. Around this time, too, the Summer Institute of Linguistics (SIL) from the United States began to operate among the Otomís of Mezquital, and in 1960 it established its headquarters in Ixmiquilpán. The SIL missionaries translated the Bible into the Otomí language and introduced the Protestant religion to the Otomís for the first time.

Despite all efforts, the expected development of the Otomís did not materialize. Most funds found their way into "the pockets of local officials, caciques, businessmen, and mestizos" (Dawson 2004:133). Lands, cattle, irrigated farms, and even schools were monopolized by the mestizo peoples of the Mezquital Valley. Although dramatic social changes have finally taken place in the Mezquital Valley in recent years, the indigenist development programs have played only limited roles in bringing about these changes. Most social change among the Otomís resulted from developments in transportation and commercial agriculture. An elaborate highway system eventually eliminated the Otomis' geographic isolation, making it possible for them to find work in the mines of Potosí, the streets of Mexico City, and the fields of Texas and California. Equally important, the development of large, irrigated vegetable farms in the valley provided convenient work opportunities for the Indians as farm laborers. The effect of these changes was to transform most Otomís from peasants to wage laborers.

Mexican scholars, such as the sociologist Roger Bartra, have documented the increasing capitalization of the Mezquital Valley and its impact on the Otomís and lower-class mestizos. They found the Otomís to be profoundly proletarianized and thus strongly integrated into the economic structure of Mexican society. In the process, it is claimed, the Indians lost the last vestiges of native Otomí culture and could no longer be distinguished from the exploited mestizo lower classes. The cacique intermediaries, some of them Otomís, began to disappear too, as rural capitalists and government agents more and more dealt directly with the Indian workers. This strategy represented a shift in native culture as well, since even though the caciques exploited the Indians, they did so as "populists" whose authority derived from the promotion of authentic native traditions. Paradoxically, the Indian culture is said to live on only in the minds of the capitalist exploiters who, as indigenists, glorify the Indians and advocate the survival of their cultures at the very time that they bring about the destruction of those same cultures. Bartra (1982:93) explains as follows:

> . . . (the capitalist) after contributing to the social disappearance of the Indian, resurrects him to a level of cultural reality; the demagoguery consists in proclaiming that the cultural Indian enters society through the main door—as the guest of honor—while the real Indian has to go through the servants' door, to be integrated—after being robbed of his culture—as a proletariat.

Bartra accurately describes the most general social condition of Indians like the Otomís of Mezquital, but two cautionary observations need to be made. First, Bartra and his followers seem to argue that all the Indians of Mexico are in a similar "proletarian" condition as are the Otomís of Mezquital. This argument is inaccurate, as we shall see in the following section of this chapter. Second, the reputed loss of native culture is stated too categorically, for it fails to give adequate attention to the efforts by the Otomís and other Mesoamerican Indians like them to reconstitute their traditional native cultures and identities. Anthropological studies of the Otomís document the loss of community solidarity and cultural patterns, but also the persistence of important elements of the native cultures at the level of family and social networks.

The Otomís have become painfully aware of their precarious social condition, and in increasing numbers they have adopted Protestantism and other forms of modern culture. Nevertheless, they have not forgotten their rich and magical Mesoamerican cultural heritage. This fact is well illustrated by the following narrative written in the Otomí language by a Mezquital Indian on behalf of his fellow Otomís (Bernard and Salinas Pedraza 1989:602–604):

> My brother! You are not alone in the world. You have had people who are your true friends for hundreds of years. Surely, you will ask, "Who are they." Brother, I must tell you, then. They are the earth that you walk on; the air that you breathe; the sun that gives you light so that you may see and walk and work, and so that you might live happily in the world. . . . The birds who sing to you out in the countryside are your friends, as are the animals that go about the surface of the earth and beneath the ground, as well. The stars are also your friends, and so is the moon, and the darkness. . . .
> Then who are your enemies? . . . Those who tell you that they respect you but who only exploit you daily for your work are your enemies. When you are young they respect you but when you grow old and can't work for them any more, they say that they don't know you. They pay you whatever they want to pay and not what your efforts demand of

them. Whenever you sell them anything, they do the same thing to you. Be careful not to make them angry when you ask them for something because they are violent when someone says anything to them that they don't like. What they pay you is not enough for you to feed your family. A salary of hunger is what they give you, and they are always poor-mouthing, saying that they have nothing to give.

Development in Central America

The Central American countries paralleled Mexico in their attempts to modernize through development after the 1940s, but they differed early on in not yet having experienced major revolutionary changes. To some extent, then, they more closely followed Paz's model of revolution that takes place as a result of (faulty) development rather than the lack of it. Growth and economic development became important goals in all the Central American countries beginning in the 1940s, spurred on by the Alliance for Progress and the Central American Common Market (CACM). Nevertheless, by mid–twentieth century, only in two countries were serious efforts made to institute lasting developmental reforms in Central America, the first in Guatemala (1944–1954) and the second in Costa Rica (1948 and thereafter).

Guatemala's major effort to modernize through development began in 1944, when students, professionals, merchants, and young military officers from the emerging urban middle class seized the reins of power from the dictator Jorge Ubico and formed their own reformist government. During the next ten years, the reformers attempted to change Guatemala from a dependent, racist country typical of the nineteenth century, to a developing, capitalist state. Under presidents Juan José Arévalo and Jacobo Arbenz, the government challenged U.S. hegemony over Guatemala, the large landowners' control of land, and the Church's hold on the people's conscience.

Much effort went into developing the economy, as forced labor was eliminated, a fair labor code enacted, and in 1952 an agrarian reform instituted. The land reform led to the expropriation of around one million acres of land from the largest plantation owners, and these lands were turned over to 100,000 landless peasant families. The Indian communities were strongly affected by the reforms, as newly formed progressive Indian leaders were pitted against traditional caciques and elders. Concurrently, the peasant leagues and agrarian councils provided opposition to the traditional authorities responsible for order within and between the Indian communities. Modernization through development was beginning to make headway in the countryside of Guatemala.

The government and its modernizing reforms were sharply contested by foreigners and ladino groups who had benefited from the past dictatorial system: large landowners, led by the United Fruit Company owners, who had lost about one-half million acres of idle lands; an older generation of army officers, who opposed the erosion of their influence in the countryside; the Church, which saw in the government a communist threat; and the U.S. State Department, which feared that its domination of the Guatemalan state was being weakened and so denounced Guatemala's leaders as Communists.

In an illegal action that had virtually nothing to do with the Indians, the U.S. Central Intelligence Agency (CIA) organized, trained, and led a clandestine band of dissident Guatemalan soldiers and mercenaries in a 1954 coup that overthrew the Arbenz government. Development and reform did not entirely end in Guatemala with the coup, but subsequent years were characterized by repressive military rule, accompanied by massive accumulation of wealth for the few but dire poverty for most Indians and lower-class ladinos.

Costa Rica's attempt to modernize through developmental reforms in the 1940s and 1950s was not as bold as Guatemala's, and as in Guatemala it failed to take into account the small number of communities still identifying themselves as Indians in that country. Nevertheless, as we see in Box 8.4, Costa Rica's development reforms turned out to be more practical and longer lasting than Guatemala's (see also Figure 8.10).

Indigenist Development in Central America. Most of the Central American countries ratified the agreements reached by the First Inter-American Indigenist Congress held in Mexico in 1940, and subsequently established national indigenist institutes of their own. Only in Guatemala, however, did this institute play much of a developmental role, and even there its influence was extremely weak compared with Mexico. For example, as already indicated, the important reforms of 1944 to 1954 in Guatemala were not strongly indigenist; as in Mexico, the Indian communities were seen as impediments to progress and therefore in need of assimilation into the broader "ladino" (mestizo) culture.

The military regimes that succeeded the reform government in Guatemala after 1954 were essentially anti-Indian. Unlike the Mexican indigenists who wanted to in-

Figure 8.10 Followers of Pepe Figueres in the 1948 Costa Rican uprising. Reprinted, with permission, from Victor Hugo Acuña, *Conflicto y Reforma en Costa Rica: 1940–1949*, Nuestra Historia (17) San José, Costa Rica: Universidad Estatal a Distancia, 1991.

Box 8.4   The Figueres Reforms in Costa Rica

In Costa Rica, a powerful populist president, Rafael Angel Calderón, managed to form alliances with both radical plantation workers and conservative coffee barons during the years leading up to 1948. This unusual coalition made it possible for Calderón to push through important social reforms, such as a labor code, social security program, and universal education. However, as Calderón began to move toward greater control of the state, opposition coalesced against him among members of the urban middle class. When Calderón and his followers attempted to annul the 1948 election results, an uprising took place under the leadership of José ("Pepe") Figueres, a mid-level coffee farmer with connections to the U.S. State Department (see Figure 8.10).

The Figueres-led rebels initiated a two-month civil war, or "revolution" as they called it, with backing from the United States (the U.S. government considered the revolt to be an anti-Communist movement). The victors went on to create a new constitution that modified the labor and electoral codes, outlawed the Communist Party, nationalized the banks, and, most dramatic of all, abolished the army. The leaders of this reform movement soon organized the National Liberation Party (PLN), and in 1952, Figueres was elected president under the new party's banner. During the years following 1952, opposition parties managed to win presidential elections from time to time, but the PLN reformers clearly dominated the political field through a series of economic, political, and social welfare reforms. As a result, Costa Rica experienced almost thirty years of relative peace, growth, and prosperity. By the 1970s, Costa Rica had surpassed not only the other Central American countries but Mexico as well, with respect to most developmental indices such as in health, education, and economic well-being. In February 2006, the former Nobel Peace Prize winner, Oscar Arias, was re-elected president of Costa Rica under the PLN banner.

---

tegrate the Indians into national life by means of culturally sensitive community development programs, the military governments of Guatemala favored the total eradication of the native cultures as quickly as possible and their replacement by a national ladino culture (a process known as "ladinoization"). Guatemala's approach to the Indian problem was assimilation with a vengeance. The government's actions toward the Indians were driven not so much by nationalist ideas as by the need to provide the country's export industries with cheap, easily available labor while at the same time maintaining strict control over the potentially rebellious Indian and ladino working classes.

The Indians of Guatemala were also subjected to extremely powerful modernization forces in the form of highly exploitative capitalist plantations and aggressive religious leaders, especially reform-minded priests imbued with the social gospel of the "Catholic Action" program. These two forces complemented one another, the plantations proletarianizing the Indians and the Church providing them with a collectivist rationale for their new social condition. By the 1970s, more than 20 percent of the Indians had joined peasant cooperative and labor organizations, many of them Church-sponsored. Other Indians residing close to large towns and cities found alternatives to work on the plantations in artisanry, especially weaving, and trade.

Despite these changes, the Indians of Guatemala, like those of Mexico, fiercely resisted the breakdown of their communities and the loss of cultural identity as Mayas. The same debate taking place in Mexico over whether the Indians should be defined in cultural rather than class terms was engaged by Guatemalan scholars and political leaders. But the stakes were much higher in Guatemala, for among those who claimed the Indians to be culturally distinct and therefore in need of "special" treatment were members of right-wing death squads; and those who saw the Indians as socially equivalent to ladino proletariats included members of left-wing guerrilla organizations. The Indians, however, were both culturally distinct *and* proletarianized, and they demonstrated this condition during the bloody revolutionary war of the 1970s and 1980s by joining the insurgent side without abandoning nativist cultural agendas. Whether a more robust Mexican-type indigenist program would have prevented the civil war in Guatemala is an open question, but its absence certainly hardened the positions of both the insurgent Indians and their military adversaries, and therefore helped initiate the Indians' vicious life-and-death struggle brought on by the civil war.

In El Salvador, Honduras, and Nicaragua the respective Indian institutes did very little either to aid the Indians in the development process or to integrate them into their respective national societies. In Nicaragua, the National Indigenist Institute may even have facilitated the loss of communal Indian lands and cultures. Costa Rica's first serious efforts to establish an indigenist organization did not take place until the 1970s, when the government set up the National Commission for Indigenous Affairs (CONAI) and decreed laws to protect Indian lands and provide for self-rule in the Indian territories. Unfortunately, CONAI proved to be ineffective, and the Indian laws were repeatedly violated by thousands of "whites" who invaded the Indian reserves.

By the 1970s, capitalist-oriented developmental reforms had already produced social conditions that precipitated the radical revolutions described earlier for the Central American region. In parallel with Mexico, these capitalist developments at first brought overall growth and prosperity to the Central American countries, although the Indian communities scarcely shared in the benefits. Gross national product (GNP) increased in the region for the three decades from 1950 to 1980 by the prodigious rate of 6 percent per year. Growth was especially high in export goods produced by commercial agriculture, the five leading products being coffee, cotton, bananas, sugar, and beef. Growth in manufactured products was almost as great, but most of the products were funneled into the region's common market (CACM). The withdrawal of Honduras from the CACM and the regional market's subsequent disintegration toward the end of the 1970s, however, was a sign of the negative growth and profound economic problems that the Central American countries began to experience in the 1980s.

The Central American revolutionary wars described before dominated political developments during the l970s and 1980s. The relatively strong support for the revolutionaries by the Indians was a clear indication that they had not generally benefited from the economic developments that seemed so promising in Central America. It is also evident that Indian participation in the civil wars brought with it a heavy developmental toll, and its impact has continued up to the present time (Spence 2004). This result is understandable, given the disasters the wars wrought on the economic, political, and cultural life in all these countries (especially in Guatemala, El Salvador, and Nicaragua). The peace accords—ended the Central American wars and promised to initiate transforming developmental patterns that would finally bring benefits to the Indians in the region.

NATIVE MESOAMERICAN ETHNIC AND NATIONAL MOVEMENTS IN MEXICO AND CENTRAL AMERICA

Most of the ethnic and national movements to be described next took place in the 1990s and early 2000s, and thus postdate the revolutionary and developmental phases of Mexican and Central American history described before. These movements have been particularly stimulated by recent neoliberal economic and political policies, greatly expanded globalization, ecological problems, and "postmodern" ideas about the importance of culture as a basis for power.

In Mexico neoliberal policies came to dominate economic and political developments there during the 1990s. Presidents such as Carlos Salinas de Gotari (1988–1994) essentially abandoned the previous state-centered model of development. They "liberalized" the market by privatizing the banking sector, joining the OPEC oil cartel (in order to improve the marketing value of oil exports), participating in the world's free-trade agreement (GATT), and allowing foreign companies once again to operate freely in Mexico (including *maquiladora* factories located along the borders with the United States). The decisive development was the 1992 signing of the free-trade agreement with the United States and Canada (NAFTA), which took effect in January 1994.

The Mexican economy soon resumed its meteoric growth, and by the twenty-first century, Mexico had achieved the eighth largest Gross National Product in the world. However, conditions for the Indians and mestizos in the rural areas of Mexico did not significantly improve, in part because of constitutional reforms that ended "government responsibility for land redistribution to peasants claiming land from private estates" (Hamnett 1999:285). Violent antigovernment rebellions broke out in states with large Indian populations such as Guerrero and Oaxaca (Tehuantepec). It has been argued that these rebellions were "prototypes" for the more lethal EZLN (Zapatista National Liberation Army) insurrection in Chiapas starting in 1994, and the resurgence of the EPR (Popular Revolutionary Army) resistance movement in Guerrero in l996. (For more on these two movements, see later and especially the detailed account of the EZLN movement in Chapter 10.)

Partly in response to such rebellious movements, Mexico's official Institutional Revolutionary Party (PRI) began to open up the electoral system by allowing minority parties to compete in elections on a fairer basis, although PRI continued to exercise virtually total control over the state apparatus. Opposition to the PRI-controlled party increased, and the power of the party was dramatically eroded. An important factor behind the party's loss of power was its failure to deal with the "Indian Problem" in the southern part of the country.

In the 1997 mid-term elections, the PRI party lost its majority in the lower house to the PRD (Democratic Revolutionary Party) and PAN (National Action Party) opposition parties. The popular PRD candidate, Cuauhtémoc Cárdenas (son of Lázaro Cárdenas), promising to alleviate the problems faced by the Indians and other rural peoples, was elected to the extremely important *Regente* (mayoralty) position of Mexico City. In addition, in the southern states of Mexico, several PRI governors were forced out before completing their terms of office because of unsettled conditions within their jurisdictions. Finally, in 2000 the PRI party for the first time lost the presidential elections, as the conservative PAN candidate, Vicente Fox, won the election with 43 percent of the votes. Like his PRI predecessors, Fox has been unable to resolve the so-called "Indian Problem."

In Central America, the peace agreements in the 1990s laid the groundwork for a series of neoliberal changes that in an uneven way have gradually unfolded throughout Central America during the past fifteen years. The modest developmental policies of the past have given way to aggressive neoliberal programs similar to those in Mexico. The economic emphasis has shifted to privatization of state industries, reduction in social spending, acceptance of multinational corporate investments, and the stabilization of private land holdings (agrarian reform has been given low priority). Following the lead of Mexico, the Central American countries appear to be on the verge of signing their own free trade agreement (CAFTA) with the United States.

One consequence of these programs is that the Gross National Product (GNP) per capita has begun to increase in the Central American countries since the end of the civil wars there (Spence 2004). For example, the per capita increases are 1.4 percent in Guatemala, 2.4 percent in El Salvador, 2.8 percent in Costa Rica (only in Nicaragua has per capita growth lagged behind at −.1 percent). Nevertheless, despite overall declines in Central American poverty rates during the postwar period, some 75 percent of Guatemalans, 36 percent of Salvadorans, and 50 percent of Nicaraguans still live in poverty (in Costa Rica the figure is 18 percent). And, as in Mexico, the Indians and poor Ladinos in general have not benefited substantially from the economic prosperity.

The most notable political achievements in Central America consist of the demise of the military dictatorships and the emergence of a variety of democratic governments in all the Central American countries (only Costa Rica was genuinely democratic prior to the 1990s). The revolutionaries who fought in the civil wars, including some Indians, have organized political parties and now participate in the electoral process. In the most recent presidential election in Guatemala, for example, the vice-presidential candidate for the leftist URNG party was Pablo Ceto, the same Mayan Indian mentioned before who joined the revolution in hopes of promoting the cause of Indians in the country (see the reference to Pablo Ceto in the earlier section on the Guatemalan revolution). Another Mayan Indian, Rigoberto Queme, announced his candidacy for the presidency, although he later withdrew from the contest prior to the election itself.

Mobilization by the native Mesoamericans in the face of these recent neoliberal developments in Mexico and Central America has taken a violent turn at times (especially in Mexico), but for the most part, it has led to the more peaceful form of protecting, and expanding, indigenous rights and ethnic and national identities. This last section, then, will be devoted to a description of the complex ethnic and national identity movements engaged in by the Mesoamerican Indians of Mexico and Central America. In order to simplify the account, these diverse forms of ethnic and national nativism are classified into three types according to their sociogeographical scope as follows:

1. Local Ethnicity, the persisting Mesoamerican local (community) cultural identities that exist by the thousands in the region.
2. Hegemonic Nationalism, the sovereign nation-state cultural identities, with emphasis on the influence that native Mesoamericans have had on the formation of state nationalisms.
3. Multiculturalism, the growing tendency by native Mesoamericans to emphasize regional ethnic cultural identities and to elevate them to autonomous "nation" status within the broader state organizations.

A fourth type, not discussed in this chapter, might be termed "Transnationalism." Transnationalism here refers to the ethnic and national cultural identities created by native Mesoamericans who have immigrated to other countries but return to their home communities and countries with new ideas about indigenous identities. This last type will be discussed in the chapter to follow on "Transnationalism and the Political Economy of Mesoamerica."

Local Ethnicity

The local or community type of ethnicity (which Aguirre referred to as being "parochial") has dominated native Mesoamerican ethnicity since the beginning of Spanish colonization. The intricate processes by which the Indians adapted Spanish and later creole and mestizo cultural features to their own elaborate Mesoamerican cultures has been the subject of numerous studies by anthropologists. This persistent type of local Indian identity calls into question the argument by some scholars that the Mesoamerican cultures were destroyed by the Spanish "conquest" and that the Indians themselves were absorbed into the emerging Mexican and Central American nation-state identities. Recently, the historian Matthew Restall (2003) has argued that among the many myths promulgated about the Spanish invasion and colonization of Mesoamerica is the myth that "the Conquest reduced the Native American world to a void." Instead, he points out, the "native cultures displayed resilience, adaptability, ongoing vitality, a heterogeneity of response to outside interference" (p.xviii).

This kind of local cultural resilience has continued in thousands of Indian communities in Mexico and Central America, and even today it probably provides the majority of the close to twenty million native Mesoamericans of the region with their primary source of ethnic identity. No community better illustrates this resilience, perhaps, than the Indian community of Chamula, located in the highlands of Chiapas, Mexico.

Chamula, a Mexican Case of Local Mesoamerican Identity.   The Chamulan Indians, who speak the Tzotzil Mayan language, have long been famous as Mexico's prototypically "closed," traditional Indian community (Figure 8.11). They have steadfastly blocked outsiders from taking up residence in their community and have carefully guarded against beliefs and customs that might deviate from the accepted traditional Mayan heritage. Indeed, community members who are thought to deviate from the accepted cultural tradition have been expelled in large numbers. The Chamulan Indians think of themselves as the "true people" and perhaps have become the best-known of Mexico's communities

Figure 8.11   Chamulan Indians carrying goods to the markets and shrines in the town of San Cristóbal de Las Casas. From Ricardo Pozas, *Juan the Chamula: An Ethnological Recreation of the Life of a Mexican Indian,* translated and edited by Lysander Kemp, with the permission of the publishers, University of California Press. Copyright © 1962 by The Regents of the University of California.

that "has chosen to be 'Indian' within the greater mestizo world of modern Chiapas and Mexico" (Gossen 1999:6).

The Chamulas' history of opposition to outside cultural influences provides powerful legitimization of the community's long-standing identity as Indians. The community followed the state of Chiapas in taking a conservative stance with respect to the Mexican revolution (a position similar to the one taken by the Oaxacan Indians as described in Box 8.2). The Chamulan Indians fought under the leadership of a cacique named Jacinto Pérez "Pajarito" on the side of the landlords who opposed the radical changes mandated by the Zapatista revolutionaries from the North (see the preceding account on the Zapatista revolution). The Chamulan rebels paid dearly for this support when later Carranza forces came to power, drove the Chamulan rebels into exile, and captured and then executed Cacique Pajarito.

During the Cárdenas period, the government began to make inroads into the community's traditional political and cultural life. Through the auspices of the PRI party, Chamula's old civil-religious hierarchy was replaced by new municipal authorities more in tune with the revolutionary program. Chamula's communal (*ejido*) lands were officially recognized, and a Department of Indian Affairs and an indigenous labor union were organized to protect the Indians against outside exploiters.

During the following years, the Chamulas experienced even more powerful pressures for change as a result of the implementation of indigenist developmental programs in Chiapas. The National Indigenous Institute's coordinating center, established in nearby San Cristóbal de Las Casas, initiated a flurry of health, education, and welfare projects designed to open up the community to more modern economic and social forces.

By the 1980s, Chamula had a growing population of over 50,000 people (it now has over 100,000 inhabitants), who are scattered across the municipal territory in well-defined hamlets. 92 percent of the economically active population still engaged in agricultural pursuits. They cultivated milpas of maize and beans, and husbanded a few animals, such as pigs, cows, and chickens, all on tiny land holdings. Almost none of the Chamulas could produce enough food to feed their families, however, and the majority of them were forced to supplement subsistence production with work for wages, either in construction or on coastal plantations. Two other means of economic survival were the growing of commercial crops, such as vegetables and flowers, and the renting of lands in the lowlands in order to produce both subsistence and commercial crops. A few families living mainly in the tiny Chamulan town center became full-time merchants, in some cases purchasing trucks for the purpose of transporting goods. One of their most lucrative commodities was locally produced "moonshine" (*pox*).

The Chamulan community has become increasingly stratified as a result of liberal and neoliberal developments in the 1980s and 1990s. A fundamental division exists between those Indians involved in commercial activities (merchants of *pox,* producers of commercial crops) and those in wage labor. The majority of the Chamulas are caught in a transitional social position between peasant farming and wage labor, although perhaps up to 30 percent of the Chamulas eventually have become full-time wage earners.

The incipient class of merchants and commercial farmers in Chamula early on was made up of Indians who were able to take advantage of the developmental programs and later expanded capitalism in Chiapas. The commercial farmers obtained credits, fertilizers, seeds, and irrigation technology from INI and other development agencies. The merchants were early collaborators with the revolutionary government and used political position to obtain the credits needed to purchase trucks and licenses to establish retail businesses in the community. Some of the commercialized Indians in Chamula, especially the merchants, became an elite group of "progressive" caciques. They gained control over key political and religious institutions, and were able to manipulate community life in such a way that it favored their own interests. It is not surprising that relations between the members of this elite group of Chamulas have been highly competitive, and this state of affairs has led to fierce factional struggles within the community.

The most serious factional conflict centered on large numbers of Chamulas who had converted to evangelical religions. The evangelicals were largely made up of disaffected wage laborers, and they resented the persisting economic and cultural limitations of the community. Because they represented a threat to the local commercial elite and the latter's guardianship of the community's Tzotzil Mayan identity and culture, they were persecuted. Those who would not renounce their evangelical beliefs were either killed or driven out of the community. Some of them formed independent agricultural communities in adjacent areas, and thousands of them settled in the marginal zones of nearby San Cristóbal and the state capital of Tuxtla Gutiérrez (for an account of the murder of a Chamulan protestant leader by the caciques of Chamula, see Gossen 1999:211ff).

The anthropologist Gary Gossen (1970; 1999) points out that Chamula culture is not an "authentic" Mesoamerican culture but a complex blending of Spanish colonial, Catholic, Mexican revolutionary, and modern developmental ideas melded with basic ideas, symbols, and practices that ultimately derive from the aboriginal Mesoamerican world. Such cultural complexity is to be expected and apparently is similar to the identifying cultures of all "Indian" communities in Mexico (and Central America). In the case of Chamula, the unique amalgam of beliefs and practices in the late modern era would appear to be the result of a synthesis worked out between the ruling Indian caciques and the more traditional rural farming sector of the community. What is extraordinary about the synthesis, however, is the extent to which it has retained profoundly Mesoamerican (Tzotzil Mayan) cultural features, despite the many cultural elements from Spanish and Mexican sources that have been incorporated into its present form.

The local Chamula cosmology, for example, retains the Mesoamerican idea of cyclic creations, in which each creation is defined by a contest between good and bad forces. The world, which centers on Chamula itself, extends upward in the form of celestial layers, each the habitat of sacred powers (for example, "Our Father" the Sun is in the third "sky," "Our Mother" the moon is in the second). The cosmos extends downward into the underworld, also layered and the habitat of the dead (such as St. Michael, the earthbearer). And the four cardinal directions provide an even more fundamental spatial division of the Chamulan world, whereby territorial sections, calendrical periods, day and night, seasons, rituals, and practically everything else that is significant in the community, are situated according to the particular cardinal direction with which they are associated (for more on these beliefs in Chamula, see Chapters 13 and 14).

The Chamulas have struggled fiercely to preserve a Mesoamerican identity and cultural orientation against all outside attempts to replace them with modern ideas. For example, in the late 1980s when the Roman Catholic Church attempted to introduce more socially oriented religious practices in the community, "in the best interests of local religious belief and practice" (Gossen 1999:5), the Chamulas withdrew from the Roman Church and sought affiliation with the Orthodox Catholic Church! Obviously, for the majority of the Chamulas their identity as (Mesoamerican) Indians was far stronger than their identity as Christians. More recently, in 1994, the radical Zapatista movement burst onto the Chiapas scene and attracted to its side many Indian communities in Chiapas. The Chamulan community, however, chose not to support the Zapatistas' nationalist agenda. Apparently, local Indian identity in Chamula counted more than the kind of "pan-Indian" identity being sponsored by the Zapatistas (for more on the Zapatista movement, see the section that follows on "Ethnic Nationalism," and especially Chapter 10).

Native Mesoamerican Communities in Central America.   In Central America, only the country of Guatemala has large numbers of local communities that are similar to those of southern Mexico in which local Mesoamerican cultures continue to provide the primary source of identity (see Box 8.5 for an account of the general nature of local identities in the Mayan communities of Guatemala).

Southeast of Guatemala—in El Salvador, Honduras, Nicaragua, and Costa Rica—only a scattering of communities have retained strong native Mesoamerican identification. Among these would be Izalco and a few other Pipil communities in western El Salvador; some 100 scattered Lencan communities in southwestern Honduras; and Monimbó and a sprinkling of other Chorotegan communities in Pacific Coastal Nicaragua and Costa Rica. The nature of native Mesoamerican local cultures in the southeastern Central American countries can be illustrated by the Monimbó community, an Indian "barrio" located in the city of Masaya, Nicaragua (see the discussion of Monimbó in connection with the Nicaraguan revolution presented in the preceding section on Central American revolutions).

The majority of Monimbó residents, more than 20,000 in number, continue to identify as Indians, even though their native Chorotegan language has been lost. Furthermore, they no longer differ significantly from other lower-class residents of Masaya in terms of occupation, marriage patterns, religion, or education. Increasingly, it would seem, Monimbó has taken on the characteristics of lower-class structure, its past communal unity being gradually replaced by a fragmented, class-stratified suburb.

The anthropologist Les Field (1998), who recently studied local identities in Monimbó, argues that their Indian identity is in flux. For some of Monimbó's leaders, Chorotegan Indian identity is based on an untenable "essentialist" view of history (that is, they argue that their Mesoamerican cultural features have persisted relatively

Box 8.5 The Cultural Logic of Local Mayan Identities in Guatemala

Many classic ethnographies have been written on Indian communities in Guatemala emphasizing the persistence there of traditional Mayan institutions and local Mayan identities. A recent description of identity in the Kaqchikel Mayan community of Tecpan by the anthropologist Edward Fischer (1999; 2001) is particularly useful because it also generalizes his findings about this community to many other Mayan communities in Guatemala.

Fischer addresses the controversial split among scholars between the ethnographic "essentialists," who tend to see Mayan cultures as a direct legacy from the original Mayan culture, and the "constructionists," who see them as the temporary outcome of continuous cultural transformation in response to changing political and material conditions. The two approaches come together, he claims, if we look at Mayan culture and identity as resulting from an underlying "cultural logic" that involves cultural construction as well as continuities of "essential" cultural elements by human agents.

The cultural logic of Mayan communities such as Tecpan provides broad and general "foundations" for thought and behavior. Mayan "logic" defines a cosmology, or metaphysics, for a culture that cannot be easily explained or subsumed by Western or any other culture. Mayan logic, for example, sees unity in diversity, balance between society and the cosmos, sacrifice as the way to achieve balance, cyclic and calendrical rejuvination operating in all spects of life. Two key Mayan terms that provide a basis for understanding the cultural logic of Tecpan and other Mayan communities of Guatemala are *k'ux* and *anima'*, which roughly translate as "heart" (or more specifically, "soul"); and "vital force."

Animá (vital force) is conceptualized as a uniquely human force laid down at birth. It is subject to outside threats and can be lost. But it survives death "and lives on as a disembodied soul in the heavens and/or earth" (p. 482). K'ux (heart, soul) is "the point of contact between individuals and the cosmic force animating the universe," and is particularly important for understanding Mayan cultural logic. It symbolizes the essence of humans and other phenomena, provides self-identity, defines normality, makes balance possible, and has regenerative power. These two concepts together provide "the foundation for individual agency and intentionality while at the same time being a product of social interaction" (p. 486). They promote balance between the social and cosmic worlds, so that even though changes occur, they remain the foundation upon which new constructions are made and identities maintained.

Similar cultural logic operates in the many other Mayan communities of Guatemala despite language differences. As in Kaqchikel-speaking Tecpan, the cultural emphasis in these communities is on finding balance in the cosmos, achieved through a symbolic covenant between humans and the cosmic forces. Similar key terms in the diverse Mayan languages provide symbols for the underlying cultural logic. Closely paralleling the *k'ux* and *anima'* Kaqchikel terms in Tecpan, the Mam Mayas employ the terms *naab'l* and *aanima,* "sense" and "soul"; and the Tz'utujil Mayan cultural logic can be illustrated by the terms *jaloj* and *k'exoj,* "maturation" and "rejuvination" (transformation and renewal).

Such deeply imbedded concepts in the local cultures of Guatemalan Mayan communities have helped sustain the continuities of these local cultures, at the same time that their highly general meanings made it possible for diverse cultural changes to take place.

unchanged through time). Indian identity in Monimbó and elsewhere in the Masaya area, Field says, is best seen as resulting from a dialectical reaction to the national myth that all Nicaraguans are mestizos. The Indian cultural identity has practical implications for the Monimboseños' present-day situation: It provides ethnic grounds for regaining long-lost Indian communal lands and for opposing government programs that in general have not been beneficial to them.

Hegemonic Nationalism

For the second type of Mesoamerican ethnic and nationalist construction, we turn to the question of how far the hegemonic nation-state (national) identities and cultures of the region have been influenced by native Mesoamericans. We are not primarily concerned here with the many surface features of native origin that historically have diffused broadly into the mestizo and national cultures of the region: for example, Mesoamerican foods, idiomatic expressions, names of geographic locations, traditional arts and crafts, iconographic themes incorporated into modern architecture, painting, and advertisement. Rather, we want to determine whether complex Mesoamerican cultural themes (including the "cultural logics" described in Box 8.5) have been embedded into the very core of national thinking in Mexico and Central America. As we will see, native Mesoamerican influence has been far greater on Mexican nationalism than on nationalism in the Central American states.

Mesoamerican Influence on Mexican Nationalism.   Within the Mesoamerican region, only in Mexico has the question of native Mesoamerica's influence on nationalism been seriously addressed, and even in Mexico the proposed answers to this question are highly controversial and vociferously disputed. Nevertheless, the anthropologist Gonzalo Aguirre's general assertion that "the cultural symbols that today serve to identify the Mexicans are in part Indian" would seem to be indisputable. Aguirre (García Moray Medina 1983:207–208) elaborates as follows:

> The absorption of the Indian personality and values by the national culture is an inexorable process that enriches that culture. . . . Unlike the U.S. and Argentina . . . Mexico elected the personality and values of the Indians to be symbols of national identity. . . . This election was transcendental because the Indian is integrated into a national world that does not discriminate against or deny him, because that would be like denying and discriminating against one's self.

Octavio Paz provided a most influential (and highly controversial) interpretation of the Indian roots of Mexican national culture in his widely acclaimed book, *The Labyrinth of Solitude* (1961), as well as in other writings. Paz claimed that following the revolution, the Mexicans created a new national culture and identity, or, as he refers to them, "hidden collective conscience." The revolution finally gave the mestizos a central place in society and a set of ideas that represented a synthesis of the traditional Indian and creole cultures. To a large extent, this synthesis was based on a dialectical process, the negation of both things creole and things Indian. Thus, the emerging national culture could be traced to the mestizo's lack of a defined national identity, whether creole or Indian, and therefore to a feeling of orphanhood or

bastardness. This has happened because the mestizo cultural identity historically derived from a residue of inferiority complexes, a certain "servant mentality" carried
over by a mestizo class that had to claw its way to power without the benefit of a proud
historical tradition or systematically worked-out culture.

Paz particularly calls attention to the collective shout made by the Mexicans each
September 15: "*Viva México, hijos de la chingada*" ("long live Mexico, you sons of the
violated mother"). This preoccupation with the violated mother, and hence bas-
tardhood, is part of the burden carried by the mestizos, a burden not born by the
Mesoamerican Indians nor by the Spanish creoles. But the deeply felt ideas that express the Mexicans' hidden conscience also have roots in the Spanish and Mesoamerican cultures. Chief among the emerging national symbols was the Cuauhtemoc
persona, remembered as the Aztec emperor who had succeeded the martyred Motecuhzoma and then led the resistance against the Spanish conquistadors (see Chapter
4). In the Mexican secular pantheon, the Cuauhtemoc persona became the long-
suffering Mesoamerican son, bloody but not bowed: the stout warrior. The dialectically opposed symbolic persona to Cuauhtemoc was Cortés, the prototype of the
Spanish conquistador. The Cortés persona stood for the Spanish "macho," symbol of
power and violation of women (his name was banned from public discussion but remained ever present in the Mexican psyche). The hidden message in this symbolism
was that the typical Mexican man had lineage from both Cuauhtemoc and Cortés,
and thus was heir to both the Indian and the Spanish heritages.

In the context of traditional Mesoamerican sexual dualism, the emerging Mexican ethos necessarily provided female symbolic equivalents to Cuauhtemoc and
Cortés. Foremost among these was the Virgin of Guadalupe persona, the saint
adopted by the Indians who represented Aztec female goddesses. The Guadalupe
persona in Mexican national culture came to stand for the mother of the poor and
weak, the orphans. Her persona became the female counterpart of Cuauhtemoc.
The dialectically opposed persona to Guadalupe was Malinche, the Mayan princess
who served as translator and mistress to Cortés and his men. The Malinche persona
became the "*chingada*," the violated woman, symbol of all those traitors who preferred foreign to Mexican ways. The hidden message behind the Guadalupe and
Malinche symbolic personae suggested that Mexican mothers, and hence their mestizo offspring, were neither Indian nor Spanish, for they could not have sprung from
either the patroness of orphans or the violated woman (on Guadalupe and Malinche,
see Chapter 5 in this text).

It is noteworthy that the Mexicans granted hero status only to the Cuauhtemoc
and Guadalupe personae, both of whom had roots in the Mesoamerican cultures.
Since one of them (Cuauhtemoc) was incorruptible, and the other (Guadalupe) vir-
ginous, it follows, says Paz, that "[t]he Mexican does not want to be either an Indian
or a Spaniard. Nor does he want to be descended from them. He denies them."

Paz's critics point out that Mexico's hegemonic national culture and identity
have been undergoing rapid changes as the country increasingly industrializes, and
in the process the underlying national culture has become more oriented to con-
sumerism and middle-class capitalist values. Even before these changes, it is argued,
Paz's "hidden" culture was too simplistic to fit the many regional, ethnic, class, and

institutional cultural variations of a large nation such as Mexico. Many Mexicans, in fact, not only do not identify with Paz's characterization of their national culture but also deeply resent it.

Although criticisms of Paz's interpretation of Mexican nationalism may be valid, it would be surprising if the Mexican national culture were not to contain important Mesoamerican elements embedded within it, even if in dialectical forms. After all, Mexico has a history that began with an aboriginal civilization of great complexity, witnessed the survival of native peoples as a significant percentage of the population for almost 500 years, and more recently experienced the active participation by millions of Mesoamerican Indians in the great modernizing events of the twentieth century. Given this historical background, the Indians and their cultural traditions necessarily were factored into the equation of modernizing Mexico. As a minimum, Paz's account of Mexico's hidden culture suggests one complex symbolic process by which Mesoamerican symbolism found its way into the emerging nationalism.

(Box 8.6 provides an account of middle-class peoples living in Mexico City who identify as Indians but who differ from each other in terms of the degree to which native Mesoamerican culture should provide the basis of Mexican nationalism.)

Mesoamerican Influence on Central American Nationalism.   Studies of national cultures and identities in the Central American countries are less well known than in Mexico, in part because nationalism in the Central American countries remains more incomplete. Furthermore, with the exception of Guatemala, the impact of the Mesoamerican cultures on national cultural identities has been relatively weak.

For example, in Nicaragua the historian Jeffrey Gould (1998) documents the ethnic persistence of Mesoamerican Indians in Nicaragua up to the modern era, followed thereafter by their ethnic transformation as "mestizos." The process was facilitated by the dominant class's creation of a "myth" that identified all Nicaraguans as ethnically mestizo. The myth was then used to justify governmental programs and policies designed to eliminate "Indian" lands, community organizations, languages, customs, and identities.

In broad terms, the same processes by which the Indians were denied important influence on Nicaragua nationalism have been at work in El Salvador, Honduras, and Costa Rica. Nevertheless, in all of these countries, along with Nicaragua, some belated recognition of the contributions made by native peoples to their national cultures and identities is taking place as part of the accommodation between neoliberalism and the currently popular notion of "multiculturalism" (see the discussion that follows on this form of ethnicity and nationalism).

Guatemala is the one Central American country where we find a stronger Mesoamerican nationalist component, no doubt because of its historically large Mayan population. Nevertheless, until recently the recognition of the Indians' contribution to Guatemalan national culture remained weak. In contrast to Mexico, the "ladinos" and "Indians" have always been ethnically and racially segregated, with the Indians considered to be too inferior to provide inspiration for the national culture. Furthermore, as already noted, the important 1944 to 1954 reforms did not strongly promote nativist symbols, certainly far less so than in Mexico for the equivalent period of time

Box 8.6   Mesoamerican Identities in Mexico City

The sociologist Alicja Iwanska in her book *The Truths of Others* (1977) describes how middle-class Indians of Mexico City vary widely with respect to how they view the significance of the native Mesoamerican tradition with respect to Mexican national culture and identity.

One group, the "Realists," adopts an indigenist position: They advocate the incorporation of the peasant Indians into Mexican society but on equitable terms and to the extent possible with preservation of the regional native cultures. Their theme is "Let's Mexicanize Indians, not Indianize Mexico." They differ from the idigenists of the National Indian Institute in claiming that educated Indians like themselves rather than governmental agents should mediate between the rural Indians and Mexican society. They are critical of certain problems faced by the native Mesoamericans in their communities, such as the machinations of caciques and other "parasites" found there. In the past the Realists organized teams of Indian professionals to visit the communities and to provide needed services.

A second group, the "Utopians," adopt a nativist position on the issue of Mesoamerica and Mexican nationalism. The so-called Utopians advocate restoring the Mesoamerican cultural traditions of the past as the basis for Mexico's identity as a progressive nation-state. They tend to glorify the Mesoamerican cultures and engage in revising native histories so as to conform more closely with their own ideas about Mesoamerica's glorious past.

One group of utopian "Aztecs," for example, argues that the Spaniards gave their Aztec forefathers a bad name by ascribing to them excessive human sacrifices. According to the leaders of this group, references to the Aztecs' practice of human sacrifice should be taken as only "poetic metaphors" and not actual literal fact. Furthermore, they claim that the Aztecs were not organized as an empire but as a genuine democratic confederacy that was founded on the communalistic *calpulli* unit. The Aztec calpulli, it is argued, became the model not only for the Mexican ejido but also for the communes of China and the kibbutzim of Israel.

This group's goals include such ideas as replacing Spanish with Nahuatl as the official national language, gaining control of the national government through the miniscule Mexicanidad party, and creating a new national ceremonial calendar based on historical events involving the Aztecs (from aboriginal times to the present day).

Despite the differences between the realist and the utopian Indians of Mexico City, they have much in common. Both have achieved middle-class status, although the Utopians tend to be wealthier, higher in social standing, and probably farther removed from their roots in the rural Indian communities. They are both cultural pluralists in the sense of wanting to preserve the native cultures within the context of Mexico's nationalism, although the Utopians go further in advocating the restoration of Mesoamerican cultural elements already lost. And both have considerable knowledge about the native Mesoamerican cultural tradition, although to a large extent their knowledge is more intellectual understanding than deeply held cultural beliefs.

The Realists insist on being called "Indians," whereas the Utopians want to be known by their ancient Mesoamerican designations: for example, as "Aztecs," "Mayas," "Purépechas" (Tarascans), and so on. Nevertheless, both groups denounce the conquest process as a result of which the term "Indian" was created; and, understandably, both strongly opposed the 1992 Quincentenary celebration of Columbus's "discovery," arguing that it should have been a time for mourning rather than for celebrating.

(see the discussion of these reforms in the preceding section on development in Guatemala). Guatemala's post–1954 indigenist programs failed to promote respect for the Indians or to successfully integrate them into national life. And with the onset of the civil war in the 1970s and 1980s, the development programs were totally scrapped as the government engaged in a genocidal attack on the Indians and their cultures (on the civil war in Guatemala and its impact on the Indians there, see the earlier section on the Guatemalan revolution).

Despite the denials of significant Mesoamerican influence on Guatemalan national culture, that influence has been substantial. This could not be otherwise, given the fact that a far larger proportion of Guatemala's people is made up of Mesoamerican Indians than in Mexico or the rest of Central America. The author of this chapter long ago called attention to influential Mesoamerican elements that found their way into Guatemala's budding national culture. For example, the country's revered name, like Mexico's, appears to have been adopted directly in memory of a powerful pre-hispanic Mayan kingdom of the area. Another of the country's most powerful symbols of national pride and identity is based on the great Mayan epic, the *Popol Wuh*, read by all the schoolchildren of Guatemala and endlessly studied and interpreted by Guatemalan scholars and writers.

Another of Guatemala's deepest and most complex national symbols derived from Mesoamerican sources is the persona of the Mayan historical hero Tekum, who led the K'iche' Mayan forces against the Spanish conquistadors in 1524. According to historical documents, Tekum was killed by Pedro de Alvarado, the Spanish captain (see the account of this historical episode in Chapter 4), and today Tekum's burial place is claimed by numerous Indian communities of the western highlands, and statues of him have been erected throughout the country. The Tekum persona can be seen as the Guatemalan equivalent of Mexico's Cuauhtemoc persona: the unbowed, valiant Indian warrior. Similarly, Alvarado is the equivalent persona to Cortés, the Spanish conquistador and violator of Indian women and political sovereignty. This Guatemalan secular pantheon is less developed and certainly more narrowly shared than Mexico's, but it does exist in diverse forms for most Guatemalans. As in Mexico it expresses profound but "hidden" native elements in Guatemala's national cultural identity.

The parallels between Guatemalan and Mexican national symbolism include similar ideas about the ladinos ("mestizos") and their origins in both countries. As Paz does for Mexico, Luís Cardoza y Aragón, one of Guatemala's main critics of indigenismo, alludes to a hidden "collective conscience" in Guatemala concerning the ladinos, which according to the anthropologist Richard Adams is so sensitive and deeply entrenched that until recently, it was almost never openly discussed. Even more so than in Mexico, the Guatemalan ladinos are defined in racial and ethnic terms, as if to provide a symbolic bridge across the historically created chasm of inequality, insecurity, and hatred between the Spaniards and Indians. Cardoza y Aragón described this aspect of the national "conscience" as follows (Adams 1991:147):

> The nation is Indian. This is the truth which first manifests itself with its enormous, sub-jugating, presence. And yet we know that in Guatemala, as in the rest of America, it is the mestizo who has the leadership throughout the society. The mestizo: the middle class. The revolution of Guatemala [reference to the 1944–1954 reforms] is a revolution of the middle class. . . . And what an inferiority complex the Guatemalan suffers for his Indian blood, for the indigenous character of his nation! . . . The Guatemalan does not want to be Indian, and wishes his nation were not.

As we explain next, the position of the Mayan Indians within the context of Guatemala's national politics and culture is dramatically changing in conjunction with newly emerging forms of "multiculturalism."

Multiculturalism

Multiculturalism, our third type of ethnic and national cultural formations in Mexico and Central America, refers to the expanded identity movements that are coalescing across the multiple local native communities of the region. Potentially, these indige-nous movements threaten the cultural hegemony of the nation states in the region, as increasingly the native leaders seek to establish pluralist national organizations whose identities fall outside (or alongside) the so-called sovereign-state nationalisms.

The anthropologist Charles Hale (2002) explains that multiculturalism in the re-gion is a response to an "extraordinary mobilization of indigenous peoples" beginning in the 1990s. Native Mesoamericans have been able to expand their indigenous orga-nizations, laying the groundwork for nexuses between Indians traditionally isolated within local community settings. This kind of mobilization was on display, and acceler-ated, by the 500-year "celebration" of the Columbus discovery, the joyous rally around Rigoberta Menchú, the winner of the 1992 Nobel Peace Prize (Figure 8.12), the dra-matic opposition to the North American Free Trade Agreement (NAFTA), and the solid support for international agreements on Indian rights and human rights in general.

Most important of all for the mobilization of the native Mesoamericans, per-haps, has been opposition to the ascendancy of neoliberal policies during this period in Mexico and Central America. Neoliberal political and economic policies have been generally destructive of the Indians' position in the market, as well as causing the loss of communal lands, access to state welfare assistance, political independence, and traditional Mesoamerican culture. As already indicated, however, the Indians have reacted strongly to the excesses of neoliberalism, in the process creating mul-tiple regional and national ethnic organizations and identities. Also, these indigenous organizations have begun to challenge the political and cultural hegemony of the nation-states themselves.

Hale (2002:492ff) argues that in the process of this mobilization, the Indians have pressured neoliberal agents, both national and international, to modify their agendas by recognizing the validity of multiculturalism. Hence, most governments and international agencies in Mexico and Central America have adopted this slo-gan: "We favor a multi-ethnic, pluri-lingual" type of society. Hale cautions, however, that "neoliberal multiculturalism" has definite limits; it inevitably stops short of the kind of "empowerment" of Indians that would allow them to challenge the funda-mental goals of the neoliberal agenda.

Figure 8.12   Artistic portrayal of Rigoberta Menchú, Nobel Laureate and leader in the Guatemalan pan-Mayan movement. Illustration by Bradley W. Russell.

Multiculturalism in Mexico   In recent decades the so-called "Indian problem" has emerged as a major issue in the political life of Mexico. The Indian population there is expanding rapidly, and it now exceeds ten million in number. In states such as Chiapas, Oaxaca, Guerrero, Puebla, and Veracruz, native Mesoamericans make up significant percentages of the population. In Chiapas, for example, they number over one million persons and constitute almost one-third of the total population. It has become clear that Mexico, like Guatemala, Ecuador, Peru, and Bolivia, should be considered an "Indo-American" rather than a "Euro-American" nation, made up of "complex mixtures (and conflicts) of many cultures of remote historical origins" (Hamnett 1999:22).

Rebellion in the Mexican countryside has become common once again, most notably in the cases of the Zapatistas (EZLN) in Chiapas, and the Popular Revolutionary Army (EPR) in Guerrero and Oaxaca (Foley 1999). The Indian rebels have particularly focused on the destructive effects of neoliberal policies adopted by the Mexican government, especially during the Salinas and Zedillo presidencies (1988–2000). These governments not only opened up the Mexican economy to global competition, culminating in the 1994 North American Free Trade agreement (NAFTA) but also curtailed agrarian reform laws and other residual revolutionary programs that had favored poor peasants, including most Indians.

The Mexican army viciously countered these native movements, relying in part on paramilitary loyalists in the regions of conflict. As negotiations broke down and the violence continued, the Indian rebels began to demand political autonomy, first for rebellious communities and then for entire Indian territories. Spearheaded by Comandante Marcos and the EZLN rebel organization, the Indians began to demand changes in the Mexican constitution that would transform Mexico from a homogeneous nation-state into a multicultural nation made up of "a series of distinct ethnolinguistic communities each striking to safeguard its identity" (Hamnett 1999:21). Despite intense efforts at negotiation and assorted agreements between the government and the rebel groups, a solution to Mexico's "Indian problem" has yet to be found (for much more on the EZLN movement in Mexico, see Chapter 10).

Just how deeply the cultural divide between the Indians and the state is in Mexico can be illustrated by Natividad Gutierrez's study (1999) of educated Indians from diverse regions of the country. Her key informants consisted of five Mayas (three from Chiapas, one from Yucatán, and one from Campeche), one Nahua, one Zapotec, and one Mixtec. Gutierrez particularly sought to understand how these elite Indians viewed their ethnic identities and what they thought about Mexican nationalism.

The views expressed by the educated Mesoamerican Indians were obtained through interviews on two key topics: (1) the founding myth of Tenochtitlan by the Aztecs, and (2) the founding myth of the mestizos through the union of the Spaniard Cortés and the Indian Malinche. What emerged from the responses was a rejection of these centralizing myths in favor of a multiculturalist perspective, which is expressed by an intense loyalty to and identification with their own respective regional ethnic groups. These "modern" Indians expressed little or no knowledge of, nor any interest in, the Aztecs as a possible integrating national symbol. Rather, they argued that the origin story of each ethnic "nation" is far more important to them. They were particularly critical of the idea of a national mestizo identity, an idea that they saw as a recent political invention designed to control and dominate the native Mesoamerican peoples. Accordingly, there was universal disapproval of the attempt in Mexico to build a unified mestizo identity, because, they explained, it only serves as an instrument for claiming and exercising superiority over the diverse Indian peoples.

It is striking how strongly these relatively urbanized, educated Mesoamerican Indians have remained loyal to their respective home communities and larger language and ethnic "nations." They make it clear that multiculturalism is strong in Mexico and that attempts to unify the Indians by adopting Aztec or mestizo symbols cannot convince, nor ethnically transform, the more than ten million native Mesoamericans scattered throughout Mexico.

One result of the almost universal rejection by the Indians of the prolonged attempt to create a unified mestizo national identity in Mexico is that the state is finally abandoning the worn-out idea of "mestizaje" (racial and cultural mixing), replacing it with a modern form of multiculturalism that encourages the development of diverse Mesoamerican literatures and languages. Gutierrez (1999:204) notes, however, that the door is closed on the possibility of self-rule by the native Mesoamerican groups. It would seem that the state's weak version of multiculturalism, and even that of the educated Indians themselves, rules out real political empowerment of the Indian peoples of Mexico.

(Box 8.7 provides a description of how one sector of the native Mesoamerican population, the Mixtecs of Oaxaca, Mexico, were able to create an expanded ethnic "nation" in the context of neoliberal Mexican economic and political policies.)

Box 8.7   Mixtec Ethnicity in Mexico

The anthropologist Michael Kearney (1996) describes the processes by which the Mixtec Indians of Oaxaca, Mexico, have reacted to developmental and neoliberal forces in Mexico by creating a greatly enlarged ethnic "nation" of their own.

Kearney narrates how in the 1960s, indigenist development projects were initiated in the Mixtec region in an attempt to "modernize" the Indians and integrate them into national life. But development failed to occur, and the result was "constant environmental deterioration and economic stagnation" (p.175).

In the face of increasing neoliberal pressures, the Mixtecs began to migrate to more developed areas in order to find wage labor opportunities. In large numbers, the Mixtecs became farm laborers in the extensive irrigated fields of Northwest Mexico and California (at one time, as many as 50,000 Mixtecs were working the California fields). Within these new settings, the Mixtecs suffered widespread exploitation and economic insecurity. Attempts to organize their own unions or join larger Farm Workers unions largely failed. As Kearney explains: ". . . for the Mixtec on both sides of the border, the proletarian route to political empowerment has proven no more successful than the peasant route" (p.176).

Many Mixtecs also migrated to urban areas such as Mexico City and Tijuana, where they found work as laborers at the bottom of the informal service sector. In such settings they sometimes attempted to organize urban squatter associations in order to better their living conditions. The more powerful Mexican mestizo classes, however, limited the Mixtecs' ability to improve their economic and social conditions.

A major reason why it has been so difficult for the Mixtecs to assert themselves has to do with the family and social fragmentation associated with moving from one area, or even country, to another. The Mixtecs found it difficult to remain unified in the context of the constant movement back and forth between their local communities in Oaxaca and the fields of Northern Mexico and California, as well as the cities of Mexico and the United States.

Thrown together in agricultural camps and urban shantytowns, and subjected to discrimination for being "Indians," the Mixtecs began to shed the imposed identities as poor Indians or lower-class workers. Instead, they identified themselves as Mixtec peoples belonging to an expanded ethnic identity that included all Mixtec Indians. Inspired by the new multiculturalism gaining ground in Mexico, they soon established relationships with other Native American "nations" from Oaxaca, such as the Zapotecs, Chinantecs, Mixes, and so on.

As Kearney (1996:180) explains, ethnic nationalism is an "identity suitable for the dispossessed, the exiled, those in diaspora, the marginal, the migrant, the diverse." And, of course, most appropriately for the native Mesoamericans of Mexico.

Multiculturalism in Central America.   Mobilization by Indians to improve their standing in society has gained momentum in all the Central American countries. Each of these states has adopted the "multicultural model," at least in its outward forms (Hale 2002:509). They have ratified the international ILO Convention 169 charter that calls for recognizing the special rights of indigenous peoples, and they have made constitutional changes to better support and accommodate their Indian peoples. Nevertheless, only in Guatemala are the issues of Indian rights and multicultural nationalism playing a central role in the political life of Central America. Indeed, during the 1990s the center of gravity for nationalist Indian movements in the larger Mesoamerican region appears to have shifted from Mexico to Guatemala.

A sign of this shift was the gathering of Indians in 1991 from all over the continent in the city of Quetzaltenango, Guatemala, where they denounced the Spanish invasion of America and celebrated 500 years of "indigenous resistance." Guatemala's centrality for the Mesoamerican Indians is understandable, given the fact that more than half the Guatemalan population (some six million strong) identify as Mayan Indians. They more easily present a unified front than Mexico's scattered Indian "nations," who make up less than one-tenth of that country's total population. The resurgence of the Mayas in Guatemala is an extraordinary development when one considers that during the recent civil war, it was dangerous even to be identified as an Indian.

In contrast to the educated Indians of Mexico mentioned before, the Indian leaders of Guatemala are probably more culturally radical and unified than their Mexican counterparts. Virtually none of them find assimilation into the ladino (mestizo) national culture a viable option, and many of them harbor the idea of a separate but equal Mayan nation (although taking over the state is still dangerous for them to advocate in public discourse). Clearly, the idea of a multicultural nation is increasingly being taken seriously by Mayan Indians from all sectors of Guatemalan society.

Scarcely had the civil war begun to wind down in Guatemala and a civilian elected president (1985), than educated Mayas began to mobilize nationwide Indian organizations. These organizations were soon linked together into postwar umbrella fronts, one of the most important of which was known as the Council of Mayan Organizations (COMG). An early leader of COMG was Demetrio Cojti Cuxil, a self-identified Kaqchikel Mayan professor in Guatemala City. Inspired in large part by events associated with the revolutionary war, Cojti proposed an ambitious agenda to create an autonomous Mayan nation within the Guatemala state, not through violence or force but by means of constitutional change and political dialogue with both the guerrillas and the government.

Cojti's plan would not have eliminated the mestizo nation of Guatemala per se but would have ended its dominance over the Indians by giving the Mayas an allied but autonomous nation of their own. Both nations would be free to promote their own languages, cultural traditions, and values, and to negotiate the kinds of political relationships that would bind them together into a new, restructured multicultural state. Cojti (1996) argued that his plan was designed to benefit all Mayan Indians in

Guatemala, including those in the rural communities whose particular languages and customs would be respected within the new Mayan nation. Although educated Mayas like himself would take the lead, Mayas from all social levels would be encouraged to develop a unified "conscience" of their own.

Much has happened in the "pan-Mayan" movement (as it is often referred to) since the original proposals by Cojti. Of special importance was the signing of Peace Accords in 1996 by the Guatemalan government and the unified guerrilla organizations (URNG). The Accords specified the rights of the Indian peoples to speak their own languages, practice their own religion and other customs, obtain political representation, and participate more equally in the economy. Even though these promised rights have been only partially honored in the years that followed, they have received important support from the many NGO's that have flooded into the country, as well as substantial backing from the Guatemalan people. Of most importance, the Accords helped lay down a (neoliberal) multicultural agenda for Guatemala's political parties and national government.

The pan-Mayan movement itself has expanded and been fortified by the previously mentioned developments. According to the anthropologist Kay Warren (1998), one of the foremost students of the movement, the educated Mayas who lead the movement have considerable "cultural capital" as a result of their knowledge of Mayan languages and cosmologies. They also have access to modern technology and media (Mayan newspapers, language books, radio stations and programs; communication through the Internet and wireless phones, etc.).

As might be expected, the greatly increased "cultural" powers of the pan-Mayanists have elicited widespread opposition. Foremost among the opponents are leftist popular organizations and ladinos of all kinds, along with an assortment of

---

Box 8.8   A Critique of the Pan-Mayan Movement.

The strongest critique of the pan-Mayan movement has come from ladino intellectuals, most prominently the journalist Mario Roberto Morales, who employs many of the "deconstructive" methods of postmodernism to disparage the movement.

Morales argues, for example, that the movement (I) is a construction by elites who do not represent the masses of Mayas in the countryside; (2) has become the tool of international neoliberal capitalism and its tourist markets, and more indirectly of development agencies and academicians; (3) excludes the many Mayas who have adopted Western ways and have assumed "hybrid identities"; (4) is racist in viewing Guatemalan society as divided between ladinos and Indians, when in reality both are differentiated by complex classes and social sectors rather than by race or ethnicity.

The anthropologist Kay Warren (1998) points out, however, that the deconstructive approach by Morales and others fails to confront important political realities that the pan-Mayan movement is trying to deal with. Morales, she says, makes "invidious ethnic discrimination and poverty dissolve before one's eyes—but, of course, only on paper" (p. 43). She thinks that much of the criticism levelled at pan-Mayan elites by critics like Morales is based on resentment over the competition that the Mayas represent to ladinos for middle-class and professional positions in Guatemalan society.

foreign intellectuals. Criticisms include the argument that the movement has polarized the diverse Mayan ethnic groups by artificially claiming cultural unity when in reality, multiple distinct regional and local Mayan identities and cultures remain. The pan-Mayanists are also accused of denying the existence of the many Mayan elements that have been incorporated into Guatemala's ladino culture, elements (it is argued) that could provide the basis for a common national cultural identity.

(Box 8.8 provides an example of one kind of criticism leveled at the pan-Mayanists, in this case by a Guatemalan journalist who is both a Ladino and former leftist sympathizer.)

In the context of harsh and often noisy criticism of the pan-Mayan movement, it is important to keep in mind that much of this criticism may be promoted by neoliberal advocates who want to prevent true Mayan "collective empowerment" (Hale 2002:523).

SUGGESTED READINGS

CARMACK, ROBERT M. 1995 *Quiche-Mayan Rebels of Highland Guatemala: A Political Ethnohistory of Momostenango.* Norman: University of Oklahoma Press.

CUMBERLAND, CHARLES C. 1972 *The Mexican Revolution: The Constitutionalist Years.* Austin: University of Texas Press.

DAWSON, ALEXANDER S. 2004 *Indian and Nation in Revolutionary Mexico.* Tucson: University of Arizona Press

DUNKERLEY, JAMES 1988 *Power in the Isthmus: A Political History of Modern Central America.* London: Verso.

GOSSEN, GARY H. (ed.) 1986 *Symbol and Meaning Beyond the Closed Community: Essays in Mesoamerican Ideas.* Studies on Culture and Society, vol. 1. Albany: Institute for Mesoamerican Studies.

GOULD, JEFFREY L. 1998 *To Die in This Way. Nicaraguan Indians and the Myth of Mestizaje, 1880–1965.* Durham, North Carolina: Duke University Press.

GUTIERREZ, NATIVIDAD 1999 *Nationalist Myths and Ethnic Identities: Indigenous Intellectuals and the Mexican State.* Lincoln: University of Nebraska Press.

JONAS, SUSANNE 2000 *Of Centaurs and Doves. Guatemala's Peace Process.* Boulder: Westview Press.

JOSEPH, GILBER M., AND TIMOTHY J. HENDERSON (eds.) 2002 *The Mexico Reader: History, Culture, Politics.* Durham, North Carolina: Duke University Press.

KENDALL, CARL, JOHN HAWKINS, AND LAUREL BOSSEN 1983 *Heritage of Conquest Thirty Years Later.* Albuquerque: University of New Mexico Press.

WARMAN, ARTURO 1980 *"We Come to Object": The Peasants of Morelos and the National State.* Baltimore: Johns Hopkins University Press.

WARREN, KAY 1998 *Indigenous Movements and their Critics: Pan-Maya Activism in Guatemala.* Princeton: Princeton University Press.

Chapter 9
Transnationalism and the Political Economy of Mesoamerica

A young Maya woman sits at a sewing machine by the open door of a small adobe room, the only source of light. She is putting together a black sport jacket. It is a shiny polyester-and-cotton blend with a fashionable style. Her employer, who likes to copy some styles and innovate others, designed it. He purchases the materials in the city, designs and cuts the pieces, and then hires young, single women and men to assemble them. The woman is using his sewing machine, whereas other workers whom he employs work at home using their own equipment. While she sews jackets, two of her brothers with their father are planting their cornfields. Her older sister and her mother are at a tourism resort, a few hours away, selling handmade textiles to foreign tourists. And her uncle is in Los Angeles, California, working as a landscaper with other men from other Mesoamerican towns.

These are examples of the wide and complex range of activities that the present-day peoples of the Mesoamerican region practice in order to make a living. Individually and collectively, native Mesoamericans engage multiple economic strategies in order to make a living and take care of their families. The most industrialized sectors currently produce for international markets, assemble goods for the most developed countries using labor-intensive programs, and produce items that require highly developed technologies. Most industrial centers are located in or around urban centers. Labor, however, is drawn heavily from rural areas. In the rural areas, we find producers of diverse crops, foodstuffs, and crafts; and smaller, labor-intensive industries, such as the garment producers of the western highlands of Guatemala, exemplified before. Just like their urban counterparts, they are dependent on the whims and fluctuations of international markets. And just like increasing numbers of their urban counterparts, they are becoming transnational workers who travel to the United States and Canada for work.

In this chapter we will introduce the various ways in which people earn a living and the ways in which they organize themselves in the process of production. In introducing the economies of Mesoamerica, our emphasis will be on the ways in which native Mesoamericans are part of the global economy. The economy is defined here as all those aspects of society related to the production, distribution, and consumption of goods and services. It is of interest to assess in this context the kinds of relations people establish among themselves as they produce a given item. Such relations are an indication of the degree of stratification found in a given society. An analysis of some of the technological, social, and cultural changes that people experience enables us to understand the nature of the changing societies in which they live. The goal, then, is to show that the different actors, producers, and consumers throughout Mesoamerica are undergoing common processes of differentiation and change.

In keeping with this text's focus, we will concentrate on the native, indigenous peoples as they participate in the national and global economy, and the strategies they devise to survive under changing and often strenuous conditions. Indigenous Mesoamerican peoples participate in a variety of ways in the economies of the region. In some settings, such as agriculture, cattle ranching, and wage labor, they share markets and opportunities with sectors of the mestizo population. The range of activities of native peoples includes traditional *milpa* agriculture (see later), semi-subsistence actions that always include some form of access to markets; various combinations of agriculture and manufactures; wage labor in small family enterprises; working in the tourism sector; and labor in larger industrial settings. We begin with a discussion of milpa agriculture, the traditional means by which Mesoamericans have survived through the centuries.

THE TRADITIONAL MILPA

From 2000 B.C. until A.D. 2000 (actually 2005), the milpa production of maize has been central to the Mesoamerican economy (Figure 9.1). The milpa has most often taken the form of swidden or slash-and-burn agriculture (see Chapter 1 for the pre-Hispanic history of maize production). In swidden agriculture, the forest and brush are cut at the end of the dry season. The slashed trees and plants are allowed to lie where they fall, whereas fruit-bearing trees and other useful plants are left standing.

Firewood is gathered, and the remaining cut brush is set on fire. In the ashes, which add nutrients to the soil—and as close to the beginning of the rainy season as possible—the farmers plant their fields. Using a digging stick, they poke holes in the enriched soil and drop in a few seeds of corn. At this time, or later, they will also plant squash and bean seeds. This combination has long formed the tripartite-basis of the Mesoamerican diet and a surplus of food sold in local and sometimes distant markets.

Milpa agriculture, primarily a male economic activity, has usually been supplemented by household-produced manufactures, garden produce, and domesticated animals, which tend to be female-based economic activities. Tomatoes, peppers, and a wide range of herbs and greens are grown in these gardens. Pottery and textiles are usually also manufactured in these households. Along with maize surpluses, garden produce, pottery, and textiles are taken to the market. Around the hearth, maize is transformed into tortillas, thus integrating the male and female economic domains

Figure 9.1   A Kaqchikel Mayan farmer from Santa María de Jesús in his milpa during harvest. Photograph provided by the authors.

of the household. When these products are taken to the market, the household is effectively linked to the broader community, even at the state and international levels.

It is easy to romanticize the self-sufficient Mesoamerican milpa household, growing and producing most, if not all of its subsistence needs. This economic form, however, is arduous, and a fine line exists between successful and unsuccessful households. The work, be it field or household, is both labor- and knowledge-intensive. Having the optimal number of individuals with the know-how to reproduce their material needs and generate a surplus beyond subsistence is often difficult to manage. Furthermore, household members need to have intimate knowledge of their fields and microclimates, all the while anticipating—but hoping against—natural disasters of draught, hurricanes, and earthquakes that frequently impact the region.

Despite these labor and natural difficulties, the Spanish invasion and colonization of Mesoamerica, and the ongoing impact of capitalism—especially its research-oriented global and transnational form—Mesoamericans cling to this form of agricultural subsistence, in actual and symbolic ways. For example, Yucatec Mayan farmers in the Mexican state of Quintana Roo plant their milpas as they have done for centuries (Anderson 2005), as do Q'eqchi' Mayas in the Alta Verapaz region of Guatemala. Rural Zapotecs and Mixtecs in the state of Oaxaca (Cohen 2004) and Nahuas living in the Huasteca region of Mexico also practice milpa agriculture. Even for those Mesoamericans who do not engage in milpa production, maize and the milpa itself have high symbolic value. For instance, Kaqchikel Mayas living near Antigua and Guatemala City are less likely to make milpas. Yet, they still grow small, more symbolic milpas in their courtyards.

Since the time of the Spanish invasion (see Chapter 5 for an account of this), the milpa-based agricultural system has been under assault. With growing populations, changing ecological conditions, and the intensification of the global economy, relatively few Mesoamerican households now have the land needed or the interest in maintaining this traditional agricultural system. In order to understand why this change has happened, it is important to keep in mind the forms of production and labor that have shaped the Mesoamerican economy since the Spanish Colonial period (see especially Chapter 5), as well as the many changes brought to the region during neocolonial and modern periods (see Chapters 7 and 8).

ECONOMIC LEGACIES OF COLONIALISM

In this section we will describe current economic practices engaged in by the Mesoamerican peoples, beginning with an account of what we consider to be the lingering legacies of colonialism.

Peasants in Mesoamerica

Since the Spanish colonial period, a great portion of the population of the region has been made up of peasants. Most people in Mesoamerica made their living by working the land and planting crops, usually for themselves and for the market. Although milpa agriculture is still close to the economic ideology of many, if not of most, indigenous people in Mesoamerica, it is being practiced by fewer and fewer people. One of the economic legacies of colonialism is a large peasant sector planting milpas for their own subsistence, but also to grow crops and make products for the dominant landowners (in colonial times, the trustees of the Spanish crown and the Catholic church). With the increased globalization of the economy, not only are there fewer *milperos* (persons who grow and subsist on maize), there are also fewer peasants.

The concept of the peasant has become quite controversial, in part because that term is used to describe very diverse social sectors, and for that reason, it is too broad to be useful. Some scholars would prefer to drop the term altogether. Contemporary scholars have tended to regard the concept of peasant in one of three ways. First, Enroghi Mayer (2002) argued that peasants continue to persist, despite the globalization of the economy, increased transnational movements of people and ideas, and neoliberal policies by Latin American governments. Although Mayer writes about indigenous peasants in Peru, the lives he describes are comparable to those in Mesoamerica in that they too have been impacted by similar Spanish-colonial legacies and have been subjected to similar neoliberal policies.

Second, as argued by Michael Kearney (1996), the term "peasant" does not properly describe an important sector of contemporary Mesoamerican economic life. On the basis of his research on transnational Mixtec and Zapotec migrants, he contends that former peasants are now wage-earning laborers and that the basic unit of production has ceased to be the household. Also working in Mesoamerica, particularly in Quintana Roo, Eugene Anderson (2005) generally agrees with Kearney and holds that the Spanish term "campesino" (rural peoples) is a better term, since the Mayas he has studied are not peasants in the classic definition although some do subsist on the land and production is organized according to household.

Third, scholars who study coffee workers and small coffee growers such as Mark Edelman (1999) argue that the concept of peasant continues to have analytical and social relevance because it is a term that serves political means. Many coffee workers and growers rally around the peasant concept in order to position themselves against unfair trade policies and large transnational coffee companies.

Clearly, the concept of peasant is debatable, as an analytical category and as an actual classificatory term. It may be that the future of "real" peasants, who base their living on subsistence farming organized according to household, is coming to an end. We suggest, however, that "peasant" continues to be a useful analytical concept and an accurate description of real Mesoamericans. At its most general (and vague) level, the term "peasant" refers to societies or sectors of societies that are linked to larger, dominant societies or sectors. Although peasants are usually discussed in the context of capitalist systems, they are present in other economic systems as well. For example, as rural inhabitants depending on and providing labor to other sectors, peasants were once a key part of feudal society. Although often associated with isolated rural settlements, some peasants live in smaller urban centers and retain some linkages to agriculture.

Most peasants own at least a small parcel of land, where they have a house and perhaps a garden. Yet many peasants have no land. They must rent land to cultivate crops or must rent a site for their house and then work for wages for other peasants in the nearest towns and cities. Some peasants work seasonally in haciendas and plantations. These people are often referred to as rural proletariats. Other peasants are engaged in commercial activities. They commercialize their own surpluses or act as intermediaries. Some combine wage labor with subsistence production. Others may fish, hunt, gather wild plants, and grow crops.

The stereotypical agricultural inhabitant who owns enough land for self-sufficiency and cooks the food he or she produces is rare in the region today. Rather, peasants represent women and men involved in multiple activities. They may be agriculturalists who are connected to other peoples through the marketing system. If this type of person owns land, Kaqchikel Mayas would refer to them as *tikonel* (Kaqchikel for farmer or agriculturalist). If a person does not own the land he or she farms, they would call the person a *campesino*. Indeed, peasants may depend strongly on items produced by others in rural towns and in national and international factories, but it is important to remember that even in feudal and capitalist systems, they relied on goods produced outside their household.

It is widely believed by scholars that the capitalist system exploits rural producers. These scholars see the system as dependent on family labor, low costs, and low prices of products produced by the peasants. When we talk about peasants, then, we need to qualify the production processes that people are involved with, and specify their relation to the larger society of which they are a part (Figure 9.2). This is important because peasants, like other economic actors in Mesoamerica, are impacted by and interact with capitalism and the larger global economy in multiple ways, not all of which are exploitative.

Rural-Urban Migration

A recent phenomenon observed in Mesoamerica that dates especially to the 1950s and 1960s is the migration of people from rural areas to the cities. The population of the cities is increasing at rates that far exceed the possibilities of absorption. Urban "primacy"—the concentration of people, resources, and services in one central city—

Figure 9.2   Day laborers in Chiapas, Mexico. JEFFREY JAY FOXX/NYC

characterizes most Latin American cities, including those of Mexico and Central America. The concentration of elites, industry, and population in cities creates centers that are spatially divided along class lines, with areas of the cities clearly marked with respect to specific socioeconomic sectors.

Owing to general population increase, rural areas are also experiencing population increases, but at lower rates than urban centers. The general migration trends have created a new sector of the economy that has been termed the "informal" economy. This sector is formed by independent vendors of a wide variety of products. It includes "chain" vendors who function as franchises of some established product, shoe shiners, and many other occupations whose economic actors were in the past classified as unemployed. In Guatemala City (Camus 2002) and in Mexico City (Cross 1998), these vendors and workers have caused politicians much consternation and anguish. Although vendors and others working in the informal economy are merely trying to earn a living, both the business owners in the formal, taxpaying sectors of the economy and the political officials often consider informal workers to be problems.

Oftentimes informal workers and vendors would welcome officially sanctioned jobs, and sometimes they provide services to urban dwellers that the formal sector does not recognize: for example, such services as washing and guarding automobiles in dangerous neighborhoods or establishing marketplaces in underserved neighborhoods. In such urban settings as Guatemala City and Mexico City, businesspersons and politicians work with the police to fine and forcibly expel informal workers and vendors from city streets. In 2004, for example, the Guatemala City police seized the merchandise of informal street vendors who were selling bootleg copies of music CDs and Hollywood movie DVDs. Although the vendors were removed from the streets and the vendors themselves acknowledge that the activity is illegal, almost immediately they returned to the streets to sell. Instead of setting up fixed stalls to sell, they became mobile vendors, carrying their goods in backpacks. These CD and DVD vendors, many of whom come from highland Mayan villages and speak Mayan languages, can be found throughout Guatemala and even in Honduras, Mexico, and El Salvador.

Often underestimated in terms of its importance to the economy, the informal sector constitutes an important part of the larger economies. Most migrants come to the cities because of the lack of land and sources of employment in their rural settings. As dispossessed peasants, they have no land and can obtain only a few days of work as day laborers in their home villages. The only other options for sustenance are occasional work in haciendas and plantations; migration to the cities; or migration to other countries, particularly the United States. We will come back to this issue later in this chapter.

Land Loss and Land Tenure

As in other parts of Latin America, land distribution patterns in Mesoamerica usually correspond to either the *latifundio* (large estates) or the *minifundio* (small farms) types. Most land in the area is owned by only a few landowners. A small fraction of land is divided into thousands of very small plots, often smaller than five acres, which are owned by the vast majority of the rural population. These small subsistence plots, where people usually grow some corn, beans, and squash, are not sufficient to provide a family with all their food needs for the year. Families often must purchase basic products. This situation results from a combination of factors, including land expropriations, population increase, and native inheritance laws.

Land dispossession on a major scale began at the moment of the European invasion and has continued until the present. Some expropriation was carried out through national legislation, whereas other expropriations took the form of land purchases from peasants who needed cash and had no other recourse. In Guatemala, the lands were used for the production of indigo (blue dye), cacao, sugarcane, cochineal (a source of red dye), and coffee during the nineteenth century; this trend was followed by cotton, bananas, and other products throughout the twentieth century. Early in the nineteenth century, Guatemalan legislation was passed permitting people to rent communal lands and forcing communities to rent "unused" lands.

Even when peasants were offered money for their lands, they resisted what they thought would be a major loss of resources. Expropriations continued, and currently some landless peasants are attempting land takeovers at the risk of their lives. In Mexico, peasants were allowed to keep some land, at least until the beginning of the nineteenth century (see the discussion of land problems in Chapter 7). However, by 1910, most rural families (96 percent of them) owned no land, with the haciendas controlling most of the land. Before the revolution, communal Indian holdings were located primarily in the south of Mexico. These holdings became the model for the contemporary ejido program, instituted by the Constitution of 1917, which expropriated land from the haciendas and allocated it to agrarian communities. This effort was accomplished in two formats. The first was individual, in which a small plot was given to one family to work; the family could pass it on to their children but could not sell it; and pasture and woodlands were community-owned and shared. The second format was collective, in which the community worked the land as a unit. Most ejido lands were given individually (see the discussion on land reform in Chapter 8).

In 1992, an amendment to the Mexican Constitution was passed that allowed for the privatization of community-held ejido land. The amendment permitted the rental of ejido land, a practice that was already in effect, and thus formally terminated land redistribution by the government. The new regulations have many implications. There are questions about the possibility of inequalities resulting from the changes: Who is going to sell their lands? Where will new investments flow? Will this encourage further migration and land concentration? In spite of the fact that half of the cultivated land is now part of ejidos, large landholdings continue in Mexico; and through leases and rental agreements, land concentration continues to be a problem for rural families.

In both Guatemala and Mexico, the existence of *minifundios* and landless peasants continue to be a major problem. Together, they constitute half the total rural population. Contributing to the minifundio system are local inheritance rules, which often demand the equal distribution of land and other resources among all children, and the further diminishing access to land for each passing generation. Coupled with population increases, this difficulty has resulted in the emergence of a large sector of landless peasants. These peasants find themselves forced to leave their towns, since they are unable to save enough money to buy or rent land. In most areas, villagers have followed the sometimes-implicit rule of not selling land to outsiders. In recent years, however, entrepreneurial peasants have decided to ignore this traditional rule in order to gain access to land at prices that they can afford. This is the case of some villages in western Guatemala, such as San Pedro Almolonga (for an economic description of this town, see Box 9.1).

Box 9.1   Agricultural Petty Commodity Production: A Case Study of the K'iche' Mayan Township of San Pedro Almolonga, "The Central American Garden"

Almolongueños can be seen selling vegetables in most markets of the central area of the marketing system of western Guatemala (particularly, the surroundings of Quetzaltenango and Totonicapán). They are quite noticeable. The women wear very bright clothes and elegant hairpieces. The men are said to dress better than others and to drive good trucks and jeeps. Located five kilometers from Quezaltenango, on what in 1983 became a paved road, a sign at the entrance of the town states: "Welcome to Almolonga, The Central American Garden (*La Huerta de Centroamérica*). At present, Almolongueños are successful traders; they sell vegetables in Guatemala, Mexico, and throughout Central America. They have diversified markets and products, and have become more prosperous than many of their neighbors.

At the present time, many Guatemalan peasants suffer from poverty and malnutrition. In fact, Almolongueños have little land: 86 percent of the plots are less than one *manzana* (about two acres). Furthermore, as is the case in other villages, Guatemalan inheritance rules stipulate that land be subdivided among a person's children in equal parts, making the few available lots insufficient for subsistence or commercial purposes. The situation in Almolonga is similar to that of the rest of the region. According to the Agricultural Census of 1979, the region holds 40 percent of the total amount of plots in the country, which in turn comprise only 19 percent of the total amount of land. In addition, population has increased in the highlands as a whole, and in Almolonga it has quadrupled in the last 100 years.

In other communities, change and capitalization brought about, for the most part, proletarianization. Almolongueños, however, chose to exploit the land by trying nontraditional crops and specializing in trade, taking advantage of their closeness to the large market in Quezaltenango. At present, there are no communal lands in Almolonga, and, with one exception, there is no memory of their existence in the past. On the contrary, many villagers denied it emphatically; Almolongueños, in their view, have always had private property, and the idea of sharing land seems totally foreign to them. Only one old man mentioned in passing that the largest extension of fertile land in the valley (approximately 9 acres) at one time might have belonged to the town, only to become the *potrero*, or grazing field, owned by a mestizo family. The family was forced to sell the land back to the Indians in very small plots of one or two *cuerdas*. Even after recovering this land, Almolonga's cultivable flat land is less than two square kilometers. To the scarcity of land, Almolongueños responded by purchasing land in Quezaltenango, Salcajá, San Cristóbal Totonicapán, and San Marcos. Almolongueños can pay prices that locals cannot, and old traditional community models that prevented selling land to outsiders were overridden by the need for cash.

(continued)

(*continued*)

Older people in Almolonga remember well the building of the Pan-American highway by Ubico in the 1930s, since they were forced to work on its construction. Mandatory work in the plantations (abolished in 1934) was replaced by a Vagrancy Law, which dictated that landless peasants had to work 100 days a year in the plantations. By then, Almolonga peasants were once again experimenting with vegetables, probably incorporating many new kinds with those that might have been grown in the past.

The earliest reports available regarding life in Almolonga come from Fuentes y Guzmán (1969), who at the end of the seventeenth century described the people as very industrious and dedicated to the production of grains, domestic fowls, and vegetables. In 1763, Almolongueños were reported to be trading bread, pigs, and cacao in the Pacific Coast region. Around the same time, they were producing corn, wheat, wool, and beans. By the end of the eighteenth century, Almolongueños were trading pork, wood, and wild herbs, and the chronicles state that they were also growing vegetables. The reports of their growing vegetables already in the seventeenth century are particularly interesting, since people today have no memory of their great-grandparents producing such crops, and our sources do not specify which vegetables they did indeed cultivate. Almolongueños now say that the production of vegetables is a new activity that developed within the last fifty years.

At the beginning of the twentieth century, the main activities in Almolonga were milpa agriculture, growing and selling flowers, and the sale of medicinal wild plants on the coast. People remember that by 1925, the main activity was growing alfalfa and oats for the animals that grazed on their lands. People from Cobán and Cabricán would bring their animals on their way to the coast.

Almolongueños say that they discovered "by accident"—some people through revealing dreams, one person from onions that spontaneously sprouted in someone's kitchen—that vegetables would grow very well on their land. They brought seeds from Sololá (Guatemala), El Salvador, and Oaxaca, Mexico. Today, 36 percent of the total production of carrots in the country is produced in Almolonga, 42 percent of the beets, 89 percent of the cabbage, and 29 percent of the onions. They have no permanent crops of significance and prefer growing vegetables to alfalfa, because the "idea of alfalfa was not ours" but came from mestizo landowners."

Almolongueños do not go to work for wages in the plantations, and they proudly emphasize that they themselves hire people from other highland towns to work for them (the workers come from such towns as Nahualá and towns in the Sololá department). The Almologueños suggest that they pay salaries that are higher than what others pay. Unlike many of their neighbors in the region, Almolongueños have changed productive activities and techniques at least twice in less than 100 years, thus capturing an important segment of the national and international markets.

The use of chemical fertilizers since the late 1960s, generalized throughout western Guatemala, was readily adopted by Almolongueños. It increased yields, but to the point of abuse and apparent detriment of their township's environmental health. They developed new and heavily specialized cash production, and new technology, sharing the monopoly over vegetables with only the peoples of the Lake Atitlán area. The Almolongueños were responding to the limited demand in Guatemala by developing new markets, and addressing production to the more solvent mestizo market, since Indians rarely consume the vegetables they produce.

The Almolongueños explain their economic success as a result of their own efforts. Their people work hard, from 4:00 or 5:00 A.M. to 6:00 or 7:00 P.M. Many are already irrigating their fields at 5:00 A.M., whereas in other places, as they say, the people do not even water or spray with fertilizers. People from neighboring villages admit that Almolongueños work hard, but many suggest that Almolongueños are rich because they obtain money from supernatural sources. Almolongueños also give credit for their success to the good weather conditions in the township.

In addition, many Almolongueños attribute their successes to the impact of evangelization, suggesting that it is because of their religion that they are able to dedicate themselves more to work than to vices, such as drinking and womanizing.

(continued)

In the process of exploring new markets and diversifying production, Almolongueños have adopted new perspectives on the world. This ideological change predisposed more people to accept the new religion and simultaneously to explore economic alternatives. As a result, the production of nontraditional crops has been accompanied by capital accumulation and economic differentiation within the town and in the region, since Almolongueños hire workers from neighboring towns. People refer to their competitiveness, individualism, and interest in profit and accumulation. However, growing economic differences and obvious resentment from their neighbors, combined with problems of environmental degradation, are now giving rise to questions about the limits of the productive strategy adopted by the people of Almolonga.

In Chiapas, Mexico, lack of land has driven peasants to become tenant farmers through a system of sharecropping. By these means, they rent lands and pay rent with part of the harvest. Gaining a livelihood by this means is increasingly difficult, since rentable parcels become scarcer. In recent years, Guatemalan agricultural workers have displaced those from Chiapas, because they are willing to work for even lower wages. The Guatemalans come from rural regions in which they have no access to land or other economic opportunities. Reluctantly, they travel to Chiapas to earn a living.

Other Mesoamericans have responded to the landless conditions and lack of economic opportunities by forming criminal organizations. One of the most infamous is the Salvadoran Salvatruchas, which operates from El Salvador to Chiapas on the Pacific coast. The Salvatruchas have engaged in a number of illicit activities from drug dealing, kidnapping, robbery, and the sale of contraband. Fortunately, most Mesoamericans do not follow this economic strategy. Instead, they migrate to other areas to seek legitimate work, try to start small businesses even if informal, and lobby through unions and professional organizations to help create more favorable economic conditions.

In summary, a large sector of the people in the Mesoamerican region is made up of rural inhabitants. Many of them are peasants who have been subjected to policies that have resulted in land loss. The increasing population, along with the loss of cultural traditions, has further contributed to their dwindling land resources. The loss of land or access to arable land has contributed to widespread migration from rural to urban areas, since many peasants try to support themselves and their families by establishing work opportunities in major urban areas. In greater numbers than in the past, however, landless peasants throughout Mexico and Central America have also opted to migrate to the cities and to other countries (especially to the United States).

LABOR AND PRODUCTION IN THE GLOBAL ECONOMY

In this section we will consider four basic labor production strategies: wage labor, petty commodity production, cottage industries, and maquiladora industries. Such production strategies point to Mesoamerica's wider connections to the global economy.

Wage Labor

Wage labor involves the payment to individuals of a wage in exchange for labor, so as to transform or produce one or more goods. A common form of rural wage labor in Mexico and Central America involves working on haciendas and plantations. Life for those who opt to migrate seasonally to coastal areas such as the Pacific Coast in Guatemala is very difficult. Relocating individuals or whole families for a few months in a totally different environment has many negative consequences. For people accustomed to highland climates, the intense heat of the coastal zones often makes them susceptible to diseases they do not encounter in their native areas. Unable to cultivate land of their own and forced to purchase food and other goods that they need for survival, they frequently suffer from malnutrition.

Plantations are often far from main towns and sources of goods. It is customary that the plantation itself has its own store to provide migrants with all their needs. Because the migrants are paid low wages and are forced to buy at the company store, they soon find themselves in debt. They then are forced to remain working for the same employer or to return the following season, often without having received any cash payments for their labor. This system of supplying migrant workers is so pervasive in Mexico, Guatemala, El Salvador, and other countries in Central America that it has its own term: "debt peonage." Once in debt, the workers lose their freedom to leave; and the longer they remain working, the more they owe the landowner. This difficult situation is combined with work that is extremely arduous, involving long hours, whether harvesting cotton, coffee beans, cacao, or fruit; cutting sugar cane; or processing sugar. (See Rigoberta Menchú's description of plantation labor in Box 9.2.)

It is not surprising that highland peasants often are reluctant to go to work on the plantations. They consider doing this a last resort. Contractors may drive through highland towns encouraging people to get on a truck that will take them to the coast. They sometimes depict misleading salaries and conditions. Contract labor is also called *enganche* ("hook up"), a term that suggests the lack of incentives people have to engage in this type of work owing to the poor labor conditions.

Petty Commodity Production

Broadly defined, petty commodity production refers to the small-scale production of agricultural or artisan goods oriented toward sale in the markets for a profit. It suggests a shift from production for sustenance to production for the market, with the corresponding intensification of labor. Petty commodity production uses occasional wage labor, whereas capitalist or petty capitalist production makes use of a permanent wage labor force from which a surplus can be extracted, thereby allowing capitalist accumulation. Examples of petty capitalist production include the treadle loom weaving industries of Teotitlán del Valle in the Oaxaca Valley, Mexico, and the garment production center of San Francisco el Alto, Guatemala.

Petty commodity production often requires the incorporation of technological changes and/or the enlargement of the labor force traditionally employed. For example, the production of textiles (cloth, table cloths, shirts, bags) in Totonicapán, Comalapa, and Chichicastenango in Guatemala, or Chamula and San Pedro Chenalhó in Chiapas, Mexico, was originally oriented toward subsistence and sale in

---

Box 9.2   Working and Living Conditions
on a Guatemalan Cotton Plantation

"I remember that from when I was about eight to when I was about ten, we worked in the coffee crop. And after that I worked on the cotton plantations further down the coast where it was very, very hot. After my first day picking cotton, I woke up at midnight and lit a candle. I saw the faces of my brothers and sisters covered with mosquitos. I touched my own face, and I was covered too. They were everywhere; in people's mouths and everywhere. Just looking at these insects and thinking about being bitten set me scratching. That was our world. I felt that it would always be the same, always the same. It hadn't ever changed. . . .

"The contracting agents fetch and carry the people from the Altiplano. The overseers stay on the fincas. One group of workers arrives, another leaves and the overseer carries on giving orders. They are in charge. When you're working, for example, and you take a little rest, he comes and insults you. 'Keep working, that's what you're paid for,' he says. They also punish the slow workers. Sometimes we're paid by the day, and sometimes for the amount of work done. It's when we work by the day that we get the worst treatment. The caporal stands over you every minute to see how hard you're working. At other times, you're paid for what you pick. If you don't manage to finish the amount set in a day, you have to continue the next day, but at least you can rest a bit without the overseer coming down on you. But the work is still hard whether you work by the day or by the amount. . . .

"Before we get into the lorry in our village, the labor contractor tells us to bring with us everything we'll need for the month on the finca; that is, plates and cups, for example. Every worker carries his plate, his cup, and his water bottle in a bag on his back so he can go and get his tortilla at mealtimes. Children who don't work don't earn, and so are not fed. They don't need plates. They share with their parents. The little ones who do earn also have plates for their ration of tortilla. When I wasn't earning anything, my mother used to give me half her ration. All the mothers did the same. We get tortilla and beans free, but they are often rotten. If the food varies a bit and we get an egg about every two months, then it is deducted from our pay. Any change in the food is deducted." (From Rigoberta Menchú, *I, Rigoberta Menchú: An Indian Woman in Guatemala,* edited by Elizabeth Burgos-Debray, translated by Ann Wright. London: Verso, 1984, pp. 22–23.)

---

regional markets. Recently, however, production has been intensified and expanded, and accompanied by the incorporation of occasional wageworkers and unpaid apprentices. There has also been a decrease in the quality of yarns and time invested in products for sale to tourists in local and national markets. In the same places just mentioned, above, laborers are hired to weave on foot looms in order to produce large quantities of fabric for inexpensive handbags and clothes for tourists (the latter, ironically, want textiles that look like traditional indigenous clothing, but they are not willing to pay even the local prices for them).

The process of intensification of production fosters stratification within and across villages as well as initiating various cultural changes. In the preceding weaving example, the owners of the looms buy the thread and hire the workers to weave for a low daily salary, and in the process they earn salaries many times that of their workers. The vendors who sell the cloth produced in these household industries sometimes earn even more money. All this contributes to the socioeconomic inequalities of Mesoamerican communities.

Similarly, in Oaxaca, Mexico, brickmakers (rural petty industrial workers studied by Scott Cook and others) have had incredible material success. Practiced since the nineteenth century, brickmaking has undergone several changes. It evolved from a temporary peasant artisan occupation practiced by just a few households to a full-time peasant capitalist industry practiced by people who have differentiated themselves into groups of businessowners, and pieceworkers who do not own their business. In San Miguel Totonicapán, Guatemala, a town studied by Carol Smith, weavers are doing quite well, since they have intensified the production of textiles for tourists and export. Totonicapán weavers do not seem to have polarized into two classes (owners and wage workers), in contrast to the trend in other petty industries.

San Pedro Almolonga in western Guatemala (see Box 9.1) is a town that specializes in the production of vegetables, and it is considered to be doing better, on average, than most other towns in the area. In that town there is widespread economic differentiation. Because of the lack of land in the township, people rented and then purchased lands in nearby townships. They diversified production strategies, including the development of new markets, new trade partners, new lands, and new cash crops. On average, those who have opted for trade and intensification of production of vegetables are doing better than those who remain dedicated to agriculture and milpa production. Traders seem to be converting to Protestantism in larger proportions than are agriculturalists, thus generating a distinct group within a town experiencing profound cultural changes. (See Box 9.3 for an illustration of the impact on community life of this kind of production.)

Box 9.3   Petty Commodity Production in the Tzeltal Mayan Township of Amatenango del Valle, Chiapas

In Amatenango del Valle, Chiapas, the intensification of the production of pottery by women has also generated internal stratification. At the same time, according to June Nash (2001), relations between men and women experienced a conflictive shift brought about by the new trend of women being independent and self-sufficient. As part of these economic developments, men and women have redefined their roles in the household. Both groups had always contributed to the subsistence of the household; but with production intensification and some degree of economic differentiation, the nature of the contributions by men and women has changed. For one thing, in most cases the hours spent working on the production of a particular commodity have increased.

Cash availability from the work of both women and men has created changes in power relations within the household and between men and women in general. Women now have access to the capital they generate owing to an expanded market for the crafts they produce. This capital has given them more power than they previously had, since they can make decisions related to production and to the household consumption that they did not make before. Men's activities yield comparable or sometimes lower returns, thus affecting intergender dynamics.

The practice of productive diversification is not new to peasant households, as already pointed out. However, with intensification, the incorporation of paid help (temporary wage workers) and a different division of labor, the economic process also has changed in nature. For example, the combination of subsistence agriculture with the practice of one or more artisan activities, along with different levels of commercialization, is now considered standard strategies for capitalization.

Of great interest to students of peasant societies is the issue of the possibilities for capital accumulation and capitalist development. Social scientists wonder whether peasants are in the process of becoming capitalists and disappearing as a group, or whether peasantry is a lifestyle that allows for only fairly limited changes (including marginal capital accumulation that would not lead to capitalist development). Are these petty producers developing larger concentrations of capital and greater intensification of both labor and technology, just as large capitalist enterprises do in the developed world? Or are they following demographic cycles that allow for periods of greater productivity and profits, to be followed by periods of decline, with no significant accumulation of capital?

The first position roughly describes the claims once made by Vladimir Lenin and came to be known as the Marxist or *de-campesinista* (de-peasantizing) perspective. According to this perspective, peasants would slowly become wageworkers for industry and service, and a few would become capitalists themselves. The second position roughly describes the argument of Alexander Chayanov, known as the *campesinista* (peasantist) perspective. According to this view, peasantries are seen as a changing but almost perpetual category, sometimes exploited by the capitalist system as they provide cheap foodstuffs to the cities, and sometimes remaining relatively marginal to the capitalist world.

Students of Mesoamerican peasants have found evidence to support both viewpoints. Some social scientists have concluded that petty commodity production as a system is limited. Because of the low level of investment, it does not allow for significant capital accumulation, nor the segregation of the population into two definite classes: one of owners of the means of production (land, labor, and capital) and the other of dispossessed people who constitute a full-time proletariat (wageworkers). Others point to the existence of a combination of full-time and part-time wageworkers with access to limited resources (that is, a small plot of land). Finally, the presence of people being capitalized and doing significantly better than the average peasant-artisan or cash-crop agriculturalist leads scholars to believe in the possibility of generating capitalist accumulation from the peasant-worker workshop or industry. These diverse positions are not necessarily in contradiction to each other, and much research is ongoing to understand and predict future developments among the peasants of Mexico and Central America.

Cottage Industries

Of the several possible ways of generating an income that are now practiced in the region, home work is a relatively recent one and is becoming quite widespread. Home work, or work done at home (also called the "putting out" system), is quite common in the garment industry, but it is also found in several other industries. It consists of work that requires simple and available technology (a sewing machine, needle and thread, and a loom). In general, the employer puts out the raw materials and specific assembling instructions for each piece. In the case of the embroidery industry of Ocotlán, Mexico, "outworkers" get the sections of material to be embroidered, and sometimes the yarn, and return the assembled piece to the merchant for a lump sum of money.

In some cases, arrangements are made to pay piece-rate, and often cash advances are given to the workers. In other cases, different members of the household will be in charge of different parts of the garment or the performance of different tasks. In Teotitlán de Valle, Mexico, for example, Cook (2004) observed workers who are independent and work with their own looms and yarn at home, as well as others who own their looms but receive yarn from the merchants. In Tecpán, Guatemala, one Kaqchikel Mayan family invested money earned from work in agricultural and teaching into mechanical sweater looms. After they learned to operate the looms, they hired workers and trained them. They then worked on marketing the sweaters, which were woven in styles typically found in the United States, Canada, and Ireland, as well as in Guatemala City, Totonicapán, and other highland Guatemalan towns. By owning the looms and the workshop and by marketing their own products, they were able to consolidate wealth. They kept expenses low by paying the current daily wage for labor—then only a couple of U.S. dollars per day—and by concentrating on sales. As a result of this strategy, they were able to make the most profit for their time and energy.

Merchants, many of whom are themselves intermediaries, take advantage of this type of work. For one thing, they do not need to supply either a space or equipment to the worker, thereby saving the expenses of electricity (when available) and upkeep. Most of the home workers are women, and this work regime allows them to continue with the daily activities of taking care of young children and various household tasks. The transition from home work to the workshop at the merchant's house or property often implies more expenses for the proprietor-merchant. It also increases his or her control over the production process. Many workers will eventually become the merchant's competitors, as they begin to buy their own raw materials and engage relatives and others with piecework. This was certainly the case with respect to the family from Tecpán previously described. When they began their sweater-making business, they were the only family in that town engaged in that enterprise. Within a few years, several other families, including some of their own workers, had their own shops.

Sol Tax (1953), who conducted research in the Guatemalan town of Panajachel in the 1930s, noted this practice of following and imitating successful economic strategies as part of his observations on Kaqchikel Mayan farmers, weavers, and vendors. Although indigenous communities are popularly conceived of as traditional, conservative, and reluctant to change, he watched the Kaqchikel Mayas of Panajachel adopt new crops and planting strategies that were successful in neighboring communities, as well as imitating weaving designs from other places and innovating new designs that would appeal to tourists. Mesoamerican businesspersons and artisans continue to innovate and make rational economic decisions.

Maquiladora Industries

The combination of lack of land and of employment opportunities for peasants and urban inhabitants in the region, and the preference of the United States and other developed countries for obtaining an unlimited supply of cheap unskilled labor, has resulted in the creation of a new type of industry: export manufacturing plants, known as *maquiladoras*. Maquiladoras are spread throughout several regions of the Third World, including Latin America and the Caribbean. Among other places, they are located in the north of Mexico, particularly near the border with the United States, and are a relatively new development in Guatemala (since the mid-1980s).

The maquiladora industries rely on migrants, some of whom are trying to immigrate to the United States, and others who are simply moving in search of jobs within their own countries. Most of the workers in these plants are women (over 85 percent). Women are considered by employers to be more docile and less inclined to protest and unionize (for a discussion of women in the labor force in Mesoamerica, see Chapter 12). In fact, owners assume that women will accept lower wages and harsher conditions than men, and will have fewer options than men. Components of goods are sent from developed countries to these Third World countries, and maquila factories assemble them into finished products to export back to the sending country (for example, the United States or South Korea), where they are finally sold.

Countries in the Third World are often eager to attract such foreign investments because they bring jobs to their countries. For that purpose they offer potential manufacturers not only an unlimited supply of labor but also different incentives in the form of tax exemptions. Labor comes in part from the rural areas, but mostly from the overpopulated urban centers. The conditions in these plants are often poor, not only by U.S. or other developed countries' standards, but by local standards as well. Women are paid little (as low as one or two dollars a day); are forced to work overtime; and are not allowed sufficient breaks, even when they are pregnant or breastfeeding. To signs of unionization, companies respond by threatening with closure of the plants. Indeed, they frequently close and move to new locations. Mesoamerican peoples, native and mestizo alike, have painfully linked themselves directly to the international arena through these export-processing enterprises.

DISTRIBUTION AND CONSUMPTION

This section will be concerned with distribution and consumption, with an emphasis on periodic markets and the culture of marketing.

Trade and Markets

Anyone traveling in Mexico and Central America will retain vivid images of the large array of colorful goods that are sold in local markets. These open markets comprise a regional commercial network with larger principal centers at greater distances from each other and smaller marketplaces in between. New markets continue to be created, in part, as a response to population increase in the region and, in part, to improved transportation infrastructure. Rural markets were an important part of pre-Columbian economies, and the frequency and number of them increased as colonial authorities would ask—often demand—Indians to hold plazas in places that would serve the Spaniards better (Figure 9.3).

Figure 9.3 Market scene in Tecpán, Guatemala. A man from Sololá sells onions and green beans, while the woman next to him, who is from a hamlet of Tecpán, sells lime, a mineral used to make tortillas. Photograph provided by the authors.

As a result of requests and impositions from Spanish authorities, enclosed market buildings began to be built in the nineteenth century. Spaniards considered enclosed markets to be more sanitary and "organized." Indians never agreed with Spaniards on this issue, thinking that their traditional open plazas with an abundance of fresh air and sunlight were not only more pleasant but also cleaner and better organized. Certainly, the preferred organizational patterns varied for both groups, and the debate over the best model for a marketplace continues today. It is common to find enclosed markets in most large towns of Guatemala, Mexico, El Salvador, and Honduras, in combination with some kind of open market that seems to spill outside the enclosed buildings. Small villages often organize the market in the main plaza in front of the church, or they create a special area (often an area covered with cement and sometimes a roof but no walls) for their market. Here, vendors from the region come to sell their products. Larger markets attract both vendors and buyers from a larger radius, whereas smaller ones attract local buyers and vendors.

It is interesting to note that while rural markets, unlike urban ones, tend to meet once a week (and historically have done so since pre-Columbian times), many markets are expanding to two or three days a week. Some towns already hold daily plazas, and the trend points to many more permanent markets. A good example of this is the market in San Francisco el Alto in western Guatemala, the largest in the region. This market used to be held only on Fridays, when over 10,000 people would crowd the hilly streets of the town early Friday morning. In 1980, vendors would arrive in San Francisco at 9:00 or 10:00 A.M. on Thursday night and sleep in the plaza to be guaranteed a space. By 1987, people were arriving early on Thursday, and the plaza would begin its activity then. In 1990, people predicted that soon Wednesdays would become an additional day of plaza. The level of commercialization, particularly in traditional textiles and male garments, is so high that San Francisco may become a permanent market center of the Western Highlands region.

Whereas many direct producers (called *propios* in Guatemala) bring small amounts of produce on each market day, a large number of intermediaries (called *regatones*) may buy from the local producers at their local market and then take them to other markets at longer distances. There is some gender differentiation in this division of labor. Most direct producers who sell at the markets are women, who prefer to sell in markets close to home and thus have to travel shorter distances. They often travel by bus, although some people in the region still walk several miles between marketplaces. Most intermediaries are men. They are long-distance merchants; many of them own trucks and cross regional and national boundaries.

Intermediaries are experimenting with new strategies that represent variations from their traditional practices. For example, many do not remain loyal to the traditional products because diversifying the items traded diminishes the risk of businesses going bad. Vendors may set a goal of reaching a distant market, even crossing national borders. They then purchase goods that will be sold at different stops throughout the trip. In turn, they acquire local specialties at each stop, which will be sold at the final destination. This practice of stepped trading, now conducted with the aid of trucks or buses, was already practiced in pre-Columbian times on foot, and during the colonial and neocolonial years with the help of mules.

Marketing Culture

The complex network of interdependent markets graphically depicts a system of social and political relations among the populations of the different regions. The closeness and intensity of the trading interactions suggest the degree of the participants' immersion in the capitalist system. As these networks expand, so does the universe of the region's inhabitants. Spanish is spoken as a trading language in most markets of Mesoamerica, even where large sectors speak Spanish only as a second language. This is the case in Chiapas, Oaxaca, and western Guatemala, among other areas.

Markets provide the means for acquiring ethnic knowledge, and as such, they have been recognized as sites for peaceful interactions, even in times of violence. The practice of bargaining, widespread in Mesoamerica, goes hand in hand with full acceptance of the market as regulator and determinant of prices. Research has shown that the resulting price of each bargaining interaction usually does not change significantly from one trading partner to another. What does change is the length and style of the bargaining itself. The negotiation is longer and more difficult, and it starts at higher prices when partners do not know each other well or at all. It is much shorter, faster, and friendlier when the partners know each other and have an established relationship (the asking price is then much closer to the expected sale price). Bargaining thus becomes a ritual of social identification that leads to more fluid economic relations.

Consumption Patterns

An examination of the distribution and consumption pattern of the commodities produced by peasant artisans, petty agricultural producers, and petty industrial producers suggests that these forms are integral to capitalism. Some would even say that capitalism heavily depends on forms like the ones described here.

Fruit and vegetables intensively produced in different areas of Central America reach the tables of most North American households. In some cases, this availability is a direct result of the efforts of thousands of migratory seasonal workers who work for large landowners on coastal estates; in others, it is the result of the combined effort of small farmers and intermediaries. Prices for those fruits and vegetables are determined by the combined forces of supply and national and international demand, that is, the world market. (Box 9.4 shows just how close the connection between the First and Third Worlds can be.)

On occasion, craft production for the world market, and in particular the sale to tourists, has compensated for the significant population losses owing to migration to the United States (which is still large). Craft production often allows peasants

---

Box 9.4   The Economic Links Between New York and Atitlán

When a woman from New York goes to a mall and purchases a pair of pants made in Lake Atitlán, Guatemala, or a blouse made in Chiapas, Mexico, she is closing a circle that began with a particular use and aesthetic context generated within the peasant household. The blouse and the pants, however, have gone through a profound transformation in use, style, intent, and (often) quality.

The weaver, embroiderer, or garment maker has adapted the product to suit a foreign taste and a foreign need. The textile, originally meant to be used in the making of a man's shirt, is now used to make pants to be worn by both men and women. The blouse, originally hand-embroidered and worn in special ceremonial occasions, is now often machine-embroidered and worn with a pair of jeans in an informal context. The quality of the pieces often has decreased to fit the demand and the pockets of the buyers. The market for peasant crafts has changed the style, dimension, and nature of their production.

Tourists visiting the region graphically reveal its producers' embeddedness in the modern world. In fact, as a vivid example of its immersion in the world economy, tourism has actually stimulated the production of craft commodities. Fewer peasants now wonder: Why would anyone want to hang a woman's blouse on the wall? Is it appropriate for men to wear women's clothes in your country? They may instead explore ways of increasing their production, while keeping costs down so that they can still compete in the market of exotic handmade goods.

Native crafts, then, are now part of the same international division of labor that includes industrial production, and their manufacture shares many of the biases and drawbacks of the larger industrial production. An example of this is the gendered division of labor, in which women increasingly constitute the majority of the lower-paid and more labor-intensive jobs.

who used to migrate to the coastal plantations to remain in their villages, as is the case of the people in many Mayan communities of Guatemala.

Cooperatives have been created in Mexico and Guatemala for the purpose of co-ordinating and managing the export of crafts (Figure 9.4). The Mexican government has sponsored cooperatives for the purchase of raw materials and the sale of artisan products. Participation in many of these cooperatives has significantly improved the standard of living of many Mesoamerican natives. Women's cooperatives in Guatemala, for example, provide some women—many widowed by the political violence of recent years—with greater skills to commercialize their products, even though their dependence on foreign markets may at some point prove dangerous (see the cases described in Chapter 12 on gender). Competition with other Third World countries may put some of the workers out of business, and it is increasingly likely that a factory worker in Asia may be producing industrial versions of hand-made native designs. Also, in the context of the tourist business and exports of artisan products, native peoples have become increasingly aware of many unjust situations. (See Box 9.5 for a discussion of how Mayas participate in international

Figure 9.4 Making necklaces for export to the United States. This woman is a member of the UPAVIM Cooperative in Guatemala, which makes handicrafts for the export market. Photograph provided by the authors.

Box 9.5   Indigenous Production for Tourists

Throughout Mesoamerica tourism has become an important part of local and national economies, some years generating more revenue than traditional plantation agriculture (coffee, sugar cane, cotton): newer nontraditional agricultural crops (broccoli and snow peas): and maquiladoras, which assemble clothes and electronics. Who reaps the most economic benefits from tourism varies greatly. In Mexico and Guatemala, tourists drawn to pre-Columbian archaeological sites tend to spend most of their money paying for pricey international chain hotels and meals in restaurants that few locals can afford. This practice generates vast sums of money for the government, which collects taxes from the businesses, the international hotel chains, and local elites that tend to provide services to the tourists.

Indigenous artisans and vendors have carved out a niche in the tourism sector by marketing handicrafts. Most of their products are based on designs that have been passed on for centuries. Weavers in Oaxaca, Chiapas, and highland Guatemala reproduce traditional designs, while continually developing new products that appeal to the changing whims of their tourist customers. Only a relatively few indigenous artisans and merchants earn enough money to purchase such items as automobiles, but many make modest livings. This income makes them economically more secure than most of their neighbors who work in agriculture.

For nearly 100 years, Kaqchikel Mayan weaver-vendors in San Antonio Aguas Calientes and neighboring Santa Catarina Barahona (Guatemala) have devised successful strategies to create new textiles and market them to tourists. One such family of weavers negotiated with the Guatemalan national tourism organization and larger tour companies to bring tourists to their home for weaving demonstrations. Another family visited Spanish-language schools in Antigua and Guatemala City, inviting students to visit their home to learn weaving, make tortillas, and eat *pepian*, a stew made with roasted tomatoes and chili peppers. Women in these households draw on traditional practices like weaving and special foods to attract customers to their hand-woven textiles.

In the previously mentioned communities, others have imitated both families' successes. Other weavers sell their textiles in a beautiful Spanish colonial-style marketplace in the San Antonio plaza. The marketplace and plaza were completely renovated between 1998 and 2003 by the local government because the mayor knew that a more attractive town center would attract more international tourists. Many other weaver-vendors from these towns travel to nearby Antigua, where they sell in marketplaces, on the streets, and in small boutiques that specialize in Mayan handicrafts. A few take their goods to Honduras, El Salvador, Panama, Mexico, and the United States.

These vendors, largely comprising of women, have a great deal of autonomy in developing new textile designs that locals and tourists recognize as traditional. One could regard this constant innovation with cynicism, because clothing styles and textiles for tourists do not remain the same over time. Such tinkering with textile designs, be they directed to tourists or local Kaqchikel consumers, frustrates textile collectors, but it also illustrates the creativity of these women to keep up with trends and to figure out ways to attract local and international customers. Although these women have international clientele and sometimes travel between their hometowns and other countries, their mode of production is the household. It is there that they weave and conceive of new strategies to sell textiles and entertain tourists. While they carry out these economic activities, their sons and husbands are tending small milpas or growing nontraditional crops. Other family members may work in maquilas, as carpenters, as teachers, and in other forms of labor. Despite the diversity of employment, many still hold fast to a peasant, or household-based mode of production. Even though few families subsist on agriculture alone, the milpa and the consumption of maize continues to be an important part of their diet and identity, alongside the production of "typical" textiles.

Figure 9.5 Tourism marketplace in Antigua, Guatemala. A vendor from Santa Catarina Palopó sells a souvenir to tourists from El Salvador. Photograph provided by the authors.

tourism.) In particular, unfair prices paid for goods sold in the cities of the region and in other countries may yield profits for the merchants that grossly exceed the payments to the producers. Artisans often feel exploited by local operators of petty capitalist workshops, or of putting-out merchants (Figure 9.5).

MESOAMERICA IN A TRANSNATIONAL WORLD

We turn now to a discussion of Mesoamerican economies in the broader context of the increasingly integrated modern world. Our focus is on the transnational economic conditions, which increasingly shape the lives of Mesoamericans.

Transnational Mesoamericans

Transnational processes include economic, political and cultural networks, the movement of people, capital, and ideas throughout the world in weblike links that keep regions of the world forever connected and transformed.

Transnational links impact class structures and ethnic identities, households and communities, in complex ways. Peoples of Mesoamerica have become linked to the world through the production and export of traditional products like coffee and cotton and nontraditional products like strawberries, melon, and redesigned arts and crafts. They are also linked through the production of labor-intensive apparel items such as shirts, dresses, or other items of clothing that we buy in the developed countries and by the constant flow of tourists who purchase Mesoamerican goods, services, and cultural representations. Production and export of goods and temporary or permanent movement of peoples are changing communities and individuals at both ends and then create transformed and complex identities.

A special case of transnationalism in Mesoamerica is the Zapatista indigenous-based social movement that originated in Chiapas, Mexico. The Zapatistas broadly call for important social and economic demands, including an end to poverty and marginalization of indigenous peoples. The movement became widely known in January 1994 at the same time that the North American Free Trade Agreement was being instituted (for a full discussion of this important movement, see Chapter 10). Once the Zapatistas began using the media to argue for justice, the international community served as a shield and often a sponsor of their plight. As the media ceased to pay as much attention to the movement and to the struggles of Mexican indigenous peoples, the influence of the movement in the area declined. June Nash (1997) referred to the media as a "third army of news reporters." The media made the difference between considering the uprising a legitimate transnational movement rather than an isolated and a local revolt. When the Zapatistas used the Internet and the news media to express their struggles and present their strategies, they were symbolizing the ultimate integration of underrepresented groups into the global landscape.

Migration to the United States

It is hard to find anyone in the rural or urban settings of Mesoamerica who does not have a relative or friend living temporarily or permanently in the United States. For many, this journey is part of the goals and dreams they hope to achieve during their lifetime. It is difficult to provide a general description of those who are more prone to migrate or to attempt migration. Research has produced diverse results. Some researchers have noted that although scarce land resources and impoverished conditions at home may motivate people to leave, it is often the middle sectors, not totally landless nor totally deprived of resources, who tend to migrate.

Individual cases point to the involvement of all socioeconomic sectors of the Mesoamerican societies, including the wealthier and/or best educated. Distribution and quality of agricultural lands certainly play a crucial role, but migrants come to the United States from areas with poor land but also from areas with intensive commercial agricultural production. When competition increases and farm incomes decline, farms tend to diversify through internal and international migration. There are also migrants who come from urban areas. The latter tend to settle in U.S. cities and remain on a more permanent basis than rural migrants, who employ more temporary migration strategies.

Gender trends are also complicated. Men are the first to migrate for practically all groups, but over time women and children follow. This pattern is somewhat different among politically motivated migrants, such as the Salvadorans and Guatemalans who tended to migrate as entire families in order to seek refuge in Mexico and the United States from highly repressive conditions in their home countries. Recent studies show a larger proportion of female migrants coming from Mexico who are younger and more educated than in earlier years, whereas other studies report no changes in the composition of the migrant population.

With respect to the origin of migrants, in the early 1980s, migrants tended to depart mostly from Mexico, but most recent waves include Latino immigrants from El Salvador, Guatemala, and Honduras. This trend is reported for many U.S. cities and rural areas of the states of Washington, Texas, Florida, and New York, and of the Midwest. Unlike migrants who originated in the communist world, many of the migrants from Guatemala and El Salvador remained in the United States without documents after having been denied political asylum or recognition as refugees by the U.S. government.

Because much of the movement into the United States is clandestine in nature, it has been difficult for students of this phenomenon to estimate migration rates. Mexico alone is the source of the largest percentage of all undocumented migrants in the United States. It is important to note, however, that much of the migration has been induced by the United States rather than by the sending countries. Southwest growers in the United States have provided incentives to Mexican agricultural workers throughout the nineteenth century and early twentieth century in order to obtain cheap, reliable labor. In this case, migration was not initiated solely by individuals in search of a better life, as often depicted, but also by North Americans trying to obtain hard labor at low wages and under conditions that few North Americans were and are willing to accept.

Migrant labor outflows were revived in 1942 when the Bracero Program was instituted by the United States. This was a temporary worker program that provided migrants with temporary documents to cross the border and work during limited periods. The program ended in 1964, but several other agreements have been instituted to allow temporary migration since then. Currently (2006), the administration of George W. Bush is proposing a new temporary permit program that would allow migrants to remain in the United States for three years. If enacted, this temporary arrangement could have lasting consequences for workers and their families, affecting the stability and education of children and possibly causing more dangerous and clandestine migration movements. In our opinion, the notion held by some that the United States does not want migrants because there is no work for them is fallacious, since U.S. growers, and not just in the South, lobby for immigration measures that will facilitate the availability of migrants who are willing to take temporary jobs.

The educational background of migrants from the Mesoamerican region is mixed. Approximately 25 percent of all migrants are professionals who expect to have a better life in the United States. Mexico sends a large number of professionals, although fewer than other countries around the world. Most of the migrants from Mexico and Central America are manual laborers. Millions of Central Americans and Mexicans have migrated to the United States, with and without documents.

They are drawn by the possibilities of work or freedom, pushed in part by uncertain economic conditions and political persecution in their own countries. But most are drawn by the processes of restructuring of the world economy, which are generating sources of labor for international capital through a new international division of labor. These same processes, including the movement of production to poor countries, have generated migration waves and have created new ethnic minorities throughout the world. These populations are struggling today to claim a space of their own in their new homelands (see Box 9.6).

Transnational Homes

Native peoples of Mesoamerica have experienced instances of voluntary and forced migration through time. They have long been accustomed to developing strategies for survival in new regions and have adopted innovations within and outside their borders to adapt to their new environments. It is common for these peoples to use traditional networks effectively to survive in new settings. Compelling testimonies from refugee camps in Mexico during the Guatemalan civil war during the early 1980s attest to some of the strategies applied. Refugees not only had to deal with the pain and stresses of departing from their homes but also had to deal with the difficulties of reintegration in their original communities. Many migrants never returned, and they formed new networks in their newly adopted home countries.

Life in the United States generally has not been easy for Mesoamerican migrants. They have experienced, and continue to experience, discrimination and exploitation in the workplaces and in daily life, in addition to other hardships related to criminal

---

Box 9.6   Celebrating an Indigenous Ritual in a Transnational Setting

In the celebration of the Christ of Esquipulas, a procession enters the church preceded by the deep and familiar smell of incense. The beautifully carved Black Christ is carried in the traditional way on the shoulders of men dressed in traditional Mayan attire. Elegantly dressed children carry candles and incense and an image of a quetzal bird, the Guatemalan national symbol. The entire audience, about 500 of them, sing familiar songs in Spanish.

The priest speaks in Spanish with a heavy accent. Being January 15, it was very cold. There is snow on the ground. This is a typical winter evening in the borough of Queens, New York City, and very few of the participants are indigenous Mayas. Those who are, are not wearing native clothes. Instead, those exhibiting the traditional Mayan attires and participating in the ceremony are non-Mayas, which is to say, ladinos (*mestizos*).

Gathered at the church are some of the several thousand Guatemalans living in the United States. They migrated at different times from the 1950s on. Some arrived in the 1980s during the Guatemalan civil war. They continue celebrating their traditional holidays, claiming the symbols of Mayan identity as part of their national identity, and reproducing elements of the life they all miss and therefore ritually reproduce on every possible occasion. The ceremony in the church is followed by food, marimba music, and dance. This is just another celebration of the yearly commemoration of the patron saint of Guatemala in their new northern home. (The preceding account is based on fieldwork by Goldin in Queens, New York.)

acts against them and loneliness. Nevertheless, many have been able to create and share strong local communities and achieve great respect from their neighbors. Migrants throughout the United States have found that they must deal with new patterns of social inequality and prestige as they work to satisfy basic needs such as housing, schooling, and health. The impact of these inequalities depend upon their alliances with various help organizations and social services, their positions in the larger economy, and their lack of understanding U.S. institutional practices. In the process of creating new communities, migrants also strengthen transnational ties with their home communities and countries.

Monetary and Cultural Remittances

Migrating to the United States has also helped people improve conditions in the sending communities by means of monetary remittances. Mesoamerican peoples rely on the remittances of those who migrated, and their home countries' economies count on the influx of those rather significant funds. Mexican estimates suggest that anywhere between two to six billion dollars are sent annually to Mexico by migrants living in the Unites States. In several countries, remittances are considered to be a preponderant share of the entire national economy. The money sent home contributes to family basic expenditures, community development, funding the education of children, and construction of new homes.

Migrants in the United States operate across borders by sending funds but also by traveling often to fulfill family and community obligations. In this way, migrants contribute to the transformation of their native communities, and in the process they constitute a new layer of prestige in the towns of origin. Circular migration, or temporary return migrants, adds a complex layer of new problems and drama to the not-so-quiet lives of sending communities. Much more than money circulates, and the impact of transnational ties is greater than can be described here. For example, cultural preferences are slowly changing: new foods, music, travel patterns, and dress styles, among many other changes, are taking place. New values, business practices, and economic ideologies are being created and operate in the context of this massive diaspora.

The process is not just an "Americanization" of Mesoamerica. Rather, it involves a clearer sense by migrants of their position in the world system and their subordination at individual and collective levels. Many of the new ideas are communicated to others in sending communities, including new forms of resistance. In addition, changing local hierarchies are being established between those who have left or live "outside" and those who remain on the "inside." Ideological changes extend to views about politics, gender relations, sexual orientations, as well as racial and ethnic identifications. A complex web of social, cultural, and economic "remittances" are transforming Mesoamerica as transnational ties permeate the full range of the diaspora.

Development and Underdevelopment

The geographic area that corresponds to ancient Mesoamerica has suffered from the effects of underdevelopment as much as, and often more so than, other countries in

Latin America. Comparative statistics show that countries like Guatemala and El Salvador compete for last place when it comes to indices of underdevelopment (Mexico and other countries in Central America follow quite closely). Countries like Mexico and Costa Rica have overall better standards of living in the region. They still experience, however, unequal distributive patterns that hurt the peasant and urban informal sectors alike.

Most attempts to explain the roots of underdevelopment in the region agree that the model of agroexport development has been detrimental to the largest sectors of the population. Commercial agriculture in the Colonial period contributed to the concentration of fertile lands in the hands of a small elite. This was by far the primary cause of the impoverishment of the rural populations, even in Mexico, where land reform and the implementation of the ejido system has not resolved land inequities. Lands were (and are) used for export crops instead of food crops for local consumption, and the proportion of lands devoted to the former is still increasing. This usage forces many of the peoples of Central America and Mexico to import food that they traditionally produced. Furthermore, the internationalization of the market has resulted in an accommodation of prices that has generated uneven terms of trade. Although some analysts thought that the concentration on a few exports would generate larger funds for investment and give the area a "comparative advantage," in practice there have been detrimental consequences of this development strategy. While prices for agricultural exports have declined, those for the manufactured goods that the people of the region must import have increased, creating uneven trading stances.

The high price of manufactured goods, combined with the great instability of prices of agricultural products, has generated the need for export diversification. The expansion of nontraditional agricultural exports, like beef, has taken over large extensions of good lands in such countries as Costa Rica and Honduras. The lack of land has generated a differentiated rural population competing among themselves for scarce resources. A most evident expression of this situation is the high level of malnutrition, especially in El Salvador, Guatemala, and Honduras.

Export agriculture, combined with population growth, has significantly contributed to environmental degradation. Soils are being exhausted because of intensification of production and excessive use of fertilizers and pesticides. Deforestation is creating further erosion as forested areas are converted to cotton or other export crops or construction timber. As a consequence of all of these factors, landlessness and unemployment have increased in the rural areas. Whereas some people have migrated to the cities, thus becoming part of the lower sectors of urban society, others have resorted to the economic strategies outlined before. Indeed, most community development alternatives seem to point to the need for some form of land reform. Costa Rica and Honduras have a somewhat more equitable land distribution program than Guatemala and El Salvador. Some steps have been taken in Mexico, but the situation there is far from resolved.

When land reform is not an option, the development programs that have proved most successful are those in which community members are allowed a greater degree of participation in the making of decisions and the setting of priorities. Furthermore, the programs that are sensitive to culturally viable initiatives, which attend not only to local needs but also to culturally meaningful means of addressing those needs, have also led to promising results. Such is the case of the relocation of Chamulans from the highlands of Chiapas to the rainforest. The immigrants from Chamula retained some of their highland patterns and introduced new ones more appropriate to the lowlands. The goal was to achieve a form of adaptation that was viable from economic, ecological, and social perspectives, and that would prevent the alienation of the resettled group.

Experiences drawn from the repertoire of local and international development agencies repeatedly point to two major consequences of violating the needs and participation of community members. On the one hand, projects that are not viewed as meaningful to the people do not represent valid alternatives for rural peoples. On the other hand, when agencies erroneously assume community homogeneity—even when the decision-making stage of governance does reach the community—the benefits often remain in the hands of local elites. The development initiative is thus truncated by the same uneven mechanisms that on a much larger scale generated underdevelopment in the first place.

ECONOMY AND CHANGE IN MESOAMERICA

Let us conclude with a brief summary of the interplay between economy and culture, as it has impacted and changed the region. Specifically, we deal with such questions as the following: In the context of the extensive economic and technological changes that we outlined before, how are people's worldviews affected, if at all? Do people's private, domestic, and social lives change along with the many other changes?

Mesoamericans have shared basic cultural assumptions since pre-Columbian times (see Chapter 2). One of these traditional Mesoamerican traits includes close ties to the earth, which is perceived as the great provider with whom people establish deep symbolic and ritual connections. The traditional person is thus identified as someone who depends heavily on the earth for resources and, given the choice, would rather have more land than any other resource. The traditional Indian expects his or her children to remain nearby, inherit the land, and keep working it.

The Mesoamerican person (idealized here) is one who, when resources are available, prefers to invest them in his or her community, often by means of participation in the communal fiestas and the civic and religious brotherhoods (*cofradías*). These investments in food, liquor, costumes for ceremonial dances, ritual paraphernalia, care of the saints, and others provide a return that translates into higher status. There is thus room for some degree of accumulation, when the culturally appropriate form it takes is prestige. Accumulation of other forms of "capital," with a lavish lifestyle and display of wealth, is frowned upon. In this worldview, emphasis is placed on community values, solidarity, and generosity. Greed and personal ambition are viewed with disdain.

Expressions of traditional beliefs and attitudes toward life, and in particular toward aspects of life related to the economy, are found in the stories people tell to each other—both in old folk accounts and in other narrations considered to be actual events that happen to people who behave in certain ways. The moral of many of these stories often suggests that ambition, greed, and desire to have more material means than others have are negative values and should be condemned by all. Such traits are perceived as detrimental to the society because they cause "envy." Envy is understood as a bad feeling, generated in part by conspicuous consumption, which, according to the traditional viewpoint, could lead to disease and even death (for a broader account of oral literature in Mesoamerica, see Chapter 13).

Within the general Mesoamerican economic ideology, there is room, of course, for notions of change and innovation. Agricultural techniques may change slightly, fertilizers may be a welcome addition to depleted soils, and acceptance of rentals or sharecropping may be necessary. The traditional native worldview is not by any means static, but it is conservative. Conversations with people who have experienced drastic changes in their lifestyles and economic practices reveal interesting perceptions about the issues outlined here. Changes in economic ideology among native Mesoamericans reveal an increasing number of people who are defining their positions differently. One transitional sector is slowly questioning some of their traditional assumptions.

Petty commodity and petty capitalist producers who have intensified production, diversified productive activities, and expanded their commercial practices come to think about the world in very different terms. Such people may indicate that they would much prefer to obtain more money than more land. They see their children leaving the township upon reaching adulthood in order to find new markets and new horizons. They are willing to try new economic ventures and take risks. Some people also indicate that accumulation is something to strive for as long as there is a degree of redistribution involved. In sum, many Mesoamericans now admit that becoming wealthy is something to aspire to, but that it is also important to be generous and not greedy. In this context, by presenting themselves as protectors of reciprocal community obligations, people facilitate the transition to a new ideological framework while trying to protect themselves from the traditional charges of envy.

Studies have shown that the native peoples who espouse new economic ideologies tend to be those whose economic status is relatively high. Many of them are heavily involved in commercial activities (as in western Guatemala) or in petty industrial production (as in Oaxaca, Mexico). Such people probably experience changes in their economic practices, as well as in how they perceive and evaluate the world around them. As these economic changes take place, other related cultural changes occur. The worldview of the larger capitalist society not only becomes familiar but also is partially adopted. Native peoples transform themselves as they transform the work they do and adjust to the changes going on around them. They become agents in this process and key links to the larger economic system.

An interesting phenomenon occurring among large sectors of Mesoamerican peoples, as well as nonindigenous people living in the region, is the high rate of conversion from Catholicism to Protestantism. This may be one of the most notable cultural change that people have been experiencing during the twentieth century. The introduction of Protestantism in the region is related to the interests of the governments in Mexico and Central America in generating capitalist development and growth, together with their conviction that by encouraging foreign investments and bringing in the ideas and styles of the developed countries, development will follow.

Ever since Max Weber elaborated his theories on the rise of capitalism, scholars have pointed to the possible relationship between Protestantism and economic improvement. There seems to be a relationship between a people's exposure to certain activities closely associated with the capitalist market (or technological innovations leading to higher economic status) and their openness to new ideas, including new religious beliefs. The ideas of Protestantism (as espoused in Mesoamerica) appear to correspond well with the new occupations and new economic practices in general, providing an articulate conceptual framework that justifies and also encourages the change. For example, Protestants usually argue that it is good to work hard, and as a result, to achieve more wealth. They stress that competition encourages well-being and growth, both individual and social. Furthermore, they tend to stress the importance of investing time in "worthwhile," constructive activities, such as economic production or healthy diversion, rather than in long ritual celebrations that include heavy drinking and several days away from economic obligations.

It should be added that Protestantism may not itself be generating change, but instead is providing people with the necessary explanatory and supportive framework for accepting general economic change.

The participation of Mexico and the countries of Central America in the capitalist world market has had a profound impact on local cultures. We have mentioned some of these developments earlier, for example, the influx of Protestantism from the United States and its related consequences on worldviews as the peoples of Mesoamerica engage in new economic activities. New political affiliations result from the combined influence of religion and production. They shape new coalitions of native and nonnative workers, and redefine old sectors in light of new problems and class affiliations. Ethnicities are also reconstructed in these new frameworks. As people engage in different economic activities and relate to other peoples in different terms, they also redefine themselves. The new autonomy of women, counterbalancing the traditional patriarchal structure, is also related to the possibilities that the new markets have created for them. As new gender relations develop, so do new family dynamics, as men and women become part of the emerging division of labor. Finally, as the products of native peoples are sold and purchased throughout the world, parts of their cultures are also disseminated, although transformed in the process.

SUGGESTED READINGS

ANNIS, SHELDON 1987 *God and Production in a Guatemalan Town.* Austin: University of Texas Press.

BROCKETT, CHARLES D. 1990 *Land, Power and Poverty: Agrarian Transformations and Political Conflict in Central America.* Boulder: Westview Press.

CAMBRANES, JULIO C. 1985 *Coffee and Peasants in Guatemala.* South Woodstock, Vermont: CIRMA.

CANCIAN, FRANK 1965 *Economics and Prestige in a Mayan Community: The Religious Cargo System in Zinacantan.* Stanford: Stanford University Press.

CHIBNIK, MICHAEL 2003 *Crafting Tradition: The Making and Marketing of Oaxacan Wood Carvings.* Austin: University of Texas Press.

COHEN, JEFFERY H. 1999 *Cooperation and Community: Economy and Society in Oaxaca.* Austin: University of Texas Press.

COLLIER, GEORGE 1989 Changing Inequality in Zinacantán: The Generations of 1918 and 1942. In *Ethnographic Encounters in Southern Mesoamerica: Essays in Honor of Evon Zartman Vogt, Jr.,* edited by V. R. Bricker and G. H. Gossen, pp. 111–123. Studies on Culture and Society vol. 3. Albany: Institute for Mesoamerican Studies.

COOK, SCOTT 2004 *Understanding Commodity Cultures. Explorations in Economic Anthropology with Case Studies from Mexico.* Lanham, Maryland: Rowman & Littlefield Publishers, Inc.

COOK, SCOTT, AND LEIGH BINFORD 1990 *Obliging Need: Rural Petty Industry in Mexican Capitalism.* Austin: University of Texas Press.

EHLERS, TRACY BACHRACH 1990 *Silent Looms: Women and Production in a Guatemalan Town.* Boulder: Westview Press.

GOLDIN, LILIANA R. (ed.) 1999 *Identities on the Move: Transnational Processes in North America and the Caribbean Basin.* Austin: University of Texas Press.

LITTLE, WALTER E. 2004 *Mayas in the Marketplace: Tourism, Globalization, and Cultural Identity.* Austin: University of Texas Press.

LITTLE, WALTER E. (ed.) 2005 Maya Livelihoods in Guatemala's Global Economy. Special Issue *Latin American Perspectives* 32(5). London: Sage Publications.

NASH, JUNE (ed.) 1993 *Crafts in Global Markets: Artisan Production in Middle America.* Albany: State University of New York Press.

SMITH, CAROL (ed.) 1990 *Guatemalan Indians and the State, 1540 to 1988.* Austin: University of Texas Press.

WASSERSTROM, ROBERT 1983 *Class and Society in Central Chiapas.* Berkeley: University of California Press.

Chapter 10
The Mayan Zapatista Movement

Readers may wonder why we have opted to devote an entire chapter to a localized indigenous social and political movement that became publicly visible only a decade ago, on January 1, 1994, in the state of Chiapas, Mexico. At midnight on that date, several thousand armed Mayas and a number of nonindigenous allies, comprising the Ejército Zapatista de Liberación Nacional (EZLN), occupied four major Chiapas towns for several days. This event constituted an acute political embarrassment for the Mexican government, for January 1, 1994, coincided precisely and not coincidentally with the beginning date of the North American Free Trade Agreement (NAFTA), whose approval by the U.S. Congress had required enormous concessions by Mexico, all of which were perceived by the Zapatistas as being against the interests of Mexico's rural poor in general and indigenous people in particular. Within days, the Mexican army drove the Zapatistas out of the urban centers and declared a victory over the insurgents, although to this day (January 2006), the Zapatistas hold de facto political control in parts of over thirty of the 100 municipios in the state. (The *municipio* is the administrative unit below the state, equivalent to the county in the United States. It is variously referred to in this chapter as township or nonitalicized municipio.)

Members and followers of the EZLN number today only a few hundred thousand, and they are impotent as a military force. Indeed, they have very recently forsworn violence as a negotiating strategy. However, their symbolic and political presence is a reality that the Mexican state cannot ignore, for they constitute an articulate and well-organized challenge to Mexico's political class itself. By "political class" they refer to the entire current political system, spanning ideological positions from right to left, that fields local, state, and national candidates. They remain at war with what they call the illegitimate Mexican state, not the Mexican nation. Many political analysts believe that the Zapatista rebellion, and the apparent inability of the Mexican state to resolve the public policy issues that it raised, had a great deal to do with the defeat of the Partido Revolucionario Institucional (PRI), Mexico's ruling party for over 70 years, in the presidential election of 2000. The winner of that election and past president, Vicente Fox, of the right-of-center Partido de Acción Nacional (PAN), has not delivered much cause for optimism. PAN in fact mustered the votes in Congress to change the original language of the San Andrés Peace Accords with the Zapatistas that government representatives signed in February 1996, so as to effectively kill the peace agreement. (We are grateful to Duncan M. Earle for his help and critical commentary on the introductory section to this chapter.)

ZAPATISTAS LAUNCH A NEW KIND OF WAR

The Zapatistas themselves declared and honored a unilateral ceasefire shortly after the original insurrection and have recently indicated their intention to participate in the national political process. Indeed, on January 1, 2006 (the twelfth anniversary of the launching their movement), they began a major public relations tour, projected to last six months, to all of Mexico's 31 states with the goal of reshaping the nation's politics and influencing the recently completed July 2 , 2006 presidential election. They have publicly declared, as of January 1, 2006, that they will "stand Mexico on its head" with a new left coalition. We know that they oppose candidates from all three major national political parties (PRI, center; PAN, right; and PRD, Partido Revolucionario Democrático, left), and that they are determined to critique the failure of the Mexican political class in general for their failure even to listen to the issues that are important to the rural and urban poor. The substance of their current position on national issues *can* at this point be inferred from their public statements and actual practice in the past. The message is simple: They insist on grassroots listening and response—a bottom-up approach to representation and governance. They demand and practice an anti-ideological stance. Zapatismo and its leadership are in constant dialogue among themselves and with their allies in "civil society" (meaning national and international allies and potential allies) about what issues need to be addressed. There is no fixed platform or ideology. Zapatismo and its leadership have in fact evolved since the beginning of the rebellion through their preferred dialectical process of listening and response, such that issues like women's rights, youth involvement, the role of labor and peasant organizations, the role of *ejido* organizations, the use of alcohol, and the encouragement of sustainable and profitable agricultural practices—not important in the beginning and centrally important now—are moving to the fore through what has been called radical democracy, in dialogue both with itself and with civil society (Earle and Simonelli 2005; Harvey 1998; Nash 1997).

So, then, what kind of war is this? The Zapatistas have publicly stated that "our word is our weapon," that radical democracy is their credo, and that their enemy is global free market capitalism—known throughout Latin America as neoliberalism. How does this rhetorical warfare work? How does one do battle with an abstract economic and political ideology? How can representative democracy work in a multiethnic society where indigenous people have been excluded from power and representation for 450 years? Zapatistas disclaim any ideology, yet they have made, via their spokesperson, Subcomandante Marcos, a remarkably postmodern policy statement, the essence of which follows, given here in the original poetic structure:

> *Zapatismo is not an ideology,*
> *is not a bought and paid for doctrine.*
> *It is . . . an intuition.*
> *Something so open and flexible that*
> *it really occurs in all places.*
> *Zapatismo poses the question:*
> *"What is it that has excluded me?"*
> *"What is it that has isolated me?"*
> *. . . In each place the response is different.*
> *Zapatismo simply states the question*
> *and stipulates that the response is plural,*
> *that the response is inclusive. (Marcos 2001:440)*

In the mode of interpreting this cryptic statement, we know that the Zapatistas are waging a new kind of war, beginning with radical reorganization of local governance and political representation in their home communities in the southeastern jungle and highlands of Chiapas, and extending to the national political arena and world stage via the Internet, a well-organized diplomatic corps, and thousands of Indian and non-Indian allies.

Hence, we are dealing with a fascinating postmodern social and political movement in which native Mesoamericans are the instrumental actors and whose cultural logic can, with effort, be unpacked and understood. Zapatismo is both a work in progress—as they would like it to be represented—and a model for other grassroots democratic movements around the world—as they would also like it to be represented. In the current shift of Latin American politics to the left (see later), Zapatista models for consultative democracy and public policy are widely cited, from the streets of Brazil, Uruguay, and Argentina, to the legislative chambers of Venezuela and Bolivia. Zapatismo, borne of local reality in Chiapas, has turned out to be a formative and highly influential voice in current Latin American politics. Our inclusion of this chapter in this textbook should be understood as a scholarly judgment call on the part of the authors—that it *is* important—and an invitation to students to apply the information that precedes this chapter to make sense of the complexity of what is happening today. We believe that the causes, strategies, and long-range goals of this movement can lead to an appreciation of how native Mesoamericans are responding to and contributing to some of the great political and economic issues of our time. We also believe that an understanding of the Maya Zapatista Movement will lead to an appreciation of how and why the forces of globalization—free trade, rapid and open communication, democratization, rational faith in what Thomas Friedman (2005) has called a "flat earth" recognition of the inevitability of global capitalism— are bringing some unexpected consequences to Mexico and Latin America. Indeed, the Maya Zapatista Movement may provide some general insights about how Third

World People—indigenous inhabitants of old European colonial societies—are responding to the post-Cold War Era all over the world. (We are grateful to Duncan M. Earle for his help and critical commentary on the introductory section to this chapter.)

CONTEXTS WITHIN WHICH THE MOVEMENT HAS EMERGED

The Current World Context

The late 1980s and early 1990s brought a sense of euphoria in the West. We had won the Cold War. The collapse of communism, the implosion of the Soviet Union, the destruction of the Berlin Wall, the emergence of democratic societies in Eastern Europe, all brought a sense glorious closure, that the West had achieved what Francis Fukuyama (1992) famously called "the end of history," by which he implied that, at last, representative democracy and capitalism had triumphed in the epic conflict of good and evil. The ensuing civil wars in the Balkan peninsula, Sri Lanka, and Timor quickly dispelled this image. It became evident that the end of the Cold War had in fact unleashed pent-up aspirations for ethnic affirmation and self-determination that had been long suppressed by the East-West conflict. In fact, the end of the Cold War marked the end of the colonial era, in which two variants of the same theme— European hegemony, Soviet and Western—were dispatched forever, only to be supplanted by a remarkable array of new players and new aspirants to power. Among these players were the Mayas of Mexico and Central America.

The unexpected paradox of Fukuyama's presumed homogenization of world economic systems and political systems on the one hand and the reality of new ethnic resurgence and balkanization all over the world on the other was of course made manifest with the disappearance of barriers such as the Iron Curtain that were intended to prohibit free movement of people. The end of the Cold War unleashed unprecedented migration and immigration, as people found themselves able to move freely in search of economic opportunity and communities of like-minded ethnic compatriots.

Also essential for understanding the new ethnic affirmation (and its extreme expression in the current world trend toward political and religious fundamentalism) is the unprecedented ease and immediacy of communication and the flow of information via the World Wide Web and the Internet. This new technology both facilitates globalization (as, for example, in making it possible to conduct international business transactions and diplomatic communications almost instantly) and thwarts it (as, for example, the clandestine maintenance of the Al Qaeda terrorist network). As this pertains to the discussion of the Mayan Zapatista Movement, the Web has been absolutely central to its funding, maintenance, public communication, even its survival.

Forty years ago, an insurrection such as the one that the Zapatistas launched on January 1, 1994, would have been put down violently by the Mexican Army. All of the hamlets that supported them would have been burned and destroyed, and the Zapatista loyalists murdered. The news and gory details would have been suppressed or "cosmetized," and the dead would have been declared "disappeared." The Mexican state did not have this option in the case of the Zapatistas, since communiqués regarding the mission of the movement and minute details of its military maneuvers were made available all over the world within hours of midnight on January 1, 1994 (for details, see Chapter 8). The government could no longer suppress dissent violently as it had in the massacre of Tlatelolco in 1968. And so it continues today, as this rebel group that is at war with the Mexican state begins its high-profile public relations tour of the republic with the confidence that instant telecommunication and public opinion will protect them and help to promote their political position.

The Current Latin American Context

Any observer of current Latin American politics will be aware that, as of 2006, over half of the South American continent has moved to the left by electing, in carefully monitored free elections, public officials who generally oppose totally free trade and open markets, the very underpinning of global capitalism. The new governments that are now in power in Argentina, Uruguay, Brazil, Venezuela, and Bolivia all favor public policies that involve the state as the guarantor of the well-being of broad sectors of the urban and rural poor. During the 1970s and 1980s, all of these countries, under pressure from the United States–controlled International Monetary Fund (IMF), imposed austerity measures aimed at balancing budgets, privatizing state-owned utilities and industries, radically curtailing state-sponsored subsidies and economic programs, and generally following IMF-recommended formulas for creating the "level playing field" that would accommodate free trade and open markets.

These golden years of *neoliberalismo* achieved their stated goals of increasing the gross domestic product and increasing foreign investment. However, the apparent economic well-being and economic stability brought by IMF-imposed policies did not reflect grassroots reality. The new wealth flowed to the white and mestizo elites and foreign investors, and generally left the urban and rural poor—in the case of Bolivia, including virtually all of the that country's indigenous majority—in worse circumstances than before. These conditions led to populist electoral rebellions that eventually repudiated the United States– and European-sponsored austerity measures and encouraged the reestablishment of state-sponsored social and economic programs in favor of disadvantaged sectors. They also forced the reassessment of foreign investors' favorable economic terms for operating in these countries.

The Mexican Context

This background may help us to understand the process that has occurred during the same period (1970 to the present) in Mexico. Without going into tedious detail (again, for details see Chapter 8), the main parallels may be summarized as follows.

First, foreign investment soared as the austerity conditions imposed by IMF were implemented. The OPEC-sponsored oil crisis (1979–1980) and the huge spike in the market price of petroleum called to the attention of Mexican government officials that they possessed, with Venezuela, the biggest proven reserves of this valuable commodity in the New World, and that they were many thousands of miles closer to the world's biggest market, the United States, than any of the African, Russian, or Middle Eastern producers. With this trump card, and with the encouragement of IMF, Mexico borrowed in the early 1980s many billions of dollars against its petroleum collateral. The oil price bubble burst in a few years, and Mexico was faced with a massive debt crisis, which led to a U.S.-sponsored emergency bailout loan in 1995. Both the impetus to get into debt and the hardship of getting out of debt were exacerbated by foreign financial and political intervention.

Second, in response to the initial conditions for massive foreign investment in the 1970s and 1980s, and as a condition for getting the North American Free Trade Agreement (NAFTA) approved by the U.S. Congress (pre-1994), and yet again as a condition for the bailout loan from the United States in 1995, Mexico was forced to privatize many of its state-owned industries, utilities, and financial institutions. Most important as a background to the Mayan Zapatista Movement, Mexico was forced to abandon its highly successful agrarian reform program—begun in the 1930s—whereby hundreds of thousands of landless peasants received state-subsidized grants of surplus and expropriated land (given and administered as *ejidos*) for their own subsistence (on the ejidos, see Chapter 8). These grants were inalienable (i.e., they could not be sold) and could be passed only to family heirs. Not only was this program cancelled as a condition for United States Congress's approval of NAFTA, but also waiting lists for land grants were annulled, and existing *ejidos* were authorized, even encouraged, to sell their land on the private market. The result? Some windfall profits from land sale, but, mostly, despair and out-migration.

A third parallel with the process that we have observed in South America involved the elimination of state-sponsored subsidies, credits, and market price controls for the production of agricultural commodities. This policy was of course aimed at opening up Mexican markets to the sale of U.S. commodities. It had the "rational" effect of driving out marginal peasant producers, who no longer had either guaranteed market prices for their own products or subsidized cheap prices for staples that they did not produce. The result of this rural impoverishment was social instability and out-migration to marginal areas (such as the Lacandon jungle, cradle of Zapatismo), cities, and, by the millions, to the United States, in search of what Mexico could no longer provide.

Fourth, even as "new wealth" was being created by these policies, it was not redistributed to the urban and rural poor via state-sponsored social and economic services; rather, it was invested in industry, transportation, infrastructure, and agribusiness, all of which tended to be in the hands of elites who lived in urban areas or in the developed intensive agricultural production areas of central and northern Mexico. The trickle-down effect generally did not reach the poor, rural south, which is home to the majority of Mexico's indigenous communities. In the decades that we are considering, these policies led to massive unemployment, impoverishment, and population displacement.

Finally, as commodities such as coffee and corn reached their "natural" export price in the world market, small producers could not compete, and they either sold out or hired "scab" field hands in the form of Guatemalan and Salvadoran refugees, whom they paid far less than the minimum wage. Many thousands of Chiapas Indians who had counted on dependable seasonal labor jobs in the 1970s were unemployed by the early 1980s. Adding salt to this wound, the government withdrew the hope and promise of new *ejido* land grants to which the unemployed and landless might have sought refuge. This scenario became one of the major sources of social instability, rural unemployment, and population exodus from the Chiapas highlands, all of which fed the constituency of the Mayan Zapatistas.

The preceding list of adverse effects of the Mexican state's embrace of *neoliberalismo* reads, not unpredictably, like pieces in the boilerplate of Zapatista rhetoric against the Mexican state and in favor of the "alternative" solution that they are seeking. All of the preceding combined in the 1980s with many other factors that are peculiar to Chiapas to make possible the gestation of the Zapatista movement.

The Chiapas Context

The last two decades of the twentieth century brought profound change to Chiapas, molded in part by the issues and Mexican state policies discussed earlier. Because Chiapas, with Oaxaca and Yucatan, has a very large (almost 50 percent) population of rural indigenous origin, it is not surprising that the problems just discussed have been felt more acutely here than in the central and northern parts of Mexico. It is also not surprising that the political and economic problems with *neoliberalismo* have assumed a racial, ethnic, and class dimension in Chiapas, since those most affected by the downturn in economic opportunity have been indigenous people of Mayan origin. Although virtually all Chiapas Mayas have an acute awareness of living in what is a de facto apartheid society (with ladino bearers of Mexican national culture enjoying both greater material well-being and higher social status than Indians), what distinguishes the new "ethnic consciousness" from the older community-specific identity (e.g., a Zinacanteco Tzotzil) is that the newer voice is pan-indigenous, pan-Mayan, and affirmative about Indianness rather than deferential to whites.

Another new dimension of Indian ethnicity in Chiapas is that it *need not be and often is not* associated with Mayan Catholic traditionalism or *costumbrismo*. The reason for this is clear: Many agents of change have been on hand in the region to mitigate the pain of massive unemployment, diminished government services, and forced internal migration (often due to expulsion from their hometowns by their own traditionalist compatriots). All have had various degrees of success in recruiting followers because they are offering belief systems, social services, and hope for the future that neither the Mexican government nor the mainstream Catholic Church is able to offer. Chief among these mediating agents have been Protestant evangelical missions of many denominations; various progressive missionary endeavors working within the liberation theology framework of the post Vatican II (1963) Roman Catholic Church; and of course, the Zapatista Movement itself. (See the recommended readings that follow for thorough coverage of the political, economic, and religion background of the Zapatistas in the context of modern Chiapas.)

GENERAL STRUCTURAL THEMES
OF THE ZAPATISTA MOVEMENT

As we move to a consideration of the chronology of events and particulars of the vision for the future that the Zapatistas have articulated, it is important to observe
some general structural themes that are new to this particular Mesoamerican movement.

Pan-Mayan/Pan-Indigenous Constituency

Only on rare occasions in colonial and modern Chiapas history—notably, the Tzeltal
Rebellion of 1712; the War of Santa Rosa of 1867 to 1870; and Pajarito's War of 1910
to 1911—have Indian political and religious movements in Chiapas crossed ethnic
and linguistic lines in terms of their constituencies and military mobilization (for
these past movements, see Chapters 5 and 8 in this text). When they have done so
in such a manner as to become active and visible, these movements have been
promptly crushed by the state. Indeed, the Spanish Crown created administrative
institutions, settlement patterns, and local civil and religious organizations that would,
in effect, segregate Indians from Spanish and mestizo communities and also from one
another. In functioning to encourage local identities, languages, customs, and loyalties, these policies served the Crown's purpose in that they discouraged pan-Indian
opposition to state policy.

In many respects, the configuration of ethnically and demographically isolated
Indian townships that are indirectly controlled by the state through the *cacique* system (see Chapter 7) has continued largely intact well into the late twentieth century
and into the present. It is particularly characteristic of municipios in highland Chiapas and highland Guatemala. It follows that Zapatista rhetoric invests particular
venom in attacking the *cacique* system as coevil with the Mexican state.

The demographic portrait of the region that spawned the Zapatista Movement,
however, is *unlike* what we have just described, and this dissimilarity matters a great
deal in making sense of the background of the rebellion. The Zapatista homeland,
in the Lacandon jungle lowlands of southeastern Chiapas, is actually a pioneer settlement area. Within the last few decades, tens of thousands of displaced individuals
have emigrated there as refugees from poverty and political and religious persecution in their Indian townships of origin. The region is also home to thousands of
Guatemalan refugees who fled there to escape the political violence in their own
country in the 1980s (on this topic, see Chapter 8). The region therefore has no established social order that is dominated by any one Mayan ethnic or linguistic group.

This is also a region of great religious diversity, comprising thousands of newly
converted Protestants and recently evangelized "progressive" Catholics who were,
over the last two decades, the subjects of intense proselytizing by lay catechists and
priests associated with Liberation Theology. The former Roman Catholic Bishop of
the Diocese of San Cristóbal, Samuel Ruiz, is known fondly as Tatik Samuel ("Our
Revered Father Samuel") by the Zapatistas, for he has, in the spirit of Liberation
Theology, steadfastly defended their interests in dealing with the Mexican state and
with local white landowning elites. Also residing in the region and committed to the

Zapatista agenda are many "traditional Mayan Catholics" who do not feel attracted to either Protestant or liberal Catholic teaching.

It is therefore not surprising that the composition of the EZLN, although generally Mayan, is actually fairly diverse in terms of ethnic, linguistic, and religious backgrounds. Tzotzil, Tzeltal, Zoque, Chol, and Tojolabal speakers, as well as Mexican Mestizos and ethnically "white" Mexicans, are all united in pursuit of common political and social goals. What is Mayan about the Zapatista Movement must therefore be sought not in particular variants of Mayan cultural identity, but rather, in general principles of values and conduct that all might share, be they Zoques, Tzotzils, Mexicans, or other Native Americans.

Although the immediate goals of the Mayan Zapatistas appear to outside observers to be primarily of an economic and a political nature, we believe that the pan-Mayan nature of this enterprise has a powerful component of postcolonial ethnic affirmation that goes well beyond political action. Well-organized pan-Mayan cooperation now extends into many arenas of activity in modern Guatemala, Chiapas, and Yucatan. The nature of these pan-Indian groups ranges from intellectual, educational, and religious organizations to crafts guilds (for example, textile and ceramic cooperatives) that cater to the tourist trade. There are also numerous writers' and artists' cooperatives whose members are working to create a corpus of literature in Mayan languages, as well as graphic and performing arts, that express traditional and contemporary Mayan themes. A current synthesis of these topics may be found in Victor Montejo's *Maya Intellectual Renaissance: Identity, Representation, and Leadership* (see the discussion of this book in Chapter 13).

Choreographic Chronology of the Zapatista Enterprise

This introduction to the background of the actual events that comprise the Mayan Zapatista Movement has seemed necessary and appropriate to us because the international media have generally ignored its existence since it was "news" back in 1994. On that occasion the occupation of the Chiapas towns by the EZLN was deemed newsworthy by major commercial and public networks in the United States. It was even covered as a feature story on PBS's McNeil/Lehrer News Hour shortly after the insurrection began. Since then, the Zapatista story has gone underground, surfacing only occasionally in Europe and the United States over the past decade. There have been moments of embarrassment and comic opera, as for example, when Subcomandante Marcos, spokesman for EZLN, published an open letter to Spanish Court Magistrate Fernando Baltasar Garzón in November 2002 in which he called the Spanish judge a "grotesque clown" and the Spanish Prime Minister Ignacio Aznar an "imbecile" for outlawing a political party that was committed to Basque political autonomy.

Marcos subsequently challenged Baltasar Garzón to a debate in the Canary Islands over the issue of state recognition of cultural and political autonomy of indigenous people, and he compared the Spanish state's persecution of its Basque people with the Mexican state's failure to recognize and deal honorably with indigenous rights and cultural autonomy at home. His comparison of the EZLN cause in Mexico and the Basque separatist movement in Spain—labeling both national governments as immoral and dishonorable for their failure to address indigenous rights—inflamed Spanish and Mexican public opinion, and even led a Mexican congressional representative to challenge Marcos to a duel to the death for having insulted the honor of Mexico.

Neither the debate nor the duel ever happened, but the controversy cost EZLN a good deal of credibility. Indeed, the Zapatista Movement is widely ridiculed in Spain today as the mad voice of a frustrated post–Cold War Marxist. Subcomandante Marcos, the critics say, is attempting to indulge his political fantasies as a "ventriloquist," ostensibly speaking for indigenous communities, but actually grandstanding for himself. Others, such as José Saramago, Nobel Laureate of Portugal, have dignified Marcos with political and literary accolades, believing that he and his cause embrace the biggest issue of the new millennium: the recognition of the political rights and cultural autonomy of minority populations. (See Saramago's Foreword to Marcos's *Our Word is Our Weapon,* 2001). Such is the diversity of opinion regarding EZLN and the Zapatista Movement.

We hope that this background information and the following chronology will allow students to form their own opinions. In considering the Zapatista historical narrative, readers are urged to take note of the social, political, religious, and calendrical symbolism of events with an eye to understanding the underlying "cultural logic" (for the meaning of these terms, see Box 8.5).

The script for specific events of the early days of the Zapatista rebellion followed a syncretically adapted version of ancient Mesoamerican time (see Box 10.1). The Zapatista critique of the state followed a preordained script. In precise accordance with the Gregorian and the ecclesiastical calendar of 1994 (augmented by the inaugural date of NAFTA on January 1 of that year), the Zapatistas mounted their carnivalesque mockery of the Mexican state, its cities, its leaders, and its institutions.

The pattern of calendrically scripted moves guided by the solar and Carnival cycles continued in subsequent developments, both positive (renewal) and negative (death). On the positive side, the comprehensive peace accord of mid-February 1996 between the Zapatistas and the Mexican government occurred immediately before Carnival. The *New York Times* announcement on February 15, 1996, that the accord had been signed appeared on the Thursday preceding the ritual enactment of the four days of Carnival for that year (Saturday 17 February–Tuesday 20 February).

On the negative side, the Indian adversaries of the Zapatistas, in league with the Mexican government, mounted the infamous massacre of Acteal on December 23, 1997. In this notorious incident, forty-three alleged Zapatista supporters (almost all of them women and children) in a Tzotzil hamlet of Chenalhó were murdered by progovernment Tzotzil Mayan enemies of the Zapatistas. This massacre coincided, we think not coincidentally, with the winter solstice. In other words, death and renewal—quintessential agrarian forces that center on the winter solstice and the early spring ecclesiastical cycle—informed ancient Mayan thought just as they appear to guide contemporary Mayan action in history in modern Chiapas. This coincidence is why we believe that Carnival, with its humor and mockery of the normative order, functions in both Zapatista and progovernment communities as much more than a sequence of curious ritual events. Carnival is a kind of script for action in history. We

---

Box 10.1 Parallels Between Mayan Calendrical Rites and Zapatista History

Beginning at midnight on January 1, 1994—the precise date and time of NAFTA's inception—the Mayan Zapatista rebels occupied and held for several days four of the major ladino towns of the Chiapas highlands, including the old colonial town of San Cristóbal de las Casas, the real and symbolic center of Spanish political, cultural, and economic presence in the highlands since the sixteenth century. Only a few days later, the Zapatistas kidnapped the ex-governor of Chiapas, General Absalón Castellanos Domínguez. Regarded by the Zapatistas as a particularly hostile force in state politics, he was a hated symbol of *neoliberalismo*, the state, the army, and the old ladino oligarchy. He was a high-ranking army officer and, as governor of Chiapas, had consistently sided with wealthy ladino landowners in response to Indian appeals for recognition of the rights to unused land that they were seeking as *ejido* grants. Castellanos was released unharmed (his considerable girth reduced after more than a month of subsisting on an Indian diet of beans and tortillas) as a token of "good faith" on Ash Wednesday, February 16, immediately following the four days of Carnival. His capture and release had been a carefully orchestrated and precisely timed joke!

Subsequent peace talks leading to a cease-fire began in San Cristóbal on Monday, February 21, the first week of Lent. In the great drama that attended this international media event, which was held in the cathedral of San Cristóbal, monkey-costumed Chamulan clowns—the quintessential Carnival entertainers of the Mayan community of San Juan Chamula—were prominent in the huge audience of onlookers outside the cathedral (for additional information on Chamula, see Chapters 8 and 13). The monkey clowns, apparently unauthorized by the government of their own town, which was anti-Zapatista, voiced unambiguous support for the Zapatista cause; that is, they did not follow the "rules" of their own community. What does all of this mean?

In part, it is resonant with what historians and anthropologists have often noted about Mayan action in history, that it is guided by a calendrical schedule, suggesting that all that happens, divine and human, is cosmically programmed to take place according to recurring cycles of actualization. The most famous historical example of this behavior was the capitulation to Spanish authority of the Peten Itza Mayan town of Tayasal on March 13, 1697, at the end of the spring planting season and the beginning of a *Katun*, the Mayan calendrical unit of twenty vague solar years (18 months of 20 days equals 360 days) ("vague" because five days are not accounted for). This cycle intercalates with other ritual cycles to form the Mayan Short Count calendar, during which prophecies stated that conquest and conversion "had" to happen (on the Mayan calendarical system, see Chapters 1 and 14).

More recent research suggests a longer, more contentious process of Mayan prophecy and politicking over several Katun cycles in the seventeenth century—and a more violent final assault—but Spanish victory ultimately did occur according to the prophecy, at spring planting time. In other words, this event took place close to Carnival time at the beginning of a Katun. This was the end of the so-called "Conquest" in Mesoamerica, and the timing happened as much on Mayan terms as on Spanish ones.

---

do not see this script, but it is there. Both the Zapatistas and their adversaries appear to subscribe to it.

And the story continues. In May 2001, The Mayan Zapatistas completed a theatrical event of nearly epic proportion. I refer to a much-publicized journey—perhaps pilgrimage is a better word—which the English and Spanish language media dubbed the "Zapatour," comparing it with a rock star caravan and its entourage. This event even had its own Web site address (Narco News 2001). The journey began in the remote Zapatista strongholds of the Lacandon jungle and proceeded by bus caravan and other conveyances to Mexico City, culminating in a rally of 150,000 on Sunday, March 11, in the Zócalo, a great plaza that is the symbolic heart of the Mexican nation. (See Figure 10.1)

Following the rally in Mexico City was still another event that will be remembered for a long time: The EZLN leaders (minus Subcomandante Marcos) addressed members of the Mexican Congress on March 28. Wearing Indian traditional costumes and their signature ski masks (symbolizing, among other things, their perception that the Mexican state regards them as "faceless"), they spoke for several hours, hoping to persuade legislators to approve new constitutional guarantees for Indian autonomy. President Fox had already presented drafts of these proposals to Congress. Predictably, there was strong opposition to these changes from within his own conservative party (PAN) and from the recently deposed ruling party (PRI). In May 2001, a watered-down version of these legislative proposals was passed by the Mexican Congress, and the Zapatistas rejected them. Stalemate continues to this day.

The pilgrimage just described was not an ordinary journey, however; nor are the rules for discussing Indian-state relations the same as before. Indeed, much has

Figure 10.1 Photograph of the Zapatista Rally in 2001 at the Zócalo, Mexico City. (Courtesy of Reuters News/Corbis.)

changed. The masked delegation of twenty-three Zapatista comandantes and Sub-comandante Marcos departed by bus from San Cristóbal de las Casas on Saturday, February 25, following a festive send-off. The itinerary included eleven stops at In-dian communities in as many states, including a four-day stop (March 1–4) in Nurio, State of Michoacán, to lend Zapatista support to and allow their participation in the Third Indigenous Congress being held there. On that occasion, representatives from dozens of Mexico's diverse native-language communities voted to make the Zapatis-tas the "official voice" of the nation's ten to fifteen million indigenous people. At the same congress, Indian representatives presented mestizo Subcomandante Mar-cos with the symbolic staff of indigenous political authority to serve as their spokesman. This constitutes a formal recognition of what Indians have long under-stood, that he truly speaks on their behalf and that his charismatic leadership carries their blessings and moral authority. These events make clear that neither the Za-patistas nor their spokesman Subcomandante Marcos can be dismissed as a distant rumble from a far corner of Mexico. They are speaking for more than 10 percent of the population of Mexico.

This carefully charted pilgrimage ended in a symbolic gesture of spiritual re-conquest, since the Zócalo in Mexico City, the site of the March 11 rally, is built over the ruins of the main ceremonial precinct of the ancient Aztec capital of Tenochti-tlán. Chiapas Mayan oral traditions remember clearly that their own conquest and defeat came from the north. The Zapatour itinerary (south-north) amounted, in their view, to nothing less than the "reconquest" of Mexico in the name of indigenous issues and causes, moving generally from the poor, predominantly Indian south and southeast, to the north and northwest, finally to the symbolic center of Mexico's mes-tizo state and its "neoliberal" prosperity. The rally in the Zócalo turned into a media spectacle comparable in magnitude to the Pope's recent visit, the 1968 Olympics, or the closely related Massacre of Tlatelolco.

In a final turn of irony, which has not yet been picked up by the media—nor publicly mentioned by the Zapatistas themselves—February 25, 2001, was not only the festive departure date of the pilgrimage from Chiapas but also the first day of the four days of Carnival. The solar calendar, as understood by Mayan Christian custom, was thus centrally involved in the script of this Carnival season pilgrimage to renew Mex-ico's Indian voice and bring it to the attention of Mexican national consciousness. This involvement means, broadly interpreted, that the Zapatistas are not secular pragmatists and that they are engaging the state in their own terms (for more on the Maya cultural logic that informs Zapatista action in history, see Gossen 1999).

Fiesta of the Word

Although the Zapatistas and their allies are accomplished and widely published in the art of rhetoric, and their statements are often signed, the best summary of the new posture of the Indian community in relation to the Mexican state appears in an ob-scure and anonymous document that was circulated in xerox format as the "Pream-ble to the Resolutions of Roundtable One" at the Zapatista-sponsored National Indigenous Forum, which was held in San Cristóbal de las Casas, January 3 to 8, 1996.

This was an extraordinary event, a kind of coming-out party for the new indigenous voice, called by the organizers "The Fiesta of the Word" (Nash 1997; Gossen 1999:251–253). In eloquent language, the gauntlet was thrown down. (Box 10.2 contains Gossen's translation of the Preamble section titled "On Autonomy".)

As a complement to this relatively abstract position statement about the Zapatista agenda at the national level, we would like to add a Zapatista position statement about democracy at the local level. The quasi-mystical link of their own agenda with Mexican "democracy" and other principles of the Mexican national idea is laid out eloquently in a communiqué, dated February 26, 1994, from the Clandestine Indigenous Revolutionary Committee High Command of the Zaptatista National Liberation Army. The following excerpt constitutes the first paragraphs of this document. We do not know from whose pen these words come; however, the poetic and opaque language bears the clear mark of contemporary Mayan oratorical style, perhaps mingled with the romantic imagery of Spanish-speaking collaborators. In reading the extract that follows, one can discern the kind of radical democracy that is envisioned by the Zapatistas and put into practice in community governance. It is clearly a mythical worldview in which the will of the community subsumes individual aspiration and desire.

> When the EZLN was only a shadow, creeping through the mist and darkness of the jungle, when the words "justice," "liberty," and "democracy" were only that: words; barely a dream that the elders of our communities, true guardians of the words of our dead ancestors, had given us in the moment when day gives way to night, when hatred and fear began to grow in our hearts, when there was nothing but desperation; when the times repeated themselves, with no way out, with no door, no tomorrow, when all was injustice, as it was, the true men spoke, the faceless ones, the ones who go by night, the ones who are in the jungle, and they said:
>
> "It is the purpose and will of good men and women to seek out and find the best way to govern and be governed, what is good for the many is good for all. But let not the voices of the few be silenced, but let them remain in their place, waiting until their thoughts and hearts become one in what is the will of the many and the opinion from within, and no outside force can break them nor divert their steps from other paths.
>
> "Our path was always that the will of the many be in the hearts of the men and women who command. The will of the majority was the path on which he who commands should walk. If he separates his step from the path of the will of the people, the heart of he who commands should be changed for another who obeys. Thus was born our strength in the jungle, he who obeys if he is true, and he who follows leads through the common heart of true men and women. Another word came from afar so that this government was named and this work gave the name 'democracy' to our way that was from before words traveled." (This text was originally published in *La Jornada*, Sunday, February 27, 1994, p. 1; English translation by Ron Nigh 1994:12; another English translation appears in Subcomandante Marcos and EZLN 1995:150–151.)

As we conclude this section on the general chronology of the Zapatista movement and the radical democratic political position that it advocates, it is appropriate to observe a final dimension of all of this that brings us to the present. As of August 2003, the Zapatistas began to dismantle their military organization and strategy, for it was obviously futile. At that time they began planning for participation in the national

Box 10.2   Preamble of the 1996 Zapatista Indigenous Forum

"We are the people who were the original inhabitants of Mexico. We have exercised, and will continue to exercise, the right to determine who we are according to our own premises. We are the bearers of our own culture and of our own common agenda. In spite of all of our losses as a conquered people, we continue to maintain an organic relationship with the land that was once ours. We feel this tie to our ancestral lands even though, in some cases, we have had to leave our homes of origin to emigrate to new areas.

"It is this link between ourselves and our home that we call 'autonomy.' We raise this flag to this cause in order to let everyone know that we continue to exist as we always have as proud and dignified communities that are different from one another just as they are also linked by the brotherhood of common Indian identity. To recognize this is the basic premise that will allow us to enjoy all of our rights and liberties.

"In a profound sense, we consider ourselves to be Mexicans. This is so even though the founders of the Mexican state and all governments that have followed in their footsteps have ignored our existence. This is so even though many Mexican men and women regard us with condescension and ignorance, virtually denying our existence. Because of this, as we reaffirm on this occasion our existence as a people, we wish to make it known that our current struggle for acknowledgment of our separate identity does not seek to launch a fight with our fellow Mexicans, nor much less to secede from a country that we consider as much our own as our separate identity as Indians. Through our act of demanding recognition of our Indian identity, we wish to contribute to the formation of a more fundamental unity of all Mexican men and women, a unity that recognizes the true diversity of the ethnic communities that make up modern Mexico. This is a fundamental condition for harmony among all Mexican men and women. Our quest for recovery of our own identity does not, in any way, constitute a challenge to national sovereignty.

"We are not asking anybody to grant us autonomy. We have always had it, and we have it today. No one can 'give' us the capacity to be ourselves, to think and act in ways that are governed by our own ways of looking at the world. However, we have not been free, either during the Spanish colonial regime or under the post-Independence Mexican State, to exercise freely our separate identity as a people. Throughout our long struggle of resistance, we have always been obliged to express our identity against the repressive backdrop of Mexican state representatives and Mexican state institutions.

"*Basta!* We have had enough of this. We will no longer continue to be the objects of discrimination, being excluded from full participation in a homeland that belongs as much to us as to the rest of Mexican men and women, a homeland that has been built with our hands, our labor, and our effort. We wish to enjoy the full freedom to continue being who we are. We wish to create conditions that will make this possible. We believe that Mexico will be truly free only when all of us are free.

"In the course of our recent struggle [the post-January 1994 Zapatista Movement], we have succeeded in establishing a number of social spaces in which to exercise our freedom. Some of us have been able to express our ethnic identity in our local communities. We have recovered local control of these communities and feel that it is there, and only there, that we are free to be ourselves. Others among us have managed to transform whole *municipios* [townships] from oppressive political units that were imposed on us during the colonial period in order to divide us and control us into space that truly belongs to us, a space where we are also free to pursue our aspirations for autonomy. Finally, some of us have managed to capture spaces of autonomy that are regional in scope, extending to the entire multi-ethnic Indian community. We refer to these advances as 'de facto autonomous entities.' Their juridical foundation is Indian law and custom, and now we intend to fight to have this de facto autonomous status recognized by the Mexican Constitution.

(continued)

(continued)

"We are committed to broadening, fortifying, and consolidating our gains. We propose to achieve this by combining our own efforts, as members of Indians communities, with those of many other fellow Mexicans who already recognize us and are allied with us in this struggle. We will mobilize to organize ourselves in order to make that which we have already achieved stronger, and also to accomplish what is still lacking. We intend to intensify our efforts at the local, municipal, and national levels.

"We intend to pursue this struggle without hesitation. We are confident that, through this struggle, our resistance will be transformed into liberation. We are prepared to do everything necessary to achieve these goals. We cannot afford to wait around for change any longer. However, we are also committed to accomplishing these things in peace and harmony. By means of this agenda, we are seeking to have our 'de facto autonomous spaces' [*autonomías de hecho*] recognized as 'de jure autonomous spaces' [*autonomías de derecho*].

"We appeal to the rule of law. The Constitution of 1917, which is the Magna Carta that governs the lives of all Mexicans, grants to the people the right to choose their own form of government. We appeal to the authority of this document (specifically, to Article 39) in order to re-found this country in such a way that all Mexican men and women may enjoy, at last, a new Magna Carta that will recognize what the Mexican nation has always been and is today: a multiethnic society."

political arena. The culmination of this planning has yielded the current (January 2006) six-month initiative to attempt to "turn Mexico on its head" by means of the six-month "listening" and informational tour of all of Mexico's 31 states. Although they are critical of all three major presidential candidates, they nevertheless hoped to influence the outcome of the July 2006 presidential election.

All of this is somewhat hard to understand, for the Zapatistas are still at war with the Mexican state because the Mexican Congress failed to ratify the 1996 San Andrés Peace Accords, which the EZLN and government negotiators signed in February of that year. So, perhaps to save face, the EZLN still exists as a clandestine militia that is prepared to defend the autonomous Zapatista villages and hamlets from harassment from the Mexican army and its paramilitary allies in Chiapas. However, the focus of the movement has now turned to a war of words and rhetoric and to a consolidation of their control of the de facto autonomous zones of Chiapas where they are now in power.

SOCIAL AND ETHNIC STRUCTURE OF THE ZAPATISTAS

Although the particulars of the Zapatistas' grassroots social organization and leadership are not officially publicized and although extended residence by outsiders is discouraged, it is possible to assemble a rough portrait of everyday and public life in the Zapatista autonomous areas. This sketch depends heavily on close reading of communiqués, some firsthand accounts via personal communication and a few published accounts by scholars who have visited the Zapatista-controlled area. The most comprehensive recent field report in English is Earle's and Simonelli's *Uprising of*

Hope: Sharing the Zapatista Journey to Alternative Development (2005), from which we have drawn particular details in the following section.

Ethnicity and Inclusion

We have already discussed the heterogeneous ethnic composition of the Zapatistas. Although primarily consisting of native people of the five principal indigenous linguistic groups of Chiapas—Tzeltal, Tzotzil, Tojolabal, Zoque, and Chol—the movement is explicitly *not* intended to encourage Indian separatism or chauvinism. Spanish is pragmatically recognized as their own lingua franca and principal language for issuing public statements. English is recognized as indispensable for achieving the high international profile that they seek via the Internet.

In countless public statements, the Zapatistas have said that their vision of a just society and good government includes everyone who has been previously excluded from representation and participation in national or community life, be it in Mexico or elsewhere. They insist that a just society should embrace everyone, including guarantees not only for their *inclusion and representation* but also for their *right to live in communities in which their individual cultural identities are respected and celebrated.* National and international observers are warmly welcomed at their public events, and their poster art exuberantly highlights international and interethnic solidarity. They are also adamant about gender equality, as one can easily observe in the scripting of public events. Of those who have the highest rank of Comandante(a) in the EZLN, approximately half are women, and they are routinely given equal time in settings of public debate and discussion (see Figure 10.2).

The ideal of *inclusion* pervades the symbolism and reality of the Zapatistas (see Box 10.3). A close reading of their elegantly constructed communiqués reveals that they consistently place their own goals within the framework of Mexico's own stated goals for itself. Zapatistas are simply demanding to be included in the Mexican national idea that states that the nation embraces all of its people. This has been a centerpiece of Mexican Revolutionary rhetoric for at least sixty years. Perhaps this link with Mexico's own story about itself explains the enigma of why a Mayan indigenous insurrection movement should be so charitably inclined toward the ideology, ethnicity, and symbols of its stated adversaries. Indeed, the maximal hero of the Mexican Revolution, Emiliano Zapata, who is the paladin of the Zapatista rebels, was himself a relatively prosperous mestizo, a son of commercial horse-breeders in central Mexico. He spoke Nahuatl as a second language and treated Indians with respect and dignity. He remains one of the few Revolutionary heroes who have not been discredited by revisionist historians (see the account of Emiliano Zapata the revolutionary in Chapter 8).

Knowledge of Zapata's own ability to transcend race and ethnicity for higher national purpose can usefully be applied to an understanding of the enigmatic role of Subcomandante Marcos, who, like Zapata, was born a child of privilege, renounced it, and turned to other—he believed—higher causes. He has been, from the beginning in 1994, the high-profile, charismatic chief spokesman for the Zapatistas, and the author of a vast corpus of Zapatista communiqués and related literary documents.

Figure 10.2 Poster from the Zapatista-sponsored National Indigenous Forum, 1996. (Based on an original poster in possession of Gary H. Gossen and modified by Bradley W. Russell.)

Now he has been elevated to the role of spokesman for all of indigenous Mexico. Even more recently (January 2006), he has dropped the Subcomandante title to assume the new title of *Delegado Cero* ("Delegate Zero"), in an effort to strip himself of symbolic authority in a movement that stresses egalitarianism and democratic consultation. Much has been made in the mode of speculation and deprecation about Marcos's role in the Zapatista Movement, for he is culturally and physically non-Indian. He is fair-skinned, light-eyed, and of European countenance. The Mexican government gleefully revealed shortly after the beginning of the insurrection that he was in fact a well-educated creole named Rafael Sebastián Guillén Vicente, a Jesuit-educated leftist instructor in philosophy at the Universidad Nacional Autónoma de México, who bailed and went to Chiapas to foment a Che Guevara–style Marxist rebellion in the early 1980s. He has neither denied nor acknowledged these revelations, only stating that he, Marcos, was born on January 1, 1994, the date of the beginning of the Zapatista insurrection.

Box 10.3   The Zapatista Ideal of Inclusion

In a commentary that may one day become famous, Marián Peres Tzu, a Chamulan Tzotzil, recorded the following impressions about the first few weeks of the Mayan Zapatista insurrection:

> For the first two weeks or so after the seizure of San Cristóbal, not a single *kaxlan* (Ladino, or non-Indian) showed his face in public: not a policeman, not a parking officer, nor a collector of fees. Not one. They disappeared! They were so terrified of the Zapatistas that they hid. But the moment they were sure the Zapatista Army was gone and wasn't coming back, Ha!, immediately the parking officers were back unscrewing license plates, the municipal police beating up drunks, and the market collectors chasing away poor women trying to sell tomatoes and lemons on the street corners. With the Zapatistas gone, suddenly they were fearless again. But when the Zapatistas were here, they stayed in their bedrooms with the shades closed, quaking with fear. They couldn't even get it up with their wives they were so scared.
>
> You see what that means? They were afraid of Indians, because that's what the Zapatistas were, Indians. When we other Indians realized that, we felt strong as well. Strong like the Zapatistas. The *kaslanetik* of San Cristóbal have always pushed us around just because we don't speak Spanish correctly. But now everything has begun to change. (Peres Tzu 1996:126–127, translated by Jan Rus.)

Marcos's own statements and ample testimony from indigenous comrades indicate that he and his Marxist colleagues in the early years (1980s) were slowly dissuaded, indeed thwarted, from trying to implement standard top-down revolutionary rhetoric in their efforts to mobilize indigenous resistance against the Mexican state. This strategy, the indigenous elders said, was old and bad news, bearing memories of more than 400 years of tutorial supervision and exploitation. They were tired of being manipulated by European agendas. The key to meaningful social change and good government, said the elders, was to start with what people themselves wanted and needed.

We understand that this learning process was aided and abetted by the extraordinary leadership of Samuel Ruiz, Bishop of the Diocese of San Cristóbal, who during the the same period (1980s) mobilized major forces—who for the most part were lay catechists—in the spirit of liberation theology, to establish base communities with strong commitment to local cooperation and collaboration that would sustain them spiritually and economically under adverse circumstances. Hundreds of these communities are vital today and constitute an important part of the Zapatista constituency (on this point, see Kovic 2005). Through these communities, with others that are more traditionally Mayan Christian and Protestant in their religious affiliation, Marcos learned to listen and realized that any meaningful social change had to begin from the roots—bottom-up—rather than from above.

There are many other details of the Zapatista movement that demonstrate that nonindigenous collaborators, human and supernatural, are welcome and essential to the cause. Among the earliest martyrs of the insurrection was Janine Pauline

Archembault Biazot, a white ex-nun known as "La Coronela" (The Colonel). Of French birth and Canadian residency, she is said to have died heroically as she led the Indian troops in the siege of the town of Las Margaritas on January 1, 1994 (Mendivil 1994:10). To this day, the Zapatista Web site is staffed by a faithful staff of technicians and translators, many of them North Americans and European. The most famous of the Zapatista translators goes by the name of La Irlandesa (The Irish Woman), suggesting that Irish is her national identity.

As has often been the case in the history of indigenous movements in the Mayan area, supernatural help has appeared in association with the Zapatista Movement. On April 30, 1994, a Tojolabal Indian woman, a Zapatista named Dominga Hernández, found herself bathed in miraculous spectral light (*rayos lucentes*), whereupon she found an image of a white Baby Jesus propped up against an oak tree. The Child of Lomantán (as the image is now called, named for the Tojolabal hamlet where the apparition occurred) spoke and declared his solidarity with the poor and requested a permanent home. Dominga built him a modest shrine in her patio, where visitors, petitioners, and visionaries now come to revere and seek intercession from the Child as a patron of the Zapatista cause. The Bishop of San Cristóbal, Samuel Ruiz, sent representatives to look for fresh signs of this miracle shortly after the apparition occurred (Ross 1995:7). The vitality of the new cult is such that both Zapatistas and progovernment Indian communities are laying claim to the Child's miraculous powers (Furbee 1996).

The non-Indian ethnic identity of the Child of Lomantán—the martyred Colonel Janine, Subcomandante Marcos, and perhaps also the emblematic memory of Zapata himself, all of them white or mestizo—reiterates the integrative, inclusive dimension of Zapatista thinking. This aspect of Zapatismo is also captured succinctly in a well-publicized poem that Marcos wrote, allegedly in response to a Chiapas PRI official's allegation in December 1997 that Marcos was gay in order to discredit his integrity. Marcos's response provides another glimpse of the global sweep of what and whom the Zapatistas seek to empower via their goal of inclusion:

> *Yes, Marcos is gay.*
> *Marcos is gay in San Francisco,*
> *Black in South Africa.*
> *An Asian in Europe,*
> *a Chicano in San Ysidro,*
> *an anarchist in Spain,*
> *a Palestinian in Israel,*
> *a Mayan Indian in the streets of San Cristóbal,*
> *a Jew in Germany,*
> *a Gypsy in Poland,*
> *a Mohawk in Quebec,*
> *a pacifist in Bosnia,*
> *a single woman on the Metro at 10 pm,*

a peasant without land,
a gang member in the slums,
an unemployed worker,
an unhappy student and, of course,
a Zapatista in the mountains.
(Subcomandante Marcos 1998, in Voces Unidas, Vol 7[4]:12)

Zapatista Community Organization

From here we proceed to offer a sketch of what is known about the grassroots political organization and leadership of the autonomous Zaptatista communities in Chiapas. Several caveats are appropriate from the outset, for we are relying on secondary,
not primary, data. For example, the Zapatistas' own published statements claim effective power in thirty to thirty-eight autonomous municipalities of more than 100
municipios that make up Chiapas. Other sources state forty.

Perhaps this discrepancy results from the fact that Zapatista *municipios autónomos*
do not necessarily correspond to the boundaries of existing official municipios. In
some cases, several autonomous municipios are found in a single official municipio.
Of the municipios where the Zapatistas hold power, most are found in the southeastern lowlands and in the central and eastern highlands. Even in these areas, Zapatista governments do not constitute the sole authority in the municipio.

Although Zapatista autonomous muncipios are always found in areas where there
is a substantial contiguous area of hamlets that are committed to the movement, the
reality is usually a scenario of parallel authority systems, such that some parts of the
population participate in government-prescribed administrative structures that are
like those that exist throughout Mexico; other parts of the population in the same
municipio—usually living in separate hamlets or settlements and sometimes following religious and ethnic markers—make up the Zapatista constituency. In these cases
of parallel authority structures, Zapatistas do not pay church, municipal, state, or
federal taxes; nor do they participate in government-sponsored elections; nor do
they accept government-sponsored social services such as schools, clinics, utilities, and
road construction and maintenance. These services, such as they exist, are privately
funded through revenue sources that come through Zapatista self-taxation, volunteer
nongovernment services from outside, and funding from sympathetic nongovernment organizations in Chiapas, Mexico, and abroad.

Further complicating the picture is the fact that there are at least four levels of
affiliation with the Zapatistas. First, turning to the EZLN itself, this was initially a well-
disciplined small army. Now, by their own designation, beginning in 2003, it has become a clandestine militia that consists of several thousand people who make up the
core of the movement. For strategic and security reasons, they do not have a permanent, publicly known headquarters. Second, many tens of thousands of people, including EZLN members, live in insular Zapatista hamlets and villages where everyone
shares a public allegiance to the movement. Third, other tens of thousands of Zapatista
sympathizers live in noncontiguous hamlets that function rather like independent
cells where there is unstated (i.e., not public) but solid support for the movement.

In these independent cells, most of them located in the highlands in areas where there are de facto parallel local governments, security reasons or religious preference for nonviolent involvement dictates the wisdom of keeping a low profile. Many dozens of these independent cells are base communities of the type organized in the 1980s and 1990s by catechists working within the liberation theology tradition of the Catholic church. Acteal, a Tzotzil community of this type located in the highlands, was the victim of the infamous massacre of December 23, 1997 (see earlier). Other independent cells are made up of Maya Christian traditionalists and Protestants.

A final type of affiliation with the Zapatistas—one that has been essential to the movement's survival—is the national and international support network. Some belong to NGOs, and others work as independent volunteers. These thousands of Zapatista sympathizers attend to fund-raising and recruiting volunteer services, staffing the Web site, as well as renting and staffing contact offices (called *enlaces civiles*) throughout Mexico, Latin America, North America, and Europe.

In addition to the EZLN itself, which now functions as a clandestine militia, there are two basic administrative units that attend to everyday life and public affairs. One is the more local *municipio autónomo* ('autonomous municipio'), of which there are thirty to forty, distributed and constituted as discussed earlier. The *caracol* ("conch shell") is a kind of regional, highest-level administrative unit, of which there are currently five units. The *caracol* is the seat of the top governing council, called the Junta de Buen Gobierno, or Council of Good Government. Together, the five Councils of Good Government make up the top decision- and policy-making body of the Zapatistas. We will discuss each of these briefly.

ZAPATISTA POLITICAL ORGANIZATION

Ejército Nacional de Liberación Nacional (EZLN)

The EZLN began to evolve from a standing army to a militia in July 2003. Although its structure is not publicly known, its key distinctive characteristic, as with all Zapatista social and administrative units, is the lateral organization of coequals at the highest level. In the case of EZLN, the highest level is the Comandante (or Comandanta). The purpose for having a relatively large number of coequals at the highest level of leadership is to achieve the Zapatista ideal of consensus and the imperative of leading by obeying the general will (usually phrased in Spanish as *mandar obedeciendo*). There were, as of the date of their public appearance before the Mexican Congress in the spring of 2001, twenty-three Comandantes, with almost equal distribution between the sexes and with proportional representation of the various linguistic and ethnic groups involved (Tzotzil, Tzeltal, Tojolabal, Chol, and Zoque).

Subcomandante Marcos ranks below the twenty-three indigenous leaders, but his role has been from the beginning that of chief spokesperson for EZLN and for the Zapatista Movement. His role has evolved, with the change in EZLN itself (see earlier), to become chief spokesperson for the political whole that is constituted by the five Councils of Good Government. He is also, as per the meeting in Michoacán

(March 1–4, 2001), the spokesperson for the whole of indigenous Mexico. What exactly this means, legally or practically, is not altogether clear.

The Autonomous Municipality

The *municipio autónomo* constitutes the local level of administrative organization above the dozens of settlements and hamlets that claim Zapatista affiliation in a given area. It is the seat of the *consejo autónomo* ("autonomous council") for each autonomous municipio. Housed in a specially designated building, the autonomous council consists of a rotating assembly of representatives from all of the constituent settlements and hamlets. The cycle of rotation is two weeks, a policy that is intended to allow the broadest possible opportunity to serve in this governing body. The short term of rotation also minimizes the amount of time that a representative must be away from home and away from work. There are no permanent or even annually elected representatives, thus minimizing any temptation on the part of anyone to consolidate his or her power and influence. A spokesperson for the whole is elected for each cycle of rotation.

The autonomous municipality, through its representative apparatus, the *consejo autónomo* (autonomous council), deals with a myriad of everyday administrative and judicial issues, such as the adjudication of disputes, allocation of labor and resources for public projects, managing the microeconomy, approval of visits from outsiders, and advising representatives of the militia about potential local threats and security problems. Among the most important functions of the autonomous council are the management, financing, and staffing of local public services (clinics, schools, road maintenance, utilities), functions that usually fall to local and state government but cannot, for obvious reasons, be taken for granted in the autonomous zones.

The Caracol (Conch Shell)
and the Council of Good Government

The five *Caracoles,* together, with their corresponding councils of good government (*Juntas de Buen Gobierno*), constitute the maximal expression of the Zapatista governance structure. These regional centers not only are the seats for the Councils of Good Government but also provide physical facilities in the form of public pavilions, bleachers, guest quarters, and ceremonial spaces that allow for major public events that can accommodate thousands of participants. It is in these regional centers that the Zapatistas receive national and international guests, and also conduct business with outside organizations such as NGOs.

The Councils of Good Government, which meet regularly at the *Caracoles,* constitute the top level of authority for the adjudication of disputes and other decision-making. They provide the most comprehensive arena for achieving consensus, particularly on issues that involve economic and political dealings with outside institutions, governments, and individuals. Each *Caracol* has a rigidly democratic and rotating representation from its constituent autonomous municipalities, each of which takes a turn at providing the spokesperson for the whole.

These centers, in their past iteration as "Nuevos Centros Aguascalientes" (see later), have been the sites of major public events in the history of the Zapatista Movement. As *Caracoles* (their new designation as of July 2003), these centers continue to embody in public architecture, its function and symbolism, what the Zapatista Movement is about. Although the five *Caracoles* are officially coequal in status and importance, the greatest and most esteemed of these symbolic centers of Zapatista power is La Realidad, located in the Lacandon jungle. Variously described by outside observers as the Zapatista capital, a tabernacle, or a Mecca, the Zapatistas themselves call it the *Caracol Madre de los Caracoles del Mar de Nuestros Suenos* [Caracol Mother of the Caracoles of the Sea of Our Dreams] (Earle and Simonelli 2005:256).

Interpretations of the meaning of the conch shell symbol vary, but all emphasize some reference to language, consensus, and continuity from the Mayan past. Duncan Earle has stated, on the basis of recent field interviews, that the Zapatistas regard the shell as part of their Mayan heritage, a symbol of time, continuity, and true speech: *la palabra,* "the word" (Earle and Simonelli 2005:257). Indeed, one hears the voice of the sea (past time and former home of the organism) by listening to the opening of the shell. One can also discern that the conch shell symbolizes the long, slow, Zapatista consultative process, one in which, following the pattern of the inner structure of the shell, the body and life of the organism curls round and round in a spiral. Each round returns to a former position, perhaps capturing the ideal of leading by obeying, being sure that all opinions are considered. The snail or conch shell is also said to symbolize the animal's capacity to retract its body for defense while also being able to extend its body for slow motion forward.

Caracoles were formerly called Nuevos Centros Aguascalientes, a name of great symbolic importance in the history of the Mexican revolution and the formation of modern Mexico (see Chapter 8). Aguascalientes was the central Mexican site of the abortive November 1914 meeting of several revolutionary leaders, including Emiliano Zapata and Pancho Villa, national icons by anybody's reckoning. The intent of this meeting was to chart the future of the Mexican Revolution and of the emerging revolutionary state. The meeting failed, the leaders went their separate ways, and the bloody civil war persisted for several more years.

The Mayan Zapatistas resuscitated the name, memory, and intent of Aguascalientes, with more optimistic expectations, in July 1994. The new Aguascalientes forum, a celebrated, revolutionary political convention called the First National Democratic Congress, was held in the Lacandon jungle, in Zapatista-controlled territory (now the site of the "capital" *Caracol* La Realidad), in a hastily improvised amphitheatre of posts and canopies. This was a deliberately provocative gesture: The Zapatista leaders invited candidates of the PRD (the principal left-of-center national political party), all of whom opposed the then-ruling PRI political establishment. They also invited a host of national and international media representatives to witness a political rally that advocated the defeat of the PRI and its so-called neoliberal policies in the ensuing state and national elections. Presumably, everyone present, including the PRD representatives, supported the political agenda of their hosts, the Zapatistas (see Figure 10.2, a Zapatista poster that commemorates this event.)

The optimism of this meeting failed, but its palpable threat to the Mexican political process, economy, and internal stability caused international tremors. The PRI candidate, Ernesto Zedillo, won the August 22, 1994, election, but he was almost immediately forced by the United States, the World Bank, and the International Monetary Fund, to "prove" that the country was under sufficient "control" for Mexico to be worthy of receiving the multi-billion-dollar bridge loan that was in the works as a bailout from the country's debt crisis. As "proof" that the Zapatista threat was under control, on February 9, 1995, the Mexican Army began a scorched earth campaign to destroy Zapatista-held settlements. Included in their operations was the total destruction and occupation of the site of the 1994 Aguascalientes convention. The rest is history. The EZLN defiantly rebuilt and rededicated the Aguascalientes center at La Realidad (along with three more regional centers at La Garrucha, Oventik, and Morelia, all also known as Aguascalientes) in January 1996, the second anniversary of the beginning of the rebellion.

Now there are five such centers, renamed *Caracoles*. We would like to note what these rustic centers mean in terms of their innovative planning and design. All of the *Caracoles* are ambitious undertakings. They are conceived on a large scale, using both traditional (dirt mounds, platforms, log buildings) and modern (plastic-laminated sheets for canopies) materials. They are for the most part constructed according to preindustrial technology, that is, shovels and pickaxes, and are reminiscent in form and function of the ancient Mayan ceremonial centers. They are, in themselves, political statements.

The *Caracol* at Oventik, located in the Chiapas highlands, was constructed entirely without modern tools: no machines, no motorized vehicles, and no petroleum products supplied by PEMEX (Petróleos Mexicanos, the Mexican government monopoly that controls production, distribution, and sale of petroleum products). In this way, the Zapatistas blocked any opportunity for quick government purchases of influence with fleets of Mercedes trucks and Japanese backhoes, a co-optation strategy for which present and past national governments are well known.

It should be added that the *Caracoles* are located, conspicuously, outside existing municipal centers, in an apparent effort to separate them symbolically from the colonial and modern seats of *cacique* rule, where local Indian elites historically exploited their own compatriots by accepting favors and gifts from the ruling Spanish and Mexican authorities in exchange for guaranteed "local control." We hope that readers will appreciate all that the *Caracoles* embody in terms of recent historical memory and also what they mean as symbols for the new society and radical democracy that the Zapatistas envision for all of Mexico, a time when ". . . Mexico itself will be truly free only when all of us are free."

THE WIDER SIGNIFICANCE OF THE ZAPATISTA MOVEMENT

Although it would be irresponsible and premature to try to "place" the Zapatista movement in modern Mesoamerican history, we do wish to suggest that parallel events in current Latin American history—notably, the high visibility that indigenous people have recently achieved in free elections in Bolivia and Guatemala, both of them nations with indigenous majorities—oblige us to take the Zapatista movement seriously as a case study in what radical democracy can mean in a post–Cold War world in which Soviet and United States interests can no longer impose their homogenizing will on client nations for reasons of "global security." At stake is what *inclusion* can mean in de facto multiethnic nations.

The Zapatistas have stated over the past few years, in both language and practice that we have attempted to glimpse at in this chapter, what they envision as the just place of indigenous people in modern Mexico. Although they are careful to state that inclusion will undoubtedly mean different things in different national contexts, their main points regarding Mexico appear to be these:

> They wish to engage the Mexican state as equals with other nonindigenous Mexicans.
>
> They no longer deplore the nation as a categorical enemy, for they realize that they are First Citizens.
>
> They are no longer willing to feign neutrality in relation to the state, for the state belongs as much to them as it does to other Mexicans.
>
> They refuse to make pragmatic deals with the subalterns of the state (that is, local political bosses), for these deals in the past have typically yielded well-being for the few (that is, the Indian elites) at the expense of the many.
>
> They realize that local resistance in the name of a single indigenous issue is futile for two reasons. First, indigenous identities and causes are plural, not unitary or homogeneous. Second, the neoliberal Mexican state is adept at using democracy (the will of the majority) to suppress any single minority appeal for an "exception to the rule of law." For that reason they are offering their own model of radical democracy that incorporates the will of the many in a single governing body. This is the de facto autonomy that they wish to have recognized by the state.

We conclude with a reference to an extraordinary work of Zapatista art (see Figure 10.3). A serigraph entitled *Por la patria,* this piece is by Dionisio (who like all Zapatistas, chooses to use no surname). The original of the work came to Gary Gossen from an art dealer in Oaxaca who received it from the artist in exchange for a piece of Aztec stone sculpture in his shop. The signed prints of this piece are for sale throughout Mexico, and the image has also become a popular subject of Zapatista poster art.

The piece has several unusual qualities, not the least of which is its quasi-anonymity. This generic ownership, or anonymity, is a pattern related to the meaning of their signature ski masks—which are said to mock the pejorative image of the "faceless" Indian that they attribute to the Mexican state—that the Zapatistas have chosen for virtually all of their public statements. The picture depicts a jungle fantasy, rendered almost in the manner of Gabriel García Márquez's fictional village of Macondo in *One Hundred Years of Solitude.*

The central subject emerging from the miasma of the jungle is a Zapatista rebel of blended physical traits, perhaps those of a generic mestizo of indigenous, European, and Asian background. The central androgynous figure has exaggerated male (hands) and female (eyes) characteristics. Staring out at us relentlessly, he or she

Figure 10.3   A Zapatista serigraph that symbolizes the indigenous and nationalist goals of the Movement. (Courtesy of Gary H. Gossen.)

proudly raises an indigenous staff of authority (*not* a gun) that is sprouting a native jungle leaf. The surrounding ambiance is also jungle vegetation; even the signature Zapatista mask (worn by the subject) is of vegetal jungle origin. The red bromeliad leaf that forms the mask merges on the guerrilla subject's left hand into the red fabric of an unfurled Mexican flag, with its well-known eagle/serpent/nopal cactus motif shown in the white field. The green section of the tricolor flag is made up of the jungle leaf sprouting from the subject's staff of authority.

Even though the piece speaks eloquently for itself, we note that the autochthonous origins of the Mexican nation and the Zapatista movement, together with the Zapatistas' desired organic integration with the Mexican national idea, are all unambiguously portrayed here. Entirely composed in the hues of the tricolor of the Mexican flag, the generic Zapatista subject seems to embody the links between the natural, the magical, the political, the social, and the heroic that also embody the Mexican nation.

SUGGESTED READINGS

COLLIER, GEORGE A. in collaboration with Elizabeth Quaratiello 1999 *Basta! Land and the Zapatista Rebellion in Chiapas.* Revised edition [original 1994]. Oakland: Food First Books.

EARLE, DUNCAN, AND JEANNE SIMONELLI 2005 *Uprising of Hope: Sharing the Zapatista Journey to Alternative Development.* Walnut Creek, California: AltaMira Press.

HIGGINS, NICHOLAS P. 2004 *Understanding the Chiapas Rebellion: Modernist Visions and the Invisible Indian.* Austin: University of Texas Press.

MARCOS, Subcomandante and EZLN 1995 *Shadows of Tender Fury: The Letters and Communiqués of Subcomandante Marcos and the Zapatista Army of National Liberation.* Trans. by Frank Bardacke, Leslie López, and the Watsonville, California, Human Rights Committee. Introduction by John Ross. New York: Monthly Review Press.

MARCOS, Subcomandante and EZLN 2001 *Our Word Is Our Weapon: Selected Writings of Subcomandante Insurgente Marcos.* Edited by Juana Ponce de León. Foreword by José Saramago. New York: Seven Stories Press.

MONTEJO, VICTOR D. 2005 *Maya Intellectual Renaissance: Identity, Representation, and Leadership.* Austin: University of Texas Press.

NASH, JUNE C. 2001 *Mayan Visions: The Quest for Autonomy in an Age of Globalization.* London: Routledge.

ROSS, JOHN 1994 *Rebellion from the Roots: Indian Uprising in Chiapas.* Munroe, Maine: Common Courage Press.

ROSS, JOHN 1995 The EZLN, A History: Miracles, Coyunturas, Communiqués. Introduction to Subcomandante Marcos and EZLN, *Shadows of Tender Fury: Letters and Communiqués of Subcomandante Marcos and the Ejército Zapatista de Liberación Nacional.* New York: Monthly Review Press.

RUS, JAN, ROSALVA AÍDA HERNÁNDEZ CASTILLO, AND SHANNAN L. MATTIACE (eds.) 2003 *Mayan Lives, Mayan Utopias: The Indigenous Peoples of Chiapas and the Zapatista Rebellion.* Lanham, Maryland: Rowman and Littlefield Publishers.

STEPHEN, LYNN 2002 *Zapata Lives! Histories and Cultural Politics in Southern Mexico.* Berkeley: University of California Press.

WATANABE, JOHN M., AND EDWARD F. FISCHER (eds.) 2004 *Pluralizing Ethnography: Comparison and Representation in Maya Cultures, Histories, and Identities.* Santa Fe: School of American Research Press, and Oxford: James Currey.

WOMACK, JOHN JR. 1999 *Rebellion in Chiapas: An Historical Reader.* New York: New Press.

Unit 4: MESOAMERICAN CULTURAL FEATURES

Chapter 11
Language and Languages
of Mesoamerica

Modern Mesoamerica is an area of great linguistic diversity. Although Spanish is the dominant language of the region, about 100 Native American languages are still spoken within its borders, and English is the official language of Belize. The study of these languages has provided a great deal of information about the cultures, histories, and relationships among Mesoamerican peoples. The native languages of Mesoamerica also share certain linguistic properties that distinguish them from languages to the north and south, and help define one part of what it is to be Mesoamerican.

THE DIVERSITY OF MESOAMERICAN LANGUAGES

The indigenous languages of Mesoamerica are listed in Figure 11.1. Any such list is to some extent subjective. Two different types of speech are considered to be the same language if speakers of one type understand speakers of the other; the two types of speech are *mutually intelligible* dialects of a single language. If speakers of the two types of speech cannot understand one another, the two languages are considered to be distinct languages. These are the clearcut cases.

The subjective element enters when people understand one another partially. People with different purposes make systematically different judgments. For example, missionaries may want to provide everyone with a Bible that they can read and understand; different languages or dialects can be defined by whether their speakers understand a single translation of the Bible well enough. For anthropologists, it may be more important to know the extent to which people in contact—for example, in markets—can make themselves understood while using their own language. The list given in Figure 11.1 reflects this general type of perspective.

The languages given in Figure 11.1 are *classified,* or grouped into *language families*. A language family is a grouping of languages based upon their degree of mutual relationship. The type of relationship involved is historical (descent from a common ancestor) and involves the idea of language change.

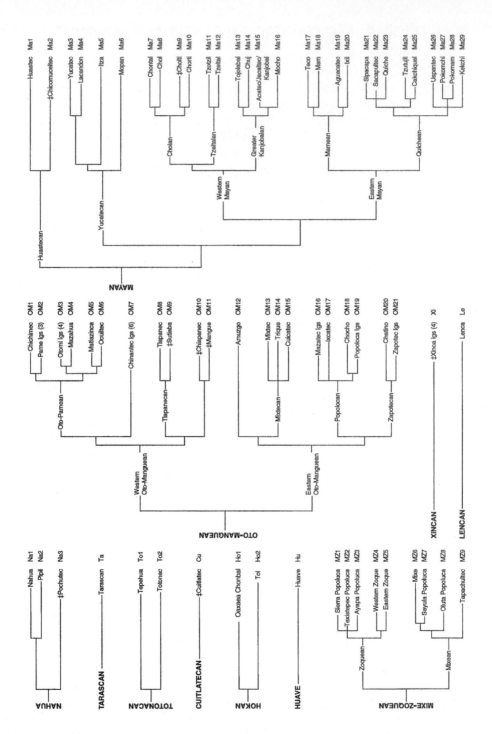

Figure 11.1 Family trees of Mesoamerican languages. Labels by language names are keys to Figure 11.2. ‡ means "extinct."

All languages are constantly changing. In time, a language changes so much that speakers of its different dialects can no longer understand each other. In cases in which we have written records over a long period of time, current speakers of a language cannot understand texts in an ancestor of that language that date from about 1,000 years ago (such as *Beowulf,* c. A.D. 900) but have only a little difficulty with texts from about 500 years ago (such as Thomas More, c. A.D. 1500).

We say that two languages are members of the same language family if they descend from a single, common ancestor language. The ancestor languages that gave rise to the different languages of Mesoamerica no longer exist, but we can draw conclusions about their properties by comparing the properties of the languages that are descended from them and *reconstructing* a hypothetical ancestral form of the language.

Linguists refer to these reconstructed versions of ancestor languages as *protolanguages.* The extinct language that gave rise to the modern Mayan languages, for example, is called *proto-Mayan;* the ancestor of the Zapotecan languages is *proto-Zapotecan;* and so on. Every indigenous Mesoamerican language is a member of one of eleven such families: Some are families of several languages, whereas others (*isolates*) consist of a single language. The locations of these units and their member languages are indicated in Figure 11.2. Their sizes, in terms of the number of languages composing them, is quite varied. The Oto-Manguean group is the largest and most diverse, consisting of at least forty distinct languages; the Cuitlatec, Huave, and **Tarascan** families have a single member each.

Two of the language groups listed here are connected to language families outside Mesoamerica. The Nahua group is a branch of a larger language family, Uto-Aztecan, whose other branches are found much further to the north, in northwestern Mexico and the southwestern United States. Many linguists believe that there is a very diverse linguistic stock called Hokan whose members are distantly related to one another. Most languages in this group are located along the Pacific coast of the United States. If Hokan is a valid genetic grouping, Tol in Honduras and Chontal of Oaxaca would be members of it. (Box 11.1 describes the history of one Native American language that falls on the margins of the Mesoamerican tradition, having arrived after the Spanish invasion.)

The languages of Mesoamerica have been written in European script since shortly after the Spanish invasion, early in the sixteenth century. The first of these records were made by Franciscan priests as part of their attempt to Christianize the indigenous population of the Americas. Beginning in the 1930s, it was again missionary linguists who mounted the first large-scale modern program of documenting Mesoamerican languages. By now most linguistic research in Mesoamerica is carried out by academic and independent anthropologists and linguists. Much of this work has been done by individual linguists, and much of it as part of large-scale academic projects. Some of these projects, as well as governments and private foundations, have devoted considerable resources and efforts to training native speakers of Mesoamerican languages as linguists. Today, several linguists working on indigenous Mesoamerican languages are in fact speakers of those languages. All of these

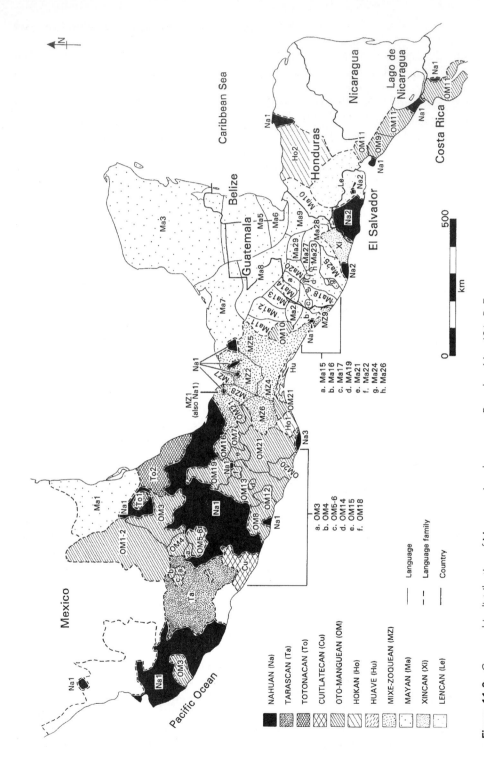

Figure 11.2 Geographic distribution of Mesoamerican languages. Based on Map 13 in R. E. Asher and Christopher Mosley's (1994) *Routledge Atlas of the World's Languages*. The key for the language labels are given in Figure 11.1.

Box 11.1 Garífuna, a Language with a Complex History

One of the most unusual languages spoken in Mesoamerica is the language known as Garífuna, or Black Carib. This language belongs to the Arawakan language family of South America, but it is currently spoken along the Caribbean coast of Belize, Guatemala, and Honduras. Before the arrival of Europeans in the Caribbean, languages belonging to two different families, Cariban and Arawakan, were spoken on the Caribbean Islands. The Arawakan people seem to have been residents of these islands for a longer period of time, but many Arawakan populations had been conquered by Cariban-speaking people.

This was the case on the island of St. Vincent, in the Lesser Antilles. An older Arawakan population had been largely overrun by Carib-speaking people. As a result of the Carib conquest, many or most Arawakan men were killed, but many Arawakan women survived and married Carib men. The women's Arawakan language (now called Garífuna) was the one that survived, but the people speaking it came to be called Black Caribs. Certain items of alternative vocabulary, stemming from Carib, are used only by men once they reach puberty.

Also on St. Vincent were a small number of European colonists and a large number of African slaves. Substantial numbers of escaped slaves mixed with the native population of the island, and there was intermarriage between the two groups. As a result, speakers of Garífuna have both African and Native American ancestry.

After revolts against the British on St. Vincent, the British government made the decision to deport all the remaining Black Carib people from St. Vincent in 1797. There were 5,080 people shipped from St. Vincent to the island of Roatán, off the coast of Honduras. The modern Garífuna people are the descendants of those who were deported from St. Vincent, and there are now tens of thousands of speakers of this language.

As a result of the unusual history of these people, a South American language spoken by people of mixed African and Native American ancestry, Garífuna, has become part of the language diversity that characterizes the Mesoamerican region today.

---

researchers have made important contributions to understanding the structures and histories of these languages.

In addition to their colonial and modern documentation, some of the languages have pre-Hispanic documentation in hieroglyphic records. The greatest number of hieroglyphic texts—a few thousand of them—come from the lowland Mayan area; and because they are so numerous, they are contributing useful information about the history of Mayan languages and writing as well as about the cultural practices they document. The texts appear to be in two different Mayan languages, Ch'olan in the south and Yucatecan in the north. It is now generally agreed that a Ch'olan language is the standard represented in texts throughout most of the lowland Mayan area. Yucatecan was the language of the northern part of the Mayan lowlands; and Yucatecan vocabulary and grammatical features appear in texts in this area, but so do some traits of the Ch'olan standard. Some scholars believe that these texts are basically written in an elite-associated Ch'olan standard, with local linguistic forms sometimes slipping through; but it is also possible that they are written in the local, Yucatecan language, with a heavy admixture of borrowed "high culture" vocabulary such as Ch'olan *ti7 y-otot* (literally "mouth of (the) house") rather than Yucatecan *chi7 y-oto:ch,* for the entrance to a temple.

A second set of hieroglyphic texts has recently been deciphered by John Juste-son and Terrence Kaufman. The texts were discovered in the region of the ancient Olmecs, but dating to the Late Preclassic period and later; the associated archaeo-logical culture, the writing system, and the language of the inscriptions has been la-beled epi-Olmec. The language of these texts is pre-proto-Zoquean, a form of Zoquean that turns out to be older than proto-Zoquean (the ancestor of the Zo-quean languages) but younger than proto-Mixe-Zoquean.

Hieroglyphic inscriptions have also been found concentrated in the Valley of Oaxaca at Monte Albán at least from Late Preclassic times, and at other sites mostly during the Classic period. Apart from some calendrical portions, these inscriptions are not as well understood as Mayan and epi-Olmec, but enough progress is being made to support the view that they are in fact written in an early form of Zapotec (see the following section on writing in ancient Mesoamerica).

THE STRUCTURE OF THE MESOAMERICAN LANGUAGES

The structure of the indigenous Mesoamerican languages is substantially different from more familiar languages like English or Spanish. Different native languages of the region also differ substantially from one another. However, the many interac-tions between speakers of different Mesoamerican languages has had an influence on the structures of the languages involved; there has been significant convergence of once-distinct features in many of these languages. In addition, many of the features shared by Mesoamerican languages are not shared with languages just across the northern or southern borders of Mesoamerica. Some of these features are discussed in this section. Many other features of Mesoamerican languages are specific to indi-vidual language families and did not spread widely. Some of these features occur fre-quently enough to merit discussion, providing a picture of the distinctiveness of the languages and cultures of the region.

It is in the rules governing the structure of sentences and phrases (*syntax*) and in the meanings of words (*semantics*) that Mesoamerican languages have converged most heavily. The systems of sounds that are used in the languages (*phonology*) and the rules governing the formation of words (*morphology*) are typically rather different from one language family to another.

Phonology

The languages of Mesoamerica tend to have consonants and vowels that are not rad-ically different from those found in familiar languages like English or Spanish. There are some exceptions, however. For example, there are cases of vowels unlike those found in most Western European languages. Many languages have a high central vowel *i*, which is somewhat like the *e* in the English word *roses*. Several Oto-Manguean languages—Otomian, Matlatzincan, and Chinantecan—have unusual vowels like *ө* and *u*, which are rare in the world's languages. They are made with the tongue in the position for *o* and *u*, but with the lips spread, rather than rounded. Such vowels are typical of languages like Vietnamese.

Distinctions are also made on the basis of the length of a vowel or whether it is followed by a glottal stop (a sound like the one that begins each syllable in the English expression "*uh-oh*"). Length and glottalization may occur on vowels in many families, such as Oto-Manguean, Mixe-Zoquean, and Mayan. Some languages make even more unusual distinctions in vowel type. For example, there are varieties of Zapotec and Totonacan that distinguish vowels according to whether they are pronounced with a creaky voice or not.

Other languages make distinctive use of tone, like that found in Chinese. In these languages, the pitch or tone with which a word is pronounced makes as much of a difference in meaning as do consonants and vowels in English. The most elaborate tone systems are found in the Oto-Manguean languages, such as Copala Trique, which has eight different tonal distinctions. Tonal distinctions are also made in a few Mayan languages, such as Yucatec. Tonal distinctions are the basis for the development of a special communicative practice called "whistled speech" (see Box 11.2).

Box 11.2 Whistled Speech in Oaxaca

Several of the native languages in the highlands of Oaxaca may take on an unusual form: They may be whistled as well as spoken! Cowan (1948) describes the following exchange, which took place in a Mazatec village:

> One day Chumi was standing idly in the doorway of our hut. Irene Flores was working around the hut. No one, it seemed, was paying any attention to the quiet, random whistlings of the boy so nonchalantly leaning against the doorpost. All of a sudden, however, Irene whirled and launched out in a terrific scolding in spoken Mazateco. The whistling had not been as aimless and innocuous as it appeared. The mischievous boy had actually been whistling very meaningful things to the girl, until she could stand the teasing no more.

Whistled speech has been observed in the Zapotec, Chinantec, and Mazatec languages. In all these languages, whistled speech relies on tonal contrasts in the language. In general, the pattern of the whistles follows the pattern of the tones in the spoken language, and is in effect a direct copy of it.

For example, in the following exchange in Mazatec, 1 shows a high tone, 4 shows a low tone, and 2 and 3 show intermediate tones:

a. Hña^1 khoa^2 ai^4-ni^3? "Where are you coming from?"
b. Ni^3.ya^2 khoa^2 ai^4-nia^3. "I'm coming from Huautla."

The whistled version of this exchange is as follows:

a. 1 2 4 3?
b. 3 2 2 4 3.

Notice that the pitch of each whistle is determined by the tone of the corresponding syllable in the spoken version of the exchange. Whistled speech is one of the features that makes Mesoamerica especially interesting as a language area.

The consonants of Mesoamerican languages also sometimes show contrasts that are unfamiliar in European languages. Totonacan languages and several Guatemalan Mayan languages include the consonant *q*, which sounds somewhat like *k* but is articulated farther back in the mouth.

Another consonant common in Mesoamerican languages is the *glottal stop*, mentioned before. It was not spelled at all in the Spanish-based orthographies adopted for most indigenous languages in the early Colonial period (a possible exception is that in some Classical Nahuatl texts, the letter *h* was used for a sound that corresponds to glottal stops of some Nahua dialects). Today it is usually spelled by an apostrophe in practical orthographies; linguists transcribe it by an apostrophe, by a *7*, or by the linguistic symbol **ʔ**.

Other consonants occur in a few Mesoamerican language families. Nahua and Totonacan languages have a consonant usually written *tl* by nonlinguists. This sound is made with the tip of the tongue firmly against the base of the upper front teeth, as for a *t*; but when moving to the next sound, air is released at one side of the tongue while the tip of the tongue remains against the teeth. This sound is distinct from both *t* and *l*. Many nouns in colonial Nahuatl ended in this *tl* sound, and when such words were borrowed into Spanish, the final *tl* was replaced with Spanish *-te;* for example, Nahuatl *tomatl* became Spanish *tomate* "tomato." There are whole classes of consonants that are found in some (but not all) Mesoamerican language families, such as glottalized (e.g., *k'*, *t'*), aspirated (e.g., *kʰ*, *pʰ*), and palatalized (e.g., *kʸ*, *pʸ*) consonants.

One feature that is common in European languages but that is rare in the languages of Mesoamerica is a contrast between consonants based on voicing. *Voicing* refers to the vibration of the vocal cords while producing a consonant, and English has many contrasts based on voicing; for example, *b* is voiced whereas *p* is voiceless; *d* is voiced whereas *t* is voiceless; and *g* is voiced, whereas *k* is voiceless. In many Mesoamerican languages, there is no contrast between these pairs of sounds; *p* and *b* are usually treated as variant pronunciations of the same basic sound.

Morphology

In all languages, the order of elements in a word is strictly defined. Words are made up of a root element plus (usually) some number of affixes (that is, prefixes, suffixes, and infixes) that must appear in a definite order. The orders of elements within a word will, of course, vary from language to language, but there are fixed rules of order for any particular language.

In almost all Mesoamerican languages, for example, a verb contains a verbal stem plus affixes that indicate the tense-aspect of the verb. In many languages, it also contains *pronominal* affixes (*agreement markers*) that indicate the person and number of the subject (in some, also the object, if there is one). Table 11.1 shows verbs with affixes in three Mesoamerican languages.

Pronouns and pronominal affixes exhibit a number of different patterns. In general, they are based on the category of *person*, defined in terms of the participants in a speech event. Some languages have rather different pronominal systems from those found in English or Spanish. In several Mesoamerican languages, there are differ-

Table 11.1 Verbs with Affixes in Three Mesoamerican Languages

---

San Dionicio Ocotepec Zapotec:
  Rr-tèh'éh=gá=rám=nì
  HABITUAL-pick:up=while=they (animal)=it
  "While the animals were picking it up"

Classical Nahuatl:
  Ō-ti-c-āltih-ca-h
  PAST-we-him-bathe-PLUPERFECT-PLURAL
  "We had bathed him."

Tzotzil:

  Stak′ ch-a-j-kolta.
  can   INCOMPLETIVE-you-I-help
  "I can help you."

Note: The = symbol in the Zapotec example precedes clitics, words which are more loosely joined to the preceding word than other morphemes.

ences between two kinds of first person plural pronoun *(we)*. The inclusive first person plural means "we (including you)," and the exclusive first person plural means "we (not including you)." Sometimes third person pronouns distinguish between humans and nonhumans, as in several Oto-Manguean languages. However, third person pronouns are rarely distinguished by sex; that is, "he" and "she" (and often "it") are all indicated by the same pronominal affix or pronoun. Differences among pronouns based on respect are also found in many languages.

In some Oto-Manguean languages—most notably Zapotec and Mixtec—third-person pronouns are differentiated according to a variety of social categories. For example, San Lucas Quiaviní Zapotec has different third person pronouns for (1) holy persons and things (e.g. God, the saints, statues in the church, the sun, and the moon); (2) respected humans (e.g., mature community members); (3) formal humans (e.g., parents, priests, and teachers); (4) animals and young people; (5) humans or things that are near or visible; and (6) humans or things that are far off or not visible. Although San Lucas Quiaviní Zapotec distinguishes six categories here, its pronouns do not distinguish gender, so there is no difference between "he" and "she" in this language.

Notice that some of these distinctions require speakers to make explicit commitments to their judgments about the social standing of people they refer to; in this way, the grammatical structure of the language is unavoidably an active element in the construction of group relationships. Other grammatical distinctions relate to the cultural outlook or cognitive orientation of speakers. For example, when speakers of Yucatec Mayan refer to an event, they mark their statement with *evidentials,* grammatical elements that indicate whether their report of the event is based on having personally witnessed it (through any of the senses), having been told about it, or its being part of the shared cultural understandings ("common knowledge") of a community. This grammatical trait requires speakers to constantly and subconsciously monitor the sources of their knowledge and beliefs.

One unusual pattern of pronoun use is widespread enough in Mesoamerica to merit mention. This pattern is one that linguists refer to as *ergative*. In English, the same pronouns are used for both transitive subjects (*He saw him*) and intransitive subjects (*He ran*). An ergative system is one that treats transitive and intransitive subjects differently, grouping the intransitive subject together with the object. If English were an ergative language, we would still have sentences like *He saw him,* but the object pronoun would be used in intransitive sentences like *Him ran.* Mayan and Mixe-Zoquean languages show this sort of ergative pattern in their pronominal affixes.

Syntax

In most Mesoamerican language families, transitive sentences are constructed with their words in a different order than in English or Spanish. Ordinary transitive sentences place the verb (V) before the subject (S) and object (O); that is, they exhibit either VOS or VSO order, rather than the SVO order of English and Spanish. Ordinary intransitive sentences place the verb before the subject; that is, they exhibit VS order, rather than the SV order of English and Spanish.

In Table 11.2, Zapotec and Copala Trique show VSO orders, and Tzotzil shows VOS. A few languages, such as Huave, Oaxaca Chontal, and Tol, have SVO as the dominant order (and some languages like Itzaj have shifted to SVO as a basic word order after centuries of Spanish influence), but few languages have SOV as their primary word order. This is a distinctive characteristic of the region, since most languages on the northern and southern borders of Mesoamerica do have SOV order.

The nearly universal occurrence of VO order in the Mesoamerican languages today is one of the features pointing to intensive intercultural interaction in this region over a long period of time. In some cases we have clear evidence that this verb-first order is a change from an earlier pattern. Nahua, for example, which now has the Mesoamerican verb-initial order, is the southernmost branch of the Uto-Aztecan language family. The other members of this rather large and diverse family generally have SOV as their basic word order, and this was probably the original order in Nahua

Table 11.2 Word Order in Three Mesoamerican Languages

San Dionicio Ocotepec Zapotec:
> Cá-ldì'í   bèh'cw   ní'=nì'.
> CONTINUATIVE-lick   dog foot=REFLEXIVE
> "The man dog is licking its own foot."

Copala Trique:
> Qui-ranj[5]   Mariaa[4] chraa[5].
> COMPLETIVE-buy Maria   tortilla.
> "Maria bought a tortilla."

Tzotzil:
> 7i-s-pet   lok'el 7antz   ti   t'ul-e.
> COMPLETIVE-it-carry away   woman the rabbit-CLITIC
> "The rabbit carried away the woman."

as well. It appears that Nahuas changed their word order after they entered the Mesoamerican world (see Box 11.7 later in the chapter). The persistence of SOV order in Tarascan is one of several ways that Tarascans' practices were somewhat independent from those of other Mesoamericans.

A similar shift can be demonstrated in the Mixe-Zoquean language family. For decades it was thought that all Mixe-Zoquean languages had verb-first word order, but other grammatical features suggested that at an earlier stage, they had SOV order. In the early 1990s, this earlier SOV stage was confirmed in epi-Olmec hieroglyphic texts, written in Zoquean, at least as late as A.D. 162. Since then, linguistic fieldwork has shown that Zoque of Santa María Chimalapa—the most conservative of the Zoquean languages—still preserves this order today. Proto-Zoquean must also have preserved SOV order, since Chimalapa Zoque descends from it; SOV order was preserved in the epi-Olmec area at least into the Classic period. It was therefore individual Zoquean languages that changed to verb-initial order, after proto-Zoquean split into separate Zoque and Gulf Zoquean branches; this was probably no earlier than the Late Classic period (on early Zoqueanspeaking Mesoamericans, see Chapter 1).

Although verb-initial orders are the most common or basic orders, it is usual for alternative orders to be used for special purposes. In the case of intransitive verbs in the epi-Olmec texts, subjects that control the action described by the verb usually precede (SV), as they do in a transitive (SOV) sentence, whereas those that undergo the action usually follow (VS). More generally, it is rather common in verb-initial languages for the subject to be moved to the front of the sentence when it is being emphasized. In many languages, *any* ordering of subject, verb, and object is possible, each order emphasizing a different notion.

Other features of the grammar of Mesoamerican languages we summarize more briefly as follows. When nouns (for example, "dog") are possessed, as in "the man's dog," the typical pattern in Mesoamerican languages is to say "(his) dog the man," or, less commonly, "the man (his) dog." The Kaqchikel and Zapotec examples in Table 11.3 show these patterns.

In many Mesoamerican languages, words that correspond in function/meaning to locative prepositions in English (for example, "on," "under," "inside") are based on or are identical to words for parts of the body. For example, one word may be used for both "head" and "on"; another may be used for both "back" and "behind." In some languages, this may mean that there are no locative prepositions, and that body-part nouns are used in their place. In other languages, it is better to say that locative prepositions are a separate part of speech, but many of these prepositions are morphologically identical to body-part nouns. The Zapotec example in Table 11.3 shows that the same word, *dèhjts*, is both "back" and "behind."

Numerals have a *vigesimal*, or base-20 structure; rather than counting in decimal units that are powers of ten (10s, 100s, 1000s), as we normally do, Mesoamericans count with vigesimal units that are powers of 20 (20s, 400s, 8000s). Thus a number like fifty-five is expressed as "two twenties plus fifteen." The Zapotec and Classical Nahuatl examples in Table 11.3 show vigesimal structure. (For more detail on this kind of counting, see Box 11.8 later in the chapter.)

Table 11.3   Other Grammatical Features in Mesoamerican Languages

San Dionicio Ocotepec Zapotec:

Zúú   béh'cw   dèhjts   yù'ù.
stand   dog   back   house
"The dog is standing behind the house"

dèhjts   Juààny
back   Juan
"Juan's back"

Gááld-bí-tsùù
twenty-with-ten
"thirty"

Kaqchikel:

ru-tz'i'   ri a   Xwan.
his-dog   the YOUNGER:MALE   Juan
"Juan's dog"

Classical Nahuatl:

ōm-pōhualli on-caxtōlli
two-twenty   and-fifteen
"fifty-five"

The words for vigesimal units are typically the names of various kinds of containers, bundles, or packages. For example, up until indigenous expressions for large numbers were largely replaced by Spanish numerical expressions, the word for "8,000" often either came from or became used for gunny sacks (or skirts) such as might have been used to carry large numbers of cacao kernels.

Other Typical Characteristics

Also widespread are idiomatic expressions that occur throughout the Mesoamerican languages through the process of *loan translation*. This is a process in which an idiomatic expression—for example, the use of "mouth of house" to mean "door"—is translated word for word into other languages and used with the same idiomatic meaning. In addition, some loan translations consist of the use of a word with one meaning for another meaning related to the first metaphorically or in an indirect way, if at all. Several such loan translations are found in Mesoamerica, but are rare beyond its language borders. Examples are "mother of hand" = "thumb," "child of hand" = "finger"; "edge" = "mouth"; "god excrement" or "sun excrement" = "gold" or "silver"; "water mountain" = "town"; "deer snake" = "boa constrictor"; "awake" = "alive"; "big star" = "Venus"; and "sun" (= "day") = "festival," with derived forms meaning "shape-shifter." Some loan translations reflect widespread Mesoamerican practices or beliefs. For example, the word for "day" often means "name," because people were named for the day of the ritual calendar on which they were born; and the ritual calendar day (or god) that named an indigenous year was referred to as the "ruler" of the year (see Chapter 1).

All of these characteristics typify the Mesoamerican language families, and all are uncharacteristic of the languages beyond the borders of the pre-Hispanic Mesoamerican region. They are ways of speaking and thinking about the world that are part of what unifies Mesoamerica culturally. Other characteristics that are widespread in Mesoamerica are found also in languages in adjacent areas; they characterize but do not distinguish Mesoamerica as a linguistic region. For example, kinship terms and body parts are normally possessed, and when they are not possessed, a special prefix or suffix is added. Semantic equivalences typical of the region, but also found outside it, include the use of the same word for "hand" and "arm;" that is, the concepts are not distinct.

Still other characteristics are widely shared among Mesoamerican languages and are rare or absent across its borders, but are missing in only one language family. In such cases, Mayan is most often the family in which the characteristic is missing; this family begins the southeastern border of the ancient Mesoamerican world.

LANGUAGE VARIATION AND CHANGE

Dialects of Native Languages

Almost all indigenous languages in Mesoamerica occur in more than one form. In some areas, linguistic diversity is so great that every town has its own dialect or even its own language. This is the case, for example, in much of the Guatemalan highlands. For example, since the late 1700s, when lists were made of the languages spoken in each town, Uspantek has been spoken in just one community; and, in general, each distinct town in the Kaqchikel region has a distinct form of Kaqchikel. The situation is similar for many of the Oto-Manguean languages, especially in Oaxaca. In other areas, linguistic diversity is quite low. The Yucatec language, for example, covers a large part of the Yucatán Peninsula.

Dialect differences are social as well as linguistic facts. When distinct forms of a language are found in different areas, people from one area may have difficulty understanding people from other areas. But this difficulty is not equally great for all participants; more often than not, tests of mutual intelligibility of dialects indicate that speakers of, say, dialect A understand speakers of dialect B more than speakers of dialect B understand speakers of dialect A. Where does this asymmetry come from? It often appears to reflect the density of communication.

Communication is pursued most with those one understands the best, all other things being equal. This structuring of communication has two effects. Linguistically, changes in poorly understood dialects are less likely to be noticed and adopted than changes in well-understood dialects, and so the least similar dialects become increasingly dissimilar. Socially, decreasing communication among communities reinforces social distance between them. This is a major trend in dialect evolution; it is the source of the origin of new languages from old, and of the development of language families out of parent languages. When this event happens, the effect of the communication bottleneck is that the most closely related languages tend to be located next to one another. The geographic pattern of location is consistent with the degree of relationship among languages unless one or more of the social groups migrates from its ancestral location.

All the changes just discussed have the effect of increasing social and linguistic distance. Some changes, however, have the effect of *integrating* social groups and *decreasing* the distance between dialects. These are changes that take place when speakers of one dialect copy the vocabulary or speech patterns of speakers of another. Those doing the copying are speakers of the *borrowing dialect;* those being copied are speakers of the *source dialect.* Eventually, some of the copying being done will be internal copying by some speakers of the borrowing dialect of the patterns acquired by other speakers of that dialect, which were ultimately acquired by copying the source language.

The differentiation between languages or dialects, and between social groups, occurs probably most often as a result of changes occurring within separate speech communities that are not interacting intensively. In some cases, however, continuing interaction helps to drive the differentiation between dialects. Leanne Hinton (1987) has shown this for the Mixtec spoken at Chalcatongo and at San Miguel, the next town along the main local highway. There is a social differentiation between the Mixtecs of San Miguel and surrounding hamlets, who are committed to and involved in traditional, local culture, and the Mixtecs of Chalcatongo, who are modernizing and ladinoizing via participation in wider economic networks. The dialects of San Miguel and Chalcatongo turn out to be most similar in the more distant parts of these communities; near the border between the municipios, the differences in the dialects are exaggerated. These Mixtec-speaking communities are using language differences to display social commitments and to call attention to social differences between them. The greater the extent of interaction among members of these groups, the greater the usefulness of devices such as the symbolism of dialect difference for reinforcing group identity and distinctness.

The process of convergence through borrowing can be illustrated by Q'eqchi', a Mayan language spoken in the highlands of Guatemala. Q'eqchi' has been spreading since the Spanish invasion and probably before. The town of Cobán is the leading economic center, and its dialect is the most highly valued by Q'eqchi' speakers generally; that is, it is the *prestige dialect.* As a result, younger speakers of other Q'eqchi' dialects are copying some of the changes that are taking place or that have already taken place in Cobán. For example, *w* is pronounced as *kw* in Cobán; this change is also being generalized, with *y* being "strengthened" in a parallel way and pronounced as *ty.* These changes are so recent that younger and older speakers of Cobán Q'eqchi' pronounce *w* and *y* differently, even as the change is spreading to other communities. Other, older changes are well entrenched throughout Cobán, and are widespread in Q'eqchi'; for example, speakers of almost all Q'eqchi' dialects have shortened their original long vowels.

These changes in Q'eqchi' are typical of patterns of language change not only in Mesoamerica but also throughout the world. A community that has a socially favored position is a center of innovations that are adopted by its neighbors. These neighbors typically lag somewhat behind the innovating center. Changed forms at first exist in variation with the original forms, but eventually replace them. Such changes may be recognized and copied not only by speakers of different dialects but even by speakers of different languages. Relatively casual contact is enough for the borrowing of vocabulary, especially for items or concepts that are newly introduced to the borrowing group. Changes in pronunciation or grammar—that is, in the structure of a language—always involve intensive interaction among speakers of the source and borrowing languages.

In ancient times, the same processes are assumed to have been at work. When linguists detect the effects of these processes, they thereby provide evidence for the existence of interaction among speakers of the languages involved, for the intensity and duration of that interaction, and for the nature of that interaction. Historical reconstruction from the imprint of culture on language is discussed later in this chapter.

Language Endangerment

There is some documentation from the early sixteenth century of languages from most of the different language families of Mesoamerica. On the basis of these and later records, we know that some languages once spoken in the region are no longer spoken. Most of the indigenous languages of Mesoamerica today are seriously endangered. We also know that language is so much a part of a people's cultural identity that they rarely give up their own language willingly, that is, without having been subjected to large-scale, invasive, and coercive social processes.

Why have so many languages of Mesoamerica died out? A partial answer is that in nation-states, minority languages that do not have political and cultural autonomy are *always* endangered. As a result, work on language rights and efforts to improve the long-term outlook for endangered languages around the world is now a priority for many governments, foundations, and human rights organizations.

In Mesoamerica, the most seriously endangered languages are *moribund (dying):* These languages are virtually restricted to private use among elderly adults. Next most seriously endangered are *obsolescent* (or *dwindling*) languages: Few or no children are learning these languages, but adults use them in a variety of both public and private contexts as in family settings, among friends, and at ceremonies such as weddings; and in civic events, such as political rallies, though usually not in speech events that are part of governmental action. The least endangered languages are *threatened:* Not all children are learning the language, and Spanish is becoming more widely known and used in response to heavy external pressure for bilingualism, but the language is used in all private and public contexts (apart from government and law). Some of these languages are moving toward obsolescence, with their transmission to children decreasing and/or the range of contexts of their use being reduced. All indigenous languages in Mesoamerica are endangered in at least this way.

The main direct cause of language endangerment and ultimately of language loss is a process called *language shift:* The speakers of one language begin using another language in place of it. Typically such speakers are at first bilingual in their native language and in Spanish, whose use is initially the only means of engaging with national and provincial institutions, and later with nonlocal commercial interests (often forced upon them through national priorities); the use of Spanish thereby becomes economically or socially advantageous. In a few cases, the second language is not Spanish, but rather an expanding native language such as Q'eqchi' Mayan or Otomi.

The use of native languages is typically associated with traditional practices and institutions, whereas the use of Spanish is associated with the penetration of mestizo (or ladino) practices and institutions, including especially regional and national political and economic systems. Survival or advancement in the local economy via participation in wider economic systems is often facilitated by the use of Spanish. Partly this is the case because Spanish aids communication among speakers of different indigenous languages, since bilingualism in Spanish is widespread across all languages of Mesoamerica. Partly, however, it is because native languages are usually stigmatized by ladinos, similar to the way nonstandard dialects of English are stigmatized among white-collar workers in the United States.

Native language use has often been discouraged by national policies. Education and scholarship in Mexico and Central America have been conducted almost entirely in European languages (mostly Spanish), so that there has been little opportunity for speakers of the native languages to achieve literacy in their own languages; and the use of indigenous languages by children in the schools has often been suppressed. Furthermore, the social infrastructure has been such that, at least until recently, relatively few of the indigenous peoples of Mesoamerica had access to any education at all.

In the twentieth century, many indigenous peoples in Mesoamerica were unfortunately caught up in political violence and were targeted for kidnapping and murder, in part because they spoke native languages and were thus viewed as subversive. In such situations, the choice of which language to use often depends upon the nature of the speech situation and on who is involved in it. Not only in Mesoamerica but also throughout the world, the range of contexts of use of the native language may be reduced. A common pattern is for the native language to be favored in private settings—for example, within the family or among close friends—whereas Spanish may be preferred in public and community-oriented settings, and in interactions with more distant acquaintances, or with strangers. An ultimately foreign *language ideology* may develop, according to which the local language is not seen as a fit instrument for formal or "important" types of communication.

Another process involved in language loss is an outgrowth of the one just described. When the native language is seen as a hindrance to social and economic advancement, parents may speak only Spanish to their children. Once children no longer learn the native language of their people, it is moribund. In Mesoamerica, this process turns out to contribute in a much more devastating way to language loss than does the act of language choice among bilinguals.

There are several native languages that few, if any, children learn. Among Mixe-Zoquean languages, for example, Texistepec Popoluca is spoken by only about 100 persons, all in their sixties or older. There are now fewer than 20 fluent speakers of Oluta Popoluca, all elderly; and less than 10 speakers of Ayapanec, a Gulf Zoquean language at the northeastern boundary of Mixe-Zoquean territory. More rarely, other languages are learned by children, but only after they learn Spanish as a second language. This situation was usual as of 1950 among the lowland Chontal of Oaxaca.

The Impact of Spanish on Native Languages

The above mentioned language choices are often tied up with ethnic identity. Bilingual speakers may choose to speak Spanish rather than an indigenous language in some contexts because they wish to identify in one way or another with those outside the native community. And when parents speak to their children in Spanish, this choice may reflect a shifting of certain kinds of social commitments, or even of ethnic identity, from the local, indigenous community to a wider regional or national level.

The potential for breakdown of ethnic identity, however, can be overemphasized. The relation between language and ethnicity may have been closer in the past, before Spanish began to replace native languages in large portions of most native groups. Today, however, language, culture, and ethnic identity cannot be equated. With the replacement of native languages by the processes just described, a native language may come to be spoken by a minority of members of the once-associated cultural and ethnic groups, with Spanish now the dominant language. Even so, those who have grown up in the community as monolingual speakers of Spanish may have a strong sense of community identity, and the indigenous language of the community may still serve as a shared, unifying *symbol* of group identity. For example, almost all of the 26,000 Sayuleños consider themselves to be Indian, and they know that they have always been different from everyone else, even though only a small proportion of them speak the Sayula Popoluca language. Similarly, in the town of San Lucas, near Antigua, Guatemala, no one speaks Kaqchikel any more, but the women still wear clothing that only indigenous people wear. Nonetheless, when a community's native language is in the process of disappearing, this condition is always a source of distress for a significant proportion of the population: There is a feeling that something important in their lives is being lost.

Since the arrival of the Europeans in Mesoamerica, then, native languages have suffered greatly in terms of numbers of speakers and social status. Many languages have become extinct, and very few of the millions of speakers of indigenous languages in Mesoamerica have been literate in native languages. However, in the last few decades, there has been an upsurge of interest in and attention to the native languages of the area. In Guatemala several million persons speak Mayan languages, and as a result of the combined efforts of native speakers and linguists, efforts are now under way to provide bilingual education in Spanish and in local Mayan languages (Q'eqchi, K'iche', Kaqchikel, Tzutujil, Poqomam, Mam, and others). Such efforts require the production of textbooks and reading materials in Mayan languages; whereas the goals of the project are to increase literacy in both Spanish and native languages. A standardized orthography for use in such materials, proposed by the Academia de Lenguas Mayas de Guatemala, has been given official status by the government. Box 11.3 provides a parallel example of how the Zapotec language is being promoted in present-day Mexico.

Box 11.3   Using the Zapotec Language Today

The Zapotec language has emerged as an important literary and political force in Oaxaca, Mexico. In Juchitán, Oaxaca, many local political figures make campaign speeches in Zapotec, and the use of the Zapotec language has become a symbol of Juchitán's resistance to Mexico's ruling government. Residents of Juchitán have also produced a Zapotec language periodical, *Guchachi Reza* ("Slit-open Iguana"), reflecting the growing Zapotec language literacy in Oaxaca. The following poem by Gabriel López Chiñas exemplifies modern pride in the Zapotec language:

> They say that Zapotec is going,
> no one will speak it now,
> it's dead they say, it's dying,
> the Zapotec language.
> The Zapotec language
> the devil take it away,
> now the sophisticated Zapotecs
> speak Spanish only.
> Ah, Zapotec, Zapotec!
> those who put you down
> forget how much their mothers
> loved you with a passion!
> Ah, Zapotec, Zapotec!
> language that gives me life,
> I know you'll die away
> on the hour of the death of the sun.

(From Gabriel López Chiñas, *El zapoteco* In *La flor de la palabra*, edited by Victor de la Cruz, pp.68–69. Mexico City: Premia Editora. English translation by Nathaniel Tarn, in *Zapotec Struggles: Histories, Politics, and Representations from Juchitán, Oaxaca*, edited by Howard Campbell, Leigh Binford, Miguel Bartolomé, and Alicia Barabas, p. 211. Washington, D.C.: Smithsonian Institution, 1993.)

Spanish has affected the vocabulary and phonology, and often the syntax, of many of the indigenous languages of Mesoamerica. Some have borrowed a great deal of Spanish vocabulary, especially for items and ideas introduced since the Spanish invasion, such as horses, chickens, and rifles. For example, the San Lucas Quiaviní Zapotec word for "horse" is *caba'i*, borrowed from Spanish *caballo*. Other languages have resisted the incorporation of Spanish vocabulary and have created new words from native roots and affixes. For example, the Kaqchikel word for "horse" is *kej*, which originally meant "deer." In Mayan languages in general, chickens were referred to by the word for turkey, whereas turkeys were referred to by this word plus a modifier or affix. Rifles were named either with the term for blowgun or with new words or expressions made of native elements as in Ch'ol *jul-on-ib'*, "shooting instrument" (based on *jul,* "to shoot, to pierce"). Today, the Academia de las Lenguas Mayas de Guatemala is promoting the replacement of some Spanish loans by Mayan-based words and expressions.

In the section on the phonology of Mesoamerican languages, we point out that the sound systems of these languages differ from that of Spanish. When Spanish words are adopted, indigenous languages often *nativize* them; that is, they adapt the pronunciation of the Spanish form to the native pattern. Tzotzil *pale* and Oluta Popoluca *pane* are examples, taken over from Spanish *padre,* "priest." This adaptation happens not only to individual Spanish sounds but also to sequences of them; for example, *cuentas,* "counters, rosary beads" was adopted as *wentax* in Yokot'an (Chontal Mayan) and several other languages. More recent borrowings, in an era of massive bilingualism in Spanish, are often not nativized as fully as in these examples.

As often happens elsewhere in the world, indigenous languages sometimes adopt Spanish words with their Spanish pronunciation, or a close approximation to it. The result is that some words in the language have *loan phonemes* and phoneme sequences (like consonant clusters) that occur only in Spanish loans to the language. When speakers use words with nonnative sounds or sound patterns, this usage marks the usage as a *hispanism.* This may orient people's attitudes toward the topic addressed through the use of the hispanic rather than nativized forms. Hispanic pronunciation is normally found only with extensive bilingualism in Spanish and the native languages.

WRITING IN ANCIENT MESOAMERICA

Ancient Mesoamerican societies were evidently unique in the New World in that most had some form of writing. Writing existed among speakers of lowland Mayan languages in southeastern Mexico, Guatemala, and Belize; among Zoquean speakers in southern Veracruz and Chiapas; among Zapotec speakers in the Valley of Oaxaca; among Mixtec speakers in Oaxaca; and among Nahuatl speakers in the Valley of Mexico. Texts are also found in other areas of Mesoamerica—at Kaminaljuyú and Izapa in Guatemala, at El Tajín in Veracruz, and at Xochicalco in Morelos, for example—but the languages associated with these scripts have yet to be determined. The content of these hieroglyphic texts is discussed in Chapter 1. In this chapter we sketch some principles of Mesoamerican writing as they relate to language.

How Languages Were Represented

All Mesoamerican scripts made use of *logograms,* signs that represented whole words or roots. This use could be through direct depiction (for example, a picture of a knot for the Zapotec day name Knot); depiction of an associated concept (for example, the wind god's face for the Aztec day name Wind); or by abstract signs. This practice may be the source of all other types of representation found earlier in Mesoamerican iconographic systems.

All well-understood Mesoamerican scripts also used *rebus* representation: Two words pronounced the same, or almost the same, could be spelled by the same sign, though that sign depicted the idea behind only one of the words. In ancient low-land Mayan languages, for example, *tu:n* meant "year-ending." Another word pronounced *tu:n* referred to cylindrical objects, including windpipes and long wooden musical instruments such as flutes, trumpets, and split-log drums. Although the similarity in pronunciation was only coincidental, the first word was sometimes spelled, like the second, using a sign that depicted a split log drum.

These principles may suffice to account for all pre-Hispanic Aztec and Mixtec writings. These representational principles, which served within complex systems of narrative pictographic iconography ("picture writing"), named the gods, peoples, and places whose depictions they accompanied, as well as the dates in the ritual calendar of the events that were shown. Although quite serviceable for conveying such information, rebus and logographic spelling was quite ambiguous from the point of view of linguistic representation, with many grammatical affixes and words left unrepresented (see Box 11.4).

Fully *textual* systems were more explicit in representing such grammatical elements, typically with *phonetic* signs that represented not words or roots, but simple syllables consisting of a consonant followed by a vowel (*CV* signs), or occasionally signs for syllables consisting of a consonant, a vowel, and another consonant (*CVC* signs). *CV* signs were heavily used in Mayan and epi-Olmec writing, and to a lesser extent in the Zapotec writing of Monte Albán and environs. In any case, for the purpose of decipherment, it is methodologically important to hypothesise at first that basic grammatical morphemes are explicitly represented.

Because words in proto-Zapotec consisted almost exclusively of *CV* syllables, writing with *CV* signs was well suited to this kind of phonetic writing. However, it was ex-

---

Box 11.4 Ethnocentrism and Writing Systems

Symbol systems that indicate some words or parts of words but do not indicate other words or grammatical suffixes are sometimes referred to as "mnemonic devices" or jogs to the memory. Others characterize such systems as failed or poor attempts to convey their languages; moreover, they remark on how surprising it is that the inadequacies could persist for centuries without being corrected by, for example, making fuller use of phonetic representation. These perspectives mistake the organization and purpose of this kind of symbolic representation, denigrating it as a defective version of our own system or of other systems that are more explicit or complete in what they represent about a language.

It seems unlikely that the Aztec and Mixtec writing systems were ever meant to represent spoken utterances. What is referred to as "writing" in these representational systems was a means of identifying gods, peoples, places, and dates. Language was a resource for this task: The roots in place names, for example, were enough to identify a place for someone who knew those names. Ambiguities in these systems do not make them any more defective than does ambiguity in word meaning; in context, we understand which meaning of a word makes the most sense, and the ancient Mixtecs and Aztecs could do the same with their system of representation. In other words, these people made effective *use* of language to help them convey important information; precise replication of the stream of speech was not their goal.

ploited mostly to spell grammatical elements, and only sparingly used to spell the stems of words.

All Ch'olan and Yucatecan words ended with a consonant, so that every word contained at least one syllable that ended in a consonant. There is an inherent structural mismatch between a spoken language whose syllables can end in consonants and a phonetic spelling using symbols for a consonant followed by a vowel (*CV* signs). Whenever a word contains a consonant that is not followed by a vowel, either a vowel will be spelled that is not actually to be pronounced (like that of the sign *pi* in epi-Olmec *7i-ki-pi-wu,* spelling Zoquean *7i-kip-wu,* "he fought him," or the sign *wa* in epigraphic Mayan *ka-ka-wa,* spelling Mayan *kakaw* "cacao"); similarly, a consonant will not be spelled that *is* to be pronounced (like *j* in Zoquean *wej-pa,* "he shouts," spelled *we-pa* in epi-Olmec, or the *h* in lowland Mayan *b'uhk,* spelled *b'u-ku,* "clothes" in epigraphic Mayan).

Rather firm rules or practices governed the choice among these alternatives in epi-Olmec writing. Weak consonants (*j, w, y,* and *7*) were not spelled out except before vowels, whereas almost all other consonants were spelled in every context; and, when an extra vowel was inserted, it matched the last preceding vowel. Practices in Mayan writing seem to have been more complex and flexible. Weak consonants (*h* and *7*) were rarely spelled before consonants and were variably spelled at the ends of words, but seemingly any consonant might not be spelled at the end of a syllable, perhaps especially before the second element of a compound. The principles governing the selection of unpronounced vowels in *CV* spellings for syllable-final consonants are debated; some scholars believe that vowel choice indicated whether the last preceding vowel was short, long (or otherwise "heavy"), whereas others believe that the vowel in these spellings was one that typically appeared in suffixes that were attached to the word.

One rather common variety of spelling combined both logographic and syllabic principles through the use of a logogram with a *phonetic complement.* In effect, the logogram spelled the word, and the syllabic sign—the phonetic component—indicated part of the pronunciation of that word. For example, the epi-Olmec word for "ten" was *mak;* that for "sky" was *tzap.* In the name of the Venus god Ten Sky, the syllabic sign *ma* was placed before the numeral *10,* indicating that the word for "ten" begins with the syllable *ma.* Phonetic complements can also spell final consonants, using the same practices as in fully phonetic spellings discussed in the previous paragraph. For example, the sign *pa* follows the sign SKY on one occasion, agreeing with the final consonant of *tzap* ("sky"), and with the extra vowel selected to agree with that of *tzap* (see Box 11.5).

How Writing Evolved

The origin of writing was a process that transformed a symbolic system in which language played no crucial role to one in which language was a significant resource for interpreting symbolic statements. The precursor system cannot have used much phonetic representation, since that kind of convention does make crucial use of language. Just what system or systems may have contributed directly to the emergence of writing

Box 11.5   Deciphering Epi-Olmec

Decipherment is a process of accounting for the patterns of sign use in a writing system. In phonetic writing, this usually means accounting for individual signs as corresponding to particular sounds, and for sequences of signs as corresponding to sequences of sounds. If the language is known, the grammatical structure and vocabulary of that language become substantial clues that can be used to decipher the script. These were major clues in the recent decipherment of a hieroglyphic script of ancient southern Veracruz by John Justeson and Terrence Kaufman.

For geographic and historical reasons, most researchers recognized that the script probably represented an ancient Mixe-Zoquean language. All verbs in these languages began with one or two of a small number of prefixes and with one of a small number of suffixes, most of which are pronounced as *CV* syllables. In fact, the most common verb prefix and the most common noun prefix were both pronounced *7i-;* the most common verb suffix was *-wʉ.* This made it easy to recognize the signs that represented these syllables. This, in turn, made it possible to begin an analysis of the text: to identify its nouns and verbs, which led to the identification of additional noun and verb affixes, which in turn led to further refinement of the analysis.

Vocabulary could also be identified. Using calendrical statements, it was possible to identify the meanings of several words in the text, including "day," "star," "ten," and "sky." The word for "day," for example, was spelled with two signs. One was postulated as representing the syllable *ja,* the next as *ma.* This *ma* reading is confirmed because the sign that spells *ma* begins the spelling of "star" (*matza7*) and "ten" (*mak*), both of which start with *ma.*

Given a number of these phonetic readings and a number of grammatical identifications, a rather complete grammatical description of epi-Olmec texts has been worked out. This resulted in the recognition of many features specific to Mixe-Zoquean grammar, which confirmed the Mixe-Zoquean family model. For example, epi-Olmec texts use SOV word order, which can be reconstructed only in Mixe-Zoquean and Tarascan among all the languages of Mesoamerica. These texts use standard ergative patterns in main clauses, but they use ergative instead of absolutive prefixes to agree with subjects in subordinate clauses. In 2004, another epi-Olmec text of 104 signs came to light, on the back of a Teotihuacan-style stone mask; this text is straightforwardly interpretable in Zoquean. Such independent tests confirm the decipherment and the Zoquean identification of the texts.

---

in Mesoamerica cannot be said with assurance. However, one early symbol system does appear to have been much like writing, using similar nonphonetic representational conventions, but without relating directly to language. This is the Olmec-style iconography on many incised celts, dating to the Early and/or Middle Formative periods.

Most incised celts in the Olmec style depict humans wearing elaborate headgear and gesturing or holding various objects that seem to indicate their social status or such offices as ruler or warrior (Figure 11.3, right). In some cases, however, most of the detail used to represent the figure was eliminated, and only those details that convey specific categories of information remain (Figure 11.3, left). For example, instead of depicting a person gesturing, the head is represented (indicating a person) with a headdress (indicating rank or office); the gesture is represented separately, as a disembodied hand or arm in the appropriate posture. Thus, iconic elements were being taken out of the usual figural context of pictorial representation, functioning as symbols for social categories, events, and probably other types of information as

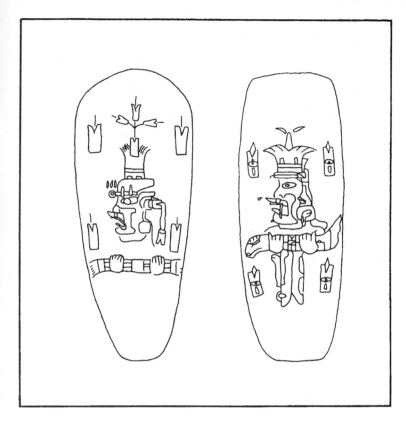

Figure 11.3   Arroyo Pesquero Celts. After Peter David Joralemon, "The Olmec Dragon: A Study in Pre-Columbian Iconography," in *Origins of Religious Art and Iconography in Preclassic Mesoamerica*, ed. H. B. Nicholson. Los Angeles, CA: UCLA Latin American Center Publications and Ethnic Arts Council of Los Angeles, 1976, p. 41, fig. 8 e and f.

well. Some of these symbols seem relatively abstract, as is often true of status symbols, whereas others seem to be depictions of something directly related to the concept; for example, weapons may indicate warrior status or battles. Thus, a subset of celt iconography uses separate symbols for the kinds of concepts that are represented by the nonphonetic conventions of later Mesoamerican writing, yet their source in standard celt iconography is apparent. The iconography of ceremonial celts is therefore a plausible precursor of writing in Mesoamerica.

It might be thought that the earliest writing resembled the Mixtec and Aztec systems, which have the most limited forms of representation of language. However, these latter systems seem to have actually developed ultimately from the Zapotec system, which was originally a more textual tradition. They contain no traces of syllabic or other phonetic spelling, except for rebus, although syllabic spelling was used in Zapotec texts. It may be that the difficulty in deciphering these early texts lies precisely in the scarcity of simple phonetic spelling, but the problem is only now being addressed with the necessary linguistic framework for analysis.

As a result of our limited knowledge of Middle Formative writing (900–400 B.C.), the nature of the earliest Mesoamerican writing systems—those from which the better-known systems emerged—is largely a matter of conjecture. It is generally thought that syllabic spelling emerged out of an earlier system or systems with rebus representation but without a substantial amount of nonrebus syllabic spelling. During the Late Formative period (400 B.C.–A.D. 200), Zapotec texts systematically use phonetic signs to spell grammatical elements, including pronouns ancestral to those discussed earlier in the section on *Morphology*, and in a more limited way as phonetic complements and possibly in fully phonetic spellings of words. By the end of the Late Formative period, when readable Mayan and epi-Olmec texts are found, syllabic spelling is firmly a part of both hieroglyphic systems. We cannot tell whether the epi-Olmec writing system evolved in any significant way during the 800 years or so that it is attested. This failure may be for lack of enough data to draw firm conclusions: Although no appreciable differences in spelling conventions have been detected, only three surviving epi-Olmec texts have enough writing to analyze. It has been determined, however, that in all six substantially legible epi-Olmec texts, syllabic signs constitute about half the total number of signs used.

In the case of Mayan writing, certain trends can be detected. Some syllabic spelling is found in the earliest datable texts. However, the amount of syllabic spelling gradually increased during the 600 to 700 years in which dated inscriptions are found. So, apparently, did the explicitness with which grammatical affixes were represented. There is a tendency to add phonetic complements first to those logograms that are ambiguous, thereby determining just which word is intended. For example, the sign for the day "Thunder" (in lowland Mayan, Ch'olan *chawuk*, or Yucatecan *kawak*) was also used for both *tu:n* ("year ending") and *ha7b'* ("year"); the word *tu:n* could be secured as the interpretation by indicating that it ends in *n*, which was done by placing the sign *ni* after it. There is also a tendency for fully syllabic spellings of a given word to occur later than logographic spellings with phonetic complements; for example, lowland Mayan *tu:n* was occasionally spelled *tu-n(i)* in the Late Classic period. So, to some extent, fully syllabic spelling seems to be a generalization from the earlier, partially syllabic and partially logographic spellings. In spite of definite trends in this direction, the story of the development of Mayan writing is much more complex than this. Some words have no known logographic spellings, and the earliest instances of such words are spelled syllabically.

LANGUAGE AND HISTORY

Linguists are able to determine a number of facts about the culture and history of Mesoamerica from the imprint that that history has left on their languages. When people interact and influence one another's cultures, their languages are among the domains that are affected. When this alteration happens, it is often possible to detect the influence, to determine its linguistic and cultural sources, and to reconstruct the nature of the interaction that brought it about. This discovery is possible because different types of social interaction lead to different types of linguistic change.

Reconstructing Culture from Vocabulary

It is possible for linguists to determine the history of the languages of Mesoamerica by comparing the present state of those languages. There are two basic approaches involved in such comparisons: reconstruction and classification. Linguists can reconstruct ancestral vocabulary and grammatical patterns by comparing the differently changed forms of these ancestral words and patterns as they survive in the modern, descendant languages. These reconstructions constitute a hypothetical description of the ancestral language. As mentioned before, such ancestral languages are known as "protolanguages." The forms that are reconstructed for protolanguages are preceded by the asterisk symbol (*) to make explicit the fact that the forms are reconstructed rather than being attested in written records. Today, a large number of proto-Ch'olan and proto-Yucatecan (Mayan) reconstructions have been verified in Mayan hieroglyphic texts, and Zoquean and Mixe-Zoquean reconstructions in epi-Olmec texts.

Cultural inferences can be drawn from reconstructed vocabularies. For example, if it is possible to reconstruct a large set of terms related to maize cultivation—e.g., corncob, cornfield, cornhusk, to double over corn, sweet corn, tortilla, and so on—then we can be quite sure that speakers of the ancestral language were maize agriculturalists. On the other hand, if the descendant languages use forms for such items that do not descend from the same words, then it is less likely that they practiced maize cultivation. As it happens, such vocabulary has been reconstructed for all Mesoamerican language families, so we suppose that ancestral Mayans, Mixe-Zoqueans, and Oto-Mangueans all practiced maize cultivation. In contrast, words for a variety of pottery vessels, for cooking and storage, are reconstructible for proto-Mayan and proto-Mixe-Zoquean, but not for proto-Oto-Manguean. We infer from this that ancestral Oto-Mangueans probably did not have pottery vessels and did not boil their food. This inference makes sense archaeologically, since pottery, including boiling pots, is only found long *after* maize agriculture began in the Oto-Manguean area, the earliest locus of maize cultivation in Mesoamerica.

Language Classification and Migration

Language classification is also a crucial key to culture history. As discussed in the section on dialects, language differences that develop among dialects result in a geographic distribution of languages that places the most closely related languages adjacent to one another; geography recapitulates phylogeny. Exceptions to this pattern result from the movement of groups from their ancestral location. Thus, classification helps us to recognize which groups have moved and where they came from. In fact, the geographic distribution of Mesoamerican languages generally agrees quite closely with the genetic relations among these languages, so that such migration has evidently been relatively rare in this part of the world.

Nonetheless, many obvious cases of the movement of peoples are known. Some linguists believe that Oaxaca Chontal and Tol are members of aHokan macrofamily, which is widespread in northern North America but rare elsewhere. Speakers of these languages must have migrated into Mesoamerica from the north.

Similarly, three Oto-Manguean languages—Sutiaba, Chiapanec, and Mangue—are outside the continuous area in which the other forty or more Oto-Manguean languages are located. Chiapanec and Mangue form a genetic grouping within Oto-Manguean. Presumably, they moved as a group, stopping first in Chiapas, and those who remained became the Chiapanecs; those who continued on to Nicaragua became the Mangues (on this migration, see Chapter 2). They must have left from the general vicinity of the Tlapanecs, linguistically their closest relatives. In fact, the Mangues were called "Chorotegas" (i.e., Cholultecas), and Terrence Kaufman proposes that they were the Early Classic inhabitants of Cholula. The closest linguistic relative of Sutiaba (in Nicaragua) is the Tlapanec language of western Mexico.

Nahua is a branch of the Uto-Aztecan family, the only one of that family to enter the Mesoamerican world. Its presence is the result of intrusion into the region, and it has been noted before that several characteristics of Nahuatl have been acquired through contact with other Mesoamerican languages (see Box 11.6). In fact, Nahuatl has spread into pockets throughout Mesoamerica, where they live among ancient language groupings of long standing; this pattern also reflects a recent radiation of Nahua peoples.

The area occupied by Zoquean languages at the arrival of the Spanish almost totally contains the Olmec heartland (on the Olmecs, see Chapter 1); Zoquean extends farther south in Chiapas, where heavily used trading routes linked Olmec sites with Pacific coast resources, as well as farther west into Oaxaca (probably as relative newcomers to the area). This area is broader than the spotty distribution of epi-Olmec texts, written in an ancestor of all Zoquean languages, but these texts verify the antiquity of this general distribution of the Zoquean languages by having surfaced near the extremes of the recent distribution of this subgroup in the northwestern part of the Gulf lowland heartland of the Olmecs, and in the south at Chiapa de Corzo in highland Chiapas. Further evidence for a Zoquean occupation of this general area is the borrowing of a great deal of Mixe-Zoquean vocabulary into neighboring cultures, almost all of it Zoquean (see the following discussion of Language Contact). Zoquean speakers, then, were the dominant cultural force in the region, and there is no straightforward alternative to Zoqueans as the bearers of the Olmec tradition and its descendants throughout this area.

Mixean languages are found on opposite sides of Zoquean territory, with Tapachultec (now extinct) to its southeast and the rest of Mixean languages to its southwest. Two Mixean languages are spoken in what is otherwise Gulf Zoquean territory in southern Veracruz, one of them in Sayula and one in Oluta, very near the old Olmec capital of San Lorenzo. In spite of the complexity of the distribution of Mixean, it basically lies to the south of the primary area of Zoquean speech. A Mixean intrusion into southern Veracruz must be relatively late, after the breakup of Mixean into different subgroups, since the language of Sayula is more closely related to the various forms of Mixe than to the language of Oluta.

Language Contact

It was noted in earlier sections that the diffusion of linguistic features from one language to another results from social interaction. One of the most obvious ways that one language influences another is through the diffusion of vocabulary. Names of animals and plants have often been borrowed by people entering an ecological zone from people already living there. For example, the Totonac language includes many loan words from Huastecan for plants and animals native to the central Veracruz

---

Box 11.6   The Mesoamericanization of Nahua

Uto-Aztecan languages share a number of characteristic features, such as SOV word order, (C)VCV root shapes; the use of separate words to refer to subjects of verbs, rather than prefixed or suffixed agreement markers; and the use of separate words rather than suffixes to indicate locations of nouns. Before its radiation out of the Basin of Mexico, Nahua was completely surrounded by Mesoamerican languages, and it was far away from every other member of the Uto-Aztecan family. It probably moved there from somewhere well to the north, in the vicinity of Cora and Huichol (see the map in Figure 11.2). These languages are each others' closest relatives, so the two are probably not far from the location of their common ancestor, and borrowings between Cora and an ancestor of proto-Nahua show that the two were formerly in contact.

Once in Mesoamerica, an ancestor of proto-Nahua borrowed a great deal of vocabulary from Huastecan, Totonacan, and Mixe-Zoquean; we know of this borrowing because this vocabulary can be reconstructed for proto-Nahua. None of these borrowings included words for lowland plants or animals, except for the widely traded cacao, so that this must have taken place in a highland context. This and other considerations make it most likely that Nahua speakers adopted these foreign features when they were in or near the Basin of Mexico.

The most dramatic effects that these languages had on Nahua were in its grammar. Original SOV word order became verb-initial, like most other languages in Mesoamerica. Locative expressions use body-part terms to show particular locations, as in most other Mesoamerican languages (see the earlier discussion on *Morphology*); the details of their structure were borrowed specifically from Mixe-Zoquean. The numeral system became vigesimal (base 20). In this, Nahua agrees with Mesoamerican languages generally, but we know that the Nahua system was modeled specifically after Mixe-Zoquean: Mixe-Zoquean numerals 6 through 9 were composed of a nonnumerical element *tujtu* combined with a preceding numeral 1 through 4; the proto-Nahua system was structurally similar, with numerals 6 through 9 composed of a nonnumerical element *chikwa* to which were added the numerals 1 through 4. Many simple noun roots were replaced by metaphorical compounds of a sort that is found in Totonacan. The distinctive *tl* sound (see the previous discussion on *Phonology*) was not original to Nahua, having replaced some instances of earlier *t*; this sound was probably adopted from Totonacan.

After proto-Nahua broke up into different speech forms, these varieties continued to be influenced by other Mesoamerican languages. However, Nahua had little or no influence on other Mesoamerican languages until the Postclassic or Epiclassic periods. Linguists can distinguish older loanwords from more recent loans by looking at the sound changes they have undergone, and by determining whether they were borrowed into early ancestors of modern languages or into individual languages or dialects. When we look at words borrowed from Nahua into other Mesoamerican languages, we find that they seem to be recent and do not show the properties associated with old loans. This finding indicates that Nahuas and their speech were not influential during the Classic period or earlier. In particular, it is not plausible that they played any prominent role at Teotihuacan.

---

coast, where many Totonacs now live. This fact suggests that the Totonacs entered the region in which they now live at a time when it was occupied by Huastecans, whom they displaced; it may be these displaced Huastecans who migrated south to become the Chicomuseltecs. Huastecan, in turn, can be shown to have occupied this area for thousands of years. Huastecan vocabulary was borrowed into a number of languages in northern Mesoamerica, and even to the north of Mesoamerica, at a very early date, before the Huastecan sound system had undergone any of the characterisitic changes that differentiate it from that of proto-Mayan.

Culturally important contacts are indicated by the borrowing of vocabulary for cultural complexes. For example, several of the names and numerals used in the ritual calendar of Oaxaca Mixes are Zoquean words, although the Mixe language has native Mixe terms in noncalendrical vocabulary that correspond in meaning to these borrowed terms. This indicates that the Oaxaca Mixe calendar was strongly influenced by Zoquean speakers, which further indicates a leading role for Zoqueans in some aspects of the ritual life of the Mixes. Mixe-Zoquean names for several important cultigens are found throughout a large number of Mesoamerican languages; these and other important loans have been taken as evidence that the Olmecs spoke Mixe-Zoquean (see Box 11.6 and 11.7 for additional cases of language contact in pre-Hispanic Mesoamerica).

Archaeological evidence shows that there was a great deal of influence of one cultural group upon another in pre-Hispanic Mesoamerica (see Chapter 1), yet, compared with other world areas, overall there has not been a lot of borrowing of vocabulary from one Mesoamerican language group by another. Almost any amount of borrowing therefore reflects a serious degree of engagement among the speakers of these languages.

Three cultural "spheres" show a level of diffusion that was massive by Mesoamerican standards. The single most active diffusion sphere was lowland Mayan civilization. Two major branches of the Mayan language family were spoken in this lowland area during the Late Preclassic and Classic periods: Greater Tzeltalan (consisting of the Ch'olan and Tzeltalan languages) and Yucatecan. These branches of Mayan are quite distinct from one another; only Huastec is more distantly related. However, there are more than 120 words that are shared exclusively by just these two groups (except that a few were later borrowed into other languages, especially Q'eqchi'), and at so ancient a time that they are reconstructible for both proto-Yucatecan and proto-Ch'olan or proto-Greater Tzeltalan. They must have been borrowed by Yucatecans from Greater Tzeltalans, or vice versa.

Many other words that are widely found in the Mayan family were also borrowed by one of these branches from the other; for example, Ch'olan *tinäm* (or Greater Tzeltalan *tinam*) 'cotton' was borrowed into Yucatecan, as were *tu:n* "stone; anniversary", *pi:k* "8000; skirt", *ku:tz* "turkey", *mu:ch* "toad", *tep'* "to wrap", *til* "to untie", and *tihti* "to shake"; proto-Yucatecan *kab'* "earth" and *kan* "to learn" were borrowed into an ancestor of proto-Ch'olan. The best estimate is that about 90 percent of these borrowings were by Yucatecans from Greater Tzeltalans or, later, from their Ch'olan descendants.

Terrence Kaufman has identified two other major diffusion spheres, which involved Mixe-Zoqueans; see Box 11.7.

Although vocabulary may be the most readily detectible reflection of linguistic diffusion, it is not the only one. As noted earlier in the discussion of language change (see also Box 11.6), one language sometimes changes grammatically by copying the grammatical structures of another. Quite intense levels of interaction must be inferred when this happens. These changes may occur when the source group switches rapidly to the language of a small target group, normally when the small group was a militarily successful elite. The source group uses its own grammatical patterns while

Box 11.7 Linguistic Diffusion from Mixe-Zoquean
(from Kaufman and Justeson in press)

About 100 Mixe-Zoquean words were borrowed into southern Mesoamerica—Mayan, Zapotec, Huave—and more southerly Central American languages like Xincan and Tol; the vast majority were probably adopted from Zoquean. About 90 Mixe-Zoquean words were borrowed in and around the Basin of Mexico, especially by Totonacans, Nahuas, Tarascans, and Matlatzincans. Most of this borrowing in both regions occurred during the Preclassic era, and most of the rest during the Early Classic.

In both areas, the borrowed vocabulary comes from all semantic domains; but most commonly borrowed were words for cultigens, especially those of lowland origin (for example, cacao, papaya, guava, manioc, sweet potato, and gourds), and words relating to the ritual calendar (for example, names for animals and plants that were names of days in the ritual calendar, and words for numbers and systems of numeration). Some of the borrowings in the south are attributable to Olmecs, others to epi-Olmecs.

A northern group of Mixe-Zoquean loans may seem surprising, given the Gulf Coast homeland of this family and their association with the Olmec civilization; but (as indicated in Chapter 1) there were small settlements of Olmec immigrants in the Basin of Mexico around 1200 B.C. Kaufman has shown that the geographic distribution of the northern loans puts their source in the eastern half of the Basin of Mexico; they were probably associated with the influence of Teotihuacan in Central Mexico.

acquiring imperfect control of the target language. Alternatively, grammatical copying occurs when two groups are in long-term, intense contact, probably the more common situation in Mesoamerica.

Such grammatical borrowing happened many times and in many places in Mesoamerica. Within the Mayan family, whereas Greater Tzeltalan and Ch'olan appear to have had a heavy influence on the vocabulary of Yucatecan, Yucatecan has probably influenced the grammar and phonology of Greater Tzeltalan and Ch'olan in such features as the development of a glottalized *p'* from some instances of earlier *b'*, and in the development of a pervasive grammatical pattern known as "split ergativity." In Oto-Manguean, the spread of sound changes among different Mixtec languages indicates that the Mixtecs of Tilantongo exerted substantial influence on neighboring kingdoms. Nahua was massively restructured after entering northern Mesoamerica, under the influence of Huastecan, Totonacan, and northern Mixe-Zoquean languages (see Box 11.6)

Glottochronology

Another tool often used in historical linguistic studies is "glottochronology." By assuming that basic vocabulary is lost at a relatively constant rate, the time elapsed since two languages had a common ancestor can be determined, provided that it is known that they are in fact related and that the basic vocabulary list has been reconstructed. The assumption that vocabulary is lost at a constant rate appears to be at best an approximation, but glottochronology can provide at least a rough estimate for when two or more languages were one. In the cases of migration just discussed, this gives an estimate for when the people speaking these languages migrated.

Box 11.8   The origin of place-value numeration and the discovery of zero (from Justeson 2001)

Mesoamerican languages express higher numbers with expressions that parallel polynomial equations in algebra: Each number is the sum of a series of terms, each of which consists of a *unit* that is a power of a base *b* (20, in vigesimal systems) multiplied by a *coefficient* that is a whole number between 1 and *b*−1; in the vigesimal system (*b* = 20). This yields expressions like "two 20s and fifteen" for 55, or "three 400s and six" for 1,206. Spoken languages have no term corresponding to zero, so 1,206 is not expressed as "three 400s, zero 20s and six."

During the Late Preclassic period, epi-Olmecs and Mayans used a system of place value notation that is effectively an abbreviation for these kinds of representation: the coefficients are listed in order, without the units, yielding a sequence like "two fifteen" for "two 20s and fifteen." So far as we know, this system was used only for counting days, and an adjustment was made to better fit this use. Instead of the expected unit of 400 days, an approximate year of 360 days was used in its place, and higher units were vigesimal multiples of that period: a year (360 days), a unit of 20 years (7,200 days), and a unit of 400 years (144,000 days). This was employed especially to record dates in the *long count,* also known as the "count of katuns" (*katu:n* and *may* were words for the 20-year period), and the system may have been developed for that specific application. Several long count dates in this system were inscribed on stone monuments between 36 B.C. and A.D. 125; among epi-Olmecs, this practice continued until at least A.D. 533.

The structure of the place-value notation system is consistent with the structure of numerals in the epi-Olmec language, but it is inconsistent with the structure of Mayan numerals. Among Mayans, the normal way to express the number 55 would be "fifteen in the third 20," and its expected abbreviation would be "three fifteen" (or "fifteen three") rather than the "two fifteen" of the actual system. So the structure of this notational system is probably owed to the epi-Olmecs. We know from its colonial survivals in the Yucatec Mayan *Books of Chilam Balam* that Mayas read these dates as written, and that this non-Mayan type of expression became a fixed formal style for expressing large counts of time: They would say something like "eight *pih,* four *ma:y,* five *ha7b'* and seventeen *k'in*" (corresponding to $8 \times 400 \times 360 + 4 \times 20 \times 360 + 5 \times 360 + 17$ days). A native Mayan expression would have been "five in the sixth *ha7b'* of the fifth *ma:y* of the ninth *pih.*"

How did this system deal with the cases in which a mathematician might use a zero coefficient, when the spoken language would simply have omitted mention of the unit? We know the answer from an early Mayan monument, Abaj Takalik Stela 5 (see Figure 11.4). It records the seating of the new year on a date that would be transcribed 8.4.5.0.17 by epigraphers (in A.D. 125). The digits in the place-value record of this date are eight, four, five, seventeen. There is simply a small extra space where the number of 20-day units would otherwise have been recorded. In this respect, the notation remained a direct if reduced transcription of the spoken version of the numeral.

By the beginning of the Classic period on, Mayans had begun using a fuller representation of these dates, recording glyphs that expressed the units used in speech as well as the coefficients of those units. In the formal speech that was used to read out these dates, the dates made use of poetic repetition, going beyond the typical couplet structure in which two parallel phrases were juxtaposed to intone five parallel phrases in a row: "There were eight *pih;* there were twelve *may;* there were fourteen *ha7b';* there were eight *winikil;* there were fifteen *k'i:n.*" Among the most formal of these occasions were the ends of katuns, when most Mayan monuments were erected in connection with katun-ending rituals. But poetically these would be the least imposing dates to recite: "There were eight *pih;* there were fourteen *ma:y*".

By A.D. 317, Mayans seem to have solved this problem by a poetic expedient: "There were eight *pih;* there were fourteen *katu:n;* there were no *ha7b';* there were no *winikil;* there were no *k'i:n.*" There is a widespread Mayan root *mih* that means "there aren't any," and a phonetic sign

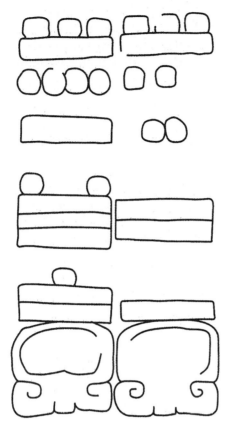

Figure 11.4 The long count dates on Abaj Takalik Stela 5. After John Justeson, "Pratiche di calculo nell'antica Mesoamerica," in Anthony F. Aveni, ed., vol. II of *Storia della Scienza*, pp. 976–990. Rome: Istituto della Enciclopedia Italiana, Fondata da Giovanni Treccani., 2001, p.988, fig.5. The long count dates are 8.4.5.(0).17 (the seating of the year in A.D. 125) and 8.3.2.(0).10; no digit is recorded where, based on later texts, a zero is expected. The second digit in the second long count is reconstructed as having been a 3 by John Graham, based on its layout.

for the syllable *mi* was used with period signs in these contexts to say, for example, "there were no *ha7b'*."

The simple place-value notation continued in use in the working almanacs used by calendar priests, judging from the screenfolds that survive from the Postclassic period, and the phonetic sign *mi* was used in the appropriate position. The contexts of use of long count dates in these manuscripts was in arithmetic tables, especially astronomical tables, where dates and time spans were generated by repeated additions of one number to another. Every other symbol in these shorthand expressions was manipulated using numerical algorithms for place-value addition. The *mi* sign would have been integrated into these algorithms. Given a numerical interpretation in these contexts, this would be the first real zero known in the history of mathematics.

Two points deserve special notice here. First, contrary to popular belief, place-value notation did not develop after the invention of zero. Just the reverse is true: A numerical zero served no practical purpose in ancient mathematics until place-value notation was in use. Second, in this particular case, the numerical zero was in the first place a linguistic practice adopted for poetic purposes. It was the embedding of the notation for this poetic device in a mathematical context that led to its reinterpretation as a numeral. The concept of zero, then, was *discovered* by Mayas; it was not "invented."

Glottochronology has been tested against hieroglyphic data in the case of Mayan and Mixe-Zoquean. Given that the underlying assumptions of the method are not universally accepted, it is remarkable how well the glottochronological dates fit the hieroglyphic evidence. In Mesoamerica, it appears that glottochronology provides a rather reliable guide for historical chronologies.

FINAL COMMENT

The languages that we have just described are crucially tied to our understanding of the Mesoamerican cultural tradition. When we attempt to understand the history of this region, the common properties of Mesoamerican languages attest to the long periods of interactions among different Mesoamerican peoples, and the hieroglyphic texts provide us with insights into ancient political systems (see Chapter 1). Glottochronology and reconstruction allow us to form hypotheses about the cultures and movements of the ancient peoples of Mexico and Central America.

The indigenous languages are also central to understanding preconquest, colonial, and contemporary Mesoamerican views of the world. The voices of native peoples in Mesoamerica have been expressed in both native and colonial languages, but the choice of languages has rarely been neutral. Choosing one or another language or dialect conveys complex messages about colonialism, community, and ethnic identity.

Finally, not only has language served as a medium for the expression of the histories, religions, and dreams of Mesoamerican people, but it has also acted as a conservative force in shaping the content of these expressions as well. Language is one of the strongest links between the achievements of ancient Mesoamerica and the struggles and accomplishments of the peoples in this part of the modern world.

SUGGESTED READINGS

BRICKER, VICTORIA R. (ed.) 1992 *Epigraphy*. Handbook of Middle American Indians, Supplement 5. Austin: University of Texas Press.

CAMPBELL, HOWARD, LEIGH BINFORD, MIGUEL BARTOLOMÉ, and ALICIA BARABAS (eds.) 1993 *Zapotec Struggles: Histories, Politics, and Representations from Juchitán, Oaxaca.* Washington, D.C.: Smithsonian Institution.

CAMPBELL, LYLE 1977 *Quichean Linguistic Prehistory.* University of California Publications in Linguistics, 81. Berkeley: University of California Press.

CAMPBELL, LYLE 1979 Middle American Languages. In *The Languages of Native America: Historical and Comparative Assessment,* edited by Lyle Campbell and Marianne Mithun. Austin: University of Texas Press.

CAMPBELL, LYLE, TERRENCE KAUFMAN, and THOMAS C. SMITH-STARK 1986 Mesoamerica as a Linguistic Area. *Language* 62:530–570.

COWAN, GEORGE M. 1948 Mazateco whistle speech. *Language* 24:280–286. Reprinted in Dell Hymes, ed., *Language in Culture and Society,* pp. 305–311. New York: Harper & Row, Publishers.

HILL, JANE H., and KENNETH C. HILL 1986 *Speaking Mexicano.* Tucson: University of Arizona Press.

JUSTESON, JOHN S., and TERRENCE KAUFMAN 1993 A Decipherment of epi-Olmec Hieroglyphic Writing. *Science* 271:1703–1711.

KAUFMAN, TERRENCE 1991 "Mesoamerican Languages." In *Encyclopaedia Britannica,* vol. 22, pp. 785–792.

SAKIYAMA, OSAMU, (ed.) 2001 Lectures on Endangered Languages: 2. From Kyoto Conference 2000–. 2 vols. Publication C003.kyoto:ELPR.

SUÁREZ, JORGE 1983 *The Mesoamerican Indian Languages.* New York: Cambridge University Press.

URCID SERRANO, JAVIER 2001 *Zapotec Hieroglyphic Writing.* Washington, D.C.: Dumbarton Oaks.

Chapter 12
Women and Gender in Mesoamerica

On October 16, 1992, Rigoberta Menchú, a Mayan woman from Guatemala, received the Nobel Peace Prize (on Rigoberta Menchú, see also Box 8.3). Menchú's selection drew worldwide attention to women's contributions to cultural, social, and political processes in Mesoamerica. It paid tribute to the new woman—indigenous and non-indigenous—emerging in the region.

On March 28, 2001, another Mayan woman, this time from Chiapas, Mexico, addressed the Mexican Congress as a representative of the EZLN (Zapatista Army of National Liberation). Comandanta Ester had come to speak to Congress about the poverty and racism that are the legacy of colonization and globalization in Mesoamerica. She spoke before a half-empty Congress because most senators refused to listen to an indigenous woman desecrate their chambers. Even many journalists emptied the room when they learned that the speaker that day would be an Indian woman, and not Marcos, the charismatic mestizo subcommander.

Rigoberta Menchú and Comandanta Esther draw attention to women's intensifying activism in Mesoamerica in the twenty-first century and to the troubling persistence of poverty, racism, and male dominance in the region. Women's recent forms of activism have their roots in over 500 years of ongoing oppression, exploitation, and forced evangelization. In the face of this legacy, women have borne major responsibility for sustaining families and communities, as well as valued cultural traditions. While indigenous men were compelled to act as intermediaries for Spanish priests and administrators, women carried on meaningful cultural traditions in the privacy of their homes. They prepared traditional foods, transmitted native languages, and passed on the arts of weaving, embroidery, and pottery-making from generation to generation. In these contexts women ensured some continuity of the Mesoamerican sacred universe while concealing the meanings of their traditions from the suspicious gaze of priests and administrators.

Women's activism takes place in the context of patriarchal national, regional, and local cultures that have endeavored to confine women's activities and lives to domestic realms. Women, especially those at lower socioeconomic levels, have always worked hard in both formal and informal economies to support their families. But the economic crisis in the region beginning in the 1980s has driven them into the labor force in unprecedented numbers. Women have also been involved in armed struggles, from the civil wars in Guatemala, Nicaragua, and El Salvador, to the low-intensity war in Chiapas (on these wars, see Chapters 8 and 10). Women's involvement in the economy and in wars has helped them realize that their input is essential to transforming society. It has also encouraged them to overcome their feelings of inadequacy, to speak up, to organize, to become leaders, and to defend their rights.

Involvement in armed struggle has raised women's consciousness about the limitations that the patriarchal order imposes on them. Although often relegated to jobs of secondary importance, both on the battlefield and in supportive activities, women nevertheless asserted their rights to equal participation; and in certain contexts, such as the Zapatista movement, they have proven themselves capable of taking on positions of highest responsibility. The new Mesoamerican woman, epitomized by Rigoberta Menchú and Comandanta Ester, has gained a sense of her own worth and her place in local, national, and international society.

This chapter consists of two main sections. The first section considers women's roles in Mesoamerican societies from pre-Hispanic to the mid–twentieth century. We describe women's active economic and political participation through the centuries as well as the central part women have played in ensuring the survival of the native cultures that give this region its distinctive shape. Such information has been missing from the record of human experience in the region; researchers and readers have assumed that women's lives unfolded exclusively within the domestic sphere, that their efforts to band together to improve their societies were prepolitical experiments, and that their roles in society were of secondary social importance. Influenced by the recent growth of feminist scholarship, ethnographers and historians have brought a critique of Eurocentric and androcentric assumptions to their studies of women and gender in Mesoamerica.

The second section explores important events and issues of the latter twentieth and early twenty-first centuries, such as the effect of the economic situation and of the politico-military crisis on women and gender, and the development of feminist movements in the various countries. Like ethnicity and class, gender configures the nature of modern Mesoamerican societies, allocating resources, rights, and privileges unequally between men and women, and creating specific controls to guarantee the reproduction of this system. Although indigenous and nonindigenous systems differ, the ideology and practice of male privilege are strongly rooted in the region, determining women's access to educational, economic, and social opportunities. Furthermore, recent economic trends—industrialization in rural areas and the emergence of *maquilas* in urban areas (see Chapter 9)—have become strongly associated with increased violence toward women and new forms of exploitation and subordination.

Throughout this chapter, complementarity and interdependence are dominant themes in the gender systems discussed. Another prevalent theme is women's activism in the face of domination and oppression. These themes challenge stereotypes of Mesoamerican women as passive and self-sacrificing.

THE PREHISPANIC MESOAMERICAN GENDER SYSTEM

What kind of gender system prevailed in Mesoamerica before the arrival of the Spaniards? In the past decade, archaeologists and ethnohistorians working in the region have made strides in interpreting codices and archaeological remains from feminist perspectives. Their findings indicate that gender systems varied widely across space, time, and ethnic group (Kellogg 2005).

The Mayan Gender System

In Classic and Postclassic Mayan imagery, noble women were portrayed as mothers or queen consorts, depicted in a lower position than men (Figure 12.1). Rulers of important cities married off their daughters or sisters to create political alliances with lesser cities. In such contexts, women were regarded highly. Mayan rulers derived

Figure 12.1 Pakal receives the divine crownship from his mother, Lady Zac Kuk, as he ascends to the throne of Palenque. Lady Zac Kuk sits in a lower position than Pacal. (Reproduced, with permission, from Linda Schele and David Friedel, A Forest of Kings, New York, NY: William Morrow and Co., 1990, p. 227.)

legitimacy from the ancestry of both their fathers and their mothers, although patrilineal descent was favored and, some authors argue, the accession of women to ruling positions indicated dynastic weakness. Noble men also dominated the religious sphere; women participated in rituals but did not act as religious functionaries. Although clearly androcentric, Mayan public art still repeatedly presented male/female pairs, thus stressing the underlying interdependence of both genders for the survival of society.

Among Mayan commoners, greater gender complementarity probably existed given the essential contribution of both genders for survival. Living in extended households, men hunted and farmed, and women prepared foods, wove, raised small animals, and cared for the children. At the household level, both noble and commoner women actively participated in the economy, providing food, textiles, and other necessities for household consumption and exchange (Joyce 2000).

The growth of urban centers and the intensification of warfare toward the late Classic Period increased the power of the nobility and reinforced male dominance, since the business of politics and war was exclusively in the hands of Mayan men. Some authors argue that despite these changes, the labor of both noble and commoner women continued to be important, as it was indispensable, not only for survival but also in market exchanges and for paying tribute.

The Mixtec Gender System

A more egalitarian gender system, based on complementarity, prevailed among the Postclassic Ñudzahuis or Mixtecs (Kellogg 2005). In their imagery, the Ñudzahuis do not use gendered images to portray gender hierarchy, female subordination, or military or class relations. Instead, their imagery conveys gender complementarity; for example, the term for rulership *yuhuitayu* combines elements referring to the reed mat (*yahui*) and the married couple (*tayu*), who were always portrayed sitting on a mat, in egalitarian fashion (Figure 12.2).

Both women and men could be rulers. Female succession was relatively common, and when both husbands and wives inherited official positions, they jointly ruled the polities that each inherited. Noble women who were not rulers also had important responsibilities in political and religious realms. For example, women were priestesses. In the division of labor, noble women supervised the production and exchange of crafts goods. Commoners replicated the complementarity of noble men's and women's political roles in their daily lives. Commoner men and women inherited property from both parents and could pass it on to their children without pooling it under a male authority.

As with Mayas, men and women also complemented each other in their roles. Mixtec men planted, transported goods, and undertook communal labor projects; women spun and wove, prepared food and drink, and gathered plants for food and ritual needs. Both private and public spaces were valued with no apparent hierarchy in the importance of work performed in either realm. After the Spanish invasion, women in Ñudzahui society increasingly lost ground, and gender hierarchy became more pronounced.

Figure 12.2   Ñudzahui husband and wife rulers sitting in an egalitarian fashion on the reed mat. Reprinted with permission from *Codex Zouche-Nuttall*. Edited by Zelia Nuttall. Graz, Austria: Akademische Druck- und Verlagsanstalt, 1987, folio 25.

The Aztec Gender System

A different gender system from that of Mayas and Ñudzahuis characterized the Mexicas or Aztecs of Central Mexico. Their gender system combined gender hierarchy with gender parallelism (men and women played different but parallel and equivalent roles). With many written sources available for this time period, a more detailed analysis of the gender system is possible. However, the authors of these documents (mainly Spanish priests) projected their own preconceptions on the unfamiliar systems they encountered. Scrutinizing their biases and problems, researchers have been able to sift through these documents in order to shed light on the lives of Postclassic and Colonial Aztec men and women (Kellogg 2005).

Gender parallelism was rooted in the kinship structures and in religious and secular ideology. Men and women were genealogically and structurally equivalent. They inherited property from both their fathers and their mothers, although the older son acted as guardian of the property for his siblings. In the Aztec pantheon, male and female deities were equally important, and deities often exhibited androgynous characteristics. Both men and women had access to priestly roles, but women did not retain this position for life as men did. Furthermore, men held the highest positions in the religious hierarchy.

Since women owned property and derived an income from their productive activities outside the household (through spinning, weaving, healing, embroidering, etc.), they maintained a measure of independence from their husbands (Figure 12.3). Before warfare came to dominate their way of life, Aztecs did not consider women as weak, dependent, or helpless. However, eventually bravery and skill became new

Figure 12.3 In addition to domestic responsibilities such as weaving (left), Mexica women held a variety of roles in their society, from trading in the markets (right) to performing agricultural and priestly duties, and prophesying the future. After Bernardino de Sahagún, *Historia General de las Cosas de Nueva España, Códice florentino.* Facsimile of the *Codex Florentinus* of the Biblioteca Medicea Laurenciana, supervised by the Archivo General de la Nación (AGN) de México, Florence, Italy, Book 10. Left figure is from "... de otros oficiales como los sastres y texedores" Chapter 10, fs. 22v and 24r; right figure is from "... de los que venden mantas" Chapter 17, fs. 44v and 45 r.

standards of behavior; men who were defeated or who acted cowardly on the battlefield were said to behave like women.

Not only did Aztec women peddle their goods in the marketplace, but they also shared market administrator positions with men; in this capacity they supervised the pricing of products, assigned tributes, and prepared war provisions. Women and men acted as leaders and administrators of their *barrios* (wards) and the song houses attached to temples or palaces. Aztec women executed important authority functions, although the highest political and religious offices were restricted to men.

Some authors argue that as Aztec society became increasingly militarized and imperialistic, women lost status (Nash 1978). Noble women saw their economic and ritual activities increasingly circumscribed when social stratification increased and royal lineages emerged. On the other hand, the productive roles of common women remained important. The dominance of Huitzilopochtli, the Sun War deity—which displaced the previous pantheon of androgynous and male-female progenitor deities—provides an important clue to changes in the gender system (see Chapter 2).

Some studies maintain that because Aztec men began to control the new sources of wealth (tribute) and the spoils of conquest, war automatically marginalized women, households, and domestic production. Others argue that although women did not fight on the battlefield and were thereby excluded from essential sources of status and wealth, their rituals and activities at home had a definite bearing upon the fate of men on the front (Burkhart 1995). Furthermore, warfare did not devalue domestic production or activities. Rather, homes and women's activities were invested with military symbolism. For example, labor in childbirth was equivalent to fighting, and the successful delivery of an infant equivalent to a warrior's taking a prisoner. A mother's death in labor was equivalent to being captured or killed. Box 12.1 provides another example of military symbolism associated with women in Aztec society.

General Pre-Hispanic Mesoamerican Gender System

Essential differences distinguished noble and common women's status and leverage within families, not only among the Aztecs but also in other Mesoamerican cultures. The productive and reproductive activities of common women were highly valued within a subsistence economy, where husbands and wives provided goods and services for each other that could not be obtained otherwise. Both men and women valued marriage as the first step to adulthood. For men, marriage often implied the beginning of their own patrilineage. In the case of nobility, however, servants and slaves performed many household tasks, and polygyny was common. Thus, women's importance hinged primarily on being bearers of legitimate offspring for rulership and as a means, through marriage, to forge political alliances.

No uniformity existed in the ways pre-Hispanic societies structured gender relations, roles, and the relative valuation of men and women. The three groups discussed before presented different degrees and forms of hierarchy, complementarity, and parallelism.

An additional aspect of pre-Hispanic gender systems of Mexico was the prominent role of homosexuality in religious life among Aztecs and its tolerance in private life by many Mesoamericans. Homosexual bonds were considered normal in many societies (Taylor 1995). The concept of a third gender may also have been prevalent in Mesoamerica as it was throughout North America before European colonization. The third gender is present in contemporary indigenous societies such as the Isthmus Zapotecs of Tehuantepec (Stephen 2002). In this society *muxe* refers to men who appear predominately male but show certain feminine characteristics. Muxe play no special religious role in their communities; however, they are considered to be gifted, and parents frequently choose to educate muxe sons (Chiñas 1995).

Although both homosexuality and flexible gender categories existed before and at the time of European contact, when the Spaniards invaded Mesoamerica, they shared much in common with the Aztecs in their celebration of male dominance and disdain for effeminate men. Homosexuality became a prime concern of the Inquisition. By executing men who defied the boundaries of a dual gender system and by destroying the social fabric of whole communities, the Spanish conquest and colonization radically transformed indigenous gender systems.

WOMEN AND GENDER IN THE COLONIAL PERIOD

The Spanish Conquest and Early Colonial Times

Sexual coercion was an intrinsic part of the process of colonization (on Spanish colonization in Mesoamerica, see Chapter 5). Spanish men saw women as objects whose bodies could be conquered and utilized as rewards for their valiant deeds as conquerors. Descriptions of violent sexual incidents during the conquest abound,

Box 12.1   Aztec Women and Ritual Sweeping

Sweeping, cooking, and weaving had important economic, symbolic, and religious connotations. Priests swept the temple, and housewives swept their homes. In both cases they defended their dwellings against chaos and dirt. The wife of a warrior had to sweep not only at dawn but also at noon, sunset, and midnight, purifying her home and marking the sun's path. The sun deity was expected to reciprocate by protecting the woman's husband in the battlefield. Warriors' wives had to prepare special foods, grind toasted maize, and place it in gourds as offerings to the deities. Women carried their weaving shuttles to the temples at night to offer food on behalf of their husbands, sons, or fathers who were fighting. Weaving shuttles symbolized warriors' weapons and the hope that they would conquer their enemies in battle. Thus, through domestic production, women ensured the survival of their families while the men were away. Furthermore, these activities carried important consequences on the battlefield. The Maya myth text to follow is on ritual sweeping.

Once the great star appeared, as we say. The sky grew bri—ght [— indicates vowel elongation in original narrative performance] from end to end. "I am the sweeper of the path. I sweep his path. I sweep Our Lord's path for him, so that when Our Lord passes by he finds [the path] already swept." [The star] travels. Then the sun appears. The sun sweeps forth as we say. But you know, first it's the morning star. Venus is a Chamulan girl. She is from Chamula.

They didn't believe the Chamulan girl when she talked about it. "We'll see what the ugly Chamulan girl is like! She says she is a star! Could she be a star? She's an awful, ugly, black Chamulan. Isn't the star beautiful? It has rays of light. The star is a beautiful bright r—ed," said the women. They ridiculed that girl for saying she was a star.

They didn't think she was. "Do you think I don't know what you're saying? You are ridiculing me. It's me. I am the one who fixes the path. I sweep off the path. When Our Lord disappears, the ocean dries up. The fish come out when Our Lord passes by there. That's when Our Lord disappears. That's why there is the monkey's sun as we call it [a red sunset]. That's when Our Lord passes over the ocean. That's when night falls. That's when the rays of light can be seen in the distance. I am the sweeper of the house. I sweep-off the path. I walk just when it grows light, at dawn again. I sweep here beneath the world. The next day when dawn comes, I appear and sweep again, because that is my work. That's what I do. I haven't any other work. That is what my work is. That's why I am a star. *Ve—nus appears early in the dawn,* say the people, but it's me. I sweep the house. [I sweep] his path, Our Lord's path. It isn't just anyone's path," she said.

She sweeps. She sweeps it off constantly. When she disappears then she is traveling inside the earth again. So the star reappears the next day again. She sweeps it off again. She passes under us, beneath the world it seems. She goes and comes out the next day again. Just the same way she appears. That's why the star appears first, it seems. "It's me, I sweep Our Lord's path," she said. The path of the holy sun.

We didn't believe it ourselves, that it was a Chamulan girl, it seems. "If I ever see what it is that sweeps, it seems to be a star, but a Chamulan, I don't believe it!" we said to ourselves. But she heard it when we were ridiculing her, when the poor girl was mocked. If it weren't so—she wouldn't have heard. But she did hear, so it's true. (Laughlin 1977:253–254) suggesting that, for the Spaniards the phallus was the extension of the sword. Indigenous people defended themselves against sexual abuse as best they could, by rejecting sex (for which women risked death), aborting fetuses of forced unions, or committing suicide.

Incidents of sexual violence continued into Colonial times combined with the ruthless exploitation of women's labor. Women's work responsibilities increased tremendously, especially for rural and nonelite women, as a result of the demographic crisis and Spanish demands for tribute and production of cloth (Kellogg 2005). Many women became widows and single mothers as a consequence of the disproportionate participation of men in the wars of conquest. Women had to work intensively to support their own households, often without the assistance of husbands and of other extended family members, while at the same time trying to earn money and to weave large quantities of cloth to satisfy increasing Spanish demands. Officials, priests, and wealthy Spanish families exploited women also through domestic work, which sometimes involved sexual coercion as well as other abusive practices such as kidnapping; forcing women to work without pay in exchange for clothing, room, and board; keeping women enclosed beyond the requirements of their domestic responsibilities; and obliging them to weave so that they could sell their cloth, a desirable commodity in colonial times.

Encomenderos (for a discussion of them, see Chapters 4 and 5) went to the extreme of renting women for domestic and sexual services to sailors who traveled to distant places for months at a time. The more attractive the women, the more money the *encomendero* could earn. In early colonial times, women from the indigenous elite were exempted by Spanish law from any of the requirements imposed on the rest of the population. A century later, having lost many of their properties and privileges, these women, too, were forced to pay tribute and to produce valuable items.

Transformations in the Colonial Aztec Gender System

By the seventeenth century, Hispanic cultural definitions and gender practices had drastically transformed women's status in Central Mexico. Aztec women lost power in the religious and political realms because many of the native institutions in which women had held posts of authority were destroyed. In addition, the imposition of Spanish ideals of women's purity and honor restricted women's freedom. Although women retained the right to litigate in court and to own and administer property, the Spanish patriarchal system encroached on every aspect of their lives, increasingly limiting their autonomy.

During the first fifty years after the conquest, native women had a strong presence in the courts defending property (see Box 12.1). By the seventeenth century, however, they were much less likely to initiate property litigation, and wills made by women were no longer as frequently used to bolster ownership claims as they had been in the sixteenth century. Likewise, the rates at which women bought, sold, or inherited property decreased dramatically, indicating a deterioration of women's status. How did this deterioration come about? The patriarchal society instituted by the Spaniards gave fathers and husbands unlimited authority over their wives and children. Two centuries after the arrival of the Spaniards, Aztec women's identity had merged with that of their husbands; women needed the support of husbands or fathers to present a claim in court. Men became the representatives of women in legal and political matters.

Although Aztec women continued to engage in productive activities crucial to their families' survival, the ideology of female purity and enclosure preached by the Catholic Church further undermined their opportunity to hold formal positions of authority. This ideology created a sharp division between a male social and political domain, and a female domestic domain. In two centuries, patriarchal ideology and its impact on the religious, social, and legal system had transformed precolonial gender parallelism into stridently hierarchical relations between men and women.

The Gender System Imposed by the Spaniards

Few colonial sources exist by or specifically about women (whether indigenous or Spanish). However, researchers are now probing colonial documents (e.g., censuses, confessional manuals, Inquisition records, and cases brought before ecclesiastical or civil authorities) for information about gender relationships in colonial society.

What were the main characteristics of the new gender system? Priests and Spanish officials alike extolled the patriarchal system as the divine design for humanity. The family epitomized this ideal and served as a model for all social relationships. A husband had control over his wife, his children, and any other members of the household. Women and children were always minors under the tutelage of fathers to whom they owed total obedience. Patriarchal ideology defined fathers as the source of authority. Their legitimacy rested upon their responsibility to support and look after the well-being of their families. They had the latitude to punish and even strike wives to correct their behavior. However, when husbands exercised excessive authority or when they did not support their families as was expected, wives could appeal to religious or secular authorities. Sometimes women opted to return to their parents' homes or seek refuge in convents, where they felt safe and were able to find work. A few court cases describe women who fought back, probably in self-defense.

Spaniards regarded virginity as an essential quality of women before marriage and when they remained single. The honor of the family was inextricably linked with female sexuality and the birth of legitimate children. A woman who engaged in premarital or extramarital affairs and who had an illegitimate child tarnished her personal reputation and brought dishonor to her family. The double standard of morality pervaded colonial society; whereas a woman's reputation suffered greatly from liaisons, neither her lover's reputation nor his family's honor suffered ill consequences. During the first two centuries of colonial rule, emphasis on family honor and concepts of women's virtue and vulnerability led to women's seclusion at home. Convents and retirement houses provided protection for older unmarried women, widows, and abandoned wives. The Church glorified celibacy as one path to perfection; women who followed the Virgin Mary's model were seen as closer to God.

On the other hand, patriarchal ideology maintained that women's will and honor were fragile; that is, men could easily convince or force women to engage in illicit relationships. In this way, society rationalized women's need for "protection" by fathers and other male relatives, as well as by authorities. When a father sought redress in court for another man's failure to make good on a marriage promise to his daughter, the father used his daughter's vulnerability to justify her behavior (e.g., eloping with the man). This strategy promoted the family's aim to force the man to marry her or to pay a dowry for having dishonored her. If the accused man rebutted by bringing up the woman's previous illicit affairs or dubious reputation, the woman and her family had no recourse; the court would protect only a woman who submitted to patriarchal behavioral codes.

Adulterous women were deemed to have committed a serious social offense. On the other hand, adultery by a man was taken lightly, especially if he was discreet and the affair did not lead to his wife's and family's humiliation. Women usually resigned themselves to their husbands' affairs and were unlikely to sue for divorce or separation based on the affairs. Because they depended economically and legally on their husbands, most women attempted to bring their errant husbands back to the family.

Women's Work in Colonial Mexico City

At the end of the eighteenth century and the beginning of the nineteenth, women accounted for one-third of the labor force in Mexico City. Whereas 46 percent of Indian women and 36 percent of "caste" women (mixed blood) were engaged in productive activities, only 13 percent of Spanish or creole women worked. These figures illustrate the contrasting situation of women in different social classes. Poor women (largely Indian and caste) could not comply with the ideal of women's enclosure. Living in conditions of extreme poverty and high mortality rates, lower-class families needed the economic cooperation of husbands and wives to survive. Most women found work as domestic servants, work that was considered degrading. Others sold fresh produce or cooked foods in corner stands and in the market; worked as waitresses in public eating houses; took in laundry; sewed, sold thread, or wove for other people, and so on.

In the early Colonial period, many middle-class women were shopkeepers. This was a more prestigious occupation than manual labor, because it enabled women to follow the rule of seclusion since these shops were usually attached to their homes. At the end of the eighteenth and the beginning of the nineteenth centuries, new possibilities opened up for middle-class women when reforms introducing women's education began to take effect. Middle-class women who pursued education were trained to care for sick or abandoned women in welfare institutions, reputable work for women at this time. As for elite women, those who wanted a career rather than marriage took religious vows. Other women from this class were involved in the management of properties they had inherited.

Feminists today draw attention to women's historical efforts to remain productive and socially involved in the face of patriarchal control. Colonial society, however, accorded high status to women who did not work, and it stigmatized those who did. Out of pure necessity, lower-class women engaged in labor considered degrading and transgressed the social precept of women's enclosure; thus, their purity and morality were called into question. Given the choice, they might have elected the path of domesticity and patriarchal protection.

Women's Responses to Patriarchal Domination

From the beginning of Spanish colonization, women resisted colonial rule. In some cases, indigenous women fought alongside men in the battlefield against the Spanish invaders. Aztec women led indigenous rebellions against colonial rule, perhaps because men worked far away from their communities. Women often insulted and vilified colonial authorities. But as the Church and state tightened their controls over women, it became increasingly difficult for women to negotiate their positions in society.

How were women able to maneuver within the limited space afforded them? In addition to political protest and outright rebellion, women sought to gain a measure of control over their lives by practicing witchcraft; seeking direct communication with supernatural beings through trance; and occasionally entering convents. These activities provided a respite from the constraints of colonial society. However, colonial authorities deemed any manifestation of power by women as disruptive and negative. Women suffered the consequences of attempting to subvert the natural and divine order requiring them to be obedient and submissive.

Women practiced witchcraft in part to gain influence over husbands or lovers. Abandoned wives, women whose husbands engaged in extramarital affairs, and those who wanted to retaliate against abusive husbands performed love magic themselves or used the services of women with esoteric wisdom. In this way, they hoped to entice their husbands back, "stupefy" them, or force the breakup of their relationships with other women. Marginalized women, such as Indian and caste women, were reputed to have extraordinary magical powers. By manipulating secret powers, women established interethnic and interclass networks; passed on secret concoctions, formulas, and prayers; and assisted other women to deal with oppressive situations (Behar 1989; Few 2002).

Spanish officials devalued and trivialized witchcraft, thus dismissing an important source of women's power. Fortunately for women, because the Spanish Inquisition regarded love magic as superstition—delusion grounded in ignorance—it was treated leniently. On the other hand, the effectiveness of Church teachings led women to internalize the notion of the evil nature of women's magical faculties and to reject their empowering effects. In documents of the time, women declared explicitly that they would rather put up with abusive or unfaithful husbands than commit the sin of entering into compacts with evil supernaturals and thus challenge the divine order. Notwithstanding, love magic continued.

During the Colonial period, many nuns and common women attempted to engage in direct communication with Jesus, the Virgin Mary, the saints, and demons. These women usually fell into raptures or trancelike states in which they heard voices or had visions of heaven, hell, or purgatory. When these women lived in a controlled environment, such as a convent, they were viewed as "mystics." Confessors enjoined women mystics to go about their lives quietly. Colonial ideology contended that women were best suited to passive contemplation rather than to intellectual analysis, the purview of men (Franco 1989). Also, mystical raptures bordered on dangerous and complex terrain, beyond the ken of women who were thought to be overcome by passion and prone to lunatic episodes. But what the confessors feared most was the direct challenge to male authority that women's communications with spiritual beings posed. Male priests were the only designated intercessors between people and God, yet women's mystical experiences gave them irrefutable authority.

Women who did not live in convents but claimed to have mystical experiences had much more difficulty legitimizing their claims. The Church dismissed their discourse as the Devil's deceptions, arguing that these women claimed to experience raptures and visions in order to make money or for other kinds of perverse reasons. Many of these women ended up in asylums. Ana de Aramburu, for example, was condemned by the Inquisition to imprisonment in a secret prison for claiming that God singled her out. An even more important female mystic was Sor Juana, a woman of renowned intellect and an acerbic critic of machismo (as her poem in Box 12.2 attests).

Native Women's Roles in Colonial Highland Chiapas, Mexico

The decimation of the native population during the first century of Spanish occupation meant that surviving men and women had to fulfill the onerous tribute and work obligations imposed by the Spaniards. Spanish priests, colonial administrators, and entrepreneurs competed among themselves to exploit Indian labor. Native women worked extremely hard to produce the yarn and woven goods demanded in the *repartimiento* system (see Chapter 5). Men had to transport the requisite goods long distances on their own beasts. Exhausted and constantly on the move, men were easy prey to sickness and died young; often, their wives survived them. Households headed by women became a common feature of indigenous life.

Women's central participation in nativist or revitalization movements illustrates the important roles women played in rural colonial communities. Through nativist movements, indigenous peoples sought to bring hope and redemption to their ravaged communities. They attempted to forge alliances with supernatural beings that, on the one hand, would help them carry on, and on the other hand, would serve as rallying points to consolidate the native struggle against invasive forces.

In highland Chiapas, a young Tzotzil-Mayan woman named Dominica López claimed that she had a vision in a cornfield of the Virgin Mary who spoke to her, requesting that her image be brought to town and a chapel be built for her there (for a shorter version of this and the rebellions to follow, see Box 5.3). The townspeople did as she wished, and Dominica and her husband were named *mayordomos* (stewards) for the Virgin. The Virgin Mary reportedly communicated only through Dominica. She stated that she would reward the people with an abundant harvest of corn and beans and many children. When word reached the Spaniards about the great stir that Dominica's vision was creating in native communities, they took decisive action. They carried the image of the Virgin off to San Cristóbal and brought Dominica López and her husband to trial.

Box 12.2   Sor Juana Inés de la Cruz (1988)

Sor Juana Inés de la Cruz, nun and talented poet and writer, lived in Mexico in the seventeenth century. She has been widely acclaimed as a precursor in defending women's rights in the region, as clearly expressed in these verses of her poem, "You Men." Sor Juana took on religious vows as a young woman to avoid marriage, the only alternative open to creole women.

Silly, you men—so very adept
at wrongly faulting womankind,
not seeing you're alone to blame
for faults you plant in woman's mind.

After you've won by urgent plea
the right to tarnish her good name,
you still expect her to behave—
you, that coaxed her into shame.

You batter her resistance down
and then, all righteousness, proclaim
that feminine frivolity,
not your persistence, is to blame.

When it comes to bravely posturing,
your witlessness must take the prize:
you're the child that makes a bogeyman,
and then recoils in fear and cries.

Presumptuous beyond belief,
you'd have the woman you pursue
be Thais when you're courting her,
Lucretia once she falls to you.

For plain default of common sense,
could any action be so queer
as oneself to cloud the mirror,
then complain that it's not clear?

Whether you're favored or disdained,
nothing can leave you satisfied.
You whimper if you're turned away,
you sneer if you've been gratified.

With you, no woman can hope to score;
whichever way, she's bound to lose;
spurning you, she's ungrateful—
succumbing, you call her lewd.

(Translated from the Spanish by Alan S. Trueblood.)

Around the time of the trial in June 1712, María López, a young woman in the Tzeltal-Mayan town of Cancuc, reported that the Virgin had appeared to her requesting that a chapel be built in her honor on the spot where she appeared. Sebastián Gómez, an indigenous man from nearby San Pedro Chenalhó, claimed to have spoken with the Virgin who demanded that a native priesthood replace the Spanish one. Following her orders, Sebastián Gómez ordained a group of Mayan men as priests. These men assumed the functions of the ousted Spanish priesthood, while María López became the *mayordoma mayor* (the main steward).

María López held the highest place of honor, standing closest to the image of the Virgin. She was flanked by two native priests who served as her scribes as she conveyed the Virgin's messages to the people.

The Spanish felt threatened by this movement, especially in August 1712, when indigenous people massacred the Spanish population of several highland towns. The Spaniards counterattacked, and after fierce fighting routed the indigenous rebels. Foreseeing a total military defeat, the rebels appealed to supernatural forces as a last resort to stop the colonial forces. They carried four women, reputedly witches, to the river, invoking female supernatural powers to destroy the enemy. Each woman represented a natural force: earthquake, lightning, flood, and wind.

What do these native uprisings reveal about gender and women in native communities during colonial times? In a general way, they allow us to assess the importance of women in these communities, at a time when severe population decline threatened the survival of the group. The deities that appeared to the young indigenous women were female, and they probably corresponded to *jme'tik*, Our Mother, who in modern Tzotzil-Mayan cosmology represents both the Moon and Mother Earth and is identified with the Virgin (Rosenbaum 1993). As the Earth, Our Mother symbolizes fertility, that is, life and renewal of population and crops. She reportedly appeared at a time of hunger and hopelessness, offering to bless the Indians with abundant food and children. Dominica López and later María de la Candelaria (the name that María López assumed when she became a spokesperson for the Virgin) could be interpreted as symbols of fertility and hope. Furthermore, the association of this cult with the female Earth is confirmed by the recruitment of women witches, representing the forces of nature, to destroy the Spaniards. To this day, Tzotzil-Mayas believe that these forces reside in the Earth. The fact that women assumed the role of stewards in these movement suggests that they were active in the religious organizations of their communities in colonial times (Rosenbaum 1992).

WOMEN IN POSTCOLONIAL MEXICO (1821–1940s)

Women's Participation in the Independence Movements

Until recently, scholars have suggested that women's participation in the struggles for independence in Mexico and Central America was restricted to a few exceptional women. However, studies of the broader participation of women in Mexico indicate that they played active roles in the independence movement, although it is difficult to assess their numbers.

In Mexico City and in Mexican provinces, women carted messages, arms, and instructions in their baskets from one place to the other. Wealthy women contributed funds to the insurgent cause. One of the most important tasks that women carried out in the independence movement was to attempt to convince soldiers to desert the Royal Army and join the insurgency. In a propaganda document dated 1812, Mexican women were enjoined to enlist in the armed struggle to avenge the deaths of their male relatives by the Spanish army. This document displayed a picture of two women wearing military hats and holding raised swords (Figure 12.4).

Although the insurgents praised women's participation as central to the success of the movement, after independence the new republic did not allow women a greater role in political life. Women were not granted the right to vote or hold office. In fact, just the opposite occurred: Books and newspapers of the period urged women to mind their homes and children.

By the end of the nineteenth century, a greater number of women entered into the labor force. At tobacco and textile factories, women were active in unions. Many unionized women later joined the opposition to Porfirio Díaz and sought membership in the various political parties and groups that opposed him.

Figure 12.4 Mexican women heeded the call of this 1812 propaganda document enjoining them to participate in the struggle for their country's independence. "Personajes de un corrido." Archivo General de la Nación (AGN) de Mexico. Peraciones de Guerra: Vol. 406, f. 195 (Catalogue no. 2648).

Women's Participation in the Mexican Revolution

Women's participation in the Mexican Revolution was extensive (Figure 12.5). They were incorporated into both the popular and the constitutionalist armies. Because of the promise of lands, peasant women overwhelmingly supported the revolution. They streamed onto battlefields in large numbers, not only following their husbands in order to care for their needs but also acting as nurses, spies, arms providers, and even as combatants. Some women dressed like men in order to get to the front lines. One woman commanded a battalion composed exclusively of sisters, daughters, and widows of dead soldiers. In a few cases, women led male soldiers in combat on specific missions. Women were startled, however, to learn that the Mexican Constitution of 1917 denied them the right to vote. Congressmen argued that, although there were exceptions, most women had not yet developed a political awareness because of having been restricted to the domestic sphere. There was no point, they argued, for women to participate in public life.

Figure 12.5 Mexican women carried out a variety of tasks during the Mexican Revolution, including fighting, nursing the wounded, spying, and providing food and arms to the combatants. Reprinted with permission from Esperanza Tuñón Pablos, *Tambien Somos Protagonistas de la Historia de México, Parte Primera* Mexico City, Mexico: Equipo de Mujeres en Acción Solidaria (EMAS), 1987, p. 8.

Box 12.3   Women in the Cuscat Uprising

In highland Chiapas, a nativistic movement developed in response to the despair and confusion that prevailed following the independence period in Mexico. It began in 1867 when Agustina Gómez Checheb, a young Chamula girl, claimed to have seen three stones falling from the sky while she pastured sheep in the fields. Pedro Díaz Cuscat, an assistant to the priest in Chamula, took over the organization of the cult. He declared that Gómez Checheb had given birth to the stones and that she was, therefore, "the Mother of God." The stones were alleged to speak to people through Gómez Checheb. She was identified with Saint Rose, an important deity in the Chamula pantheon.

Díaz Cuscat incorporated the cult into the traditional festival cycle and *cofradía* (religious confraternities) organization. He established a market that attracted a large number of people, who were then recruited into the cult. The movement ended in open confrontation with mestizo authorities, as nine Tzotzil-Mayan towns participated in the revolt. The confrontation between the Indian and the mestizo armies left many people dead on both sides. Like the Virgin cults of 1712, this so-called "War of Saint Rose" expressed the aspirations of native peoples to establish a cult that would unite them in the worship of a distinct, native deity.

The stones that ignited the spark for the rebellion may be interpreted as another expression of the female Earth and her wealth, defined in terms of crops, animals, or money. Tzotzil-Mayas today tell of how in the past, people received money magically from the earth. Sometimes they found it under a stone. In contemporary prayers to restore health to problem drinkers, healers refer to money and stone interchangeably (Eber 2000:189).

The participation of women went beyond igniting the spark for the rebellion. They fought alongside their husbands in the battles against mestizo soldiers. According to highland Chiapas folklore, women decided to join in the struggle with the hope that their "cold" female genitals would "cool" the guns ("hot" male object) of the Mestizos. This account substantiates the contemporary view held in many highland Chiapas indigenous communities that female genitals are cold in nature, in direct association with the coldness of the Earth's womb. The account also reveals the solidarity of husbands and wives and the decision of men and women to fight their oppressors jointly in a final attempt to rescue their society from seemingly inevitable destruction.

Women's groups began to emerge in the 1920s. One was the *Consejo Feminista Mexicano* (Mexican Feminist Council), affiliated with the Mexican Communist Party, which tried to engage women, especially those working in factories, in the fight to radically transform the country's socioeconomic structures. The major aim of this group was not the liberation of women but the triumph of the proletariat over the bourgeoisie. The Council dismissed the feminist quest to improve the situation of women, claiming that this pursuit played into the hands of conservative powers weakening the revolutionary movement.

Another women's group was attached to the ruling revolutionary party. This group's platform pursued the vindication of women's rights, promising to fight against the exploitation of Mexican women. The group pledged to improve women's working conditions and to organize day-care centers, health centers, communal houses, and legal advice centers for women. The two groups clashed with each other as they endeavored to win the hearts and minds of Mexican women.

Lázaro Cárdenas's ascent to power in 1934 brought the promise of new possibilities for women in the political arena (on Cárdenas, see Chapter 8). In 1935, women organized the National Conference of Women, which gave birth to the United Front Pro-Women's Rights (FUPDM), an organization that united Mexican women of diverse ideological, religious, and social backgrounds. After Cárdenas left office, women had a difficult time regrouping an effective social movement in the confluence of international forces of the early 1940s and the dramatic expansion of industrialization and its concomitant social changes.

Politically active women's groups redirected their efforts to charitable organizations, working to improve the situation of the most needy segments of the population. Not until 1947 did women have the right to participate in municipal elections both as voters and as office-holders. Finally, in 1953, President Ruiz Cortínes modified the Mexican constitution to grant women full citizen's rights on a par with men (see Box 12.3 for an example of women's participation at the local level in postindependence Chiapas, Mexico).

Rural Native Women in the Mexican Republic 1821–1940: The Case of Highland Chiapas

Not much changed for the better in the lives of indigenous peoples after independence. In fact, in the second half of the nineteenth century in both Mexico and Central America, their economic situation worsened as the infusion of foreign investment in export products intensified the exploitation of indigenous labor. Furthermore, Catholic priests continued to press the Indians to give up their native beliefs and practices (see Box 12.3)

During the Mexican Revolution, the contending sides recruited, manipulated, and mistreated indigenous peoples of highland Chiapas, resulting in the loss of thousands of native lives. The revolution's promise of land to peasants began to bear fruit in the region only after 1936, when the Cárdenas government embarked on large-scale land reform (see Chapters 8 and 9). From Cárdenas's time to the present, the Mexican government has sought to control and mobilize the indigenous population by effecting changes in native communities' government structure.

By law, each community was required to establish a Constitutional Council that would represent it before state and national authorities. Whereas previously these communities had been governed by civil and religious organizations (the "cargo systems") headed by respected monolingual elders, during Cárdenas's term the Mexican government required that costitutional councils be made up of educated bilingual men. These conditions led to a drastic transformation of the traditional structure of government in indigenous communities and to the entrenchment of mestizo power within the communities (Rus 1994).

The political changes described earlier inflicted a severe blow on women who for centuries had been actively engaged in religious cargo services and had important religious obligations complementary to their husbands' civil positions. In the newly created offices, women had no place: first, because since early colonial times Mexican officials were accustomed to dealing exclusively with male leaders in indigenous communities; and second, because most indigenous women in highland Chiapas were, and continue to be, monolingual. Women's knowledge of and contact with mestizo society and government was minimal. Even women actively involved in politics in the urban areas had no prospect of gaining public office or suffrage.

After the 1940s, constitutional councils came to stand for a new kind of power in indigenous communities: a totally male elite, strongly secularized, and with much greater economic resources than the majority of the population. The complementary presence of women, customary in the native cargo systems, was lost within the new councils. Women's presence continues today only in the cargos related to spiritual matters, particularly the festival of carnival and festivals in honor of the Catholic saints (Eber 2000).

CONTEMPORARY MESOAMERICAN GENDER RELATIONS

Machismo

Machismo, variously defined, but always implying a hypermasculine ideal in which manhood rests on controlling or dominating women, continues to shape gender roles and relations in contemporary Mesoamerica. Although in this chapter we focus on women's experiences, it is important to note that machismo also shapes power relationships among men. For example, effeminate men are particularly vulnerable to prejudice and violence because they do not appear or act manly. They defy the strict boundaries of women's and men's roles, that dictate that men should be active, dominant and independent while women should be passive, submissive, and dependent (Carrier 1995; Lancaster 1992). The focus on masculinity and strict gender roles throughout Mesoamerica places homosexual men and women in the difficult position of keeping their sexuality a secret while fulfilling traditional gender roles in public. Nevertheless, in some areas, such as Yucatán, young men in their teens and twenties are not ostracized for engaging in homosexual relationships (Wilson 1995).

Despite the persistence of a macho ideal, many scholars have found the concept of machismo too general to embrace diversity and change across categories of class, ethnicity, and race (Navarro 2001). Today men in a range of social and ethnic groups in both rural and urban areas spend significant amounts of time in activities that were not considered manly before, for example, caring for children and doing household chores such as shopping and cleaning (Guttman 1998). And as we show next, women are increasingly assuming roles that were traditionally filled only by men.

Most women continue to be economically dependent on men and to have less access to job training and education. These conditions often mean that women who have no way to support themselves or their children will put up with abusive behavior from their spouses. Domestic violence against women and children, common in the region, is one of the most serious consequences of machismo, leading to psychological and physical trauma for victims, and sometimes even to death.

Students of Mexican and Central American societies argue that machismo and paternal irresponsibility are less of a problem among indigenous people (especially those living in traditional contexts) than among mestizos or ladinos. Although indigenous men engage in extramarital affairs, social norms in their communities stress responsible behavior toward families (Bossen 1984; Eber 2000). Relatives and neighbors are reluctant to condone the behavior of men who have affairs or abandon their families. Although abandonment occurs in indigenous communities, it is less common than in the mestizo population. Domestic violence, on the other hand, is a serious problem in both indigenous and nonindigenous households.

Women and Economics

Women have played a central role in the struggle to effect radical changes in the socioeconomic structures of their countries, a struggle that led to civil wars in Guatemala, El Salvador, and Nicaragua from the late 1970s to the late 1980s, and to the Zapatista rebellion and subsequent indigenous autonomy movement in Chiapas, Mexico, in the 1990s and early twenty-first century (see Chapters 8, 9, and 10).

Coinciding with civil wars in the 1980s, Mexico and Central America suffered the impact of an international recession, debt crisis, and the ultimate triumph of the market over the state. Under the direction of the IMF, governments in the region initiated structural adjustment programs that involved privatizing state-owned industries, reversing agrarian policies, and cutting back government spending. Although regional economic integration has provided some opportunities for women's advancement, it continues to aggravate conditions for the poorest sectors of the population of which women and children constitute the majority. In addition, the tendency of structural adjustment policies to privilege men—as a result of the interplay between modernizing forces and the ideology of machismo—has contributed to lowering women's authority in indigenous societies, and to a dramatic increase in femicides (gender-based murder of women) throughout Mexico and Central America.

Gender and Modernization of Indigenous Societies

Gender studies conducted among Zapotec Indians of Oaxaca and Mexico and among Mayan Indians of Chiapas and Guatemala indicate that indigenous populations living in traditional communities enjoy aspects of a more egalitarian gender system than their corresponding socioeconomic class within the mestizo population (Ehlers 2000; Stephen 1991). For example, among Tzotzil-speaking Chamulas of highland Chiapas, women and men contribute equally to the household economy. While men tend the milpas and engage in wage labor in distant places, women take care of children and domestic animals and devote many hours to producing textiles for sale (Eber 2000; Rosenbaum 1993). In addition, they assume responsibility for milpa production while their husbands work away from home. Women's cash contributions (as well as other services they provide) are indispensable to their families' survival (Rus 1990).

Interdependence between husbands and wives strengthens their relationships in indigenous communities. Again, in Chamula, men and women are not considered adults until they marry. A man cannot opt for political or religious office unless he has a wife to fulfill the required complementary duties of his position. Although women are barred from civil office, the joint participation of husband and wife in the religious cargo system (cofradía service) enhances communication and cooperation between them, and strengthens the marital bond. Chamulans say that the deities that couples serve grant them blessings, bringing them material well-being and improving their relationship. In this way, Chamulan culture encourages the interdependence of husbands and wives (Rosenbaum 1993).

Interdependence is especially relevant in the lower socioeconomic sectors of indigenous societies. Among higher-income indigenous people, interdependence between spouses diminishes. As mentioned before, the male bias of the larger society enhances men's greater access to education, credit, and contacts with the outside world. Some indigenous men are able to benefit from these privileges. Women whose husbands' cash earnings are much greater than theirs lose leverage in their households. Their economic value to their household diminishes as their dependence on their husbands increases.

In the past twenty years, the intense penetration of modern capital into indigenous communities has radically altered gender systems. For example, in the Mam Mayan town of San Pedro Sacatepéquez, Guatemala, the introduction of capitalism brought about a remarkable rise in living standards. Similar processes took place among Zapotec Indians of Teotitlán del Valle with the entry of artisan production into international markets, and among Zapotecs of the Sierra de Oaxaca when coffee (a major commercial crop) replaced a household-oriented system of production. In these three relatively egalitarian communities, social classes and gender stratification gradually crystallized over time leading to a dramatic deterioration in women's status.

How did this change occur? Because of their advantages, men were able to secure loans; buy trucks; engage in more modern, industrialized production; or forge links with national and international markets to sell their products. As the demand for industrial goods began to replace demand for traditional products of cottage industries largely in women's hands, women's income often diminished. Whereas women have been valued as defenders of identity and continuity in traditional communities, in rapidly modernizing societies, women become identified with backwardness. In these societies women become increasingly dependent on their husbands who have ultimate control of cash earnings. Frequently this dependency means that women lose power. They are less likely to be influential in important family decisions and often have no alternative but to tolerate their husbands' infidelity or abuse.

Chan Kom, a Mayan Indian village in Yucatan, presents a contrasting case (Re Cruz 1998). The traditional way of life in Chan Kom has been centered around milpa production characterized by interdependence between husbands and wives. In recent decades both men and women have emigrated to the tourist center of Cancun in search of jobs. In Cancun, women work as domestics, and men work in construction. Migrants return periodically to Chan Kom to visit family, take care of business, and reconnect with their community.

As a consequence of this social transformation, both traditionalists and migrants have come to hold differing views of what constitutes Mayan identity and the right way to live. Traditionalists are concerned to preserve land and community, whereas migrants push to introduce changes into Chan Kom's social and cultural life. In this conflictive context, women have ironically benefited from their association with being guardians of tradition and symbols of the proper Mayan person.

In elections held at the end of the 1990s, traditionalists supported a woman candidate for mayor, an unprecedented move since only men have previously held formal authority positions in Chan Kom. The woman candidate offered as her political platform reconciliation between the opposing groups. She was bolstered in her platform by traditional female symbols and women's new positions of leverage as decision-makers and guardians of house, land, and children in the absence of migrant husbands. Although she did not win, the woman candidate projected a new vision of women as leaders of Chan Kom. Her story draws attention to the diversity of effects that modernization can have on gender systems, and as we will see next, on the strategies that women create to resist the negative effects of these forces.

Responses to the Economic Crisis

As mentioned before, the region experienced a drastic economic recession during the 1980s (see Chapter 9). Decreasing standards of living hit the lower classes disproportionately hard, and among them women suffered more than men. Several factors contributed to women's vulnerability, lack of schooling being one of the most significant. A large proportion of poor women never attend school, or they do so for only a few years. Additionally, large families prevent women from seeking formal employment, and lack of access to property and credit minimizes their entrepreneurial possibilities. Malnourishment tends to be twice as high among women as among men, making their overall health more precarious. These factors push women into the "informal" sector, which is characterized by low returns, lack of insurance benefits, and little or no job security. This state of affairs perpetuates women's dependence on their husbands, forcing them to put up with abuse.

How have women responded to the increasing impoverishment? The case of Marta Sandoval, a single mestizo mother of three living in a squatter settlement on the outskirts of San Salvador, El Salvador, illustrates survival strategies common to many poor women. To reduce costs and help with child care, Marta invited her sister Manuela and her two children to move in with her. Several months before Marta had lost her janitorial job at a nearby plant and was leaving at dawn with her six-year-old son to sell newspapers on a busy street corner. Before she found work selling newspapers, Marta had tried her hand unsuccessfully at many different jobs in the informal sector (Figure 12.6). All the while she paid a neighbor to keep an eye on her children.

Living together, the sisters were able to pool their meager resources by sharing rent, cooking and eating together, and helping each other with child care. When Marta returns home at noon, Manuela leaves for her job washing clothes for a middle-class family three times a week. Although the women barely have enough money for their own needs, they send some money to their parents who live in a rural village. The two sisters are happy that they have not had to reduce their food intake as some

Figure 12.6   In the various economic crises that have gripped the region, women's ingenuity has proved fundamental to survival. Photograph provided by the authors.

of their neighbors have. In their settlement, some of the poorest families have begun to search for food in garbage dumps. One of the most difficult aspects of life for women in Marta's and Manuela's situation is that mothers bear primary responsibility for their children. Living together, the two women are able to alleviate some of this burden by sharing their resources and making critical decisions together about their own and their children's welfare.

Intensifying household production has become another important survival strategy (see Box 12.4). In contrast to poor mestizo women, indigenous women—although poor and not formally educated—are often trained at a young age in their community's traditional arts, such as weaving and pottery making (Greenfield 2004). In recent decades, artisan cooperatives have become a way for many women to survive the economic crisis. Women's cooperatives have proliferated in the Mayan Indian areas of Chiapas and Guatemala. Although earnings through cooperative sales are not sufficient for most women, their symbolic importance cannot be underestimated. Women state that working in cooperatives gives them moral and material support in their struggle to remain on their lands while living with more dignity than would be possible as displaced workers in the United States or other parts of Mexico (Eber and Rosenbaum 1993; Eber and Tanski 2001;) (see Figure 12.7).

Women also find solidarity with other women and support for problems with domestic violence and spousal abandonment in the many Protestant church com-

Figure 12.7   Women making bread in a Zapatista breadmaking co-op in San Pedro Chenalhó, Chiapas, 1996. Photo by Heather Sinclair.

munities that have grown throughout Mesoamerica. Women who join Protestant churches speak about how they find in their new spiritual communities support to help them deal with alcoholism, illness, domestic violence, and poverty. In general, modernization has influenced many indigenous and poor Mestizo women to explore alternatives to traditional spiritual practices. However, studies of women's conversion to Protestant religions suggests that they seldom occupy leadership roles in their new church communities (Robledo Hernández 2003; Rostas 2003).

Emigration to urban areas of Mesoamerica and to the United States has become an increasingly popular strategy to alleviate poverty and to escape the armed conflicts of the region (see Chapter 9). Although migration is not new in Mesoamerica, it has intensified dramatically in recent decades. For many small farmers, migrating to farms or cities used to be a means to supplement farming in their home communities. Increasingly, migrants find that their only real option is to continue migrating north to the United States.

Transnational migration is on its way to becoming the principal employment for the younger generation in many poor communities of Mesoamerica (for more on this topic, see Chapter 9). Although men migrate in greater numbers than women, in some communities, such as the Zapotec town of Cotecas Altas, women make up half of all seasonal migrants to the vegetable and fruit production zones of the northern states of Mexico. In certain areas of El Salvador, women constitute one-third of the migrants. Single women migrate in larger numbers than married women with children.

Box 12.4   Mayan Women
Ease the Economic Crisis Through Domestic Production

Dominga Quej, an Achí Maya woman from Guatemala, and her family were deeply affected by the economic crisis. Seasonal work in Guatemala's coffee plantations, her family's main source of cash, dwindled considerably. However, Dominga has an advantage over her mestiza counterparts. Her skills in weaving provide some protection in difficult economic times. Dominga and thousands, perhaps millions, of indigenous women responded to the economic crisis by intensifying domestic production of textiles, pottery, wooden objects, and other craft goods (Figure 12.8). Indeed, although in the past Dominga had always woven some items for sale in addition to her family's clothing, she began to spend many hours weaving for the tourist market in order to compensate for her family's lost income from seasonal plantation work. This strategy not only enables women like Dominga to improve their economic situation somewhat during times of crisis but also lets them do so without giving up control over tools, techniques, and work schedules. By working at home or close by, women are able to structure their domestic chores and child care around productive activities. By intensifying artisan production, women resist total incorporation into the capitalist sector.

Figure 12.8   Practicing the ancient arts of spinning and weaving, indigenous women contribute to the survival of their family while preserving valued aspects of their ancestors' cultures. Photograph provided by the authors.

The social and economic effects of migration are mixed. Although remittances may alleviate the worst extremes of poverty, the social, emotional, and physical costs are often great for both the migrants and their families who stay behind. Emigrants who enter the migrant stream from throughout Mesoamerica face many dangers on the journey across the borders into Mexico and the United States. Women risk being raped or trafficked into prostitution by smugglers as they cross borders or try to find jobs in cities. Although some migrants have established communities in the United States composed of fellow villagers who have also migrated, migration tends to loosen people's connections to families, meaningful places, ancestral histories, and communal traditions.

Once in the United States, both men and women migrants work very hard, sometimes holding two or three jobs simultaneously and living in crowded conditions. Back home, women often work longer hours as they assume more of the responsibilities of daily survival. Families are separated by migration with one or both parents working in the United States while children are cared for by family or friends in sending communities. Families are divided at great emotional cost. For example, Mesoamerican domestic workers do the reproductive work of more privileged American women while being unable to nurture their own children (Hondagneu-Sotelo 2001). It is often difficult for migrants to return home to visit; sometimes they do not return home for many years. In the worst case scenario for those left behind, migrants establish second families abroad and stop sending remittances home.

Researchers report that both men and women migrants acknowledge that women have become more empowered living and working in the United States because they can earn as much money as their husbands and can contribute equally to the household economy. Women also enjoy freedom of mobility, a concomitant of employment outside the home. Although their undocumented status often prevents them from calling the police in instances of domestic violence, the awareness of this option seems to have some restraining effect on abusive men (Hirsch 1999).

Many women whose husbands have migrated also report that they have become empowered by transcending traditional female roles and venturing into male spheres, for example, of planting and harvesting. Studies on migration further suggest that the transformation of gender concepts and practices among migrants impact those of the sending communities, as young men and women realize that there are new opportunities for women and different ways of organizing relationships between men and women (Mahler 1999).

The Incorporation of the Region into the Global Economy

Many international companies have set up assembly operations (*maquilas*) in Mesoamerica as part of the drive to capitalize on the abundant and inexpensive labor supplies in Third World countries (see the discussion of maquilas in Chapter 9). Although Mexican and Central American industries have traditionally employed men, maquilas began by recruiting mainly women workers. The explanation for the different employment strategies is found in the prevailing gender ideology in Mesoamerica: Considered the chief breadwinners, men are afforded greater opportunities for education and technical training and consequently greater access to jobs with benefits, security, and stability. In contrast, women are conceptualized primarily as housewives and mothers whose productivity is inevitably and properly limited by these roles. Hence, any income they bring in is supplemental, and formal training is unnecessary. Although change has occurred in this area, many parents still argue that education is wasted on daughters since their future domestic roles make it unnecessary. This ideology and the practices it generates have led to the concentration of women in the informal, self-employed sector of the economy or in unskilled work in factories.

Ironically, women's "comparative disadvantages"—including their culturally shaped submissiveness and docility, and their willingness to accept a lower wage for lack of alternatives—make them the most desirable workers for maquilas. Mexican economists Lourdes Arizpe and Josefina Aranda (1986:193) argue that the "comparative disadvantages" of women have been translated into "comparative advantages" for companies, capitals, and governments in the international markets.

In towns in the central highlands of Guatemala located near maquilas, approximately half of the households send some members to work in maquilas. Both men and women work in these factories, but women ages sixteen to twenty-four are the preferred workers. Working in maquilas provides women alternatives to self-employment, domestic service, or wage-labor in farming. Women workers state that working in the maquilas enables them to give their families monetary assistance and that it makes them feel stronger and more independent. Married women state that their cash income decreases their dependence on their husbands. Young women report enjoying greater freedom to dress as they please, to wear make up, and to go out with coworkers in groups (Goldin 1999).

Other women report that maquila work is difficult and that they experience many injustices and abuses in this kind of work (Pickard 2005). Women are required to take pregnancy tests as a condition of employment—they are often fired if they become pregnant or try to unionize; they have to work through the night to finish urgent orders; they are often not paid for overtime; and supervisors sometimes harass them, verbally abuse them, and even strike them with rulers or other objects.

In general, maquila work represents a temporary palliative for young women in need of an income. These jobs do not create the conditions for long-term development that could bring about major changes in women's lives. Neither do they pose a challenge to the existing social and economic structures that privilege men. In addition, women who have migrated to the U.S.-Mexico border in search of work in maquilas have discovered that many factories are closing in order to relocate to Asia where workers demand less pay and are less likely to organize for their rights.

Violence Against Women

Violence against women, a problem throughout the world, has increased in recent years in Mesoamerica. International attention has focused mainly on the murders of women in Ciudad Juarez on the Mexican/U.S. border. However, the numbers in Guatemala are higher (Amnesty International 2005). Why is this increase happening? And how are these murders different from crimes against men?

The term femicide, like genocide, refers to systematic targeting of a specific population, in this case women. Researchers in Costa Rica, for example, found that in 1999, about 56 percent of the women murdered were victims of domestic violence and "passional problems," a euphemism that explains away femicides and lessens the severity of the crimes (Carcedo and Sagot 2001). Only 11 percent of the homicides of men fall into these categories. Many murders of women take place when the women attempt to leave their partners, when they reject men's sexual advances, or when they are sexually assaulted. Femicide thus occurs as a consequence of the aggressor trying to control the woman's body and/or her behavior.

The causes of femicide are complex. The underpinnings of the phenomenon are to be found in persistent gender inequality in Mesoamerica. Women continue to be regarded as objects that men have a right to control. Violence toward women is exacerbated by the armed conflicts in the region (see Chapter 8). Military and paramilitary groups used rape and sexual violence as a strategy of war; women were tortured, terrorized, brutally murdered, and "disappeared" (Green 1999).

In the aftermath of the armed conflicts, violence remains strong in these societies. It is accentuated by access of the civilian population to weapons; by the fact that thousands were trained to murder, torture, and rape; by the displacement of entire populations; and by the torn social fabrics of communities, with the attendant internal factionalism. Fractured and fragile communities, particularly in impoverished urban areas, have become fertile soil for the proliferation of youth gangs. Gangs terrorize the populations of the region. Among their tactics, they use rape and sexual violence.

Researchers have also noted a relationship between violence and ongoing changes in the region due to globalization processes. In the past twenty years, neoliberal policies have resulted in widespread unemployment, underemployment, an increase in the informalization of the economy, an overall increase in poverty, and marked pauperization of women and children. These conditions coupled with cuts in government programs to assist poor families generate marginality, tension, and despair in families and communities, and they fuel the cycle of violence. The most violent areas in the region, in terms both of femicides and of general violence, are the most economically depressed and marginalized, that is, the misery belts around cities (Goldin and Rosenbaum, forthcoming). These areas are settled by migrants from rural areas desperate to find jobs or by extremely poor urban people working in the informal sector.

Women's groups in the region demand reforms to the antiquated legal and judicial systems in these countries. They call for domestic violence to be considered a crime and for all crimes against women to be prosecuted and punished severely (De la Fuente and Chachón 2001). Nevertheless, impunity continues to be a serious problem as most often criminals literally get away with murder. When the 1996 Law Against Intrafamilial Violence was being discussed in Guatemala, many congressmen protested losing their rights to chastise their wives and argued that the proposed law represented a state violation of family privacy. Some Guatemalan leaders involved in both the women's rights movement and the Peace Accords suggest that some of the violence against women may be due to a backlash against the gains that the women's movement has made. This assertion is confirmed by reports of threats and attacks suffered by many individuals working for women's rights in Guatemala as well as in Chiapas, Mexico.

Social Movements and Armed Conflicts

In the early 1960s, participating in *campesino* (peasant) organizations and in the Catholic church laid the foundation for women's growing awareness of the structural roots of their poverty and subordination to men. As a result of changes instituted through the reforms of the Second Vatican Council (1962–1965) and the Conference of Latin American Bishops in 1968, the Catholic church became active throughout Mesoamerica in raising poor people's awareness of the roots of their oppression (Kovic 2005).

Throughout the region the social justice projects of the Catholic church have been known by various names, including Liberation Theology, "the popular church," "the church of the poor," and "The Word of God." Although the Church's option for the poor was more concerned with class oppression than gender oppression, women began to transform gender norms by participating in increasing numbers in workshops and reflection groups in their local communities. For example, in Chiapas, Mexico, under the auspices of the Diocesan Coordination of Women (CODIMUJ), thousands of women participate in local women's groups in which they critique unequal gender relation and develop their leadership and other skills. In these groups women also explore how their subordination as women is related to the structural forces of racism and the neoliberal economic policies of their nation (Kovic 2003).

The focus on women's empowerment in these groups contrasts to the more limited focus on emotional, spiritual, and material support of women's groups in Protestant church communities, in which a strong critique of male dominance has seldom developed (see Box 12.5).

When armed struggles erupted in Guatemala, El Salvador, and Nicaragua, many women eagerly joined the rebel forces (see Chapter 8). Among them were poor peasant women, including indigenous women in Guatemala; urban working-class women; and middle-class, educated mestizo women. Many women joined the insurgency as a result of appalling actions perpetrated against their families and communities by the military. Being victims of rape, their villages razed to the ground, their close relatives kidnapped and murdered, women felt compelled to protect themselves and their families from the army and avenge the deaths of their loved ones.

Women "joined the struggle" in a variety of ways: Some went to the front as combatants; others produced propaganda material, occupied local radio stations to gain support for the insurgency, and wrote communiqués for newspapers. In the mountains and villages, women acted as doctors and nurses, and they fed, clothed, and sheltered combatants. Women also acted as messengers, provided infrastructural support, allowed the insurgents to convene in their homes, and transported explosives and guns (Kampwirth 2002).

Women had to overcome major obstacles in order to become active in the insurgency. They needed first to establish child care arrangements that would enable

---

Box 12.5   Women's Awakening to Gender Oppression

"When I started working with the mothers' clubs in the Catholic Church, it was the first time I realized that we women work even harder than the men do.

"We get up before they do to grind the corn and make tortillas and coffee for their breakfast. Then we work all day—taking care of the kids, washing the clothes, ironing, mending our husband's old rags, cleaning the house. We hike to the mountains looking for wood to cook with. We walk to the stream or the well to get water. We make lunch and bring it to the men in the field. And we often grab a hoe and help in the fields. We never sit still one minute. . . .

"Men may be out working during the day, but when they come home they usually don't do a thing. They want their meal to be ready, and after they eat they either lie down to rest or go out drinking. But we women keep on working—cooking the corn and beans for the next day's meal, watching the children.

"I don't think it's fair that the women do all the work. Maybe it's because I've been around more and I've seen other relationships. But I think that if two people get together to form a home, it should be because they love and respect each other. And that means that they should share everything." From Medea Benjamin, trans. and ed., *Don't Be Afraid Gringo: A Honduran Woman Speaks from the Heart. The Story of Elvia Alvarado.* New York: HarperCollins, 1989, pp. 51–52.

---

them to join the struggle. It was not easy to prevail over their husbands' resistance to their involvement. Even revolutionary men made it difficult for their wives to join in the fight, claiming that women who did this were disregarding the needs of their children and husbands. On the battlefront, leaders and combatants alike opposed women's participation in combat, and instead they gave women tasks such as caring for the sick, cooking, covering for a male combatant, and preparing a mission. Women, however, did not acquiesce; they demanded equality of participation and jobs of greater responsibility.

According to many female insurgents, women had to work twice as hard as men and be twice as courageous to be allowed into important positions. Eventually, as the war intensified and women became indispensable, men realized the need to incorporate them fully into the fight and opened the way for their participation at all levels. In the struggle to overthrow Somoza in Nicaragua, and in some of the areas controlled by the guerrillas in El Salvador, women accounted for about a third of the insurgent forces. Some women were even able to rise to leadership positions.

Many widows, and women whose husbands, fathers, or children had been kidnapped and disappeared, joined human rights organizations such as GAM and CONAVIGUA in Guatemala (Figure 12.9); Mothers and Relatives of the Disappeared in El Salvador; Relatives of Jailed and Disappeared People in Honduras; and Mothers of Heroes and Martyrs in Nicaragua. Women, who constitute the majority of the membership of these organizations, initially entered to seek economic and emotional support and to gain some leverage by functioning within a group (see Box 12.6). Many of them came from the ranks of indigenous peasant women, illiterate and humble. The traumas they suffered and their work in these organizations brought about the politicization of motherhood. These women now stage public protests,

Figure 12.9   Like thousands of women in Guatemala, El Salvador, and Nicaragua, this woman, holding a picture of her missing son, joined the opposition movement in her country as a result of a personal tragedy. Jim Tynan/Impact Visuals.

pressuring governments to find the whereabouts of their loved ones and to punish the people responsible for their deaths or disappearances.

Through their accusations of human rights violations to the international forum, women have procured worldwide support for their cause. Through their activism, they have gained a deeper understanding of the roots of poverty and violence in

---

Box 12.6   How CONAVIGUA Came to Life.

"Since I was fourteen I joined groups of young Catholics, cooperative groups and literacy groups. We taught women using their own experiences, employing the milpa, a hoe, a broom, to teach them to read and write in connection with their reality.

"Our lives changed after the earthquake of 1976. We devoted our energies to reconstruct our town and villages. Our communal organization was increasingly stronger because everybody participated in the work of reconstruction.

"Then the violence came, in 1979. We were disbanded. Our work became extremely difficult, many women disappeared, others were murdered. The whole population was terrorized. The groups disintegrated. Everybody felt persecuted. . . .

"In 1984, while I was living in the city with my family, my husband was kidnapped and I was left alone with two children. . . . I had to sell vegetables in the city every day with my children. It is thus that I had the opportunity to meet other sisters that were also widows. We supported each other, we began to weave together and our work grew.

"We were here in Guatemala City, all of us widows, when we learned about similar groups in Chimaltenango. There were groups all over the country and we began to communicate. That is how CONAVIGUA came to life; it was not the work of one or two women, but of many, seeking help, seeking corn. In the first Assembly of Widows there were one hundred representatives of the different groups. I was chosen as a member of the board because I was one of the three women, among those 100, who knew how to read, write and speak Spanish. This Assembly opened the eyes of many women. Sharing our problems strengthened us." From "Rosalina Tuyuc: Our Lives Changed Since the Earthquake," interview published in *Siglo Veintiuno*, April 20, 1993. Translated by Brenda Rosenbaum.

---

their countries and now seek to transform their societies so that their children may have a better future. A similar process of awareness and development of activism took place in the refugee camps in Mexico, where thousands of Guatemalan Maya widows fled in terror with their children.

In contrast to the movements in Guatemala, El Salvador, and Nicaragua, from its inception women found a place in the Zapatista rebellion in Chiapas as combatants and in positions of leadership in support bases in their local communities (see Chapter 10). Mayan women constitute about one-third of the combat forces and 55 percent of the popular support of the Zapatista National Liberation Army that came onto the world's stage in January 1994. During the peace talks between rebel leaders and representatives of the Mexican government, female commanders Ana María, Ramona, and Maribel shared the negotiating table with Subcomandante Marcos; and journalists witnessed the internationally renowned Marcos taking orders from Ramona, a slight woman wearing a multicolored, handwoven *huipil*.

Local Zapatista support bases and regional councils are structured to have equal numbers of male and female representatives. In reality it is often difficult to find women willing to fill leadership positions, since most women are married and have children and cannot afford to take on unpaid service outside the home (Eber 1999). Men have yet to assist their wives sufficiently with household work and child care to enable women to serve in leadership positions. In many communities only unmarried, divorced, or widowed women serve in leadership positions.

Box 12.7   Women's Organizations in Contemporary Central America

At the beginning of the 1990s, women's organizations turned their attention from supporting insurgency movements to advancing agendas for women in the transition to democracy. They pressured their governments to create specific institutions for women, such as special offices and national institutes to denounce discrimination and violations of women's rights and to investigate and prosecute crimes against women. Laws against intrafamily violence were enacted as a result of the demands of women's organizations. Although these laws have not been fully enforced, their existence represents a major victory; they tear down the boundaries between public and private, and force the state to assume responsibility for what happens inside the walls of the home. Women's proposals for other important laws regarding reproductive rights, sexual harassment, equality of opportunities for women, and protection for domestic and maquila workers have yet to become a reality.

Over the past decade, many women's organizations have dedicated their efforts to helping women become political subjects. This effort is a major contribution to the democratization processes in Central America. In Guatemala, for example, AMVA (Association Woman Let's Move Forward) offers workshops on gender, leadership, and political awareness to hundreds of indigenous and rural women. When these women return to their villages, they organize local women's groups. AMVA began by assisting women to obtain their ID papers, a process that took several years to complete and became a sine qua non for the political participation of women (Castillo Godoy 2003).

Women's groups are having a major impact at the local level; women are making their voices heard within and outside their communities. They are presenting proposals, demanding accountability from authorities, and voting and participating as candidates in elections. In addition, organizing in groups has empowered women to search for economic avenues to alleviate the precarious conditions of their households. Many groups have created links with NGOs to procure microcredit or find markets for their artisan products.

GENDER AWARENESS AND CONTEMPORARY WOMEN'S MOVEMENTS

Women's organizational efforts in Mesoamerica have been increasing in numbers and complexity since the 1950s. Women's organized activities on local, state, and national levels demonstrate the integration between their "feminine" or practical needs as mothers and wives with their feminist or strategic goals of transforming public spheres (Stephen 1997).

Although charitable and politically active women's groups began to emerge in Central America after the 1950s, women's groups did not appear in great numbers until the 1970s (Box 12.7). The impetus to create these groups originated in the international sphere, with the United Nation's declaration of the Decade of Women. Professional women's organizations proliferated in the region, and several women's groups emerged to support the insurgency movements in the area.

Political activists and insurgents in Mesoamerica in the 1970s and 1980s expected women to subordinate the quest to further their rights as women to the larger revolutionary goals of class struggle. Yet, in the process of facing the limitations imposed by machismo and gender discrimination, women have come to realize their strength, competence, and worth in a variety of contexts, and to confront the male bias of their societies. In the process, they are articulating unique forms of feminism that merge class, gender, and cultural interests.

Several factors have influenced indigenous women to intensify their activism in Mesoamerica since the 1970s. Two of the most important are the suffering that poor women have experienced as a result of the effects of neoliberal economic policies in the region and the human rights abuses they have endured as a result of the current low-intensity war in Chiapas and the civil wars of the region in the 1970s and 1980s. In their communities and also as insurgents in armed struggles, women have woven together new social structures out of diverse threads, from the social justice programs of the Catholic Church; to experiments in self-governance in autonomous Zapatista townships of Chiapas; and to the development of multiethnic regional and national indigenous movements directed at land rights, democracy, and self-determination (Eber and Kovic 2003; Speed, Hernández-Castillo, and Stephen, 2006).

From its inception early in the twentieth century, the Mexican feminist movement has ebbed and flowed in consonance with national and international political climates. The movement has made great strides in the past twenty-five years. Hundreds of women's organizations work at both state and national levels to promote in-depth analyses of women's situations at regularly held feminist conventions and through media campaigns. Mexican women follow with interest feminist discussions presented in magazines, radio, television, and newspapers. Feminist organizations in Mexico have forced men and women alike to pay attention to issues of rape, birth control, voluntary pregnancy, sterilization, homosexuality, decriminalization of abortion, sexual harassment, and domestic violence. As evidence of gains made to bring the rights of homosexuals to public attention, on June 26, 1999, ten thousand gays, lesbians, bisexuals, and sympathizers marched through Mexico City to the city's historic center. Gay and lesbian organizing has been spreading throughout Mexico, facilitated by increased access to telephones and the Internet.

Dealing with issues of gender inequality openly has furthered the awareness of women in all Mexican social classes of the need to confront patriarchal domination. Thousands of women—especially middle-class, professional, and unionized women, and to a lesser degree women in rural areas—are demanding the right to control their bodies, equality in the job market, and access to decision-making in public life. They are pressuring political parties to deal systematically with women's issues in government programs and to include women as candidates in their slates. Even though women and gays and lesbians are still grossly underrepresented in the highest and medium-rank political positions, they have begun to increase their presence in national and state political bodies. In Mexico since the late 1990s, openly homosexual or bisexual men have served in important political posts, such as secretary of tourism, governor of Quintana Roo, and ambassador to Cuba (Reding 2000).

The Zapatista movement represents a dramatic development in terms of indigenous women's organizing (Hernández Castillo 1997). This movement stands out among social and revolutionary movements in Mesoamerican history for its willingness to identify women's oppression as a central problem of society. On January 1, 1994, at the beginning of the uprising, the EZLN (Ejército Zapatista de Liberación Nacional) made public the "Women's Revolutionary Law." (See Box 12.8.)

Box 12.8   The Women's Revolutionary Law

In the just fight for the liberation of our people, the EZLN incorporates women into the revolutionary struggle, regardless of their race, creed, color or political affiliation, requiring only that they share the demands of the exploited people and that they commit to the laws and regulations of the revolution. In addition, taking into account the situation of the woman worker in Mexico, the revolution supports their just demands for equality and justice in the following Women's Revolutionary Law.

First: Women, regardless of their race, creed, color or political affiliation, have the right to participate in the revolutionary struggle in a way determined by their desire and capacity.

Second: Women have the right to work and receive a just salary.

Third: Women have the right to decide the number of children they will have and care for.

Fourth: Women have the right to participate in the affairs of the community and hold positions of authority if they are freely and democratically elected.

Fifth: Women and their children have the right to primary attention in matters of health and nutrition.

Sixth: Women have the right to an education.

Seventh: Women have the right to choose their partner, and are not to be forced into marriage.

Eighth: Women shall not be beaten or physically mistreated by their family members or by strangers. Rape and attempted rape will be severely punished.

Ninth: Women will be able to occupy positions of leadership in the organization and hold military ranks in the revolutionary armed forces.

Tenth: Women will have all the rights and obligations elaborated in the Revolutionary Laws and regulations. The Women's Revolutionary Law was distributed by members of the EZLN on January 1, 1994. This translation to English is from Zapatistas! Documents of the New Mexican Revolution, New York: Autonomedia (1994).

The rights laid out in the document hold great symbolic importance for women in a variety of organizations in Mexico and beyond. The demands range from detailing the rights of women within the Zapatista movement to demands of the state for gender equity in wages and in access to education and health care (Hernández Castillo, 1994). However, the most progressive feminist demands, given the conservative nature of the gender system in Chiapas, concern the rights of women to determine the size of their families, to choose their own husbands, and to be free not to marry against their will. The laws also call for implementing severe punishments for alcohol abuse and domestic violence.

The Zapatista movement is unique in enabling women, who traditionally do not participate in public assemblies, to take part in community assemblies and committees. The Women's Laws were the result of numerous consultations held among women of different ethnic groups throughout the state of Chiapas. Since their first experiments with law-making, Zapatista women have been carrying their collective process of decision-making to regional and national meetings of women from diverse civil society organizations throughout Mexico. In these meetings, women—who do not speak each others languages or know each others' cultural traditions—are creating new forms of discourse to articulate their common concerns and hopes as indigenous women. Together they are inserting their demands for change, such as changing aspects of their traditions that exclude or oppress them, into the national indigenous movement in Mexico (Speed, Hernández Castillo, and Stephen 2006). In the process these women are creating a new conception of cultural citizenship that integrates ethnic and cultural rights with women's rights. They break new ground in Mesoamerican history by successfully adding their own claims as women to the demands of a national indigenous movement.

In general, much needs to be done in Mesoamerican nations to make the social systems more gender-equitable. Because of the military conflicts in Central America and the devastating poverty of the majority of the population in the region, awareness of gender inequality has been slow to develop. Neither men nor women have viewed the effort to liberate women from the oppressive conditions imposed by patriarchy as a priority. Nevertheless, the relative political stability and better economic situation of a wider sector of the population in Mexico and Costa Rica have opened windows for women and men to rethink patriarchal ideologies and practices. The examples of Rigoberta Menchú and Comandante Ester, indigenous women who dared to challenge the established order, will unquestionably remain an inspiration to Mesoamerican women for years to come.

SUGGESTED READINGS

BURKHART, LOUISE 1995 Mexica Women on the Home Front: Housework and Religion in Aztec Mexico. *In Indian Women in Early Mexico: Identity, Ethnicity and Gender Differentiation,* edited by Susan Schroeder, Stephanie Wood, and Robert Haskett. Norman: University of Oklahoma Press.

EBER, CHRISTINE, and CHRISTINE KOVIC (eds.) 2003 *Women of Chiapas: Making History in Times of Struggle and Hope.* Austin: University of Texas Press.

GREEN, LINDA (1999) *Fear as a Way of Life: Mayan Widows in Rural Guatemala.* New York: Columbia University Press.

GUTMANN, MATTHEW 1998 "The Meanings of Macho: Changing Mexican Male Identities." In *Situated Lives: Gender and Culture in Everyday Life,* edited by Louise Lamphere, Helena Ragoné, and Patricia Zavella, pp. 223–234. New York: Routledge.

JOYCE, ROSEMARY A. 2000 *Gender and Power in Prehispanic Mesomerica.* Austin: University of Texas Press.

KAMPWIRTH, KAREN 2002 *Women and Guerrilla Movements: Nicaragua, El Salvador, Chiapas, Cuba.* University Park: The Pennsylvania University Press.

KELLOG, SUSAN 2005 *Weaving the Past: A History of Latin America's Indigenous Women from the Prehispanic Period to the Present.* New York: Oxford University Press.

McLUSKY, LAURA 2001 *"Here Our Culture Is Hard: Stories of Domestic Violence from a Mayan Community in Belize.* Austin: University of Texas Press.

MENCHÚ, RIGOBERTA 1984 *I, Rigoberta Menchú: An Indian Woman in Guatemala,* edited by Elizabeth Burgos-Debray. London: Verso.

NASH, JUNE 1993 Maya Household Production in the World Market: The Potters of Amatenango del Valle, Chiapas, Mexico. In *Crafts in the World Market: The Impact of Global Exchange on Middle American Artisans,* edited by June Nash. Albany: State University of New York Press.

PAST, AMBAR, with XUN OKOTZ and XPETRA ERNÁNDEZ 2005 *Incantations by Mayan Women.* San Cristóbal de Las Casas, Mexico: Taller Leñateros

SPEED, SHANNON, R. AIDA HERNANDEZ CASTILLO, and LYNN STEPHEN (eds.) 2006 *Dissident Women: Gender and Cultural Politics in Chiapas.* Austin: University of Texas Press.

Chapter 13

The Indian Voice in Recent Mesoamerican Literature

THE NINETEENTH-CENTURY HIATUS

With all of the extraordinary legacy of texts and commentary on colonial Mesoamerican verbal arts that we have considered in Chapter 6, it may come as something of a surprise to the reader to find that the nineteenth century appears, by comparison, to be relatively weak with regard to serious scholarly works either by or about Mesoamerican native people. This does not mean that Mesoamerican verbal arts were either moribund or inert in the nineteenth century. Ample testimony to the contrary comes from the powerful role played by oral traditions and underground native books of prophecy in such political movements as the Caste War of Yucatán (1848) (see Chapter 7). One can also infer, from the extraordinary documentation of Indian oral traditions that has been achieved in the twentieth century, that these forms were no doubt thriving in both the formal and the informal fabric of life in Indian communities of the nineteenth century. They simply did not get recorded, either by mestizo or creole scholars, for they generally lacked interest in the subject, or by the Indians themselves, for they were for the most part nonliterate in either Spanish or their native languages.

To make sense of this pattern, one should recall that the nineteenth century was a period of creole ascendancy in the political, social, and economic arena. The same was true of the arts. The last thing that interested the new creole masters was artistic representation of their region as composed of an ancient or a contemporary Indian substratum; this emphasis would merely testify to their "backwardness," both to themselves and to the world community. The name of the artistic game in the period therefore became self-conscious imitation of European and U.S. literary fashions. Such as they were considered, Native Americans in nineteenth-century Mexican and Guatemalan literature, like that of the United States in the same period, came to symbolize the vanquished primitive world, with both its romantically attributed virtues (the "noble savage" theme) and its (then) scientifically and historically assigned vices and afflictions (irrational, prelogical thought; sensuality; cruelty; paganism, etc.). In the end, nineteenth-century representation of Indians, such as it existed, was not about Indians, but about creole views of themselves and of what they were not.

THE REPRESENTATION OF INDIAN VOICES IN RECENT MESOAMERICAN ART AND LITERATURE

Mexico

The beginning of the twentieth century marks both a political and a methodological change in approaches to recording, understanding, and representing the Indian voice in Mesoamerican verbal arts and literature. The political backdrop of this change is manifest in the Mexican Revolution of 1910 to 1918, which sought nothing less than a redefinition of Mexico, to itself and to the world at large. Along with the radical reforms in land tenure, labor laws, church-state relations, and government stewardship of vital natural resources and industries, the revolution brought massive ideological changes that were reflected in the arts, sciences, and literature. The unifying theme of this intellectual transformation was the celebration of Mexico's Indian past and present as the soul of its national identity (See Chapter 8).

Indigenista themes came to permeate national life, from public policy to creative work in the arts: for example, the symphonic music of Carlos Chávez and the great school of muralist painters, Diego Rivera, José Clemente Orozco, and David Siqueiros. Popular and academic interest in Indian and peasant art forms flourished. Pre-Columbian architecture and decorative art, as well as contemporary folk art, provided the models and inspiration for expressive forms as diverse as government buildings, schools, clinics, novels, calendar arts, and formal painting. Indeed, the proletarian political focus of the revolution found perhaps its optimal expression in the graphic, plastic, and verbal arts, for these forms were thought to communicate the new revolutionary order more effectively than formal written tracts and abstract public policy statements (Figures 13.1, 13.2, and 13.3).

Not only did Indian and peasant themes enjoy a vogue in popular and academic culture, but there was also abundant public funding to support the scientific collection, study, and publication of native art forms. Nationalism and nation-building justified massive public investment in archaeological and ethnographic research and in restoration of pre-Columbian monuments. These same nationalistic efforts encouraged scholarship in the area of native languages and oral literatures, as well as research on colonial documents written in these languages. Not only Mexicans, but also foreign scholars—including anthropologists, historians, and Protestant missionaries—acquired sophisticated knowledge of Indian languages, thus enabling them to record and document, from live field settings, a substantial archive of modern Indian art and literature. Some of this contemporary material was transcribed and translated from Indian languages that had never before, prior to the twentieth century, enjoyed a written literature of any kind.

Another important trend in twentieth-century Mexico has been the revitalization of scholarship on the Indian languages and literatures that have a significant

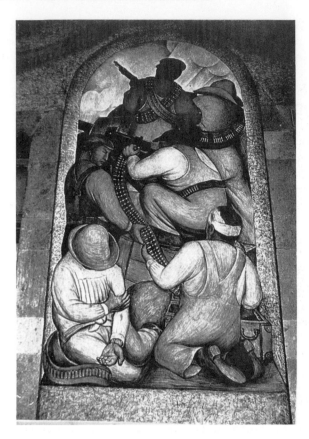

Figure 13.1   "En las trincheras" [In the Trenches], fresco by Diego Rivera in the Ministerio de Educación Pública in Mexico City. Reproduced with permission of the Instituto de Investigaciones Estéticas, Universidad Nacional Autónoma de México.

corpus of texts dating from the Colonial period. The most important work in this area has concerned the vast corpus of Nahuatl (Aztec) language texts that were set down in the Colonial period. Beginning in the early twentieth century with Fray Angel Garibay and continuing in the present with the work of his student Miguel León-Portilla and many others, there is now a continuing tradition of scholarship in both classic and modern Nahuatl literature at major Mexican universities. Other major linguistic groups whose colonial and modern languages and literatures are regularly taught in Mexican universities are Mixtec and Zapotec (from the Valley of Oaxaca) and Yucatec Maya.

Guatemala

To a certain extent, twentieth-century developments in the study and recording of Guatemalan Indian literatures have until recently lagged behind those of Mexico, in large part because the popular revolutionary setting that provided the impetus for collection and scholarly creativity on these materials in Mexico developed later in Guatemala and did not become institutionalized as part of the national agenda. A partial revolutionary parallel in Guatemala occurred in 1944 and lasted only through

Figure 13.2   "Día de los muertos: la ofrenda" [Day of the Dead: the Offering], fresco by Diego Rivera in the Ministerio de Educación Pública in Mexico City. Reproduced with permission of the Instituto de Investigaciones Estéticas, Universidad Nacional Autónoma de México.

1954, at which time the U.S.-backed counterrevolution both directly and indirectly discouraged *indigenista* political and cultural programs (as discussed in Chapter 8). During this brief decade, however, the Guatemalan government sponsored major research projects focusing on the nation's majority Indian population; from that period forward to our time, anthropologists, linguists, and ethnohistorians, many of them foreign, have been relatively free to conduct research there.

Although Indian themes in the arts and in popular and institutional culture have never achieved the huge popularity that they have in Mexico, the middle and late twentieth century have produced major discoveries and studies of Guatemalan colonial ethnohistoric documents written in Indian languages. In addition, a significant corpus of ethnographic literature and important collections of Indian oral traditions have also appeared during this period. In spite of these scholarly advances in the post-1954 era, local and national government interest in the Indian past and present has been, until the past few years, largely focused on the value of Indian "folkloric" themes (for example, Indian festivals and architectural monuments) for promoting tourism.

Figure 13.3 "Orgía: noche de los ricos" [Orgy: Soiree of the Rich], fresco by Diego Rivera in the Ministerio de Educación Pública in Mexico City. Reproduced with permission of the Instituto de Investigaciones Estéticas, Universidad Nacional Autónoma de México (UNAM).

On the other hand, Indian themes early on found their way into Guatemalan literature, as evidenced in Miguel Angel Asturias's *Men of Maize* (1949), which is based on symbolic ideas that come from the *Popol Wuh*. He received the Nobel Prize in Literature for this work, among others, in 1967. More recently, Rigoberta Menchú, herself a Mayan, received the 1992 Nobel Peace Prize for her work in promoting social and political justice for the nation's still-oppressed Maya Indian population. Her book *I, Rigoberta Menchú* (1983), an autobiography that documents her life and the dawn of her political consciousness, was a key item of evidence that entered into the decision-making process that led to this great honor. It is symptomatic of the political differences between Mexico and Guatemala that Rigoberta Menchú and her work achieved international fame not for their celebration of traditional Indian themes as a rediscovered part of national identity, but for the author's vivid personal testimonial of the tragic victimization of Indians by the ruling white government in the current climate of civil violence (for more on Rigoberta Menchú, see Box 8.3, Chapter 8).

Other Central American Nations

It is perhaps a reflection of the mestizo demographic composition of El Salvador, Honduras, Nicaragua, and Costa Rica, together with the still-evolving ethnic composition of Belize, that none of these countries has produced what might be called a distinctively Mesoamerican voice in the arts in the twentieth century (as pointed out in the Introduction). Literary creators of such international fame as Rubén Darío and Ernesto Cardenal, both of Nicaragua, have both, for radically different artistic reasons, spoken to issues larger than the nation. Darío self-consciously and very successfully imitated early-twentieth-century European literary fashions in his modernist poetry; the Nicaraguan imagery, though often present, was nevertheless not central to his poetic vision or to his international fame.

Ernesto Cardenal's great poetic corpus has been tied closely to the theme of Liberation Theology as a cause that pertains to all of Latin America's urban and peasant poor. The Nicaraguan setting in which he lived and worked (eventually as President Daniel Ortega's Minister of Culture) was not really significant as Nicaraguan or Mesoamerican reality per se, but was, rather, emblematic of social and political problems that might be situated anywhere in Latin America. In this sense, both Darío and Cardenal are major literary voices from the region that speak of issues and causes and themes that are beyond, but also pertinent to, Mesoamerica. (for a description of Indians in Nicaragua, see Chapter 8).

THE NATIVE VOICE IN NATIONAL WRITTEN LITERATURES OF MESOAMERICA

In attempting to generalize about the Indian voice in the national literary traditions of Mesoamerica in the twentieth century, it is important to keep in mind that Mexico and Guatemala—fundamentally unlike the United States and also, for reasons just discussed, unlike the rest of Central America—are nations whose cultural, social, and biological identities are profoundly linked to their Indian past and present. It therefore became imperative, as writers sought in the twentieth century to represent national reality and aspirations through literary creations, that the Indian body and soul of these nations be addressed. As noted before, both Mexico and Guatemala have undergone violent civil upheavals in this century, focusing on the issue of *pan y libertad,* "bread and liberty," which, roughly interpreted, means economic and political justice for all, including marginalized Indians and mestizos. If the nineteenth century was a period of suppression, both political and symbolic, of the Indian cultural component of these nations in the effort to create modern states in the image of France and the United States, the twentieth century has radically reversed this trend, and many of the emblematic literary creations of the modern era clearly reflect this change.

What now follows is a small sampler of such works, with brief introductions. It is hoped that the texts will speak clearly for themselves.

Octavio Paz (1914–1998)

Octavio Paz is among the foremost of many writers and artists in the twentieth century who have sought to define Mexico's singular identity as a modern mestizo nation whose roots are both Indian and Western. In addition to his being an acclaimed national poet, philosopher, and social commentator, he has held major diplomatic posts abroad as well as visiting professorships in Europe and the United States. His book *The Labyrinth of Solitude* (1950, revised in 1959), from which the following excerpt is taken, was certainly not the first postrevolutionary work to make the point that Mexico's future as a modern nation requires an ongoing dialogue with its Indian past and present. However, it was, without a doubt, one of the most influential statements of this theme, both at home and abroad.

The following excerpt is from the chapter entitled "The Sons of Malinche." In it, Paz deals with two national icons: Mexico's patron saint, the Virgin of Guadalupe, and La Malinche (or Doña Marina, as Spaniards called her), who was Cortés's Indian mistress and interpreter. She is viewed by most Mexicans ambivalently: both as a traitor to the nation's Indian past and as the Mexican Eve (Figure 13.4) (for more on La Malinche, see Chapters 5, 8, and 14).

Figure 13.4   "Cortés y la Malinche" [Cortés and Malinche], mural by José Clemente Orozco in the Escuela Nacional Preparatoria, No. 1, Mexico City. Reproduced with permission of the Universidad Nacional Autónoma de México (UNAM).

In contrast to Guadalupe, who is the Virgin Mother, the Chingada [Malinche] is the violated Mother. Neither in her nor in the Virgin do we find traces of the darker attributes of the great goddesses: the lasciviousness of Amaterasu and Aphrodite, the cruelty of Artemis and Astarte, the sinister magic of Circe or the bloodlust of Kali. Both of them are passive figures. Guadalupe is pure receptivity, and the benefits she bestows are of the same order: she consoles, quiets, dries tears, calms passions. The Chingada is even more passive. Her passivity is abject: she does not resist violence, but is an inert heap of bones, blood and dust. Her taint is constitutional and resides, as we said earlier, in her sex. This passivity, open to the outside world, causes her to lose her identity: she is the Chingada. She loses her name; she is no one; she disappears into nothingness; she is Nothingness. And yet she is the cruel incarnation of the feminine condition.

If the Chingada is a representation of the violated Mother, it is appropriate to associate her with the Conquest, which was also a violation, not only in the historical sense but also in the very flesh of Indian women. The symbol of this violation is doña Malinche, the mistress of Cortés. It is true that she gave herself voluntarily to the conquistador, but he forgot her as soon as her usefulness was over. Doña Marina becomes a figure representing the Indian women who were fascinated, violated or seduced by the Spaniards. And as a small boy will not forgive his mother if she abandons him to search for his father, the Mexican people have not forgiven La Malinche for her betrayal. She embodies the open, the chingado, to our closed, stoic, impassive Indians. Cuauhtémoc and Doña Marina are thus two antagonistic and complementary figures. There is nothing surprising about our cult of the young emperor—"the only hero at the summit of art," an image of the sacrificed son—and there is also nothing surprising about the curse that weighs against La Malinche. This explains the success of the contemptuous adjective *malinchista* recently put into circulation by the newspapers to denounce all those who have been corrupted by foreign influences. The malinchistas are those who want Mexico to open itself to the outside world: the true sons of La Malinche, who is the Chingada in person. Once again we see the opposition of the closed and the open.

When we shout "¡Viva México, hijos de la chingada!" we express our desire to live closed off from the outside world and, above all, from the past. In this shout we condemn our origins and deny our hybridism. The strange permanence of Cortés and la Malinche in the Mexican's imagination and sensibilities reveals that they are something more than historical figures: they are symbols of a secret conflict we have still not resolved. When he repudiates La Malinche—the Mexican Eve, as she was represented by José Clemente Orozco in his mural in the National Preparatory School—the Mexican breaks his ties with his past, renounces his origins, and lives in isolation and solitude. (Paz 1961:85–87)

Ricardo Pozas Arciniega (1912–1994)

Ricardo Pozas began in the 1940s, along with many others, to contribute to what would be by the late twentieth century a tidal wave of Mexican scholarly interest in *indigenista* topics in the social sciences. Pozas, a social anthropologist, was among the first Mexican mestizo scholars to conduct extended field research in Indian communities. Pozas's major monograph on the Chamula Tzotzil Mayas was published in 1959; unlike most other social scientists, Pozas had a literary bent, and he contributed, in addition to his ethnographic reports, an extremely popular ethnological reconstruction of the life of a Chamula Tzotzil. The book, entitled *Juan Pérez Jolote* (for the name of the hero), was first published in Spanish in 1952. Pozas used this historical individual (who is, by the way, buried in a marked grave in San Juan Chamula) as a literary and scientific medium to bring to life for a broad sector of the Mexican public the culture of Indian Mexico. The book was even made into a fairly successful motion picture.

In the following excerpt (from the 1962 English translation *Juan the Chamula*), Juan Pérez Jolote tells of his homecoming to his Indian village of birth after a ten-year absence during which he fought as a conscripted soldier in the Mexican Revolution (see Figure 8.10).

I went into the house and greeted my father, but he didn't recognize me. I'd almost forgotten how to speak Tzotzil, and he couldn't understand what I was saying. He asked me who I was and where I came from.

"You still don't know me? I'm Juan!"

"What? . . . You're still alive! But if you're Juan, where have you been? . . . I went to the farm twice to look for you."

"I left the farm and went to Mexico City to be a soldier." I was kneeling down as I said this.

"Did you really become a soldier?"

"Yes, papacito."

"Well, I'll be damned! But how come you didn't get killed?"

"Because God took care of me."

Then he called to my mother. "Come here and see your son Juan! The cabrón has come back to life!"

My mother came in and my father asked her, "Do you know who this is?"

I knelt down again. "I'm your Juan, mamacita."

My mother began to cry and said to my father, "Look at him, he's grown up! If you hadn't hit him so much, he wouldn't have run away from us."

My father said, "Well, he's back now, so that's that. Let's go inside."

They gave me a chair and I sat down and looked at them. I couldn't make any conversation because I'd forgotten too much of our language.

They called my brother Mateo and my sister Nicholasa to come see me. "Come here! It's Juan who ran away!"

My brother and sister came in to greet me, but I couldn't talk with them, all I could do was look at them. They didn't remember me, because they'd been so little when I left home.

"He's your older brother," my mother told them. "The one that ran away because his father kept beating him."

Then my sister said, "We thought you must be dead."

"No, thanks to God. He took care of me."

Some of the words I used were Tzotzil, but the rest were Spanish. Everybody laughed at me because I couldn't say things correctly in our language.

And I stayed here, I lived in my own village again. The first night I woke up when my father started blowing on the embers of the cooking fire. I was afraid he'd come over and wake me up by kicking me. But he didn't, because I was a man now! My mother got out of bed and gave him some water so he could wash his hands. She washed hers, too, and began to grind the dough for the tortillas.

We all gathered around the fire to warm ourselves, and I watched the flames, how they surround the comal [tortilla griddle] on which the tortillas were baking. . . . While my mother was making the tortillas I remembered a lot of things I'd forgotten: my mother's dreams, the stories the old people like to tell, their joys and sorrows.

Three hours later the sky grew bright and the sun came up from behind the mountains. My mother put some coals into the clay incense burner and went out to greet the first rays of the sun. She dropped some pieces of copal into the burner, knelt down to kiss the ground, and begged the sun to protect us and give us health. (Pozas Arciniega 1962:44–47)

Ermilo Abreu Gómez (1894–1971)

Ermilo Abreu Gómez was a novelist, poet, journalist, critic, scholar, and educator who taught in Mexico, the United States, and several Latin American universities. His work *Canek: History and Legend of a Maya Hero* (originally published in 1940, and excerpted in Box 13.1), is a short but complex mosaic of vignettes that take place on a great Yucatec estate in the late nineteenth century. Although it is ostensibly about the peculiar and moving friendship between an invalid creole boy (Guy) of old, aristocratic family background, and a Mayan boy (Jacinto Canek) who works as a peon on his aunt's and uncle's henequen plantation, the book is in reality a fictional reconstruction of the living Mayan memory of a tragic and terrible moment in White-Indian relations in colonial Yucatán, dating from 1761.

Box 13.1   Canek: History and Legend of a Mayan Hero

Abreu Gómez's story of Canek actually takes place in multilayered cyclical time: Canek was a pre-Columbian royal title; it was the name of a messianic prophet who lived early in the Colonial period; it was the name of the martyred hero of 1761 and thus the rallying cry symbolizing all Mayan heroes from 1761 to 1900; and it was the name of Guy's Mayan friend who lived at around the time of the historical present that is portrayed in the novel. It is not difficult to read the novel as both an indictment of white Mexico and a bid for Mexican reconciliation with its Indian past.

The following passage, depicting the tenderness of Canek's last days with his frail White friend, evokes several possible interpretations:

When Guy came back from the field he was bent over like a broken cornstalk and was drowsy. Canek laid him down on the grass. He sat beside him and kept watch over his sleep. In the shelter of his care, Canek could feel the boy was resting. Without speaking it, in the peace of his closed eyes, Canek read the message of innocence that lived in Guy's spirit.

Guy can't sleep. The night is sour and the winds from the south beat heavily on the limy earth. A yellow dust clouds the stars. Guy can't stop coughing. Resting his head in Canek's hands he sometimes smiles. Canek tells him ancient tales.

As soon as he woke up, Guy asked for water. He had spent the night sweating and in pain. Canek took the jug with water collected from the morning dew and gave it to him. Guy drank with an almost painful anxiousness. Afterward he asked, "Jacinto, why is dew water so good?" "Because it is filled with light from the stars, and starlight is sweet."

"Is it true, Jacinto, that children who die are turned into birds?"

"I don't know, Guy."

"Is it true, Jacinto, that children who die become flowers?"

"I don't know, Guy."

"Is it true, Jacinto, that children who die go to heaven?"

"I don't know, Guy."

"Then Jacinto tell me what does happen to children who die?"

"Children who die, little Guy, awaken."

In the morning Guy was gone. Nobody saw him die. Between the strands of his hammock, he looked asleep. On his pale, delicate lips a light smile also slept. In the corner, not making any noise, Canek cried like a child.

Tía Charo came near, touched his shoulder and said, "Jacinto, you're not family. Why are you crying?" (Abreu Gómez 1979:29–30)

The year 1761 was the date of a rebellion in which the Mayas—subscribing to a prophecy (set down in the famous underground book, the *Chilam Balam*) of the imminent return of an Itza king of the royal lineage of Canek to rescue them from their Spanish oppressors—sought, under just provocation, to make the prophecy come true and to drive the Whites into the sea. The leader, for this reason, assumed the name of the prophet, Jacinto Canek. Canek's uprising was squelched, and the hero was publicly drawn, quartered, and burned in the plaza of Mérida. From that time forward "Jacinto Canek" became the rallying cry of Yucatec Mayan rebellion and separatism, which again flowered in the well-known Caste Wars of Yucatán, which began in 1848 and lasted in one form or another almost to the end of the nineteenth century (see the account of the Caste War of Yucatán in Chapter 7).

Gregorio López y Fuentes (1897–1966)

Gregorio López y Fuentes, like Ermilo Abreu Gómez, belongs to the great generation of early-twentieth-century Mexican writers who considered Indian themes to be centrally important in the valuation of postrevolutionary national identity. He was both a novelist and a journalist, and his novel *El Indio*, from which the following extract is taken, won for him in 1935 Mexico's first National Prize of Literature. The original edition and current English translations are illustrated by Diego Rivera. This book reveals López y Fuentes to be an artist of both historical and ethnographic sensitivity, yet the book itself is odd in that it is about no particular place or time. The events depicted fictionally suggest that its ethnographic time and place are "somewhere in East Central Mexico sometime before, during and after the Revolution."

The novel is tragic and ironic in that its protagonist is not a person but the collective identity of marginalized Indian Mexico. The village represented here is a Nahuatl-speaking community that could symbolize hundreds of other Indian communities. For centuries the protagonists and their ancestors had fled from the land-grabbing and labor exploitation of White and mestizo Mexicans into the mountain fastnesses. Now, however (at the time of the novel), they are sought out, at the edge of nowhere, by Whites and mestizos who demand that the Indians provide knowledge of alleged hidden treasure. Subsequently they also demand from the Indians labor service for public works related to the revolution in progress, which is intended to "liberate" them.

In the passage that follows, the Indians have slain one of these abusive Mexicans with a well-engineered rockslide, and they gird themselves for the consequences:

> All that night the rancheria buzzed with excitement. It was evident that the old men were in council, and the villagers crowded around them, droning like a disturbed beehive.
>
> The men who had just returned from work were told what had happened. Those who had been in their own fields, those who had come up from the valley after their daily labor in the haciendas, and those who had just finished their week as servants in the houses of rich townspeople—all heard and gave their opinions, but they carried no weight. The council of elders would decide.
>
> The most important information was brought by one of the Indians just back from service in the town. He had met two whites on horseback, one of them leading a pack mule, and the other a riderless mount. It was clear from this that the fugitive treasure

hunters had abandoned the one who was hit by the rock—maybe buried it—at the bottom of the canyon.

The old men remained sunk in thought for a long time. Beyond question the white man was dead; therefore, they could expect reprisals. The paper the strangers had shown them was proof of their influential connections. And, just as they had been able to obtain credentials, so they would get an order to capture and punish the killers.

The oldest of the huehues [elders] got up from the stone where he had been sitting. The moon rose like a yellow mirror catching the fading light of the sun. The old man's eyes ran over the crowd.

Few, if any, were missing. He beckoned those farthest away to come closer. They all looked alike in the first light of the moon. Their color was the same and their features identical, as if cast by one impulse, the reason for their meeting.

Everybody was silent as the old man spoke. He said the town would take its revenge even if the rancheria was in the right. As had happened before, the death of the white man would be a pretext for annihilation and pillage.

A new cycle of suffering had begun, he explained, and they could survive it only if the whole tribe faced it together, just as they had punished the white man together. He and the other elders, although they were part of the rancheria and had witnessed the act, could not say who pushed the rock that, plunging down the mountainside, had caused the death. Furthermore—and he raised his voice in resentment and anger—to give up the avenger would be an insult to the women of the tribe, for the pursuit of the girl was an outrage to all of them. Likewise, it would be an affront to the men, for the misfortune of the youth who served as guide through the mountains was an injury to them all.

The speaker concluded with an outline of his plan of campaign: abandon the rancheria; take refuge in the mountains as in past epochs of persecution; resist when the situation was favorable; beware of the neighboring tribes whose hatred made them allies of the strangers; and finally, for whoever fell into the hands of the whites, this order—sealed lips. That was their strength!

"No matter," he told them, "if they burn your feet to make you confess our hiding-places. Not a word! If they hang you on a tree to tear from your lips the names of those who took part in the fight with the whites—not a word! If they twist your arms till they break, to make you tell where we have our provisions—not a word!"

The huehue then turned to the other old men, and they nodded their heads in approval; for in his mouth, the tongue of experience had spoken. The crowd was silent. And silently they scattered. (López y Fuentes 1981:61–64)

Miguel Angel Asturias (1899–1974)

Miguel Angel Asturias, of Guatemala, was awarded the 1967 Nobel Prize for Literature. Widely regarded as one of the great artistic voices of twentieth-century Latin America, he also served in his country's diplomatic corps, including a period as ambassador to France. His literary innovation has been extraordinary. Indeed, he is regarded as the major Mesoamerican voice (along with García Márquez in Colombia and Carpintier in the Caribbean) of the great twentieth-century Latin American literary movement known as magical realism. His novel *Mr. President (Señor Presidente)* has also been credited with the creation of a whole new genre of Latin American fiction, that which deals artistically and politically with the persona of the military dictator.

His many works have focused on two central themes: the literary re-creation of themes in Indian mythology and folklore, and the systematic indictment of the economic, social, and political privilege of the creole elite. The work *Men of Maize,* from which the following excerpt is taken, mounts what is essentially an epic framework for addressing both of these themes. The imagery of the book is borrowed from the *Popol Wuh* (see Chapter 6 for a discussion of this work); yet this contact-period K'iche' Mayan symbolism is cast against a twentieth-century backdrop of social and political conflict over Maya Indian rights to their land, which for them has both sacred and economic value. The overall plot of this quasi-mythical epic story concerns the Indians' heroic quest for repatriation of their lands from their ruthless ladino (mestizo) usurpers.

The following passage evokes the mood of a Mayan village religious observance:

> Each woman stopped beneath the portico to lift her shawl over hair strummed by the wind from the mountains, each man paused briefly to spit out the butt of a maize-leaf cigarette and take off a hat like a cold tortilla. They were frozen, like hailstones. The church, inside, was a mass of flames. The confraternities, men and women, the oldest of them with bands around their heads, held small bundles of candles between fingers streaming sweat and hot wax. Other candles, a hundred, two hundred, were burning on the floor, fixed directly to the ground, on islands of cypress branches and *choreque* petals. Other candles of various sizes, from highborn ones with silver paper decorations and votive offerings pinned to them, down to the smallest tapers, waxes of less value, in candleholders which looked like tinplate flowerpots. And the candles at the altar adorned with pine branches, *pacaya* leaves. In the center of all this veneration stood a wooden cross painted green and spotted with red to represent the precious blood, and a white altar cloth draped hammock-style over the arms of the cross, also spotted with blood. The people, the color of hog-plum bark, motionless in front of those rigid timbers, seemed to root their supplication in the holy sign of suffering with a whispering of leached ashes. (Asturias 1975:127)

TRADITIONAL INDIAN VERBAL ARTS IN THE TWENTIETH CENTURY

Major works of Mesoamerican Indian literature in a number of genres—narrative, song, poetry, ritual language, and public discourse—have been known and published for centuries (as discussed in Chapter 6). That Mesoamerica has by far the earliest documentation of native verbal expressive culture of any region of the Americas is no doubt related to the fact that the cultures from which most of these texts come (the Nahua, Mixtec, K'iche' Maya, Kaqchikel Maya, and Yucatec Maya) had writing systems and the tradition of books and literacy long before contact with the Spanish missionaries under whose aegis their texts were set down in the Latin alphabet in the Colonial period. Although these colonial texts have been rediscovered, studied, and translated in the modern era, the cultural and linguistic traditions from which they come have been limited to those areas that were subject to early and continuing missionary presence, notably the Mexican Central Valley, the Valley of Oaxaca, highland Guatemala, and Yucatan.

A major addition to this circumscribed pattern of areal coverage of historical texts has emerged only recently with the important breakthroughs in the decipherment of hundreds of Classic lowland Mayan hieroglyphic texts. These developments, discussed elsewhere in this text (see Chapter 11), have already revealed a written

Mayan historical tradition that dates at least to the first century of the Christian era in lowland Chiapas and Guatemala. At least in the Mayan area, therefore, the presence of written texts available for study now spans a period of almost 2,000 years.

The twentieth century has provided both the political and the scientific infrastructure to greatly expand our knowledge of Native American art forms to include regions that were hitherto not well known. Indeed, many of the eighty-plus Indian languages still surviving in Mesoamerica (including, as of 2005, about 18 million speakers, living primarily in Mexico, Guatemala, and Belize) did not have, even in the mid–twentieth century, any published accounts of their contemporary verbal arts. Now, however, much is known of both the variety and the complexity of this expressive and spiritual world.

It may come as a surprise to the reader to find that oral traditions are not easy to record, transcribe, translate, and interpret in written form. We are dealing not only with spoken languages that may not even have a standardized written form, but also with a fluid set of art forms that are always changing as they are re-created and used in new contexts. There are no fixed texts, sometimes not even fixed genres, as in, say, the Bible's Genesis 1, verses 1 to 8. What is spoken in what we might classify as verbal art is carried in traditional knowledge that exists only as it is re-created by the pragmatic dictates of myriad social settings that require use of stylized language in an oral culture. These may be everyday events like the following: morning prayers; joke-telling banter among young men as they walk on a mountain path; requests for a loan or a favor from a relative; a toast to ritual kin who offer a friendly drink of rum; a recounting of the day's gossip around the fire at night, with casual reference to similar events in time past; or a warning to children about a spook that will capture them and turn them into tamales if they wander too far from home.

Special forms of language also occur as an accompaniment to ritual events at festivals: for example, long sacred songs, prayers, and ritual language. It is often the case during ritual proceedings that sacred narratives are implicitly present in participants' background knowledge, although they may not be formally recited; they are assumed to be part of everyone's common knowledge. Thus, the task of setting down an oral tradition as a "written literature" and the quest for native theories of language and poetics that characterize these traditions are, necessarily, somewhat artificial undertakings, for, from an oral performer's point of view, that which is useful and beautiful in the spoken word is simply learned and known from cultural experience; it is never a circumscribed, fixed corpus of knowledge.

The quest for adequate descriptions of these fleeting art forms is nevertheless worth the effort, since modern Mexican and Guatemalan Indians, like their pre-Columbian forebears, take accomplished and poised use of language extremely seriously. Eloquence in the spoken word, in fact, often ranks as the single most important qualification for leadership and public service in Indian communities. Why and how is this so?

Mesoamerican mythological accounts, past and present, link acquisition of language and dialogue with the dawn of consciousness in the creation of the human condition. In time present as in time past, language, with its wide range of poetic and musical embellishments, has functioned as a sacred symbol that allows humans to share qualities with gods and to communicate with them. In effect, beautifully executed speech and song are the only substances, with the possible exception of blood, that the human body can produce that are accessible to and worthy before divine beings.

Ancient and modern Nahuatl theory of language, song, and poetics was expressed in the metaphor of plants and flowers. Flowers, according to this theory of "flower and song," are the most beautiful, perfect achievement of plants, and also their medium for continuity through seed production. So also, song and poetry are the most beautiful realization of the human spirit, making these "verbal essences" worthy before the deities. If divine beings are pleased, human life is allowed to continue. A variant of these ideas occurs among the Chamula Tzotzil Mayas, whose metatheory of language links high poetic and musical forms of the language to the qualities of divine heat, which are required for communication with, and about, the Sun-Christ deity.

Closely linked to Mesoamerican ideas about the sacred qualities of poetic language are the stylistic conventions through which this elevated quality is achieved. As in many parts of the world, Mesoamerican poetry, ritual speech, and sacred narrative are highly redundant. Moreover, this redundancy is most typically expressed in variants of couplet poetry. Munro S. Edmonson has described this stylistic pattern for K'iche' Mayan narrative as follows:

> A close rendering of the Quiché will inevitably give rise to semantic couplets, whether they are printed as poetry or prose. In no case, so far as I can determine, does the Quiché text embellish this relatively simple poetic device with rhyme, syllabification or meter, not even when it is quoting songs. The form itself, however, tends to produce a kind of "keying," in which two successive lines may be quite diverse but must share key words which are closely linked in meaning (Edmonson 1971:xii).

The couplet may be merely semantic in structure, as in this example from a Zinacantec Tzotzil narrative:

> *He was very sick now,*
> *He wasn't at all well now;*

or it may follow closely parallel syntax, as in these lines from a Zinacanteco court declaration:

> *What do they say is my crime, Sir?*
> *What do they say is my evil, Sir?*

or it may be expressed in fixed formulaic couplets, as in this typical introductory invocation that is used in Chamula Tzotzil prayers:

> *I have come before your feet,*
> *I have come before your hands,*
> *With my spouse,*
> *With my companion.*

It is important to note that the couplet pattern and multiple forms of such redundancy do not by any means characterize all of Mesoamerican verbal art. Readers will see in the examples that follow in this section that different linguistic traditions and different performers within these traditions do not follow couplet structure with any rigidity or absolute consistency. Furthermore, different scholars who have collected and transcribed oral texts from Mesoamerican traditions do not always agree on how best to translate the pattern of native oral style into Western languages. There is, however, a "center of gravity" to Mesoamerican oral literary style that tends, like so many aspects of their expressive and spiritual universe, to complementarity, duality, and opposition.

Three examples of contemporary Mesoamerican verbal art are provided in the pages that follow. The first case study, from the Chamula Tzotzil of Chiapas, Mexico, provides a broad portrait of the content, structure, and poetics of a living oral tradition. The second case study, from the Huichol of Western Mexico, presents a long didactic or instructional text dictated by a shaman. The purpose is to explain the meaning of a native ritual practice, that of the peyote vision quest. In this case study, we will see how different genres of stylized language move freely in and out of the flow of ordinary conversational language. The third example, from the Nahuatl-speaking people of Central Mexico, presents an extract from what is now regarded as one of the first major Nahuatl-language texts to be transcribed in the twentieth century. Transcribed and translated by Fernando Horcasitas from a remarkable narrator, Doña Luz Jiménez, it recounts a Nahua Indian view of the Mexican Revolution.

The Tzotzil Mayas of Chiapas, Mexico

This case study comes from the research of Gary H. Gossen. The goal of the description that follows is to illustrate the importance and the extraordinary diversity and coherence of stylized language use in a Mesoamerican Indian community, San Juan Chamula, the largest (over 100,000 people) of twenty Tzotzil Maya–speaking *municipios* found in highland Chiapas today. (See the account on Chamula in Chapter 8).

What is a literature? The term becomes feeble when one tries to apply it to non-literate oral traditions. For literate traditions, the term carries some evaluative nuance; literature contains exemplary works of recognized genres: short story, poetry, essay, and so forth. For oral traditions, the task of considering them as literatures becomes enormously more difficult, for although there may be a native view of what counts as a native genre in the tradition, it is ultimately up to those of us who care to take them seriously as literatures to classify culturally significant genres and provide good examples of them. One cannot provide the wood smoke and laughter or adequately transcribe the delight that listeners find in a well-turned sexual pun. Nor can one reproduce the complex cadence of spoken Tzotzil in the silent fog on a muddy mountain path as an old man tells you of his father's encounter with an earth lord. Much, therefore, is lost in sketching an oral tradition whose very life is ephemeral, highly variable, and always linked to a particular performance context that will never again be quite the same.

Whether you look or whether you listen, you cannot spend time even as a casual visitor in a Tzotzil community without coming away impressed by the intensity and vitality of public ritual life. There are no scripts or notes, of course: only knowledge, precedent, and advisers. All that is done—the processions, the songs, the seemingly endless prayers and exchanges of ritual language—is carried in the oral tradition. In similar fashion, the daily round of domestic life in Tzotzil households typically begins with prayers to the Sun-Christ and other deities at the household shrine, and ends with tortillas, beans, gossip, and joking around the fire.

Most narrative accounts of Tzotzil history emphasize the learning of *batz'i k'op* (the "true language," or Tzotzil) and its specialized forms—such as prayer, ritual speech, and song—as the diagnostic moment in human "progress" through the four-period creation cycle. As it was in progress as a species, so it is with Tzotzils as they move through the life cycle. Infants are classified as monkeys *(mashetik),* precultural beings without language, until they are named and baptized, usually in the first two years of life. According to Tzotzil theories of self and individual being, a human life is a cycle of heat, beginning as a cold fetus and acquiring ever-increasing measures of spiritual heat as the individual moves through the life cycle.

Language-learning and increasing sophistication in language use, particularly in punning and joking behavior, are signs of increasing social maturity. Skillful use of language, like sexual maturity and wealth, is likened to powerful heat, the desired and the desirable. Those men and women who achieve rank and status in shamanistic careers and public ritual life do so in part through their linguistic competence. So complex are the specialized linguistic requirements of civil and religious office-holders and shaman that formal and informal apprenticeship is the norm.

Major civil and religious offices carry as a requirement the engagement of ritual advisers *(yahvotik),* typically past holders of the office, whose task is to accompany the officials and to teach them proper ritual behavior, prayers, songs, and ritual formulas. Aspiring shamans must not only dream to receive their calling but also find (and sometimes pay) a mentor from whom to learn prayers and other specialized knowledge. Musicians (those of string ensembles, harp, and guitar) occupy a culturally important role as ritual accompanists and as informal ritual advisers. A prestigious musician not only knows song sequences involving hundreds of formal couplets but also is able to prompt ritual officials and assistants about matters of etiquette, protocol, and specialized language use.

If specialized language use is crucial to the success of a "public service" career, it is also laced into the fabric of countless everyday social transactions. To borrow money, to ask a favor, to ask for help, to share a drink of rum, to enlist a ritual kinsman *(compadre)* for the baptism of one's child, even to pay a visit to one's neighbor's house, all require the use of formal language, a style of speech that is formulaic and fixed rather than spontaneous and free-form.

Box 13.2 is a transcription of a casual visit of two *compadres* (ritual kinsmen), as recorded in Zinacantan by Robert Laughlin. There has apparently been a misunderstanding. The visitor seeks to assuage bad feelings by offering rum, talk, and camaraderie. A bewildering number of processes, abstractions, and things can be

---

Box 13.2   Formal Speech Between Compadres of Zinacantán

Maryan: (He offers a bottle of rum to Romin.) I am paying you a visit here. Grant a little pardon for our tiny bit of cold water [ritual deprecation of the gift of rum], since you suffered the pain and the hardship. You sustained the lowly soul, the lowly spirit of God's humble angel.

Romin: God, are your lordly heads still anxious, your lordly hearts, My Father, My Lord? That should have been all, I wish nothing. My Father, I wish nothing. My Lord, I wish nothing, my holy companion, my holy compadre. Thank you so much. May God repay you a little. It isn't that I have said a thing, it seems.

Maryan: This way it has always been from the beginning, from the start, grant a very little pardon. God, compadre, grant the holy pardon, a little, a bit. I have come holding in my possession, the sunbeams, the shade of Our Lord [another ritual reference to rum]. Thanks for suffering the lordly pains, enduring the lordly hardship, you sustained the lowly soul, the lowly spirit of God's humble angel [speaker reference to himself in the mode of self-deprecation], the way you, too, are measured as a lordly man, as a lordly person.

Romin: God, thanks, then, thanks. They say there is still a little, a bit. Well, see here, compadre, it seems that now you offered me the little, the bit, it seems. I partook of the lordly liquor at your table. Let's share the little, the bit, it seems of what you offered me, too. It's not as if I am fine, by myself, proper by myself. It won't happen that I will go by myself to drink next to the house, of course [meaning that he does not regard this merely as an opportunity to have a casual drink of rum]. (Laughlin 1975:17)

The reader can easily infer that the formal use of language matters a great deal in Tzotzil everyday life. To gain some understanding of the complexity of this sphere of human affairs is indispensable for an appreciation of the vitality of this community.

---

glossed as *k'op,* which refers to nearly all forms of verbal behavior, including oral tradition. The term *k'op* can mean word, language, argument, war, subject, topic, problem, dispute, court case, or any number of forms of verbal lore.

Chamulas recognize that correct use of language (that is, their own dialect of Tzotzil) distinguishes them not only from nonhumans but also from their distant ancestors, and from other contemporary Indian- and Spanish-speaking groups. According to Chamula narrative accounts, no one could speak, sing, or dance in the distant past. These were among the reasons why the sun creator destroyed the experimental people of the First and Second creations. The more recent people learned to speak Spanish, and then everyone understood one another. Later, the nations and *municipios* were divided because they began quarrelling. The sun deity changed languages so that people would learn to live together peacefully in small groups. Chamulas came out well in the long run, for their language, *batz'i k'op* ("the true language"), was the best of them all.

The taxonomy of *k'op,* which appears as Box 13.3 and in Figure 13.5, was elicited several separate times from six male assistants ranging in age from eighteen to sixty-five over the period of one year. The information contained therein should be more or less self-explanatory.

Box 13.3   A Folk Taxonomy of Chamula Verbal Behavior

"Ordinary Language" is restricted in use only by the dictates of the social situation and the grammaticality or intelligibility of the utterance. It is believed to be totally idiosyncratic and without noteworthiness in style, form, or content; it is everyday speech. As one moves from left to right in this taxonomy, progressively more constraints of various sorts apply to what one says (content) and how one says it (form) (Figure 13.5).

The intermediate category ("language for people whose hearts are heated") contains kinds of verbal behavior that are neither "ordinary language" nor "pure words." They are restricted with regard to form (that is, how people will speak), but are unpredictable as far as content is concerned. A common Chamula explanation for this kind of emotional speech emphasizes the individual idiosyncratic qualities of the performance: "It comes from the heart of each person." The term referring to all of these intermediate forms ("language for people whose hearts are heated") implies an elevated, excited, but not necessarily religious attitude on the part of the speaker.

Within "pure words," the criterion of time association is the most important one in distinguishing the secular forms ("recent words," associated with the Fourth Creation) from those having greater ritual and etiological significance ("ancient words," associated with the First, Second, and Third creations). "Recent words" are colder, for they do not refer to the full four-cycle period of creations, destructions, and restorations. "Ancient words" are hotter, for they refer to events and supernatural beings that date from the very beginning of time. "Ancient words," therefore, comprise the sacred narratives and forms of language used for religious transactions (see Figure 13.5).

The following prayer text exemplifies the great beauty of Chamula "ancient words." The prayer comes from the induction ceremony of the Steward for San Juan. This is among the most prestigious of many religious offices held by members of the community, for San Juan is the patron saint of the community. The date is December 22, and the new official stands before the home of the outgoing Steward for San Juan. An assistant places a lighted censer before the patio shrine, and the whole party together—with the ritual adviser and incoming steward (*martoma*, from Spanish *Mayondomo*) leading—begins to pray for the success of their coming year of ritual service:

> *Have mercy, Lord.*
> > *Great Juan,*
> > *Great Patron.*
> *How is it that I come before your feet?*
> > *How is it that I come before your hands?*
> *With my spouse,*
> > *With my companion.*
> > *With your guitar,*
> > *With your gourd rattle,*
> > *With your servant, the musician,*
> > *With your servant, the gruel-maker,*
> > *With your servant, the cook,*

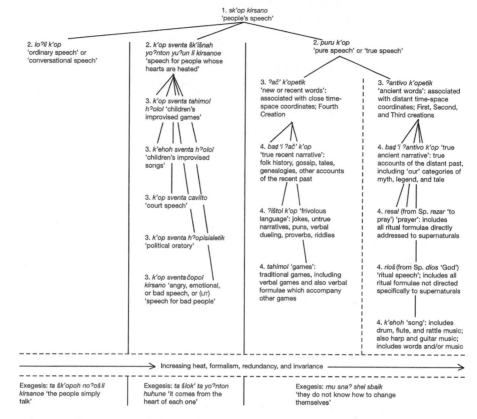

Figure 13.5   A Folk Taxonomy of Chamula Verbal Behavior. After Gary H. Gossen, "Tzotzil Literature," in *The Handbook of Middle American Indians Supplement, Volume 3: Literatures,* volume editor Munro S. Edmonson, general editor Victoria R. Bricker. Austin, TX: University of Texas Press, 1985, p. 81.

> *With your fireworks,*
> *With your hand cannons.*
> *Your children are gathered together,*
> *Your offspring are gathered together,*
> *For you to see,*
> *For you to witness.*
> *Great San Juan,*
> *Great Patron.*
> *Now you are to be delivered at my feet.*
> *Now you are to be entrusted to my hands.*
> *Now I am your new servant;*
> *Now I am your new attendant.*

I shall be as father to you,
> *I shall be as mother to you.*
> *For one year the same as for one day.*

Great San Juan,
> *Great Patron,*

There is incense for you,
> *There is smoke for you.*

I shall lift you,
> *I shall carry you,*
> *For one year the same as for each day.*

My Lord, Jesus, your children are gathered together,
> *For you to see,*
> *For you to witness.*

One alone cannot assume your care;
> *A man alone cannot do your will.*

What a good thing it is!
> *What an undertaking!*

That your children are gathered together,
> *That your offspring are gathered together,*

To stand up for you,
> *To stand firmly for you.*

May nothing befall us,
> *May nothing harm us.*

May your flowery countenance shine in white radiance,
> *May your flowery face shine in soft brilliance.*

That you may watch over us,
> *That you may care for us,*
> *And your musicians*
> *And your cannoneers*
> *And your cook.*

May nothing befall us,
> *May nothing harm us.*

Great San Juan,
> *Great Patron.*

Now you are to be delivered at my feet,
> *Now you are to be delivered into my hands,*
> *And those of my spouse, my companion;*
> *And those of my father and my mother;*
> *And those of your children, your offspring,*

For you to witness,
> *For you to see,*
> *For one year as for each day.*

Great San Juan,
      Great Patron,
I search over the earth,
      I search over the heavens,
Man of the cane of authority,
      Ladino of the staff.
Patron of Heaven,
      Lord of Glory.
Our Father Saint Matthew, Our Lord,
      Our Father Saint Matthew, Jesus.
Mother of Heaven,
      Mother of Glory.
Father of the Cross,
      Father of the Passion.
How is it that you come before my feet?
      How is it that you commend your self to my hands?
Great San Juan,
      Great Patron.
      For one year as for each day.
(Adapted from Gossen 1970:330–334; Gossen 1985:64, 76–82)

The Huichol of Western Mexico

The Huichol, numbering some 40,000 in the late twentieth century, live in the relatively remote mountainous areas of the states of Nayarit, Jalisco, Durango, and Zacatecas. In the pre-Columbian era they lived at the northwestern periphery of the Mesoamerican heartland. Being mountain dwellers and seminomads, they did not in the pre-Columbian or Colonial periods, nor do they today, participate fully in the centralized political and social arrangements that have long characterized the region. Their social, political, and economic world has always been an order somewhat separate from that of the heartland, sharing certain elements with it but remaining nevertheless at the margins of it.

The following text excerpt in Box 13.4 is about the sacred journey into the Huichol past that they reenact ritually via their ceremonial peyote hunt. This material, recorded by Barbara Myerhoff in the 1970s, constitutes a formal instructional speech that interprets the meaning of this ritual practice to children. Dictated by a shaman named Ramón Medina Silva, this account reveals the central importance of this sacred pilgrimage to the desert, their legendary homeland. Small groups of Huichols undertake this journey at great personal cost, in order to "find their life," past and present, via prayer, song, and vision quest as they "hunt" and consume the sacred peyote cactus. Through this sacred hallucinogenic substance, which is closely linked with maize and deer symbolism in their cosmology, Huichols affirm their social bonds with one another and with their ancestors and founding deities.

Box 13.4 Huichol Journey to Find Their Life

The text to follow, though cast in somewhat complex metaphorical language, nevertheless succeeds in communicating the religious urgency of the sacred journey. The "birds" of the text refer both to the pilgrims who actually participate and to the listeners who, via the narrative, participate vicariously and magically. The text provides a fine example of the manner in which sacred narrative, exegesis of text, and ritual language all occur together in a single discourse.

"Look," he tells them, "it is this way. We will fly over this little mountain. We will travel to Wirikuta, where the sacred water is, where the peyote is, where Our Father comes up." And from there they fly, like bees, straight, they go on the wind as one says, this way. As though they were a flock of doves, very beautiful, like the singing turtle doves. They fly evenly. You can see that they become as little tiny bees, very pretty. They continue from hill to hill. They fly from place to place as the mara'akame [shaman] tells them. The mara'akame goes with Kauyumari, Kauyumari who tells him everything. He protects them all. A little girl is missing a wing because the father or the mother have committed many sins. If they are missing a wing, the mara'akame puts it back on. Then she flies with the rest of them.

So they continue to travel. As they come to a place, the mara'akame points it out. So that they will know of it, how it was when Our Grandfather, Our Father, Our Great Grandparent, Our Mothers, when they went to Wirikuta, when Elder Brother Deer Tail, Maxa Kwaxí-Kauyuimari, crossed over there and the children of the first Huichols went there, so that they became cured.

That is what the drum says on our rancho. When it is beaten. There the children fly. The mara'akame leads them on the wind. They land on one of the rocks. It is as though they were clinging to the rock, very dangerous. The mara'akame tells them, "Look, children, you are not familiar with these paths. There are many dangers, there are many animals that eat children, that threaten people. You must not separate, you must stay close together, all of you." And the children are very glad, very happy. . . .

"At last," he prays, "Our Mother, Our Fathers, all you who are in Wirikuta, those who are eaten as peyote, we are on our way to Wirikuta." He says to the children, "Act and feel like eagles, you will go there on your wings." They give instructions to one another, they learn. One tells the other, "Light your candle," and he answers, "Yes, very well." Mara'akame takes tinder, he takes flint, he takes steel for striking fire. They do this five times and they light the candles and worship there and go on their way. They travel and come to a place they call Las Cruces, where the cross is. They exclaim, "Oh, look, we really have come far, yes we have come far. And how will we be able to go on?" And they say, "Well, it is because we are going to Wirikuta, where the peyote grows, where our ancestors traveled. We have to get rid of our sins, everything. . . ."

Where it is called Wirikuta, where Our Mother Peyote dwells, there they arrive. When he has beaten the drum, when he stands by the sacred pools, when he has spoken to the Mothers and the Fathers, to Our Father, to Our Grandfather, to Our Great Grandparent, when he has laid his offerings down, when their votive bowls are in their place, when their arrows are in their place, when their wristbands are in their place, when their sandals are in their place, then it will be good, then we will have life.

The children are happy, all, they are contented. Because now they are blessed. The offerings are made, the deer tail plumes are in their place, the arrows are to the south, to the north, to the east, up above. He holds them out. The horns of the deer are in their place, no matter what kind. The mara'akame says, "Oh, Our Father, Our Grandfather, Our Mothers, you all who dwell here, we have arrived to visit you, to come and see you here. We have arrived well." And when they arrive, they kneel and Our Father, Our Grandfather, Our Elder Brother, embrace them.

"What did you come for, my children?" they ask. "You have come so far, why did you travel so far?" They answer, "We came to visit you so that we will know all, so that we will have life." "All right," they say, "it is well," and they bless them. And there they remain but ten minutes, a very few minutes, to speak with Our Father, Our Grandfather, with all of them there. And then the Mother gives them the blessing and they leave. (Myerhoff 1974:179–184)

The Sierra Nahuatl of Central Mexico

The text excerpt that is presented next comes from one of the first major Nahuatl language testimonies transcribed in the twentieth century. The source is Fernando Horcasitas's transcription and translation of an oral historical account of the time of the Mexican Revolution. Dictated by a virtuoso narrator, Doña Luz Jiménez, the entire large text from which the extract is taken (*Life and Death in Milpa Alta: A Nahuatl Chronicle of Díaz and Zapata,* originally published in Nahuatl and Spanish in 1968) illustrates the extraordinary value of listening to historical accounts of key events from diverse points of view.

The eyewitness perspective of the Mexican Revolution from the point of view of a small Nahua village will make any "authentic" version of this event seem just that: official history. In particular, Doña Luz Jiménez's account reveals that President Porfirio Díaz (on Díaz, see Box 7.6 in Chapter 7), known to most of the revolutionaries (and to most modern Mexicans) as a ruthless dictator and hated symbol of the old order, was in fact well respected in her village. Furthermore, Emiliano Zapata, the great revolutionary leader of central and southern Mexico (see Chapter 8), emerges from Doña Luz's chronicle with mixed reviews: handsome and well-spoken, but nevertheless responsible for actions and policies that she finds reprehensible.

Here begins her account of how the first events related to the Revolution came to Milpa Alta, located in the mountains just south of Mexico City:

> The heavens did not thunder to warn us that the tempest was coming. We knew nothing about the storms nor about the owlish wickedness of men.
> One day gunfire was heard between the hills of Teuhtla and Cuauhtzin. We were told that it was the Federals fighting against the men of Morelos. There was a lot of shooting. It was the first time we had heard such a thing, and all of Milpa Alta trembled.
> The men of Morelos kept passing through the village and it was said they were on their way to Xochimilco. I do not know why they were against Porfirio Díaz.
> These men from Cuernavaca and Tepoztlan spoke our language. They were only peasants, and we did not know why the Federals were afraid of them.
> This was the first thing we heard of the Revolution. One day a great man by the name of Zapata arrived from Morelos. He wore good clothes—a fine broad hat and spats. He was the first great man to speak to us in Nahuatl. All his men were dressed in white—white shirts, white pants, and they all wore sandals. All these men spoke Nahuatl more or less as we spoke it. Señor Zapata also spoke Nahuatl. When all these men entered Milpa Alta, we understood what they said. Each of the Zapatistas carried pinned to his hat a picture of his favorite saint, so that the saint would protect him. Each bore a saint in his hat.
> Zapata stood at the head of his men and addressed the people of Milpa Alta in the following way: "Come join me! I have risen in arms, and I have brought my countrymen

with me. We don't want Our Father Díaz to watch over us any more. We want a better president to care for us. There isn't enough to eat or to buy clothes. I want every man to have his own plot of land. He will sow it and reap corn, beans, and other grains. What do you people say? Will you join us?"

Nobody answered. The days passed. The barracks of Zapata and Everardo González were set up in the village. González was told to stay in Milpa Alta to watch over the village. General Zapata was received in the following way. Everyone in the village went out to receive him. Crowds of men and women came with flowers in their hands. A band played and fireworks burst; and when he had entered, the band played the diana [a Mexican patriotic song].

Several months went by, and Our Father Porfirio Díaz and the Secretary Justo Sierra were not worried about the Revolution. Their great passion was the Mexican people. Wherever there were four children, they were given clothing. Girls were given a blouse and skirt, and boys were given a shirt and trousers.

Perhaps Señores Díaz and Sierra believed this: "Fathers and mothers will thus learn how to give an education to their children. They will send them to school." The hopes of these great men were fulfilled, and everybody in the village obeyed them. . . .

One day the Zapatistas came down and burned the town hall, the courthouse, and several homes. One of these houses belonged to a rich man by the name of Luis Sevilla. His house was burned to the ground. It was enough to break your heart to hear the bursting of the grains of corn and the beans. All his domestic animals died in the burning of that house. The next day, the Zapatistas came down again to the village and forced our men to take fodder and water to their horses. All of these things were caused by the Zapatistas.

When the men of Zapata entered the town, they came to kill. They killed the rich because they asked for large amounts of money which the rich were not willing to give up. Then they would take the rich men to the woods and murder them there. They also carried off girls. People said that they took them to the woods and raped them there. These maidens were abandoned forever in the woods, never to return to their homes. No one knew whether they were devoured by wild animals or whether the Zapatistas murdered and buried them there. (Doña Luz Jiménez, from the transcription and translation of Fernando Horcasitas 1972:125–135)

NEW INDIAN WRITING IN MESOAMERICA

In addition to the incorporation of Native Mesoamerican voices into the national literatures, ethnohistories, and anthropological studies in the late twentieth century and early twenty-first century, it must also be noted that Indian scholars and artists are now increasingly active in producing their own historical and literary texts. In both Guatemala and Mexico, this new generation of Indian writers became visible in the 1980s with the founding of such organizations as the *Academia de Cultura Maya* and the *Instituto Lingüístico Francisco Marroquín* in Guatemala, and the Tzotzil Writers' Cooperative *(Sna Jtz'ibahom)*, located in San Cristóbal de las Casas, Chiapas, Mexico. These organizations and others like them have encouraged not only the creation of literature in native languages—including readings and performances of their work at home and abroad—but also the teaching of literacy in these languages.

It should be noted that local and national governments of both Mexico and Guatemala have recognized these organizations, but that funding has been hard to obtain, since their goals are in some respects at odds with other government policies that encourage acculturation and literacy in Spanish. Still other opposition has come from Protestant missionary organizations that, prior to the rise of these native cultural movements, held a virtual monopoly (largely in the form of Biblical and other religious texts) on the production of written materials in native languages. For these reasons, the new Indian cultural organizations have been for the most part self-supporting, depending on funds generated by the sale of their publications and by private donations. The published works of these organizations are available in low-cost editions and usually carry a dual language text in the Indian language and Spanish. The subject matter varies from the retelling of traditional folktales, to the interpretation of recent historical events, to extensive biographical and autobiographical texts. In some cases, ancient Mayan and Spanish colonial texts are being translated and interpreted in modern Indian languages. The following brief excerpts will provide a sampling of this "new" Indian literary creation.

"About Pajarito and Chamula in 1911"

This work, dated 1991, is Publication 8 of the Writers' Cooperative (*Sna Jtz'ibahom*, or *Cultura de los Indios Mayas, A. C.*) of San Cristóbal de las Casas. This organization was founded in the late 1970s by a group of Tzotzil, Tzeltal, and Tojolabal Indian writers, with the assistance of Robert Laughlin of the Smithsonian Institution of Washington, D.C. Although initially supported by private donors (notably Cultural Survival, Inc., and the *Fundación Interamericana*), the organization has become to a certain extent self-supporting. The publication series is supported by the Mexican government's *Consejo Nacional para la Cultura y las Artes*.

The book whose preface is reproduced next derives from oral sources about a famous Chamula Tzotzil historical figure, Jacinto Pérez Chishtot, who was the leader of a violent political and religious movement of 1910 and 1911. He and his followers sought, under the tutelage of the conservative Bishop Francisco Orozco y Jiménez, to place the town of San Juan Chamula in the political camp of the counterrevolutionary forces of the Chiapas theater of the early years of the Mexican Revolution.

"Pajarito," as the leader was known in Spanish (meaning "Little Bird," from his Tzotzil surname Chishtot), has not fared well in Mexican official history, for he was eventually executed as a counterrevolutionary by the Mexican army. However, the following introduction to the Tzotzil retelling of these violent events of 1911 leads us to entertain a more complex reading of his life and political career than that given in official histories, where he is simply written off as a counterrevolutionary "crazy." As in the case of Doña Luz Jiménez's Nahuatl chronicle, the rendering of historical events depends a great deal on where one stands in the flow of these events, and, above all, who one is in terms of local identities and affiliations.

> As we shall now see, one person's counterrevolutionary is another's ethnic hero. Pajarito emerges from this account as an Indian ethnic martyr who tragically died at the hands of self-interested and deceitful ladinos, both revolutionaries and counterrevolutionaries. This account of the life and work of the famous "Pajarito" presents another facet of this well-known historical figure. We see here both an ironic and ambiguous side to his character that differs somewhat from the official accounts of him that appear in history books. This point of view is possible because the account recorded here was narrated by the son of one of Pajarito's closest political allies and co-religionists who fought side by side with him in his ill-fated uprising against the Mexican authorities.

Because of the personal anecdotal origin of what is told here, we are able to understand that Pajarito's violent military activities were in fact being manipulated by other non-Indian political interests. In fact, goals quite opposite those that Pajarito believed he was fighting for, were in fact pushing him onto the field of battle. Now, as we stand some 95 years removed from these events, we must be aware that the circumstances have become clouded with false framing and contextualization. We are now in a position to free ourselves from these assertions about our past, for we begin to sense a feeling of liberation from the long tradition of racism that Ladinos have imposed on us and our own past.

Although it can hardly be argued that Pajarito's people were justified in perpetrating all of their bloody activities, it is nevertheless the case that they were in fact being manipulated, however briefly, by Ladino power plays. (Sna Jtz'ibahom 1991:5; translation by Gary H. Gossen)

Victor Montejo's Testimony:
Death of a Guatemalan Village (1987)

Victor Montejo, a Jacaltec Maya from Guatemala, has become one of the more prominent members of a new generation of Mesoamerican Indian writers and artists whose work has appeared in Spanish and English editions. His most recent major work considers generally and synthetically the Mayan intellectual renaissance of which he is a part:*Maya Intellectual Renaissance: Identity, Representation, and Leadership* (2005). He has published a recent retelling of the Popol Wuh (the sixteenth-century Mayan classic) for young audiences in both Spanish and English editions: *Popol Wuh: A Sacred book of the Maya* (1999). At heart a storyteller, Montejo has also published a poetic rendering of a Jacaltec sacred narrative (*El Kanil, Man of Lightning* (1982) and a retelling of Jacaltec children's stories (*The Bird Who Cleans the World*, 1991).

The text extract that we offer here records Montejo's hair-raising eyewitness account of a local event in Guatemala's recently concluded civil war—known as the "the violence"—that convulsed national life in the 1970s and 1980s) (see the account of this war in Chapter 8). This important work, entitled *Testimony: Death of a Guatemalan Village* (1987), is extracted here not only for its artistic merit but also for its political content. It reflects the plain social historical truth that Mesoamerican Indians have spent centuries as the de facto underclass of New Spain and of the modern nations of the region. *Testimony* records Montejo's eyewitness account of the Guatemalan army's massacre of a Jacaltec Indian village on September 9, 1982, when the civil patrol of Tzalala, where Montejo was a schoolteacher, mistook an army detachment dressed in olive fatigues for leftist guerillas and fired on them. This massacre included members of Montejo's own family. These events took place in a period in which many of the departments of northwestern Guatemala (most of them with a majority Mayan population) were under military occupation. The justification, from the military point of view, was that all of the region's inhabitants, being Indians, were subject to leftist insurgency or were themselves guerilla sympathizers.

Reproduced here are the final passages of *Testimony:*

I returned innumerable times to report to the base commander, until he was relieved from his post. He was replaced by another lieutenant who had stored up in his being all the deadly poisons. I hesitated to present myself before him but finally had to do it to avoid intrigues and greater dangers. "I know nothing of you," he said to me the first time, which was fine with me. But some days later I learned he was carrying out a probe about me and my associations in town and in the village.

When I next reported to the commander, he said to me: "You will have to report here without fail. And don't duck out on me because I'm not one to be fooled with, as you did with my predecessor. I just came from el Quiché and I know how to clean up towns infested by guerrillas."

"Be assured, I will comply with the order."

Around this time the school semester was coming to a close. I had written final evaluations for my pupils and prepared to fill out the end of term reports and lead the closing ceremonies. The last days of October resembled a sick burro reluctant to move a step. More corpses kept appearing in the outskirts of town, and machine gun volleys shattered the silence every night. The army infested the town with secret agents who sowed distrust and fear among the neighbors. Once more I began to fear the prospect of a late-night kidnapping; my sleep grew fitful and my dreams were stalked by nightly terrors.

With the rise to power of Efraín Ríos Montt, all remaining human rights were abolished, and the army became the sole arbiter of the lives of Guatemalans. As the situation deteriorated day by day, I became convinced that I had to protect my life somewhere else, and so one dark night I fled with my wife and children in the firm expectation of returning when peace and tranquility will have returned to the beloved land of the quetzal. (Montejo 1987:112)

Rigoberta Menchú's *I, Rigoberta Menchú* (1983)

It is fitting to conclude this chapter with the voice of Rigoberta Menchú, the K'iche' Mayan woman of Guatemala who won the 1992 Nobel Peace Prize (for more on Rigoberta, see Box 8.3 in Chapter 8). Chief among the credentials that won for her this well-deserved honor was her autobiographical account *I, Rigoberta Menchú*. In this work she recorded, via oral testimony in Spanish (her second language), her extraordinary life as an Indian peasant woman who saw her own family (mother, father, and brother) cruelly murdered by the Guatemalan army for their alleged involvement in antigovernment activities under the military regime of President Romeo Lucas García, who came to power in 1978. (The reader will note that Menchú is responding to the same period and the same national tragedy as Montejo, whose work is discussed and excerpted immediately before.)

The social context of Rigoberta Menchú's testimony is considered elsewhere in this volume (see Chapters 8 and 9). However, for the present context, it is useful to recall that Guatemala in the late twentieth century retains many features of a caste society. A minority population of Hispanic identity ("ladinos") controls most of Guatemala's land and means of production, and behind the scenes it continues to suppress political expression and ethnic affirmation of the majority population of Mayan Indian identity. Although she addresses her Guatemalan experience in particular, she regards her testimony as a manifesto on behalf of all of Latin America's marginalized indigenous peoples (for an opposing ladino view, see Box 8.8 in Chapter 8).

In the following extract from *I, Rigoberta Menchú*, the author considers the political and ethnic power of Mayan views of the human soul. This discussion is directly related to the concept of individual coessences (discussed in Chapter 14) as a key trait of native Mesoamerican religious belief and practice. The author concurs with our assertion that coessences are important, but she takes it a step further, suggesting that Indian "souls" provide an esoteric language of self-definition that helps Indian communities to affirm their identity, even in circumstances of oppression and discrimination:

> Every child is born with a *nahual*. The *nahual* is like a shadow, his protective spirit who will go through life with him. The *nahual* is the representative of the earth, the animal world, the sun and water, and in this way the child communicates with nature. The *nahual* is our double, something very important to us. We conjure up an image of what our *nahual* is like. It is usually an animal. The child is taught that if he kills an animal, that animal's human double will be very angry with him because he is killing his *nahual*. Every animal has its human counterpart and if you hurt him, you hurt the animal too. . . .
>
> We Indians have always hidden our identity and kept our secrets to ourselves. This is why we are discriminated against. We often find it hard to talk about ourselves because we know we must hide so much in order to preserve our Indian culture and prevent it being taken away from us. So I can only tell you very general things about the *nahual*. I can't tell you what my *nahual* is because that is one of our secrets. (Menchú 1984:18–20)

With Rigoberta Menchú's commentary we come, in a sense, full circle. Native Mesoamericans, once a literate people before contact with Europe, are regaining this form of independent empowerment through literacy and through artistic and scholarly activity in both Native American and Western languages.

SUGGESTED READINGS

BIERHORST, JOHN 1990 *The Mythology of Mexico and Central America*. New York: William Morrow.

BURNS, ALLAN F. 1983 *An Epoch of Miracles: Oral Literature of the Yucatec Maya*. Austin: University of Texas Press.

EDMONSON, MUNRO S. (ed.) 1985 *Literatures*. Supplement to the Handbook of Middle American Indians, vol. 5, Victoria R. Bricker, general editor. Austin: University of Texas Press.

GOSSEN, GARY H. 1974 *Chamulas in the World of the Sun: Time and Space in a Maya Oral Tradition*. Cambridge: Harvard University Press.

GOSSEN, GARY H. 1993 On the Human Condition and the Moral Order: A Testimony from the Chamula Tzotzil of Chiapas, Mexico. In *South and Meso-American Native Spirituality: From the Cult of the Feathered Serpent to the Theology of Liberation*, edited by Gary H. Gossen and Miguel León-Portilla, pp. 414–435. New York: Crossroad.

GOSSEN, GARY H. 2002 *Four Creations: An Epic Story of the Chiapas Mayas*. Norman: University of Oklahoma Press.

KARASIK, CAROL (ed.), and ROBERT M. LAUGHLIN (trans.) 1988 *The People of the Bat: Mayan Tales and Dreams from Zinacantán*. Washington, D.C.: Smithsonian Institution Press.

LAUGHLIN, ROBERT M. 1977 *Of Cabbages and Kings: Tales from Zinacantán*. Smithsonian Contributions to Anthropology, No. 23. Washington, D.C.: Smithsonian Institution Press.

MONTEJO, VICTOR 2005 *Maya Intellectual Renaissance: Identity, Representation, and Leadership*. Austin: University of Texas Press.

PAZ, OCTAVIO 1961 *The Labyrinth of Solitude: Life and Thought in Mexico*. New York: Grove Press. (English translation of the revised Spanish edition, 1959) *El laberinto de la soledad*. Mexico City: Fondo de Cultura Económica.

TAGGART, JAMES M. 1983 *Nahuat Myth and Social Structure*. Austin: University of Texas Press.

TEDLOCK, DENNIS 1993 *Breath on the Mirror: Mythic Voices and Visions of the Living Maya*. San Francisco: Harper.

Chapter 14
The Religious Traditions
of Mesoamerica

THE ANCIENT WORLD

From at least 2000 B.C., Mesoamerican religious traditions, like the region itself, began to evolve a distinctive identity. In fact, one of the strongest early expressions on the archaeological record that suggests incipient political and social integration above the level of village cultures occurs in the form of supernatural motifs in what is known as the Olmec Style. This is most clearly expressed in hundreds of objects—rendered in such diverse media as monumental sculpture, carved jade figurines, ceramics, and mosaic pavements—that depict a "baby-faced" human-jaguar motif (Figure 14.1).

Originating around 1150 B.C. in the Central Gulf Coast of Mexico, this distinctive iconography appears to be associated with the ascendancy and expansion of a major cult that came to wield considerable political and ideological influence over large parts of Central and Eastern Mexico by the time of Christ. This iconography appears to link political authority with divine ancestors via the half human–half animal deity. So sudden was the rise of this great style and so notable were the large ceremonial sites from which it emanated, such as San Lorenzo and La Venta, that the Mexican scholar Miguel Covarrubias (see the Introduction) advanced in the 1950s the hypothesis that the Olmec civilization and its associated theocratic state apparatus constituted the major formative culture from which multiple subsequent expressions of Mesoamerican civilization evolved (on the rise of Mesoamerican civilization, see Chapter 1). There is now increasing evidence that leads us to believe that it was not just the Olmec culture, but rather several such influential Formative period polities, that provided the foundation of Mesoamerican civilization. We can assert with a high degree of certainty that Mesoamerica as we know it, from its inception in the Formative period as a great regional configuration of common ideas and adaptations, did not acquire its singular character through surplus-producing agriculture and village life alone. Mesoamerican civilization evolved, perhaps like all

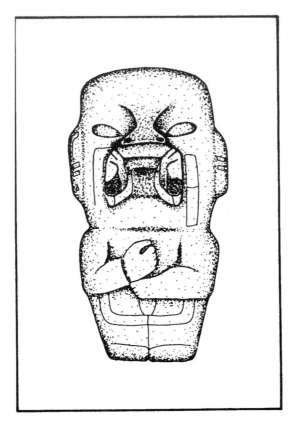

Figure 14.1   A jade effigy axe (the "Kunz Axe") in the Olmec style. Provenance and date unknown, though central Tabasco, Mexico, circa fifth century B.C. is plausible. Drawing by Ellen Cesarski from a photograph of the original piece in the American Museum of Natural History, New York.

other civilizations, as the complex product of *both* the political and economic means to form larger, integrated polities *and* the symbolic forms that rationalized and legitimated the existence of these greater units of integration. To borrow Clifford Geertz's well-known paraphrase of Max Weber, Mesoamericans, past and present, have lived in webs of significance they themselves have spun. Religion clearly ranked as a major political and ideological force in this "created" universe of meaning in ancient Mesoamerica.

Here, then, we will synthesize some of the templates by whose agency life and death, well-being and suffering, plenty and poverty, continuity and destruction of life, moral authority and corruption, were understood. We begin with informed speculation about the spiritual traditions of the earliest period of human occupation of the region and then trace patterns in Mesoamerican religious traditions that continue into the present.

Shamanic Roots

The earliest Americans arrived on the continent as fishers, hunters, and gatherers. They lived in small nomadic bands, and it is assumed that they had spiritual beliefs and practices that were possibly similar to the shamanic traditions that survive today among the Eskimos of Arctic North America and among the nomadic hunters and gatherers of Amazonia. Such communities as these were scattered throughout Mexico and Central America in what is known as the Paleo-Indian period (40,000 to 10,000 B.C.) (see Chapter 1). Although any effort to reconstruct their spiritual life must be speculative, modern ethnographies of domestic curing and divination practices in Mesoamerica and elsewhere in the Americas suggest that shamanic belief and supernatural mediation formed a substratum of spirituality in which all Amerindian cultures participated to some degree. We therefore infer that shamanism is a very old, elementary practice that was probably present in ancient Mesoamerica.

Consider, for example, the title of a major recent book on the Mayas: *Maya Cosmos: Three Thousand Years on the Shaman's Path* (Freidel, Schele, and Parker: 1993). Shamanism is thought, in its ancient form, to have been a highly individualistic and pragmatic form of spirituality, the goal of the religious quest being essentially to underwrite human well-being, food supply, and health through interacting with the spirits of animals, plants, geographical features, and deities that were believed to be responsible for hunting, gathering, and fishing resources, and also for human destiny. Practitioners were probably not full-time specialists nor members of organized cults, but were individuals who, for their own ends and on behalf of family members, sought to communicate by trance, vision quest, and dream interpretation with the spirits of the natural world.

The Rise of Agriculture and Its Supernatural Charters

The slow process of domestication of food and fiber cultigens during the Archaic period (8000–2000 B.C.) (see Chapter 1) brought with it a vastly increased food-production capacity, a dramatic population increase, and a concomitant evolution of sedentary village life. As new technologies evolved in relation to food production, more complex social forms developed to regulate, defend, and renew the vulnerable infrastructure of settled life: homes, equipment, storage facilities, fields, and water supplies. Among these new social forms, a new configuration of agricultural and ancestral cults appeared. Agricultural practice demanded propitiation of earth, water, and solar and lunar deities, along with cults devoted to achieving supernatural protection of domestic plants and to ensuring their continuing fertility. In support of this inference, scholars have noted the extraordinary prominence, in the symbolic representation of this period, of ceramic figurines that portrayed females, sometimes with exaggerated genitalia and breasts (Figure 14.2). This theme has been interpreted to signify a cultural concern with both human and agrarian fertility.

Agriculture and sedentary life also required social control related to property rights. The most typical expression of these new forms of social control was the expanded importance of kin groups as the basis of permanent residential patterns and of genealogical reckoning as the basis of ancestral rights to property and access to water for irrigation. These "goals" appear to find expression in the rise of totemic ancestor cult affiliation, the ritual maintenance of the "founder's memory" being closely

Figure 14.2 A Tlatilco ceramic figurine in what is known as the "Pretty Lady" style. Provenance: Central Mexico, circa 1200 B. C. Courtesy of Gillett G. Griffin.

linked to the identity, property rights, and social status of the corresponding social group.

These patterns probably came to form the ideological foundation of the city-states, kingdoms, and empires that followed in subsequent periods.

The Rise of the Mesoamerican Theocratic States

Upon the base of thousands of village cultures there evolved in what is known as the Preclassic or Formative period (2000 B.C.–A.D. 200) composite and large units of social integration. Characterized by expanding ideological, economic, and political influence, these larger polities built impressive administrative and ritual centers that expressed their growing dominance in regional affairs. Whether or not these urban centers can be called true "cities," it is clear that they evolved as the "greater among equals" in their respective regions with regard to elaborate architectural features such as large pyramids, temples, fortifications, and monumental sculpture. These early centers served not only as administrative and trade foci, but also as seats for the ruling families' ancestor cults and for increasingly centralized celestial, earth, and rain deity cults.

It was during this period that the important early centers, such as La Venta and San Lorenzo, began to exercise religious and political influence over areas far greater than their immediate environs. In such ceremonial centers, we see the expression of the trend, as noted before, toward increasing complexity and integration of regional traditions. This was reflected in the emergence and wide diffusion of cults dedicated to major deities. One such case of this pattern can be observed in the ubiquitous distribution of the famous Olmec "were-jaguar" images in the central Gulf Coast and in adjacent regions. It is inferred that these strange beings may have represented divine ancestors by whose moral and political authority the Olmec elite exported their tradition via trade and other, possibly more aggressive, forms of contact. Furthermore, evidence from the Gulf Coast site of Tres Zapotes and other sites farther south and west suggests that the unique Mesoamerican calendrical system, whose sacred astronomical and solar cycles underwrote the political authority of later (Mayan) theocratic states, originated with the Olmecs and other Formative peoples.

Classic Period Mesoamerican Religion

The Classic period (A.D. 200–900) is considered elsewhere in this text (Chapter 1). Here it is reiterated that we attribute to this period the consolidation of theocratic statecraft throughout Mesoamerica, in hundreds of variants, stretching from Central Mexico to Honduras and possibly farther south. All of the city-states of this period were administratively focused on carefully planned ceremonial centers that were characterized by monumental religious architecture and elaborate subsidiary structures. All of the polities appear to have been ruled by hereditary divine kings who lived surrounded by architectural and artistic expressions of their grandeur. The arts, sciences, and writing flourished, all in the service of centralized, divine kingship. It can be said without exaggeration that Mesoamerica's remarkable cultural achievements of this period—running the gamut from astronomy, mathematics, architecture, and urban design to calendrics, writing, sculpture, mural painting, and sophisticated polychrome ceramic art—were all focused on the symbolic representation and legitimation of centralized and unified religious and political authority systems.

Indeed, as far as we have been able to interpret the meaning of the great urban centers of this period, it seems clear that their overall spatial design and major structures expressed nothing less than divine cosmograms. For example, Teotihuacan, which at its peak (circa A.D. 500) had a population of 150,000 and thus ranked as one of the handful of the world's great cities at that time, commemorated the very birthplace of the gods. The Aztecs, who rose to power almost 1,000 years later, remembered Teotihuacan with the greatest of awe. Davíd Carrasco notes that the Aztecs attributed the creation of the fifth age of the cosmos, their own era, to mythical events that took place at Teotihuacan:

> It is told that when yet [all] was in darkness, when no sun had shown and no dawn had broken—it is said—the gods gathered themselves there at Teotihuacan. They spoke. . . . "Who will take it upon himself to be the sun, to bring the dawn?" (Sahagún 1952–1982, Book VII:4)

It is not surprising, therefore, to find many of the urban centers of the Classic period dedicated to divine ancestors and their spatial layout to be a replication of the cosmos. For example, the important east-west axis of ceremonial centers was often delimited by major architectural features, just as the central ceremonial plazas were typically laid out in a four-part plan that replicated the four sectors, associated with the cardinal directions of the divine cosmos. Furthermore, individual structures appear to have been identified with specific deities and parts of the cosmos. For example, in addition to the well-known massive pyramids dedicated to the sun and moon deities, Teotihuacan has an entire temple structure whose iconography is dedicated to a deity whom later cultures identified as Quetzalcoatl (the Feathered Serpent). Murals and other structures at Teotihuacan suggest that supernatural beings associated with rain, water, and vegetation—most prominently a female water deity—were also revered in the great capital.

Sacred ceremonial architecture also dominated the urban centers of the Classic Mayas. For example, Palenque, one of the best studied and most thoroughly understood of the ancient Mayan cities, contains several elegant temple structures (notably the Temple of the Cross and the Temple of the Foliated Cross; see Figure 1.10 and Figure 14.3) that are dedicated to the cosmic tree, from whose trunk and leaves spring maize deities who are in turn linked to sacred ancestors and, ultimately, to the sun deity.

Mayan rulers embodied the very life force of the universe and were called Mah K'ina (Great Sun Lord) or Ahau (Lord). Thus, not only the temple centers from which they ruled but also the rulers' bodies themselves constituted living terrestrial cosmograms.

Another prominent feature of Mayan urban centers was the ball court, an architectural form whose spatial distribution spans almost all reaches of ancient Mesoamerica (Figure 14.4). In the Mayan area, the ball court was, like the cities themselves, a model of the sacred cosmos. This ball court was invariably recessed in the earth or was structurally designed to provide a sunken pavement, often in the shape of a capital "I". The cosmic region represented was the underworld (Xibalba) from whose precincts primordial life itself sprang via the sun deity's battle with the forces of darkness and death. Hence it was both the Place of Death and the Place of Regenerative Power. The ball game itself appears to have been played as a ritual of cosmic renewal whose purpose was to drive the sun, represented by a heavy natural rubber ball, through a hoop or other structural feature that represented the point of emergence of the sun at dawn. The consequences for the losing team ranged from rituals of humiliation to sacrifice.

Figure 14.3 The central tablet in the interior of the Temple of the Foliated Cross at the Classic-period Mayan city of Palenque, Chiapas, Mexico. Drawing by Linda Schele. Reproduced, with permission, from David Freidel, Linda Schele, and Joy Parker, *Maya Cosmos: Three Thousand Years on the Shaman's Path*. New York, NY: William Morrow and Co., 1993, p. 282.

It can therefore be said without exaggeration that much of the social, intellectual, and artistic energy of Mesoamerican states of this period focused on highlighting the sacred cosmic authority that ordained and underwrote their existence.

The Postclassic Period

The "Postclassic" designation of the period (A.D. 850–1521) is a Eurocentric misnomer, for it attributes to this phase a general "decline" in quality of the arts, engineering, and statecraft. In reality, the beginning of this period in the Mayan area is actually an arbitrary date at which the lowland Mayas stopped making inscriptions in what is known as their long count calendrical system. This abrupt change in the calendrical recording was also associated with the so-called Mayan "collapse," a time at which many of the major lowland Maya cities were apparently abandoned and in some cases destroyed. Whatever the radical shift of fortune of lowland Mayan elite and why it happened (for details, see Chapter 1), life went on; and the subsequent cultural expressions of all parts of Mesoamerica, including the lowland and highland Mayas, were substantial to extraordinary. It was, for example, in the Early Postclassic period that the renowned Toltec civilization began its ascendancy as a quasi-mythical "golden age" culture to which many subsequent Mesoamerican cultures, both Mayan and Mexican, would look back with reverence and awe.

If the Postclassic was a period of warfare and political expansion on the part of numerous states in their effort to establish larger spheres of interest, it was obviously

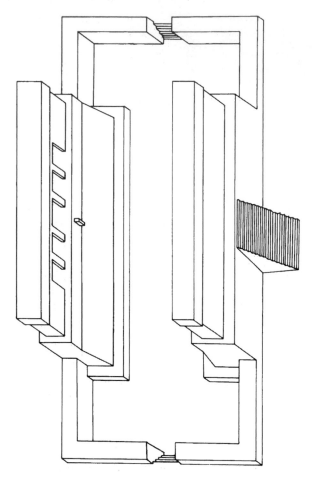

Figure 14.4 A schematic drawing of a Mesoamerican ball court in the shape of a capital "I." Redrawn from *The Quiché Mayas of Utatlán: The Evolution of a Highland Guatemala Kingdom,* by Robert Carmack. University of Oklahoma Press, 1981.

not a period devoid of political finesse, ideological sophistication, or remarkable achievement in social engineering, trade and marketing, public works, and urban design. To this period of course belong the rise and consolidation of the Aztec empire as well as a great number of lesser imperial initiatives in other parts of Mexico and Guatemala (see the account of the Late Postclassic period in Chapter 2).

This period is of particular importance to this text because it is, of course, this phase of ancient Mesoamerican history that is best known to us, for contact-period Spanish observers and chroniclers actually witnessed and recorded minute details of this world even as they were destroying it in order to create colonial New Spain. Furthermore, as has been discussed in a previous chapter (see Chapters 6), the contact period itself produced massive documentation of ancient Mesoamerican religion, much of it written by Indians themselves in native languages rendered in Latin characters, together with drawings, translation, and commentary in Spanish. Thus,

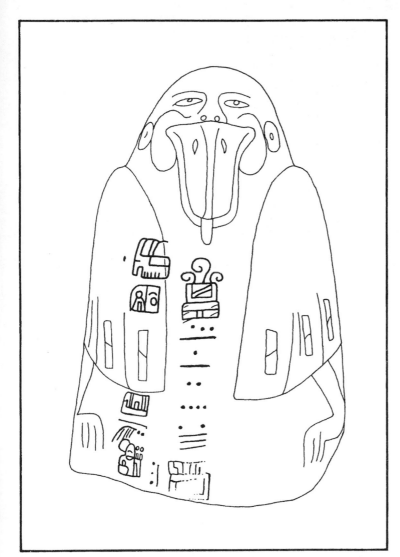

Figure 14.5   The Tuxtla Statuette. Iconography, writing, and long count date are in the Epi-Olmec style. Provenance: San Andrés Tuxtla, Veracruz, Mexico. The date in the inscription corresponds to A.D. 162. The lower four glyphs in the column on the left side of the figure can be translated as "The animal soul companion is powerful" (Justeson and Kaufman 1993: 1703). Redrawn after W. H. Holmes, "On a Nephrite Statuette from San Andrés Tuxtla, Mexico," *American Anthropologist* 9 (1907), 691–701.

although Indian "autoethnography" was undoubtedly biased (in that it was "sponsored" by the Crown and was under the tutelage of priests for reasons having to do with facilitating the missionary enterprise), we can with certainty claim to know a great deal more of sixteenth-century Indian religious thought and practice than we can pretend to know of earlier periods.

For this reason, we are able to offer brief sketches of the main precepts in two contact-period religions, those of the Mexica (Aztecs) and, in Box 14.1, of the Mayas of Yucatan, based in large part on native testimonies and written texts.

Box 14.1   Precepts of Mayan Religion

If Aztec spirituality was preoccupied primarily with the problem of fulfilling and paying for cosmically ordained destiny, the dominant motif of Mayan religion was the preoccupation with cosmic time and the organization of human affairs in accordance with the sacred dictates of the many cycles, natural and arbitrary, that comprised it. Ultimately, divine rulership and, hence, the political order, were linked to the creator Sun God and his cosmic pantheon. It is thus to the issue of divinized time that much of the energy of Mayan spirituality was directed. The concept of the Mayan "chronovision" is here summarized by León-Portilla:

> From at least the time of the first inscriptions of Maya Classic (A.D. 300), the concept of time as an abstraction, derived from the cyclical nature of the sun and the related "day" unit, had primacy in the sphere of Maya culture. Proof of this comes from the ancient word *kinh*, whose meaning is identical in different groups. . . . *Kinh* is primordial reality, divine and without limit. *Kinh* includes, conceptually, all of the cycles and all of the cosmic ages that have existed. . . . The universe of time in which the Maya lived was an ever-changing stage in which one was able to feel the sum of influence and actions of the various divine forces which coincided in a particular period. . . . Since the essence of the nature of *kinh* was cyclical, it was important above all to understand the past in order to understand the present and predict the future. . . . The faces of time, that primordial reality which obsessed the Maya, were objects of veneration. . . . The Maya sages invented a cosmovision. Since it was history, measure of, and prediction about the total reality whose essence was time, it would be more appropriate to call the Maya world view a chronovision. . . . To ignore the primordial importance of time would be to ignore the soul of this culture. (León-Portilla 1968:62–63, 109–110; translated by G. Gossen)

To this discussion must be added the caveat that time itself was not a deity for the Mayas. Time did, however, form the very complex cyclical matrix in which deities acted and therefore, in logical sequence, time also dictated the schedule of human propitiation to them. Finally, it should be noted that Mayan chronovision was *both* cyclical and linear: cyclical, in that what was will be again *in pattern,* but will also move forward, as a weaver moves back and forth along the warp, repeating a pattern, but also moving forward, producing variation on the pattern.

It is further worth noting that these fundamental Mayan precepts, as with those of the Aztecs, functioned as powerful underlying forces that entered actively into the process of subsequent Christian missionization. Furthermore, there is abundant evidence from the modern era that demonstrates that centuries of contact with Christianity have not eliminated these ancient Mesoamerican ideas: restructured them, yes; transformed them, perhaps; supplanted them, not at all.

Of Human Destiny in Ancient Mexico. Bernardino de Sahagún's Nahuatl-speaking assistants recorded their soul beliefs in the middle of the sixteenth century as follows:

> *It was said*
> *that in the thirteenth heaven*
> *[in the uppermost of the heavens]*
> *our destinies are determined.*

When the child is conceived,
when he is placed in the womb,
his destiny (tonalli) comes to him there;
it is sent by the Lord of Duality. (Florentine Codex 1969, Book VI, Chapter XXII)

In a recent commentary on this text, the historian Miguel León-Portilla writes the following:

> In several of the books where divine presences are depicted one finds also the hiero-glyphs which denote the *tonalli,* the individual human destinies which, at given moments and places, are brought by the gods. These *tonalli,* destinies, will determine everything in each human life, from birth to death. The tonalli is essentially an individual's *i-macehual,* "that which is granted to one, that which one deserves." Thus, the *tonalli* bears, for all people on earth, the consubstantial origin and imprint of the divine source of life; it is this essence that determines what is going to happen in accordance with prearranged schemes. The unveiling of this predestined plan and propitiation of its divine source are vital to the human condition. (León-Portilla 1993:46)

When this belief system came into contact with Christianity, its fundamental "otherness" became apparent to the missionaries and other Spanish observers. Jorge Klor de Alva has recently summarized these differences:

> . . . there was no autonomous will at the core of the self since every human being was a microcosm reflecting the forces that made up the cosmos at large. Furthermore, there was no clear boundary between personal will and the supernatural and natural forces that governed the universe. Consequently, acts that were believed truly to harmonize the contrary influences of the gods (saints, spirits, "devils"), rather than right intentions per se, mapped out the terrain of the ethical individual. Therefore, behavior, performance and punctiliousness, rather than will, contemplation or motivation were the key concerns of the Nahua who strove to be moral. (Klor de Alva 1993:183–184)

Although Aztec state religion was of course enormously more complex than this native theory of self alone reveals, it has been argued that Aztec spirituality as a whole was fundamentally preoccupied with the problem of ascertaining and fulfilling the destiny that humans were given, individually and collectively, by the Lord of Duality. From this logically follows the need for humanity to propitiate and reciprocate for the gift of life. This requirement underlies the theme of human sacrifice, for which the Aztecs were noted but little understood.

THE MESOAMERICAN SPIRITUAL WORLD MEETS THE WEST

By the end of the sixteenth century, well before the Puritans arrived on the rocky shore of what is now Massachusetts, Mesoamerica had been profoundly transformed. New Spain—as Mexico and Central America were called by the Spaniards—was fully established as one of the two linchpins (with Peru) of Spain's New World empire.

Hundreds of churches sat on or near the ruins of pyramid mounds that had been the foundations of ancient Mexican and Mayan temple shrines. Often, in fact, these ruins provided the building materials for the new colonial structures. Mexico's National Cathedral was built close to the very foundation of the central temple of what had been Tenochtitlan, the Aztec capital. Mexico City, the economic hub of Spain's massive New World operation, had a major university, numerous seminaries, convents, hospitals, plazas, and palaces, all situated in a neatly conceived grid plan. Antigua, Guatemala, also resembled a Renaissance template of ordered colonial life, housing the convent headquarters of a number of religious orders that had the mission of evangelizing America for the Crown. Vast tracts of Mexico and Guatemala had been granted as *encomiendas,* along with their surviving Indian communities, to soldiers and servants of the conquest. Silver mines, cattle ranches, and great estates had emerged in the countryside, all staffed by forced Indian labor (for details, see Chapters 4 and 5).

Implementing the Missionary State

The cost of all of this to the Indians of Mesoamerica had been exceedingly high. The physical structures of their temple centers, their books and art forms, lay in ashes and ruins, and their population had been reduced by more than 90 percent, from an estimated 27,000,000 in 1521 (a figure disputed by some scholars) to around 1,200,000 by 1600. European-introduced diseases, to which Mesoamericans were not resistant, along with the abuses of forced labor and forced relocation, were factors in this demographic cataclysm that far outweighed outright slaughter (see the Introduction and Chapter 4). The demographic decline was a matter of practical concern to the Spaniards, for they, unlike the Puritans in North America, needed both bodies and souls of Indians to fulfill the ambitious goals that the Crown had set for itself in America.

The Laws of the Indies, promulgated in 1542, specifically stipulated that all representatives of the Crown in America were de facto bearers of responsibility for the missionary enterprise; this responsibility could not be separated from the more pragmatic goals of the political and economic agenda. Therefore, all Crown officials were formally obliged to encourage and support the "spiritual conquest" of America by persuasion and nurture, for the pope had declared in a bull entitled *Sublimus Deus* that Amerindians were humans with souls worthy of cultivation and redemption who could not be legally or justly enslaved. Although the discrepancies between this ideal on the one hand and local practice on the other were surely great, it was nevertheless the case that the Crown was deeply concerned with carrying out the duties of Spain as a "missionary state." This intention was perhaps nowhere in Spanish colonial history better symbolized than in the triumphal arrival in Mexico of twelve Franciscan priests (popularly known as "apostles") in 1524. In a great state ceremony, they were received by their compatriots as the very architects of a millennial kingdom, the New Jerusalem on earth. This earthly Christian community, heralding the return of Christ on earth, would be achieved by the conversion of the masses of natives into Christians.

Religious Syncretism and Local Realities

In 1531 (according to a legend that became "canonized" in subsequent centuries; see Chapter 5), just ten years after the Spaniards destroyed the Aztec capital of Tenochtitlan, an Indian named Juan Diego declared that the Mother of Jesus had revealed herself to him. At first, Church authorities were incredulous and scoffed at the very idea that the Virgin might appear to an Indian. Juan Diego returned to the site of the initial apparition of the Virgin to ask her assistance. She told him (in Nahuatl) to take roses from a nearby bush that was in bloom out of season and roll them up in his cloak. Davíd Carrasco narrates this miracle and its consequences in the following passage:

> He did as he was told, and when he unrolled the cloak a magnificent color image of the Virgin was imprinted upon it. When Juan Diego took the cloak to the Archbishop of Mexico, according to popular legend, the astonishing miracle was accepted and the site of the revelation was chosen for the future cathedral. Today, Mexico's greatest basilica stands at the bottom of the hill [Tepeyac] and is visited every day by thousands of the faithful, who gaze upward at the glass-encased cloak with its miraculously painted image. (Carrasco 1990:136)

That the site of the apparition of the Virgin was a sacred site that was of significance to the Aztecs and that she chose to reveal herself to an Indian are parts of the story that deserve further discussion, for they have to do with the pragmatics of Spain's colonial agenda. Whether or not the miraculous apparition occurred as legend and Church doctrine narrate the event, it nevertheless illustrates a typical phenomenon of situations of cultural encounter. Both the dominant culture and the vanquished seek—no doubt for different reasons—the means, often articulated through religion, to make sense of the inevitable present by mingling parts of prior cultural forms with new forms, thus creating new syntheses that address new political realities (see Chapter 5). Christianity itself was born this way out of the turmoil of the encounter of Judaism with the expanding Roman Empire, and "Mesoamerican Christianity," in its myriad variants, was born this way.

The original founding of a different cult of the Virgin of Guadalupe, a small dark-skinned image of a Madonna and Child, long antedated the events at Tepeyac Hill, having miraculously appeared, according to legend, to the Spanish faithful several centuries before. Her image is today enshrined in western Spain (in the town of Guadalupe) and was deeply revered long before the conquest. However, her manifestation as a Nahuatl-speaking Mother of Jesus, with Indian features, was something new. Indeed, some scholars note that there is no historical link whatsoever between the two images. Whatever the ironies and accidental convergences in the history of this image, Mexico's Virgin of Guadalupe became nothing less than the patron of Mexico and "Queen of America," and she is revered by tens of millions today. Her story bears significant elements of both the conqueror and the vanquished. In some ways, she can be said to integrate the tensions of Indian and Spaniard, mestizo and Indian, Spaniard and mestizo, into one community of faith and devotion (for more on the Virgin cult, see Box 5.1).

The cult of the Virgin of Guadalupe is but one of the thousands of "encounter themes" in postcontact Mesoamerican religion that bear elements that are syncretic. By *syncretic,* we refer to the nature of ideas, deities, and practices that derive from historically distinct traditions but become reinterpreted and transformed in situations of cultural encounter. It is extremely difficult to learn with any certainty just how these myriad syncretic forms took shape in Mesoamerica. The reasons for caution are several.

The process of encounter between Christianity and Mesoamerican spirituality involved hundreds of variants of religious belief and practice, and this pluralism no doubt characterized all types of actors in the American crucible. These variants derived not only from different religious orders and different statuses of individuals in the socioeconomic hierarchy of Spain, but also from different personal biographies. The same muddiness and subjectivity undoubtedly characterized the religious views of Indians who encountered the Europeans. These subjects of Christian evangelism were, in origin, highly diverse: aristocrats and slaves, peasant farmers and traders, artisans and priests, all with different attitudes and loyalties toward former state religions, if any, in their respective roots. Indeed, they often carried no loyalty whatsoever to a former "great tradition." To expect, therefore, an easily isolable new phenomenon (that is, the "new Mesoamerican Christianity") is wishful thinking. At best, we can hope for an enlightened dialogue about the subjective expectations and responses of the different types of actors in the encounter in relation to those of the others.

Where have these concerns about the concept of religious syncretism taken us? It is to the recognition that an understanding of the transformed religious order of Mesoamerica in the wake of the conquest is exceedingly complex. The region was, in the first place, a sophisticated and cosmopolitan scene. Mesoamerica, at the time of contact, was the seat of dozens of state theocracies, the Aztec empire being only one of these. All of these ideological power centers constituted "great traditions," in Robert Redfield's sense of the term, signifying that they represented the official ideological canon of the ruling elite and the associated priesthood that controlled the destinies of millions of people of diverse ethnic and linguistic backgrounds who were forced to live as economic tributaries and dependencies of the urban administrative centers. However, the local village cultures that constituted the peasant peripheries of the theocratic states were themselves bearers of religious customs and beliefs that reflected their own local experiences of memory and practice. These local religions expressed what Redfield has called "little traditions" in the sense that they continued to practice highly local spiritual activities even as they had to adapt to larger state demands in terms of their public ceremonial life. Thus, in addition to maintaining obligatory cult affiliations that emanated from the urban centers, precontact Mesoamericans also engaged in local shamanic, ancestral, and agricultural cult practices.

It is therefore reasonable to expect that when the Spanish missionary state decapitated and destroyed the major public foci of pre-Columbian religious practice, and obliged local elites to become lay catechists—or, at the least, local sponsors—of the new Christian doctrine, they did so in highly diverse ways that were subject to local practice (on this topic, see again Chapter 5). In effect, Christianity became the new great tradition to which all were obliged to pay lip service. Little traditions, whose religious practices had been for millennia focused on rituals of home, lineage, field, and waterhole, did not lose their vitality, though these local foci of religious practice received a new overlay of Christian ideas.

Even God and associated central doctrines of Christianity did not reach the newly converted in ways that the missionaries expected, for they (the Christian concepts) often merged as new semantic overlays with what were already, prior to the conquest, complex, polyvalent ideas. Thus, for example, throughout Mesoamerica in the Colonial period and even today in thousands of Indian communities, Jesus Christ has become one of several manifestations of the ancient sun god. Similarly, the Virgin Mary has become merged with multiple expressions of the ancient moon goddess and other female deities. The Christian saints also became associated with various pre-Christian concepts and deities (as they had in Spain when Christianity encountered native Iberian belief systems).

A good example of this syncretic phenomenon comes to us from Chiapas, where the contemporary Tzotzil Mayas have assigned to Saint Jerome the care of people's animal soul companions in the mountains and in the sky (for more on the Tzotzil Mayas, see Chapters 8 and 13). This association appears to be related to the popular Spanish iconographic portrayal of Saint Jerome in the company of a docile lion, an image that is linked to the medieval legend of the saint's life. However, the "success" of this Spanish saint among the Tzotzil Mayas appears to be tied less to his virtues as a Christian martyr than to his affinity with the lion. The belief in supernatural coessences (among them, animals) that share with individuals a kind of predestination was, even in the sixteenth century, a very ancient Mesoamerican concept, being manifest in written hieroglyphic texts dating from around A.D. 150. Saint Jerome's association with this belief system is thus a relatively recent facet of an old and a complex Native American spiritual idea. Similar local transformations occurred as the Christian concepts of Satan and the angels were assimilated into local belief and practice. Satan has merged with countless pre-Columbian forces and beings that were hostile to the order-giving power of the sun god. Christian angels have been assimilated in diverse regions of modern Mesoamerica into various pre-Columbian cults to the earth and rain. Thunder and lightning, for example, are known in many contemporary Indian communities of Mesoamerica by some form of the Spanish word for angel ("*ángel*").

When one multiplies all of the preceding by a factor of many thousands of villages that were subject to Christianization, it becomes clear that the new great tradition, Christianity, was just that and only that. Local practices, little traditions, assimilated Christianity in countless different ways, often with minimal doctrinal maintenance and daily offices left in the hands of Indian sacristans of the village churches. Thus, although some church authorities spoke publicly of the success of the "spiritual conquest," many local priests themselves realized that they were dealing with unfavorable odds (as seen in Box 14.2).

Box 14.2   Gage's Account of a Little Tradition

The following account is from a famous seventeenth-century English traveler and Catholic missionary, Thomas Gage, who lived and ministered as a parish priest in highland Guatemala around 1640. The extract given here (originally published in 1648) records a bizarre set of events that surrounded his pious ministry to a dying Maya Indian named Juan Gómez:

> They told me that the report went that Juan Gómez was the chief wizard of all the wizards and witches in the town, and that commonly he was wont to be changed into the shape of a lion, and so to walk about the mountains. That he was ever a deadly enemy to one Sebastián López, an ancient Indian and head of another tribe, and that two days before they had met in the mountain, Gómez in the shape of a lion and López in the shape of a tiger, and that they had fought must cruelly till Gómez, who was the older and weaker, was tired, much bit and bruised, and died of it. And further, that I might be assured of this truth, they told me that López was in prison for it, and that two tribes were striving about it, and that the tribe and kindred of Gómez demanded from López and his tribe and kindred satisfaction, and a great sum of money, or else threatened to make the case known unto the Spanish power and authority. . . .
>
> This struck me to the very heart, to think that I should live among such people, who were spending all they could get by their work and labor upon the church, saints, and in offerings, and yet were so privy to the counsels of Satan. It grieved me that the world I preached unto them did no more good, and I resolved from that time forward to spend most of my endeavors against Satan's subtlety, and to shew them more than I had done the great danger to the souls of these who had made any compact with the Devil. I hoped that I might make them abandon and abjure his works, and close with Christ by faith. . . .
>
> Whilst I was thus musing, there came unto me at least twenty of the chiefest of the town with the two majors, jurats and all the officers of justice, who desired me to forbear that day the burying of Juan Gómez, for that they had resolved to call a crown officer to view his corpse and examine his death, lest they all should be troubled for him, and he be exhumed. I made as if I knew nothing, but enquired of them the reason. Then they related to me how there were witnesses in the town who saw a lion and a tiger fighting, and presently lost the sight of the beasts, and saw Juan Gómez and Sebastián López much about the same time parting one from another, and that immediately Juan Gómez came home bruised to his bed, whence he never rose again, and that he declared upon his deathbed unto some of his friends that Sebastián López had killed him. For this reason they had López in safe custody. . . .
>
> The crown officer was sent for and came that night and searched Gómez' body. I was present with him, and found it all bruised, scratched, and in many places bitten and sore wounded. Many evidences and suspicions were brought in against López by the Indians of the town, especially by Gómez' friends, whereupon he was carried away to Guatemala [City], and there again was tried by the same witnesses, and not much denying the fact himself, was there hanged. And though Gómez' grave was opened in the church, he was not buried in it, but in another made ready for him in a ditch. . . . (Gage 1958:275–277)

From an examination of this text, it is evident that Thomas Gage witnessed the tragic aftermath of what, in the view of the Indian community, had been a supernatural battle between the animal soul companions of two powerful shamans. The "lion" and the "tiger" (perhaps a careless English reference to the puma and the jaguar, which are native to Guatemala) were the co-essences of Gómez and López, and hence, their battle in the woods involved both their bodies and the bodies of their human counterparts. Gage's narrative leads us to believe that neither he nor the crown officials fully understood what was going on, though all parties, in the end, ironically concurred in believing that López was guilty as accused.

The Social Organization of the Colonial Church

In a profound sense, Spain stacked its cards against achieving a massive, unified King-dom of God in New Spain. In the first place, the Crown implemented in Mexico and Central America the policy that it practiced elsewhere in America. Two "states," based on caste and color, were established in the New World: a creole state for Spaniards and their mixed offspring, and an Indian state for Indians. Thus, from local organi-zation to representation before Crown institutions, there were two juridically, spiri-tually, and demographically separate entities within Spain's New World empire. Separate and unequal Crown laws, civil and ecclesiastical codes, and tax schedules ap-plied to Spanish and Indian communities.

Indians were encouraged, even obliged by the laws of caste, to live in, pay trib-ute from, and attend mass in their own communities through their own Indian pup-pet authorities. In a system not unlike the system of home rule practiced by the British in India, the local elites were encouraged by the Crown to remain in power as long as they facilitated legal and tributary obligations of Indian subjects to Crown authorities. In exchange for their services in keeping local villages docile and com-pliant with Crown demands, local caciques (chiefs or bosses) received substantial privileges and tax benefits, often even access to higher education (on this topic, see also Chapter 5).

In terms of Christian religious organization, belief, and practice, this separate and unequal arrangement also prevailed. With the paucity of clergy necessary to service thousands of Indian parishes, Indian lay catechists, often drawn from the old elite classes, were trained in doctrine by the missionaries. They typically received in-struction in Spanish and were taught the basic elements of the catechism, with the expectation that they would carry on day-to-day maintenance of the faith in the In-dian communities when the Spanish clergy were not present. Known in Mesoamer-ica as *sacristanes* (sacristans) and *maestros de capilla* (chapel choir masters), these Indian representatives of the Church were often responsible for assisting with the daily office, for translating prayers and canticles into Indian languages, and for serv-ing as the link of the local communities with regional representatives of the Church and with the Crown representatives of the Inquisition who were responsible for over-seeing the purity of the faith. The sacristans and choir masters thus became, with the local Indian political elite, individuals who had something to gain in terms of privileges and exemptions from serving as proxy representatives of the Crown. They also had a great deal to do with molding church doctrine and practices to the dic-tates of local custom.

In another ironic twist of colonial history—ironic in that it contributed to the maintenance of limited Indian authority even under Crown dictates—Spain insisted that local Indian communities organize themselves according to highly prescribed formulas of civil administration and religious cult sponsorship (see Chapter 5). Ex-pressing a certain Renaissance compulsion for bureaucratic symmetry, this was the colonial prototype (later reinterpreted and reinstituted for similar reasons under secular governments in the nineteenth century) for the well-known civil-religious hi-erarchies (also known as "cargo systems") that survive today in hundreds of Indian communities throughout Mexico and Central America.

Religious organization below the occasionally present parish priest (usually a Spaniard or mestizo) and the trusted continuing lay assistants (sacristans and choir masters) consisted of sodalities of local people who were designated—sometimes on a continuing and sometimes on a rotating basis—to sponsor and maintain images of saints, to care for their accoutrements and clothing, and to be responsible for paying for annual festivals in their honor. These cult-maintenance groups had been encouraged by the Church in medieval Spain and became even more popular with the Church authorities during the Counter-Reformation as a means of maintaining approved forms of local community devotion. The system was vigorously encouraged in Mesoamerica as well. Typically, the leaders would bear titles such as *mayordomo* ("steward") and *alférez* ("standard bearer"). They received honor and prestige for their contributions to community life and for their sponsorship of particular saints who were identified as being special patrons and protectors of local health, prosperity, and well-being. These cults also contributed significantly to the maintenance of highly local identities and loyalties, a situation that the Crown favored because it kept Indians separate from creole and mestizo populations and also discouraged the formation of pan-Indian political solidarity against colonial authorities.

Thus, the civil-religious hierarchies gave the appearance of relative homogeneity throughout colonial Mesoamerica, which was, of course, in part their administrative rationale. Indians could be taxed, baptized, indoctrinated, and conscripted for forced labor and other services through an efficient and a uniform local authority system: efficient, precisely because it was in the hands of Indian petty officials who had something to gain from compliance. The other side of the coin, of course, was that religious events and festivals could be conceived and staged, mingling themes from precontact beliefs and practices, with relative autonomy from Crown and Church authorities. If the cults to the saints—ubiquitous in the Colonial period as they are today—served the purpose of mobilizing individual communities in corporate celebration of approved icons, they also functioned to maintain the new forms of Indian Christianity as highly distinct from one another and from creole and mestizo beliefs and practices. Even today in many Mesoamerican villages that have mixed ladino (mestizo) and Indian populations, the annual liturgical cycle is staged and understood by both parties to be a parallel and separate, not unified, event.

These organizational factors help to account for the amazing mosaic of local expressions of Indian Christianity that evolved in the Colonial era and continue into our time. The emphasis on public celebration also allows us to understand how easily nonpublic beliefs and practices might continue to express significant pre-Columbian content and ideas, since the fields, homes, gardens, and pastures were not the preferred foci for staging the Christian liturgical cycles. It is thus the case that highly localized precontact rituals and practices associated with the individual life cycle, family, and domestic life could, with relative ease and impunity, persist and successfully coexist with the more prescribed content of public devotion. This circumstance helps to account for the persistence of hundreds of forms of shamanic curing and divination practices in the Modern era. Agricultural and fertility rituals, along with related beliefs and practices associated with ancestors and rain, wind, and earth deities, constituted an area in which precontact customs could continue in relative isolation from the vigilance of Crown authorities.

It is helpful, therefore, to consider the myriad syncretic forms that evolved in the colonial era as expressing both prescribed uniformity in the structure (if not content and practice) of public devotion and relatively unmonitored particularity of domestic and individual religious practice, much of which was veiled discreetly from church vigilance. The many expressions of this public-domestic mix of spiritual beliefs and practices are further multiplied by the fact that the linguistic and cultural mosaic of colonial Mesoamerica was, as it is today, enormously diverse.

INTO THE MODERN ERA

If the diverse cultural geography of Mesoamerica—mestizo, Amerindian, European, and Afro-American—was already forged at the time of the independence movements of the early nineteenth century, this pattern of cultural and religious diversity has become more rather than less complex in the nineteenth and twentieth centuries. The reasons for this outcome involved both internal and external forces.

Local Communities under Secular States

Much of the impetus leading to Mesoamerica's increasing religious pluralism came from the detachment of the new nations of the region from the centralized political and religious institutions of Europe. These new nations were avowedly secular and "progressive" in their self-definition. In most of the national constitutions, based as they were on French and U.S. models, the Church was disestablished juridically (if not always in practice). This event meant that political authority (once one-and-the-same with the Church) no longer had responsibility for the spiritual nurture and protection of Indian communities. This fundamental change, combined with "liberal" land reform legislation that encouraged private as opposed to communal ownership of land, led to massive encroachment of mestizos and creoles on traditional communal landholdings. Whether by legal or illegal means, this erosion of the land and economic base of Indian communities forced large-scale displacement of Indian populations.

Many Indian communities were forced into the paradoxical situation of becoming more demographically and socially isolated—their truncated landholdings being in marginal areas deemed undesirable for cattle ranching, commercial agriculture, and mining—just as they were increasingly forced to become migrant laborers in mestizo- and creole-owned ranching and farming operations. Often, economic circumstances forced whole families to abandon their home communities altogether to become debt-slaves on cattle ranches and plantations (see Chapter 7).

One route of escape from this situation—one that continues unabated in certain parts of Mexico and Guatemala even today—was massive migration to urban areas, where better economic opportunities were thought to exist. Urban migration has typically led to assimilation of Indians into the national culture, usually at the lower end of the socioeconomic spectrum (see Chapter 8). As members of the town and city underclasses, newly acculturated Indians have proven to be particularly attractive and willing subjects for Protestant evangelical and Roman Catholic lay missionary activity in our time. These recent urban immigrant populations, together with the rural proletariat, have also emerged as an important constituency of the reform-oriented Theology of Liberation, a radical Roman Catholic movement that developed in Latin America in the wake of the Vatican II reforms of the 1960s.

Nativism, Revitalization, and Separatism

Another internal force that has led to an increasingly complex mosaic of religious belief and practice in the nineteenth and twentieth centuries has been local Indian nativistic or revitalization activity. As liberal, secular governments came to power and (sometimes inadvertently) forced acute economic hardship upon Indian communities, there were several types of local response. One, already noted, was massive migration to ranches, plantations, and cities to find employment in the wake of the alienation of their communal and private landholdings that had been their subsistence base. This typically led to assimilation and "development" (modernization). The counterface, one that occurred with some frequency, was a reactionary force in the remaining, increasingly marginalized Indian communities.

It will be recalled from previous discussions in this and other chapters that Crown authority and also the postindependence secular governments had deliberately created and encouraged socially and ethnically separate Indian townships with strong local religious and civil hierarchies (the so-called "closed corporate communities"). The social infrastructure and demographic mass of people who shared an Indian identity were therefore present in such force as to allow Indian towns to seal themselves off socially and spiritually from those whom they regarded as their oppressors. For these reasons, among others, the nineteenth and twentieth centuries saw hundreds of articulate and violent religious movements that focused on Indian nativism and autonomy.

Perhaps the best known of these movements was the "Caste War" of 1848 in Yucatán, Mexico (see the discussion of this war in Chapter 7). The uprising created national panic as Mayan Indian communities—which clearly comprised the majority population of Yucatán—mobilized syncretized Mayan Christian and pre-Columbian religious symbols and underground books of prophecy, together with an impressive military force, to assert their identity as sovereign people in the region. This movement is widely recognized as the most successful native-controlled, quasi-Christian, separatist alternative religion ever invented by Mesoamericans. Indeed, they came remarkably close to driving the mestizos out of the region altogether.

Another such movement, loosely related to the Caste War, was the so-called War of Saint Rose (1867–1870) of highland Chiapas, Mexico. Tzotzil Mayan Indians of the area laid siege to San Cristóbal (the mestizo trade and administrative center of the region) in the name of a cult dedicated to Indian religious separatism. In addition to worshipping a set of sacred images that had been acquired by a woman who declared herself to be the "Mother of God," the cult focused symbolically on the coming of a new Indian Christ. Both Mexican and Indian accounts of the movement affirm that the Chamula Tzotzil people crucified a young man on Good Friday, 1869, claiming that only a newly martyred Indian Sun-Christ was worthy of their homage and respect. The national Catholic establishment was irrelevant to them, as was the political authority of Mexico.

Although this movement, like many others in Mexico and Guatemala, was effectively suppressed by state military intervention, it expressed in powerful terms that Mesoamerica had a hidden minority—the Indian community—that was excluded from economic opportunity, political expression, and religious freedom. Far from being passive and unconscious of their oppressed situation, they recognized their circumstances and, in seeking autonomy, created an Indian political consciousness that was bound inextricably with local religious symbols. This is a pattern that remains clearly visible in our time.

New Tutelage: Indigenismo and Foreign Missionization

Still another internal phenomenon that has contributed, albeit indirectly, to increasing religious diversity has been *indigenismo* (see the discussion on indigenist "development" in Chapter 8). Typically associated with periods of secular political reform at the national level (particularly Mexico since the 1930s and Guatemala between 1944 and 1954), indigenismo is a body of public policy aimed at addressing the educational, economic, health, and social needs of long-ignored Indian communities. Although the agenda is ostensibly one of providing social and economic opportunities for Indians, the "subtext" is aimed at accelerated assimilation of Indian communities into the mainstream of national culture. Indigenismo has produced mixed results, the most important of them being the following: (1) the expected tendency of acculturation of Indians into the rural and mestizo mainstream of the respective nations; (2) the resistance to acculturation, as expressed in ideological and religious separatism as discussed before; and (3) the open-door policy extended to the activities of European and U.S. missionaries.

Missionary activity, it is argued, must necessarily be tolerated under the premise of freedom of religious affiliation that is guaranteed by most Latin American constitutions, including those of the modern nations of Mesoamerica. Thus, as early as the mid–nineteenth century, U.S. Protestant missionaries began their labors in the area, particularly in Guatemala. In an ironic twist that brings the policy template of indigenismo in the twentieth century together with accelerated missionary activity in our time, governments have perceived that foreign missionary work typically shares the goals of indigenismo: teaching of literacy in Spanish, providing better health care, advocacy of development and "progress," and integration of isolated communities into national cultures and economies. In this manner, national "goals" are achieved at little or no cost to the governments themselves. Thus, beginning in the mid–nineteenth century, foreign missionaries have been tolerated, even encouraged by cash-strapped national governments, in that they are thought to bring foreign-financed "community development," the goals of which mesh with those of the nation.

The policy link between various government policies aimed at rural and urban development, on the one hand, and the tolerance and encouragement of missionary activity, on the other, has had an enormous impact on the religious configuration of the modern nations that constitute the formal Mesoamerican world. Dozens of U.S. and European Protestant denominations, Mormons, post–Vatican II reform Catholics, and militant "people's church" advocates within the Theology of Liberation can all claim extraordinary success in the late twentieth century. Their faithful number in the many millions, almost none of whom can be claimed as loyal to the old order state Catholicism. Already extraordinarily diverse at the time of independence from Europe, Mesoamerican religious belief and practice in the modern period have splintered even further with the successes of the new evangelism. The much sought-after "national integration," in whose name missionary activity has sometimes been encouraged, has not always been achieved; indeed, the converts sometimes achieve the power and influence to change the quality of the national culture itself.

New Immigration

Another force that has contributed to the increasing religious pluralism of Mesoamerican is the substantial non-Iberian immigration into the region, beginning in the early nineteenth century and continuing, though at a diminished rate, in our time. This new immigration of the postindependence era has brought many new strains of religious belief and practice: West Indian Afro-Caribbean cult practitioners; English Protestants; Irish Catholics; Italian Catholics; German Protestants, Jews, and Catholics; Eastern European Roman Catholics, Jews, and Orthodox Christians; Middle Eastern Jews, Moslems, and Christians; Chinese Buddhists; Vietnamese Catholics; even North American Kickapoo Indian traditionalists; and U.S. and Canadian Mennonites. All came in quest of economic opportunity and, in some cases, religious and political asylum. Several of the region's major cities, such as Mexico City, Monterrey, Guadalajara, Guatemala City, and San José (Costa Rica), have hundreds of non–Roman Catholic practicing religious groups. Thus, from city to remote Indian hamlet, modern Mesoamerica does not permit easy generalizations about traits that characterize the whole.

If one adds to all of the preceding the especially important role of nations like Mexico and Costa Rica in granting political asylum to refugees from other parts of the Hispanic world in the twentieth century, the region begins to look increasingly international in terms of the national and religious traditions represented. Hundreds of thousands of Spanish Republicans, Cubans, Chileans, Salvadorans, Nicaraguans, Argentines, and, most recently, Guatemalan Indians, have found refuge in Mexico, almost all of them for reasons related to political upheavals in their own countries. Costa Rica has also, in proportion to its small size, received enormous numbers (in the hundreds of thousands) of political refugees in the late twentieth century, most recently from Nicaragua and El Salvador.

Thus, the crucible of life and belief has become, in our time, enormously complex in terms of who's who. Like much of the world, Mesoamerica—for millennia a region mingling many variants of great and little traditions—continues in the twentieth century to be a borderland of spiritualities, now involving much of the hemisphere and the globe rather than merely the extent of pre-Hispanic trade networks.

IS THERE A COMMON CORE
OF MESOAMERICAN SPIRITUALITY?

Although it is relatively easy to speak of certain themes that unify Mesoamerican spirituality, one is confounded at every turn by millions of people for whom the generalization does not hold true. If the Virgin of Guadalupe is called the Patron of Mexico, and indeed the Queen of America, about whom is one speaking in terms of believers? Mexico's approximately 11 million Indians and several million Protestants cannot be said to "revere" the Virgin of Guadalupe as the soul of their belief. She is often relegated to the status of a minor, though duly recognized and respected, deity in Mesoamerican Indian communities that practice variants of Indian Christianity. She is a neutral, secular symbol, sometimes even a threatening pagan icon, to millions of Protestants, Indian and mestizo. Guatemalan and Salvadoran Catholics may or may not take her seriously as a powerful intermediary with God. Many Afro-Caribbean religious practitioners on the Gulf Coast rimland have never heard of her. To complicate things even further, there are, as of 2005, several communities of recently converted Mayan Muslims in Chiapas who are the product of Spanish Muslim missionary activity in the last decade. As for the Virgin of Guadalupe, they regard her as a pagan symbol that is best forgotten. Where, then, does one turn for generalization?

All of this said, we feel that generalization is possible about a relatively circumscribed segment of Indian Mesoamerica that has been the primary focus of this text. If the limitations are clearly stated, we think that the following sketch of core features of Mesoamerican Indian religions, past and present, will be useful. What we assert here is that these spiritual concerns have dramatic temporal and spatial persistence in Mesoamerican thought, so much perhaps that some of these ideas may be found to color the tone of other traditions found in the area.

The Concept of Individual Coessences

Perhaps linked to a deep shamanic past, Mesoamerican spiritual traditions throughout the region carry a fundamental commitment to the idea that each individual carries a predestined fate that is expressed by a coessence that is given at the time of conception. Sometimes merely an abstract "destiny," but more often embodied in the person of a deity or an animal or a spirit companion, this coessence experiences the life journey of the human counterpart through good and ill, often determining, in the supernatural world, what will befall the individual: power or wealth, sickness or health, early death or a fulfilled life, humility or power. The documentation of this spiritual idea dates now (on the basis of hieroglyphic texts) from at least A.D. 150 and has been recently asserted to be the fundamental principle underlying Mesoamerican Classic period rulers' claim to power (on the hieroglyphic text, see Chapter 11).

Known as the *tonalli* in the Mexican Central Valley (see the discussion earlier in this chapter), past and present, and as the *nagual, chanul,* or *wayel* in the Mayan area, this coessence of the individual plays a powerful role in both affirmative and therapeutic rituals—as in curing—and in negative and aggressive transactions—as in witchcraft (see Box 14.2 on Thomas Gage's seventeenth-century report from Guatemala). The coessence and its role in individual destiny were once, apparently, determined by calendrical reckoning (birthdate and associated deities). Today, this belief system is made to "speak" via dream interpretation, pulsing of the wrist (allowing the blood to speak), and divination. In both the ancient and the modern eras, the coessence embodies, exalts, and constrains individual power and destiny, for these forces are in essence "from elsewhere." Since this idea constitutes a conceptual foundation for a kind of predestination, it is not unreasonable to link it with a certain skepticism about the capacity of individuals to "make their own way in the world" through their own volition. We know that this belief is strong in Indian communities of the region today. It may also be found to characterize certain aspects of the world view of non-Indians, particularly in Mexico and Guatemala.

Cyclical Time as a Sacred Entity

Whether in its macroform as a four- or five-part grand creation and restoration cycle that constitutes all of history, or in its microform as the metaphor of the day as a minimal cycle of heat, in its calendrical mode, in its astronomical mode, in its ritual mode, or in the smallest nuances of verbal metaphor and poetics, it is clear that sacred, cyclical solar time has held powerful sway in both the ancient and the contemporary Mesoamerican universe. (See the earlier extract from Miguel León-Portilla.) Other natural and cultural cycles—such as the human life cycle, the human gestation cycle, the agricultural cycle, and the festival cycle—are all laced into the daily and annual solar cycles to create a cosmos that places humankind in an inherited, a sacred, a temporal order that demands human maintenance. This is not a system in which the human will is free to indulge its whims or to innovate in the hope of achieving personal or collective gain. It is obvious that this ideological premise occupies a key position in questions of continuity and change in the Mesoamerican present and future, for it possesses, in addition to its cyclical principles, a cumulative, progressive component. But this progressive, linear component is not selfishly pragmatic and not necessarily subject to the human will. It is a spiral that cannot move forward without contemplating and retracing its past positions and prior forms. Competing ideologies, such as Protestantism, Marxism, Reform Catholicism, and Developmentalism, must either acknowledge and accommodate this ancient ideology or must demand its eradication. Comfortable coexistence is unlikely, for many of the new ideologies are linear, progressive, secular, and pragmatic. The old Mesoamerican temporal order, in both its cyclical and linear modes, is sacred and highly patterned.

The Structure of the Vertical and Horizontal Cosmos

Both ancient and modern Mesoamerican communities recognize a consistent delimitation of sky, earth, and underworld in the spatial layout of the cosmos, with mediation among these realms as a key intellectual, political, and religious activity. With successful mediation come power, wisdom, even personal health and community survival. Some variant of this spatial structure, with subunit segmentation and corresponding cardinal directional symbolism, occurs throughout pre-Columbian

Mesoamerica and in hundreds of contemporary communities. Shamanism, heroic narratives, key integrating symbols, and deities themselves (particularly Sun, Moon, Jaguar, Wind, Lightning, Earth Lords, Serpents, Jesus Christ, the Virgin Mary and the saints, even the individual coessences) all depend for their power and efficacy on spatial mobility within all or parts of the tripartite vertical cosmos (sky, earth, and underworld) and the related quadripartite (four-part) horizontal cosmos. Through the mediation of supernatural forces that traverse this spatio-temporal whole, the individual gains access to, and is also constrained by, the whole.

Supernatural Combat and Secular Conflict as Creative and Life-Sustaining Forces

From grand mythical commentaries on the creation and early phases of the universe, to the structure and content of sacred narrative, to the ordering of everyday life—conflict is the genesis and precondition for order. This theme has countless permutations, from the battles of the underworld in the *Popol Wuh* (the sixteenth-century K'iché Maya epic; see the discussion in Chapter 6), to the dialectic of the male and female principle in everyday life, to the problem of Indian ethnicity in the complex modern societies of the region today. The theme of conflict as part of creation and life-maintenance does not impress one at first as distinctive. Is it not part of the human condition?

What makes the conflict motif peculiarly Mesoamerican is twofold. First, conflict is divinely ordained. Thus, it is primordial, ubiquitous, and easy to rationalize. Second, the parties in the conflicts are often dual aspects of the same supernatural being, social unit, or person. For example, the Passions, who are ritual personages who sponsor the cult to the Sun-Christ deity in the Chamula Tzotzil (Mayas) ritual of annual renewal, simultaneously sponsor the ritual warfare that is intended to kill the Sun-Christ deity. The Passions' ritual accomplices, the Monkeys, in the same festival simultaneously represent the precultural forces that helped to kill the Sun-Christ before the First Creation of the mythic era, and that function as the policemen who keep order at the festival and defend the sacred symbols of the Sun-Christ's cult. This of course echoes the dual nature of countless deities of the pre-Columbian Mesoamerican pantheon (for example, the founding deity of the Aztec cosmos: the Lord of Duality).

The issue of duality and subsequent dialogue and conflict between these dual principles is indeed the dynamic force that creates the cosmos in the Mayan world, ancient and modern. Dennis Tedlock has noted that the peculiar Mesoamerican twist to this idea is not only that this dynamic tension is sacred but also that it is complementary rather than oppositional, contemporaneous rather than sequential. This reading of Mesoamerican dualism meshes intelligibly with the principles of cyclical time (noted before) in that the elements in temporal cycles that are not currently active always remain latent, ready to express themselves again in the same formal manner, though perhaps in a different code. Latent elements do not disappear, nor do they get permanently transcended or defeated.

The pattern of complementary dualism also recalls and illuminates the ubiquitous Mesoamerican custom of addressing ancestors, deities, and ritual personages with a bisexual honorific title, for example, "Fathers-Mothers" or "Grandmothers-Grandfathers." Power, divinity, age, and honor seem to evoke the complementary whole (male and female), rather than the everyday mode in which the male has primacy over the female in the public arena of community life and the female dominates the male in many spheres of domestic life. Obviously, public and domestic life coexist now, as they always have, in the Mesoamerican world (see the discussion of gender in Chapter 12).

Complementary Dualism as a Key to Understanding Religious Process and Social Change in Mesoamerica

Is it not plausible that the male-dominated public arena has been the active assimilator of new codes (new languages, economic systems, political authority systems, state religions) and, thus, seemingly able to respond quickly, even apparently capitulating to the winds of change; whereas the female-dominated domestic sector simultaneously guards the older order (native languages, agricultural ritual, curing and divinatory knowledge, ancestor cults, shamanistic knowledge) for present and future reference and security? This arrangement renders intelligible the enigma that has impressed many scholars and casual observers of Indian communities in Mesoamerica: People seem at once to be modern Mexican or Guatemalan peasants and living shadows of a vanished pre-Columbian world.

Which is the "true" identity? This may well be a moot question; surely it does not concern the average Mesoamerican rural family. Yet we are, as students and scholars, interested in making sense of what we observe. It seems clear that both identities—Mexican and Indian, Guatemalan and Indian—are, simultaneously, true identities, for Mesoamerican ideology accommodates such complementary duality easily. Perhaps it has also always been so in the ebb and flow of Mesoamerican history, as the little communities of the hinterland absorbed wave after wave of new state ideas and religions that emanated from the urban centers. The public sector voluntarily adapted or involuntarily capitulated to the ideological demands of the more inclusive system, while the domestic sector held fast. This is not unrelated to the fact that female deities have played a singularly important role in the initial moments of Mesoamerican nativistic movements and major syncretic adjustments. The Virgin of Guadalupe herself may be usefully interpreted in this light, for she chose to make her appearance on Tepeyac, a hill that, according to legend, housed a shrine dedicated to the Aztec Tonantzín, an honorific title referring to "Our Dear Mother" (see Box 5.1 in Chapter 5). New political authority and new religions were pragmatically accommodated, yet the integrity of local identity and local knowledge was not annihilated; rather, it was, somewhat conservatively, transformed.

The Extraordinary Power of Spoken and Written Language as a Symbolic Entity in Itself, Beyond Its Neutral Role as Medium for Routine Communication

The great American linguist Edward Sapir wrote long ago of language as "those invisible garments that drape themselves about our spirit." He, of course, was writing about language in general. Mesoamericans, reflecting on their own languages, would agree with Sapir, but would be likely to force the issue to greater hyperbole. Throughout the region, Mesoamericans linked language and dialogue to the dawn of consciousness in the creation of the human condition. In time present as in time past, language, with its wide range of rhetorical, poetic, and musical embellishments, has behaved as a sacred symbol that allows humans to share qualities with, and to communicate with, gods.

In effect, beautifully executed speech and song are the only substances, with the possible exception of blood, that the human body can produce that are accessible to, and worthy before, divine beings. The Aztec theory of language, song, and poetics was expressed in the metaphor of plants and flowers. Flowers are the most beautiful, perfect achievement of plants, and also their medium for continuity through seed production. Flowers are also symbols of the transforming sacred power of the sun. So also, song and poetry are the most beautiful realization of the human spirit, making this essence worthy before the deities. If divine beings are pleased, human life is allowed to continue. A variant of these ideas occurs among the Chamula Tzotzil, in which the metatheory of language links high poetic and musical forms of the language to the qualities of divine heat, which are required for communication to and about the Sun-Christ (for a detailed discussion of Tzotzil metatheory about language, see Chapter 13).

It is well known that ancient Mesoamerican writing and mnemonic systems were used to record calendrical, dynastic, and astronomical information of the highest order of political and religious importance. Books were in fact produced, kept, and used by a priestly class. The spiritual and political power that the native Mesoamericans attached to pictographic and hieroglyphic books was such that the conquering Spaniards destroyed them as a first order of business, and did so with particular zeal (native writing in Mesoamerica is discussed in Chapter 6).

The native languages of Mesoamerica retain today not only their remarkable vitality (over 15 million contemporary Mesoamericans continue to speak over eighty native languages as their first or only language) but also their importance as an art form and as a passive and active political force (again, see Chapter 13). The late anthropologist Eva Hunt observed, with understatement, that the conservative character of Mesoamerica's native languages may be the single best way to account for the continuity in the region's distinctive symbolic order in our time.

It is also worth noting that the written form of language continues to be important in Mesoamerican Indian communities, even in those that are largely nonliterate either in their own languages or in Spanish. For example, the charter proclamation of the Festival of Games in San Juan Chamula, a community that is largely monolingual in Tzotzil and over 90 percent nonliterate, exists only in written form. This document, called the "Spanish letter," is "read" (actually recited from memory) at key moments in the ritual sequence. The Spanish letter itself is a regional historical synthesis of the conquest, incorporating references to Spanish soldiers who come from Guatemala and Mexico City. The paper on which it is written is a potent ritual symbol and mnemonic device. This function is not unlike the role of the written word in ancient Mesoamerica (see Chapter 11). This also recalls the sacred "Books of Chilam Balam," written in Maya utilizing the Latin alphabet, which persisted throughout the colonial and early modern periods (perhaps even today) as underground books of prophecy.

All of this could be dismissed as a mere curiosity were it not for the fact that literacy and the written word, as symbols of political and religious power and ethnic consciousness, matter a great deal in the ideological warfare that pervades Mesoamerica in our time. All of the major purveyors of new ideology—Protestants, Marxist revolutionaries, Roman Catholic reform-oriented missionaries affiliated with the Theology of Liberation, and advocates of national integration and development—promise some form of political entitlement through literacy. This is old soil, well trodden for 2,000 years. However, two new issues are apparent. First, in all cases, the focus is upon shared entitlement; literacy is not destined to empower only the elite. The second issue is, of course, whether the written word will empower in Spanish or in native languages. Interested parties disagree here. However, there is at least good reason to speculate that victory in the new spiritual warfare of Mesoamerica will go to those who offer literacy (and something to read) in native languages. This eventuality may partly account for the extraordinary recent success of Protestantism in many of the predominantly Indian areas of Guatemala and Mexico.

We have concluded this chapter by sketching six core features of spirituality that span the linguistic diversity and the ethnic, political, and ecological boundaries of Mesoamerica across several millennia. Because these traits are so widespread and apparently so durable, it is not unreasonable to assert that religion, cosmology, and related symbolic constructions may be among the more important features that unify the native peoples of the region as a distinctive cultural space ("civilization") in both past and present. Although this may be true, we have noted earlier that there are now tens of millions of Mexicans and Central Americans for whom the core features we have described as characterizing Indian-derived spiritual components of the region certainly do not apply, at least insofar as people would consciously identify themselves. However, although cultural space and individual identity are not necessarily related, it is nevertheless the case that the Indian past and present color the quality of life throughout the region.

From minishrines that adorn the front of buses and taxis, to the coins in their pockets, to the murals painted on public buildings, Mexicans daily encounter sacred symbols from their Indian past. Guatemala's greatest literary classics—the sixteenth-century K'iche' Mayan *Popol Wuh* and Miguel Angel Asturias's twentieth-century epic novel *Men of Maize,* for which he received the Nobel Prize in literature, are nothing more and nothing less than root and branch of Maya spiritual ideas (for citations from these sources, see Chapter 13). Thus, the realm of spiritual and religious traditions does not lie far removed from the lives of all contemporary peoples residing in the bounds of the ancient Mesoamerican lands.

SUGGESTED READINGS

ANNIS, SHELDON 1987 *God and Production in a Guatemalan Town.* Austin: University of Texas Press.

BROWN, LYLE C., AND WILLIAM F. COOPER 1980 *Religion in Latin American Life and Literature.* Waco, Texas: Markham Press Fund of Baylor University Press.

CARRASCO, DAVÍD 1990 *The Religions of Mesoamerica: Cosmovision and Ceremonial Centers.* San Francisco: Harper & Row.

FARRISS, NANCY M. 1987 Remembering the Future, Anticipating the Past: History, Time and Cosmology among the Maya of Yucatán. *Comparative Studies in Society and History* 29:566–593.

GOSSEN, GARY H. (ed.) 1986 *Symbol and Meaning Beyond the Closed Community: Essays in Mesoamerican Ideas.* Studies on Culture and Society, Vol. 1. Albany: Institute for Mesoamerican Studies.

GOSSEN, GARY H., AND MIGUEL LEÓN-PORTILLA (eds.) 1993 *South and Mesoamerican Native Spirituality: From the Cult of the Feathered Serpent to the Theology of Liberation.* Vol. 4. *World Spirituality: An Encyclopedic History of the Religious Quest.* New York: Crossroad.

INGHAM, JOHN M. 1986 *Mary, Michael and Lucifer: Folk Catholicism in Central Mexico.* Austin: University of Texas Press.

LEÓN-PORTILLA, MIGUEL 1980 *Native Mesoamerican Spirituality.* New York: Paulist Press.

MENDELSON, E. MICHAEL 1967 Ritual and Mythology. In *Social Anthropology,* edited by Manning Nash, pp. 392–415. Handbook of Middle American Indians, vol. 6, Robert Wauchope, general editor. Austin: University of Texas Press.

MYERHOFF, BARBARA G. 1974 *Peyote Hunt: The Sacred Journey of the Huichol Indians.* Ithaca, New York: Cornell University Press.

SANDSTROM, ALAN R. 1991 *Corn Is Our Blood: Culture and Ethnic Identity in a Contemporary Aztec Indian Village.* Norman: University of Oklahoma Press.

STOLL, DAVID 1990 *Is Latin America Turning Protestant? The Politics of Evangelical Growth.* Berkeley: University of California Press.

TEDLOCK, BARBARA 1992 *Time and the Highland Maya,* Revised edition. Albuquerque: University of New Mexico Press.

VOGT, EVON Z. 1993 *Tortillas for the Gods: A Symbolic Analysis of Zinacanteco Rituals.* New Edition. Norman: University of Oklahoma Press.

WATANABE, JOHN 1992 *Maya Saints and Souls in a Changing World.* Austin: University of Texas Press.

Glossary

acculturation: the process by which a subordinate culture changes to become more like the dominant culture during culture contact situations.

Alcalde Mayor: Spanish royal official charged with the administration of a district known as an Alcaldía Mayor. Other district officials were known as Corregidores.

altepetl: Nahuatl term for a town or city (city-state) that had its own deities, religious and civil administrative structures, markets, and land base.

amaranth: a short, bushy plant with small black seeds that were an important source of food in Precolumbian Mesoamerica.

Archaic period: the period from around 8000 B.C. to 2000 B.C. when many plants were domesticated and people became more sedentary.

Aztec: a general term used for Nahuatl-speaking peoples of Late Postclassic Central Mexico; people from Aztlán.

Bajío: a highland basin located along the drainage of the Lerma River around Guanajuato, historically important for agricultural production and mining.

ball game: a game played with a rubber ball on a formal court throughout ancient Mesoamerica. The game was played primarily for ritual purposes.

barrio: territorial division of a town or city.

cabildo: town council and municipal office building.

cacao: the beans from the cacao tree from which chocolate is made.

cacique: in the Colonial period, a native ruler or chief (from the Arawak language); in modern times, a small-town political boss.

calmecac: the schools for the children of the Aztec nobility.

calpulli: Aztec territorial unit corresponding to a village, a town, or a neighborhood (barrio) within a city.

castas: in the Colonial period, categories in a social hierarchy based on biological heritage with respect to European, African, and Native American ancestry and combinations thereof.

caudillo: a military or political leader or dictator.

centralist: in nineteenth-century Mesoamerica, those who supported the traditional power of large landholders, the army, and the Catholic Church, and favored centralized political and economic power.

chia: a sage plant whose seeds were used in ancient Mesoamerica for oil and in a drink.

Chichimec: a general term applied to the nomadic peoples originally from, in some cases, the northern desert area of Mexico. The term was used to denote ethnic groups in ancient Mesoamerica.

chiefdom: a complex society characterized by social inequality, limited full-time occupational specialization, and economic and political institutions headed by hereditary authority (a chief).

chinampa: Nahuatl term for raised field, a highly productive farming method in which artificial plots are created in swamps or shallow lake-beds from layers of mud and vegetation.

chronicle: a historical record; annals.

científicos: generally, the elite scientists and technicians who created the economic infrastructure in nineteenth-century Mesoamerica; in nineteenth-century Mexico, the group of intellectuals, landowners, and bankers who served as advisers under the Porfirio Díaz regime in Mexico.

Classic period: the period from approximately A.D. 200 to A.D. 900, marked in many areas by the development of large-scale political states and a florescence in the arts.

codex (plural, codices): generally, any preconquest or colonial manuscript with pictorial content produced by native artists. Codices are frequently named for their location, discoverer or former owner, or place of origin. Preconquest codices were constructed of fig tree bark paper (amate) or deerhide, coated with a layer of plaster, and then painted and rolled up like a scroll or folded up accordion-style into a screenfold. Codices dating to the Colonial period may be painted on European paper and bound like a book. Known codices record historical, religious, astronomical, or economic information.

cofradía: religious confraternity dedicated to the cult of a particular saint or aspect of the Christian deity.

compadrazgo: ritual kin ties between godparents and biological parents.

CONAVIGUA: National Coordinator of Guatemalan Widows. Human rights group formed by widows from Chimaltenango, Guatemala. The group was founded in 1988 in order to counter the "abuse, rape, and exploitation" by the Guatemalan right wing military forces.

congregación: Spanish colonial policy of concentrating Indian populations of different and dispersed communities into a single new community.

conversos: Jewish converts to Christianity.

core: in world-system theory, the dominant region or regions that are the recipients of resources (luxury goods and labor) from the peripheral regions.

corregidor: Spanish royal official charged with the administration of a district known as a Corregimiento; corregidor de indios was in charge of an Indian district; similar in functions to the acalde mayor.

creoles: Spaniards born in the New World.

dialect: variation within one language.

doctrina: a parochial or parish district made up of Indian communities.

domestication: the process by which humans select for specific traits thereby causing the evolution of wild plants or animals into forms advantageous to human use.

ejido: community lands; in twentieth-century Mexico, the program that expropriated land from large landholders and redistributed the land to agrarian communities.

encomienda: system that rewarded certain individuals (encomenderos) with the rights to goods and labor of a specific group of native people; the encomendero was responsible for Christianizing the natives.

epistemology: the study of theories or the theory of knowledge.

estancia: farm or ranch, usually for livestock.

ethos: the characteristic spirit and cultural patterns of a people.

expropriate: taking control of productive goods, as when a government takes control of what was once private property.

extensive agriculture: agricultural practices that utilize relatively simple technology; requires large areas for cultivation. An example is swidden or slash-and-burn agriculture; contrasts with intensive agriculture.

federalist: in nineteenth-century Mexico and Central America, those who supported liberal ideals of social progress, a secular state, and regional political and economic power.

feminism: a movement that promotes equal rights and opportunities for women; an approach that analyzes the concept of gender and the meaning of sexual differences.

fiscal: in indigenous communities, a religious official who acts as the priest's assistant and oversees the affairs of the local church.

Formative period: the period from around 2000 B.C. to A.D. 200, during which many societies in the Mesoamerican region became more complex; Preclassic period.

friar: a member of a Catholic religious order such as the Franciscans or Dominicans; may be an ordained priest or a lay brother.

GAM: Mutual Support Group. Human rights group originally formed by Indian widows of men who were killed or "disappeared" as part of the violence (1970s and 1980s) in Guatemala.

gender: culturally prescribed behaviors, roles, and relationships between the sexes.

genre: class or category, such as speech genres.

halach uinic: prehispanic Mayan term for the ruler of a town or region; governor.

henequen: a plant that produces fiber used for cordage.

indigenismo: public policy and institutions that address the educational, economic, health, and social needs of the Indian population, with the underlying goal of assimilating Indians into the national culture.

indigo: a plant from which blue dye is produced.

intensive agriculture: agricultural practices that use labor-intensive techniques to produce high yields. Examples include terracing, irrigation, and raised fields; contrasts with extensive agriculture.

ladino: in the Colonial period, an acculturated or Spanish-speaking Indian; in the modern period, a non-Indian, a mestizo, or a person of European or mixed descent.

latifundio: a large rural estate; plantation.

Liberation Theology: movement within the Catholic Church in which criticism of oppression and exploitation is central to the practice of theology.

long count: a dating system used primarily by the lowland Classic Maya in which a particular day was defined as occurring in a specific baktun (cycle of about 400 years), katun (cycle of about twenty years), tun (cycle of 360 days), uinal (cycle of twenty days), and kin (day), also including the appropriate date in the 260-day secular calendar.

macehual (plural, macehualtin): Nahuatl term for commoner or vassal.

machismo: an ideology and its practices that place a high value on male dominance and virility.

maestro de cantor: Indian official in charge of liturgy and catechism; choirmaster.

maize: corn (*Zea mays*); the staple food of Mesoamerica.

maquiladora: export manufacturing factories.

mayordomo: caretaker or custodian (steward).

mendicants: members of Catholic religious orders who live by a vow of poverty and are dependent on donations, such as the Franciscans, Augustinians, and Dominicans.

mestizaje: the process by which a mestizo population is created through biological and cultural mixing.

mestizo: a person of mixed white, Indian, and in many cases African descent; as used in colonial *casta* system, a mestizo would *not* have African ancestry.

Mexica: the Nahuatl-speaking group that founded Tenochtitlan and came to dominate Central Mexico; the Aztecs of Tehochtitlán.

milpa: a plot of land planted with maize and beans and often chile as well.

minifundio: a small rural estate or farm plot.

modernization: the practice of emulating European models for progress based on the assumption that Latin American countries could catch up with Europe and the United States through capitalist economic development.

moriscos: Moorish converts to Christianity.

morphology: in linguistics, the system for the formation of words in a language.

mulatto: person of mixed white and African/African-American ancestry.

myth: a narrative, usually involving supernatural forces, that accounts for historical and natural phenomena and expresses deeply held cultural values.

nagual (nahual): the magical companion animal or force of humans, and the individual who is believed to have the power to transform him/herself into that magical entity.

nativistic movement: an attempt by native groups and their charismatic prophet leaders to achieve religious and/or political autonomy and recognition of ethnic identity. These movements often turn violent when efforts are made to suppress them by force.

obraje: textile workshop or factory, primarily for woolens, in which forced labor is typical.

obsidian: a volcanic glass-like rock used to make sharp tools like arrow points and knives.

orthography: in linguistics, the use of phonetic symbols to express sounds and words.

Paleoindian period: the period that began with the earliest arrival of humans (40,000 to 20,000 years ago) in the Americas and ended around 8000 B.C. This period was characterized by populations with a nomadic lifestyle.

patriarchy: a social system in which fathers are dominant in the family relations.

peasant: a person belonging to a society or sectors of society subject to providing surpluses to a larger, dominant society; they support themselves to some extent through agricultural labor.

peninsulares: Spaniards born in Spain and living in the New World.

periphery: in world-system theory, the subordinate regions that supply the core with resources.

petty commodity production: small-scale production of agricultural or artisan goods for sale in markets for profit.

phonology: the sound systems of a language.

pilli (plural, pipiltin):   Nahuatl term for a noble.

Pleistocene: the geological period of colder climate that began about 100,000 years ago and ended about 10,000 years ago.

polygyny: marriage pattern in which one man has two or more wives simultaneously.

positivism: the ninteenth-century philosophy that maintains that no knowledge is possible beyond that which can be discovered through empirical facts and hypothesis testing.

Postclassic period: the period from approximately A.D. 900 to the time of Spanish contact (ca. 1520).

Preclassic period: same as the Formative period.

proletariat: wage laborers.

pulque: a native Mesoamerican alcoholic beverage made from the fermented juice of the maguey plant (also called agave or century plant).

reconquista: the process by which Christian Spaniards reconquered the Iberian Peninsula from the Muslim Moors of North Africa (who had conquered the peninsula in the early eighth century).

reducción: same as congregación.

repartimiento: in the Colonial period, various institutions for exploiting Indian goods, labor, and wealth; a labor draft, forced distribution of goods, or forced production of goods.

rural proletariat: individuals from traditional agricultural rural areas who rely on wage labor.

secular clergy: Catholic priests who do not belong to a religious order.

sedentism: a way of life characterized by permanent or semi-permanent settlements.

semantics: in linguistics, relations among meanings of different words or grammatical constructions.

semi-periphery: in world-system theory, the regions that mediate between core and periphery, often through trade.

shaman: part-time religious specialist who possesses magical powers through links with a supernatural source.

sharecropping: the system by which farmers rent land and pay owners with part of their harvest.

state: a large, complex society characterized by social stratification, full-time occupational specialists, and political and economic institutions that allow the central authorities to monopolize the use of force.

stela (plural, stelae):   stone slab erected as a monument, often sculpted with hieroglyphic texts and scenes depicting ceremonies or mythical events.

subaltern: generally, someone of inferior status, especially relative to the ruling class.

swidden: slash-and-burn agriculture, an extensive agricultural method in which the vegetation of a plot is cut and burned, cultivated until the soil is depleted, and left fallow to recover before the cycle begins again.

syncretism: ideas and practices derived from distinct traditions that are reinterpreted and transformed during the process of cultural contact.

syntax: in linguistics, rules governing the order and use of words.

Tlaloc: Aztec rain god, same as the rain deity in other regions of Mesoamerica; Chac (Maya), Cocijo (Zapotec).

tlamene: Nahuatl-derived term for Indian carriers; they usually employed the tiempline.

tlatoani (plural, tlatoque):   Nahuatl term for the ruler of a town or region (literally, "speaker").

tonalli: an individual's destiny or co-essence as indicated by the calendar; also a day-sign in the Aztec 260-day calendar.

Treaty of Tordesillas: 1493 treaty between Spain and Portugal that gave Spain the rights to all lands to the west of a certain line and Portugal the rights to all lands to the east of the line; in the Americas only Brazil lies to the east of this line.

vigesimal: base-20 numerical system; the typical system in ancient Mesoamerica.

world-system: a model articulated by Immanuel Wallerstein and others of a social system that supersedes political boundaries and is characterized by unequal exchange between core, semi-peripheral, and peripheral regions, and an international division of labor.

Bibliographic References

ABREU GÓMEZ, ERMILO 1979 *Canek: History and Legend of a Maya Hero*, translated with an introduction by Mario L. Dávila and Carter Wilson. Berkeley: University of California Press. (English translation of the original, 1940, *Canek*. Mexico City: Ediciones Canek.)

ACOSTA, JOSE DE 1987 *Historia natural y moral de las Indias*. José Alcina Franch, ed. Madrid: Crónicas de América, Historia 16.

ADAMS, RICHARD N. 1991 Strategies of Ethnic Survival in Central America. *Nation-States and Indians in Latin America*, edited by Greg Urban and Joel Sherzer. Austin: University of Texas Press.

AGUIRRE BELTRÁN, GONZALO 1983 Indigenismo en México: Confrontación de problemas. In *La Quiebra Política de la Antropología Social en México*, edited by A. Medina and Carlos Garcia Mora, pp. 195–212. Mexico City: Universidad Nacional Autónoma de México.

AMNESTY INTERNATIONAL 2005 No Protection, No Justice: Killings of Women in Guatemala. Online publication at Amnestyusa.org/countries/Guatemala

ANDERSON, ARTHUR J. O., FRANCES BERDAN, AND JAMES LOCKHART (eds. and trans.) 1976 *Beyond the Codices: The Nahua View of Colonial Mexico*. Berkeley: University of California Press.

ANDERSON, E. N. 2005 *Political Ecology in a Yucatec Maya Community*. Tucson: University of Arizona Press.

ARIZPE, LOURDES, AND JOSEFINA ARANDA 1986 Women Workers in the Strawberry Agribusiness in Mexico. In *Women's Work, Development and the Division of Labor*, edited by Eleanor Leacock and Helen I. Safa, pp. 174–193. Greenwood, MA: Bergin and Garvey Publisher.

ASHER, R. E. AND MOSLEY, CHRISTOPHER 1994 *Routledge Atlas of the World's Languages*. Second edition. London: Routledge.

ASTURIAS, MIGUEL ANGEL 1949 *Men of Maize*, translated by Gerald Martin. New York: Delacorte Press/St. Lawrence. (English translation of the original Spanish edition, 1949, *Hombres de Maíz*. Buenos Aires: Editorial Losada, S. A.)

ASTURIAS, MIGUEL ANGEL 1975 *Men of Maize*. Gerald Martin, translator. New York: Delacorte Press / S. Lawrence.

BARTRA, ROGER 1982 *Campesinado y poder político en México*. Mexico City: Ediciones Era.

BEHAR, RUTH 1989 Sexual Witchcraft, Colonialism and Women's Powers: Views from the Mexican Inquisition. In *Sexuality and Marriage in Latin America*, edited by Asunción Lavrin, pp. 178–206. Lincoln: University of Nebraska Press.

BENJAMIN, MEDEA (ed. and trans.) 1989 *Don't Be Afraid Gringo: A Honduran Woman Speaks from the Heart. The Story of Elvia Alvarado*. New York: HarperCollins Publishers.

BERDAN, FRANCES F. 1982 *The Aztecs of Central Mexico: An Imperial Society*. New York: Holt, Rinehart and Winston.

BERDAN, FRANCES F., RICHARD E. BLANTON, ELIZABETH H. BOONE, MARY G. HODGE, MICHAEL E. SMITH, AND EMILY UMBERGER 1996 *Aztec Imperial Strategies*. Washington, D.C.: Dumbarton Oaks.

BERNARD, H. RUSSEL, AND JESUS SALINAS PEDRAZA 1989 *Native Ethnography: A Mexican Indian Describes His Culture*. Newberry Park, California: Sage Publications.

BIERHORST, JOHN (ed. and trans.) 1985 *Cantares Mexicanos: Songs of the Aztecs*. Stanford: Stanford University Press.

BLANTON, RICHARD E., GARY M. FEINMAN, STEPHEN A. KOWALEWSKI, AND LINDA M. NICHOLAS 1999 *Ancient Oaxaca: The Monte Albán State: Case Studies in Early Societies*. New York: Cambridge University Press.

BLANTON, RICHARD E., S. A. KOWALEWSKI, GARY FEINMAN, AND LAURA FINSTEN 1992 *Ancient Mesoamerica: A Comparison of Change in Three Regions,* 2nd ed. New York: Cambridge University Press.

BLANTON, RICHARD, AND GARY FEINMAN 1984 The Mesoamerican World System. *American Anthropologist* 86:673–682.

BOONE, ELIZABETH HILL 2000 *Stories in Red and Black: Pictorial Histories of the Aztecs and Mixtecs.* Austin: University of Texas Press.

BOSSEN, LAUREL 1984 *The Redivision of Labor: Women and Economic Choice in Four Guatemalan Communities.* Albany: State University of New York Press.

BRETTELL, CAROLINE 2000 Theorizing Migration in Anthropology the Social Construction of Networks Identities Communities and Globalscapes. In *Migration Theory: Talking across Disciplines,* edited by Caroline B. Brettell and James F. Hollifield, pp. 97–136. London: Routledge.

BRICKER, VICTORIA REIFLER 1981 *The Indian Christ, The Indian King: The Historical Substrate of Maya Myth and Ritual.* Austin: University of Texas Press.

BURKHART, LOUISE 1995 Mexica Women on the Home Front: Housework and Religion in Aztec Mexico. *In Indian Women in Early Mexico: Identity, Ethnicity and Gender Differentiation,* edited by Susan Schroeder, Stephanie Wood and Robert Haskett, pp. 25–54. Norman: University of Oklahoma Press.

BURKHART, LOUISE M. 1989 *The Slippery Earth: Nahua-Christian Moral Dialogue in Sixteenth-Century Mexico.* Tucson: University of Arizona Press.

———. 2001 *Before Guadalupe: The Virgin Mary in Early Colonial Nahuatl Literature.* Albany: Institute for Mesoamerican Studies.

BURNS, ALAN 1993 *Maya in Exile: Guatemalans in Florida.* Philadelphia: Temple University Press.

BYLAND, BRUCE E., AND JOHN M. D. POHL 1994 *In the Realm of 8 Deer: The Archaeology of the Mixtec Codices.* Norman: University of Oklahoma Press.

CAMUS, MANUELA 2002 *Ser Indígena en Ciudad de Guatemala.* Guatemala City: FLACSO.

CARCEDO, ANA Y MONTSERRAT SAGOT 2001 *Costa Rica, Balance Mortal.* Online publication at Malostratos.org #32

CARMACK, ROBERT M. 1981 *The Quiché Mayas of Utatlan: The Evolution of a Highland Guatemalan Kingdom.* Norman: University of Oklahoma Press.

———. 1995 *Rebels of Highland Guatemala: The Quiche-Mayas of Momostenango.* Norman: University of Oklahoma Press.

CARRASCO, DAVID 1990 *The Religions of Mesoamerica: Cosmovision and Ceremonial Centers.* San Francisco: Harper & Row.

CARRIER, JOSEPH 1995 *De Los Otros: Intimacy and Homosexuality among Mexican Men.* New York: Columbia University Press.

CASTILLO GODOY, DELIA 2003 *Mujeres Excluidas.* Guatemala City: Asociación Mujer Vamos Adelante, Ediciones Papiro SA.

CHAPMAN, ANA 1960 *Los Nicaraoy los Chorotega según las Fuentes históricas.* San Jose: Universidad de Costa Rica.

CHAPMAN, ANN M. 1957 Port of Trade Enclaves in Aztec and Maya Civilization. In *Trade and Market in the Early Empires,* edited by Karl Polanyi, M. Conrad Arensberg, and Harry W. Pearson. New York: The Free Press.

CHIÑAS, BEVERLY 1995 *Isthmus Zapotec Attitudes Toward Sex and Gender Anomalies.* In *Latin American Male Homosexualities,* edited by Stephen O. Murray, pp. 293–302. Albuquerque NM: University of New Mexico Press.

CLARK, JOHN E., AND MICHAEL BLAKE 1994 The Power of Prestige: Competitive Generosity and the Emergence of Rank Societies in Lowland Mesoamerica. In *Factional Competition and Political Development in the New World,* edited by E. M. Brumfiel and J. W. Fox, pp. 17–30. Cambridge: Cambridge University Press.

COBOS PALMA, RAFAEL 2004 Chichén Itzá: Settlement and Hegemony During the Terminal Classic Period. In *The Terminal Classic in the Maya Lowlands: Collapse, Transition, and Transformation,* edited by A. A. Demarest, P. M. Rice, and D. S. Rice, pp. 517–544. Boulder: University of Colorado Press.

COCKCROFT, JAMES D. 1983 *Mexico, Class Formation, Capital Accumulation, and the State.* New York: Monthly Review Press.

COE, MICHAEL D., AND GORDON WHITTAKER (eds. and trans.) 1982 *Aztec Sorcerers in Seventeenth Century Mexico: The Treatise on Superstitions by Hernando Ruiz de Alarcón.* Albany: Institute for Mesoamerican Studies.

COHEN, JEFFREY H. 2001 Transnational Migration in Rural Oaxaca, Mexico: Dependency, Development and the Household. *American Anthropologist* Vol.103(4): 954–967.

———. 2004 *The Culture of Migration in Southern Mexico.* Austin: University of Texas Press.

COJTI CUXIL, DEMETRIO 1996 The Politics of Maya Revindication. In *Maya Cultural Activism in Guatemala,* edited by Edward F. Fischer and R. McKenna Brown. Austin: University of Texas Press.

COLLIER, GEORGE A., in collaboration with ELIZABETH QUARATIELLO 1999 *Basta! Land and the Zapatista Rebellion in Chiapas.* Revised edition [Original 1994]. Oakland: Food First Books.

CONRAD, GEOFFREY W., AND ARTHUR A. DEMAREST 1984 *Religion and Empire: The Dynamics of Aztec and Inca Expansionism.* Cambridge: Cambridge University Press.

CONTRERAS, J. DANIEL 1951 *Una Rebelión Indígena en el Partido de Totonicapán en 1820: El Indio y la Independencia.* Guatemala City: Imprenta Universitaria.

COOK, SCOTT 2004 *Understanding Commodity Cultures: Explorations in Economic Anthropology with Case Studies from Mexico.* Lanham, Maryland: Rowman & Littlefield Publishers, Inc.

CORTÉS, HERNANDO 1962 *Five Letters of Cortés to the Emperor,* translated by J. Bayard Morris. New York: W. W. Norton.

COVARRUBIAS, MIGUEL 1957 *Indian Art of Mexico and Central America.* New York: Alfred A. Knopf.

COWAN, GEORGE M. 1948 Mazateco whistle speech. *Language* 24:280–286. Reprinted in Dell Hymes, ed., *Language in Culture and Society*, pp. 305–311. New York: Harper & Row, Publishers.

CROSS, JOHN 1998 *Informal Politics: Street Vendors and the State in Mexico City*. Stanford: Stanford University Press.

CUMBERLAND, CHARLES C. 1968 *Mexico: The Struggle for Modernity*. London: Oxford University Press.

DÍAZ DEL CASTILLO, BERNAL 1956 *The Discovery and Conquest of Mexico*, edited and translated by A. P. Maudslay. New York: Farrar, Straus and Giroux.

DAWSON, ALEXANDER S. 2004 *Indian and Nation in Revolutionary Mexico*. Tucson: University of Arizona Press.

DE LA FUENTE, NURIA Y ALMA ODETTE CHACHÓN 2001 *El Feminismo como una opción de vida para las mujeres*. Guatemala: Agrupación de Mujeres Tierra Viva.

DEMAREST, ARTHUR A., PRUDENCE M. RICE, AND DON S. RICE 2004 *The Terminal Classic in the Maya Lowlands: Collapse, Transition, and Transformation*. Boulder: University of Colorado Press.

DURAND, JORGE, AND DOUGLAS MASSEY 1992 Mexican migration to the U.S. *LARR* vol.27(2):3–42.

EARLE, DUNCAN, AND JEANNE SIMONELLI 2005 *Uprising of Hope: Sharing the Zapatista Journey to Alternative Development*. Walnut Creek, California: AltaMira Press.

EBER, CHRISTINE, AND BRENDA ROSENBAUM 1993 "That We May Serve Your Hands and Feet": Women Weavers in Highland Chiapas Mexico. In *Crafts in the World Market: The Impact of Global Exchange on Middle American Artisans*, edited by June Nash, pp. 155–179. Albany: State University of New York Press.

EBER, CHRISTINE 1999 Seeking our own food: Indigenous Women's Power and Autonomy in San Pedro Chenalhó, 1980–1998. *Latin American Perspectives* 26(3):6–36.

———. 2000 *Women and Drinking in a Highland Maya Town: Water of Hope, Water of Sorrow*. Austin: University of Texas Press.

EBER, CHRISTINE, AND CHRISTINE KOVIC (eds.) 2003 *Women of Chiapas: Making History in Times of Struggle and Hope*. Austin: University of Texas Press.

EBER, CHRISTINE, AND JANET TANSKI 2001 Women's Cooperatives in Chiapas, Mexico: Strategies of Survival and Empowerment in Times of Struggle. *Social Development Issues* 24(3):33–40.

EDELMAN, MARC 1999 *Peasants Against Globalization: Rural Social Movements in Costa Rica*. Sanford: Stanford University Press.

EDMONSON, MUNRO S. 1971 *The Book of Counsel: The Popol Vuh of the Quiché Maya of Guatemala*. Middle American Research Institute Publication 35. New Orleans: Tulane University.

EHLERS, TRACY 2000 [1990] *Silent Looms: Women and Production in a Guatemalan Town*. Rev. ed. Austin: University of Texas Press.

EVANS, SUSAN T., AND DAVID L. WEBSTER (eds.) 2001 *Archaeology of Ancient Mexico and Central America: An Encyclopedia*. New York: Garland.

FANON, FRANTZ 1968 *The Wretched of the Earth*. Hamondsworth, England: Penguin Publishers.

FARRISS, NANCY 1984 *Maya Society under Colonial Rule: The Collective Enterprise of Survival*. Princeton: Princeton University Press.

FEW, MARTHA 2002 *Women who live evil lives: gender, religion, and the politics of power in colonial Guatemala*. Austin: University of Texas Press.

FIELD, LES W. 1999 *The Grimace of Macho Ratón: Artisans, Identity, and Nation in Late-Twentieth-Century Western Nicaragua*. Durham: Duke University Press.

FISCHER, EDWARD 1999 Cultural Logic and Maya Identity. *Current Anthropology* 40:473–499.

———. 2001 *Cultural Logics & Global Economies: Maya Identity in Thought & Practice*. Austin: University of Texas Press.

FLANNERY, KENT V. (ed.) 1976 *The Early Mesoamerican Village*. New York: Academic Press.

FLORES, JUAN 2005 The Diaspora Strikes Back: Reflections on Cultural Remittances. *NACLA* 39(3):21–26.

FOLEY, MICHAEL W. 1999 *Southern Mexico: Counterinsurgency and Electoral Politics*. United States Institute of Peace, Special Report 43.

FRANCO, JEAN 1989 *Plotting Women: Gender and Representation in Mexico*. New York: Columbia University Press.

FREIDEL, DAVID A., AND JEREMY A. SABLOFF 1984 *Cozumel: Late Maya Settlement Patterns*. New York: Academic Press.

FREIDEL, DAVID A., AND LINDA SCHELE 1988 Kingship in the Late Preclassic Maya Lowlands: The Instruments and Places of Ritual Power. *American Anthropologist* 90: 547–567.

FREIDEL, DAVID, LINDA SCHELE, AND JOY PARKER 1993 *Maya Cosmos: Three Thousand Years on the Shaman's Path*. New York: William Morrow and Co.

FREYERMUTH ENCISO, GRACIELA 1995 Migration, Organization and Identity: The Women's Group Case in San Cristóbal de Las Casas. *Signs* 20: 970–995.

———. 2001 The Background to Acteal: Maternal Mortality and Birth Control, Silent Genocide? In *The Other Word: Women and Violence in Chiapas before and after Acteal*, edited by Aída Hernández Castillo, pp. 57–73. Copenhagen: International Work Group on Indigenous Affairs.

FRIEDMAN, THOMAS L. 2005 *The World Is Flat: A Brief History of the 21st Century*. New York: Farrar, Straus & Giroux.

FRONTERA NORTE SUR "A Town of Women Migrants." Available on-line at www.nmsu.edu/%7Frontera/. Accessed October 11, 2005.

FUENTES Y GUZMÁN, FRANCISCO 1969 [1690] *Recordación Florida*. Madrid: Biblioteca de Autores Españoles, No. 230, 259.

FUKUYAMA, FRANCIS 1992 *The End of History and the Last Man*. New York: Free Press.

FURBEE, N. LOUANNA 1996 The Religion of Politics in Chiapas: Founding a Cult of Community Saints. Unpublished paper presented the the 95th Annual Meeting of the American Anthropological Association, San Francisco, November 23.

GAGE, THOMAS 1958 [1648] *Thomas Gage's Travels in the New World,* edited with an introduction by J. Eric S. Thompson. Norman: University of Oklahoma Press.

GANN, THOMAS W. 1900 *Mounds in Northern Honduras.* Nineteenth Annual Report of the Bureau of American Ethnology 1897–1898, Part 2:655–692.

GARCIA MORA, CARL Y MEDINA ANDRES 1983 *La quiebra política de la antropología social en México.* Mexico City: UNAM.

GILL, RICHARDSON B. 2000 *The Great Maya Droughts: Water, Life, and Death.* Albuquerque: University of New Mexico Press.

GOLDIN, LILIANA R. 1999 Identities in the (Maquila) Making: Guatemalan Mayas in the World Economy. In *Identities on the Move: Transnational Processes in North America and the Caribbean Basin,* edited by Liliana Goldin, pp. 151–167. Albany: Institute for Mesoamerican Studies.

GOLDIN, LILIANA, AND BRENDA ROSENBAUM Forthcoming. The Everyday Violence of Exclusion: Women in Precarious Neighborhoods of Guatemala City. In *Harvest of Violence Revisited,* edited by Walter Little and Timothy Smith. Baton Rouge: LSU Press.

GOLDIN, LILIANA, BRENDA ROSENBAUM, AND SAMANTHA EGGLESTON In Press. Women's Participation in Non-Government Organizations: Implications for Poverty Reduction in Precarious Settlements of Guatemala City.

GOSNER, KEVIN 1992 *Soldiers of the Virgin: The Moral Economy of a Colonial Maya Rebellion.* Tucson: University of Arizona Press.

GOSSEN, GARY H. 1970 *Time and Space in Chamula Oral Tradition.* Unpublished Ph.D. Dissertation, Department of Anthropology, Harvard University.

———. 1985 Tzotzil Literature. In *Literatures,* edited by Munro S. Edmonson, pp. 64–106. Supplement to the Handbook of Middle American Indians, vol. 3. Austin: University of Texas Press.

———. 1999 *Telling Maya Tales: Tzotzil Identities in Modern Mexico.* London: Routledge.

———. (ed.) 1986 Symbol and Meaning beyond the Closed Community: Essays in Mesoamerican Ideas. Albany: Institute for Mesoamerican Studies.

GOULD, JEFFREY L. 1998 *To Die in This Way: Nicaraguan Indians and the Myth of Mestizaje, 1880–1965.* Durham: Duke University Press.

GRANT WOOD, ANDREW 2000 Writing Transnationalism: Recent publications on the US Mexico Borderlands. *LARR* vol. 35 (3):251–265.

GREEN, LINDA 1999 *Fear as A Way of Life: Mayan Widows in Rural Guatemala.* New York: Columbia University Press.

GREENFIELD, PATRICIA 2004 *Weaving Generations Together: Evolving Creativity in the Maya of Chiapas.* Santa Fe: School of American Research.

GUTIERREZ, NATIVIDAD 1999 *Nationalist Myths and Ethnic Identities: Indigenous Intellectuals and the Mexican State.* Lincoln: University of Nebraska Press.

GUTMANN, MATTHEW C. 1998 "The Meanings of Macho: Changing Mexican Male Identities." In *Situated Lives: Gender and Culture in Everyday Life,* edited by Louise Lamphere, Helena Ragoné, and Patricia Zavella, pp. 223–234. New York: Routledge.

HAGAN, JAQUELINE, AND NÉSTOR RODRÍGUEZ 1992 Recent Economic Restructuring and Evolving Intergroup Relations in Houston. In *Structuring Diversity: Ethnographic Perspectives on the New Immigration,* edited by Louise Lamphere, pp. 145–172. Chicago: University of Chicago Press.

HALE, CHARLES R. 2002 Does Multiculturalism Menace? Governance, Cultural Rights and the Politics of Identity in Guatemala. *Journal of Latin American Studies* 34:485–524.

HAMMOND, NORMAN 1991 *Cuello: An Early Maya Community in Belize.* Cambridge: Cambridge University Press.

HAMNETT, BRIAN 1999 *A Concise History of Mexico.* Cambridge: Cambridge University Press.

HARVEY, NEIL 1998 *The Chiapas Rebellion: The Struggle for Land and Democracy.* Durham: Duke University Press.

HERNÁNDEZ CASTILLO, R. AÍDA 1994 Reinventing Tradition. *Akewkon Journal* 18(1): 67–70.

———. 1997. Between Hope and Adversity: The Struggle of Organized Women in Chiapas Since the Zapatista Uprising. *Journal of Latin American Anthropology* 3(1):102–120.

HINTON, LEANNE 1987 Sound Change on Purpose: A Study of Highland Mixtec. In *Variation in Language: NWAV-XV,* edited by Keith Denning, Sharon Inkelas, Faye McNair-Knox, and John Rickford, pp. 197–211. Stanford, Calif.: Department of Linguistics, Stanford University.

HIRSCH, JENNIFER 1999 En el Norte la Mujer Manda: Gender, Generation and Geography in a Mexican Transnational Community. *The American Behavioral Scientist* 42(9):1332–1348.

HIRTH, KENNETH G. (ed.) 2000 *Archaeological Research at Xochicalco. Volume 1, Ancient Urbanism at Xochicalco: The Evolution and Organization of a Pre-Hispanic Society. Volume 2, The Xochicalco Mapping Project.* Salt Lake City: University of Utah Press.

HODGE, MARY G., AND MICHAEL E. SMITH (eds.) 1994 *Economies and Polities in the Aztec Realm.* Albany: State University of New York, Institute for Mesoamerican Studies.

HONDAGNEU-SOTELO, PIERRETTE 2001 *Doméstica: Immigrant Workers Cleaning and Caring in the Shadows of Affluence.* Berkeley: University of California Press.

HORCASITAS, FERNANDO (eds. and trans.) 1972 *Life and Death in Milpa Alta: A Nahuatl Chronicle of Díaz and Zapata.* Norman: University of Oklahoma Press. (Translation of the original Spanish edition, 1968, *De Porfirio Díaz a Zapata.* Universidad Nacional Autónoma de México, Instituto de Investigaciones Históricas, Mexico City.)

HOSLER, DOROTHY 2003 Metal Production. In *The Postclassic Mesoamerican World,* edited by Michael E. Smith and Frances F. Berdan, pp. 159–171. Salt Lake City: University of Utah Press.

HUMBOLDT, ALEXANDER VON 1814 *Researches Concerning the Institutions and Monuments of the Ancient Inhabitants of America.* 2 vols. London: Longman, Hurst, Rees.

INGHAM, JOHN M. 1986 *Mary, Michael and Lucifer: Folk Catholicism in Central Mexico.* Austin: University of Texas Press.

IWANSKA, ALICJA 1977 *The Truths of Others.* Summerset, New Jersey: Transaction Publishers.

JONAS, SUSANNE 1974 Guatemala: Land of Eternal Struggle. In *Latin America: The Struggle with Dependency and Beyond,* edited by R. H. Chilcote and J. C. Edelstein, pp. 93–219. New York: John Wiley & Sons.

———. 2000 *Of Centaurs and Doves: Guatemala's Peace Process.* Boulder: Westview Press.

JONES, GRANT D. 1989 *Maya Resistance to Spanish Rule.* Albuquerque: University of New Mexico Press.

———. 1999 *The Conquest of the Last Maya Kingdom.* Stanford: Stanford University Press.

JOYCE, ROSEMARY A. 2000 *Gender and Power in Prehispanic Mesoamerica.* Austin, TX: University of Texas Press.

JUSTESON, JOHN 2001 Pratiche di calculo nell'antica Mesoamerica. In *Storia della Scienza:* vol. II, edited by Anthony F. Aveni, pp. 976–990. Rome: Istituto della Enciclopedia Italiana, Fondata da Giovanni Treccani.

KAMPWIRTH 2002 *Women and Guerrilla Movements: Nicaragua, El Salvador, Chiapas, Cuba.* University Park, Pennsylvania: The Pennsylvania University Press.

KARTTUNEN, FRANCES 1994 *Between Worlds: Interpreters, Guides, and Survivors.* New Brunswick, New Jersey: Rutgers University Press.

KAUFMAN, TERRENCE AND JOHN JUSTESON, In press The Epi-Olmec language and its neighbors. In Classic Veracruz: Cultural Currents in the Ancient Gulf Lowlands, edited by Philip J. Arnold and Christopher A. Pool. Washington, D.C.: Dumbarton Oaks.

KAUFMAN, TERRENCE 1994 The prehistory of the Nawa language group from the earliest times to the sixteenth century. Available online at http://www.albany.edu/pdlma/nawa.pdf.

———. 2000–2005 *Olmecs, Teotihuacaners, and Toltecs: Language History and Language Contact in Meso-America.* Unpublished manuscript.

KEARNEY, MICHAEL 1996 *Reconceptualizing the Peasantry: Anthropology in Global Perspective.* Boulder: Westview Press.

KEEN, BENJAMIN (trans.) 1959 *The Life of the Admiral Christopher Columbus by his son, Ferdinand.* New Brunswick, New Jersey: Rutgers University Press.

KELLOGG, SUSAN 2005 *Weaving the Past: A History of Latin America's Indigenous Women from the Prehispanic Period to the Present.* New York: Oxford University Press.

KIRCHOFF, PAUL 1943 Mesoamerica. In *Heritage of Conquest,* edited by S. Tax. Glencoe: The Free Press.

KLOR DE ALVA, J. JORGE 1993 Aztec spirituality and Nahuatized Christianity. In *South and Meso-American Native Spirituality: from the Cult of the Feathered Serpent to the Theology of Liberation,* edited by Gary H. Gossen and Miguel Leon-Portilla, pp. 173–197. World Spirituality: An Encyclopedic History of the Religious Quest. New York: Crossroads Press.

KOVIC, CHRISTINE 2003 Demanding Their Dignity as Daughters of God: Catholic Women and Human Rights. In *Women of Chiapas: Making History in Times of Struggle and Hope,* edited by Christine Eber and Christine Kovic, pp. 131–148. Austin: University of Texas Press.

———. 2005 *Mayan Voices for Human Rights: Displaced Catholics in Highland Chiapas.* Austin: University of Texas Press.

KRAMER, WENDY, W. GEORGE LOVELL, AND CHRISTOPHER H. LUTZ 1991 Fire in the Mountains: Juan de Espinar and the Indians of Huehuetenango 1525–1560. In *Columbian Sequences,* vol. 3, edited by David Hurst Thomas, pp. 263–282. Washington, D.C.: Smithsonian Institution Press.

KRAUSE, ENRIQUE 1997 Mexico, *Biography of Power. A History of Modern Mexico, 1810–1996.* Hank Heifetz, translator. New York: HarperCollins Publishers.

LÓPEZ y FUENTES, GREGORIO 1981 *El Indio.* New York: Frederick Ungar. (English translation of the original Spanish edition, 1935, *El Indio.*)

LANCASTER, ROGER 1992 *Life Is Hard: Machismo, Danger and the Intimacy of Power in Nicaragua.* Berkeley: University of California Press.

LAUGHLIN, ROBERT M. 1975 *The Great Tzotzil Dictionary of San Lorenzo Zinacantán.* Smithsonian Contributions to Anthropology No. 19. Washington, D.C.: Smithsonian Institution Press.

———. 2003 *Beware the Great Horned Serpent!: Chiapas under the Threat of Napoleon.* Albany: Institute for Mesoamerican Studies.

LEON-PORTILLA, MIGUEL 1963 *Aztec Thought and Culture: A Study of the Ancient Nahuatl Mind.* Norman: University of Oklahoma Press.

———. 1968 *Tiempo y realidad en el pensamiento maya.* Instituto de Investigaciones Históricas, Universidad Nacional Autónoma de México, México City. (English translation, 1973. *Time and Reality in the Thought of the Maya.* Boston: Beacon Press.)

———. 1992 Have We Really Translated the Mesoamerican 'Ancient Word'? In *On the Translation of Native American Literatures,* edited by Brian Swann, pp. 313–338. Washington, D.C.: Smithsonian Institution Press.

———. 1993 Those Made Worthy by Divine Sacrifice: The Faith of Ancient Mexico. In *South and Meso-American Native Spirituality: From the Cult of the Feathered Serpent to the Theology of Liberation,* edited by Gary H. Gossen and Miguel León-Portilla, pp. 41–64. New York: Crossroad.

LEWIS, OSCAR 1963 *Life in a Mexican Village: Tepoztlán Restudied.* Urbana: University of Illinois Press.

LITTLE, WALTER E. 2004 *Mayas in the Marketplace: Tourism, Globalization, and Cultural Identity.* Austin: University of Texas Press.

LOCKHART, JAMES 1991 *Nahuas and Spaniards: Postconquest Central Mexican History and Philology.* Stanford, California: Stanford University Press.

————. (ed. and trans.) 1993 *We People Here: Nahuatl Accounts of the Conquest of Mexico*. Berkeley: University of California Press.

LOCKHART, JAMES, FRANCES BERDAN, AND ARTHUR J. O. ANDERSON (eds. and trans.) 1986 *The Tlaxcalan Actas: A Compendium of the Records of the Cabildo of Tlaxcala (1545–1627)*. Salt Lake City: University of Utah Press.

LOHSE, JON C., AND FRED VALDEZ, JR. (eds.) 2004 *Ancient Maya Commoners*. Austin: University of Texas Press.

LOUCKY, JAMES, AND MARILYN M. MOORS (eds.) 2000 *The Maya Diaspora: Guatemalan Roots, New American Lives*. Philadelphia: Temple University Press.

LOVE, BRUCE 1994 *The Paris Codex: Handbook for a Maya Priest*. Austin: University of Texas Press.

LA FEBER, WALTER 1983 *Inevitable Revolutions: The United States in Central America*. New York: W. W. Norton.

LAS CASAS, BARTOLOMÉ DE 1958 *Apologética historia de Indias*. Nueva Biblioteca de Autores Españoles, vol. 13. Madrid.

MAHLER, SARA J. 1999 Engendering Transnational Migration: A case study of Salvadorans. *The American Behavioral Scientist:* 42(4):690–719.

MANZANILLA, LINDA (ed.) 1993 *Anatomía de un Conjunto Residencial Teotihuacano en Oztoyahualco*. 2 vols. Mexico City: Instituto de Investigaciones Antropológicas, Universidad Autónoma de México.

MARALLI, ENRICO A., AND WAYNE A. CORNELIUS 2001 The Changing Profile of Mexican Migrants to the U.S.: New Evidence from California and Mexico. *LARR* vol. 36(3):105–131.

MARCOS, SUBCOMANDANTE 1998 Marcos Is Gay. *Voces Unidas* 7(4):12. Albuquerque: Southwest Organizing Project. Reprinted from Michigan Peace Team, 12/97, Lansing, Michigan.

————. 2001 *Our Word Is our Weapon: Selected Writings of Subcomandante Insurgente Marcos*, edited by Juana Ponce de León. New York: Seven Stories Press.

MARCOS, SUBCOMANDANTE, AND EZLN 1995 *Shadows of Tender Fury: The Letters and Communiqués of Subcomandante Marcos and the Zapatista Army of National Liberation*, translated by Frank Bardacke, Leslie López, and the Watsonville, California, Human Rights Committee. New York: Monthly Review Press.

MARCUS, JOYCE, AND KENT V. FLANNERY 1996 *Zapotec Civilization: How Urban Society Evolved in Mexico's Oaxaca Valley*. New York: Thames and Hudson.

MARTIN, SIMON, AND NIKOLAI GRUBE 2000 *Chronicle of the Maya Kings and Queens: Deciphering the Dynasties of the Ancient Maya*. London: Thames and Hudson.

MASSON, MARILYN A. 2000 *In the Realm of Nachan Kan: Postclassic Maya Archaeology at Laguna de On, Belize*. Boulder: University Press of Colorado.

MASTACHE, ALBA GUADALUPE, ROBERT H. COBEAN, AND DAN M. HEALAN 2002 *Ancient Tollan: Tula and the Toltec Heartland*. Boulder: University Press of Colorado.

MAYER, ENRIQUE 2002 *The Articulated Peasant: Household Economies in the Andes*. Boulder CO: Westview Press.

MCANANY, PATRICIA A. 2004 *K'axob: Ritual, Work, and Family in an Ancient Maya Village*. Los Angeles: Cotsen Institute for Archaeology, University of California, Los Angeles.

MCCLUSKY, LAURA 2001 *Here Our Culture Is Hard: Stories of Domestic Violence from a Mayan Community in Belize*. Austin: University of Texas Press.

MCCREERY, DAVID J. 1989 Atanasio Tzul, Lucas Aguilar, and the Indian Kingdom of Totonicapán. In *The Human Tradition in Latin America: The Nineteenth Century*, edited by J. Ewell and W. H. Beezley, pp. 39–58. Wilmington, Delaware: SR Books.

MELENDRERAS MARROQUIN, LLEANA Y MANUEL ESSAU PÉREZ 2003 *Así Nos Hicimos Ciudadanas*. Guatemala: Asociación Mujer Vamos Adelante, Ediciones Papiro SA.

MELTZER, D. J., D. K. GRAYSON, G. ARDILA, A. W. BARKER, D. F. DINCAUZE, C. V. HAYNES JR., F. MENA, L. NUÑEZ, AND D. J. STANFORD 1997 On the Pleistocene Antiquity of Monte Verde, Southern Chile. *American Antiquity* 62: 659–663.

Meltzer, David J. 2004 The Peopling of North America. In *The Quaternary Period in the United States*, A. R. Gillespie, S. C. Porter, and B. I. Atwater (eds.), pp. 539–563. Elsevier Science, NY. MENCHÚ, RIGOBERTA 1984 *I, Rigoberta Menchú: An Indian Woman in Guatemala*. London: Verso. (English translation of the original Spanish edition, 1983, *Me llamo Rigoberta Menchú y así me nació la conciencia*. Barcelona: Editorial Argos Vergara.)

MENDEVIL, LEOPOLDO 1994 ¡Murió Janine! La monja, cabeza de los "Zapatistas", murió en combate. *¡Alarma!* 143 (February 8): 10–14. Mexico City.

MONTEJO, VICTOR D. 1987 *Testimony: Death of a Guatemalan Village*, translated by Victor Perera. Willimantic, Conn.: Curbstone Press.

————. 2005 *Maya Intellectual Renaissance: Identity, Representation, and Leadership*. Austin: University of Texas Press.

MYERHOFF, BARBARA G. 1974 *Peyote Hunt: The Sacred Journey of the Huichol Indians*. Ithaca: Cornell University Press.

NASH, JUNE C. 1978 The Aztecs and the Ideology of Male Dominance. *Signs* 4:349–362.

————. 1997 The Fiesta of the Word: The Zapatista Uprising and Radical Democracy in Mexico. *American Anthropologist* 99(2):261–271.

————. 2001 *Mayan Visions: The Quest for Autonomy in an Age of Globalization*. London: Routledge.

NATIONAL INDIGENOUS FORUM 1996 On Autonomy: Preamble to the Resolutions of Roundtable One. Unpublished document circulated at the meeting of January 3–8 in San Cristóbal de las Casas, Chiapas, Mexico.

NAVARRO, MARYSA 2001 Against Marianismo. In *Gender's Place: Feminist Anthropologies of Latin America*, edited by Rosario Montoya, Lessie Jo Frazier, and Janise Hurtig, pp. 257–272. New York: Palgrave.

NICHOLSON, H. B. 1971 Religion in Pre-Hispanic Central Mexico. In *Archaeology of Northern Mesoamerica*, Pt. 1., edited by Gordon F. Ekholm and Ignacio Bernal, pp. 395–446. Handbook of Middle American Indians, vol. 10, Robert Wauchope, general editor. Austin: University of Texas Press.

NIGH, RON 1994 Zapata Rose in 1994: The Indian Rebellion in Chiapas. *Cultural Survival Quarterly* 18(1): 9–13.

OFFNER, JEROME A. 1983 *Law and Politics in Aztec Texcoco.* Cambridge: Cambridge University Press.

PAIGE, JEFREY 1983 Social Theory and Peasant Revolution in Vietnam and Guatemala. *Theory and Society,* vol. 699–737.

PAZ, OCTAVIO 1961 *The Labyrinth of Solitude: Life and Thought in Mexico.* New York: Grove Press. (English translation of the revised Spanish edition, 1959, *El laberinto de la soledad.* Mexico City: Fondo de Cultura Económica.)

———. 1972 *The Other Mexico: Critique of the Pyramid.* New York: Gove Press, Inc.

———. 1985 *The Labyrinth of Solitude and the Other Mexico.* New York: Grove Press, Inc.

PERES TZU (translated by Jan Rus). 1996 The First Two Months of the Zapatistas: a Tzotzil Chronicle. In *Indigenous Revolts in Chiapas and the Andean Highlands,* Kevin Gosner and Arij Ouweneel, editors. Amsterdam: Center for Latin American Research and Documentation.

PIÑA CHAN, ROMAN 1978 Commerce in the Yucatec Peninsula: The Conquest and Colonial Period. In *Mesoamerican Communication Routes and Culture Contacts,* edited by Thomas A. Lee and Carlos Navarrete, pp. 37–48. Papers of the New World Archaeological Foundation 40. Provo, Utah: Brigham Young University.

PICKARD, MIGUEL 2005 Florinda's Story: A Woman of the Maquiladora in San Cristóbal, Chiapas. *Chiapas Today,* Bulletin No. 473, August 10th. CIEPAC: San Cristóbal de Las Casas, Chiapas: Mexico. On-line publication at http://www.ciepac.org.

POHL, JOHN. M. D. 2003 Creation Stories, Hero Cults, and Alliance Building: Confederacies of Central and Southern Mexico. In *The Postclassic Mesoamerican World,* edited by Michael E. Smith and Frances F. Berdan, pp. 61–66. Salt Lake City: University of Utah Press.

POLLARD, HELEN PERLSTEIN 1993 *Tariacuri's Legacy: The Prehispanic Tarascan State.* Norman: University of Oklahoma Press.

POZAS ARCINIEGA, RICARDO 1962 *Juan the Chamula: An Ethnological Re-creation of the Life of a Mexican Indian.* Berkeley: University of California Press. (English translation of the original Spanish edition, 1952, *Juan Pérez Jolote: Biografía de un tzotzil.* Mexico City: Fondo de Cultura Económica.)

PRIEUR, ANNICK 1998 *Mema's House, Mexico City: On Transvestites, Queens and Machos.* Chicago: University of Chicago Press.

QUEZADA, SERGIO 1993 *Pueblos y Caciques Yucatecos, 1550–1580.* Mexico City: El Colegio de México.

RE CRUZ, ALICIA 1998 Maya Women, Gender Dynamics, and Modes of Production. *Sex Roles* 39(7/8):573–587.

RECINOS, ADRIAN 1980 *Memorial de Solola, Anales de los Cakchiqueles.* Mexico City: Fondo de Cultura Económica.

RECINOS, ADRIAN 1984 Título de la Casa Ixcuin-Nehaib, Señora del Territorio de Otzoya. In *Crónica Indígenas de Guatemala.* Second edition. Guatemala City: Academia de Geografía e Historia de Guatemala.

REDING, ANDREW 2000 Mexico: Update on Treatment of Homosexuals. QA/MEX/00.001. New York: INS Resource Information Center

REED, NELSON 1964 The Caste War of Yucatan. Stanford, Calif.: Stanford University Press.

REINA AOYAMA, LETICIA 2004 Historia de los pueblos indígenas de México. Historia indígena de Oaxaca en el siglo XIX. Mexico City: Centro de Investigaciones y Estudios Superiores en Antropologia Social.

RESTALL, MATTHEW 1995 *Life and Death in a Maya Community: The Ixil Testaments of the 1760s.* Lancaster, California: Labyrinthos.

———. 1997 *The Maya World: Yucatec Culture and Society, 1550–1850.* Stanford: Stanford University Press.

———. 1998 *Maya Conquistador.* Boston: Beacon Press.

———. 2001 The People of the Patio: Ethnohistorical Evidence of Yucatec Maya Royal Courts. In *Royal Courts of the Maya, Volume Two: Data and Case Studies,* edited by Takeshi Inomata and Stephen D. Houston, pp. 335–390. Boulder: Westview Press.

———. 2003 *Seven Myths of the Spanish Conquest.* Oxford: Oxford University Press.

RICE, PRUDENCE M. 2004 *Maya Political Science.* Austin: University of Texas Press.

RINGLE, WILLIAM M. 2004 On the Political Organization of Chichén Itzá, *Ancient Mesoamerica* 15:167–218.

RINGLE, WILLIAM M., AND GEORGE J. BEY III 2001 Post-Classic and Terminal Classic Courts of the Northern Maya Lowlands. In *Royal Courts of the Maya, Volume Two: Data and Case Studies,* edited by Takeshi Inomata and Stephen D. Houston, pp. 266–307. Boulder: Westview Press.

RINGLE, WILLIAM M., TOMAS GALLARETA NEGRON, AND GEORGE J. BEY III 1998 The Return of Quetzalcoatl: Evidence for the Spread of a World Religion during the Epiclassic Period. *Ancient Mesoamerica* 9:183–232.

ROBLEDO HERNANDEZ, GABRIELLA PATRICIA 2003 Protestantism and Family Dynamics in an indigenous Community of Highland Chiapas. In, *Women of Chiapas: Making History in Times of Struggle and Hope.* Christine Eber and Christine Kovic, eds. London: Routledge.

ROSENBAUM, BRENDA 1992 Mujer, Tejido e Identidad Etnica en Chamula: Un ensayo Histórico. In *Indumentaria y el tejido mayas a través del tiempo,* edited by Linda Barrios and Dina Fernández, pp. 167–169. Guatemala City: Museo Ixchel.

ROSENBAUM, BRENDA 1993 *With Our Heads Bowed. The Dynamics of Gender in a Maya Community.* Studies in Culture and Society, V. 5. Albany, New York: Institute for Mesoamerican Studies.

ROSENSWIG, ROBERT M. 2000 Some Political Processes of Ranked Societies. *Journal of Anthropological Archaeology* 19: 413–460.

ROSS, JOHN 1995 The EZLN, A History: Miracles, Coyunturas, Communiqués. Introduction. In *Shadows of Ten-*

der Fury: The Letters and Communiqués of Subcomandante Marcos and the Zapatista Army of National Liberation. New York: Monthly Review Press.

ROSTAS, SUSANNA 2003 Women's Empowerment Through Religious Change in Tenejapa. In *Women of Chiapas: Making History in Times of Struggle and Hope,* edited by Christine Eber and Christine Kovic, pp. 171–187. Austin TX: University of Texas Press.

ROYS, RALPH L. 1933 *The Book of Chilam Balam of Chumayel.* Washington, D.C.: Carnegie Institution of Washington, Publication 438.

———. 1957 *The Political Geography of the Yucatan Maya.* Washington, D.C.: Carnegie Institution of Washington, Publication 613.

———. 1962 *A Review of Historic Sources for Mayapán. In Mayapán, Yucatan, Mexico,* edited by H. E. D. Pollock, R. L. Roys, T. Proskouriakoff, and A. L. Smith. Washington, D.C.: Carnegie Institution of Washington, Publication 619.

RUGELEY, TERRY 1996 *Yucatan's Maya Peasantry & the Origins of the Caste War.* Austin: University of Texas Press.

RUS, DIANE 1989 "La Crisis Económica y la mujer indígena: El caso de Chamula, Chiapas. San Cristóbal de Las Casas, Chiapas: Instituto de Asesoría Antropológica para la Región Maya.

RUS, JAN 1994 "The Comunidad Revolucionaria Institucional: The Subversion of Native Government in Highland Chiapas, 1936–1968. In *Every-day Forms of State Formation and the Negotiation of Rule in Modern Mexico,* edited by Gilbert Joseph and Daniel Nugent, pp. 265–300. Durham: Duke University Press.

RUS, JAN, ROSALVA AÍDA HERNÁNDEZ CASTILLO, AND SHANNAN L. MATTIACE (eds.) 2003 *Mayan Lives, Mayan Utopias: The Indigenous Peoples of Chiapas and the Zapatista Rebellion.* Lanham, Maryland: Rowman and Littlefield Publishers.

SAHAGÚN, BERNARDINO DE 1950–1982 *Florentine Codex: General History of the Things of New Spain,* edited and translated by Arthur J. O. Anderson and Charles E. Dibble. 12 books. Santa Fe and Salt Lake City: School of American Research and the University of Utah Press.

———. 1993 *Psalmodia Christiana (Christian Psalmody).* Edited and translated by Arthur J. O. Anderson. Salt Lake City: University of Utah Press.

SANDERS, WILLIAM T., ALBA GUADELUPE MASTACHE, AND ROBERT H. COBEAN (editors) 2003 *El urbanismo en mesoamérica/Urbanism in Mesoamerica. Proyecto Urbanismo de Mesoamérica/The Mesoamerican Urbanism Project,* vol. 1. Pennsylvania State University and Instituto Nacional de Antropología e História, University Part and Mexico City.

SANDERS, WILLIAM T., JEFFREY R. PARSONS, AND ROBERT S. SANTLEY 1979 *The Basin of Mexico: Ecological Processes in the Evolution of a Civilization.* New York: Academic Press.

SANDERS, WILLIAM, AND BARBARA PRICE 1968 *Mesoamerica: The Evolution of a Civilization.* New York: Random House.

SANDROM, ALAN R. 1991 *Corn Is Our Blood: Cultural and Ethnic Identity in a Contemporary Aztec Indian Village.* Norman: University of Oklahoma Press.

SARAMAGO, JOSÉ 2001 Chiapas, a Name of Pain and Hope. Foreword to Subcomandante Marcos, *Our Word Is Our Weapon: Selected Writings of Subcomandante Insurgente Marcos,* pp. xix–xxii. New York: Seven Stories Press.

SCHELE, LINDA, AND PETER MATHEWS 1998 *The Code of Kings: The Language of Seven Sacred Maya Temples and Tombs.* New York: Simon and Schuster.

SCHROEDER, SUSAN, STEPHANIE WOOD, AND ROBERT HASKETT (eds.) 1997 *Indian Women of Early Mexico.* Norman: University of Oklahoma Press.

SCHWARTZ, NORMAN B. 1983 *The Second Heritage of Conquest; Some Observations. Heritage of Conquest, Thirty Years Later,* edited by Carl Kendall, John Hawkins, and Laurel Bossen. Albuquerque: University of New Mexico Press.

SELL, BARRY D., AND LOUISE M. BURKHART (eds.) 2004 *Nahuatl Theater Volume 1: Death and Life in Colonial Nahua Mexico.* Norman: University of Oklahoma Press.

SHARER, ROBERT J., AND DAVID C. GROVE (eds.) 1989 *Regional Perspectives on the Olmec.* New York: Cambridge University Press.

SMALLEY, JOHN, AND MICHAEL BLAKE 2003 Sweet Beginnings: Stalk Sugar and the Domestication of Maize. *Current Anthropology* 44:675–703.

SMITH, MICHAEL E. 1996 *The Aztecs.* Oxford: Blackwell.

SMITH, MICHAEL E. 2003 *The Aztecs.* Second Edition. Oxford: Blackwell Publishers.

SMITH, MICHAEL E., AND FRANCES F. BERDAN (eds.) 2003 *The Postclassic Mesoamerican World.* Salt Lake City: University of Utah Press.

SNA JTZ'IBAHAM 1991 *Sventa Pajaro ta Chamula ta l9ll* [Spanish translation: *Los pajaritos de Chamula*]. Sna Jtz' Ibaham [Cultura de los Indios Mayas, A. C.] Publication 8, San Cristóbal de las Casas, Chiapas.

SOR JUANA INÉS DE LA CRUZ 1988 *A Sor Juana anthology.* Translated by Alan S. Trueblood. Cambridge, Mass.: Harvard University Press.

SOUSA, LISA, AND KEVIN TERRACIANO 2003 The "Original Conquest" of Oaxaca: Nahua and Mixtec Accounts of the Spanish Conquest. *Ethnohistory* 50:349–400.

SPEED, SHANNON 2003 "Actions Speak Louder than Words: Indigenous Women and Gendered Resistance in the Wake of Acteal." In *Women of Chiapas: Making History in Times of Struggle and Hope,* edited by Christine Eber and Christine Kovic, pp. 47–65. Austin: University of Texas Press.

SPEED, SHANNON, R. AIDA HERNANDEZ CASTILLO, AND LYNN STEPHEN (eds.) 2006 *Dissident Women: Gender and Cultural Politics in Chiapas.* Austin: University of Texas Press.

SPENCE, JACK 2004 *War and Peace in Central America: Comparing Transitions toward Democracy and Social Equity in Guatemala, El Salvador, and Nicaragua.* Brookline, Massachusetts: Hemisphere Initiatives.

SPENCE, LEWIS 1908 *The Mythic and Heroic Sagas of the K'ichés of Central America.* London: David Nutt.

SPENCE, LEWIS 1925 *Atlantis in America.* London: E. Benn.

STARK, BARBARA L., AND PHILIP J. ARNOLD, III (eds.) 1997 *Olmec to Aztec: Settlement Patterns in the Ancient Gulf Lowlands.* Tucson: University of Arizona Press.

STEPHEN, LYNN 1991 *Zapotec Women.* Austin: University of Texas Press.

STEPHEN, LYNN 1997 *Women and Social Movements in Latin America: Power From Below.* Austin: University of Texas Press.

STEPHEN, LYNN 2002 Sexualities and Genders in Zapotec Oaxaca. *Latin American Perspectives* 29(2):41–59.

STEPHENS, JOHN L. 1841 *Incidents of Travel in Central America, Chiapas and Yucatan.* 2 vols. New York: Dover Publications.

STEPHENS, JOHN L. 1843 *Incidents of Travel in Yucatan.* 2 vols. London: J. Murray.

STEWARD, JULIAN 1949 Cultural Causality and Law. *American Anthropologist* 51.

STOLL, DAVID 1999 *Rigoberta Menchú and the Story of All Poor Guatemalans.* Boulder: Westview Press.

SULLIVAN, THELMA 1980 O Precious Necklace, O Quetzal Feather! Aztec Pregnancy and Childbirth Orations. *Alcheringa/Ethnopoetics* 4:38–52.

SYMONDS, STACEY, ANN CYPHERS, AND ROBERTO LUNAGÓMEZ 2002 *Asentamiento prehispánico en San Lorenzo Tenochtitlán.* Serie San Lorenzo. Mexico City: Instituto de Investigaciones Antropológicas, Universidad Nacional Autónoma de México.

TAX, SOL (ed.) 1952 *Heritage of Conquest: The Ethnology of Middle America.* Viking Fund Seminar in Middle American Ethnology. Glencoe: The Free Press.

———. 1953 *Penny Capitalism: A Guatemalan Indian Economy.* Smithsonian Institute of Social Anthropology, No. 16. Washington, D.C.

TAYLOR, CLARK 1995 "Legends, Syncretisms, and Continuing Echoes of Homosexuality from Pre-Columbian and Colonial Mexico." In *Latin American Male Homosexualities,* edited by Stephen O. Murray, pp. 80–99. Albuquerque: University of New Mexico Press.

TEDLOCK, DENNIS (trans. and ed.) 1996 *Popol Vuh: The Mayan Book of the Dawn of Life.* 2nd ed. New York: Simon and Schuster.

TERRACIANO, KEVIN 1998 Crime and Culture in Colonial Mexico: The Case of the Mixtec Murder Note. *Ethnohistory* 45:709–745.

———. 2001 *The Mixtecs of Colonial Oaxaca: Ñudzahui History, Sixteenth through Eighteenth Centuries.* Stanford: Stanford University Press.

TORQUEMADA, JUAN DE 1943 *Monarquía Indiana,* 3 vols. Mexico: Chávez Hayhoe.

TOWNSEND, RICHARD F. 1993 *The Aztecs.* London: Thames and Hudson.

TUTINO, JOHN 1986 *From Insurrection to Revolution in Mexico: Social Bases of Agrarian Violence, 1750–1940.* Princeton: Princeton University Press.

VAN WEY, LEAH K., CATHERINE M. TUCKER, AND EILEEN DIAZ MCCONNEL 2005 Community Organization, Migration and Remittances in Oaxaca. *LARR* 40(1):83–107.

VILLACORTA, J. ANTONIO, AND CARLOS A. VILLACORTA 1971 *Códices Mayas.* Tipográfía Nacional, Guatemala. [1930].

VOORHIES, BARBARA 2004 *Coastal Collectors in the Holocene: The Chantuto People of Southwest Mexico.* Gainesville: University Press of Florida.

WALLERSTEIN, IMMANUEL 1976 *The Modern World-System: Capitalist Agriculture and the Origins of the European World-Economy in the Sixteenth Century.* New York: Academic Press.

WARREN, KAY 1998 *Indigenous Movements and Their Critics: Pan-Maya Activism in Guatemala.* Princeton: Princeton University Press.

WATANABE, JOHN 2000 Neither as They Imagined nor as Others Intended: Mayas and Anthropologists in the Highlands of Guatemala Since the 1960s. *Ethnology. Supplement to the Handbook of Mesoamerican Indians,* vol. 6. Austin: University of Texas Press.

WATERBURY, RONALD 1975 Non-revolutionary Peasants; Oaxaca Compared to Morelos in the Mexican Revolution. *Comparative Studies in Society and History,* vol. 17:410–442.

WEST, ROBERT C. 1964 The Natural Regions of Middle America. In *Natural Environment and Early Cultures,* edited by Robert C. West, pp. 363–383. Handbook of Middle American Indians, vol. 1. Austin: University of Texas Press.

WEST, ROBERT C., AND JOHN P. AUGELLI 1989 *Middle America: Its Land and Peoples.* 3rd ed. Englewood Cliffs, New Jersey: Prentice Hall.

WILLEY, GORDON R. 1966 Mesoamerica. *An Introduction to American Archaeology.* Englewood Cliffs, New Jersey: Prentice Hall, Inc.

WILSON, CARTER 1995 *Hidden in the Blood: A Personal Investigation of AIDS in the Yucatán.* New York: Columbia University Press.

WILSON, RICHARD 1995 *Maya Resurgence in Guatemala: Q'eqchi' Experiences.* Norman: University of Oklahoma Press.

WOLF, ERIC R. 1959 *Sons of the Shaking Earth.* Chicago: University of Chicago Press.

WOLF, ERIC R. 1969 *Peasant Wars of the Twentieth Century.* New York: Harper & Row.

Index